Hazel.

Summer 2011.

ARAMAIC PESHITTA NEW TESTAMENT TRANSLATION

With explanatory footnotes marking variant readings, customs and figures of speech

By
Janet M. Magiera

Light of the Word Ministry
LWM Publications

Light of the Word Ministry
813 Pershing St.
Truth or Consequences NM 87901
505-894-7475
619-920-2503

www.lightofword.org
www.aramaicresearch.org

ISBN #0-9679613-5-1

CONTENTS

INTRODUCTION

A Brief History of the Aramaic Language

The Aramaic language has its beginning with the sons of Noah. The first biblical clue to the origin of Aramaic is found in Genesis 10:22, which informs us that Aram was the youngest son of Shem. What Aram spoke has been called "the Mesopotamian language." This was the language that was then transmitted down to Abraham. It is the precursor of all the Semitic languages.

Abraham left his home in Ur of the Chaldeans and traveled with his father Terah and his brother Nahor to Haran in Syria. The son of Nahor was also called Aram (Genesis 22:21). This area of land in Syria became known as the land of the Arameans, or Aram. By 1000 BC, the people lived in strong city-states and had developed a cursive version of the North Semitic alphabet. The language and alphabet has continued in use until the present.

Abraham left Haran and crossed the Euphrates River and traveled to Canaan. There is a reference to Jacob as a "wandering Aramean" in Deuteronomy 26:3. His descendants were called "Hebrews," a term derived from the Aramaic word *abar*, meaning, "to cross over." Gradually, a unique dialect and script called Hebrew was developed. Moses and the subsequent authors of the Old Testament scriptures probably originally wrote these books in this Old Hebrew, which was not far removed from Aramaic.

Around 1000-800 BC, there were several major powers in the Near East: Assyria, Babylonia and Syria. They adopted the alphabet and language of the Arameans and Aramaic became the *lingua franca* throughout the Mesopotamian area. It was the language of commerce, trade and communication. It became the vernacular language of Assyria, Babylonia (Chaldee) and Syria. There was then a split in dialects between the east, consisting of Babylonia and Assyria and west, consisting of Syria. The eastern Aramaic was further divided into two dialects, Assyrian (northern) and Babylonian (southern).

The Assyrians conquered the northern ten tribes of Israel in 721 BC and transported the Israelites to Assyria. Those who came from Assyria to settle in Galilee and Samaria spoke this northern dialect of Aramaic. This dialect continued until the time of Christ.

5

INTRODUCTION

The Babylonians conquered Judea in 586 BC and transported them to Babylon, where Eastern or Chaldean Aramaic was spoken. Daniel was written in Aramaic. When the people under Ezra and Nehemiah went back to Jerusalem to rebuild the temple, they spoke this dialect. This dialect of Aramaic continued down through the 1st century and is sometimes called Palestinian Aramaic.

That is how there came to be two different dialects spoken during the time of Christ in Palestine. The difference was not great, perhaps similar to the difference between the northern and southern parts of the United States. Jesus Christ and his disciples (all except for Judas Iscariot) spoke the northern dialect of Aramaic because they were from Galilee. Paul was born and raised in Tarsus (western Aramaic), but he was educated in Jerusalem (eastern Aramaic), so he must have been fluent in both dialects. Paul also spoke Greek (Acts 21:37).

The Gospels were most certainly written in Aramaic and, most likely, Paul's letters were also. But as the gospel reached out in the 1st century from Jerusalem into Antioch of Syria and then on into Achaia and Macedonia, which were Greek-speaking areas, the Gospels and other letters were probably almost immediately translated into Greek. The transmission of the text then developed in parallel lines.

Constantinople was the capital of Babylon in the 3rd and 4th centuries, where Aramaic was still the *lingua franca*. Christianity was declared the official religion, so manuscripts of the scriptures in Aramaic were copied and passed on. There was a very careful preservation of the text and that is the reason for the integrity among the various Peshitta manuscripts.

Since the original split in the dialects to western and eastern Aramaic, Syria had grown in power and, after the 1st century, a center of teaching developed in Edessa near Haran. It is from here that the Peshitta version was compiled. The oldest complete manuscripts in Aramaic are this Peshitta version. The word Peshitta means "straight, simple, sincere, or true." The earliest manuscripts used a script called Estrangelo and this script reached the height of its development by the 4th century.

INTRODUCTION

There was a great controversy in the church at Ephesus and Chalcedon in 431 and 451 AD because of the Monophysite bishops and about the issue of Mary as the mother of God. The church split into two separate entities in the east and west and has never recovered from this controversy. The Aramaic language was already divided into dialects, but now each side also developed new scripts from the Estrangelo letters to differentiate them from the other side.

Jacob was the leader in the school in Edessa and the script in the west became known as the Jacobite script. At this time, vowel markings were also established. Almost all of the grammar books we have today and many manuscripts were written in this script.

The other script developed in the east is called Nestorian. It is squarer and uses dots for the vowel markings. The differences in the scripts were in the formation of the letters or characters, not in the words. Thus, we use the dictionaries such as Payne Smith and Jennings to translate the Estrangelo manuscripts, even though they are written in Jacobite script. There are differences in the script, not the language.

Aramaic continued as the *lingua franca* until Arabic and Islam replaced it in the 9th century. There are still some people today in Turkey and Kurdistan who speak Aramaic. Aramaic was the native language of Dr. George Lamsa.

The Peshitta Text

The text used in this translation as the base text is taken from *The Syriac New Testament and Psalms*, published by the United Bible Societies. In 1905, the British and Foreign Bible Society published an edition of the Peshitta, reprinted by permission from a critical edition prepared by Rev. G. H. Gwilliam in 1901. This is a critical text of the Peshitta, meaning that it is a composite of readings from different manuscripts that were located in the British Museum. It is known as a western text of the Peshitta and varies to a small degree from other eastern versions of the Peshitta. In the footnotes, these differences from the eastern version are noted as variant readings. In this translation, the text is called the Peshitta. However, some would distinguish that the Peshitta is the name for only the eastern version and that the western text should be called Peshito. In order to simplify the reference in this translation, both versions are called the Peshitta.

INTRODUCTION

Peshitta is an Aramaic word that means "simple" or "straight." Although there are some alternative arguments, the best estimate is that the Peshitta was first written around 150 AD. The primary center that was responsible for its dissemination was Edessa in Syria. It is written in the Aramaic dialect of that region, which is called Syriac. This dialect differs from the Palestinian Aramaic of Judea and Galilee, but not to the extent that both parties would have not understood each other. Perhaps the best comparison would be between British and United States English. Since there are no surviving manuscripts of the New Testament in Palestinian Aramaic from the first century, it is very clear that the Peshitta is the closest text that we have readily available to study the Scriptures in Aramaic.

There is a particular reason why it is evident that the Peshitta must have been completed early in the 2nd century. It does not include the books of II Peter, II John, III John, Jude and Revelation, which were added to the Peshitta manuscripts later. These books were not completely accepted as canon until after the middle of the 2nd century, and their origin was in the area of Ephesus. This translation utilizes the later versions of these books to complete the New Testament text.

Why a New Translation?

There are two prominent translations that are out of print from the middle 1800's. One was by James Murdock and the other by J. W. Etheridge. Murdock based his work on the western text and Etheridge on the eastern text. Both of them are still very useful in studying the Peshitta. In the 1930's, Dr. George Lamsa, a native speaker of Aramaic, completed a translation of the eastern manuscripts of the Peshitta and began to travel extensively in the United States, teaching about the value of studying Aramaic. From that time until the present, there has been a renewed interest in fundamental Christianity to know about the language of Jesus and what it has to contribute to biblical study.

INTRODUCTION

Today there are several works available that employ different methods of translation of the New Testament or portions of the New Testament. The Hebraic Roots Version by Dr. James Trimm emphasizes the Messianic beliefs of his branch of Nazarene Judaism. Herb Jahn published a very literal translation using cognate definitions in his Exegeses Bible from a computerized lexicon along with distinctive interpretations and grammatical constructions incorporated by Jahn. The Disciples New Testament by Victor Alexander, a native Aramaic speaker, uses an idiomatic approach to the translation and contributes much in this area. The American Christian Press has produced an interlinear version of the New Testament in 3 volumes. Dr. Rocco Errico has translated the Gospel of Matthew in a parallel edition with useful footnotes. Lamsa's translation is still available for purchase through HarperCollins Publishers. Another work of great value is by Paul Younan of peshitta.org, which is an interlinear version. Each of the above works represent the distinctive beliefs of the translator.

Light of the Word Ministry has developed this particular translation to fill in a need for a very accurate literal translation, but in modern English. The method employed in this translation is to preserve as much as possible the Semitic usage and sentence structure, but in readable English. Idioms are translated with dynamic equivalency. It adds many footnote explanations, providing a way for the biblical student to begin study from the Aramaic. There is a system of marking common expressions and idioms so that the footnotes can be clear and not repetitious. It is meant to be utilized with the complete database which is available through BibleWorks software.

It is my sincere wish that each Bible student who is able to read these pages will grow in understanding of the language of Jesus, its idioms and figures of speech and will be blessed with further understanding of the message of the New Testament.

Janet M. Magiera, April 2006.

INTRODUCTION

Coding and Idioms

A system of coding the text is used throughout this translation. Various typefaces distinguish particular construction or grammatical phrases of note.

1. **Bold type** shows a proleptic or emphatic pronoun. This grammatical construction is common in Syriac, where a pronoun, such as *he*, precedes the verb, which also is translated with the pronoun. It emphasizes and marks a change in address or the noun in action. An example is from Matthew 4:20, *And **they** immediately left their nets.* Literally, this would read, "And they, immediately, they left their nets." Another example is found in Matthew 3:15, *But **Jesus** answered and said...* Literally, this would be, "But he, Jesus answered..."

2. SMALL CAPS BOLD INDICATE OLD TESTAMENT QUOTATIONS

3. SMALL CAPS (NO BOLD) HIGHLIGHT HEBREW WORDS THAT ARE RETAINED IN THE TEXT. Please refer to the first use for explanation.

LORD is *MARYA*, meaning LORD of the Old Testament, YAHWEH

BEELZEBUB	MATT 10:25
GEHENNA	MATT 5:22
HOSANNA	MATT 21:9
MAGI	MATT 2:1
MESSIAH	MATT 1:16
RABBI	MATT 23:7
RABBULI	JOHN 20:16
SABBATH	MATT 12:1
SATAN	MATT 4:10
SHEOL	MATT 11:23

4. [ ] All bracketed words are added to the text to make sense in English or to show the ellipsis in the verse.

5. Holy Spirit is always capitalized, and Spirit is capitalized, except when spirit is in construct form (no "aleph" ending) and then it is translated either "in" or "by spirit" or "spiritually".

10

INTRODUCTION

6. Outline type notes idioms and common expressions. The definition of idioms used in this translation is from Webster's Dictionary, "an expression in the usage of a language that is peculiar to itself either grammatically or in having a meaning that cannot be derived form the conjoined meanings of its elements." It is limited to primarily grammatical constructions that need to be translated in English to communicate the sense of the phrase, not its literal components. Other broader types of sentence structure or implications that could be called idioms are explained in the footnotes and are considered to be "Semitisms" instead of idioms. The following is a chart in alphabetical order of the phrases outlined in this type.

Idiom Chart			
English	**Aramaic**	**Literal Translation**	**Scripture Example**
__ years old	ܒܪ ... ܫܢܝܢ	son of ___ years	Mat 2:16
a little	ܩܠܝܠ ܡܢ ܣܓܝ	little by much	Rom 15:24
a little while	ܩܠܝܠ ܐܚܪܝܢ	little another	Joh 12:35
accuse, accuser, slanderer	ܐܟܠ ܩܪܨܐ	eater of pieces	Mat 4:4
adoption	ܣܝܡܬ ܒܢܝܐ	placing as sons	Rom 8:15
adversary, opponent at law	ܒܥܠ ܕܝܢܝ	lord of my judgment	Luk 18:3
after	ܡܢ ܒܬܪ	from after	Mat 26:32
again	ܡܢ ܕܪܝܫ	from above, from the beginning	Joh 3:3
almost	ܩܠܝܠ ܚܣܝܪ	wanting or lacking a little	2Co 2:5
already, even now	ܡܢ ܟܕܘ	by now, sometime about now	Luk 12:49
always	ܒܟܠ ܥܕܢ	at every moment	Joh 7:6
always (2)	ܒܟܠܙܒܢ	at all times	Mat 18:10
answer	ܬܦܩܘܢ ܪܘܚܐ	go out in breath (make a defense)	Luk 12:11
anxiety, embarrassment	ܦܘܫܟ ܐܝܕܝܐ	wringing of the hands	Luk 21:25

11

INTRODUCTION

English	Aramaic	Literal Translation	Scripture Example
Idiom Chart			
archangel	ܪܫ ܡܠܐܟܐ	head angel	1Th 4:16
at all	ܐܦ ܠܐ ܚܕ	even not one	Joh 19:11
babbler	ܡܠܩܛ ܡܠܐ	picker up of words - "seed picker"	Act 17:18
banquet	ܒܝܬ ܡܫܬܘܬܐ	house of the banquet	Luk 14:8
banquet house	ܒܝܬ ܡܫܬܝܐ	house of wedding	Mat 22:10
banquet, banquet hall	ܒܝܬ ܚܠܘܠܐ	house of festivity	Mat 25:10
best seat	ܪܫ ܣܡܟܐ	head of the meal or company	Luk 14:7
beyond	ܠܗܠ ܡܢ	over from	Act 7:43
birthday	ܒܝܬ ܝܠܕܗ	house of his birth	Mat 14:6
book-carrier	ܒܝܬ ܟܬܒܐ	house of books	1Ti 4:13
brotherly kindness	ܪܚܡܬ ܐܚܘܬܐ	compassion of the brotherhood	2Pe 1:7
by way of	ܒܝܕ	by the hand of	Mat 1:22
captain, guard	ܪܫ ܚܝܠܐ	chief of the strong ones	Luk 22:4
cemetery, tomb	ܒܝܬ ܩܒܘܪܐ	house of the graves	Mat 8:28
censor	ܒܝܬ ܒܣܡܐ	house of incense	Heb 9:4
chief priests	ܪܒܝ ܟܗܢܐ	heads of the priests	Mat 16:21
citizen	ܒܢܝ ܡܕܝܢܬܐ	sons of the city	Luk 19:14
clergy	ܒܢܝ ܥܕܬܐ	sons of the church	Act 11:22
companions	ܒܢܝ ܠܘܬܗ	sons toward him	Act 19:29
contemporaries	ܒܢܝ ܫܢܝ	sons of my years	Gal 1:14
council	ܒܝܬ ܟܢܘܫܬܗܘܢ	house of their synagogues or assemblies	Luk 22:66
counselor	ܡܪܐ ܡܠܟܐ	lord of the counsel	Rom 11:34
counselors	ܒܢܝ ܡܠܟܐ	sons of counsel	Act 25:12
countrymen	ܒܢܝ ܥܡܐ	sons of the people	Joh 18:35

12

INTRODUCTION

English	Aramaic	Literal Translation	Scripture Example
cousin		son of his uncle	Col 4:10
curtain, veil		face of the door	Mat 27:51
customs-house		house of taxes	Mat 9:9
daily, everyday		all day	Mat 26:55
dead		house of the dead	Mat 14:2
detention hall		house of confinement	Rev 2:10
each and every one		all one to one	Luk 19:15
each man, each one		a man, a man	Mar 13:34
empty-handed		being empty	Luk 20:10
ever since		what from	Col 1:4
every year		all year	Luk 2:41
everyone		all men	Mat 19:29
everything		all what	Mat 8:33
except		outside of	Act 8:1
except, unless		but if	Mat 11:27
extraordinary		full of distinctions	Eph 3:10
faint-hearted [ones]		little [ones] of soul	1Th 5:14
farewell		being healthy or whole	Act 23:30
fellow-heirs		sons of the inheritance	Rom 8:17
follow		come after	Mat 4:19
fool, ignorant [one], stupid		lacking sense or mind	Luk 12:20
footstool		stool of the feet	Jam 2:3
for a minute		the fullness of an hour	Gal 2:5
for a while		up to a time	Luk 4:13

The title row "Idiom Chart" spans the table.

13

INTRODUCTION

Idiom Chart			
English	**Aramaic**	**Literal Translation**	**Scripture Example**
for your sake, for you	ܠܐܦܝܟܘܢ	for your faces	Eph 1:16
forbid it to you	ܠܗ ܣܘ	be it far from you or spare you	Mat 16:22
foreheads (their)	ܒܝܬ ܥܝܢܝܗܘܢ	between their eyes	Rev 7:3
foreknowledge	ܡܩܕܡܘܬ ܝܕܥܬܗ	his preceding knowledge	Act 2:23
foresaw	ܩܕܡ ܚܙܐ	see before	Act 2:25
forever and ever	ܠܥܠܡ ܥܠܡܝܢ	to the age of the age	Rom 9:1
foster brother	ܒܪ ܡܪܒܝܢܘܬܗ	son of his upbringer	Act 13:1
freemen, free	ܒܢܝ ܚܐܪܐ	sons of freedom	Mat 17:26
go	ܙܠ ܠܟ	go to you	Mat 4:10
grandchildren	ܒܢܝ ܒܢܝܐ	sons of the sons	1Ti 5:4
grandmother	ܐܡܗ ܕܐܡܟ	mother of your mother	2Ti 1:5
greet	ܫܐܠ ܫܠܡܐ	ask peace	Mat 5:47
guest house	ܒܝܬ ܡܫܪܝܐ	house of visiting	Phm 1:22
guest, friend of the wedding feast	ܒܢܝ ܓܢܘܢܐ	son of the wedding feast	Mat 9:15
handwriting	ܟܬܒܐ ܕܐܝܕܝ	writing of my hand	2Th 3:17
have nothing to do	ܠܐ ܠܟ	not to you	Mat 27:19
her years were past	ܠܐ ܒܙܒܢܐ ܕܫܢܝܗ	not in the time of her years	Heb 11:11
high priest	ܪܒ ܟܗܢܐ	the great [one] of the priests	Mat 26:32
homosexuals	ܫܟܒܝ ܥܡ ܕܟܪܐ	lying [ones] with males	1Co 6:9
house to house	ܒܝܬ ܒܝܬܐ	house of house	1Ti 3:6
household	ܒܢܝ ܒܝܬܐ	sons of the house	Mat 10:36
how long	ܥܕܡܐ ܠܐܡܬܝ	until when	Mat 17:17
how much more	ܟܡܐ ܚܕ	one how much	Phm 1:16

14

INTRODUCTION

English	Aramaic	Literal Translation	Scripture Example
hypocrites, respecter of persons	ܣܒ̈ܝ ܐܦ̈ܐ	receiver or taker of faces	Mat 6:2
idol worshippers	ܦܠܚܝ ܦܬܟܪ̈ܐ	servers of idols	1Co 5:10
idolatry	ܕܚܠܬ ܦܬܟܪ̈ܐ	reverence of idols	1Th 1:9
immediately, at that moment	ܒܗ ܒܫܥܬܐ	in that hour	Mat 13:5
in order	ܒܬܪ ܒܬܪ	after after	Act 11:4
in part	ܡܢ ܐܬܪ ܩܠܝܠ	from a little place	Rom 11:25
in the presence of	ܡܢ ܠܘܬ	from toward	Luk 1:45
in the presence of (2)	ܠܥܝܢܝ ܐܢܫܐ	to the eyes of the man	Mat 17:9
in various times	ܙܒܢ ܙܒܢ	in times times	Joh 5:4
insane	ܒܪ ܐܓ̈ܪܐ	son of a rooftop	Mat 4:24
integrity	ܫܪܝܪܘܬܗܘܢ ܛܒܬܐ	their good truth	Tit 2:10
judgment hall	ܒܝܬ ܕܝܢܐ	house of judgment	Act 17:19
lawgiver	ܣܐܡ ܢܡܘܣܐ	setter of the law	Jam 4:12
lest	ܐܢ ܠܐ ܕܠܡܐ	and if not, unless	Luk 5:37
long-suffering, patient	ܐܓܝܪ ܪܘܚܐ	length of spirit	Mat 18:26
man, men	ܒܪ ܐܢܫܐ	son of man, son of men	Mat 4:19
never	ܠܐ ܡܢ ܡܬܘܡ	not ever, not from the moment	Mat 7:23
nobleman	ܒܪ ܛܘܗܡܐ	son of nobility	Luk 19:12
not yet	ܠܐ ܥܕܟܝܠ	not still	Act 9:1
obedience	ܡܫܡܥ ܐܕܢܐ	hearing of the ear	Rom 10:17
of age	ܥܠ ܥܠ ܠܫܢܬܗ	concerning him for his year	Joh 8:21
of noble birth	ܒܢܝ ܛܘܗܡܐ ܪ̈ܒܐ	sons of a great family	1Co 1:26

15

INTRODUCTION

Idiom Chart			
English	**Aramaic**	**Literal Translation**	**Scripture Example**
of old	ܕܗ̣ܘ ܥܠܡ	that are from the age	Act 3:21
once and again	ܚܕܐ ܙܒܢ ܘܬ̈ܪܬܝܢ	one time and two	Phi 4:16
one another, each other	ܚܕ ܥܡ ܚܕ	one with one	Mar 1:27
one by one	ܚܕ ܚܕ	each one	Mar 14:19
one to another, to each other	ܚܕ ܠܚܕ	one to one	Mar 4:41
one-tenth	ܚܕ ܡܢ ܥܣܪܐ	one from ten	Rev 11:13
openly, boldly	ܒܥܝܢܐ ܓܠܝܬܐ	with eye open	Act 2:29
our report	ܒܪܬ ܩܠܢ	daughter of our voice	Rom 19:16
partly	ܡܕܡ ܡܕܡ	what what	1Co 11:18
patriarch	ܪܝܫ ܐܒ̈ܗܬܐ	head of the fathers	Act 2:29
poll tax, tribute	ܟܣܦ ܪܝܫܐ	head money	Luk 20:22
previously	ܡܢ ܒܪܝܫܝܬ	from the beginning	Mat 19:8
prison	ܒܝܬ ܐܣܝ̈ܪܐ	house of captives	Mat 5:25
privately	ܒܝܢܘܗܝ ܘܠܗܘܢ	alone and with them	Mat 20:17
privately	ܒܝܢܝ ܘܠܗܘܢ	between me and them	Gal 2:2
punishment	ܣܝܡ ܒܪܝܫܐ	a laying on the head (capital punishment)	Act 22:5
relatives	ܒ̈ܢܝ ܛܘܗܡܐ	sons of the family	Luk 1:58
residents	ܒ̈ܢܝ ܐܬܪܐ	sons of the place	Act 21:12
sanctuary	ܒܝܬ ܩܘܕܫܐ	house of holiness	Rom 2:22
seize	ܐܪܡܝܘ ܐܝ̈ܕܝܐ ܥܠ	place hands on	Act 4:3
sergeant	ܐܚܝܕ ܚܒܘܫܝܐ	holder of the captives	Act 16:35
show-bread	ܠܚܡ ܐ̈ܦܐ	bread of the face	Heb 9:2
soldier	ܦܠܚܐ ܕܩܪܒܐ	worker of warfare	Luk 3:14

16

INTRODUCTION

Idiom Chart			
English	**Aramaic**	**Literal Translation**	**Scripture Example**
sown fields	ܒܝܬ ܙܪܥܐ	house of seeds	Luk 6:1
steward	ܪܒ ܒܝܬܐ	head of the house	Mat 20:8
stewardship	ܪܒ ܒܝܬܘܬܐ	head of the household	Luk 16:2
storehouse	ܒܝܬ ܩܦܣܐ	house of collection (or storage)	Luk 12:18
suddenly	ܡܢ ܫܠܝܐ	from quiet	Mar 9:8
tetrarch	ܪܝܫܐ ܕܪܒܝܥܘܬܐ	ruler of fourth part	Luk 3:1
thanksgiving	ܩܘܒܠ ܛܝܒܘܬܐ	acceptance of a kindness	Rev 4:9
they did not have	ܠܝܬ ܗܘܐ ܠܗܘܢ	it was not to them	Luk 1:7
they have nothing	ܠܝܬ ܠܗܘܢ ܡܕܡ	there is not to them anything	Luk 12:4
this very day	ܝܘܡܐ ܕܝܘܡܢܐ	day of this day	Act 20:26
together	ܡܢ ܚܕ	from one	Jam 2:10
tomb	ܒܝܬ ܩܒܘܪܐ	house of the grave	Mat 8:28
treasury	ܒܝܬ ܩܘܪܒܢܐ	house of offerings	Mat 27:6
treasury (2)	ܒܝܬ ܓܙܐ	house of treasure	Luk 21:1
two by two, in pairs	ܬܪܝܢ ܬܪܝܢ	two two	Luk 9:1
two-edged	ܬܪܝܢ ܦܘܡܝܗ	of two mouths	Heb 4:12
until	ܐܠܐ ܐܢ ܠܐ	but if what	Mar 9:9
until now, still	ܥܕܡܐ ܠܗܫܐ	up to now	Mar 8:17
very diseased	ܒܝܫܐܝܬ ܐܬܚܫܡ	evilly afflicted or done	Mat 8:16
very nearly	ܩܠܝܠ ܩܕܡ	by a little before	Act 26:28
very sick, ill, afflicted	ܒܝܫ ܒܝܫ ܥܒܝܕܝܢ	evilly done	Mat 4:24
we have	ܐܝܬ ܠܢ	there is to us	Mat 3:9
what does it appear to you	ܡܢܐ ܡܬܚܙܐ ܠܟ	how seems it to you	Mat 17:25

17

INTRODUCTION

<table>
<tr><th colspan="4">Idiom Chart</th></tr>
<tr><th>English</th><th>Aramaic</th><th>Literal Translation</th><th>Scripture Example</th></tr>
<tr><td>what have we to do with you, what do we have in common</td><td>ܡܢ ܠܢ ܘܠܟ</td><td>what to us and to you</td><td>Mat 8:29</td></tr>
<tr><td>whatever, whomever</td><td>ܟܠ ܡܐ</td><td>all what, all something</td><td>Mat 17:12</td></tr>
<tr><td>whoever</td><td>ܟܠ ܡܢ</td><td>all who</td><td>Mat 5:19</td></tr>
<tr><td>with various tongues, with various languages</td><td>ܒܠܫܢ ܠܫܢ</td><td>with tongues tongues</td><td>Act 10:46</td></tr>
<tr><td>yokefellow</td><td>ܒܪ ܙܘܓܝ</td><td>son of my yoke</td><td>Phi 4:7</td></tr>
<tr><td>you will have</td><td>ܬܗܘܐ ܠܟ</td><td>it will be to you</td><td>Luk 1:14</td></tr>
</table>

Footnote Abbreviations

Var: variant reading
OS (Aph): Aphraat, from *Patrologia Syriaca*
OS (LG): Liber Graduum
OS (Efr): St. Ephrem of Syria
OS (c): Curetonian manuscript of gospels
OS (s): Sinaitic manuscript of gospels
H: Harklean Version
Pal Syr: Palestinian Syriac
Pal Lex: Palestinian Lectionary
W: edition of Peshitta by B. Walton, 1657
S: edition of Peshitta by C. Schaaf, 1709
L: edition of the Peshitta by S. Lee, 1816
M: Mosul 1898 text of the Peshitta
Mr: Mosul 1891 text of Revelation (from the New Covenant text)
P: Peshitta manuscript
Fig: Figure of speech
Culture: regarding orientalisms or customs that help to explain the verse
Lit: Literal translation

INTRODUCTION

Grammar Notes

The following is a list of more common grammatical constructions that will explain some other phrases that are noted either in the footnotes or by use of a certain font type.

1. Enclitic verbs: Use of ܗܘܐ plus verb communicates the present tense or a participle, e.g. "he was saying." These are so common that they are not particularly noted.
2. Proleptic Pronoun: Repetition of pronoun with the verb, marks change in address or noun. This change is noted and marked with **bold type**.
3. Noun put in apposition: this is translated in common English. An example is *all the people,* literally, "the people, all of them." These are not particularly noted, except in the interlinear.
4. Repetition of noun: denotes diversity or multitude, also can be distributive. Matthew 20:9, ܕܝܢܪ ܕܝܢܪ, denar, denar, means *each a denarius.* This construction is marked in the footnotes or on the idiom chart.
5. Conjunction not expressed, but understood: shows asyndeton, e.g.: *went [and] gave.* This is noted in outline type.
6. *Truly I say to you*: a very solemn phrase used by Jesus in the Gospels to take special note of what follows. It is the figure of speech, asterism, and is marked with an * preceding the phrase. This phrase is also set off by a comma to indicate that the following phrase is like direct speech.
7. Interrogative *lema* ܠܡܐ is not translated, because it introduces a question, most often implying a negative answer or doubt. It is marked in the interlinear as <?> and marked in the footnotes under the figure of speech, erotesis.
8. Conjunction *deyn* ܕܝܢ is always translated *and, but* or *now.*
9. When the accusative is missing, most often after verbs, e. g. *to hear [it], to see [it],* the implied object is put in brackets to show the addition and highlighted in outline type.

19

ARAMAIC PESHITTA NEW TESTAMENT
MATTHEW

Chapter 1

1   The book of the genealogy[1] of Jesus Christ, the son of David, the son of Abraham;

2   Abraham fathered Isaac, Isaac fathered Jacob, Jacob fathered Judah and his brothers,

3   Judah fathered Perez and Zerah by Tamar. Perez fathered Hezron, Hezron fathered Aram,

4   Aram fathered Aminadab, Aminadab fathered Nahshon, Nahshon fathered Salmon,

5   Salmon fathered Boaz by Rahab, Boaz fathered Obed by Ruth, Obed fathered Jesse, [and]

6   Jesse fathered David the king. David fathered Solomon by the wife of Uriah,

7   Solomon fathered Rehoboam, Rehoboam fathered Abijah, Abijah fathered Asa,

8   Asa fathered Jehoshaphat, Jehoshaphat fathered Joram, Joram fathered Uzziah,[2]

9   Uzziah fathered Jotham, Jotham fathered Ahaz, Ahaz fathered Hezekiah,

10 Hezekiah fathered Manasseh, Manasseh fathered Amon, Amon fathered Josiah,

11 Josiah fathered Jechoniah and his brothers in the captivity of Babylon.

12 And after the captivity of Babylon, Jechoniah fathered Shealtiel,[3] Shealtiel fathered Zerubbabel,

13 Zerubbabel fathered Abiud,[4] Abiud fathered Eliakim, Eliakim fathered Azor,

---

[1] Or "nativity," from root verb, to give birth, father; repeat *fathered*, vs. 2-16

[2] Three generations are missing between Joram and Uzziah, the sons of Athaliah, Ahab's daughter, who were wiped out of the genealogy to the 3rd generation (Exodus 20:5) because of her evil deeds – Ahaziah, Joash (Jehoash) and Amaziah. OS (c): these three are added back in the text.

[3] Jechoniah (also known as Jehoiachin) was actually the grandson of Josiah and only reigned for three months. Josiah's sons were Shallum (Jehoahaz), Eliakim (Jehoiakim), and Mattaniah (Zedekiah), each reigning during the Babylonian captivity. Zedekiah was the last king to reign. See clear explanation in Thiele, *A Chronology of the Hebrew Kings*, pp. 65-72.

[4] Additional name in genealogy in Heb. Dutillet MS, Abior. OS (cs): 'Abior' for *Abiud.*

21

ARAMAIC PESHITTA NEW TESTAMENT
MATTHEW

Chapter 1

14 Azor fathered Sadoc, Sadoc fathered Achim, Achim fathered Eliud,

15 Eliud fathered Eleazer, Eleazer fathered Matthan, Matthan fathered Jacob,

16 Jacob fathered Joseph, the husband of Mary, from whom Jesus, who was called the MESSIAH, was born.[1]

17 Therefore, all the generations from Abraham until David, [e][were] fourteen generations, and from David until the captivity of Babylon, fourteen generations, and from the captivity of Babylon until the MESSIAH, fourteen generations.

18 Now the birth of Jesus Christ was like this: when Mary his mother was engaged[2] to Joseph, before they were joined in marriage, she was found [to be] pregnant from the Holy Spirit.

19 But Joseph her husband was upright and was not willing to disgrace her and he was thinking that he would dismiss her privately.

20 But while he was considering these [things], an angel of the LORD appeared to him in a dream and said to him, "Joseph, son of David, do not be afraid to take Mary your wife, for he that is fathered in her [is] from the Holy Spirit.

21 And she will give birth to a son and she will call his name Jesus,[3] for he will give life to his people from their sins."

22 Now all this that happened [was] that it would be fulfilled what was spoken from the LORD by way of the prophet:[4]

23 ***BEHOLD, A VIRGIN WILL CONCEIVE AND WILL GIVE BIRTH TO A SON AND THEY WILL CALL HIS NAME EMMANUEL, WHICH IS INTERPRETED, OUR GOD [IS] WITH US.**

24 And when Joseph rose up from his sleep, he did as the angel of the LORD had commanded him and he took his wife.

---

[1] *Messiah* is the English rendering of **mashikha** ܡܫܝܚܐ in Aramaic and is derived from root verb meaning to anoint. Old Syriac has two variant readings for this verse, OS (c): 'Joseph, to whom was espoused Mary, the Virgin, she who bare Jesus the Messiah.' See Wilson, p. 6 and Lewis, *Light on the Four Gospels*, p. 37.

[2] Root verb is **makar** ܡܟܪ, meaning to purchase, acquire for a price, hence to be engaged.

[3] OS (s): 'you will call,' OS (c): 'his name shall be called'

[4] OS (cs): add 'Isaiah'

ARAMAIC PESHITTA NEW TESTAMENT
MATTHEW

Chapter 1
25   And he did not know her[1] until she had given birth to her firstborn son. And she called his name Jesus.

Chapter 2
1   Now when Jesus was born in Bethlehem[2] of Judea in the days of Herod the king, MAGI[3] came from the east to Jerusalem
2   and said, "Where is the king of the Judeans who was born? For we have seen his star in the east[4] and we have come to worship him."
3   And Herod the king heard and was troubled and all [m]Jerusalem with him.
4   And he gathered all of the chief priests and scribes of the people and was asking them where the MESSIAH was [to be] born.
5   And **they** said, "In Bethlehem of Judea," for so it is written in the prophet:
6   YOU **ALSO, BETHLEHEM OF JUDEA,** [t]**YOU WILL NOT BE THE LEAST AMONG THE KINGS OF JUDEA, FOR FROM YOU WILL GO OUT A KING WHO WILL SHEPHERD[5] MY PEOPLE ISRAEL.**
7   Then Herod secretly called the MAGI and learned from them at what time the star appeared to them.
8   And he sent them to Bethlehem and said to them, "Go, search for the boy diligently and when you have found him, come, inform me that I may also go [and] worship him."
9   And when they had heard from the king, they went away and *behold, the star that they had seen in the east went before them, until it came [and] stood over[6] where the boy was.
10   And when they saw the star, they rejoiced [with] very great joy.
11   And they entered the house and they saw the boy with Mary his mother and they fell down [and] worshipped him and they opened their treasures and offered him gifts, gold [P]and myrrh and incense.┐ ✓

---

[1] Culture: *know* is to know intimately. OS (s): adds 'and he was purely dwelling with her until...'
[2] Lit: house of bread
[3] The English word *Magi* is from Aramaic, **magoshey** ܡܓܘܫܐ. These men were learned astronomers from the Persian Empire, Edersheim, *Life and Times of Jesus the Messiah*, Book II, pp. 202-203.
[4] OS (s): 'from the east'
[5] Or "rule"
[6] OS (c): 'above the place *where...*'

ARAMAIC PESHITTA NEW TESTAMENT
MATTHEW

Chapter 2

12 And it was shown to them in a dream that they should not return to Herod and by another way, they went to their country.

13 And when they had gone, an angel of the LORD appeared in a dream to Joseph and said to him, "Get up. Lead the child and his mother and flee to Egypt and stay there until I tell you, for Herod is going to seek for the child in order to destroy him."

14 Now Joseph rose up, took up the child and his mother in the night, and fled to Egypt.

15 And he remained there until the death of Herod, so that it would be fulfilled what was spoken from the LORD by the prophet[1] who said: **FROM EGYPT I HAVE CALLED MY SON.**

16 Then Herod, when he saw that he was mocked by the MAGI, was very angry and sent [and] killed all the boys of Bethlehem and of all its borders from two years old and under, according to the time that he had investigated from the MAGI.

17 Then was fulfilled what was spoken by way of Jeremiah the prophet, who said:

18 **A VOICE WAS HEARD IN RAMA, CRYING AND GREAT MOURNING, RACHEL CRYING FOR HER SONS AND NOT WANTING TO BE COMFORTED, BECAUSE THEY WERE NOT.**

19 Now when Herod the king died, an angel of the LORD appeared in a dream[2] to Joseph in Egypt.

20 And he said to him, "Get up. Lead the child and his mother and go to the land of Israel, for those who were seeking the life of the child have died."

21 And Joseph rose up [and] led the child and his mother and came to the land of Israel.

22 But when he heard that Archelaus was king in Judah in place of Herod his father, he was afraid to go there and it was shown to him in a dream that he should go to the land of Galilee.

23 And he came [and] lived in the city that is called Nazareth, so that it would be fulfilled what was spoken by the prophet: "He will be called a Nazarene."[3]

---

[1] OS (s): 'by the mouth of the prophet Isaiah'

[2] OS (s): omit *in a dream*

[3] Nazarene may be derived from **nzr** ܢܨܪ – branch, or may refer to the sect of John the Baptist, Black, pp. 197-200.

ARAMAIC PESHITTA NEW TESTAMENT
MATTHEW

Chapter 3

1   Now in those days John the baptizer came and was preaching in the desert of Judea.

2   And he said, "Repent. The kingdom of [m]heaven[1] is near."

3   For this is he about whom it was said by way of Isaiah the prophet: **THE VOICE OF ONE CRYING IN THE DESERT: PREPARE THE WAY OF THE** LORD **AND MAKE STRAIGHT HIS PATHS.**

4   Now [this] **John**, his clothes were of the hair of camels and a girdle[2] of skin [was] on his loins and his food [was] locusts and honey of the desert.[3]

5   Then [m]Jerusalem went out to him and all [m]Judea and all the [m]region that was around the Jordan.

6   And they were baptized by him in the Jordan River when they confessed their sins.

7   And when he saw many from the Pharisees and from the Sadducees who came to be baptized, he said to them, "[j]Generation of [h]vipers! Who has informed you to flee from the [m]wrath that will come?[4]

8   Produce, therefore, the [m]fruits that are proper for repentance.

9   And do not think or say within yourselves that we have Abraham [e][as a] father, for *I say to you, God is able from these stones to raise up sons to Abraham.

10   [al]Now *behold, the ax is placed on the root of the trees. Therefore, every tree that does not bear good fruit will be cut down and thrown into the fire. ⌐

11   [al]I baptize you with water for repentance, but **he** who comes after me is stronger than I [am], **whose** sandals I am not worthy to carry. **He** will baptize you with the Holy Spirit and with [m]fire,[5]

12   **he** whose winnowing fan [is] in his hand and he will cleanse his threshing floors. And he will gather the wheat to his granaries, and he will burn the chaff in a fire that does not go out."[6]⌐

---

[1] Fig: metonymy, *heaven* stands for God. Used often in the gospel of Matthew.

[2] Lit: holder of loins

[3] OS (s): 'honey of the mountain' is wild honey

[4] Fig: erotesis, obvious answer "no one". Culture: this viper as a black scorpion. When the scorpion is conceived, the father dies and when the viper is born, it eats its way out of the side of the mother, causing her death. Thus, here John is calling the Pharisees spiritual orphans, Lamsa, *Gospel Light*, p. 16.

[5] Repeat *with* (not hendiadys)

[6] Repeat *he will* 3x, same beginning sound – Pael & Aphel active participles

ARAMAIC PESHITTA NEW TESTAMENT
MATTHEW

Chapter 3

13 Then Jesus came from Galilee to the Jordan to John to be baptized by him.

14 But **John** restrained him and said, "**I** need to be baptized by you and are **you** coming to me?"

15 But **Jesus** answered and said to him, "Allow [it] now, for so it is proper for us to fulfill all uprightness." And then he allowed him ᵉ[to baptize him].

16 And when Jesus was baptized, immediately he came out of the water and heaven was opened to him and he saw the Spirit of God that was descending ˢas a dove and it came on him.

17 And *behold, [there was] a voice from ᵐheaven that said, "This is my beloved Son in whom I am pleased."

Chapter 4

1 Then Jesus was led by the Holy Spirit to the wilderness to be tempted by the ACCUSER.¹

2 And he fasted forty days and forty nights and afterwards he was hungry.

3 And **he** who was tempting came near and said to him, "If you are the Son of God, say that these stones should become bread."

4 But **he** answered and said, "It is written: MAN **DOES NOT LIVE BY BREAD ALONE, BUT BY EVERY WORD THAT COMES OUT OF THE ᶜMOUTH OF GOD.**"

5 Then the ACCUSER led him to the holy city and placed him on the outer edge of the temple.

6 And he said to him, "If you are the Son of God, throw yourself down, for it is written: **HE WILL COMMAND HIS ANGELS CONCERNING YOU,** and **ON THEIR HANDS THEY WILL BEAR YOU UP, SO THAT YOU SHOULD NOT STRIKE YOUR FOOT ON A STONE.**"

7 Jesus said to him, "Again it is written: **YOU SHOULD NOT TEMPT THE LORD YOUR GOD.**"

8 Again, the ACCUSER² took him to a mountain that was very high. And he showed him all the kingdoms of the world and their glory.

---

¹ *Accuser* is the name for Devil, lit: "eater of bread." Bread was pulled to pieces, hence the meaning, accusation or biting words. Also can be translated "devourer." OS (c): 'Satan'

² OS (s): 'Satan'

26

ARAMAIC PESHITTA NEW TESTAMENT
MATTHEW

Chapter 4

9   And he said to him, "All these ^e[kingdoms] I will give to you if you will fall down [and] worship me."

10   Then Jesus said to him, "Go, SATAN![1] For it is written: **YOU SHOULD WORSHIP THE** LORD **YOUR GOD AND FOR HIM ALONE YOU SHOULD WORK**."

11   Then the ACCUSER[2] left him and *behold, angels came near and ministered to him.

12   Now when Jesus heard that John had been delivered up, he went away to Galilee.

13   And he left Nazareth and came [and] lived in Capernaum by the shore of the sea in the territory of Zebulun and of Naphtali,

14   that it would be fulfilled what was spoken by way of Isaiah the prophet who said:

15   **THE LAND OF ZEBULUN, THE LAND OF NAPHTALI, THE WAY OF THE SEA, THE CROSSINGS OF THE JORDAN, GALILEE OF THE GENTILES,**

16   **THE PEOPLE WHO SIT IN DARKNESS HAVE SEEN A GREAT LIGHT AND A LIGHT HAS ^hDAWNED TO THEM WHO SIT IN THE ^{he}LAND[3] AND THE SHADOWS OF DEATH.**

17   From then [on], Jesus began to preach and to say, "Repent, for the kingdom of ^mheaven is near."

18   And while he was walking along the shore of the Sea of Galilee, he saw two brothers, Simon who was called Peter and Andrew his brother, who were casting nets into the sea, for they were fishermen.

19   And Jesus said to them, "Follow me and I will make you to be fishermen of men."[4]

20   And **they** immediately left their nets and went after him.

21   And when he crossed over from there he saw two other brothers, James, the son of Zebedee, and John, his brother, in a ship with Zebedee, their father, who were mending their nets and he called them.[5]

---

[1] *Satan* is a transcription of the Heb. word **shatan** and means lit: an opponent, adversary. Derived from root verb, **sata** ܣܛܐ, to go aside, turn away, Jennings, p. 150.

[2] OS (s): 'tempter'

[3] OS (s): for *sit in the land,* 'sitting in mourning or sadness'; fig: hendiadys, *land and shadows,* "dark regions"

[4] Culture: Talmudic expression (Maimonides, *Torah,* cap. I) meaning a fisher of the law. See further explanation, Bullinger, *Companion Bible,* p. 1315.

[5] Eastern txt: for *he called them,* 'Jesus called them'

ARAMAIC PESHITTA NEW TESTAMENT
MATTHEW

Chapter 4

22 And immediately **they** left the ship and their father[1] and they went after him.

23 And Jesus traveled around in all Galilee [P]and taught in their synagogues and preached the gospel of the kingdom and cured every disease and sickness among the people.⌐

24 And his fame was heard in all Syria[2] and they brought to him all those who were very sick with various diseases [P]and those who were oppressed with severe pains and possessed [ones] and [those] who were insane and paralyzed [ones] and he healed them.⌐ [3]

25 And large crowds followed him from Galilee and from the Decapolis and from Jerusalem and from Judea and from[4] beyond the Jordan.

Chapter 5

1 And when Jesus saw the crowd, he climbed a mountain and when he sat down, his disciples came near to him.

2 And he opened his mouth and was teaching them and said,

3 "Blessed [are][5] the poor in spirit,[6] because **theirs** is the kingdom of [m]heaven.

4 Blessed [are] the mourners, because **they** will be comforted.

5 Blessed [are] the meek, because **they** will inherit the earth.

6 Blessed [are] those who hunger and thirst for uprightness,[7] because **they** will be satisfied.

7 Blessed [are] the merciful, because on them will be mercies.

8 Blessed [are] those who are pure in their heart[s], because they will see God.

9 Blessed [are] the peacemakers,[8] because they will be called the sons of God.

---

[1] OS (c): 'nets'

[2] OS (s): omit *and his fame was heard in all Syria*

[3] OS (cs): add 'and on each one he was laying his hand and healed them all.'

[4] Repeat *and from,* emphasis on the distance people came to see Jesus.

[5] Repeat beginning phrase vs. 1-10, *Blessed are,* lit: Blessed [are] they

[6] *In spirit* is construct form of word, can be translated spiritually.

[7] *Uprightness* is the word used throughout this translation for **canutha** ܟܐܢܘܬܐ, righteousness, to distinguish it from **zadikutha** ܙܕܝܩܘܬܐ, justification.

[8] Lit: servers of peace

ARAMAIC PESHITTA NEW TESTAMENT
MATTHEW

Chapter 5

10 Blessed [are] those who are persecuted because of uprightness, because theirs is the kingdom of ^mheaven.

11 You are blessed when they curse you and persecute you and say every evil word against you falsely because of me.

12 Then rejoice and be glad, because your reward is great in heaven, for so they persecuted the prophets who [were] before you.

13 ^{me}**You** are the salt of the earth, but if the salt should go flat, with what will it be salted? It is not fit for anything, but to be thrown outside and to be trampled on by man.

14 ^{me}**You** are the light of the world. It is not possible to hide a city that is built on a mountain.

15 ^{al}And they do not light a lamp and place it under a basket, but on a lampstand and it lights all those who are in the house.

16 Likewise, your light should shine before men, so that they will see your good works and will glorify your Father who is in heaven.⌐

17 Do not think that I have come to change[1] the law or the prophets. I have not come to change, but to fulfill [them].

18 For *truly I say to you,[2] until heaven and earth pass away, not one jot or one stroke[3] will pass from the law until everything happens.

19 Therefore, whoever[4] changes one ^e[jot] of these small commandments ^{pa}(and will teach so to men) will be called little in the kingdom of ^mheaven. But all who will do and teach this ^e[law] will be called great in the kingdom of ^mheaven.

20 For *I say to you, unless your uprightness exceeds [that] of the scribes and Pharisees, you will not enter the kingdom of ^mheaven.

---

[1] *Change*, vs. 17, 19, lit: to loosen, untie, break down, disannul, Jennings, p. 230.

[2] Repeat phrase (*truly*) *I say to you*, vs. 18, 20, 22, 26, 28, 32, and 34. This fig: asterismos is a solemn expression that means to take note and pay attention to what is following. In the translation it is marked with *.

[3] *Jot* is the smallest letter in the alphabet, a **yod**. A *stroke* is a mark on the top of a Hebrew letter similar to a serif in English type, Bullinger, *Figures of Speech*, p. 678.

[4] Eastern txt: *whoever* as one word -- ܟܠܡܢ

ARAMAIC PESHITTA NEW TESTAMENT
MATTHEW

Chapter 5

21 You have heard that it was said to the ancient [ones][1]: **YOU SHOULD NOT KILL.** And **ANYONE WHO KILLS IS CONDEMNED TO JUDGMENT.**

22 But *I say to you, whoever provokes his brother to anger without cause is condemned to judgment. And anyone who says to his brother, '[I] spit [on you]!'[2] is condemned to the assembly. And he, who says, 'Fool,' is condemned to the ^an^GEHENNA[3] of fire.

23 If, therefore, you offer your offering[4] on the altar and there you remember that your brother holds a certain grudge against you,

24 leave your offering there before[5] the altar and first go, be reconciled with your brother and then come, offer your offering.

25 Reconcile with your opponent at law[6] quickly while you [are] with him on the journey, so that your opponent at law will not deliver you to the judge and the judge deliver you to the officer and you fall [into] prison.

26 And *truly I say to you, you will not come out from there until you give back the last coin.[7]

27 You have heard that it was said: **YOU SHOULD NOT COMMIT ADULTERY.**

28 But *I say to you, anyone who looks at a woman as desiring her immediately commits adultery with her in his heart.

29 Now if your right ^m^eye causes you to offend,[8] tear it out and throw it from you. For it is better for you that one of your members should be lost and not [that] your whole body should fall into GEHENNA.

---

[1] Lit: those before you

[2] **Raca** is term of disgust, lit: "Spit!" See Lamsa, *Gospel Light*, pp. 60-61, also, Wilson, p. 38.

[3] *Gehenna* is an English rendering of the Heb. word **Hinnom.** Originally the name of a gorge SE of Jerusalem, which was a place of sacrifice to Molech and then became a place where refuse and trash was burned. It is a real place that is the picture of the lake of fire in the end times, Jennings, p. 47.

[4] Same root: *offer, offering*, vs. 23, 24.

[5] Eastern txt: 'on'; OS (c): 'before,' OS (s): 'on'

[6] Lit: master of your judgment

[7] *Coin* is a **shamuna,** a small copper coin, often called "mite." See Mk 12:42 and Appendix 2.

[8] Culture: "If you have a habit of envying, cut it out, stop it." The eye is the symbol of desire and envy. The hand is the agent of what the person does, Lamsa, *Idioms in the Bible Explained*, p. 51.

Chapter 5

30 And if your right hand causes you to offend, cut [it] off [and] throw it from you. For it is better for you that one of your members should be lost and not [that] your whole body should fall into GEHENNA.[1]

31 It was said: **HE WHO DISMISSES HIS WIFE MUST GIVE HER A WRITING OF DIVORCE.**

32 But *I say to you, anyone who dismisses his wife outside of the case of fornication makes her commit adultery and he who marries a dismissed woman[2] commits adultery.

33 Again, you have heard that it was said of the ancient [ones]: **DO NOT BE FALSE IN YOUR OATH, BUT COMPLETE YOUR OATH TO THE** LORD.

34 But *I say to you, you should not swear at all, neither by heaven, [me]which is the throne of God,

35 nor by earth, [me]which is the footstool that is under his feet, not even by Jerusalem, which is the city of the great king.

36 You should not even swear by your head, because you are not able to make one separate hair [either] black or white.

37 But your word should be yes, yes, and no, no.[3] Anything that is apart from these [things] abounds from evil.[4]

38 You have heard that it was said: **EYE FOR EYE AND TOOTH FOR TOOTH.**

39 But *I say to you, you should not oppose an evil [one], but he who strikes you on your right cheek, turn to him the other also.[5]

40 And he who wants to go to court with you and to take your coat, give him your cloak also.

41 He who compels you [to go] one mile, go with him two.

42 Whoever asks you, give to him. And he who wants to borrow from you, you should not refuse him.

43 You have heard that it was said: **LOVE YOUR NEIGHBOR AND HATE YOUR ENEMY.**

---

[1] Repeat whole phrase, *one of your members…Gehenna*, vs. 29, 30.

[2] Culture: *A dismissed woman* is one who is forsaken, but not given a writing of divorce. In our culture, this would be equivalent to not being legally divorced.

[3] Fig: epizeuxis, means to consider your words carefully, solemn repetition.

[4] Or the Evil [one]

[5] Fig: hyperbole, means you should not to be contentious or hard in insisting on your rights, Neil, *Palestine Life*, p. 202; also, vs. 40-42.

ARAMAIC PESHITTA NEW TESTAMENT
MATTHEW

Chapter 5

44   But *I say to you, love your enemies ᴾand bless those who curse you and do that which is pleasing to him who hates you and pray for those who take you by force and persecute you,⌐

45   so that you may be the sons of your Father who is in heaven, who causes his sun to rise on the good and on the bad and causes his rain to come down on the upright and on the wicked.[1]

46   For if you love those who love you, what is the reward for you? *Behold, [do] not even the tax collectors do the same?[2]

47   And if you greet only your brothers, what extraordinary [thing] are you doing? *Behold, [do] not even the tax collectors do this?

48   Therefore, be made perfect, as your Father who is in heaven is perfect.'[3]

Chapter 6

1   And take heed with regard to your almsgiving that you should not do it before men, so that you may be seen by them, otherwise[4] you [will] not have a reward from your Father who is in heaven.

2   Therefore, whenever you do almsgiving, do not ʰsound a trumpet[5] before you as the hypocrites do in the synagogues and in the marketplaces, so that they may be praised by men. And *truly I say to you, they have received their reward.[6]

3   But when **you** do almsgiving, you should not let your ᵖᵉleft hand know what your right hand does,

4   so that your almsgiving may be in secret and your Father, who sees in secret, shall repay you openly.

5   And when you pray, you should not be as the hypocrites, who love to stand in the synagogues and on the corners of the marketplaces to pray, to be seen by men. And *truly I say to you, they have received their reward.[7]

---

[1] Parallel structure: *good and bad, upright and wicked*, ABAB

[2] Fig: erotesis, obvious answer "yes," repeat as refrain in v. 47.

[3] Repeat *perfect*, Aram. **gamir** ܓܡܝܪ means *perfect* in the sense of full-grown, mature or complete,.

[4] Eastern txt: *otherwise* is two words, ܘܐܢ ܠܐ, lit: "and if not"

[5] Fig: hypocatastasis, *sound a trumpet* is put for being ostentatious, as heralds making a public announcement, Freeman, p. 339.

[6] Repeat *And truly I say to you, they have received their reward*, vs. 5, 16, as refrain.

[7] OS (s): omit whole verse

32

6   But when **you** pray, enter your room and close your door and pray to your Father, who is in secret, and your Father, who sees in secret, [1] will repay you openly.

7   And when you are praying, you should not talk idly as the heathens[2] [do], for they think that they are heard by much speaking.

8   Therefore, do not imitate them, for your Father knows what is needed by you before you ask him.

9   Therefore pray like this: 'Our Father, who is in heaven, may your name be holy.

10 May your kingdom come. May your will occur, as in heaven, also on earth.

11 Give us the [m]bread of our need today[3]

12 and forgive us our debts, as also we have forgiven our debtors.[4]

13 And do not let us enter into trial, but deliver us from the Evil [one], because the kingdom and the power and the glory is yours, forever and ever.'[5]

14 For if you forgive men their offenses, your Father who is in heaven will also forgive you,

15 but if you do not forgive men, your Father will also not forgive you your offenses.

16 Now when you fast, you should not be sad as the hypocrites, for they distort their faces so that they may be seen by men that they are fasting. And *truly I say to you, they have received their reward.

17 But when you fast, wash your face and anoint your head,

18 so that [e][the fact that] you are fasting may not be seen by men, but by your Father who is in secret. And your Father, who sees in secret, will reward you.

---

[1] Repeat *in secret*, vs. 4-6, 18.

[2] OS (s): 'saying useless things as the heathens,' OS (c): 'babbling as the hypocrites'

[3] Lit: day by day

[4] Repeat *forgive*, vs. 12-15; The word for *debt* can mean debt or sin, cf. Luke 11:4, Black, p. 140.

[5] Lit: to the age of the ages; fig: hendiatris, *kingdom and the power and the glory*, meaning, "powerful glorious kingdom"

Chapter 6

19 ^{al}You should not place for yourself treasures on earth, where moth and rust corrupt and where thieves break in and steal.

20 But place for yourself treasures in heaven, where neither moth nor rust corrupt and where thieves do not break in and do not steal.

21 For where your treasure is, there is also your heart.⌐

22 ^{al}The ^{me}lamp of the body is the eye. Therefore, if your eye will be simple, your whole body also is enlightened.

23 But if your eye will be evil,[1] your whole body will be dark. If then the light that is in you is darkness, how great will be your darkness.⌐

24 No man is able to serve two lords. For either he will hate the one and will love the other or he will honor the one and will treat the other with contempt. You are not able to serve God and wealth.[2]

25 Because of this, *I say to you, you should not be worried about your life, what you will eat and what you will drink and not about your body, what you will wear. *Behold, is not life more than food and the body [more] than clothing?[3]

26 Look at the birds in the sky that do not sow nor[4] reap nor gather into storehouses, yet your Father who is in heaven feeds them. *Behold, are not **you** more important than they?

27 And who among you, while worrying, is able to add one cubit to his height?

28 And why are you worried about clothes? Consider the lilies of the field, how they grow without toil and without spinning.

29 But *I say to you, not even Solomon in all his glory was clothed like one of these.

30 Now if God so clothes the grass of the field that today is and tomorrow falls into the oven, [will he] not much more ^e[clothe] you, oh little of faith?

---

[1] Culture: *simple* is to be generous, *evil eye* is greedy, Bivin, pp. 144-145.

[2] *Wealth* is the meaning of the word mammon, which is an English rendering of Heb. and Aram. words, wrongly spelled with 2 'm's and means, accumulation of riches and substance, Black, p. 139, Jennings, p. 125.

[3] Fig: erotesis, vs. 25, 26, 27, 28 and 30. These questions are designed to cause us to ponder the truth of the teaching.

[4] Repeat *nor*, lit: and not

Chapter 6

31 Therefore, do not be worried or say, 'What will we eat?' or, 'What will we drink?' or, 'What will we wear?'

32 For the nations of the world seek all these [things]. And your Father who is in heaven knows that even all these [things] are needed[1] by you.

33 But seek first the kingdom of God and his justification and all these [things] will be added to you.

34 Therefore, do not be worried about tomorrow, for tomorrow will care for itself. Sufficient for the [sy]day is its [own] evil.

Chapter 7

1 You should not judge, so that you will not be judged.

2 For with the judgment that you judge, you will be judged and by the measure that you measure, it will be measured to you.[2]

3 [al]And why do you see the straw that is in the eye of your brother and you do not observe the beam that is in your eye? [3]

4 Or how do you say to your brother, 'Allow [me] to take out the straw from your eye,' and *behold, a beam [is] in your eye?

5 [i]Hypocrite! First take out the beam from your eye and then you will be proved capable to take out the straw from the eye of your brother.⌐

6 You should not give a holy [thing] to dogs and you should not throw your pearls before pigs, so that they will not trample them with their feet and turn [and] attack you.[4]

7 Ask and it will be given to you. Seek and you will find. Knock and it will be opened to you.[5]

8 For everyone who asks will receive and he who seeks will find and to him who knocks, it will be opened to him.

9 Or what man among you, whose son asks him for bread, will hold out a stone to him? [6]

10 And if he asks him for a fish, will he hold out a snake to him?

---

[1] Same root: *needed, seek,* vs. 32, 33

[2] Repeat forms of *judge* and *measure*

[3] Fig: erotesis – question to ponder, also vs. 4, 9, 10, 11.

[4] Fig: proverb or maxim. Alternate interpretation of *give a holy thing* is to hang earrings, Black, pp. 200-202. Structure of verse is ABBA.

[5] Fig: climax, progression of actions.

[6] Culture: flat loaf of bread looks very similar to a stone; series of fig: erotesis – questions to ponder, vs. 9-11.

Chapter 7

11 And if therefore **you** who are evil know to give good gifts to your sons, how much more will your Father who is in heaven give good [e][gifts] to those who ask him?[1]

12 All that you desire that men should do to you, so also do to them, for this is the law and the prophets.

13 [al]Enter by the straight door because wide is the door and broad [is] the road[2] that leads to loss and many are those who go in it.

14 How narrow the door and straight the road[3] that leads to life and few are those who find it.⌐

15 Beware of false prophets, who come to you in the clothing of lambs,[4] but within are savage [h]wolves.

16 [al]Now by their [m]fruit you will know them. Do they pick grapes from thorns or figs from thistles?[5]

17 So every healthy tree bears beautiful fruit, but a diseased tree bears diseased fruit.

18 A healthy tree is not able to bear diseased fruit and a diseased tree [is not able] to bear healthy fruit.[6]

19 Every tree that does not bear healthy fruit is cut down and thrown into the fire.

20 So then, by their [m]fruit you will know them.⌐ [7]

21 Not all who say to me, 'My Lord, my Lord,' will enter the kingdom of [m]heaven, but he who does the will of my Father who is in heaven.

22 Many will say to me in that [sy]day, 'My Lord, my Lord, in your name[8] have we not prophesied [P]and in your name cast out demons and in your name done many miracles?'⌐

23 And then I will confess to them, 'I have never known you. Go away from me, workers of wickedness.'

24 [al]Therefore, everyone, who hears these words of mine and does them, will be compared to a wise man who built his house on a rock.

---

[1] Fig: erotesis, **kema** question, answer in the affirmative

[2] Word play: *broad,* **awraykha** ܐܘܪܝܟܐ *road,* **awurkha** ܐܘܪܚܐ

[3] Fig: antithetic parallelism: *wide and narrow, broad and straight. Straight* can be translated "constricted, enclosed."

[4] Culture: wearing a sheepskin garment was the distinctive outward mark of a prophet, cf. Zech. 13:4, II Kings 1:8.

[5] Fig: erotesis, obvious answer "no", also vs. 10, 16

[6] Parallel structure: *healthy and diseased,* lit: good and bad, ABBA

[7] Repeat *by their fruit you will know them* from v. 16, encircling the passage

[8] Repeat *in your name*

ARAMAIC PESHITTA NEW TESTAMENT
MATTHEW

Chapter 7

25 ^{P}And the rain fell and the floods came and the winds blew and they beat against the house[1] but it did not fail, for its foundations were set on a rock.

26 And everyone, who hears these words of mine and does not do them, will be compared to a foolish man who built his house on the sand.

27 And the rain fell and the floods came and the winds blew and they beat against the house and it fell and its fall was great."⌐

28 And it happened that when Jesus finished these words, the crowds were amazed at his teaching.

29 For he was teaching them as [one having] authority and not as their scribes and the Pharisees.

Chapter 8

1 Now when he came down from the mountain, large crowds followed him.

2 And *behold, a certain leper came [and] worshipped him and said, "My Lord, if you desire, you are able to cleanse me."

3 And Jesus stretched out his hand [and] touched him, and said, "I desire. Be cleansed." And immediately his leprosy was cleansed.

4 And Jesus said to him, "See. [that] you tell no one, but go, show yourself to the priests and offer an offering,[2] as Moses commanded for their witness."

5 Now when Jesus entered Capernaum, a certain centurion[3] approached him and was entreating him.

6 And he said, "My Lord, my child is lying at home and is paralyzed and seriously tortured with pain."

7 Jesus said to him, "I will come and heal him."

8 The centurion answered and he said, "My Lord, I am not worthy that you should enter under my roof, but only speak a word and my child will be healed.

9 For I also am a man who is under authority and there are soldiers under my ^{m}hand.[4] And I say to this one, 'Go,' and he goes, and to another, 'Come,' and he comes and to my servant, 'Do this,' and he does [it]."

---

[1] Repeat exact sentence in v. 27. The conditions are the same.

[2] Same root: *offer, offering*

[3] OS (s): 'chiliarch' (ruler of 1000), vs. 5, 8, 13.

[4] Fig: metonymy, *hand* represents authority

ARAMAIC PESHITTA NEW TESTAMENT
MATTHEW

Chapter 8

10   And when Jesus heard [this], he marveled and said to those who had come with him, "*Truly I say to you, not even in Israel have I found faith like this.

11   And *I say to you, many will come from the east and from the west and will lie down to eat with Abraham and Isaac and Jacob in the kingdom of ᵐheaven,

12   but the sons of the kingdom will go out to outer ᵐdarkness. There will be crying and gnashing of teeth."[1]

13   ᴾAnd Jesus said to the centurion, "Go! As you have believed, it will be to you." And his child was healed immediately.

14   And Jesus came to the house of Simon and saw his mother-in-law who was lying down, and a fever had taken hold on her.

15   And he touched her hand and the fever left her and she got up and was serving him.

16   And when it became evening, they brought to him many possessed of devils and he cast out their devils by a word and he healed all those who were very diseased,

17   so that it would be fulfilled what was spoken by way of Isaiah the prophet who said: HE WILL TAKE OUR SORROWS AND HE WILL BEAR OUR SICKNESSES.

18   And when Jesus saw the many crowds that were surrounding him, he commanded that they should go to the opposite shore.

19   And a certain scribe approached and said to him, "My Master,[2] I will follow you to the place where you are going."

20   Jesus said to him, "Foxes have holes and the bird of heaven [has] a nest, but the Son of Man has no ᵉ[home] where he may lay his head."[3]

21   And another of his disciples said to him, "My Lord, allow me first to go [and] bury my father."[4]

22   But Jesus said to him, "Follow me and ᵃᵗleave the dead[5] to bury their dead."

23   And when Jesus boarded a boat, his disciples boarded with him.

---

[1] Culture: idiomatic way to say, "every range of emotion."

[2] Title of address, Rabbi (English spelling), or **rabi**, means, my Master, translated as this throughout this version; OS (c): 'Teacher'

[3] Fig: proverb or maxim

[4] Culture: *bury my father* means to take care of him until he dies, Lamsa, *Idioms*, p. 51.

[5] Or could be translated "town." The only difference between town and dead is the vowel.

Chapter 8

24 And *behold, a great earthquake occurred in the sea, so that the boat was covered by the waves. Now **Jesus** was asleep.

25 And his disciples came near [and] they woke him and said to him, "Our Lord, save us. We are being destroyed."

26 Jesus said to them, "Why are you afraid, oh little of faith?" Then he stood and rebuked the wind and the sea and there was a great calm.

27 And the men were amazed and said, "Who is this whom the winds and the sea obey?"[1]

28 And when Jesus had come to the opposite shore to the place of the Gadarenes, two [men] possessed of devils[2] met him, who were coming out from the tombs,[3] very evil, so that no one was able to pass by that road.

29 And they cried out and said, "What have we to do with you, Jesus,[4] Son of God? Have you come here before the time to torment us?"

30 Now there was a herd of many pigs a distance from them that was feeding.

31 And those demons were begging him and said, "If you cast us out, allow us to go to the herd of pigs."

32 Jesus said to them, "Go!" And immediately they went out and attacked[5] the pigs and that whole herd went straight over a steep rock and they fell into the sea and died in the water.

33 Now those who were tending [the herd] fled and went to the city and made known everything that had occurred and about those possessed of devils.[6]

34 And the whole city went out for a meeting with Jesus. And when they saw him, they begged him to leave their borders.

Chapter 9

1   And he boarded the ship and crossed [and] came to his city.

2   And they brought to him a paralytic[7] lying on a pallet. And Jesus saw their faith and said to the paralytic, "Take courage, my son, your sins are forgiven."

---

[1] Fig: erotesis – question to ponder, also v. 26.

[2] OS (s): 'on whom were devils'

[3] Lit: house of the graves

[4] OS (cs): omit *Jesus*

[5] Lit: entered in, ܠ + ܒ can mean *attack*, Payne Smith, pp. 412-413.

[6] OS (s): for *possessed of devils*, 'on whom a demon rode'

[7] From **shra** ܫܪܐ, loosed, drooping, broken

Chapter 9

3   But some of the scribes said among themselves, "This one blasphemes."

4   But Jesus knew their thoughts and said to them, "Why do you think evil in your heart[s]?[1]

5   For what is easier to say, 'Your sins are forgiven,' or to say, 'Get up [and] walk?'

6   But that you will know that the Son of Man[2] has authority to forgive sins on earth," he said to that paralytic, "Get up, take up your pallet and go to your house."

7   And he got up [and] went to his house.

8   Now when the crowds saw [this], **they** were frightened and glorified God, who gave authority such as this to men.

9   And when Jesus passed over from there, he saw a man who was sitting [at] the customs-house,[3] whose name [was] Matthew. And he said to him, "Follow me." And he rose up [and] went after him.

10   And as they were sitting to eat in the house, many tax collectors and sinners came and sat to eat with Jesus and with his disciples.

11   And when the Pharisees saw, they said to his disciples, "Why does your master eat with tax collectors and sinners?"

12   But Jesus when he heard said to them, "The healthy have no need for a doctor, but those who are very diseased.[4]

13   Go, learn what this is: **I REQUIRE COMPASSION AND NOT SACRIFICE**, for I did not come to call the just [ones], but sinners."

14   Then the disciples of John approached him and said, "Why do **we** and the Pharisees fast much and your disciples do not fast?"

15   Jesus said to them, "Are the guests of the wedding feast able to fast as long as the bridegroom [is] with them?[5] But the days are coming when the bridegroom will be taken from them and then they will fast.

16   [al]No one places a new patch on a worn-out garment, lest the patch should tear away from the garment and the hole become greater.

---

[1] Fig: erotesis – questions to ponder, vs. 4, 5

[2] The phrase *Son of Man* is always referring to judgment and dominion, "He is God's Man to redeem man. He is God's answer to Satan to guarantee his defeat and restore man's original dominion," Dakes' Annotated Bible, p. 94, Bullinger, *Figures of Speech*, pp. 219, 408-409.

[3] Lit: house of taxes

[4] Fig: proverb

[5] Fig: erotesis – question to ponder

Chapter 9

17 And they do not place new wine in worn-out wineskins, lest the wineskins should rip and the wine would be poured out and the wineskins be ruined. But they place new wine in new wineskins and both of them are preserved."ᵈ [1]

18 Now while he was speaking these [things] to them, a certain ruler[2] came near [and] worshipped him and said, "My daughter is now dead. But come, place your hand on her and she will live."

19 And Jesus got up and his disciples followed him.

20 And *behold, a woman, whose blood had flowed [for] twelve years, came from behind him and touched the edge[3] of his clothes,

21 for she was saying within herself, 'If I only touch his clothing, I will be healed.'

22 Now Jesus turned [and] saw her and said to her, "Be comforted, my daughter, your faith has given you life." And that woman was healed immediately.

23 And Jesus came to the house of the ruler and saw the musicians and the crowds, who were troubled.

24 And he said to them, "Go away, for the girl is not dead, but is asleep." And they were laughing at him.

25 And when he dismissed the crowds, he entered in, took her by the hand and the girl got up.

26 And this news went out into all this land.

27 And when Jesus passed over from there, two blind men followed him, who were crying out and saying, "Have compassion on us, Son of David."

28 And when he came to the house, those blind men approached him. Jesus said to them, "Do you believe that I am able to do this?" They said to him, "Yes, our Lord."

29 Then he touched their eyes and said, "As you have believed will it be to you."

30 And immediately their eyes were opened and Jesus rebuked them and said, "See [that] no man should know [about this]."

31 But they went out [and] spread his fame in all that land.

---

[1] Parallel structure, *patch* and *wine,* this passage called a parable in Luke.

[2] OS (s): 'one of the leaders of the synagogue'

[3] Culture: *edge,* **qarna** ܩܪܢܐ, could be the fringe or tassel at one of the four corners of the garment, Bullinger, *Companion Bible*, p. 1327.

Chapter 9

32 And when Jesus went out, they brought to him a mute in whom was a devil.

33 And after the devil went out, that mute spoke and the crowds were amazed and said, "Never was it seen so in Israel."

34 But the Pharisees were saying, "By the chief of devils, he casts out devils."

35 And Jesus journeyed into all the cities ᴾand into the villages and was teaching in their synagogues and preaching the gospel of the kingdom and healing all their diseases and all their pains.⌐

36 And when Jesus saw the crowds, he had compassion on them, because they were weary and scattered ᵃas sheep that do not have a shepherd.

37 And he said to his disciples, ᵃˡ"The harvest is great, and the workers, few.

38 Entreat, therefore, the Lord of the harvest that he would send workers for his harvest."⌐

Chapter 10

1 And he called his twelve disciples and gave them authority over unclean spirits to cast [them] out and to heal every pain and disease.

2 Now the names of the twelve apostles are these: first, Simon, who was called Peter, ᴾand Andrew, his brother, and James, the son of Zebedee, and John, his brother,

3 and Philip and Bartholomew and Thomas and Matthew, the tax collector, and James, the son of Alphaeus, and Lebbaeus, who was called Thaddaeus,

4 and Simon, the Canaanite, and Judas Iscariot, who betrayed him.⌐

5 Jesus sent these twelve and commanded them and said, "Do not go on the road of the heathens and do not enter the city of the Samaritans.

6 But go rather to the ʰsheep that are lost¹ from the house of Israel.

7 And as you are going, preach and say, 'The kingdom of ᵐheaven is near.'

8 Heal the sick ᴾand cleanse the lepers and cast out devils.⌐ Freely you have received, freely² give.

---

¹ Fig: hypocatastasis, *sheep* representing those who need to be led.

² Repeat *freely*, Aram, **magan** ܡܓܢ has same meaning as Grk, **dorean**, "without a cause"

Chapter 10

9   Do not have gold or silver or brass in your purses[1]

10   or a wallet for the journey or two coats or shoes or staff, for a worker is worthy of his food.

11   And into whatever city or village you enter, ask who in it is worthy and there stay until you leave.

12   And when you enter a house, greet the household

13   and if the house is worthy, your peace will come on it. But if it is not worthy, your peace will return on you.

14   And whoever does not receive you and does not hear your words, when you leave the house or that village, shake off the dust from your feet.[2]

15   And *truly I say to you, it will be [more] pleasant for the land of Sodom and Gomorrah in the [sy]day of judgment than for that city.

16   *Behold, I send you [s]as a lamb into the middle of wolves. Be therefore wise [s]as snakes and harmless [s]as doves.

17   And beware of men, for they will deliver you to the courts[3] and they will beat you in their synagogues.

18   And they will bring you before governors and kings for my sake, for a witness to them and to the Gentiles.

19   Now when they deliver you up, do not be concerned how or what you should speak, for it will be given to you immediately what you should speak.

20   For it will not be you speaking, but the Spirit of your Father speaking in you.

21   But brother will deliver his brother to death and father[4] his son. And children will rise up against their parents and they will kill them.

22   And you will be hated by all men, because of my name. But he who endures until the end will live.

23   Now when they persecute you in this city, flee to another, for *truly I say to you, you will not complete all the cities of the house of Israel before the Son of Man will come.

---

[1] Repeat *or*, vs. 9, 10, lit: and not. Culture: *purses* were Oriental girdle, double-folded and sewn together with opening to put in money. A *wallet* is a small bag called a **tarmala**, Ribhany, *The Syrian Christ*, pp. 179-180, Lamsa, *Gospel Light*, p. 119.

[2] Culture: *shake the dust off your feet* means not to retain any animosity.

[3] Lit: house of judgments

[4] Fig: ellipsis, add [will deliver]

Chapter 10

24 There is no disciple who is greater than his master, nor a servant [e][who is greater] than his lord.

25 It is sufficient for a disciple to be as his master and for a servant [to be] as his lord. If they call the lord of the house BEELZEBUB,[1] how much more[2] the sons of his house?

26 Therefore do not be afraid of them, for there is not anything that is covered that will not be revealed, or that is hidden that will not be made known.[3]

27 What I say to you in darkness, you speak in the light. And what you hear in your ears,[4] preach on the roofs.

28 And do not be afraid of those who kill the body, but are not able to kill the soul. But be afraid rather of him who is able to destroy the soul and body in GEHENNA.

29 Are not two sparrows sold for a copper coin?[5] And one of them does not fall on the earth without your Father.

30 Now **yours**, even all the hairs of your head are numbered.[6]

31 Therefore do not be afraid. You are more important than many sparrows.

32 Everyone therefore who confesses me before men, I will confess him also before my Father who is in heaven.

33 But he who denies me before men, I will deny him also before my Father who is in heaven.

34 Do not think that I have come to bring harmony on earth. I have not come to bring harmony, but a [m]sword.[7]

35 For I have come to separate a man from his father and a daughter from her mother and a daughter-in-law from her mother-in-law.

36 And the enemies of a man [will be] his household.

---

[1] *Beelzebub* is an English rendering of Hebrew phrase, lit: lord of the flies. Possibly corruption of Aramaic word **beldabba** ܒܥܠܕܒܒܐ, enemy, lit: master of slander, Jennings, p. 39.

[2] Fig: ellipsis, [will they call] *the sons of the house* [Beelzebub]; fig: erotesis, **kema** question, answer in the affirmative

[3] Fig: antithetic parallelism: *covered and hidden*, ABAB.

[4] Fig: redundancy, *hear in your ears.* "The roof was also the natural place to make public announcements," Thompson, p. 67.

[5] *Copper coin* is a Roman coin called assarion, Aram. ܐܣܪ Appendix 2.

[6] Word play: *hairs,* **mene** and *numbered,* **manyan**, Black, p. 161.

[7] Fig: metonymy, sword represents differences or conflict. OS (c): add phrase, 'difference of opinion and a sword'

ARAMAIC PESHITTA NEW TESTAMENT
MATTHEW

Chapter 10

37 He who loves father or mother more than me is not worthy of me and he who loves son or daughter more than me is not worthy of me. [1]

38 And everyone who does not take up his cross and follow me is not worthy of me.

39 He who finds his life will lose it, and he who will lose his life because of me will find it. [2]

40 He who receives you receives [3] me, and he who receives me receives him who sent me.

41 He who receives a prophet in the name of a prophet will receive the reward of a prophet, and he who receives a just [man] in the name of a just [man] will receive the reward of a just [man].

42 And everyone who gives one of these little ones only a cup of cold [water] [4] to drink in the name of a disciple, *Truly I say to you, he will not lose his reward."

Chapter 11

1 And it happened that when Jesus completed directing the twelve disciples, he went away from there to teach and to preach in their cities.

2 Now when John, [being in] prison, heard of the deeds of the MESSIAH, he sent [word] by way of his disciples

3 and said to him, "Are you he who will come or should we expect another?"

4 Jesus answered and said to them, "Go. Relate to John those [things] that you have heard and seen.

5 The blind see ᴾand the lame walk and the lepers are cleansed and the deaf hear and the dead are raised and the poor are given good news.⌐

6 And he who is not offended by me is blessed."

7 Now when they had gone, Jesus began to speak to the crowds about John, "What did you go out to the wilderness to see? A ʰreed that is shaken by the wind?[5]

---

[1] Repeat *more than me is not worthy of me*

[2] Fig: oxymoron, wise saying

[3] Repeat *receive*, vs. 40, 41

[4] OS (cs): omit *only*, add 'of water,' cf. most Latin texts

[5] Fig: erotesis – questions to ponder, vs. 7-9; repeat *what did you go out to see*, to emphasize that although they were attracted to John yet they rejected his ministry, Bullinger, *Figures of Speech*, p. 202; culture: a reed was used figuratively meaning a "weak or unstable support," Brown, Driver, Briggs, p. 889.

Chapter 11

8   And if not, what did you go out to see? A man who is clothed in soft robes? *Behold, those who are clothed in soft [robes] are [in] the house of kings.[1]

9   And if not, what did you go out to see? A prophet? Yes, *I say to you, even [one] greater than the prophets.[2]

10   For this is he about whom it was written: *BEHOLD, I WILL SEND MY MESSENGER BEFORE YOUR [m]FACE THAT HE WOULD ESTABLISH THE WAY BEFORE YOU.

11   *Truly I say to you, among those born of women has not stood one who is greater than John the baptizer, but the least in the kingdom of [m]heaven is greater than him.

12   Now from the days of John the baptizer and until now, the kingdom of [m]heaven was being guided with restraint and the restrainers were robbing it.[3]

13   For all the prophets and the law[4] have prophesied until John.

14   And if you desire, accept that this is Elijah who was to come.

15   He who has ears to hear should hear.[5]

16   [al]But to what should I liken this generation? It is like children who sit in the marketplace and call out to their friends

17   and say, 'We sang for you and you did not dance, and we mourned for you and you did not lament.'[6]

18   For John came not eating and not drinking, and they said, 'There is a devil in him.'

19   The Son of Man came eating and drinking and they said, '*Behold, a gluttonous man and [one who] drinks wine and a friend of tax collectors and of sinners.' Yet wisdom is justified by its works."[7]

---

[1] Or "among kings," Cureton, *Four Gospels in Syriac*, p. xxi.

[2] Eastern txt: 'prophet' (singular)

[3] Lit: "...heaven is taken with fastening or violence and the fastener or violent plunder it." Whenever there is a move of God, it is set upon by restraint and oppression to bind it up. Same root: *restraint, restrainer*. For further study, see Bivin, pp. 123-135.

[4] *Law* is the Aram. equivalent of **Torah**

[5] Fig: proverb or maxim

[6] Word play: *dance*, **raqditon** ⲁⲇⲙⲟⲣ⳨, *lament*,**araqditon** ⲁⲇⲙⲟⲣ⳨ Black, p. 161.

[7] Greek and OS (cs): 'her children,' cf. Luke 7:35.

ARAMAIC PESHITTA NEW TESTAMENT
MATTHEW

Chapter 11

20 Then Jesus began to berate the cities, those in which his many miracles occurred and yet they did not repent.

21 And he was saying, "[d]Woe to you, [m]Chorazin! [i]Woe to you, [m]Bethsaida! Because if the miracles that were done in you had been done in Tyre and Sidon, doubtless they [would have] repented in sackclothes and in ashes.

22 But *I say to you, it will be [more] pleasant for [m]Tyre and [m]Sidon in the [sy]day of judgment than for you.

23 And you [m]Capernaum, who has been raised up to heaven, will be brought down to SHEOL.[1] Because if the miracles had been done in Sodom that were done in you, she would stand to [this] [sy]day.

24 But *I say to you, it will be [more] pleasant for the land of Sodom in the [sy]day of judgment than for you."[2]

25 At that time, Jesus answered and said, "I give thanks to you my Father, Lord of heaven and of earth, that you have hidden these [things] from the [he]wise and intelligent and you have revealed them to babies.

26 [i]Yes, my Father, because such was the desire before you.

27 Everything has been delivered to me from my Father and no man knows the Son, except the Father. Also, no man knows the Father, except the Son and he whom the Son desires to reveal [him].

28 Come to me, all of you [who] labor and bear burdens and I will refresh[3] you.

29 Bear my [m]yoke on you and learn from me that I am restful and I am meek in my heart, and you will find rest for your souls.

30 For my [m]yoke is pleasant and my burden is light."

Chapter 12

1 At that time Jesus was walking on the SABBATH [in] the sown fields[4] and his disciples were hungry and began picking grain and eating [it].

2 Now the Pharisees, when they saw them, said to him, "*Behold, your disciples are doing what is unlawful to do on the SABBATH."

---

[1] *Sheol* is the transliteration of Hebrew word, meaning simply, the grave, cf. Gen. 37:35

[2] Repeat whole phrase *but I say…to you* from v. 22

[3] Same root: *find rest, refresh, restful,* vs. 28-30

[4] Lit: in the house of seeds; OS (c): adds 'and rubbing it in their hands.' This was permitted according to Deut 23:25, but not harvesting with a tool. *Sabbath* is the transliteration of the Hebrew word, meaning, rest, day of rest.

Chapter 12

3　But **he** said to them, "Have you not read what David did when he was hungry and those who were with him,

4　how he entered the house of God and ate the bread of the table of the LORD, that which was not lawful for him, nor for those who were with him to eat, but only for the priests?

5　Or have you not read in the law that the priests in the temple break the SABBATH and are without blame? ¹

6　But *I say to you, a greater [one] than ᵉ[a priest of] the temple is here.

7　Now if you would have known what ᵉ[was meant by], I DESIRE MERCY AND NOT SACRIFICE, you would not have condemned those who are without blame,

8　for the Lord of the SABBATH is the Son of Man."

9　And Jesus went away from there and came to their synagogue.

10　And a certain man was there whose hand was withered, and they were asking him and said, "Is it lawful to heal on the SABBATH?" so that they could accuse him.

11　Now he said to them, "What man among you who has a certain sheep, and if it falls into a pit on the SABBATH day, would not grab [it] and lift it out?

12　Now how much more important [is] a man than a sheep? So then is it lawful on the SABBATH to do that which is good?"²

13　Then he said to that man, "Stretch out your hand." And he stretched out his hand and it was restored like the other.

14　And the Pharisees left and took counsel about him, so that they could destroy him.

15　But Jesus knew [of it] and he went away from there. And large crowds followed him and he healed all of them.

16　And he charged them that they should not reveal him,

17　that it would be fulfilled what was spoken by way of Isaiah the prophet, who said:

18　*BEHOLD, MY SERVANT WITH WHOM I AM WELL PLEASED, MY BELOVED, FOR WHOM MY SOUL LONGS. I WILL PLACE MY SPIRIT ON HIM AND HE WILL DECLARE JUDGMENT TO THE NATIONS.

---

¹ Fig: erotesis, "not" question, answer in the affirmative

² Fig: erotesis, 1ˢᵗ **kema** question, emphasizing the importance of taking care of people, even if on the Sabbath, 2nd – question to ponder

Chapter 12

19 HE WILL NOT DISPUTE AND HE WILL NOT CRY OUT AND NO MAN WILL HEAR HIS VOICE IN THE MARKETPLACE.

20 THE ʰBROKEN REED, HE WILL NOT BREAK DOWN, AND THE ᵐLAMP THAT IS DYING OUT, HE WILL NOT EXTINGUISH, UNTIL JUDGMENT COMES TO PASS FOR VICTORY

21 AND THE NATIONS WILL TRUST IN HIS NAME.

22 Then they brought to him a certain [one] possessed of a devil that was mute and blind and he healed him so that the mute and blind[1] man could talk and could see.

23 And all the crowds were marveling and said, "Is this not the Son of David?"

24 But the Pharisees, when they heard [this], were saying, "This [man] does not cast out demons, but by BEELZEBUB, the chief of devils."

25 Now Jesus knew their thoughts and said to them, "Every kingdom that is divided against itself will be destroyed. And every house and city that is divided against itself will not stand.

26 And if SATAN casts out SATAN, he is divided against himself. How then does his kingdom stand?[2]

27 And if by BEELZEBUB I cast out devils, in what way do your sons cast them out? Because of this, they will be judges of you.

28 And if by the Spirit of God I cast out devils, the kingdom of God has come near to you.

29 ᵃˡOr how is a man able to enter into the house of a strong man and to rob his possessions, except first he will bind the strong man and then rob his house?⌐

30 He who is not with me is against me. And he who does not gather with me indeed scatters.[3]

31 Because of this, *I say to you, all sins and blasphemies will be forgiven to men, but blasphemy that is against the Spirit will not be forgiven to men.

---

[1] Repeat *mute and blind*, opposite: *talk and see*

[2] Fig: erotesis – questions to ponder, vs. 27, 29; repeat *is divided against itself*, vs. 25, 26.

[3] Fig: polyptoton, *indeed scatters*, lit. scattering, he scatters

ARAMAIC PESHITTA NEW TESTAMENT
MATTHEW

Chapter 12

32 And anyone who will say a word against the Son of Man will be forgiven. But anyone who will speak against the Holy Spirit will not be forgiven, neither in this age nor in the age that is to come.

33 [al]Either make the tree fine and its fruit fine or make the tree bad and its fruit bad, for a tree is known by its fruit.

34 [i]Generation of [h]vipers! How are you who are bad able to speak good [things]?[1] For from the fullness of the heart the mouth speaks.

35 A good man from good treasures produces good [things] and a bad man from bad treasures produces bad [things].[2]

36 For *I say to you, [for] every idle[3] word that men speak, they will give an account of it in the [sy]day of judgment.

37 For by your words you will be justified and by your words you will be condemned."¬ [4]

38 Then answered some of the scribes and of the Pharisees and said to him, "Teacher, we desire to see a sign from you."

39 But **he** answered and said to them, [al]"An evil and adulterous generation seeks a sign, yet a sign will not be given to it, except the sign[5] of Jonah the prophet.

40 For as Jonah was in the belly of the fish three days and three nights, so will the Son of Man be in the heart of the earth three days and three nights.¬ [6]

41 The Ninevite men will stand in judgment[7] with this generation and will condemn it, because they repented at the preaching of Jonah. And *behold, one who is greater than Jonah is present.

42 The queen of the south will stand in judgment with this generation and she will condemn it, because she came from the ends of the earth to hear the wisdom of Solomon. And *behold, one who is more[8] than Solomon is here.

---

[1] Fig: erotesis – question to ponder

[2] Antithetic parallelism, *good and bad*

[3] *Idle* could be translated "unprofitable," Payne Smith, p. 41.

[4] Repeat *by your words*

[5] Repeat *sign*

[6] Repeat *three days and three nights*

[7] Culture: among Jews and Romans, witnesses rise from their seats when they give evidence against an accused criminal, Burder, vol I, p. 271.

[8] Fig: ellipsis, *one who is* [wiser] *than Solomon*

Chapter 12

43 Now when an unclean spirit goes out from a man, it wanders in places in which there is no water and it seeks rest, yet does not find [it].

44 Then it says, 'I will return to my house from where I came out.' And it comes [and] finds that it is empty and swept and set in order.

45 Then it will go [and] lead with it seven other spirits who are more evil than it and they will enter and dwell in it. And the end of that man will be more evil than his beginning. So it will be to this evil generation."

46 Now while he was speaking to the crowds, his mother and his brothers came [and] they were standing outside and requesting to speak with him.

47 Now someone said to him, "*Behold, your mother and your brothers are standing outside and requesting to speak with you."

48 But **he** answered and said to the one who had spoken to him, "Who is my mother and who are my brothers?"[1]

49 And he stretched out his hand toward his disciples and said, "*Behold, my mother and *behold, my brothers.

50 For everyone who does the will of my Father who is in heaven is my brother and my sister and my mother."

Chapter 13

1 Now on that day, Jesus went out from the house and sat by the shore of the sea.

2 And large crowds were gathered around him so that he boarded a ship to sit down and the whole crowd was standing on the shore of the sea.

3 And he was speaking many [things] with them in parables and said, pb"*Behold, a sower went out to sow.[2]

4 And while he was sowing, it happened that e[some seed] fell by the side of the road. And a bird came and ate it.

5 And other e[seed] fell on rocky ground where there was not much soil and immediately it sprouted, because there was no asdepth of earth.

6 But when the sun came up, it became hot and because it had no root, it dried up.

---

[1] Fig: erotesis – question to ponder

[2] Same root: *sower, seed*; fig: ellipsis of seed throughout whole passage.

ARAMAIC PESHITTA NEW TESTAMENT
MATTHEW

Chapter 13

7 And other ^e[seed] fell among thorns[1] and the thorns grew up and choked it.

8 And other ^e[seed] fell on good earth and bore fruit, some a hundred and some sixty and some thirty[fold].

9 He who has ears to hear should hear."┐

10 And his disciples came near and said to him, "Why do you speak in parables with them?"

11 Now **he** answered and said to them, "To you it is given to know the mystery of the kingdom of ^mheaven, but it is not given to them.

12 For to him who has, it will be given to him and he will have abundance,

13 and to him who has not, even that which he has will be taken from him.[2] Because of this, I speak with them in parables, because they see and do not see, and they hear and do not hear and they do not understand.

14 And the prophecy of Isaiah is fulfilled in them, who said: **HEARING YOU WILL HEAR AND YOU WILL NOT UNDERSTAND AND SEEING YOU WILL SEE AND YOU WILL NOT KNOW.**

15 **FOR THE HEART OF THIS PEOPLE IS BEEN HARDENED AND WITH THEIR EARS THEY ARE HARD OF HEARING AND THEIR EYES ARE CLOSED, LEST THEY WOULD SEE WITH THEIR EYES AND WOULD HEAR WITH THEIR EARS[3] AND WOULD UNDERSTAND WITH THEIR HEART AND WOULD REPENT AND I [WOULD] HEAL THEM.**

16 But blessed are your eyes, because they see and your ears, because they hear.

17 For *truly I say to you, many prophets and just [men] have longed to see what you see and they did not see [them], and to hear what you hear and they did not hear [them].

18 But hear the parable of the seed.

19 [From] everyone who hears the message of the kingdom and does not understand, the Evil [one] comes and grabs the word that was sown in his heart. This is ^{me}that which was sown by the side of the road.

20 And ^{me}that which was sown on rocky ground is he who hears the message and immediately receives it with joy.

---

[1] Lit: house of thorns, also v. 22.

[2] Eastern txt: v. 13 begins here. Repeat forms of *see, hear*, vs. 13-18.

[3] Fig: redundancy --*see with their eyes and hear with their ears*

ARAMAIC PESHITTA NEW TESTAMENT
MATTHEW

Chapter 13

21 Yet he has no root in him, but is transient.[1] And when trouble or persecution comes because of the word, he is offended quickly.

22 Now ᵐᵉthat which was sown among thorns is he who hears the word and the care of this world and the deception of riches choke the word and it becomes without fruit.

23 But ᵐᵉthat which was sown on good earth is he who hears my word and understands [it] and produces ᵐfruit and yields some a hundred and some sixty and some thirty[fold]."

24 He spoke another parable to them and he said, ᵖᵇ"The kingdom of ᵐheaven is compared to a man who sowed good seed in his field.

25 And when the people were asleep, his enemy came and sowed weeds[2] in the middle of the wheat and [then] left.

26 And when the plant sprouted and bore fruit, then the weeds also were seen.

27 And the servants of the master [of] the house came near and said to him, 'Our lord, *behold, did you not sow good seed in your field? From where are the weeds in it?'

28 But **he** said to them, 'A man [who is] an enemy did this.' His servants said to him, 'Do you want us to go to pick them out?'

29 But **he** said to them, '[No], lest while you are picking out the weeds, you will uproot the wheat with them also.'

30 Allow both to grow together until the harvest. And in the time of harvest, I will say to the reapers, 'Pick out the weeds first and bind them [into] bundles to be burned.' But gather the wheat into my granaries.'"┐

31 He spoke another parable to them. And he said, ᵖᵇ"The kingdom of ᵐheaven is compared to a grain of mustard seed that a man took [and] sowed in his field.

32 And this [seed] is smaller than all the small seeds,[3] but when it grows, it is greater than all the small herbs and it becomes a tree, so that a bird of heaven will come [and] nest in its branches."┐

---

[1] OS (cs): 'he persists in it a short time,' or 'it (the seed) abides in him a short time'

[2] Culture: *weeds* throughout the passage is Aramaic word **zizaney**, a weed called darnel. The darnel before it comes into ear is very similar in appearance to wheat. If it remains with the wheat, it causes the flour to be bitter and may even cause convulsions and death, Peloubet, *Bible Dictionary*, p. 674, Walker, *All the Plants of the Bible*, pp. 208-209.

[3] Word play: *seed,* **zara** and *small,* **zora**

Chapter 13

33 He spoke another parable to them. ^{pb}"The kingdom of ^mheaven is compared to leaven that a woman took [and] hid in three measures of flour, until all of it was leavened."⌐

34 All these [things] Jesus spoke in illustrations to the crowds. And without illustrations he did not speak with them,

35 so that it would be fulfilled what was spoken by way of the prophet, who said: **I WILL OPEN MY MOUTH WITH PARABLES AND I WILL BRING FORTH HIDDEN [THINGS] THAT WERE FROM BEFORE THE FOUNDATIONS OF THE WORLD.**

36 Then Jesus left the crowds and came to the house and his disciples came near to him and said to him, "Explain to us that parable of the weeds and of the field."

37 And **he** answered and said to them, "^{me}He who sowed the good seed is the Son of Man.

38 And ^{me}the field is the age and ^{me}the good seed are the sons of the kingdom. And ^{me}the weeds are the sons of the Evil [one].

39 And ^{me}the enemy who sowed them is SATAN. And ^{me}the harvest is the culmination of the age and ^{me}the reapers [are] the angels.

40 As therefore the weeds are picked out and burned in the fire, so it will be in the culmination of this age.

41 The Son of Man will send his angels and they will pick out from his kingdom all the stumbling blocks and all the servants of wickedness

42 and they will throw them into the furnace of fire. In that place will be crying and gnashing of teeth.[1]

43 Then the just [ones] will shine as the sun in the kingdom of their Father. He who has ears to hear should hear.

44 Again, ^{pb}the kingdom of ^mheaven is compared to a treasure that is hidden in a field that a man found and hid. And from his joy, he went [and] sold everything he had and bought[2] that field.⌐

45 Again, ^{pb}the kingdom of ^mheaven is compared to a merchant[3] who was seeking expensive pearls.

46 And when he found a certain precious[4] pearl, he went [and] sold everything that he had and bought it.⌐

---

[1] Culture: *crying and gnashing teeth* means that the whole range of emotions will be exhibited, everything from weeping and crying to fierce anger.

[2] Repeat whole phrase, *he went [and] sold everything he had and bought*, v. 46

[3] Lit: man of business

[4] Lit: heavy of price

ARAMAIC PESHITTA NEW TESTAMENT
MATTHEW

Chapter 13
47 Again, [pb]the kingdom of [m]heaven is compared to a net that was thrown into the sea and gathered together [e][fish] of every kind.
48 And when it was full, they pulled it out to the shore of the sea and sat down [and] sorted [it]. And the good [e][fish] they placed in containers and the bad they threw away.¬
49 So it will be in the culmination of the age. The angels will go out and separate the evil [ones] from among the just [ones]
50 and they will throw them into the furnace of fire. In that place will be crying and gnashing of teeth.
51 Jesus said to them, "Do you understand all these [things]?" They said to him, "Yes, our Lord."
52 He said to them, [pb]"Because of this, every scribe who is instructed for the kingdom of [m]heaven is compared to a man [who is] a master [of] a house, who brings out from his treasures the new and old."¬
53 And it happened that when Jesus completed these parables, he went away from there.
54 And he came to his [own] city and was teaching them in their synagogues, so that they marveled and were saying, "From where [does] this wisdom and [these] miracles [e][come] to this [man]?[1]
55 Is not this the son of the carpenter?[2] Is not his mother called Mary [P]and his brothers, James and Joses and Simon and Judas?¬
56 And all his sisters, *behold, are they not with us? So from where [do] all these [things] [e][come] to this [e][man]?"
57 And they were offended by him. And Jesus said to them, "There is no prophet who is despised, except in his [own] city and in his [own] house."
58 And he did not do many miracles there because of their unbelief.

Chapter 14
1 Now in that time, Herod the Tetrarch heard a report[3] about Jesus.
2 And he said to his servants, "This is John the baptizer. He has risen from the dead. Because of this, miracles are done by him."
3 For Herod had arrested John and bound him and threw him into prison because of Herodias, the wife of his brother Philip.

---

[1] Fig: erotesis – question to ponder, also v. 56
[2] Fig: erotesis, "not" questions, answer in the affirmative, also 1st question, v. 56
[3] Lit: a hearing

Chapter 14

4   For John was saying to him, "It is unlawful that she be a wife to you."

5   And he was desiring to kill him, but he was afraid of the people, who were regarding him as a prophet.

6   Now when the birthday of Herod occurred, the daughter of Herodias danced before the guests and she pleased Herod.

7   Because of this, with an oath he swore to her that he would give her anything that she asked.

8   And because **she** was instructed by her mother, she said, "Give me here on a plate the head of John the baptizer."

9   And it saddened the king, but because of the oath and the guests, he commanded that it be given to her.

10   And he sent [and] cut off the head of John [in] the prison.

11   And he brought his head on a plate and it was given to the girl and she brought it to her mother.

12   And his disciples came near, took up his corpse, buried [it] and came [and] made ᵉ[his death]¹ known to Jesus.

13   Now when Jesus heard [this], he went away from there in a ship to a desert place alone. And when the crowds heard [this],² they followed him by dry land from the cities.³

14   And Jesus went out [and] saw the large crowds. And he had compassion on them and he healed their diseases.

15   Now when it was evening, his disciples came near to him and said to him, "[This] is a desert place and the time has passed. Dismiss the crowds of people that they may go on to the villages and buy food for themselves."

16   But **he** said to them, "It is not necessary for them to leave. Give them ᵉ[food] to eat."

17   But **they** said to him, "We have nothing here, except five [loaves of] bread⁴ and two fish."

18   Jesus said to them, "Bring them here to me."

---

¹ Fig: ellipsis, emphasis on the bad news
² Repeat *heard [this]*
³ OS (c): add 'and from the towns'
⁴ Lit: breads

Chapter 14

19 ^PAnd he commanded the crowds to recline on the ground and he lifted up those five [loaves of] bread and two fish and looked into heaven and blessed and broke [them] and gave [them] to his disciples and the disciples set ^e[the food] before the crowds.

20 And all of them ate and were satisfied. And they took up the rest of the fragments, twelve baskets full.┐

21 Now those men who ate were five thousand, besides women and children.

22 And immediately he urged his disciples to board the ship and to go before him to the opposite side, while he dismissed the crowds.

23 And when he dismissed the crowds, he went up to a mountain alone to pray. And when it became dark, he was alone there.

24 And the ship was many furlongs away from land, being tossed greatly[1] by the waves, for the wind was against it.

25 Now in the fourth watch of the night, Jesus came toward them, walking on the water.

26 And his disciples saw him that he was walking on the water. And they were troubled and were saying, "It is false vision." And they cried out because of their fear.

27 But Jesus immediately spoke with them and said, "Be encouraged,[2] it is I. Do not be afraid."

28 And Peter answered and said to him, "My Lord, if it is you, command me[3] to come to you on the water."

29 And Jesus said to him, "Come." And Peter got down from the ship and walked on the water to go to Jesus.

30 And when he saw the wind was rough, he feared and began to sink. And he raised his voice and said, "My Lord, save me."

31 And immediately our Lord reached out his hand and grasped him and said to him, "Little of faith, why did you doubt?"[4]

32 And when they boarded the ship, the wind quieted.

33 And those who were in the ship came [and] worshipped him and said, "*Truly you [are] the Son of God."

34 And they traveled on and came to the land of Gennesaret.

---

[1] Same root: *many, greatly*

[2] OS (cs): 'be strong'

[3] Word play: *command me* **pqad li** and *save me* (v. 30) **priqini**

[4] Fig: erotesis, **lema** question, obvious answer "yes", could be translated, "are you doubting?"

Chapter 14

35 And the men of that place knew him and they sent ᵉ[word] to all the villages of the surrounding area. And all those who were very sick came near to him.

36 And they were begging him that they might touch [him], even if only the outer edge of his clothing. And those who touched were healed.

Chapter 15

1 Then the Pharisees and scribes, who were from Jerusalem, came near to Jesus and said,

2 "Why do your disciples cross against the tradition of the elders and do not wash their hands when they eat bread?

3 Jesus answered and said to them, "Why do **you** also cross against the commandment of God because of your tradition?

4 For God said: **HONOR YOUR FATHER AND YOUR MOTHER AND HE WHO REVILES HIS FATHER AND HIS MOTHER SHOULD INDEED BE PUT[1] TO DEATH.**

5 But **you** say, 'Anyone who will say to a father or to a mother, [Let] whatever you have gained by me [be] my offering,[2] and [then] he does not ᵉ[need to] honor his father or his mother.'

6 And you nullify the word of God because of your tradition.

7 ⁱHypocrites! Well did Isaiah prophesy concerning you and say:

8 **THIS PEOPLE HONORS ME WITH THEIR ᵐLIPS, BUT THEIR ᵐHEART IS VERY FAR FROM ME.**

9 **AND VAINLY THEY REVERENCE ME, WHILE TEACHING THE DOCTRINES OF THE COMMANDMENTS OF MEN."**

10 And he cried out to the crowds and said to them, "Hear and understand.

11 ᵖᵇIt is not what enters the mouth [that] corrupts a man, but what comes out of the mouth, that corrupts a man."┐ [3]

12 Then his disciples came near and said to him, "Do you know that the Pharisees who heard this saying were offended?"

---

[1] Fig: polyptoton, lit: putting, be put

[2] Culture: *offering* is the word **qurbana**, English rendering, Corban. This offering was in fulfillment of a vow. Once it was vowed, it could not be used for oneself. That was how many got out of taking care of their parents and family, Freeman, pp. 400-401, cf. Mark 7:11.

[3] Parallel structure, ABAB

Chapter 15

13 Now **he** answered and said to them, "Every plant that my Father who is in heaven has not planted[1] will be uprooted.

14 Leave them alone. They are blind leaders of the blind. And if the blind lead the blind,[2] both will fall into a pit."

15 And Simon Peter answered and said to him, "My Lord, explain to us this parable."

16 And **he** said to them, "Until now do **you** also not understand?

17 Do you not know that whatever enters the mouth goes to the stomach and from there is cast out ᵉ[of the body] by a bowel movement?[3]

18 But what goes out of the mouth goes out of the heart and becomes corrupting to the man.

19 For from the heart go out ᵃevil thoughts: adultery, murder, fornication, theft, false witness, [and] blasphemy.⌐

20 These are [the things] that corrupt a man. But if a man eats while his hands are not washed, he is not corrupted."

21 And Jesus went out from there and came to the border of Tyre and Sidon.

22 And *behold, a woman of Canaan from those borders came out crying and saying, "Have compassion on me, my Lord, Son of David. My daughter is seriously oppressed by a demon."

23 But **he** did not answer her a word. And his disciples came near [and] begged him and said, "Send her away, because she cries after us."

24 But **he** answered and said to them, "I have not been sent, except to the ʰsheep that have strayed from the house of Israel."

25 And she came [and] worshipped him. And she said, "My Lord, help me."

26 ᵃˡHe said to her, "It is not proper to take the bread of the children and to throw [it] to the dogs."[4]

27 Now she said, "Yes, my Lord, [but] even the dogs eat from the crumbs that fall from the tables of their lords and live."⌐

28 Then Jesus said to her, "ⁱOh woman, great is your faith. Let it be to you as you desire." And her daughter was healed at that moment.

---

[1] Same root: *plant, planted*

[2] Repeat *blind*

[3] Fig: erotesis, "not" question, answer in affirmative

[4] Culture: *Dogs* are puppies. Otherwise dogs were not allowed in houses, Neil, *Everyday Life*, p. 179. Gentiles were considered to be "dogs" by the Israelites.

Chapter 15

29 And Jesus went away from there and came to the shore of the Sea of Galilee. And he climbed a mountain and sat there.

30 And large crowds came near to him in which there were the lame ᴾand blind and dumb and the maimed and many others.⅂ And they laid them at the feet of Jesus and he healed them,

31 so that those crowds were amazed who saw the dumb who spoke ᴾand the maimed who were made whole and the lame who walked and the blind who saw.⅂ And they praised the God of Israel.

32 But **Jesus** called to his disciples and said to them, "I have compassion for this crowd, because, *behold, three days they have stayed with me and they do not have anything to eat. And I do not want to send them away fasting, so that they will not lose strength during the journey."

33 His disciples were saying to him, "Where is there ᵐbread for us in the desert to satisfy this whole crowd?"

34 Jesus said to them, "How many [loaves of] bread do you have?" They said to him, "Seven and a few small fish."

35 And he commanded the crowds to recline on the ground.

36 And he took those seven [loaves of] bread and the fish and gave thanks and broke [them] into pieces and gave [them] to his disciples and the disciples gave [them] to the crowds.

37 And all of them ate and were satisfied. And they took up the rest of the fragments, seven baskets full.

38 Now those who ate were four thousand men, besides women and children.

39 And when he sent away the crowds, he boarded a ship and came to the border of Magdala.[1]

Chapter 16

1 And the Pharisees and Sadducees came near, tempting him and asking him to show them a sign from ᵐheaven.

2 But **he** answered and said to them, "When it becomes evening, you say, 'It [will be] fair, for the sky is red.'

---

[1] OS (cs): 'Megiddo'

ARAMAIC PESHITTA NEW TESTAMENT
MATTHEW

Chapter 16

3   And in the morning you say, 'Today it [will be] stormy for the sky is a gloomy red.' ᶦHypocrites! You know [how] to investigate the appearance of the sky, [but] you do not know [how] to discern the signs of this time.[1]

4   An evil and adulterous generation seeks for a sign and a sign[2] is not given to it, except the sign of Jonah the prophet." And he left them and went away.

5   And when his disciples came to the other side, they had forgotten to take bread with them.

6   Now **he** said to them, "Watch. Beware of the ʰleaven[3] of the Pharisees and the Sadducees."

7   And **they** were reasoning among themselves and said that they had not taken bread.

8   But Jesus knew and said to them, "What are you thinking to yourselves, little of faith, that ᵉ[it is because] you did not bring bread?

9   Do you not yet[4] understand? Do you not remember those five [loaves of] bread for the five thousand and how many baskets you took up?[5]

10 Nor those seven [loaves of] bread for the four thousand and how many baskets you took up?

11 How do you not understand that it was not about bread [that] I spoke to you, but that you should beware of the leaven of the Pharisees and of the Sadducees?"

12 Then they understood that he did not say that they should beware of the leaven of bread, but of the doctrine of the Pharisees and of the Sadducees.

13 And when Jesus came to the region of Caesarea of Philippi, he was asking his disciples and said, "What are men saying about me, who is the Son of Man?"[6]

14 And they said, "Some say [that you are] John the baptizer, but others [that you are] Elijah and others Jeremiah or one of the prophets."

15 He said to them, "But who do you say that I am?"

---

[1] OS (c+s) omit v. 2b and 3

[2] Repeat *sign*, 3x

[3] Fig: hypocatastasis, explained in v. 12 = doctrine

[4] Lit: up to or until now

[5] Fig: erotesis, series of "not" questions, vs. 8-11, must be answered in the affirmative; repeat *how many baskets*.

[6] Eastern txt: 'that I am the son of man?' OS (s): 'who then is this Son of Man?'

Chapter 16

16 Simon Peter answered and said, "You are the MESSIAH, the Son of the living God."

17 Jesus answered and said to him, "You are blessed, Simon, son of Jonah, because ^{sy}flesh and blood[1] did not reveal [this] to you, but my Father who is in heaven.

18 Also *I say to you, ^{me}you are a rock and on this rock I will build my church and the gates[2] of SHEOL will not subdue it.

19 To you I will give the ^mkeys of the kingdom of ^mheaven and anything that you bind on earth will be bound in heaven. And that which you loose on earth will be loosed[3] in heaven."

20 Then he commanded his disciples that they should not tell anyone that he was the MESSIAH.

21 And from then [on], Jesus began to show his disciples that he would go to Jerusalem and suffer much from the elders and from the chief priests and scribes and [that] he would be killed and on the third day would rise up.

22 Yet Peter took him and began to berate him. And he said, "Forbid it to you, my Lord, that this [thing] should happen to you."

23 But **he** turned and said to Peter, "Go behind me, SATAN! You are a stumbling block to me, because you do not think ^e[the things] of God, but of men."

24 Then Jesus said to his disciples, "He who wants to follow me should deny himself and take up his ^mcross and follow me.[4]

25 For he who wants to save his life will lose it. And he who will lose his life because of me will find it.

26 For what does a man profit if he gains the whole world and loses his life? Or what [thing of] exchange will a man give for his life?

27 For **THE SON OF MAN IS ABOUT TO COME IN THE GLORY OF HIS FATHER WITH HIS HOLY ANGELS**. And then he will reward each man according to his works.

28 *Truly I say to you, there are men who are standing here who will not ^htaste death until they will see the Son of Man come in his kingdom."

---

[1] Fig: synecdoche, *flesh and blood,* meaning people

[2] Zimmerman, p. 25, says *gates* should be translated attackers.

[3] *Bind* means to forbid, *loose* means to permit, Bivin, pp. 145-149, Freeman, pp. 353-354.

[4] Parallel structure, vs. 24, 25, fig: oxymoron, wise saying

ARAMAIC PESHITTA NEW TESTAMENT
MATTHEW

Chapter 17

1 And after six days, Jesus led Peter and James and John his brother and took them up to a high mountain alone.

2 And Jesus was transformed before them and his face was bright ˢlike the sun. And his clothes became white ˢlike light.

3 And [there] appeared to them Moses and Elijah speaking with him.

4 And Peter answered and said to Jesus, "My Lord, it is good for us that we were here. And if you want, we will make here three booths, one for you and one for Moses and one for Elijah."

5 And while he was speaking, *behold, a bright cloud overshadowed them. And a voice came from the cloud that said, "This is my beloved Son in whom I am pleased. Hear him."

6 And when the disciples heard [this], they fell on their faces and were very afraid.

7 And Jesus came near to them and touched them and said, "Stand up. Do not be afraid."

8 And they raised their eyes and did not see anyone, except Jesus alone.

9 And while they were coming down from the mountain, Jesus commanded them and said to them, "Do not speak [about] this vision in the presence of anyone until the Son of Man rises from the dead."

10 And his disciples asked him and said to him, "Why then do the scribes say that Elijah ought to come first?"

11 Jesus answered and said, "Elijah comes first to fulfill everything.

12 But *I say to you, *behold, Elijah has come and they did not know him and they did with him whatever they desired. So also the Son of Man is about to suffer from them."

13 Then the disciples understood that he spoke to them about John the baptizer.

14 And when they came to the crowd, a man came near to him and ᵖʳbowed down on his knees[1]

15 and said to him, "My Lord, have compassion on me. My son is one who is insane and he is seriously afflicted, for many times he has fallen into the fire and many times[2] in the water.

16 And I brought him to your disciples and they were not able to heal him."

---

[1] Lit: kneeled on his knees, same root

[2] Repeat *many times*

Chapter 17

17 Jesus answered and said, "[i]Oh faithless and perverted generation! How long must I be with you and how long must I endure you?[1] Bring him here to me."

18 And Jesus rebuked it and the demon went out of him and the child was healed at that moment.

19 Then the disciples came near to Jesus alone and said to him, "Why were we not able to heal him?"

20 Jesus said to them, "Because of your unbelief. For *truly I say to you, if you have faith [s]like a grain of mustard seed, you can say to this mountain, 'Move from here,' and it will move and nothing will overcome you.

21 But this kind does not go out, except by fasting and by prayer."

22 Now while they were traveling[2] in Galilee, Jesus said to them, "The Son of Man is about to be betrayed into the [m]hands of men.

23 And they will kill him and on the third day, he will rise up." And [the saying] saddened them very much.

24 And when they came to Capernaum, those who were receiving the two drachmas for the poll tax[3] came near to Peter. And they said to him, "Does not your master give his two drachmas?"

25 He said to them, "Yes." And when Peter entered the house, Jesus anticipated him and said to him, "What does it appear to you, Simon? The kings of the earth, from whom do they receive tribute and the poll tax, from their children or from strangers?"

26 Simon said to him, "From strangers." Jesus said to him, "Then the children are free.[4]

27 But so that [this] should not offend them, go to the sea and cast a fishhook. And the first fish that comes up, open its mouth and you will find a stater. Take that and give [it] for me and for you."

Chapter 18

1 At that time, the disciples came near to Jesus and said, "Who is indeed great in the kingdom of [m]heaven?"

2 And Jesus called a child[5] and set him among them

---

[1] Fig: erotesis – question to ponder

[2] Lit: walking

[3] *Two* drachmas, lit: two each; the *poll tax* is the temple head tax, Appendix 2.

[4] Lit: sons of freedom

[5] OS (c): add 'one boy or child,' cf. Old Latin texts

Chapter 18

3 and said, "*Truly I say to you, if you do not change and become ˢlike children, you will not enter into the kingdom of ᵐheaven.

4 Therefore, he who humbles himself ˢlike this child will be great in the kingdom of ᵐheaven.

5 And he who receives [one] ˢlike this child in my name receives me.

6 And anyone who causes one of these little ones who believe in me to stumble, it would be better for him that the millstone of a donkey would be hung on his neck and he be sunk in the depths of the sea.

7 ⁱWoe to the world because of offenses! For it is necessary that offenses should come. But ⁱwoe to the man by whose ᵐhand the offenses come![1]

8 Now if your hand or your foot causes you to stumble, cut it off and throw it away from you.[2] It is better for you to enter life while you are lame or while maimed, and not, while you have two hands or two feet, to fall into everlasting fire.

9 And if your eye causes you to stumble, tear it out and throw it away from you. It is better for you that you enter life with one eye and not, while you have two eyes, to fall into the GEHENNA of fire.

10 See, you should not despise one of these little ones, for *I say to you, their angels that are in heaven always see the face of my Father who is in heaven.

11 For the Son of Man has come to make alive that which was perishing.[3]

12 What does it appear to you? ᵃˡIf a man had one hundred sheep and one of them strayed, does he not leave the ninety-nine on the mountain and go [and] seek that which has strayed?

13 And if he finds it, *truly I say to you, he rejoices at it more than the ninety-nine that did not stray.

14 Likewise, it is not the will before[4] your Father who is in heaven that one of these little ones should perish.⌐

15 Now if your brother offends you, go [and] reprove him between you and him alone. If he hears you, you have gained your brother.

---

[1] Repeat *offenses*

[2] Culture: Lamsa explains that this means to "stop stealing, stop trespassing" or envying, Lamsa, *Idioms*, p. 54.

[3] OS (s), Pal Syr: omit verse.

[4] Lit: has no desire, or does not wish

Chapter 18

16 And if he does not hear you, take with you one or two [others] that, AT THE [m]MOUTH OF TWO OR THREE WITNESSES EVERY WORD WILL BE ESTABLISHED.

17 Now if he will not hear them also, tell the church.[1] And if he will not hear the church also, he will be to you [s]like a tax collector and [s]like a heathen.

18 And *truly I say to you, anything that you bind on earth will be bound in heaven. And that which you loose on earth will be loosed in heaven.

19 Again *I say to you, if two of you agree on earth concerning every matter that they will ask, they will have [e][an answer][2] from the presence of my Father who is in heaven.

20 For where two or three are gathered in my name, there I am among them."

21 Then Peter came near to him and said, "My Lord, if my brother offends me, how many times should I forgive him? Up to seven times?"

22 Jesus said to him, "I do not say to you up to seven [times], but up to seventy times, by sevens.[3]

23 Because of this, [pb]the kingdom of [m]heaven is compared to a certain king, who wanted to take an accounting of his servants.

24 And when he began to take [e][the accounting], they brought to him one who owed ten thousand talents.

25 And when he had no [way] to repay, his lord commanded that he should be sold and his wife and his children and everything that was his and [that] he should repay [e][the debt].

26 And the servant fell down [and] worshipped him and said, 'My lord, be patient with me and I will repay everything to you.'

27 And the lord of that servant had compassion and sent him away and forgave him his debt.

28 Now that servant went out and found one of his fellow-servants, who owed him one hundred denarii, and he grabbed him and was choking him, and said to him, 'Give me that which you owe me.'

---

[1] OS (s): 'synagogue.' The word *church* here must be understood in the sense of assembly, Errico, *Aramaic Light of the Gospel of Matthew*, p. 234.

[2] Fig: ellipsis, the implied word could be "it" or "what they asked," but since we do not always get what we ask, this is a more conservative insertion.

[3] *By sevens*, means "every seven," Noldeke, p. 186.

Chapter 18

29 And that [man], his fellow-servant, fell at his feet, begged him and said to him, 'Be patient with me and I will repay you.'

30 And **he** did not want [to], but went [and] threw him into prison, until he would pay him what he owed him.

31 Now when their fellow-servants saw what had happened, it saddened them very much. And they came [and] made known to their lord all that happened.

32 Then his lord called him and said to that evil servant, "I forgave you all of the debt because you begged me.

33 Was it not proper for **you** also to have mercy toward your fellow-servant, as I had mercy on you?"[1]

34 And his lord was angry and delivered him to the torturers,[2] until he would repay everything that he owed him.

35 Likewise my Father who is in heaven will do to you, unless you each forgive his brother his offense from your heart."ﻗ

Chapter 19

1 And it happened that when Jesus finished these words, he started from Galilee and came to the border of Judea on the other side of Jordan.

2 And large crowds followed him and he healed them there.

3 And the Pharisees came near to him and were tempting him and saying, "Is it lawful for a man to put away his wife on any occasion?"

4 Now he answered and said to them, "Have you not read that he who made [them] from the beginning made them male and female?"

5 And he said, "Because of this, **A MAN SHOULD LEAVE HIS FATHER AND HIS MOTHER AND SHOULD CLEAVE TO HIS WIFE AND THE TWO OF THEM WILL BECOME ONE** [SY]**FLESH.**[3]

6 Therefore, they will not be two, but rather, one [SY]flesh. Therefore, that which God has united, man should not separate."

7 They said to him, "Why then did Moses command to give a writing of divorce and to dismiss her?"

8 He said to them, "Moses, because of the hardness of your heart, allowed you to dismiss your wives. But previously it was not so.

---

[1] Fig: erotesis – question to ponder

[2] Culture: *torturers* were jailors who were allowed to beat and torture the debtor, so that his friends would come and "bail" him out, Freeman, p. 355.

[3] Lit: body

ARAMAIC PESHITTA NEW TESTAMENT
MATTHEW

Chapter 19

9 But *I say to you, he who forsakes his wife, except [for] adultery, and takes another, commits adultery. And he who takes a forsaken woman, commits adultery."[1]

10 His disciples said to him, "If such is the case between husband and wife, it is not advantageous to take a wife."

11 But he said to them, "Not every man is fit for this arrangement,[2] except he to whom it is given.

12 For there are believers[3] who were born so from the womb of their mother and there are believers who became believers by men and there are believers who made themselves believers for the sake of the kingdom of [m]heaven. He who is able to understand should understand."

13 Then children came near to him that he would lay his hand on them and pray. And his disciples berated them.

14 But **Jesus** said to them, "Allow the children [to] come to me and do not hinder them. For of those who are like these is the kingdom of [m]heaven."

15 And he laid his hand on them and went away from there.

16 And a certain [man] came [and] approached and said to him, "Good teacher, what good [thing] should I do that I might have eternal life?"

17 Now he said to him, "Why do you call me good?[4] There is no good [one], except one, God. Now if you want to enter life, keep the commandments."

18 He said to him, "Which [ones]?" And Jesus said to him, "**DO NOT KILL** and **DO NOT COMMIT ADULTERY** and **DO NOT STEAL** and **DO NOT GIVE FALSE TESTIMONY.**[5]

19 And **HONOR YOUR FATHER AND YOUR MOTHER** and **LOVE YOUR NEIGHBOR AS YOURSELF.**"

20 That young man said to him, "All these [things] I have kept from my youth. What do I lack?"

21 Jesus said to him, "If you want to be mature, go, sell your possessions and give [them] to the poor and you will have treasure in heaven and follow me."

---

[1] OS (cs): omit *and he who takes...adultery*; cf. note on Matt. 5:32.

[2] Lit: word

[3] Or "eunuchs," see Wilson pp. l, li and p. 176, Cureton, p. xxxiii. Context is not of marriage versus celibacy, but remaining married to the same woman.

[4] OS (cs): 'Why are you asking me concerning the good one?'

[5] Lit: testify false testimony; repeat *and not*

ARAMAIC PESHITTA NEW TESTAMENT
MATTHEW

Chapter 19

22 And that young man heard this word and went away, feeling sorry for himself, for he had many possessions.

23 Now Jesus said to his disciples, "*Truly I say to you, it is difficult for a rich man to enter into the kingdom of ᵐheaven.

24 And again *I say to you, it is easier for a camel[1] to enter into the eye of a needle than [for] a rich man to enter into the kingdom of God."

25 And when the disciples heard [him], they were very amazed and said, "Who is indeed able to ᵉ[gain] life?"

26 Jesus looked at them and said to them, "With men, this is not possible, but with God everything is possible."

27 Then answered Peter and said to him, "*Behold, we have left everything and have followed you. What indeed will we have?"

28 Jesus said to them, "*Truly I say you, you who have followed me, when the Son of Man sits on the ᵃⁿthrone of his glory in the new age, you will also sit on twelve seats of state. And you will judge the twelve tribes of Israel.

29 And everyone who has left houses or brothers or sisters or father or mother or wife or children or fields[2] on account of my name will receive one hundred[fold] and will inherit eternal life.

30 But many [are] first, who will be last, and ᵉ[many are] last, ᵉ[who will be] first.

Chapter 20

1 ᵖᵇFor the kingdom of ᵐheaven is compared to a man, the lord of a house, who went out in the morning to hire laborers for his vineyard.

2 And he made an agreement with the laborers for a denarius per day. And he sent them to his vineyard.

3 And he went out in the third hour and saw others who were standing in the marketplace and were idle.

4 And he said to them, 'Go also to the vineyard and I will give to you whatever is right.'

5 And they went away. And again he came out in the sixth and in the ninth hour and did the same.

---

[1] *Camel* is **gamla**, can be translated rope. For explanation of saying regarding camel, see Schor, pp. 19-22, Lamsa, *Gospel Light*, pp. 167-168.

[2] Repeat *or,* emphasis on all relationships.

Chapter 20

6   And toward the eleventh hour, he went out and found others who were standing and were idle. And he said to them, 'Why are you standing all day and are idle?'

7   They said to him, 'No man has hired us.' He said to them, 'Go also to the vineyard and you will receive whatever is right.'

8   Now when it was evening, the lord of the vineyard said to his steward, 'Call the laborers and give them their wage and begin from the last and [proceed] up to the first.'

9   And those of the eleventh hour came [and] each received a denarius.[1]

10   And when the first came, they thought that they would receive more. And they each received a denarius also.

11   And when they received [it], they murmured against the lord of the house.

12   And they said, 'These last [ones] worked one hour and you made them equal with us who bore the burden of the day and its heat.'

13   Now **he** answered and said to one of them, 'My friend, I did not wrong you. Did you not agree with me for a denarius?

14   Take your own and go. But I desire to give to this last [one] as to you.

15   Or is it not lawful for me to do with my own[2] what I want? Or is your eye evil[3] because I am good?

16   So the last will be first and the first last. For many are called and few chosen."[4]

17   And Jesus was about to go up to Jerusalem. And he took [aside] his twelve disciples privately on the journey and said to them,

18   "*Behold, we are going up to Jerusalem and the Son of Man will be delivered to the chief priests and to the scribes ᴾand they will condemn him[5] to death.

19   And they will deliver him to the Gentiles and they will mock him and they will beat him and they will crucify him and on the third day, he will rise up."⌐

---

[1] *Each...a denarius* is lit: a denarius, a denarius, also in v. 10.

[2] OS (s): 'in my house'

[3] Semitism: *evil* eye is an idiomatic way to say "envious or jealous," Lamsa, *Idioms*, p. 54.

[4] *Chosen* could be translated, approved or elected.

[5] Repeat *him*, vs. 18, 19.

ARAMAIC PESHITTA NEW TESTAMENT
MATTHEW

Chapter 20

20 Then the mother of the sons of Zebedee came to him, she and her sons. And she worshipped him and was asking him something.

21 Now he said to her, "What do you want?" She said to him, "Say that these, my two sons, will sit one on your right and one on your left in your kingdom."

22 Jesus answered and said, "You do not know what you ask. Are you able to drink the ^mcup that I am about to drink or to be baptized [with] the baptism [with] which I [will be] baptized?" They said to him, "We are able."

23 He said to them, "You will drink my ^mcup and be baptized [with] the baptism [with] which I [will be] baptized.[1] But that you should sit at my right and at my left is not mine to give, except to those [for] whom it is prepared by my Father."

24 And when the ten heard [of this], they were angry at those two brothers.

25 And Jesus called them and said to them, "You know that the rulers of the Gentiles are their lords and their nobles are in authority over them.

26 It should not be so among you. But rather, whoever among you wants to be great should be a minister to you.

27 And whoever among you wants to be first should be a servant to you,

28 even as the Son of Man did not come to be served, but to serve and to give himself [as] a payment on behalf of many."[2]

29 And when Jesus went out of Jericho, a large crowd was following him.

30 And *behold, two blind men were sitting on the side of the road. And when they heard that Jesus passed by, they gave a cry and said, "Have compassion on us, my Lord, Son of David."

31 But the crowds were admonishing them to be quiet. And they raised their voice more and said, "Our Lord, have compassion on us, Son of David."

32 And Jesus stopped and called them and said, "What do you want me to do for you?"

33 They said to him, "Our Lord, that our eyes be opened."[3]

---

[1] Parallel structure

[2] OS (c): adds a lengthy verse here regarding sitting in the best seats at a banquet, Wilson, p. 192.

[3] OS (c): adds 'and we may see you'

Chapter 20

34 And Jesus had compassion on them and touched their eyes and immediately their eyes were opened and they followed him.

Chapter 21

1 And when he came near to Jerusalem and came to Bethphage[1] by the side of the Mount of Olives, Jesus sent two of his disciples

2 and said to them, "Go to this village that is opposite you and immediately you will find a donkey that is tied and a colt with her. Loose [them and] bring [them] to me.

3 And if anyone says anything to you, say to him that they are needed for our Lord. And immediately he will send them here."

4 Now this which happened [was] so that what was spoken by way of the prophet would be fulfilled, who said:

5 SAY TO THE DAUGHTER OF ZION, *BEHOLD, YOUR KING COMES TO YOU MEEK AND MOUNTED ON A DONKEY AND ON A COLT, THE FOAL OF A DONKEY.[2]

6 And the disciples went and did as Jesus had commanded them.

7 And they brought the donkey and the colt and placed their garments on the colt and Jesus mounted it.

8 And a large number of crowds were spreading out their clothes in the road. And others were cutting branches from the trees and throwing [them] on the road.[3]

9 And the crowds, who were going before him and were following him, were crying out and saying: HOSANNA[4] TO THE SON OF DAVID. BLESSED IS HE WHO COMES IN THE NAME OF THE LORD. HOSANNA IN THE HIGHEST!

10 And when he entered Jerusalem, the entire city was in turmoil. And they were saying, "Who is this [man]?"

11 And the crowds were saying, "This is Jesus, the prophet, who is from Nazareth of Galilee."

---

[1] Lit: house of unripe figs, Jennings, p. 36.

[2] Two different words for female donkey

[3] Culture: spreading garments and branches on the road was done for kings, and as a sign of honor and respect. This procession was in honor of "choosing the lamb" Freeman, p. 358.

[4] *Hosanna* is the transliteration of Hebrew words for, "Save now!"

Chapter 21

12 And Jesus entered the temple of God and threw out all who were buying and selling in the temple. And he overturned the tables of the moneychangers and the chairs of those who were selling doves.

13 And he said to them, "It is written: **MY HOUSE WILL BE CALLED A HOUSE OF PRAYER.** But you have made it a [h]den of thieves."

14 And the blind and lame came near to him in the temple and he healed them.

15 Now when the chief priests and the Pharisees saw the wonders that he did and the children who were crying out in the temple and saying, "HOSANNA to the Son of David," they were displeased.[1]

16 And they said to him, "Do you hear what these are saying?" Jesus said to them, "Yes. Have you never read: **FROM THE [m]MOUTH OF CHILDREN AND INFANTS YOU HAVE FASHIONED PRAISE?**"

17 And he left them and went away outside of the city to Bethany[2] and lodged there.

18 Now in the morning when he returned to the city, he was hungry.

19 And he saw a certain fig tree by the road and came to it. And he did not find anything on it, except leaves only. And he said to it, "There will not be fruit on you again forever." And immediately that fig tree dried up.

20 And the disciples saw and marveled and said, "How quickly the fig tree dried up!"

21 Jesus answered and said to them, "*Truly I say to you, if you have faith and do not doubt, not only will you do this [e][miracle] of the fig, but even if you say to this mountain, 'Be removed and fall into the sea,' it will happen.

22 And everything that you ask for in prayer and believe, you will receive."

23 And when Jesus came to the temple, the chief priests and the elders of the people came near to him while he was teaching and said to him, "By what authority do you do these [things]? And who gave you this authority?"

24 Jesus answered and said to them, "I will ask you also a certain question and if you answer me, I will also tell you by what authority I do these [things].

---

[1] Lit: it was evil to them

[2] Lit: house of echo, Jennings, p. 36.

Chapter 21

25 The baptism of John, from where is it? Is it from ᵐheaven or from men?" Now **they** were reasoning among themselves and said, "If we say from ᵐheaven, he will say to us, 'Why[1] did you not believe him?'

26 And [if] we say from men, we are afraid of the crowd, for all of them regarded John as a prophet."

27 They answered and said to him, "We do not know." Jesus said to them, "Neither will **I** tell you by what authority I do these [things].

28 But what does it seem to you? ᵖᵇA certain man had two sons. And he came near to the first and said to him, 'My son, go today [and] work in the vineyard.'

29 Now he answered and said, 'I do not want to.' But later, he regretted [it] and went.

30 And he came near to the other and said to him the same. Now he answered and said, 'I am [going], my lord,' and did not go.

31 Which of these two did the will of his father?" They said to him, "That first [son]." Jesus said to them, "*Truly I say to you, tax collectors and harlots will precede you in the kingdom of God.

32 For John came to you in the way of uprightness and you did not believe him. But the tax collectors and harlots believed him. But not even when **you** saw [him], did you finally repent[2] that you might believe in him.⌐

33 Hear another parable. ᵖᵇA certain man was a lord of a house. And he planted a vineyard. And he set a fence around it[3] and dug a winepress in it. And he built a tower in it and handed it over to laborers and went on a journey.

34 Now when the time of harvest arrived, he sent his servants to the laborers that they might send [some] of the fruit of his vineyard to him.

35 Yet the laborers grabbed his servants and some[4] they beat and some they stoned and some they killed.

36 And again he sent other servants, more than the first, and they did the same to them.

37 And lastly, he sent them his son, saying, 'Perhaps they will respect my son.'

---

[1] Lit: on or concerning what

[2] OS (cs): 'you repented afterward'

[3] Repeat *it*

[4] Repeat *some*

ARAMAIC PESHITTA NEW TESTAMENT
MATTHEW

Chapter 21

38 But the laborers, when they saw the son, said among themselves, 'This is the heir. Come, let us kill him and obtain his inheritance.'

39 And they grabbed [him and] took him outside of the vineyard and killed him.

40 When, therefore, the lord of the vineyard comes, what should he do to those laborers?"

41 They said to him, "He will utterly[1] destroy them and he will hand over the vineyard to other laborers, those who will give him the fruit in its season."⌐

42 Jesus said to them, "Have you never read in the scripture of [al]THE STONE THAT THE BUILDERS REJECTED? IT HAS BECOME THE HEAD OF THE CORNER. THIS [STONE] CAME FROM THE PRESENCE OF THE LORD AND IT IS A WONDER IN OUR EYES.

43 Because of this, *I say to you, the kingdom of God will be taken away from you and be given to a people who bear [m]fruit.

44 And whoever falls on this stone will be bruised, and whomever it falls on, it will blow him away [e][as chaff]."⌐ [2]

45 And when the chief priests and Pharisees heard his parables, they knew that he spoke against them.

46 And they sought to arrest him, yet they were afraid of the crowd, because they regarded him as a prophet.

Chapter 22

1 And Jesus answered again in parables and said,

2 [pb]"The kingdom of [m]heaven is compared to a certain king who prepared a wedding feast[3] for his son.

3 And he sent his servants to call the invited [ones] to the wedding feast and they did not want to come.

4 Again he sent other servants and told [them] to say to the invited [ones], '*Behold, my feast is prepared and my oxen and my fat [ones] are killed and everything is ready. Come to the wedding feast.'

---

[1] Lit: evil evil

[2] Culture: winnowing was done on a high flat location so that the wind would take the chaff away.

[3] Could be just a feast, not necessarily a wedding feast. Then v. 11 would be translated "banquet clothes."

Chapter 22

5   But they scorned ^e[the servants] and went away, one to his field and another to his business.

6   Now the rest grabbed his servants and disgraced and killed [them].

7   Now when the king heard [this], he was angry and sent his armies [and] destroyed those murderers and burned their city.

8   Then he said to his servants, 'The wedding feast is prepared and those who were invited were not worthy.

9   Go, therefore, to the limits of the roads and call whomever you find to the wedding feast.'

10 And those servants went out to the roads and gathered all whom they found, bad and good, and the banquet house was filled with guests.

11 And the king entered to see the guests. And he saw there a man who was not wearing wedding clothes.

12 And he said to him, 'My friend, how did you enter this place, having no wedding garments?' And he was speechless.

13 Then said the king to the servers, 'Bind his hands and his feet and throw him into the outer darkness. Crying and gnashing of teeth will be there.[1]

14 For many are called, yet few chosen."

15 Then the Pharisees went away [and] took counsel how they might trap him with a question.

16 And they sent him their disciples with the Herodians and said to him, "Teacher, we know that you are true and you teach the way of God with truthfulness and you are not moved by anyone, for you are not a respecter of persons.[2]

17 Tell us, therefore, how does it seem to you? Is it lawful to give the poll tax to Caesar or not?"

18 Now Jesus knew their evil ^e[counsel] and said, "Why do you tempt me? ⁱHypocrites!

19 Show me the denarius[3] of the poll tax." And they brought to him a denarius.

20 And Jesus said to them, "Whose is this image and inscription?"

---

[1] See note on Mat. 13:42.

[2] Lit: receive faces of men, same construction as the phrase, hypocrite, see Idiom list.

[3] OS (s): 'seal' or 'stamp'

Chapter 22

21 They said, "Caesar's." He said to them, "Give, therefore, Caesar's to Caesar and God's to God."

22 And when they heard [this], they were amazed and they left him and went away.

23 On the same day, the Sadducees came near and said to him, "There is no resurrection of the dead." And they asked him

24 and said to him, "Teacher, Moses said to us, IF A MAN DIES WHILE HE HAS NO SONS, HIS BROTHER SHOULD TAKE HIS WIFE AND RAISE UP SEED FOR HIS BROTHER.

25 Now there were seven brothers with us. The first took a wife and died and since he had no sons, he left his wife to his brother.

26 Likewise also, the second and also the third, even up to the seventh.

27 Now finally, all of them died [and] the woman also.

28 In the resurrection, therefore, to which of those seven [brothers] will she be a wife? For all of them married her."

29 Jesus answered and said to them, "You err, because you do not know the scriptures nor[1] the power of God.

30 For in the resurrection of the dead, ᵉ[men] do not marry women, nor are women [given] to husbands, but they are ˢas the angels of God in heaven.

31 Now concerning the resurrection of the dead, have you not read that which was spoken to you by God, who said:

32 I AM THE GOD OF ABRAHAM, THE GOD OF ISAAC, [AND] THE GOD OF JACOB. And he is not the God of the dead, but of the living."

33 And when the crowds heard [this], they were amazed by his teaching.

34 Now when the Pharisees heard that he had silenced the Sadducees, they assembled together.[2]

35 And one of them who knew the law asked, tempting him,

36 "Teacher, what commandment is great in the law?"

37 And Jesus said to him, "YOU SHOULD LOVE THE LORD YOUR GOD WITH ALL YOUR HEAR AND WITH ALL YOUR SOUL AND WITH ALL YOUR STRENGTH AND WITH ALL YOUR MIND.

38 This is the great and first commandment.

---

[1] Lit: and not

[2] OS (cs): 'they were assembled against him'

ARAMAIC PESHITTA NEW TESTAMENT
MATTHEW

Chapter 22

39 And the second is like it: YOU SHOULD LOVE YOUR NEIGHBOR AS YOURSELF.

40 On these two commandments suspend[1] the law and the prophets."

41 Now while the Pharisees were assembled, Jesus asked them[2]

42 and said, "What do you say about the MESSIAH? Whose son is he?" They said to him, "The Son of David."

43 He said to them, "Yet how does David spiritually call him LORD? For he said:

44 THE LORD SAID TO MY LORD, SIT AT MY RIGHT UNTIL I PLACE YOUR ENEMIES UNDER YOUR FEET.

45 Therefore, if David called him 'LORD,' how is he his son?"

46 And no man was able to give him an answer. And no man dared to question him again from that day [on].

Chapter 23

1 Then Jesus talked with the crowds and with his disciples.

2 And he said to them, "The scribes and the Pharisees sit on the seat of Moses.

3 Everything, therefore, that they say that you should keep, keep and do. But you should not do according to their deeds. For they speak and do not act.[3]

4 And they bind heavy burdens and place [them] on the shoulders of men, but do not want to touch them with their finger[s].

5 And they do all of their deeds to be seen by men. For they broaden their phylacteries[4] and lengthen the fringes of their mantles.

6 And they love the chief places at festivals and the chief seats in the synagogues

7 and a greeting in the marketplaces and that they are called RABBI[5] by men.

8 But you should not be called RABBI. For one is your RABBI and all of you are brothers.

---

[1] Or "hang, hinge"

[2] This passage is a great example of Jesus' method of questioning and answering a question with a question.

[3] Repeat *keep;* same root: *do, deeds, act*

[4] Culture: phylacteries were worn on foreheads and arms, a small box with Scripture written on paper within, cf. Ex. 13:1-16; Deut. 11:13-23. OS (cs): add 'the straps of their phylacteries.'

[5] Lit: my master, or my great [one]. OS (s): 'Rabbi, Rabbi'

Chapter 23

9 And do not call yourselves father on earth. For one is your Father, who is in heaven.

10 And you should not be called leaders, because one is your leader, the MESSIAH.

11 But he who is great among you should be a minister to you.

12 For he who elevates himself will be humbled and he who humbles himself will be elevated.

13 [i]Woe to you,[1] scribes and Pharisees! [i]Hypocrites! Because you consume the houses of widows with the occasion that you would lengthen your prayers. Because of this, you will receive greater judgment.

14 [i]Woe to you, scribes and Pharisees! [i]Hypocrites! Because you have held the kingdom of [m]heaven closed before men.[2] For you are not entering and those who would enter, you do not allow to enter.

15 [i]Woe to you, scribes and Pharisees! [i]Hypocrites! Because you travel over sea and land to make one convert. And when he has become [e][a convert], you make him the son of GEHENNA more than you.

16 [i]Woe to you, blind guides! Because you say that whoever swears by the temple, it is nothing. But he who swears by the gold that is in the temple is guilty.

17 [i][You are] fools and blind! For what is greater,[3] the gold or the temple? Which sanctifies, the gold?

18 And [e][you say], whoever swears by the altar, it is nothing. But he who swears by the offering that is on it is guilty.

19 [i][You are] fools and blind! What is greater, the offering or the altar that is sanctified by the offering?

20 Therefore, he who swears by the altar swears by it and by everything that is on it.

21 And he who swears by the temple swears by it and by him who dwells in it.

22 And he who swears by heaven swears by the throne of God and by him who sits on it.

---

[1] Series of interjections of woe, combined with *Hypocrites*. Notice parallel structure of lines.

[2] OS (s): 'you hold the key of the kingdom of heaven before men.' OS (cs): reverse vs. 13 and 14.

[3] Repeat *what is greater*; repeat *swears by*, vs. 16-22.

Chapter 23

23 [i]Woe to you, scribes and Pharisees! [i]Hypocrites! Because you tithe mint and dill and cummin and you overlook the more important [things] of the law, judgment and mercy and faith. Now these were necessary for you to have done and you should not have overlooked those.

24 [i][You are] blind guides, who strain gnats and swallow camels![1]

25 [i]Woe to you, scribes and Pharisees! [i]Hypocrites! For you cleanse the outside of the cup and of the dish, but inside are full of violence and wickedness.

26 [i]Blind Pharisees! Cleanse first the inside of the cup and of the dish, so that their outside may also be clean.

27 [i]Woe to you, scribes and Pharisees! [i]Hypocrites! Because you are [s]like white graves that on the outside appear beautiful, but on the inside are full of the bones of the dead and all corruption.[2]

28 So also, on the outside **you** appear to men as just and on the inside you are full of wickedness and hypocrisy.

29 [i]Woe to you, scribes and Pharisees! [i]Hypocrites! Because you maintain the graves of the prophets and you adorn the tombs of the just [ones]

30 and you say, 'If we had been in the days of our fathers, we would not have been participants with them in the [m]blood of the prophets.'

31 Thereby you witness against yourselves that you are the sons of those who killed the prophets.

32 And you also fill up the measure[3] of your fathers.

33 [i][You] snakes! Offspring of [h]vipers! How will you flee from the judgment of GEHENNA?[4]

34 Because of this, *behold, I send to you prophets and wise men and scribes. Some of them you will kill and you will crucify and some of them you will beat in your synagogues and you will pursue them from city to city,

---

[1] Fig: proverb or maxim, meaning they had exactness about little matters, but not important ones, Burder, vol I, pp. 281-282.

[2] Culture: graves were whitewashed so that they were outwardly beautiful and also so that no one would step on them and accidentally become unclean, Freeman, p. 370.

[3] Culture: *fill up the measure of your fathers* means, "you are as evil as your father," Lamsa, *Idioms*, p. 54.

[4] Fig: erotesis – question to ponder

Chapter 23

35 so that all the blood of the just [ones] that has been shed on the earth will come on you, from the blood of Abel the just up to the blood of Zechariah, the son of Barachiah, whom you killed between the temple [and] the altar.

36 *Truly I say to you, all these [things] will come on this generation.

37 Jerusalem, Jerusalem,[1] you have killed the prophets and you have stoned those who were sent to her. How many times have I wanted to gather your sons ⁵like a hen gathers her chicks under her wings and you did not want ᵉ[to be gathered]?

38 *Behold, your house is left to you desolate.

39 For *I say to you, you will not see me from now until you say, BLESSED IS HE WHO COMES IN THE NAME OF THE LORD."

Chapter 24

1 And Jesus came out of the temple to go away. And his disciples came near [and] were showing him the construction of the temple.

2 And he said to them, "*Behold, do you not see all these [things]? *Truly I say to you, [one] stone here will not be left on [another] stone that will not be demolished."

3 And when Jesus sat on the Mount of Olives, his disciples came near and said among themselves and to him, "Tell us when these [things] will be and what is the sign of your coming and of the end of the age."

4 Jesus answered and said to them, "Beware, [so that] no one will deceive you.

5 For many will come in my name and they will say, 'I am the MESSIAH.' And they will deceive many.

6 Now you are about to hear of battles and a report of wars. See [that] you are not disturbed. For it is necessary that all these [things] occur, but the end [is] not yet.

7 For people will rise against people ᴾand kingdom against kingdom and famines and pestilence and earthquakes will occur in various places.⌐

8 But all these [things] are [only] the beginning of sorrows.

9 Then they will deliver you to trials and they will kill you and you will be hated by all nations because of my name.

10 Then many will be caused to stumble and will hate one another and will betray one another.

---

[1] Fig: epizeuxis, very solemn repetition

Chapter 24

11 And many false prophets will rise up and deceive many.

12 And because of the ^{as}abundance of wickedness,[1] the love of many will grow cold.

13 But he who endures until the last will have life.

14 And this gospel of the kingdom will be preached in the entire world for a testimony to all of the nations and then the end will come.

15 Now when you see the abominable sign of desecration that was spoken of by Daniel the prophet that will stand in the holy place ^{pa}(he who reads should understand),

16 then those who are in Judah should flee to the mountain.

17 And he who is on the roof should not come down to take that which is in his house.

18 And he who is in the field should not turn back behind himself to take his clothing.

19 But ⁱwoe to the pregnant women and those who are nursing in those days!

20 Now pray, so that your flight will not be in the winter, nor on the SABBATH.

21 For then a great ordeal will occur, such as has not been from the beginning of the world until now, nor will be.

22 And if those days were not cut short, no ^{sy}flesh would live. But because of the chosen [ones], those days will be cut short.

23 Then if anyone should say to you, '[2]Here is the MESSIAH or [over] here,' do not believe [him].

24 For[3] false messiahs and lying prophets will rise up and they will produce signs [and] wonders in order to deceive even the chosen [ones], if possible.

25 *Behold, I have told you beforehand.

26 Therefore, if they say to you, '*Behold, he is in the wilderness,' do not go out, or '*behold, he is in an inner chamber,' do not believe [them].

27 For as the lightning comes out of the east and is visible into the west, so the arrival of the Son of Man will be.

28 Wherever the carcass will be, there the eagles will be gathered.

---

[1] Fig: antiptosis, "great wickedness or evil"

[2] Eastern txt: add 'behold'

[3] Eastern txt: ܘܐܢ instead of *for*

Chapter 24

29 [P]And immediately after the ordeal of those days, THE SUN WILL
GROW DARK AND THE MOON WILL NOT SHINE ITS LIGHT AND STARS
WILL FALL FROM HEAVEN AND THE POWERS OF HEAVEN WILL BE
SHAKEN.

30 And then the standard[1] of the Son of Man will be seen in heaven.
And then all the tribes of the earth will mourn and they will see THE SON
OF MAN WHO COMES ON THE CLOUDS OF HEAVEN WITH [he]POWER AND
GREAT GLORY.

31 And he will send his angels with a great trumpet and they will gather
his chosen [ones] from the four winds, from one end of heaven to the
other.⌐ [2]

32 [al]Now learn an illustration from the fig tree. Immediately when its
branches are tender and its leaves bud, you know that summer has
arrived.

33 So also **you**, when you have seen these [things], will all know that I
have arrived[3] at the door.⌐

34 *Truly I say to you, this generation will not pass until all these
[things] occur.

35 Heaven and earth will pass away, yet my words will not pass away.

36 But about that [sy]day and about that[4] [sy]hour, no man knows, not even
the angels of heaven, but the Father only.

37 And as the days of Noah, so will be the arrival of the Son of Man.

38 For as they were before the flood, eating [P]and drinking and marrying
women and giving [women in marriage] to men,⌐ up to the day [in]
which Noah entered the ark,

39 and they did not know until the flood came and took all of them, so
will be the arrival of the Son of Man.

40 Then two [men] will be in the field.[5] One will be taken and one will
be left.

---

[1] *Standard* is the Aram. word, **nish**, cf. Heb. **nissi**, meaning ensign or banner,
Wilson, p. 234.

[2] Lit: from the beginning of heaven and up to the beginning [of the earth], cf.
Mark 13:27.

[3] OS (s): 'I am near' or 'it is near.' The verb could be either 1st pers sing or 3rd
fem sing. Most likely it is 1st person.

[4] Repeat *about that*

[5] OS (s): 'on the mountain'

Chapter 24

41 And two [women] will be grinding at the mill. One will be taken and one will be left.[1]

42 Therefore, watch, because you do not know in what [sy]hour your Lord will come.

43 But know this, if the master of the house had known in what watch the thief would come, he would have watched and would not have allowed his house to be broken into.

44 Because of this, **you** should be prepared also, because in an [sy]hour that you do not expect, the Son of Man will come.

45 Who truly is the faithful and wise servant whom his lord has set over his household, to give them food in its time?[2]

46 Blessed [is] that servant who, [when] his lord comes, finds him doing so.

47 *Truly I say to you, he will set him over all that he has.

48 But if a servant, [being] evil in his heart, says, 'My lord is delaying to come,'

49 [P]and begins to beat his fellow-servants and is eating and drinking with drunkards,[⌐]

50 the lord of that servant will come in a [sy]day that he does not expect and in an [sy]hour that he does not know.

51 And he will cut him in pieces[3] and assign [him] his portion with the hypocrites. Crying and gnashing of teeth will be there.

Chapter 25

1 [pb]Then the kingdom of [m]heaven will be compared to ten virgins, those who took their lamps and went out for the arrival of the bridegroom and bride.

2 Now five of them were wise and five were foolish.

3 And those foolish [virgins][4] took their lamps, but did not take oil with them.

4 But those wise [virgins] took oil in vessels with their lamps.

5 Now when the bridegroom was delayed, all of them tired and went to sleep.

---

[1] Repeat entire phrase, *one will be taken...left*, from v. 40

[2] Fig: erotesis – question to ponder

[3] Or could be translated, 'divide it,' i.e. the portion.

[4] Or [ones], feminine adjective

Chapter 25

6 And at midnight there was a shout, '*Behold, the bridegroom comes. Go out to meet him.'

7 Then all those virgins got up and put their lamps in good order.

8 And those foolish [virgins] said to the wise, 'Give us [some] of your oil, because, *behold, our lamps have gone out.'

9 These wise [virgins] answered and said, 'Will there be enough for us and for you?[1] But rather, go to those who sell and buy [some] for yourselves.'

10 And while they went to buy, the bridegroom came. And those who were prepared entered with him into the banquet hall and the door was shut.

11 Now later, those other virgins also came and said, 'Our Lord, our Lord, open [the door] for us.'

12 But **he** answered and said to them, '*Truly I say to you, I do not know you.'

13 Therefore, watch, for you do not know that ^{sy}day or ^{sy}hour.⌐

14 ^{pb}For [the kingdom of ^{m}heaven is][2] as a man who went on a journey. He called his servants and delivered his possessions to them.

15 There was one to whom he gave five talents and another two and another one, each according to his ability. And immediately he went on a journey.

16 Now he who received five talents went, engaged in business with them, and gained five others.

17 And in the same manner also, he who ^{e}[received] two engaged in business ^{e}[and gained][3] two others.

18 But he who received one [talent] went [and] dug in the ground and hid the money of his lord.

19 Now after a long time the lord of those servants came and received an accounting from them.

20 And he who received five talents came near and brought five others and said, 'My lord, you gave me five talents. *Behold, I have engaged in business ^{e}[and gained] five others with them.'

---

[1] Fig: erotesis, **lema** question, obvious answer "no"
[2] Probably an omission in the text
[3] Or "added by trade"

Chapter 25

21 His lord said to him, 'Well done, good and faithful servant. You have been faithful over little. I will place you over much. Enter into the joy of your lord.'

22 And he who ^e[received] two talents came near and said, 'My lord, you gave me two talents. *Behold, I have engaged in business ^e[and gained] two others with them.'

23 His lord said to him, 'Well done, good and faithful servant. You have been faithful over little. I will place you over much. Enter into the joy of your lord.'

24 Now he who received one talent also came near and said, 'My lord, I know[1] that you are a hard man and [that] you reap where you have not sown and [that] you gather from where you have not scattered.

25 And I was afraid and went [and] hid your talent in the ground. *Behold, you have [what is] yours.'

26 His lord answered and said to him, 'Wicked and lazy servant, you know that I reap where I have not sown and gather from where I have not scattered.

27 It would have been right for you to have put my money on the exchange table and I would have come and demanded my own with its interest.

28 Take from him, therefore, the talent and give it to him who has ten talents.

29 For to him who has[2] it will be given and it will be added to him. But he who does not have, even that which he has will be taken from him.

30 And throw the useless servant into outer darkness. Crying and gnashing of teeth will be there.'⌐

31 ^PAnd when the Son of Man comes in his glory and all of his holy angels with him, then he will sit on the throne of his glory.

32 And all the nations will be gathered before him. And he will separate them one from another ^sas a shepherd who separates the sheep from the goats.

33 And he will set the sheep on his right and the goats on his left.⌐ ³

---

[1] Lit: it is known to us, also v. 26

[2] Repeat *has, has not*

[3] Culture: In the Sanhedrin, the Judeans placed those to be acquitted on the right, and those to be condemned, on the left, Burder, vol I, p. 287.

Chapter 25

34 Then the king will say to those who are on his right, 'Come, blessed of my Father, inherit the kingdom that has been prepared for you from the foundations of the world.'

35 For I was hungry[1] and you gave me to eat. And I was thirsty and you gave me to drink. I was a stranger and you took me in.

36 I was naked and you covered me. I was sick and you visited me. And I was in prison and you came to me.

37 Then those just [ones] will say to him, 'Our Lord, when did we see that you[2] were hungry and feed you, or that you were thirsty and give you drink?

38 And when did we see that you were a stranger and take you in or that you were naked and cover you?

39 And when did we see you sick or in prison and come to you?'

40 And the king will answer and say to them, '*Truly I say to you, whatever you did for one of these, my little brothers, you did for me.'

41 Then he will say also to those who are on his left, 'Go away from me, cursed [ones], to the eternal fire that is prepared for the ACCUSER[3] and his angels.

42 For I was hungry and you did not[4] give me to eat and I was thirsty and you did not give me drink.

43 And I was a stranger and you did not take me in and I was naked and you did not cover me. And I was sick and I was in prison and you did not visit me.'

44 Then they will also answer and say, 'Our Lord, when did we see you hungry or[5] thirsty or a stranger or naked or sick or in prison and not minister to you?'

45 Then he will answer and say to them, '*Truly I say to you, whatever you did not do for one of these little ones, you did also not do for me.'

46 And these will go to eternal torment and the just [ones] to eternal life."

---

[1] Parallel structure, vs. 34-46, repeat *I was*.

[2] Repeat *you*

[3] OS (Aph): 'for the Evil one,' Chase, *Syro-Latin Text of the Gospels*, p. 16.

[4] Repeat *and not*

[5] Repeat *or*

ARAMAIC PESHITTA NEW TESTAMENT
MATTHEW

Chapter 26

1 And it happened that when Jesus completed all of these sayings, he said to his disciples,

2 "You know that after two days will be the Passover and the Son of Man will be betrayed to be crucified.

3 Then the chief priests and scribes and elders of the people were gathered at the court of the high priest, who was called Caiaphas.

4 And they held counsel against Jesus that they might arrest him by deceit and kill him.

5 And they were saying, "Not during the festival, lest a riot should occur among the people."

6 And while Jesus was in Bethany in the house of Simon the leper,[1]

7 a woman approached him who had with her an alabaster vase of oil that was very costly perfume. And she poured it on the head of Jesus while he was lying down [to eat].

8 And his disciples saw [it] and it displeased them. And they said, "Why [was there] this waste?

9 For this e[oil] could have been sold for much and e[the money] given to the poor."

10 But Jesus knew [this] and said to them, "Why are you troubling the woman? She has done a good deed[2] for me.

11 For you will always have the poor with you, but you will not always have me.

12 Now this [act], that she poured this oil on my body, she did as though for my burial.

13 And *truly I say to you, wherever this my gospel is preached in all the world, what she has done will be spoken also for her remembrance."

14 Then one of the twelve, who was called Judas[3] Iscariot, went to the chief priests.

15 And he said to them, "What do you want to give me? And I will deliver him to you." Now they promised him thirty [pieces] of silver.[4]

16 And from that time on, he was seeking an occasion to betray him.

---

[1] Or "jar-maker," the difference between jar maker and leper are only vowels, a leper would not have been having company, unless he was formerly a leper, Black, p. 9.

[2] OS (s): 'a beautiful and good work'

[3] Same name as Judah

[4] Culture: 30 drachmas of silver was the price of a slave. Arabic Tatian (Hill, p. 218; Chase, p. 18) inserts mention of the coin – thirty drachmas.

ARAMAIC PESHITTA NEW TESTAMENT
MATTHEW

Chapter 26

17 Now on the first day of the Feast of Unleavened Bread, the disciples came near to Jesus and said to him, "Where do you want us to prepare for you to eat the Passover?"

18 And **he** said to them, "Go to the city to a certain [one] and say to him, 'Our Master says, my ^{sy}time comes.' With you I will serve the Passover with my disciples."

19 And his disciples did as Jesus had commanded them and they prepared the Passover.

20 And when it was evening, he was lying down [to eat] with his twelve disciples.

21 And while they were eating, he said, "*Truly I say to you, one of you will betray me."

22 And it made them very sad. And each one of them began to say to him, "Is it I, my Lord?"

23 But he answered and said, "He who dips his hand with me in the dish, he will betray me.

24 And the Son of Man will ^{eu}go as it is written about him. But woe to the **man** by whose ^mhand the Son of Man is betrayed! It would be better for that man if he had not been born."

25 Judas, the betrayer, answered and said, "Is it I, my Master?" Jesus said to him, "**You** have said [it]."

26 And while they were eating, Jesus took up bread and blessed [it] and broke [it] and gave to his disciples and said, "Take, eat, ^{me}this is my body."

27 And he took up a cup and gave thanks and gave [it] to them. And he said, "Take, drink from it, all of you.

28 ^{me}This is my blood of the new covenant[1] that is poured out for many for the forgiveness of sins.

29 And *I say to you, I will not drink from now [on] from this fruit of the vine until the ^{sy}day in which I drink it with you anew in the kingdom of my Father."[2]

30 And they offered praise and went out to the Mount of Olives.

31 Then Jesus said to them, "All of you will be offended by me in this night, for it is written: **I WILL STRIKE THE SHEPHERD AND THE SHEEP OF HIS FLOCK WILL BE SCATTERED.**

---

[1] OS (s): 'this is my blood, the new covenant'
[2] Eastern txt: 'of God'

Chapter 26

32 But after I have risen, I [will go] before you into Galilee."

33 Peter answered and said to him, "Even if everyone be offended by you, I will never be offended by you."

34 Jesus said to him, "*Truly I say to you, in this night before the rooster crows three times, you will deny me."

35 Peter said to him, "If it be [necessary] for me to die with you, I would not deny you." And so also said all the disciples.

36 Then Jesus came with them to a place that was called Gethsemane.[1] And he said to his disciples, "Sit here while I go [and] pray."

37 And he took Peter and the two sons of Zebedee. And he began to be sad and wearied.

38 And he said to them, "There is sadness to my soul unto death. Remain with me here and watch with me."

39 And he went on a little and fell down on his face and was praying and said, "My Father, if it is possible, let this ᵐcup pass by me.[2] Nevertheless not as I want, but as you ᵉ[want]."

40 And he came to his disciples and found them asleep. And he said to Peter, "What, were you not able to watch with me one ˢʸhour?

41 Watch and pray, so that you will not enter into temptation. The spirit is ready, but the body is weak."

42 Again he went a second time [and] prayed. And he said, "My Father, if it is not possible for this ᵐcup to pass over, except I drink it, your desire will be [done]."

43 And he came again [and] found them asleep, for their eyes were heavy.

44 And he left them and went again [and] prayed a third time and he said the same thing.

45 Then he came to his disciples and said to them, "Sleep now and be rested. *Behold, the ˢʸhour has arrived and the Son of Man will be delivered into the ᵐhands of sinners.

46 Rise up, we will go. *Behold, he who has betrayed me has arrived."

47 And while he was speaking, *behold, Judas the betrayer, one of the twelve, came and with him [was] a large crowd with swords and staffs, from before the chief priests and elders of the people.

---

[1] From Heb: **Gath Shemen**, oil press, OS (s): alt. sp. GOSMNI, ܓܘܣܡܢܝ

[2] Fig: metonymy, cup represents what it contains, not liquid, but the responsibility of taking man's sins on himself, Burder, vol I. pp. 275-276.

Chapter 26

48 And Judas the betrayer had given them a sign and said, "It is he whom I kiss. Arrest him."

49 And immediately he came near to Jesus and said, "Peace, my Master." And he kissed him.

50 And **Jesus** said to him, "Did you come for this [purpose], my friend?" Then they came near and placed their hands on Jesus and arrested him.

51 And *behold, one of those who [were] with Jesus stretched out his hand and drew a sword and struck a servant[1] of the high priest and cut off his ear.

52 Then Jesus said to him, "Return the sword to its place, for all those who take up swords by swords[2] will die.

53 Or do you think that I am not able to ask of my Father and would he [not] assign to me now more than twelve legions of angels?

54 How then would the scriptures be fulfilled that so it must be?"[3]

55 At that moment Jesus said to the crowds, "Have you come out as against a robber with swords and with staffs to arrest me? I was sitting and teaching everyday with you in the temple and you did not arrest me.

56 Now this has occurred so that the writings of the prophets would be fulfilled." Then all the disciples deserted him and fled.

57 And those who arrested Jesus led him to Caiaphas, the high priest, where the scribes and elders were gathering.

58 And Simon Peter was following him from a distance up to the courtyard of the high priest. And he entered [and] sat inside with the guards that he might see the end.

59 Now the chief priests and elders and all the assembly were seeking witnesses against Jesus so that they might kill him

60 and they did not find [them] and many false witnesses came. But finally, two came near

61 and said, "This [man] said, 'I am able to destroy the temple of God and to rebuild it in three days.'"

62 And the high priest stood up and said to him, "Do you not answer anything [to this] matter? Why do these [men] witness against you?"

---

[1] OS (s): lit: the boy, ܛܠܝܐ

[2] Repeat *swords*

[3] Fig: erotesis – questions to ponder, vs. 53, 54

ARAMAIC PESHITTA NEW TESTAMENT
MATTHEW

Chapter 26

63 But Jesus was silent. And the high priest answered and said to him, "I command you by the living God that you tell us if you are the MESSIAH, the Son of God."

64 Jesus said to him, "You have said. But *I say to you, from now on you will see **THE SON OF MAN SITTING AT THE RIGHT HAND OF POWER AND COMING ON THE CLOUDS OF HEAVEN.**"

65 Then the high priest tore his clothes and said, "*Behold, he has blasphemed. Why, therefore, do we need witnesses? *Behold, now you have heard his blasphemy.

66 What do you want [to do]?" They answered and were saying, "He is deserving of death."

67 Then they spit in his face and they were striking him. And others were beating him.

68 And they said, "Prophesy to us, MESSIAH. Who is the one who beat you?"

69 Now Peter was sitting outside in the courtyard and a certain maid came near to him. And she said to him, "You also were with Jesus the Nazarene."

70 But **he** denied [it] before all of them and said, "I do not know what you are saying."

71 And when he went out to the porch,[1] another [maid] saw him and said to them, "This [man] also was there with Jesus the Nazarene."

72 And again he denied [it] with oaths, "I do not know the man."

73 And after a little while, those who were standing by came near and said to Peter, "Surely also you are one of them, for your speech also makes you known."

74 Then he began to curse and to say, "I do not know the man." And immediately the rooster crowed.

75 And Peter remembered the word of Jesus who said to him, "Before the rooster crows three times, you will deny me." And he went outside [and] cried bitterly.

Chapter 27

1 Now when it was morning, all the chief priests and elders of the people took counsel against Jesus so that they might put him to death.

---

[1] OS (s): 'he went up to the door of the courtyard'

ARAMAIC PESHITTA NEW TESTAMENT
MATTHEW

Chapter 27

2   And they bound him and took him and delivered him[1] to Pilate the governor.

3   Then Judas, the betrayer, when he saw that Jesus was condemned, repented and went [and] returned those thirty [pieces] of silver to the chief priests and to the elders.

4   And he said, "I have sinned, because I have betrayed innocent[2] blood." But they said to him, "What [is it] to us? You know [what to do about it]."[3]

5   And he threw down the silver in the temple and left and went [and] strangled himself.

6   Now the chief priests picked up the silver and said, "It is not lawful to put [this] in the treasury, because it is the price of blood."

7   And they took counsel and bought with it the field of the potter as a cemetery for strangers.

8   Because of this, that field is called "The Field of Blood"[4] until today.

9   Then it was fulfilled what was spoken by way of the prophet,[5] who said: **I TOOK THE THIRTY [PIECES] OF SILVER, THE PRICE OF THE PRECIOUS [ONE] WHICH [THOSE] FROM THE SONS OF ISRAEL AGREED ON,**

10   **AND I GAVE THEM FOR THE FIELD OF THE POTTER AS THE** LORD **COMMANDED ME.**

11   Now **Jesus** stood before the governor. And the governor asked him and said to him, "Are you the king of the Judeans?" Jesus said to him, "You have said."

12   And while the chief priests and elders were accusing him, he did not give any answer.

13   Then Pilate said to him, "Do you not hear how much they testify against you?"

14   And he did not give him an answer, not even with one word. And he greatly marveled at this.

---

[1] Repeat *him*, suffix

[2] OS (s): 'just' or 'righteous'

[3] Idiomatic way to say, "That is your problem," Younan interlinear translation.

[4] Aram. word for *field* is **qritha** ܩܪܝܬܐ meaning "village, land, country or field." OS (s): spelled ܩܘܪܝܬ

[5] Notice omission of "Jeremiah," cf. OS (s), Diatesseron and Old Latin

Chapter 27

15 Now at every feast, the governor was accustomed to free one prisoner[1] to the people, whomever **they** were desiring.

16 And they had imprisoned a well-known prisoner who was called Barabbas.[2]

17 And when they were gathered, Pilate said to them, "Whom do you want me to free to you, Barabbas or Jesus, who is called the MESSIAH?"

18 For Pilate was realizing that they had delivered him up because of envy.

19 Now while the governor sat on his judgment seat, his wife sent to him and said to him, "Have nothing to do with that just [man], for I have suffered much today in my dream because of him."

20 But the chief priests and elders persuaded the crowds to ask for Barabbas and to destroy Jesus.

21 And the governor answered and said to them, "Whom do you want me to free to you from the two?" And **they** said, "Barabbas."

22 Pilate said to them, "And what should I do to Jesus, who is called the MESSIAH?" All of them said to him, "He should be crucified!"

23 The governor said to them, "For what has he done that is evil?" But **they** cried out all the more and said, "He should be crucified!"

24 Now Pilate, when he saw that nothing helped, but [that] the clamor was increased, he took water [and] washed his hands before the crowd and said, "I am absolved of the blood of this just [man]. You should do ᵉ[what you will]."

25 And all the people answered and said, "His blood [be] on us and on our children."

26 Then he released Barabbas to them and scourged Jesus with whips and delivered him up to be crucified.

27 Then the soldiers of the governor took Jesus to the Praetorium and assembled all the company[3] of soldiers against him.

28 ᴾAnd they stripped him and clothed him with a robe of purple.

---

[1] Same root: *prisoner, imprisoned*, vs. 15, 16

[2] *Barabbas* means lit: son of the father. Irony that the people chose Barabbas over Jesus. OS (s): 'Jesus Bar-abba.'

[3] Culture: Aram word **espira** ܐܣܦܝܪܐ, cf. Grk **speira**, ordinarily 600 soldiers, the tenth part of a legion, Freeman, p. 392.

Chapter 27

29 And they wove a crown of thorns and placed [it] on his head and a reed in his right hand and they bowed down on their knees[1] before him and were mocking him and said, "Hail,[2] king of the Judeans."

30 And they spit in his face and they took the reed and were striking him on his head.

31 And after they had mocked him, they stripped him of the robe and dressed him in his clothes and led him[3] away to be crucified.

32 And while they were going out, they found a man, a Cyrenian, whose name [was] Simon. They compelled this [man] to carry his cross.

33 And they came to the place that is called Golgotha, which is interpreted, "The Skull."

34 And they gave him vinegar that was mixed with gall[4] to drink. And he tasted [it], yet did not want to drink [it].

35 And when they crucified him, they divided his clothes by lot.

36 And they were sitting and watching him there.

37 And they placed over his head the cause of his death in an inscription, "This is Jesus, king of the Judeans."

38 And two thieves were crucified with him, one on his right and one on his left.

39 And those who were passing by were insulting him and were shaking their heads.[5]

40 And they said, "e[You who would] tear down the temple and rebuild it in three days, save yourself if you [are] the Son of God and come down from the cross."

41 Likewise, also, the chief priests were mocking [him] with the scribes and elders and Pharisees.

42 And they said, "He saved others, [but] is not able to save himself. If he is the king of Israel, let him come down now from the cross and we will believe in him.

43 He put his trust in God. Let him save him now if he is pleased with him, for he said, 'I am the Son of God.'"

---

[1] Lit: kneeled on their knees
[2] Lit: Peace
[3] Repeat *him* as pronoun and suffix
[4] Root verb means, "to be bitter"
[5] Culture: *shaking their heads* is extreme disapproval.

Chapter 27

44 Likewise, also, those robbers[1] who were crucified with him were insulting him.

45 Now from the sixth hour there was darkness over all the land until the ninth hour.

46 And about the ninth hour, Jesus cried with a loud voice and said, "God, God,[2] why have you left me?"

47 And some of those who were standing there, when they heard, were saying, "This [man] calls to Elijah."

48 And immediately one of them ran and took a sponge and filled it with vinegar and placed it on a reed and offered [a drink] to him.

49 But the rest were saying, "Leave [him]. We will see if Elijah comes to rescue him."

50 Now Jesus again cried out with a loud voice and gave up his spirit.

51 **P**And immediately the curtains of the temple[3] were torn in two from the top to the bottom and the earth was shaken and the rocks were split.

52 And the tombs were opened and many bodies of the holy [ones] who were asleep rose up

53 and went out. And after his resurrection they entered the holy city and were seen by many.

54 And the centurion and those who were watching Jesus with him, when they saw the earthquake and those [things] that had occurred, they were very afraid and said, "*Truly this was the Son of God."⌐

55 Now there were also there many women who were watching from a distance, those who had followed Jesus from Galilee and had ministered to him.

56 One of them [was] Mary Magdalene, and Mary, the mother[4] of James and John, and the mother of the sons of Zebedee.

57 Now when it was evening, a rich man from Ramath came, whose name [was] Joseph, who also was taught by Jesus.

58 This [man] came near to Pilate and asked for the body of Jesus. And Pilate commanded that the body be given to him.

59 And Joseph took the body and wrapped it in a cloth of clean linen.

---

[1] Different word than v. 38

[2] Text has **Eil, Eil**, from Hebrew word for mighty God, **El.** In Aramaic, it would have easily sounded like "Elijah;" could be quote from Ps 22:1.

[3] OS (s): for *temple* is 'house of holiness' or 'holy of holies.'

[4] OS (s): 'daughter,' agrees with Mk 15:40, 16:1, also in Pal Syr.

ARAMAIC PESHITTA NEW TESTAMENT
MATTHEW

Chapter 27

60 And he placed it in his new tomb that was hewn in rock. And they rolled a large stone [and] placed [it] over the opening of the tomb and they went away.

61 Now Mary Magdalene was there and the other Mary, who were sitting opposite the grave.

62 And on the next day that was after the preparation, the chief priests and the Pharisees were gathered with Pilate

63 and said to him, "Our lord, we are reminded that that ^h deceiver was saying while he was alive, 'After three days, I will rise up.'

64 Command therefore to guard the grave until the third day, so that his disciples will not come [and] steal him in the night and say to the people that he has risen from the dead and the last deception should become more evil than the first."

65 Pilate said to them, "You have soldiers. Go, watch as you know [how]."

66 And they went [and] set a watch on the tomb and sealed that stone, with the soldiers.

Chapter 28

1 Now in the evening of the SABBATH, as it was twilight [on] the first of the week, Mary Magdalene and the other Mary came to see the grave.

2 And *behold, a great earthquake occurred, for an angel of the LORD came down from heaven and came near [and] rolled the stone from the opening and he was sitting on it.

3 And his appearance was ^s like lightning and his clothes were white ^s like snow.

4 And those who were watching, trembled with fear of him and became ^s like dead [men].

5 Now the angel answered and said to the women, "Do not fear, for I know that you seek Jesus who was crucified.

6 He is not here, for he has risen, as he said. Come, see the place in which our Lord was laid.

7 And go quickly [and] tell his disciples that he has risen from the dead, and *behold, ^e [he goes] before you to Galilee. There you will see him. *Behold, I have told you."

8 And they went away quickly from the grave with fear and with great joy and ran to tell his disciples.

Chapter 28

9   And *behold, Jesus met up with them and said to them, "Peace to you." And they came near [and] clasped his feet and worshipped him.

10   Then Jesus said to them, "Do not fear! But go [and] tell my brothers that they should go to Galilee and there they will see me."

11   Now when they had gone, some of those soldiers came to the city and told the chief priests everything that had occurred.

12   And they were gathered with the elders and took counsel and gave no little¹ money to the soldiers

13   and said to them, "Say that his disciples came [and] stole him in the night while we were asleep.

14   And if this is heard before the governor, **we** will persuade him and we will not make trouble for you."

15   Now **they**, when they had received the money, did as they had instructed them. And this report has gone out among the Judeans up to today.

16   Now the eleven disciples went to Galilee to the mountain where Jesus had arranged [for] them to meet.

17   And when they saw him, they worshipped him. But some of them were doubting.

18   And Jesus came near [and] spoke with them and said to them, "All authority is given to me in ᵐʳheaven and on earth.² And as my Father sent me, I send you.

19   Go, therefore, disciple all nations and baptize them in the name [of] the Father and the Son and the Holy Spirit.

20   And teach them to keep all that I commanded you. And *behold, **I** am with you all the days until the end of the world." Amen.³

---

¹ Lit: not a small [amount]

² Fig: merismos, meaning "everywhere"

³ Lit: let it be so, from Hebrew.

ARAMAIC PESHITTA NEW TESTAMENT
MARK

Chapter 1

1   The beginning of the gospel of Jesus Christ, the Son of God.

2   As it is written in Isaiah the prophet: *BEHOLD I WILL SEND MY MESSENGER BEFORE YOUR ᵐFACE THAT HE MIGHT PREPARE YOUR WAY.

3   A VOICE THAT CRIES IN THE WILDERNESS: PREPARE THE WAY OF THE LORD AND MAKE STRAIGHT HIS PATHS.

4   John was in the wilderness, baptizing and preaching the baptism of repentance for the forgiveness of sins.

5   And the whole ᵐregion of Judah went out to him and all the sons of ᵐJerusalem, and he was baptizing them in the Jordan [river] as they confessed their sins.

6   Now **John** was clothed with clothing[1] of the hair of camels and was bound with a leather girdle around his loins and his food was locusts and wild honey.

7   And he was preaching and said, "*Behold, one comes after me who is more powerful than I, the straps of whose sandals I am not worthy to stoop [and] loosen.

8   I have baptized you with water, but **he** will baptize you with the Holy Spirit."

9   And it was in those days [that] Jesus came from Nazareth of Galilee and was baptized in the Jordan [River] by John.

10 And immediately[2] when he came up from the water, he saw the heavens[3] split and the Spirit, ˢas a dove, came down on him.

11 And there was a voice from the heavens: "You are my beloved Son. I am pleased with you."

12 And immediately the Spirit led him out into the wilderness.

13 And he was there in the wilderness [for] forty days, being tempted by SATAN. And he was with the wild beasts and angels were ministering to him.

14 Now after John was delivered up, Jesus came to Galilee and was preaching the gospel of the kingdom of God.

15 And he said, "The ˢʸtime is complete and the kingdom of God has arrived. Repent and believe in the gospel."

---

[1] Same root: *clothed with, clothing*

[2] Lit: at once (not idiom), very common usage in Mark

[3] Eastern txt: *heaven* (singular)

Chapter 1

16 And while walking round about the Sea of Galilee, he saw Simon and Andrew, his brother, who were casting nets into the sea, for they were fishermen.

17 And Jesus said to them, "Follow me and I will make you fishermen of men."[1]

18 And immediately they left their nets and followed him.

19 And as he passed on a little further, he saw James, the son of Zebedee, and John, his brother, and they also [were] in a boat mending their nets.

20 And he called them and immediately they left Zebedee, their father, in the boat with the hired servants and followed him.

21 And when they entered Capernaum, immediately he was teaching[2] on the SABBATHS in their synagogues.

22 And they were amazed at his teaching, for he was teaching them as an authority and not as their scribes.

23 And in their synagogue there was a man in whom was an unclean spirit. And he called out

24 and said, "What have we to do with you, Jesus, the Nazarene? Have you come to destroy us? I know who you [are]. You are the holy one of God."

25 And Jesus rebuked him and said, "Close your mouth and come out of him."[3]

26 And the unclean spirit threw him down and cried out with a loud voice and went out of him.

27 And all of them were amazed and were asking each other and saying, "What is this? And what is this new teaching? For with authority he commands even the unclean spirits and they obey him."

28 And immediately his fame went out into all the land of Galilee.

29 And they went away from the synagogue and came to the house of Simon and of Andrew, with James and John.

30 And the mother-in-law of Simon was sick with a fever and they told him about her.

31 And he came near [and] took her by her hand and raised her up. And immediately her fever left her and she was ministering to them.

---

[1] See note on Mat 4:19

[2] Repeat *was teaching, teaching,* vs. 21, 22

[3] Word play: *mouth,* **pemakh** ܦܘܡܟ and *come out,* **puwaq** ܦܘܩ

ARAMAIC PESHITTA NEW TESTAMENT
MARK

Chapter 1

32 Now in the evening at the setting of the sun, they brought to him all those who were very ill and possessed.

33 And the entire city was gathered at the door.

34 And he healed many that were very ill with diverse sicknesses and he cast out many devils. And he did not allow the devils to speak, because they knew him.

35 And in the morning he got up very early[1] and went to a desert place and was praying there.

36 And Simon and those with him were searching for him.

37 And when they found him, they said to him, "Everyone is searching for you."

38 He said to them, "Walk into the villages and into the cities that are nearby, for I will also preach there, for I have come to [do] this."[2]

39 And he was preaching in all their synagogues in all of Galilee and cast out demons.

40 And a leper came to him and fell at his feet and was begging him and said to him, "If you want to, you can cleanse me."

41 And **Jesus** had compassion on him and stretched out his hand, touched him and said, "I want to. Be cleansed."

42 And immediately his leprosy went away from him and he was cleansed.

43 And he charged him and sent him out

44 and said to him, "See [that] you do not speak to anyone, but go, show yourself to the priests and offer an offering for your purification,[3] as Moses commanded for their testimony."

45 But when **he** went away, he began much preaching and made known the event, so that Jesus was not able to openly enter the city, but was outside in a deserted place. And they were coming to him from every place.

Chapter 2

1 And Jesus again entered into Capernaum after [some] days. And when they heard that he was in the house,

---

[1] Lit: before

[2] Lit: for to this [reason] I have come

[3] Same roots: *offer, offering; purification, he was cleansed*, v. 42

Chapter 2

2   many gathered, so that ᵉ[the house] was not able to contain them, not even in front of the door. And he was speaking the word with them.

3   And they came to him and brought him a paralytic, bearing him between four [men].

4   And because they were not able to draw near to him because of the crowd, they climbed up to the roof and lifted the covering of the place where Jesus was and they lowered the bed on which the paralytic was laid.

5   And when Jesus saw their faith, he said to that paralytic, "My son, your sins are forgiven you."

6   Now there were there some scribes and Pharisees, who were sitting and reasoning in their heart[s],

7   "Why does this [man] speak blasphemy? Who is able to forgive sins, except one, God?"

8   But Jesus knew in his spirit that they were reasoning these [things] in themselves and he said to them, "Why do you reason these [things] in your heart[s]?

9   Which is easier to say to the paralytic, 'Your sins are forgiven you' or to say, 'Rise, take up your bed and walk?'

10   But that you might know that it is lawful [for] the Son of Man to forgive sins on earth," he said to the paralytic,

11   "*I say to you, Rise, take up your bed, and go to your house."

12   And he got up immediately and took his bed and went away in the sight of all, so that all of them were amazed and praised God, saying that they had never seen such.

13   And he went again to the sea and all the crowds were coming to him and he was teaching them.

14   And while passing by, he saw Levi the son of Alphaeus, who was sitting at the customs-house and he said to him, "Follow me." And he got up [and] followed him.

15   And it happened that when he was seated [to eat] in his house, many tax collectors and sinners[1] were seated [to eat] with Jesus and with his disciples, for there were many and they followed him.

16   And the scribes and the Pharisees, when they saw that he was eating with the tax collectors and with sinners, said to his disciples, "Why does he eat and drink with tax collectors and sinners?"

---

[1] Repeat *publicans and sinners*, vs. 15-17

ARAMAIC PESHITTA NEW TESTAMENT
MARK

Chapter 2

17 But when Jesus heard [this] he said to them, "The whole do not have need for a physician, but those who are very ill. I have not come to call the just, but rather the sinners."

18 Now the disciples of John and the Pharisees were fasting and came and said to him, "Why do the disciples of John and of the Pharisees fast and your disciples do not fast?"[1]

19 Jesus said to them, "Are the guests of the wedding feast able to fast as long as the bridegroom is with them?[2] No!

20 But the days will come when the bridegroom will be taken away from them. Then they will fast in that [sy]day.

21 [al]No man lays a new patch and sews [it] on an old garment, lest the new addition takes away from the old and the tear becomes worse.[3]

22 And no man puts new wine into old wineskins, lest the wine burst the wineskins and the wineskins are ruined and the wine is poured out. But they put new wine into new wineskins."

23 And it happened that when Jesus went [through] the sown fields on the SABBATH, his disciples were walking and picking the heads of grain.

24 And the Pharisees said to him, "See, why are they doing something that is not lawful [to do] on the SABBATH?"

25 Jesus said to them, "Have you never read what David did when he had need and was hungry, [both] he and those with him,

26 how he entered the house of God, while Abiathar [was] high priest,[4] and ate the bread of the table of the LORD, which was not lawful to eat except for the priests, and gave also to those who were with him?"

27 And he said to them, "The SABBATH was made for[5] man and man was not [e][made] for the SABBATH.

28 So also, the Son of Man is the Lord of the SABBATH."

Chapter 3

1 And again Jesus entered into the synagogue, and there was there a certain man whose hand was withered.

2 And they were watching him, so that if he healed him on the SABBATH, they might accuse him.

---

[1] Repeat *fast*

[2] Fig: erotesis, **lema** question, obvious answer "no"

[3] Or "larger"

[4] OS (S): omit *while Abiathar [was] high priest*

[5] Lit: because of

103

Chapter 3

3 And he said to that man whose hand was withered, "Stand up in the middle."

4 And he also said to them, "Is it lawful on the SABBATH to do that which is good or that which is evil? To save life or to destroy [it]?"[1] But **they** were silent.

5 And he looked on them with anger, being saddened by the hardness of their heart[s]. And he said to that man, "Stretch out your hand." And he stretched [it] out[2] and his hand was restored.

6 And the Pharisees went out immediately with the Herodians[3] and took counsel against him, how they might destroy him.

7 And Jesus went with his disciples to the sea and many people were joining with him from Galilee and from Judah

8 and from Jerusalem and from Idumaea and from beyond Jordan and from Tyre and from Sidon.[4] Many crowds who had heard all that he had done came to him.

9 And he told his disciples to bring him a boat because of the crowds, so that they would not press on him.

10 For he had healed so many up until then that they were falling on him in order to touch him.

11 And those who had torments of unclean spirits, when they saw him, were falling down and crying out and saying, "You are the Son of God."

12 And he severely rebuked them that they should not reveal him.

13 And he climbed up a mountain and called those whom he wanted and they came to him.

14 And he chose twelve to be with him ᴾand to send them to preach

15 and to be authorities to heal the sick and to cast out devils.┐

16 And he named Simon the name[5] Peter,

17 and to James the son of Zebedee and to John the brother of James, he gave them the name Boanerges, which is, sons of thunder.[6]

---

[1] Fig: erotesis – question to ponder

[2] Repeat *stretched out*, he obeyed exactly

[3] Lit: sons of Herod

[4] Repeat *and from*

[5] Same root: *named, name*; notice the polysyndeton in this chapter.

[6] Idiom of use with *sons* shows characteristics or description. *Boanerges* is **bnay-raghshee,** from Heb. and means sons of noise, rage, or turbulence. OS (s): omit explanation.

Chapter 3

18 And [he chose] Andrew and Philip and Bartholomew[1] and Matthew and Thomas and James, the son of Alphaeus, and Thaddeus and Simon the Canaanite,[2]

19 and Judas Iscariot, who betrayed him. And they came to a house

20 and the crowds gathered again, so that they were not able to eat bread.

21 And his relatives heard and went out to seize him, for they were saying that he had gone out of his mind.

22 And those scribes who had come down from Jerusalem were saying, "BEELZEBUB is in him, and he casts out devils by the chief of the devils."

23 And Jesus called them and in parables said to them, "How is SATAN able to cast out SATAN?

24 For if a kingdom will be divided against itself, that kingdom is not able to stand.[3]

25 And if a house will be divided against itself, that house is not able to stand.

26 And if SATAN stands against himself and is divided, he is not able to stand, but is [at] his end.

27 No man is able to enter the house of a strong man and to grab his possessions, except he first binds the strong man and then robs his house.

28 *Truly I say to you, all the sins and blasphemies that men will blaspheme[4] will be forgiven them,

29 but he who blasphemes against the Holy Spirit has no forgiveness forever, but is guilty before the judgment that is eternal."[5]

30 [This was] because they were saying, "He has an unclean spirit."

31 And his mother and his brothers came, standing outside, and they sent [someone] to call him to them.

32 Now the crowd was sitting around him and they said to him, "*Behold, your mother and your brothers [are] outside seeking you."

33 And he answered and said to them, "Who is my mother? And who are my brothers?"

34 And he looked at those who sat with him and said, "*Behold, my mother, and *behold, my brothers.

---

[1] *Bartholomew* is **Bar-Tulmay**, also known as Nathaniel.

[2] Or "zealot"

[3] Repeat *is not able to stand*, vs. 24-26; this passage could be an allegory

[4] Same root: *blasphemies, blaspheme*

[5] Lit: for the age, *forever* is the same word as *eternal*

Chapter 3

35   For he who does the will of God is my brother ^Pand my sister and my mother."⅂

Chapter 4

1   And again he began to teach by the shore of the sea. And large crowds were gathered around him so that he boarded [and] sat in a boat on the sea. And the entire crowd was standing on the land by the shore of the sea.¹

2   And he was teaching them in many parables and said in his teaching,

3   ^{pb.}"Listen. *Behold, a sower went out to sow²

4   and while he sowed, one ^e[seed] fell by the side of the road and a bird came and ate it.

5   And another ^e[seed] fell on rock where there was not much earth, and immediately it sprouted ³because there was no depth of earth.

6   But when the sun came up, [the plant] withered and because it had no root, it dried up.

7   And another ^e[seed] fell among the thorns.⁴ And the thorns grew up and choked it and it did not bear fruit.

8   But another ^e[seed] fell on good earth and grew up and matured and bore fruit, some thirty and some sixty and some one hundred[fold]."

9   And he said, "He who has ears to hear should hear."

10 Now when they were alone, those who were with him with his twelve asked him about that parable.

11 And Jesus said to them, "To you is given to know the mystery of the kingdom of God. But to [those] outside, everything is in parables,

12 so that **WHEN THEY SEE, THEY WILL SEE YET NOT SEE, AND WHEN THEY HEAR, THEY WILL HEAR⁵ YET NOT UNDERSTAND, LEST THEY SHOULD RETURN AND THEIR SINS WOULD BE FORGIVEN THEM.**"

13 And he said to them, "Do you not understand this parable? Then how will you understand all parables?⁶

---

¹ Repeat *by the shore of the sea*, encircling the passage
² Same root: *sower, sow*
³ OS (s): add 'And' (to start new sentence here)
⁴ Lit: house of thorns, also v. 18
⁵ Same root: *see, hear*
⁶ Fig: erotesis – question to ponder

Chapter 4

14 The sower, who sowed, sowed the word.[1]

15 And those [e][seed] that were by the side of the road are those in whom the word is sown. And when they have heard, immediately SATAN comes and takes away the word that was sown in their heart[s].

16 And those that were sown on rock are those that when they have heard the word, immediately receive it with joy.

17 And they have no root in themselves, but they are temporary.[2] And when trouble or persecution happens on account of the word, they are quickly offended.

18 And those that were sown among thorns are those who have heard the word

19 and the care of this world and the [as]deceit of riches and the rest of the other lusts enter [and] choke the word, and they are without fruit.

20 And those that were sown on good ground are those who have heard the word and receive [it] and bear fruit thirty and sixty and one hundred[fold]."⌐

21 And he said to them, "Is there any profit for a lamp to be placed under a basket or under a couch?[3] Should it not be placed on a lamp stand?

22 For [t]there is not anything that is hidden that will not be revealed or [anything] occurring in secret and is not revealed.

23 If a man has ears to hear, he should hear."

24 And he said to them, "Notice what you hear. With that measure that you measure, it will be measured to you, and it is accumulated to you who hear.

25 For he who has, it will be given to him. And he who has not, even that which he has will be taken from him."

26 And he was saying, "Such is the kingdom of God [pb]as a man who throws seed on the ground.[4]

27 And he will sleep and rise in the night and in the day, and the seed will grow and be tall, as **he** does not know [how],

---

[1] Same root: *sower sowed*, repeat *sown,* vs. 15-20

[2] Lit: of a [short] time

[3] *Couch* is the Aram word, **'arsa,** meaning, bed, couch, divan, bier. Common idea is that of a wooden frame, cf. Strongs #6200, 6210. fig: erotesis, **lema** question, obvious answer "no"

[4] Word play: *seed,* **zoara** ܙܪܥܐ, *ground,* **ar'aa** ܐܪܥܐ throughout this parable

Chapter 4

28 for the ground brings forth the fruit. And first comes the plant, and after it the ear,[1] and finally the full grain in the ear.

29 And when the fruit is ripe, immediately [pe]the sickle comes, because the harvest has arrived."⅂

30 And he said, "What is the kingdom of God like and with what parable can we compare it?[2]

31 [pb]It is as a grain of mustard, which, when it is planted in the ground, is the least of all the small seeds that are on the earth.[3]

32 And when it is planted, it grows up and becomes greater than all the herbs and produces great branches, so that a bird is able to nest in its shade."[4]

33 With parables such as these, Jesus was speaking with them, parables[5] such as they were able to hear.

34 And without parables, he was not speaking with them. But he was explaining everything to his disciples privately.

35 And he said to them on the same day at evening, "Let us cross over to the other shore."

36 And they left the crowds and conducted him away in a boat, and there were other boats with them.

37 And there was a great storm and wind, and waves were falling into the boat, and [e][the boat] was about to be filled.

38 And **Jesus** was asleep on a cushion[6] in the stern of the boat, and they came [and] woke him and said to him, "Our Master, do you not care that we are being destroyed?"

39 And he rose up and rebuked the wind and said to the sea, "Cease; be restrained." And the wind ceased and a great calm occurred.

40 And he said to them, "Why are you fearful in this manner? And why do you not have faith?"[7]

---

[1] Or "spike"

[2] Fig: erotesis – question to ponder; same root: *parable, compare*, could be translated: "illustration can we illustrate it."

[3] Word play: *least*, **zairey** ܙܥܘܪܝ, *seeds*, **zeruney** ܙܪܥܘܢܝ. *ground* and *earth*, same word.

[4] Culture: the mustard seed is not the smallest of all the seeds, but it makes the largest plant, a tree, from the small seed.

[5] Repeat *parables*, v. 34 also

[6] Or "blanket"

[7] Fig: erotesis, **lema** questions, obvious answer "yes"

ARAMAIC PESHITTA NEW TESTAMENT
MARK

Chapter 4
41 And they feared a great fear[1] and were saying one to another, "Who indeed is this [man] that the winds and sea obey him?"

Chapter 5
1 And he came to the opposite side of the sea to the region of the Gadarenes.[2]
2 And when he disembarked from the boat, he met a man from the tombs who had an unclean spirit.
3 And he was living in the tombs and no man was able to bind him with chains,
4 because whenever he was bound with shackles and with chains, he would break the chains and would cut the shackles. And no man was able to subdue him.
5 And always in the night and in the day, he was in the tombs and in the mountains and he was crying and cutting himself with stones.
6 And when he saw Jesus from a distance, he ran [and] worshipped him.
7 And he cried with a loud voice and said, "What have I to do with you, Jesus, Son of the Most High God? I urge you by God that you do not torment me."
8 For he was saying to him, "Come out from the man, unclean spirit."
9 And he asked him, "What is your name?" He said to him, "Our name [is] Legion, because we are many."
10 And he was begging him very much not to send him out of the country.
11 Now there was there near the mountain a large herd of pigs that were feeding.
12 And those demons were begging him and saying, "Send us against those pigs that we may attack[3] them."
13 And he allowed them. And those unclean spirits went away and attacked the pigs, and that herd ran to a steep place and fell into the sea and about two thousand [pigs] were drowned in the water.
14 And those who were tending them fled and reported [it] in the city and also in the villages. And they came out to see what had happened.

---

[1] Same root: *feared, fear*, also *fearful*, v. 40
[2] OS (s): 'Gargasia'
[3] Lit: enter into them, but this use of 𐎹 with 𐎹 means attack

Chapter 5

15 And they came to Jesus and saw him, the one possessed of demons, in whom Legion had been, dressed and sober and sitting. And they were afraid.

16 And those who had seen related to them how it happened to the one possessed of demons and also about those pigs.

17 And they began begging him to leave their border.

18 And when he boarded a boat, he who had been possessed of demons was begging him that he might be with him,

19 yet he did not allow him. On the contrary, he said to him, "Go to your house to your people and tell them what the LORD did for you and how he had compassion on you."

20 And he went and began preaching in the Decapolis[1] what Jesus had done for him, and all of them were amazed.

21 And when Jesus had crossed over by boat to that other side, large crowds again were gathered around him while he was by the shore of the sea.

22 And a certain [man] whose name [was] Jairus came from the rulers of the synagogue.[2] And when he saw him, he fell down at his feet.

23 And he was begging him very much and said to him, "My daughter is very sick. Come [and] place your hand on her and she will be made whole and live."

24 And Jesus went away with him and a large crowd followed him and they were pressing on him.

25 And a certain woman, who had a flow of blood [for] twelve years,

26 who had suffered much from many doctors and had spent everything that she had and was not helped some, but was afflicted even more,

27 when she heard about Jesus, came through the press of the crowd [and] from behind him touched his clothing,

28 for she was saying, "If only I can touch his clothing, I will live."

29 And immediately the flow of her blood dried up and she felt in her body that she had been healed of her sickness.

30 Now Jesus immediately knew within himself that power had gone out of him. And he turned to the crowd and said, "Who touched my garments?"

---

[1] Lit: ten cities

[2] OS (s): 'one of the leaders of the synagogue'

Chapter 5

31 And his disciples said to him, "Do you see the crowds that are pressing you, and you say, who touched me?"

32 And he was looking to see who had done this.

33 And that woman, being afraid and trembling, because she knew what had happened to her, came [and] fell down before him and told him all the truth.

34 And **he** said to her, "My daughter, your faith has given you life. Go in peace and be healed from your sickness."

35 And while he was speaking they came from the house of the ruler of the synagogue and were saying, "Your daughter is dead. Why therefore are you troubling the teacher?"

36 But Jesus heard the word that they said and said to the ruler of the synagogue, "Do not fear; only believe."

37 And he did not allow anyone to go with him, except Simon Peter and James and John, the brother of James.

38 And they came to that house of the ruler of the synagogue and saw that they were troubled and weeping and wailing.[1]

39 And he entered and said to them, "Why are you troubled and weeping? The girl is not dead, but she is asleep,"

40 and they were laughing at him. But **he** sent all of them out and he took the father of the girl and her mother and those who were with him and entered where the girl was laid.

41 And he took the hand of the girl and said to her, "[Young] girl, rise."[2]

42 And immediately the girl rose up and walked, for she was twelve years old. And they were amazed [with] great amazement.[3]

43 And he commanded them very much that no one should make this known. And he said that they should give her [something] to eat.

Chapter 6

1 And he went away from there and came to his city and his disciples were following him.

---

[1] Fig: onomatopoeia, *wailing* is **mililin**, from **alia**. The mourners cried "al-a-lai, al-a-lai," hence also Grk: **alalazo**.

[2] **Talitha** means girl, **kumi** means stand or rise up.

[3] Same root: *amazed, amazement*

ARAMAIC PESHITTA NEW TESTAMENT
MARK

Chapter 6

2   And when it was the SABBATH, he began to teach in the synagogue. And many who heard were amazed and were saying, "Where [did] this man [e][learn] these [things]?[1] And what is [this] wisdom that was given to him, that miracles such as these might be done by his [m]hand?

3   Is this not the carpenter, the son of Mary [P]and the brother of James and of Joses and of Judas and of Simon? And *behold, are not his sisters here with us?" And they were offended at him.

4   And Jesus said to them, "There is [t]no prophet who is dishonored, except in his own city and among his own relatives and in his own house."

5   And he was **not** able to do even one miracle there, except that he laid his hand on a few sick and healed [them].

6   And he was amazed by the lack of their faith. And he was traveling in the villages while teaching.

7   And he called his twelve and began to send them in pairs. And he gave them authority over unclean spirits, to cast [them] out.

8   And he commanded them that they should not carry anything for the journey, except only a staff, no bag and no bread and no brass in their purses,[2]

9   but [that] they should wear sandals and not wear two coats.

10   And he said to them, "Into that house, which you enter, there be until you leave there.

11   And whoever does not receive you and does not hear you when you leave from there, shake off the dust that is under the sole of your feet[3] for their witness. And *truly I say to you, it will be [more] pleasant for Sodom and for Gomorrah in the [sy]day of judgment than for that city.

12   And they went out and preached that [men] should repent.

13   And many demons were cast out. And they were anointing with oil[4] many sick [people] and were healing [them].

14   And Herod, the king, heard about Jesus, for his name was made known to him. And he was saying [that] John the baptizer had risen from the dead, [and] because of this, miracles are done by him.

---

[1] Fig: erotesis, series of questions to ponder, vs. 2, 3.

[2] Repeat *no*

[3] Culture: *shake off the dust* means "do not retain any animosity."

[4] Same root: *anointing, oil*

Chapter 6
15 Others were saying that he was Elijah, and others[1] that he was a prophet like one of the prophets.
16 Now when Herod heard [this] he said, "[It is] John, the one whose head **I** cut off. **He** has risen from the dead."
17 For **Herod** had sent [and] arrested John and bound him [in] prison because of Herodias, the wife of Philip, his brother, whom he had taken.
18 For John had told Herod, "It is unlawful for you to take the wife of your brother."
19 Now **Herodias** was threatened by him and she wanted to kill him and was not able,
20 for Herod was afraid of John, because he knew that he was a just and holy man. And he observed him, and [in] many [e][things] heard him and did [these things], and gladly heard him.
21 And there was a notable day when Herod made a banquet on his birthday for his nobles and chiliarchs[2] and rulers of Galilee.
22 And the daughter of Herod entered [and] danced and pleased Herod and those who were sitting to eat with him. And the king said to the girl, "Ask me anything that you want and I will give [it] to you."
23 And he swore to her, "Whatever you ask, I will give to you, up to half of my kingdom."
24 And **she** went away and said to her mother, "What should I ask of him?" She said to her, "The head of John the baptizer."
25 And immediately she entered with care to the king and said to him, "I desire right now that you would give me on a platter the head of John the baptizer."
26 And it made the king very sad, but because of the oaths and because of the guests, he did not want to deny her.
27 But immediately the king sent the executioner and commanded that he should bring the head of John. And he went [and] cut off the head of John [in] prison.[3]
28 And he brought [it] on a platter and gave [it] to the girl, and **the girl** gave [it] to her mother.
29 And his disciples heard and came [and] took his body and placed [it] in a grave.

---

[1] Repeat *others*
[2] Lit: rulers of a thousand
[3] Fig: polysyndeton, begins lengthy passage all connected with *and*...

Chapter 6
30 And the apostles were gathered around Jesus and told him everything they had done and everything they had learned.
31 And he said to them, "Come, let us go into the desert by ourselves and rest a little," for there were many who were going and coming and they had no opportunity even to eat.
32 And they went away to a deserted place in a boat by themselves.
33 And many saw them as they were going away and recognized them. And they ran by land before him, from all the cities, to the place.
34 And Jesus disembarked [and] saw the large crowds and had compassion on them because they were [5]like sheep that did not have a shepherd. And he began to teach them many [things].
35 And when the time grew late,[1] his disciples came to him and said to him, "This is a barren place and the time is late.
36 Dismiss them to go to the surrounding fields and villages and let them buy bread for themselves, for they do not have anything to eat."
37 But **he** said to them, "Give them to eat." They said to him, "Should we go [and] buy bread [worth] two hundred denarii and give them to eat?"
38 And **he** said to them, "Go [and] see how much bread you have here." And when they saw, they said to him, "Five [loaves of] bread[2] and two fish."
39 And he commanded them to seat everyone by groups on the grass.
40 And they sat [to eat] by groups of hundreds and fifties.[3]
41 And he took those five [loaves of] bread and two fish, and looked into heaven and blessed and broke the bread, and gave [it] to his disciples to place before them. And they distributed those two fish to all.
42 And all ate and were full.
43 And they took up the fragments [of bread] and of fish, twelve baskets full.
44 And those who ate bread were five thousand men.
45 And immediately he pressed his disciples to board a boat and to precede him to the opposite shore to Bethsaida[4] while he dismissed the crowds.
46 And when he had dismissed them, he went to a mountain to pray.

---

[1] Lit: the hour is much; repeat *time is late*, with slight variation
[2] Lit: breads
[3] Lit: hundred hundreds, fifty fifties, group groups
[4] Lit: house of fisherman, **Bet Sayyada**

Chapter 6

47 And when evening came, the boat was in the middle of the sea and he [was] alone on the land.

48 And he saw them straining while rowing, for the wind was against them. And in the fourth watch of the night, Jesus came to them, walking on the water. And he wanted to pass by them.

49 But **they** saw him walking on the water, and they thought to themselves that it was a false vision, and they cried out,

50 for all of them saw him and were afraid. And immediately he spoke with them and said to them, "Take courage,[1] it is I. Do not be afraid."

51 And he climbed into the boat with them and the wind ceased. And they were greatly amazed and astonished among themselves,

52 for they had not gained insight from that bread, because their heart was hardened.

53 And when they had crossed to the other side, they came to the land of Gennesaret.

54 And after they had disembarked from the boat, immediately the people of the place recognized him.

55 And they ran into that entire region and began to bring those who were very ill, carrying them on pallets to where they heard that he was.

56 And wherever he entered into the villages and cities, the sick were placed in the streets. And they were begging him that they might touch even the border of his clothes. And all those who touched him were healed.

Chapter 7

1 And the Pharisees and scribes gathered around him who came from Jerusalem.

2 And they saw some of his disciples who were eating bread while their hands were not washed, and they complained.

3 For all the Judeans and the Pharisees do not eat unless they wash their hands carefully, because they hold to the tradition of the elders.

4 And they do not eat [things] from the marketplace unless they are washed. And there are many other ᵉ[traditions] that they have received to observe, washings of cups ᴾand of pots and of brass vessels and of beds.˥

---

[1] OS (s): 'be strong'

Chapter 7

5   And the scribes and the Pharisees asked him, "Why do your disciples not walk according to the tradition of the elders, but they eat bread while their hands are not washed?"

6   And **he** said to them, "Well did Isaiah the prophet prophesy concerning you. [i]Hypocrites! As it is written: **THIS PEOPLE HONORS ME WITH ITS LIPS BUT THEIR HEART IS VERY FAR FROM ME.**

7   **AND WITHOUT RESULTS THEY REVERENCE ME WHILE TEACHING THE TEACHINGS**[1] **OF THE COMMANDMENTS OF MEN.**

8   For you have left the commandment of God and you have held to the tradition of men, washings of cups and of pots and many things that resemble these."

9   He said to them, "Well[2] did you reject the commandment of God that you might establish your tradition.

10   For Moses said: **HONOR YOUR FATHER AND YOUR MOTHER.**[3] And **HE WHO REVILES FATHER AND MOTHER SHOULD INDEED DIE.**[4]

11   But **you** say [that] if a man should say to his father or to his mother, 'My offering[5] [is] what you have gained from me,'

12   then you allow him not to do anything for his father or his mother.

13   And you despise the word of God because of the tradition that you have handed down and you do many [things] that resemble these.

14   And Jesus called to the entire crowd and said to them, "Hear me, all of you, and understand.

15   There is nothing that is outside of a man that enters him that is able [to] defile him. But what goes out from him, that defiles a man.[6]

16   He who has ears to hear should hear."

17   And when Jesus entered the house [away] from the crowd, his disciples asked him about that saying.

18   He said to them, "Are **you** likewise also slow to understand? Do you not know that everything that enters a man from the outside cannot defile him,

---

[1] Same root: *teaching, the teachings*

[2] Repeat *well* from v. 6, fig: irony, not to be commended at all

[3] Repeat *father and mother*, vs. 10-12

[4] Fig: polyptoton, lit: should die the death

[5] Culture: regarding "Corban" offering, see note on Matt. 15:5, Freeman, p. 400, Lamsa, *Gospel Light*, p. 251.

[6] Eastern txt: one word, 'men'(plural)

Chapter 7

19 because it does not enter his heart, but into his stomach and is cast off by excretion, which purifies all the food?[1]

20 But anything that goes out from a man, that defiles the man.

21 For from within, from the heart of men, evil thoughts proceed: [a]adultery, fornication, theft, murder,

22 injustice, wickedness, deceit, filthiness, an evil eye,[2] blasphemy, boastfulness, foolishness.┐

23 All these evils proceed from within and defile a man."

24 From there Jesus rose up and came to the border of Tyre and Sidon. And he entered a certain house. And he did not want anyone to know about him, yet he was not able to conceal [himself],

25 for immediately a certain woman, whose daughter had an unclean spirit, heard about him and came [and] fell down before his feet.

26 Now the **woman** was a foreigner[3] from Phoenicia of Syria, and she was begging him to cast out the demon from her daughter.

27 And Jesus said to her, [al]"Allow first the children to be satisfied, for it is not proper to take the bread of the children and to throw [it] to the dogs."

28 And **she** answered and said to him, "Yes, my Lord. Yet even the dogs eat the crumbs of the children from under the tables."┐ [4]

29 Jesus said to her, "Go! Because of this saying, the demon has gone out from your daughter."

30 And she went to her house and found her daughter lying on a pallet and her devil had left her.

31 Again Jesus went out from the border of Tyre and Sidon and came to the Sea of Galilee, on the border of the Decapolis.

32 And they brought him a certain deaf man, a stammerer, and were asking him to place a hand on him.

33 And he led him away from the crowd privately and placed his fingers in his ears and he spit and touched his tongue.

34 And he looked into heaven and sighed and said to him, "Be opened."[5]

---

[1] Fig: erotesis – question to ponder, what is the application?

[2] Semitism: *evil eye* means, greed or envy

[3] OS (s): 'widow'

[4] Word play: *crumbs,* **paretothey** ܦܪܬܘܬ̈ܐ, *tables,* **pethorey** ܦܬܘܪ̈ܐ

[5] The correct pronunciation is **ethpatakh**. It is passive.

Chapter 7

35 And immediately his ears were opened and the restriction of his tongue was loosed and he spoke plainly.

36 And he admonished them not to tell anyone. And the more that **he** was admonishing them, the more **they** were proclaiming.

37 And they were exceedingly amazed and were saying, "He does everything well. He makes the deaf to hear, and those not speaking to speak."[1]

Chapter 8

1   Now in those days when there was a large crowd and there was nothing to eat, he called his disciples and said to them,

2   "I have compassion on this crowd because, *behold, they have remained with me three days and they do not have anything to eat.

3   And if I dismiss them to their homes while they are fasting, they will faint along the road, for some of them have come from far away."

4   His disciples said to him, "[From] where can a man find here in the wilderness bread to satisfy all these [people]?"

5   And he asked them, "How many [loaves of] bread[2] do you have?" They told him, "Seven."

6   And he commanded the crowds to recline on the ground, and he took those seven [loaves of] bread and blessed and broke [them] and gave [them] to his disciples to set forth, and they set [the food] before the crowds.

7   And there were a few fish and he also blessed them, and said to set them out.

8   And they ate and were satisfied. And they took up the remains of the fragments, seven baskets.

9   And the men who ate were about four thousand.

10   And he dismissed them, and immediately boarded a boat with his disciples, and came to the region of Dalmanutha.

11   And the Pharisees came out and began to dispute with him. And they were asking him [for] a sign from ᵐheaven, tempting him.

12   And he sighed in his spirit and said, "Why does this generation seek a sign? *Truly I say to you, a sign will not be given to this generation."

13   And he left them and boarded a boat and they went to the other side.

---

[1] Lit: *deaf* is plural: deaf [ones]; same root: *speaking, to speak*
[2] Lit: breads

Chapter 8

14 And they forgot to take bread. And except [for] one loaf, there was nothing with them in the boat.

15 And he commanded them and said to them, "Watch out![1] Beware of the [h]leaven of the Pharisees and of the [h]leaven[2] of Herod."

16 And they were reasoning with each other and saying, "[It is] because we have no bread."

17 But Jesus knew [this] and said to them, "Why are you thinking [it is] because you have no bread? Do you still not know and do you not understand? How long will you have a hard heart?

18 [P]And you have eyes and you do not see, and you have ears and you do not hear,[3] and you do not remember.

19 When I broke those five [loaves of] bread for the five thousand, how many baskets[4] full of fragments did you take up?" They told him, "Twelve."

20 He said to them, "And when[5] seven [loaves] to the four thousand, how many baskets full of fragments did you take up?" They said, "Seven."

21 He said to them, "Why is it [that] still you do not understand?"

22 And he came to Bethsaida. And they brought him a blind man and were begging him to touch him.

23 And he took the hand of the blind man and led him outside of the village. And he spat on his eyes and laid his hand [on him] and asked him what he saw.

24 And he looked and said, "I see men [s]as trees that are walking."

25 Again he laid his hand on his eyes and he was restored and was seeing everything clearly.

26 And he sent him to his house and said, "Neither enter the village nor tell anyone in the village."

27 And Jesus and his disciples went out to the villages of Caesarea Philippi. And he was asking his disciples along the way and said to them, "What do men say about me, who I am?"

---

[1] Lit: See!

[2] Repeat *of the leaven*, fig: hypocatastasis,, leaven represents doctrine, cf. Mat. 16:12.

[3] Repeat *you have, you do not*, vs. 16-18

[4] Different word than v. 20, meaning large baskets, cf. Grk: **kophinos**

[5] Fig: ellipsis, add [I broke]

Chapter 8

28 And **they** said, "John the baptizer, and others Elijah, and others,[1] one of the prophets.

29 Jesus said to them, "But what do **you** say about me, who I am?" Simon[2] answered and said to him, "You are the MESSIAH, the Son of the living God."

30 And he charged them not to tell anyone about him.

31 And he began to teach them that the Son of Man would suffer much, and be rejected by the elders and by the chief priests and by the scribes, and be killed and after three days, rise up.

32 And he was speaking publicly [about this] matter. And Peter took him and began to rebuke him.[3]

33 But **he** turned and looked at his disciples and rebuked Simon and said, "Go behind me, SATAN, because you do not think about e[the things] of God, but e[the things] of men!"

34 And Jesus called the crowds with his disciples and said to them, "He who wants to follow me should deny himself and take up his mcross and follow me.

35 For everyone who wants to save his soul[4] will lose it. And anyone who will lose his soul because of me and because of my gospel will save it.

36 For what is a man profited if he should gain the entire world and should lose his soul?[5]

37 Or what will a man give in exchange of his soul?

38 For anyone who is ashamed of me and my words in this sinful and adulterous generation, the Son of Man will also be ashamed[6] of him when he comes in the glory of his Father with his holy angels."

Chapter 9

1 And he was saying to them, "*Truly I say to you, there are some that are standing here who will not petaste death until they see the kingdom of God that has come in power."

---

[1] Repeat *others*

[2] OS (s): 'Peter'

[3] OS (s): 'Simon Peter, who pitied him, said, May it be far from you!'

[4] Or "life," vs. 35-37

[5] Fig: erotesis – questions to ponder, vs. 36, 37.

[6] Repeat *ashamed*

ARAMAIC PESHITTA NEW TESTAMENT
MARK

Chapter 9

2 And after six days, Jesus led Peter and James and John and took them up into a high mountain privately and he was changed before their eyes.

3 And his clothing was bright[1] and became very white ˢlike snow, such that men are not able to make white[2] on earth.

4 And Elijah and Moses were seen by them, speaking with Jesus.

5 And Peter said to him, "My Master, it is good for us to be here. And let us make three booths, one for you and one for Moses and one[3] for Elijah."

6 And he did not know what he was saying, for they were in fear.

7 And a cloud came and overshadowed them, and a voice [came] from the cloud that said, "This is my beloved Son; hear him."

8 And suddenly, when the disciples looked up, they did not see anyone except Jesus only with them.

9 And while they were descending from the mountain, he was commanding them that they should not tell anyone what they saw until after the Son of Man had risen from the dead.

10 And they kept the saying to themselves and were inquiring, "What is this saying, 'When he is raised from the dead?'"

11 And they were asking him and saying, "Why then do the scribes say that Elijah must come first?"

12 He said to them, "Elijah will come first in order to prepare everything and as it is written about the Son of Man: **HE WILL SUFFER MUCH AND BE REJECTED.**

13 But *I say to you, indeed Elijah has come and they did with him whatever they desired, as it was written about him."

14 And when he came to the disciples, he saw a large crowd with them and the scribes disputing with them.

15 And immediately all the crowds saw him and were amazed, and they ran [and] greeted him.

16 And he asked the scribes, "What are you disputing with them?"

17 And one of the crowd answered and said, "Teacher, I brought my son to you, because he has a spirit that does not speak.

---

[1] OS (s): 'he shone brightly'

[2] Same root: *white, make white*

[3] Repeat *one*

Chapter 9

18 And whenever it grabs him, it knocks him down ᴾand he foams and gnashes his teeth and he languishes.⌐ And I asked your disciples to cast it out, and they were not able."

19 Jesus answered and said to him, "ⁱOh faithless generation! How long must I be with you and how long must I endure you? Bring him to me."

20 And they brought him to him. And when the spirit saw him, immediately it knocked him down ᴾand he fell on the ground and was violently shaken, and he foamed.⌐

21 And Jesus asked his father, "How long [has it been] since ᵉ[he was] this way?" He said to him, "Since his youth.

22 And many times it has thrown him into the fire and into the water to destroy him, but whatever you are able [to do], help me and have compassion on us."¹

23 Jesus said to him, "If you are able to believe, everything will be possible to him who believes."

24 And immediately the father of the boy cried out, mourning, and said, "I believe, my Lord! Help the lack of my faith."

25 And when Jesus saw that the people ran and gathered about him, he rebuked that unclean spirit and said to it, "Dumb spirit that does not speak, I command you, come out of him and do not enter him again."

26 And that demon cried out and he bruised him much and came out. And he was ˢlike a dead man, so that many said, "He is dead."

27 But Jesus took him by his hand and raised him up.

28 Now when Jesus entered the house, his disciples asked him privately, "Why were we not able to cast it out?"

29 He said to them, "This kind cannot be cast out by anything except by fasting and by prayer."

30 And when he went away from there, they were passing through Galilee. And he did not want anyone to know about him,

31 For he was teaching his disciples and said to them, "The Son of Man will be delivered into the ᵐhands of man,² and they will kill him, and after he has been killed, on the third day he will rise up."

32 And they did not understand the meaning, yet were afraid to ask him.

---

¹ Eastern txt: 'on me'
² Eastern txt: 'men'

ARAMAIC PESHITTA NEW TESTAMENT
MARK

Chapter 9

33 And they came to Capernaum and when they had entered the house, he asked them, "What were you discussing among yourselves on the way?"

34 But **they** were silent, for they were arguing on the way with each other, who was the greater among them.

35 And Jesus sat down and called the twelve and said to them, "He who wants to be first should be the last of all men and a servant of all men."[1]

36 And he took a certain child and set him in the middle [of them] and took him into his arms and said to them,

37 Whoever receives ˢlike this child in my name receives me. And **he** who receives me does not receive me, but him who sent me.

38 John said to him, "My Master, we saw a man who was casting out demons in your name and we stopped him, because he did not follow us."

39 Jesus said to them, "Do not stop him, for there is no one who does miracles in my name and is readily able [to] speak wickedly about me.

40 Therefore, he who is not against you is for you.

41 But anyone who gives you only a cup of water to drink because you are in the name of the MESSIAH, *truly I say to you, 'ᵗhe will not lose his reward.'

42 And whoever causes one of these little ones who believe in me to stumble,[2] it would be better for him if the millstone of a donkey were placed on his neck and he were thrown into the sea.

43 Now if your hand offends you, cut it off.[3] It is better for you to enter life maimed, than although you have two hands, to go to GEHENNA,

44 where their worm does not die and their fire does not go out.[4]

45 And if your foot offends you, cut if off. It is better for you to enter life lame, than although you have two feet, to fall in GEHENNA,

46 where their worm does not die and their fire does not go out.

47 And if your eye offends you, pick it out. It is better for you to enter into the kingdom of God with one of your eye[s], than though you have two eyes, to fall in the GEHENNA of fire,

48 where their worm does not die and their fire does not go out.

---

[1] Repeat *of all men*, lit: of every man
[2] Same root: *stumble, offend*, v. 43
[3] Parallel structure regarding *hand, foot and eye*, see note on Matt 5:22.
[4] Repeat exact phrase, vs. 46, 48.

Chapter 9

49 For everything[1] will be salted with fire and every sacrifice will be salted with salt.[2]

50 Salt is good, but if the salt should lose its flavor, with what will it be salted?[3] Let salt be in you, and be in harmony with each other."

Chapter 10

1 And he rose up from there and came to the border of Judea to the crossing of the Jordan and large crowds went there with him. And[4] he was teaching them again, as he was accustomed.

2 And the Pharisees approached, tempting him, and were asking if it was lawful for a man to divorce his wife.

3 He said to them, "What did Moses command you?"

4 And **they** said, "Moses allowed us to write a decree[5] of divorce and to send [her] away."

5 Jesus answered and said to them, "In contrast to the hardness of your heart, he wrote this commandment for you,

6 but from the beginning **GOD MADE THEM MALE AND FEMALE.**

7 Because of this, **A MAN WILL LEAVE HIS FATHER AND HIS MOTHER AND JOIN TO HIS WIFE**

8 **AND THE TWO OF THEM WILL BECOME ONE** [sy]**FLESH.** So then, they are not two, but one [sy]flesh.

9 Therefore, that which God has joined together, man should not separate."

10 And his disciples asked him again in the house about this [matter].

11 And he said to them, "Whoever dismisses his wife and takes another commits adultery.

12 And if a woman should dismiss her husband and be [e][a wife] to another, she commits adultery."[6]

---

[1] OS (s): 'everyone'

[2] Word play: *sacrifice,* **bekhta** ܕܒܚܐ, *salt,* **melkha** ܡܠܚܐ. Salt was both a preservative and poison. The phrase *salted with fire* implies destruction, Bivin, www.jerusalemperspective.com

[3] Perhaps a well known proverb, Black, pp. 166-167, cf. Luke 14:34, 35.

[4] OS (s): add 'he healed...*and taught them*'

[5] Lit: write a writing

[6] OS (s): 'he commits adultery', and adds: 'and any man who divorces his wife and takes another commits adultery.'

ARAMAIC PESHITTA NEW TESTAMENT
MARK

Chapter 10

13 And children were approaching him so that he would touch them, but his disciples were rebuking those who were bringing them.

14 And Jesus saw [it] and was offended and said to them, "Allow the children [to] come to me and do not hinder them, for because of those who are as these are, the kingdom of God exists.

15 *Truly I say to you, anyone who does not receive the kingdom of God ˢlike a child will not enter it."

16 ᴾAnd he took them into his arms and placed his hand on them and blessed them.⌐

17 And while he was traveling on the road, a certain [man] ran [and] fell on his knees and asked him and said, "Good teacher, what should I do to gain eternal life?"

18 Jesus said to him, "Why do you call me good? There is no [one] good, except one, God.

19 You know the commandments: **DO NOT COMMIT ADULTERY, DO NOT STEAL, DO NOT KILL AND DO NOT BEAR FALSE WITNESS,**[1] **DO NOT DEFRAUD, HONOR YOUR FATHER AND YOUR MOTHER.**"

20 And **he** answered and said to him, "Teacher, I have kept all of these [things] from my youth."

21 And Jesus looked at him and loved him and said to him, "You lack one [thing]. Go [and] sell everything that you have and give to the poor and you will have treasure in heaven and take up a cross[2] and follow me."

22 And **he** was sad at this saying and went away, being grieved, for he had many possessions.

23 And Jesus looked at his disciples and said to them, "How difficult [it is] for those who have possessions to enter the kingdom of God."

24 And the disciples were wondering at his words, and Jesus answered again and said to them, "My sons, how difficult [it is] for those who trust in[3] their possessions to enter the kingdom of God.

25 It is easier for a camel[4] to enter through the eye of the needle than [for] a rich man to enter the kingdom of God."

---

[1] Lit: witness a witness falsely

[2] Eastern txt: your cross

[3] Only difference with v. 23 (*who have*), is *who trust in*

[4] Or "rope". There are several explanations for this verse, Lamsa, *Gospel Light*, pp. 167-168, Schor, pp. 19-22; could be proverb.

Chapter 10

26 And **they** were all the more wondering and saying among themselves, "Who is able to ᵉ[gain] life?"

27 And Jesus looked at them and said to them, "With men this is not possible,[1] but with God ᵉ[it is]. For everything is possible with God."

28 And Peter began to say, "*Behold, we have left everything and followed you."

29 Jesus answered and said, "*Truly I say to you, there is no man who has left houses or[2] brothers or sisters or father or mother or wife or children or fields because of me and because of my gospel,

30 and will not receive a hundredth part[3] now in this time, houses and brothers and sisters and mothers and children and fields with persecution. Yet in the age to come, ᵉ[he will receive] eternal life.

31 And ᵉ[there will be] many first who will be last, and last,[4] first."

32 And while they were climbing up on the road to Jerusalem, Jesus was before them. And they were amazed and were following him, although they were afraid. And he took his twelve and began to tell them what would happen to him.

33 "*Behold, we will go up to Jerusalem, and the Son of Man will be delivered to the chief priests and to the scribes, ᴾand they will condemn him[5] to death and deliver him to the Gentiles.

34 And they will mock him and beat him and spit in his face and kill him and on the third day, he will rise up."

35 And James and John, the sons of Zebedee, approached him and said to him, "Teacher, we want you to do for us all that we ask."

36 He said to them, "What do you want me to do for you?"

37 They said to him, "Grant us that one sit on your right and one on your left in your glory."

38 But **he** said to them, "You do not know what you ask. Are you able to drink the ᵐcup that **I** drink and to be baptized with the baptism [with] which **I** am baptized?"[6]

---

[1] Same verb: *is possible, is able,* v. 26
[2] Repeat *or*
[3] Lit: one in a hundred
[4] Fig: ellipsis, add [who will be]
[5] Repeat suffix *him,* also v. 34
[6] Same root: *baptized, baptism*

Chapter 10

39 They said to him, "We are able." Jesus said to them, "The ᵐcup that I drink, you will drink, and the baptism [with] which I am baptized, you will be baptized,

40 but that you may sit at my right and at my left is not mine to give, except to those for whom it is prepared."

41 And when the ten heard [it], they began murmuring against James and John.

42 And Jesus called them and said to them, "You know that those who are counted as chiefs of the nations are their lords and their great men are in authority over them.

43 But it should not be so among you, but rather he who wants to be great among you should be a minister to you.

44 And whoever of you wants to be first should be a servant of everyone.

45 For even the Son of Man did not come to be served, but rather to serve[1] and to give himself [as] a ransom for many."

46 And they came to Jericho. And when Jesus went out from Jericho and his disciples and a large crowd, Timaeus, the son of Timaeus,[2] a blind man, was sitting by the side of the road and begging.

47 And he heard that it was Jesus the Nazarene and he began to cry out and to say, "Son of David, have compassion on me."

48 Many were reproving him to be silent, but **he** was crying out all the more and said, "Son of David, have compassion on me."

49 And Jesus stopped and commanded that they call him. And they called the blind man and said to him, "Take courage [and] rise up. He calls you."[3]

50 And the blind man threw off his garment[4] and rose up [and] came to Jesus.

51 Jesus said to him, "What do you want me to do for you?" And the blind man said to him, "My Master, that I may see."

52 And Jesus said to him, "See! Your faith has made you whole." And immediately he received sight[5] and went on [his] way.

---

[1] Same root: *serve, minister*, v. 43

[2] Bartimeus means literally, *son of Timaeus*

[3] Repeat forms of *call*, 3x

[4] OS (s): 'took up.' Culture: the blind man's garment was the symbol of his "license" to beg.

[5] Lit: it was seen to him

ARAMAIC PESHITTA NEW TESTAMENT
MARK

Chapter 11

1   And when he came near to Jerusalem by the side of Bethphage[1] and Bethany[2] toward the Mount of Olives, he sent two of his disciples

2   and said to them, "Go to that village opposite us. And immediately when you enter it, you will find a colt that is tied that no man[3] has ridden. Untie[4] [it] [and] bring it.

3   And if anyone should say to you, 'Why are you doing this?' say to him, 'It is necessary for our Lord,'[5] and immediately he will send it here."

4   And they went [and] found a colt that was tied at the door outside on the street. And while they were untying it,

5   some of those who were standing [there] said to them, "What are **you** doing untying the colt?"

6   And **they** said to them as Jesus had commanded them and they allowed them.

7   And they brought the colt to Jesus and placed their garments on it and Jesus rode on it.

8   And many were spreading their garments on the road and others were cutting branches from trees and spreading [them] on the road.[6]

9   And those who were before him and those who were behind him were crying out and saying: "HOSANNA! BLESSED IS HE WHO COMES IN THE NAME OF THE LORD.

10 AND BLESSED IS THE KINGDOM OF OUR FATHER DAVID THAT IS COMING! HOSANNA ON HIGH!

11 And Jesus entered Jerusalem [and] the temple and saw everything. And when evening time came, he went out to Bethany with the twelve.

12 And on the next day, when he went out from Bethany, he was hungry.

13 And he saw a certain fig tree from a distance that had leaves on it. And he came to it [e][to see] if he could find anything on it. And when he

---

[1] Lit: house of young figs
[2] Derivation uncertain, could mean, "house of echo or song"
[3] Lit: no man from men
[4] Lit: loosen [it]
[5] OS (s): 'his lord' or 'his owner'
[6] See note Matt 21:8

ARAMAIC PESHITTA NEW TESTAMENT
MARK

Chapter 11

arrived, he did not find ᵉ[anything] on it except leaves, for the time of figs had not ᵉ[yet] come.¹

14 And he said to it, "Now and forever man will not eat fruit from you." And his disciples heard [it]. And they came to Jerusalem.

15 And Jesus entered the temple of God and began to drive out those who were buying and selling² in the temple. And he turned over the tables of the moneychangers and the seats of those who were selling doves.

16 And he did not allow anyone to carry goods inside the temple.

17 And he was teaching and said to them, "Is it not written: **MY HOUSE**³ **WILL BE CALLED A HOUSE OF PRAYER FOR ALL NATIONS?** But **you** have made it a ʰden of robbers."

18 And the chief priests and scribes heard [it] and were seeking how they might destroy him, for they were afraid of him because all the people were astonished at his teaching.

19 And when it was evening, they went out of the city.

20 And in the morning while they were passing by, they saw that fig tree dried up from its root.

21 And Simon remembered and said to him, "My Master, *behold, that fig tree that you cursed has dried up."

22 And Jesus answered and said to them, "You should have faith of⁴ God.

23 For *truly I say to you, whoever says to this mountain, 'Be lifted up and fall into the sea,' and is not divided in his heart, but believes that what he said will happen, he will have what he said.

24 Because of this, *I say to you, everything that you pray and you ask⁵ [for], believe that you will receive [it], and you will have [it].

---

¹ Culture: If a tree had leaves, but no fruit (buds) it would be barren. The lesson is that "the Jews, professing to be first...[were] as the rustling leaves of a religious profession, the barren traditions of the Pharisees, the ostentatious display of the law, and vain exuberance of words, without the good fruit of works," Tristram, *Natural History*, pp. 350-353.

² Repeat same root: *buying and selling*, different tenses

³ Repeat *house*, lit: my house, a house of prayer will be called

⁴ Or "because of"

⁵ Repeat *you*

Chapter 11

25 And when you stand to pray, forgive anything that you have against anyone, so that your Father, who is in heaven, will also forgive you your transgressions.

26 And if **you** do not forgive, neither will your Father who is in heaven forgive you your transgressions."

27 And they came again to Jerusalem. And while he was walking in the temple, the chief priests and scribes and elders came to him.

28 And they said to him, "With what authority do you do these [things]? And who gave you this authority to do these [things]?"

29 And **Jesus** said to them, "**I** will ask you also a certain question[1] that you might answer me. And **I** will tell[2] you with what authority I do these [things].

30 The baptism of John, from where was it, from ᵐheaven or from men? Tell me."

31 And they reasoned among themselves and said, "If we say to him that [it was] from ᵐheaven, he will say to us, 'Then why did you not believe him?'

32 And [if] we say from men, there is the fear of the people, for all of them were regarding John to be truly a prophet."

33 And they answered and said to Jesus, "We do not know." He said to them, "Neither will **I** tell you by what authority I do these [things]."

Chapter 12

1 And he began to speak with them in parables. ᵖᵇ"A certain man planted a vineyard and surrounded it [with] a hedge, and dug a wine press in it, and built a tower in it, and handed it over to workers and went on a journey.

2 And in time he sent[3] his servant to the workers to receive from the fruit of the vineyard.

3 But **they** beat him and sent him away empty.

4 And he sent again to them another servant and they also stoned and wounded that one and they sent him away in shame.

---

[1] Lit: one word

[2] Same verb: *answer, tell*

[3] Repeat *he sent, he sent again*, vs. 2-6

Chapter 12

5   And he sent again another[1] also, whom they killed. And he sent many other servants and they beat some and killed some.

6   And [at] the end, he had one beloved son and he sent him to them finally,[2] for he said, 'Perhaps they will respect my son.'

7   But those workers said among themselves, 'This is the heir. Come, let us kill him and the inheritance will be ours.'

8   And they took [and] killed him and they drove him outside of the vineyard.

9   What then will the lord of the vineyard do? He will come to destroy those workers and give the vineyard to others.⌐

10   And have you not even read this scripture: **THE STONE THAT THE BUILDERS REJECTED HAS BECOME THE HEAD OF THE CORNER?**

11   **THIS CAME FROM THE PRESENCE OF THE LORD AND IT IS A WONDER IN OUR EYES."**

12   And they sought to arrest him, yet they were afraid of the people, for they knew that he spoke this parable about them, and they left him and went away.

13   And they sent him some of the scribes and [e][some] of the Herodians to ensnare him in speech.

14   And **they** came and asked him, "Teacher, we know that you are true and [that] you are not moved by anyone, for you do not look on the faces of men, but in truth you teach the way of God. Is it lawful to give the poll tax to Caesar or not? Should we give or should we not give [it]?

15   But **he** knew their trickery and said to them, "Why do you tempt me? Bring me a denarius to see."

16   And they brought [one] to him. He said to them, "Whose image and inscription is this?" And **they** said, "Caesar's."

17   Jesus said to them, "That which is of Caesar give to Caesar and that which is of God[3] to God." And they were marveling at him.

18   And the Sadducees came to him, those who say that there is no resurrection, and were asking him and saying,

19   "Teacher, Moses wrote to us: **IF THE BROTHER OF A MAN DIES AND LEAVES A WIFE AND DOES NOT LEAVE SONS, HIS BROTHER SHOULD TAKE HIS WIFE AND RAISE UP SEED FOR HIS BROTHER.**

---

[1] Fig: ellipsis, add [servant]

[2] Repeat forms of ܪܚܡ, *the end, finally*

[3] Fig: ellipsis, add [give]

ARAMAIC PESHITTA NEW TESTAMENT
MARK

Chapter 12

20 There were seven brothers. The first took a wife and died and did not leave [any] seed.

21 And the second took her and died, although also he did not leave [any] seed, and the third likewise.

22 And the seven of them took her and did not leave [any] seed. Last of all of them, the wife also died.

23 Therefore, in the resurrection, whose wife will she be? For the seven of them took her."

24 Jesus said to them, "Is it not because of this you err?[1] For you do not know the scriptures nor the power of God.

25 For when they rise up from the dead, they do not marry women nor are women with men, but rather they are ˢas the angels that are in heaven.

26 Now about the dead who will rise up, have you not read in the book of Moses how God spoke to him from the bush: I AM THE GOD OF ABRAHAM AND THE GOD OF ISAAC AND THE GOD OF JACOB?

27 And he is not the God of the dead, but of the living. Therefore **you** err greatly."

28 And one of the scribes approached and heard them disputing and saw that he answered the matter[2] well for them. And he asked, "What is the most important[3] commandment?"

29 Jesus said to him, "The most important of all the commandments [is]: HEAR, ISRAEL, THE LORD OUR GOD IS ONE LORD

30 and YOU SHOULD LOVE THE LORD YOUR GOD WITH ALL[4] YOUR HEART AND WITH ALL YOUR SOUL AND WITH ALL YOUR MIND AND WITH ALL YOUR MIGHT. This is the most important commandment.

31 And the second that is like it [is]: YOU SHOULD LOVE YOUR NEIGHBOR AS YOURSELF. There is no other commandment that is greater than these."

32 The **scribe** said to him, "Well [said], my Master. You have spoken in truth, because he is one and there are no others outside of him.

33 And that a man should love him with all the heart and with all the mind and with all the soul and with all might, and that he should love his neighbor as himself, greater is [this] than all the burnt offerings and sacrifices."

---

[1] Fig: erotesis – "not" question, answer in the affirmative
[2] Lit: he gave them an answer
[3] Lit: the first of all, also vs. 30, 31
[4] Repeat *with all*, also v. 33

Chapter 12

34 And Jesus saw that he responded to the matter wisely. He answered and said to him, "You are not far from the kingdom of God." And no man dared to question him again.

35 And Jesus answered and said while [he was] teaching in the temple, "In what way do the scribes say that the MESSIAH is the Son of David?

36 For **David** spoke by the Holy Spirit: THE LORD SAID TO MY LORD, SIT ON MY RIGHT [HAND] UNTIL I PLACE YOUR ENEMIES [AS] A FOOTSTOOL UNDER YOUR FEET.

37 Since **David** called him, 'My Lord,' then how is he his Son?" And the whole crowd was hearing him gladly.

38 And in his teaching he was saying to them, "Beware of the scribes who want to walk in robes[1] and love a greeting in the streets

39 and the chief seats[2] in the synagogues and the chief places at banquets,

40 those who devour the house of widows with the pretext that they lengthen their prayers. Those will receive the greater judgment."

41 And when Jesus sat near the treasury, he considered how the crowds were putting[3] money into the treasury. And many rich men were putting in much.

42 And a certain poor widow came [and] put in two minas that are very small coins.[4]

43 And Jesus called his disciples and said to them, "*Truly I say to you, this poor widow has put in more than everyone who has put in the treasury.

44 For all of them put in from what abounded to them, but this one, from her need, put in everything that she had, her entire wealth."

Chapter 13

1 And when Jesus went out from the temple, one of his disciples said to him, "Teacher, *behold, look at those stones and those buildings."

2 But Jesus said to him, "Do you see these great buildings? One stone on another[5] will not be left here that will not be torn down."

---

[1] OS (s): 'in the porches' (as of public buildings), same as Luke 20:46.

[2] Repeat *and the chief*

[3] Repeat forms of verb, *to put in,* vs. 41-44

[4] Lit: **shamuna**, see Appendix 2.

[5] Lit: a stone on a stone

Chapter 13

3   And while Jesus sat on the Mount of Olives opposite the temple, Peter and James and John and Andrew asked him privately,

4   Tell us when these [things] will be. And what [is] the sign when all these [things] are close to being fulfilled?

5   And **Jesus** began to say to them, "¹Beware,¹ so that no one will deceive you.

6   For many will come in my name and say, 'I am [he],' and will deceive many.

7   But when you hear of wars and a rumor of battles,² do not be afraid, for it is about to occur, but the end [is] not yet.

8   For people will rise up against people and kingdom against kingdom. And there will be earthquakes in various places and there will be famines and riots. These [things] are the beginning of sorrows.

9   But watch out for yourselves, for they will deliver you to the judges, and in the synagogues you will be beaten, and you will stand before kings and governors³ because of me, as a testimony to them.

10   But first my gospel will be preached among all the nations.

11   And when they bring you to deliver you up, do not be anxious beforehand about what you will say or think, but what is given to you at that moment, that speak. For you are not speaking, but the Holy Spirit.

12   And brother will deliver his brother to death and a father⁴ his son and children will rise up against their parents and will put them to death.

13   And you will be hated by all men because of my name. But he who endures until the end will live.

14   And when you see the abominable sign of desecration that was spoken of by Daniel the prophet that will stand where it should not be ᵖᵃ(he who reads should understand) then **those** who are in Judah should flee to the mountain.

15   And **he** who is on the roof should not come down nor enter to take anything from his house.

16   And **he** who is in the field should not turn back to pick up his clothing.

---

¹ Lit: See!

² Or 'crisis', from Greek loanword

³ OS (s): 'you will be beaten before governors...', omit *in the synagogues*

⁴ Fig: ellipsis, add [will deliver]

Chapter 13

17 And ⁱwoe to pregnant women and to those who are nursing in those days!

18 Now pray, so that your flight will not be in winter.

19 For an ordeal will come in those days such as has not occurred from the beginning of the creation that God created until now, nor will be [again].

20 And if the LORD had not shortened those days, no ˢʸflesh would live. But because of the chosen [ones] that he chose,¹ he shortened those days.

21 Then, if anyone says to you, '*Behold, here is the MESSIAH and *behold, [over] here,' do not believe [him].

22 For false messiahs and lying prophets will rise up and they will produce signs and wonders and will deceive even the chosen [ones], if possible.

23 But watch out! *Behold, I have told you everything beforehand.

24 And in those days after that ordeal, THE SUN WILL DARKEN AND THE MOON WILL NOT GIVE ITS LIGHT.

25 AND THE STARS WILL FALL FROM HEAVEN AND THE POWERS OF HEAVEN WILL BE SHAKEN.

26 And then they will see THE SON OF MAN COMING IN THE CLOUDS WITH GREAT POWER AND WITH GLORY.

27 Then he will send his angels and gather his chosen [ones] from the four winds, from one end of the earth to the end of heaven.²

28 Now learn an illustration from the fig tree that when its branches are tender and its leaves bud, you know that summer has arrived.

29 So also, when **you** have seen these [things] that are going to be, know that it is near, at the door.

30 *Truly I say to you, this generation will not pass away³ until all these [things] occur.

31 Heaven and earth will pass away, yet my words will not pass away.

32 But about that ˢʸday and about that ˢʸhour, no man knows, not even the angels of heaven, nor the Son, but only the Father.

33 Watch, be alert⁴ and pray, for you do not know when the time is.

---

¹ Same root: *chosen, chose*

² Lit: from the beginning of the earth and up to the beginning of heaven

³ Repeat *pass away*, v. 31

⁴ Repeat *be alert*, vs. 35, 37. Repetition encircles the passage.

ARAMAIC PESHITTA NEW TESTAMENT
MARK

Chapter 13

34 ᵖᵇFor [it is] like a man who went on a journey and left his house and gave authority to his servants and to each man his work, and commanded the porter to be alert.

35 Be alert, therefore, because you do not know when the lord of the house will come, in the evening or[1] in the middle of the night or at the rooster crow or in the morning,

36 lest he comes suddenly and finds you sleeping.⌐

37 Now what I say to you, *I say to all of you: 'Be alert.'"

Chapter 14

1 Now after two days was the Passover of the unleavened bread, and the chief priests and scribes were seeking how they might arrest [him] with trickery and kill him.

2 And they were saying, "Not during the feast, so that a riot will not occur among the people."

3 And while he was in Bethany in the house of Simon the leper[2] while reclining, a woman came who had near her an alabaster box of perfume of spikenard, the best,[3] very costly, and she opened it and poured it on the head of Jesus.

4 And there were some of the disciples who were offended among themselves and said, "Why was [there] the waste of this perfume?

5 For it was possible to be sold [for] more than three hundred denarii and be given to the poor." And they were angry with him.[4]

6 But **Jesus** said, "Leave her alone. Why are you troubling her? She has done a proper act for me.

7 For you always have the poor with you, and whenever you want, you are able to do for them what is proper, but I am not always with you.

8 She did this of what she had and she has perfumed my body as for burial beforehand.

9 And *truly I say to you, wherever this, my gospel, is preached in all the world, also the thing that she has done will be spoken for her remembrance."

10 And Judas Iscariot, one of the twelve, went to the chief priests to betray Jesus to them.

---

[1] Repeat *or*

[2] Or "jar-maker," cf. Mat. 26:6

[3] OS (s): 'pure', from Greek loanword

[4] Or "about it"

ARAMAIC PESHITTA NEW TESTAMENT
MARK

Chapter 14

11 And they, when they heard [him], rejoiced and promised to give him money. And he was seeking for himself an opportunity to betray him.

12 And on the first day of unleavened bread on which the Judeans slay the Passover, his disciples were saying to him, "Where do you want us to go to prepare for you to eat the Passover?"

13 And he sent two of his disciples and said to them, "Go to the city and *behold, a man who is carrying a vessel of water will meet you. Follow him.

14 And wherever he enters, say to the lord of the house, 'Our Master said, where is the guest house where I may eat the Passover with my disciples?'

15 And *behold, he will show you a large upper room that is furnished and prepared. There make ready for us."

16 And his disciples went out and came to the city and found as he had said to them and they prepared the Passover.

17 And when evening came, he came with his twelve.

18 And while they were reclining and eating, Jesus said, "*Truly I say to you, one of you who eats with me will betray me."

19 And **they** began to be grieved and were saying to him, one by one, "Is it I?"[1]

20 And **he** said to them, "^e[It is] one of the twelve who dips with me in the dish.

21 And the Son of Man will die[2] as it is written about him. But ⁱwoe to that man by whose ^mhand the Son of Man is delivered up! It would be better for that man if he had not been born."

22 And while they were eating, Jesus took bread and blessed [it] and broke [it] and gave [it] to them. And he said to them, "Take, ^{me}this is my body."[3]

23 And he took a cup and gave thanks and blessed [it] and gave [it] to them, and they all drank from it.

24 And he said to them, "^{me}This is my blood of the new covenant that is shed on behalf of many.

25 *Truly I say to you, I will not drink again from the fruit of the vine until that ^{sy}day in which I will drink it anew in the kingdom of God."

---

[1] Fig: erotesis, **lema** question, implying "yes"
[2] Lit: will go
[3] Or "corpse," see note, Wilson, p. 362.

Chapter 14

26 And they offered praise and went out to the Mount of Olives.

27 And Jesus said to them, "All of you will be offended at me in this night, for it is written: **I WILL STRIKE THE SHEPHERD AND HIS LAMBS WILL BE SCATTERED.**

28 But when I have risen, I will go before you into Galilee."

29 Peter said to him, "Though all of them be offended, I [will] not [be]."[1]

30 Jesus said to him, "*Truly I say to you, today in this night, before the rooster will crow two times, **you** will deny me three [times]."

31 And all the more **he** was saying, "If I must die with you, I will not deny you, my Lord." And all of them[2] also spoke likewise.

32 And they came to a place that was called Gethsemane,[3] and he said to his disciples, "Sit here while I pray."

33 And he took with him Peter and James and John and began to be sad and to grieve.

34 And he said to them, "It is grievous to my soul unto death. Remain here and be watchful."

35 And he went on a little and fell on the ground and was praying that if it was possible, [this] [sy]hour might pass from him.

36 And he said, "Father, my Father, you can [do] everything.[4] Make this [m]cup pass from me. Yet not my own will, but yours."

37 And he came [and] found them sleeping. And he said to Peter, "Simon, are you sleeping? Are you not able to be watchful for one [sy]hour?

38 Be watchful[5] and pray, so that you do not enter into temptation. The spirit is willing and ready, but the body is weak."

39 And he went again [and] prayed and he said the same thing.[6]

40 And he returned [and] came [and] again found them sleeping, because their eyes were heavy, and they did not know what to say to him.

41 And he came a third time and said to them, "Sleep now, and rest. The end has arrived and the [sy]hour has come and *behold, the Son of Man is delivered into the [m]hands of sinners.

---

[1] Lit: but not I

[2] Eastern txt: add 'the disciples'

[3] See note on Matt 26:36, OS (s): alt sp. ܓܕܣܡܢܐ gdsmna

[4] Lit: everything is possible for you

[5] Repeat *be watchful* as next word from v. 37

[6] Lit: the same word

Chapter 14

42 Rise up, let us go. *Behold, he who has delivered[1] me draws near."

43 And while he was speaking, Judas Iscariot, one of the twelve, and many people with swords and rods, came from being with the chief priests and scribes and elders.

44 And the traitor who betrayed[2] [him] had given them a sign and had said, "Whomever I kiss is he. Arrest him securely and take him away."

45 And immediately he drew near and said to him, "My Master, my Master,"[3] and he kissed him.

46 And **they** placed [their] hands on him and arrested him.

47 And one of those who were standing [there] drew a sword and struck the servant of the high priest and took off his ear.

48 And **Jesus** answered and said to them, "Do you come out as against a robber with swords and rods to arrest me?

49 Every day I was with you while I was teaching in the temple and you did not arrest me. But this has occurred that the scriptures would be fulfilled."

50 Then his disciples left him and fled.

51 And a certain young man followed him, and a linen cloth was wrapped around [his] naked [body], and they grabbed him.

52 And **he** left the linen cloth and fled naked.

53 And they took Jesus to Caiaphas, the high priest, and all the chief priests and scribes and elders were gathered with him.

54 And Simon was following him from a distance as far as the inside of the courtyard of the high priest. And he was sitting with the servants and was warming [himself] near the fire.

55 And the chief priests and all their assembly were seeking testimony against Jesus, so that they might kill him, but they did not find [any].

56 For although many were testifying against him, their testimony was not agreeing.

57 And some false witnesses[4] stood up against him and said,

58 "We heard him when he said, 'I will destroy this temple that was made with hands, and after three days I will build another that is not made with hands.'"[5]

---

[1] Repeat *has delivered*, from v. 41, also same root as *betrayed*, v. 44
[2] Same root: *traitor, betrayed*
[3] Fig: epizeuxis, very solemn repetition
[4] Same root: *testifying, testimony, witnesses*
[5] Repeat *not made with hands*

Chapter 14

59 But even so, their testimony was not agreeing.[1]

60 And the high priest stood up in the middle [of them] and questioned Jesus and said, "Do you not answer the accusation? Why are they testifying these [things] against you?"

61 But **he** was silent and did not answer him anything. And again the high priest questioned him and said, "Are you the MESSIAH, the Son of the Blessed One?"

62 And **Jesus** said to him, "I am. And you will see THE SON OF MAN WHEN HE SITS ON THE RIGHT [HAND] OF POWER and COMES UPON THE CLOUDS OF HEAVEN."

63 And the high priest tore his robe and said, "Why now are we seeking witnesses?

64 *Behold, from his ᵐmouth you have heard blasphemy. What do you think?" And all of them judged that he was deserving of death.

65 And some began spitting in his face. And they covered his face and were striking him and saying, "Prophesy!" And the guards were striking him on his cheeks.

66 And while Simon was below in the courtyard, a certain maiden of the high priest came.

67 She saw him while he was warming [himself] and she looked at him and said to him, "And **you** also were with Jesus the Nazarene."

68 But **he** denied [it] and said, "I do not know what you are saying." And he went outside to the porch and the rooster crowed.

69 And again the maiden saw him and **she** began to tell those who were standing [there], "This one also is one of them."

70 But again **he** denied [it]. And after a little [time] again those who were standing [there] said to Peter, "Truly you are one of them, for you are also a Galilean and your speech is like [theirs]."

71 And **he** began to curse and swore, "I do not know this man of whom you speak!"

72 And immediately, the rooster crowed the second time, and Simon remembered the saying of Jesus, who had said to him, "Before the rooster crows two times, you will deny me three [times]," and he began to cry.

---

[1] Repeat from v. 56, encircling the passage

ARAMAIC PESHITTA NEW TESTAMENT
MARK

Chapter 15

1 And immediately in the morning the chief priests took counsel with the elders and with the scribes and with the entire assembly. And they bound Jesus and led him away. And they delivered him to Pilate.

2 And Pilate asked him, "Are you the king of the Judeans?" And **he** answered and said to him, "**You** have said [it]."

3 And the chief priests were accusing him of many things.[1]

4 And **Pilate** again asked him and said to him, "Will you not answer the accusation? See how many are testifying against you!"

5 But **Jesus** did not give any answer, so that Pilate was amazed.

6 Now he was accustomed during every feast to release one prisoner to them, whomever they requested.

7 And there was one who was called Barabbas[2] who was a prisoner with the ones who had caused an insurrection, those who had committed murder in the insurrection.

8 And the people cried out and began to request he do [this] for them as he was accustomed.

9 But **Pilate** answered and said, "Do you want me to release to you the king of the Judeans?"

10 ᵖᵃ(For Pilate knew that the chief priests had delivered him up out of envy.)

11 And the chief priests[3] all the more exhorted the crowds ᵉ[to ask] that he should release Barabbas to them.

12 And **Pilate** said to them, "What then do you want me to do to this one whom you call king of the Judeans?"

13 And again **they** cried out, "Crucify him!"

14 And **Pilate** said to them, "What evil has he done?" And **they** were crying out all the more, "Crucify him!"

15 And Pilate wanted to do the will of the crowds and he released Barabbas to them and he delivered Jesus to them, after he had scourged [him], to be crucified.

---

[1] OS (s): adds, 'but he gave them no answer,' found also in Ferrar Grk MS and Old Latin.

[2] Lit: son of the father. This is ironic that he was the counterfeit to the true son of the Father.

[3] Repeat *chief priests* as next word from v. 10

Chapter 15

16 And the soldiers led him[1] away inside the hall that was the Praetorium, and they called the whole company of soldiers.

17 And they put purple clothes on him and wove [and] placed on him a crown of thorns.

18 And they began to salute him [with], "Hail,[2] king of the Judeans."

19 And they were striking him on his head with a reed and were spitting in his face and were kneeling on their knees[3] and bowing to him.

20 And after they had mocked him, they stripped off the purple clothes and put on his own garments and took him out to crucify him.

21 And they compelled one who was passing by, Simon, a Cyrenian, who had come from the country, the father of Alexander and of Rufus, to carry his cross.

22 And they brought him to Golgotha, the place that is interpreted, The Skull.

23 And they gave him wine in which was mixed myrrh to drink, but **he** did not take [it].

24 And after they had crucified him, they divided his garments and cast lots for them, what each should take.

25 And it was the third hour when they crucified him.

26 And the cause of his death was written in the inscription, "This is the king of the Judeans."

27 And they crucified with him two robbers,[4] one on his right and one on his left.

28 And the scripture was fulfilled that said: HE WAS COUNTED WITH THE WICKED.

29 And also those who were passing by were reviling him and shaking their heads and saying, "ᵈOh indeed! ᵉ[He said] he will destroy the temple and build it after three days.

30 Save yourself and come down from the cross."

31 And likewise also the chief priests and the scribes were laughing with each other and saying, "Others he saved. Himself he is not able to save.

---

[1] Beginning here and throughout vs. 16-25, repeat suffix *him* with many verbs describing the crucifixion, particularly v. 20.

[2] Lit: peace

[3] Same root: *kneeling, knees*

[4] Compare Greek word, **lestai**

Chapter 15

32 Let the MESSIAH, the King of Israel, come down now from the cross that we might see and believe in him." And those also who were crucified with him were reviling him.

33 And when the sixth hour came, there was darkness over all the land until the ninth hour.

34 And in the ninth hour Jesus cried out with a loud voice and said, "Eil, Eil,[1] lmana shavaqtani," which is [interpreted], **"My God, My God,** why have you left me?"

35 And some of those who were standing [there] who heard were saying, "He calls to Elijah."

36 And one ran and filled a sponge [with] vinegar and fastened [it] on a reed to give him to drink. And they said, "Leave [him]! Let us see if Elijah will come to take him down."

37 And **Jesus** cried out with a loud voice and died.[2]

38 And the veil[3] of the temple was torn into two [pieces], from the top to the bottom.

39 Now when the centurion who was standing near him saw that he cried out so and died, he said, "Truly this man was the Son of God."

40 And there were also women who were watching from afar, Mary Magdalene and Mary the mother[4] of James the less and of Joses and Salome,

41 those who, when he was in Galilee, were following him and ministering to him, and many others who had gone up with him to Jerusalem.

42 And when the evening of the preparation had come, that was before the SABBATH,[5]

43 Joseph who was from Arimathaea,[6] an honorable counselor who also was waiting for the kingdom of God, came and was bold and approached Pilate and requested the body of Jesus.

---

[1] The reason for the need for interpretation is the use of the Hebrew, *Eil* or El. The Aramaic word for God is **Alaha**, which is in the interpretation. Could be quote from Psalm 22:1.

[2] Lit: he finished. ܫܠܡ means, "completed, fulfilled," and also, "died or expired," also used in v. 39.

[3] Lit: the face of the door

[4] OS (s): 'daughter'

[5] Culture: sunset began the Sabbath or high day, cf. Luke 23:54.

[6] OS (s): 'and it was on the Sabbath and Joseph came from Ramatha.'
Arimathaea is a place in the hill country of Ephraim, cf. I Sam 1:1.

Chapter 15

44 And Pilate marveled that he had already[1] died. And he called the centurion and asked him if he had already died.

45 And when he learned [it], he gave his body to Joseph.

46 And Joseph bought linen cloth and took him down and wrapped him in it and placed him in a grave that was hewn out in the rock and he rolled a stone on the door of the grave.

47 And Mary Magdalene and Mary the ᵉ[mother] of Joses saw where he was laid.

Chapter 16

1 And when the SABBATH had passed, Mary Magdalene and Mary [the mother][2] of James and Salome bought spices that they might come to anoint him.

2 And early on the first [day] of the week, they came to the tomb while the sun was rising.

3 And they were saying among themselves, "Who [will] roll the stone from the door of the tomb for us?"[3]

4 And they looked [and] saw that the stone was rolled away, for it was very great.

5 And they entered the tomb and saw a young man who was sitting on the right [side] and wrapped around [him] was a white robe, and they were amazed.

6 And **he** said to them, "Do not be afraid. You seek Jesus the Nazarene who was crucified. He has risen. He is not here. *Behold the place where he was laid.

7 But go [and] tell his disciples and Peter that *behold, ᵉ[he goes] before you to Galilee. There you will see him as he said to you."

8 And when they had heard, they fled and went out of the grave, for ʰᵉamazement and trembling had taken hold on them[4] and they did not speak anything to anyone, for they were afraid.

9 And early on the first of the week he had risen and appeared first to Mary Magdalene from whom he had cast out seven devils.

---

[1] Different phrase from second *already,* lit: if by [now] it was enough

[2] OS (s): 'daughter'

[3] OS (s): add 'for it was very great' and omit phrase in v. 4, also found in Codex Bezae and Pal Syr.

[4] OS (s): omit *of the grave, for amazement and trembling had taken hold on them*

Chapter 16

10 And **she** went [and] brought hope to those who had been with him who were mourning and weeping.

11 And when **they** heard what they were saying, that he was alive and had appeared to them, they did not believe them.

12 After these [things] he appeared to two of them in another form while they were walking and traveling to a village.

13 And those went [and] told the rest. They did not even believe them.

14 And finally he appeared to the eleven while they were eating.[1] And he reproved the lack of their faith and the hardness of their heart, since they had not believed those who had seen that he had risen.

15 And he said to them, "Go to all the world and preach my gospel in all of creation.

16 Whoever believes and is baptized will live, and whoever does not believe is condemned.

17 And these signs will follow those who believe, in my name they will cast out demons and they will speak with new tongues.

18 And they will capture [h]snakes,[2] and if they should [h]drink a deadly [h]poison,[3] it will harm not them and they will place their hands on the sick and they will be made whole."

19 And Jesus, our Lord, after speaking with them, went up to heaven and sat on the right [m]hand[4] of God.

20 And **they** went out [P]and preached in every place and our Lord was helping them and establishing their words by the signs that they were doing.⌐

---

[1] Lit: reclining

[2] Not normal word for serpent, from verb, ܚܘܐ, to show, could be translated "pretenders," could also be referring to the devil and his spirits; *capture* is literally "take," but in war is translated "capture"

[3] Lit: a poison of death; fig: hypocatastasis, meaning "words," cf. Rom 3:13, Jam. 3:8, Psalm 140:3.

[4] Culture: the right hand is the hand of blessing

ARAMAIC PESHITTA NEW TESTAMENT
LUKE

Chapter 1

1 Because many have wanted to write the accounts of the works of which **we** are persuaded,

2 according to what they delivered to us, those who were eye-witnesses and ministers of the word at the first,

3 it seemed [good] to me also, because I had carefully attended to all of them that I should write down everything in order for you noble Theophilus,

4 that you would know the truth of the words by which you were taught.

5 In the days of Herod, the king of Judea, there was a certain priest, whose name was Zachariah, from the course of the house of Abia,[1] and his wife, from the daughters of Aaron, whose name was Elizabeth.

6 Now both of them were just before God and were walking in all his commandments and in the uprightness of the LORD without blame.

7 But they had no son because Elizabeth was barren and both of them were advanced[2] in their days.

8 [P]And it happened, while he was serving as priest in the order of his ministering before God,

9 in the custom of the priesthood, it arrived that he was to place the incense. And he entered the temple of the LORD

10 and the whole assembly of people was praying outside at the time of the incense.

11 And an angel of the LORD appeared to Zachariah, who stood on the right [side] of the altar of incense,

12 and Zachariah was agitated when he saw him, and fear fell on him.

13 And the angel said to him, "Do not fear, Zachariah, because your prayer has been heard, and your wife, Elizabeth, will bear you a son, and you will call his name John,

14 and you will have [he]joy and gladness, and many will rejoice at his birth.

15 For he will be great before the LORD, and he will not drink wine or strong drink, and he will be filled with the Holy Spirit while he is in the womb of his mother,

16 and he will turn many of the sons of Israel to the LORD their God,

---

[1] OS (cs): 'Abium' ܐܒܝܘܡ

[2] Lit: many, also v. 18

Chapter 1

17 and **he** will go before him in the spirit and in the power of Elijah the prophet that he might turn the heart of the parents to the children and those who are disobedient to the knowledge of the upright, and he will prepare a mature people for the LORD."

18 And Zachariah said to the angel, "How will I know this? For **I** am old and my wife is advanced in her days."

19 And the angel answered and said to him, "I am Gabriel, for I stand before God. And I have been sent to speak with you and to declare to you these [things].

20 From now on, you will be silent and not able to speak until the [sy]day that these [things] occur, because you did not believe my words that will be fulfilled in their season."

21 Now the people were standing and waiting for Zachariah and they were wondering about his delay in the temple.

22 And when Zachariah came out, he was not able to speak with them and they perceived that he had seen a vision[1] in the temple. And he continually made signs[2] to them, yet remained mute.

23 And when the days of his service were completed, he went to his house.

24 And it happened after those days [that] Elizabeth, his wife, conceived. And she hid herself [for] five months, and she said,

25 "These [things] the **LORD** has done for me in the days that he looked on me to remove my reproach that was among men."

26 Now in the sixth month, the angel Gabriel was sent from before God to Galilee, to a city by the name of Nazareth,

27 to a virgin who was engaged to a man whose name [was] Joseph from the house of David. And the name of the virgin [was] Mary.

28 And the angel approached her and said to her, "Peace to you, [one] full of grace! Our Lord [is] with you, blessed [one] of women."

29 Now when **she** saw [him], she was shocked at his saying and wondered, "What is[3] this greeting?"

30 And the angel said to her, "Do not be afraid, Mary, for you have found grace with God.

---

[1] Same root: *seen, vision*

[2] Fig: polyptoton, lit: *signing, he signed*

[3] Eastern txt: one word for *what is*

Chapter 1

31 For *behold, you will conceive and give birth to a son and you will call his name Jesus.

32 He will be great, ᴾand he will be called the Son of the Most High, and the LORD God will give to him the throne of David, his father,

33 and he will reign over the house of Jacob forever, and there will not be a boundary to his kingdom."ܕ

34 Mary said to the angel, "How can this be? Because no man has known me."[1]

35 The angel answered and said to her, "The Holy Spirit will come and the power of the Most High will overshadow you. Because of this, the one who is begotten in you will be holy and will be called the Son of God.

36 And *behold, Elizabeth, your kinswoman, is also pregnant with a son in her old age and this [is] the sixth month for her who was called barren,

37 because ᵗnothing [is] difficult for God."

38 Mary said, "*Behold, I am the handmaid of the LORD. It will happen to me according to your word." And the angel left her.

39 And Mary rose up in those days and went quickly to a mountain, to a city of Judea.

40 And she entered the house of Zachariah and greeted Elizabeth.

41 And it happened that when Elizabeth heard the greeting of Mary, the baby leaped in her womb, and Elizabeth was filled with the Holy Spirit

42 and she cried out in a loud voice and said to Mary, "You are blessed among women, and blessed is the ᵐfruit that is in your womb.

43 How did this [happen] to me that the mother of my Lord would come to me?

44 For *behold, when the sound of your greeting fell on my ears, the baby in my womb leaped with great joy.

45 And blessed [is] she who believed,[2] because there will be a completion of those [things] that were spoken with her in the presence of the LORD."

46 And Mary said, "My soul magnifies the LORD

47 and my spirit has rejoiced in God, my Life-giver,

48 because he has looked at the humiliation of his handmaid. For *behold, from now on, all generations will give me a blessing,

---

[1] Semitism: *to know* means to be intimate with
[2] OS (s): 'believes'

ARAMAIC PESHITTA NEW TESTAMENT
LUKE

Chapter 1

49 because he who is mighty has done great [things] with me and his name [is] holy

50 and his mercy [is] on those who fear him for ages and generations.

51 He has accomplished victory with his arm and has scattered the proud in the thought of their heart[s].

52 He has thrown down the mighty from the ᵐseats and elevated the humble.

53 The hungry he has satisfied with good [things] and the rich he has sent away empty-handed.

54 He has aided Israel his servant[1] and remembered his mercy,

55 as he spoke with our fathers, with Abraham and with his seed forever."

56 And Mary stayed with Elizabeth for three months and she returned to her house.

57 Now [concerning] Elizabeth, the time came that she should give birth and she bore a son.

58 And her neighbors and her relatives heard that God had increased his mercy toward her and they rejoiced with her.

59 And it happened on the eighth day and they came to circumcise the young boy and they were going to call him by the name of his father, Zachariah.

60 But his mother answered and said to them, "Not so, but he will be called John."

61 And they said to her, "There is no man in your tribe who is called by this name."

62 And they made signs to his father as to what he wanted to name him.

63 And he asked for a writing tablet and wrote and said, "His name is John." And everyone marveled.

64 And immediately his mouth was opened and his ᵐtongue ᶜ[was loosed] and he spoke and blessed God.

65 And fear came over all their neighbors, and in all the mountain of Judea these [things] were spoken.

66 And all that heard were pondering in their heart[s] and saying, "What indeed will this child be?" And the ᶜhand of the LORD was with him.

---

[1] OS (s): 'his son'

ARAMAIC PESHITTA NEW TESTAMENT
LUKE

Chapter 1

67 And Zachariah, his father, was filled with the Holy Spirit and prophesied and said,

68 "The LORD is blessed, the God of Israel, who has visited his nation and brought redemption for it.

69 And he has raised up for us a ^mhorn of redemption in the house of David his servant,

70 as he spoke by the ^mmouth of his holy prophets who were from old,

71 that he would redeem us from our enemies and from the ^mhand of all our adversaries.

72 And he has performed his mercy with our fathers and has remembered his holy covenants

73 and the oaths that he swore to Abraham, our father, that he would give to us,

74 so that we would be redeemed[1] from the ^mhand of our enemies and [that] without fear we might serve before him

75 all our days in uprightness and justification.

76 And **you**, [oh] child, will be called the prophet of the Most High, for you will go before the face of the LORD to prepare his way,

77 so that he may give the knowledge of life to his people in the forgiveness of their sins,

78 by the ^mbowels of mercy of our God, by which the ^hdawn[2] from on high will visit us,

79 to enlighten those who sit in darkness and in the shadows of death, that he may direct our ^mfeet in the way of peace."

80 And the child grew and was strengthened by the Spirit and he was in the wilderness until the ^{sy}day of his appearance to Israel.

Chapter 2

1 And it happened [that] in those days a decree went out from Caesar Augustus that every nation of his jurisdiction should be enrolled.[3]

2 This was the first enrollment during the governorship of Quirinius in Syria.

3 And everyone went to his city to be enrolled.

---

[1] Repeat forms of *redeem, redemption,* vs. 69, 71, 74

[2] Fig: metonymy, *bowels* meaning compassion, *dawn* meaning John the Baptist

[3] Same root: *enrollment, enrolled,* vs. 1-5, root picture: to write down

150

ARAMAIC PESHITTA NEW TESTAMENT
LUKE

Chapter 2

4 And Joseph also went up from Nazareth, a city of Galilee, into Judea to the city of David that is called Bethlehem, because he was from the house and from the tribe of David,

5 with Mary, his pregnant wife, to be enrolled there.

6 And it happened that while they were there, her days were fulfilled that she should give birth,

7 and she bore her firstborn son and wrapped him in swaddling clothes and laid him in a manger, because they had no place where they were staying.

8 And there were shepherds in that region who were abiding there and keeping watch over their flocks at night.[1]

9 And *behold, an angel of God came to them and the glory of the LORD shone on them and they were very afraid.[2]

10 And the angel said to them, "Do not be afraid, for *behold, I announce to you great joy that will be to all the world.

11 For today the deliverer, who is the LORD the MESSIAH,[3] is born to you in the city of David.

12 And this [is] a sign to you, you will find a baby who is wrapped in swaddling clothes and laid in a manger."

13 And suddenly the great hosts of heaven appeared with the angel, praising God and saying,

14 "Glory to God in the highest and on earth, peace and a good hope[4] to men."

15 And it happened that after the angels had gone away from them to heaven, the shepherds spoke with each other and said, "Let us journey to Bethlehem and see this matter that has happened as the LORD has made known to us."

16 And they came quickly and found Mary and Joseph and the baby, who was laid in the manger.

17 And after they had seen [him], they made known the message that had been told to them about the child.

18 And all who heard [it] marveled at those [things] that were spoken to them by the shepherds.

---

[1] OS (s): omit *at night*
[2] Lit: feared a great fear
[3] OS (s): 'the anointed Lord'
[4] OS (s): 'reconciliation'

Chapter 2

19 But Mary kept all those words and was pondering [them] in her heart.

20 And those shepherds returned, glorifying and praising God for all that they had seen and heard as it was told to them.

21 And when eight days were completed so that the boy could be circumcised, his name was called Jesus as he had been named by the angel before he was conceived in the womb.

22 And when the days of their purification were fulfilled according to the law of Moses, they took him up to Jerusalem to present him to the LORD,

23 according to what was written in the law of the LORD: **EVERY MALE [WHO] OPENS THE WOMB WILL BE CALLED A HOLY ONE OF THE LORD,**

24 and to give a sacrifice, as is said in the law of the LORD, **A PAIR OF TURTLEDOVES OR TWO CHICKS OF A DOVE.**

25 Now there was a certain man in Jerusalem whose name was Simeon. And this man was [he]upright and just and was waiting for the [m]comfort of Israel and the Holy Spirit was on him.

26 And it had been spoken to him by the Holy Spirit that he would not see death until he would see the MESSIAH of the LORD.

27 This [man] came by the Spirit to the temple and when his parents brought the child Jesus to do for him as was commanded in the law,

28 he took him up in his arms and blessed God and said,

29 "Now, my Lord, dismiss your servant in peace according to your word.

30 For *behold, my eyes have seen your [m]mercy

31 that you have prepared in the presence of all nations,

32 a [m]light for a revelation to the Gentiles and a glory to your people, Israel."

33 And Joseph and his mother marveled at these [things] that were spoken about him.

34 And Simeon blessed them and said to Mary his mother, "*Behold, this [man] is set for the [mr]fall and the rising of many in Israel and for a [an]sign of contention,

35 [pa](and a [m]spear will pass through your soul) so that the thoughts of many hearts may be revealed."

ARAMAIC PESHITTA NEW TESTAMENT
LUKE

Chapter 2

36 And Anna, a prophetess, the daughter of Phanuel, from the tribe of Asher, was also advanced in her years.[1] And she had lived [for] seven years with her husband from her maidenhood.

37 And she was a widow for about eighty-four years and she did not go out of the temple and she served in fasting and in prayer both [mr]day and night.[2]

38 And she also stood up immediately and gave thanks to the LORD and spoke about him to everyone who waited for the [m]redemption of Jerusalem.

39 And when they had completed everything according to in the law of the LORD, they returned to Galilee, to their city Nazareth.

40 And the child grew and was strengthened by the Spirit and was filled with wisdom and the grace of God was on him.

41 And his relatives, during every year, went to Jerusalem for the celebration of the feast of Passover.

42 And when he was twelve years old, they went up, as they were accustomed, for the celebration.

43 And after the [feast] days were completed, they returned. But the child Jesus remained in Jerusalem and Joseph and his mother did not know [it],

44 for they thought that he was with their companions. And after they had journeyed one day, they searched for him among their relatives and among anyone who knew them

45 and they did not find him. So they returned again to Jerusalem and searched for him.

46 And after three days, they found him in the temple, sitting in the middle of the teachers. And he was listening to them and questioning them.

47 And all those who heard him were amazed [he]by his wisdom and his answers.

48 And when they saw him, they were amazed and his mother said to him, "My son, why have you acted toward us in this manner? For *behold, your father and I[3] have been searching for you with much anxiety."

---

[1] Lit: older in her days
[2] Lit: by day and by night, fig: merismos
[3] Eastern txt: 'I and your father'

ARAMAIC PESHITTA NEW TESTAMENT
LUKE

Chapter 2

49 He said to them, "Why were you searching for me? Do you not know that it is necessary for me to be in the house of my Father?"[1]

50 But **they** did not understand the saying that he had told them.

51 And he went down with them and came to Nazareth and was subject to them. And his mother kept all the words in her heart.[2]

52 And Jesus grew in his stature and in his wisdom and in[3] favor with God and men.

Chapter 3

1 Now in the fifteenth year of the reign of Tiberius Caesar, in the governorship of Pontius Pilate in Judea, while Herod [was] tetrarch in Galilee and Philip, his brother, [was] tetrarch in Ituraea and in the region of Trachonitis, and Lysanias [was] tetrarch of Abilene,[4]

2 during the high priesthood of Annas and Caiaphas, the word of God came to John, the son of Zachariah, in the wilderness.

3 And he came into all the region that was around the Jordan, proclaiming the baptism of repentance for the forgiveness of sins,

4 as it is written in the book of the words of Isaiah the prophet who said: **THE VOICE THAT CALLS IN THE WILDERNESS: PREPARE THE WAY OF THE LORD AND MAKE STRAIGHT PATHS IN THE PLAIN FOR OUR GOD.**

5 **ALL THE VALLEYS WILL BE FILLED AND ALL THE MOUNTAINS AND HILLS WILL BE LEVELED AND THE RUGGED [PLACE] WILL BE CLEARED AND THE ROUGH LAND, A PLAIN.**

6 **AND ALL [sy]FLESH WILL SEE THE LIFE OF GOD.**[5]

7 And he said to those crowds that had come to him to be baptized, "Generation of [h]vipers,[6] who has shown you to flee from the wrath that is to come?

---

[1] Fig: erotesis – question to ponder; *house of my Father* refers to the temple

[2] OS (s): omit *in her heart*

[3] Repeat *in*

[4] OS (s): alt sp. HBLINA

[5] OS (c): 'Restore *the way of the Lord*,' OS (cs): add 'and the glory of the Lord will be revealed;' OS (c): add at end of verse, 'because the mouth of the Lord has spoken it'.

[6] Fig: hypocatastasis, meaning men who bring poisonous words and acts; erotesis – question to ponder

Chapter 3

8   Produce therefore ^mfruit that is worthy for repentance and do not begin to say within yourselves, 'We have Abraham [for] a father.' For *I say to you, 'From these stones, God is able to raise up sons to Abraham.'

9   ^{al}And *behold, the ax is laid on the root of the trees. Therefore, every tree that does not produce good fruit will be cut off and will fall into the fire."⌐

10   And the crowds were asking him and saying, "What then should we do?"

11   He answered and said to them, "He who has two coats should give to him who does not have [any] and he who has food should do likewise."

12   And the tax collectors also came to be baptized and were saying to him, "Teacher, what should we do?"

13   And **he** said to them, "Do not require anything more than what is commanded to you to require."[1]

14   And the soldiers were asking him and said, "What should we also do?" He said to them, "Do not deal harshly with anyone and do not accuse anyone and let your rations be sufficient for you."

15   And as the nation was thinking about John and all were considering in their heart that perhaps he was the MESSIAH,

16   John answered and said to them, "*Behold, **I** baptize you with water, but one who is greater than I will come, the straps of whose sandals I am not worthy to loosen. **He** will baptize you with the Holy Spirit and with ^mfire.[2]

17   ^{al}he who holds a winnowing fan in his hand and has cleaned his threshing floors. And he will gather the wheat into his granaries and he will burn the chaff with a fire that will not go out."⌐

18   Now also many other [things] he was teaching and declaring to the people.

19   But Herod, the tetrarch, because he had been reproved by John on account of Herodias, the wife of Philip, his brother, and on account of all the evil [things] that he had done,

20   added this also above all of them, that he shut up John [in] prison.

21   Now it happened while he baptized all the people, he also baptized Jesus. And while he prayed, the sky opened,

---

[1] Repeat *require*, OS (c): 'collect'

[2] Eastern txt: add '*come* after me;' repeat *with* (not hendiadys)

Chapter 3

22 and the Holy Spirit came down on him in the likeness of the form of a dove. And a voice came from heaven that said, "You are my beloved Son in whom I am pleased."

23 And Jesus was about thirty years old and was thought [to be] the son of Joseph, the son of Heli,

24 the son of Matthat, the son of Levi, the son of Melki, the son of Janni, the son of Joseph,

25 the son of Mattathias, the son of Amos, the son of Nahum, the son of Esli, the son of Naggai,

26 the son of Maath, the son of Mattathias, the son of Semein, the son of Joseph, the son of Judah,

27 the son of Joanan, the son of Rhesa, the son of Zerabbabel, the son of Shealtiel, the son of Neri,

28 the son of Melki, the son of Addi, the son of Cosam, the son of Elmodam, the son of Er,

29 the son of Jose, the son of Eliezer, the son of Jorim, the son of Matthat, the son of Levi,

30 the son of Simeon, the son of Juda, the son of Joseph, the son of Jonam, the son of Eliakim,

31 the son of Melea, the son of Menna, the son of Mattatha, the son of Nathan, the son of David,

32 the son of Jesse, the son of Obed, the son of Boaz, the son of Salmon, the son of Nahshon,

33 the son of Aminadab, the son of Aram, the son of Hezron, the son of Perez, the son of Judah,

34 the son of Jacob, the son of Isaac, the son of Abraham, the son of Terah, the son of Nahor,

35 the son of Serug, the son of Reu, the son of Peleg, the son of Eber, the son of Shelah,

36 the son of Cainan, the son of Arphaxad, the son of Shem, the son of Noah, the son of Lamech,

37 the son of Methuselah, the son of Enoch, the son of Jared, the son of Mahalalel, the son of Kenan,

38 the son of Enosh, the son of Seth, the son of Adam, who [was] from God.[1]

---

[1] Repeat *the son of*, vs. 23-38

ARAMAIC PESHITTA NEW TESTAMENT
LUKE

Chapter 4

1 And Jesus, being full of the Holy Spirit, returned from the Jordan. And the Spirit led him to the wilderness

2 [for] forty days to be tempted by the Accuser. And he did not eat anything in those days, and when he had completed them, at the end he was hungry.

3 And the Accuser said to him, "If you are the Son of God, tell this stone to become bread."

4 Jesus answered and said to him, "It is written: MAN SHOULD NOT LIVE BY BREAD ALONE, BUT BY EVERY ANSWER OF GOD."

5 And SATAN took him up to a high mountain and showed him all the kingdoms of the earth in a short period of time.

6 And the Accuser said to him, "I will give you all this authority and its glory that is delivered to me and to whom I want, I give it.

7 Therefore, if you worship before me, all of it will be yours."

8 Jesus[1] answered and said to him, "It is written: YOU SHOULD WORSHIP THE LORD YOUR GOD AND YOU SHOULD SERVE HIM ALONE."

9 And he brought him to Jerusalem and placed him on the edge of the temple and said to him, "If you are the Son of God, throw yourself down from here to the bottom.

10 For it is written: HE WILL COMMAND HIS ANGELS CONCERNING YOU TO KEEP YOU

11 AND BEAR YOU IN THEIR ARMS, SO THAT YOUR FOOT WILL NOT STUMBLE ON A STONE."

12 And Jesus answered and said to him, "It is said: YOU SHOULD NOT TEMPT THE LORD YOUR GOD."

13 And after the Accuser had finished all his temptations, he left his presence for a while.

14 And Jesus returned in the power of the Spirit to Galilee and a report about him went out into every region around them.

15 And he was teaching in their synagogues and was being praised by everyone.

16 And he came to Nazareth where he had been raised. And he entered into the synagogue as he was accustomed on the day of the SABBATH and stood up to read.

---

[1] Eastern txt: add 'But *Jesus answered*'

157

ARAMAIC PESHITTA NEW TESTAMENT
LUKE

Chapter 4

17 And the scroll of Isaiah the prophet was given to him and Jesus opened the scroll and found the place where it was written:

18 **THE SPIRIT OF THE LORD [IS] ON ME AND BECAUSE OF THIS, HE HAS ANOINTED ME TO PREACH TO THE POOR AND HAS SENT ME TO HEAL THE BROKEN-HEARTED AND TO PREACH FORGIVENESS TO THE CAPTIVES AND SIGHT TO THE BLIND AND TO STRENGTHEN THE BROKEN WITH FORGIVENESS**

19 **AND TO PREACH THE ACCEPTABLE YEAR OF THE LORD."**

20 And he rolled up the scroll and gave it to the minister and went [and] sat down. And the eyes of all of them in the synagogue were fixed on him.

21 And he began to speak to them, "Today this scripture is fulfilled in your ᵐears."

22 And all were witnessing to him and were amazed at the words of blessing that were coming out of his ᵐmouth. And they were saying, "Is not this [man] the son of Joseph?"[1]

23 Jesus said to them, "Perhaps you will tell me this proverb: 'Physician, heal yourself,' and all that we have heard that you did in Capernaum, do also here in your city."

24 But **he** said, "*Truly, I say to you, there is no prophet that is received in his city.

25 For *I tell you the truth, that there were many widows in Israel[2] in the days of Elijah the prophet, while the heavens were closed [for] three years and six months and a great famine was in all the land.

26 And Elijah was not sent to one of them, except to Zarephath of Sidon, to a widow woman.

27 And there were many lepers [in] Israel in the days of Elisha the prophet, yet not one of them was cleansed, except Naaman the Syrian."

28 And when they heard[3] these [things], all that were in the synagogue were filled with anger.

29 And they rose up [and] threw him outside of the city. And they brought him up to the top of the mountain on which their city was built to throw him down from the steep place.

30 But **he** passed through them and went away.

---

[1] Fig: erotesis, "not" question, answer in the affirmative

[2] Eastern txt: add '*in* the house of *Israel*'

[3] Eastern txt: add '*they* had *heard*'

ARAMAIC PESHITTA NEW TESTAMENT
LUKE

Chapter 4

31 And he went down to Capernaum, a city of Galilee, and taught them on the SABBATHS.

32 And they were astonished at his teaching, because his message had power.

33 And there was in the synagogue a man who had the spirit of an unclean demon and he cried out with a loud voice

34 and said, "Leave me. What do we have in common, Jesus the Nazarene? Have you come to destroy us? I know you, who you are, the Holy [one] of God."

35 And Jesus rebuked him and said, "Shut your mouth and go out of him." And the demon threw him down in the middle and went out of him, not harming him at all.

36 And great amazement took hold of everyone and they were speaking with each other and saying, "What indeed is this message, because with he authority and power he commands the unclean spirits and they go out?"[1]

37 And a report went out about him into the entire region surrounding them.

38 And after Jesus went out of the synagogue, he entered the house of Simon, and the mother-in-law of Simon was tormented with a great fever, and they begged him on account of her.

39 And he stood over her and rebuked her fever and it left her. And immediately she rose up and served them.

40 And [at] the setting of the sun all those who had sick who were sick with various sicknesses[2] brought them to him. And **he** placed his hand on each of them and healed them.

41 And also demons were going out of many, crying out and saying, "You are the MESSIAH, the Son of God." And he rebuked them and did not allow them to say that they knew he was the MESSIAH.

42 And on the morning of the day he went out [and] journeyed to a deserted place. And the crowds were seeking him and came up to him and were holding him captive so that he would not go away from them.

43 But **Jesus** said to them, "It is necessary for me also to preach to other cities the kingdom of God, because for this I was sent."

44 And **he** was preaching in the synagogues of Galilee.

---

[1] Fig: erotesis – question to ponder

[2] Same root: *sick, were sick, sicknesses*

Chapter 5

1 And it happened [that] as the crowd gathered around him[1] to hear the word of God and **he** was standing on the shore of the lake of Gennesaret,

2 he saw two ships that were standing at the edge of the lake and the fishermen that had come down from them and they were washing their nets.

3 And one of them belonged to Simon Peter. And Jesus boarded [and] sat in it and told [them] to take him a little way from dry land on the water. And he sat and taught the crowd from the ship.

4 And after he stopped speaking, he said to Simon, "Row to deep [water] and cast your net for a catch."

5 Simon answered and said to him, "My Master, we have labored all night and have not caught anything. But at your word I will cast the net."

6 And after they did this, they caught a great many fish and their net was tearing.

7 And they made signs to their friends who were in the other ship to come to help them. And after they had come, they filled both ships, so that they were close to sinking.

8 And when Simon Peter saw [this], he fell down before the feet of Jesus and said to him, "I beg you, my Lord, go away from me, for I am a sinful man."

9 For amazement had taken hold of him and all who were with him, because of that catch of fish that they had caught,[2]

10 and so also James and John, the sons of Zebedee, who were partners of Simon. And Jesus said to Simon, "Do not be afraid. From now on, you will catch men to life."[3]

11 And they brought those ships to land and left everything and followed him.

12 And when Jesus was in one of the cities, a man who was completely covered with leprosy came. He saw Jesus and fell on his face and begged him and said to him, "My Lord, if you want to, you are able to cleanse me."

13 And Jesus stretched out his hand [and] touched him and said to him, "I want to. Be cleansed." And immediately his leprosy went away from him and he was cleansed.[4]

---

[1] OS (s): 'was crushing together'
[2] Same root: *catch, caught*
[3] See note on Mat 4:19.
[4] Eastern txt: omit *and he was cleansed*

Chapter 5

14 And he commanded him, "Do not tell anyone, but go [and] show yourself to the priests and offer for your purification, as Moses commanded for their witness."

15 And a report about him went out all the more and a large crowd was gathered to hear from him and to be healed from their sicknesses.

16 And **he** went away to the desert land and was praying.

17 And it happened [that] on a certain day while Jesus was teaching, Pharisees and teachers of the law were sitting [there] who had come from all the villages of Galilee and of Judea and of Jerusalem,[1] and there was the power of the LORD to heal them.

18 And men brought on a pallet a certain paralyzed man and were seeking to bring [him] in to lay him before him.

19 And when they could not find how to bring him in because of the multitude of people, they went up to the roof and let him down on his pallet from the roof floor into the middle before Jesus.

20 And when Jesus saw their faith, he said to that paralyzed man, "Your sins are forgiven."

21 And the scribes and Pharisees began reasoning and saying, "Who is this [man] who speaks blasphemy?[2] Who is able to forgive sins, except God alone?"

22 But Jesus knew their reasonings and answered and said to them, "Why are you reasoning in your heart?

23 Which [thing] is easier to say, 'Your sins are forgiven' or to say, 'Rise up, walk?'

24 But that you will know that it is lawful for the Son of Man to forgive sins on earth," he said to the paralytic, "*I say to you, rise up, take up your pallet and go to your house."

25 And immediately he rose up before their eyes and took up his pallet and went to his house, praising God.

26 And amazement took hold of everyone and they were praising God and were filled with fear and were saying, "We have seen wonders today."

27 After these [things], Jesus went out and saw a tax collector, whose name was Levi, who was sitting at the customs-house,[3] and he said to him, "Follow me."

---

[1] Repeat *and of*

[2] Fig: erotesis – questions to ponder, vs. 21-23

[3] Lit: house of the tax; culture: tax collectors were despised, Freeman, pp. 411-412.

Chapter 5

28 And he left everything and stood up [and] followed him.

29 And Levi made for him a great feast in his house, and there was a large crowd of tax collectors and of others who were eating with them.

30 And the scribes and Pharisees were murmuring and saying to his disciples, "Why are you eating and drinking with tax collectors and sinners?"

31 And Jesus answered and said to them, "The physician is not needed by the healthy, but by those who are very sick.

32 I did not come to call the just, but sinners to repentance."

33 And those were saying to him, "Why are the disciples of John, also of the Pharisees, fasting and praying continually, but yours are eating and drinking?"

34 And **he** said to them, "You cannot make the wedding guests fast as long as the bridegroom [is] with them.

35 But the days will come when the bridegroom will be taken up from them. Then, in those days, they will fast."

36 And he told them a parable: [al]"No one cuts off a piece of cloth from a new garment and lays [it] on an old garment, lest he cuts off the new and the patch that is from the new does not repair the old.

37 And no one puts new wine into old wineskins, lest the new wine will burst the wineskins and the wine should be poured out and the wineskins ruined.

38 On the contrary, they put new wine into new wineskins and both of them are preserved.

39 And no one drinks old wine and immediately desires new, for he says, 'The old is delicious.'"[1]

Chapter 6

1 And it happened [that] on the SABBATH, while Jesus was walking [in] the sown fields, his disciples were picking the heads of grain and rubbing [them] in their hands and eating [them].

2 And some of the Pharisees were saying to them, "Why are you doing that which is not lawful to do on the SABBATH?"

3 Jesus answered and said to them, "And have you not read what David did when he was hungry, and those who were with him,

---

[1] Parallel structure, vs. 36-39, *patch, wine*

162

Chapter 6

4 how he entered the house of God and took the bread of the table of the LORD [and] ate and gave to those who were with him, that which was not lawful for [anyone] to eat, but only the priests alone?"

5 And he said to them, "The Lord of the SABBATH is the Son of Man."

6 And it happened [that] on another SABBATH he entered the synagogue and was teaching. And there was there a man whose right hand was withered.

7 And the scribes and Pharisees were watching him, if [1] he would heal on the SABBATH, so that they would be able to accuse him.

8 And **he** knew their thoughts and said to that man whose hand was withered, "Stand up. Come to the middle of the synagogue." And when he came and stood,

9 Jesus said to them, "I will ask you, is it lawful on the SABBATH to do good[2] or evil, to cause a soul to live or to destroy [it]?"

10 And he gazed at all of them and said to him, "Stretch out your hand." And he stretched [it] out and his hand was restored like the other.

11 And **they** were filled with envy and were speaking with each other about what they should do to Jesus.

12 And it happened [that] in those days Jesus went out to a mountain to pray. And there he spent the night in prayer to God.

13 And when [day] dawned, he called his disciples and chose twelve of them, those whom he named apostles:

14 Simon, whom he called Peter, [P]and Andrew, his brother, and James and John and Philip and Bartholomew

15 and Matthew and Thomas and James, the son of Alphaeus, and Simon, who was called the zealot,

16 and Judas, the son of James, and Judas Iscariot, who was the betrayer.┐

17 And Jesus came down with them and stood in the plain with a large crowd of his disciples and a multitude of a crowd of people from all Judea and from Jerusalem and from[3] the sea coast of Tyre and of Sidon,

18 who had come to hear his message and to be healed of their sicknesses, and those who were tormented by unclean spirits, and they were healed.

---

[1] Eastern txt: *if* is one word
[2] Eastern txt: 'to do evil or good,' reverse word order
[3] Repeat *and from*

Chapter 6

19 And the whole crowd was seeking to touch him, for power was going out of him, and he was healing all of them.

20 And he ᴾʳlifted up his eyes to his disciples and said, "Blessed are you¹ poor, because yours is the kingdom of God.

21 Blessed are you who are hungry now, because you will be satisfied. Blessed are you who are weeping now, because you will laugh.

22 Blessed are you when men hate you ᴾand discriminate against you and reproach you and cast out your name as evil for the sake of the Son of Man.⌐

23 Rejoice in that ˢʸday and leap for joy, because your reward is great in heaven, for their fathers did the same to the prophets.

24 But ⁱwoe to you, rich [ones], because you have received your comfort!

25 ⁱWoe to you, satisfied [ones], because you will hunger! ⁱWoe to you who are laughing now, because you will cry and you will mourn!

26 ⁱWoe to you, when men will speak what is good about you, for their fathers did so to the false prophets!²

27 But to you who hear, I say, 'Love your enemies and do that which is good to those who hate you.

28 And bless those who curse you and pray for those who take you by force.

29 And to him, who strikes you on your cheek, offer to him the other, and from him who takes away your outer cloak, do not hold back your tunic also.

30 To everyone who asks you, give to him, and from him, who takes away your [things], do not demand [them] back.³

31 And whatever you desire men to do to you, do the same to them also.

32 For if you love those who love you, what is your goodness?⁴ For even sinners love those who love them.

33 And if you do that which is good to those who do good to you, what is your goodness?⁵ For even sinners do the same.

---

¹ Repeat *blessed are*, repeat suffix *you*, vs. 20-22
² Repeat *woe to you*, vs. 24-26
³ Parallel structure, vs. 27-30, opposites
⁴ Repeat *what is your goodness,* and *even sinners,* vs. 33, 34; fig: erotesis – questions to ponder; repeat *love*
⁵ Same root: *do good, goodness*

Chapter 6

34 And if you lend to [those] from whom you expect to be repaid, what is your goodness? For even sinners lend to sinners, that in the same way they might be repaid.

35 But love your enemies ᴾand do good to them and lend and do not cut off the hope of anyone, and your reward will be increased and you will be the sons of the Most High,⌐ because **he** is kind to the evil and to the unthankful.

36 Therefore be merciful, as your Father also is merciful. [1]

37 Do not judge and you will not be judged. Do not condemn and you will not be condemned. Forgive and you will be forgiven.

38 Give and it will be given to you. With good and pressed down and abundant measure they will throw into your laps.[2] For with the same measure that you measure, it will be measured to you."

39 And he told them a parable, ᴾᵇ"Are the blind able to lead the blind? Would not they both fall in a ditch?[3]

40 There is no disciple who is greater than his master, for everyone who is mature should be as his master [is].[4]⌐

41 ᵃˡAnd why do you see the straw that is in the eye of your brother, but the plank that is in your [own] eye is not seen by you?[5]

42 Or how are you able to say to your brother, 'My brother, allow me to take out the straw from your eye,' when *behold, the plank that is in your own eye is not seen by you? ⁱHypocrite! First take out the plank from your [own] eye and then it will be clear for you to take out the straw from the eye of your brother.⌐

43 ᵃˡThere is not a good tree that produces bad fruit or a bad tree that produces good fruit.

---

[1] Repeat forms of same roots: *merciful, judge, condemn, forgive, give, measure,* vs. 36-38

[2] Culture: A lap is part of a natural pocket in the loose Eastern outer garment. *Pressed down…running over* means to give a generous amount, Freeman, p. 412, Neil, *Palestine Explored*, pp. 30-34.

[3] Fig: erotesis, 1ˢᵗ, **lema** question, obvious answer "no", 2ⁿᵈ question, "not" question, obvious answer "yes", also vs. 39, 41, 42

[4] OS (s): entire verse is different: 'No student is as accomplished as his master in learning,' Wilson, p.432.

[5] Fig: erotesis – question to ponder

Chapter 6

44 For every tree is known by its ^mfruit. For they do not gather figs from thorn-bushes, nor do they gather grapes from a bramble-bush.

45 A good man, from the good treasures that are in his heart, produces good things, and an evil man, from the evil treasures that are in his heart, produces evil things. For from the abundant [things] of the heart the ^mlips speak.[1]ך

46 Why do you call me, 'My Lord, my Lord,'[2] and you do not do what I say?

47 I will show you what each one who comes to me and hears my words and does them is like.

48 ^{al}He is like the man who built a house and dug and went deep and laid the foundations on rock. And when there was a flood, the flood beat on that house and it was not able to shake it, for its foundation was placed on rock.

49 And whoever hears ^e[my words] and does not do [them] is like the man who built his house on ground without a foundation. And when the river beat on it, immediately it fell, and the fall of that house was great."

Chapter 7

1 And when he completed all the sayings for the ^mhearing of the people, Jesus entered Capernaum.

2 And the servant of a certain centurion, who was dear to him, was very sick and was about to die.

3 And he heard about Jesus and sent to him elders of the Judeans and was begging him to come [and] give life to his servant.

4 And when **they** came to Jesus, they were begging him earnestly and saying, "He is worthy that you do this for him,

5 for he loves our people and has even built a synagogue for us."

6 And Jesus went with them. And when he was not very far from the house, the centurion sent his friends to him and said to him, "My Lord, do not trouble [yourself], for I am not worthy that you should come under my roof,

7 [and] on account of that, **I** am not worthy[3] to come to you. But speak with a word and my young man will be healed,

---

[1] Parallel structure, vs. 43-45, opposites; repeat forms of *good, evil*
[2] Fig: epizeuxis, solemn repetition
[3] Repeat *I am not worthy,* cf. v. 4

Chapter 7

8   for **I** also am a man who is subject to authority and there are soldiers under my ^m^hand. And I say to this one, 'Go,' and he goes, and to another, 'Come,' and he comes, and to my servant, 'Do this,' and he does [it]."

9   [1]And when Jesus heard these [things], he marveled at him. And he turned and said to the crowd that was following him, "*I say to you, not even [in] Israel[2] have I found faith like this."

10   And those who were sent returned to the house and found that servant who was sick made whole.

11   And it happened on the day that followed, [that] he went to a city by the name of Nain and his disciples and a large crowd [were] with him.

12   And when he approached the gate of the city, he saw a dead man being brought who was the only [son] of his mother, and his mother was a widow, and a large crowd of citizens [was] with her.

13   And Jesus saw her and had compassion on her and said to her, "Do not cry."

14   And he went [and] touched the pallet. And those who were carrying it stood, and he said, "Young man, *I say to you, rise up."

15   And that dead man sat up and began to speak and he gave him to his mother.

16   And fear took hold of all men and they were praising God and saying, "A great prophet has risen up among us and God has visited his people."

17   And this saying went out about him into all Judea and into all the region around them,

18   and his disciples reported all these [things] to John.

19   And John called two of his disciples and sent them to Jesus and said, "Are you that one who is to come or should we wait for another?"

20   And they came to Jesus and said to him, John the baptizer sent us to you and said, "Are you that one who is to come or should we wait for another?"[3]

21   And in that same ^sy^hour he healed many of sicknesses and of plagues and of [4] evil spirits and he gave sight to many blind.

---

[1] Fig: polysyndeton, begin extensive passage connected with many "ands"
[2] Lit: the house of Israel
[3] Repeat entire phrase from v. 19
[4] Repeat *and of*

ARAMAIC PESHITTA NEW TESTAMENT
LUKE

Chapter 7

22 And Jesus answered and said to them, "Go [and] tell John everything that you have seen and heard, that the blind see ^Pand the lame walk and the lepers are cleansed and the deaf hear and the dead rise up and the poor receive good news.[1]┐

23 And blessed is he who is not offended at me."

24 And when the disciples of John went away, he[2] began to speak to the crowds about John: "What did you go out to the desert to see, a reed that was shaken by the wind?[3]

25 And if not, what did you go out to see, a man clothed with soft garments? *Behold, those who are with fancy clothes and luxuries are [in] the house of kings.

26 And if not, what did you go out to see, a prophet? Yes, *I say to you, even greater than the prophets.[4]

27 This is he about whom it is written: *BEHOLD, I WILL SEND MY MESSENGER BEFORE YOUR FACE TO PREPARE THE WAY BEFORE YOU.

28 *I say to you, there is no prophet among those born of women who is greater than John the baptizer, but the least in the kingdom of God is greater than he."

29 And all the people who heard, even the tax collectors, declared God [to be] just, because they had been baptized [with] the baptism[5] of John.

30 And the Pharisees and the scribes rejected in themselves the will of God, because they were not baptized by him.

31 "To what therefore can I liken the men of this generation and to what are they like?

32 ^{al}They are like young boys who sit in the marketplace and call out to their friends and say, 'We have played music for you and you did not dance and we mourned for you and you did not weep.'

33 For John the baptizer came neither eating bread nor drinking wine and you said, 'There is a demon in him.'

34 The Son of Man came eating and drinking and you say, '*Behold, a gluttonous man and [one] drinking wine and a friend of tax collectors and sinners.'

---

[1] Verbs are all participles
[2] Eastern txt: 'Jesus'
[3] See note on Mat 7:11.
[4] Repeat *what did you go out to see?*, vs. 24-26; fig: erotesis –questions to ponder
[5] Same root: *baptized, baptized, baptizer*, vs. 28, 33

Chapter 7

35 Yet ^{pe}wisdom is declared just by all its ^hchildren."[1]

36 Now one of the Pharisees came [and] begged him to eat with him. And he entered the house of that Pharisee and[2] sat to eat.

37 And there was a woman [who was] a sinner in that city. And when she learned that he was reclining in the house of that Pharisee, she took an alabaster box of ointment

38 and stood behind him at his feet and she was crying. And she began washing his feet with her tears and wiping them with the hair of her head. And she was kissing his feet and anointed [them] with ointment.

39 Now when that Pharisee who had invited him saw [this], he reasoned within himself and said, "This man, if he were a prophet, would have known who she is and what her reputation [is], because the woman who touched him is a sinner."

40 But Jesus answered and said to him, "Simon, I have something to say to you." And **he** said to him, "Speak, my Master." Jesus said to him,

41 "There were two debtors to a certain lender.[3] One owed five hundred denarii and the other fifty denarii.

42 And because they had no way to repay, he forgave both of them. Now then, which of them will love him more?"[4]

43 Simon answered and said, "I suppose that the one who was forgiven the most." Jesus said to him, "You have judged correctly."

44 Then he turned to that woman and said to Simon, "Do you see this woman? I entered your house [and] you did not give [me] water for my feet, but this ^e[woman] has washed my feet with her tears and she has dried them with her hair.

45 **You** did not kiss me, but *behold, this [woman], since I entered, has not ceased to kiss my feet.

46 **You** did not anoint my head [with] oil, but this [woman] has anointed[5] my feet with perfumed ointment.

47 Because of this *I say to you, her many sins are forgiven, because she has loved much. But he to whom little is forgiven loves little."[6]

---

[1] Different word than in Mat 11:19; fig: hypocatastasis, *children*, meaning "results" or "works"

[2] Eastern txt: omit *and*

[3] Lit: master of a debt

[4] Fig: erotesis – question to ponder

[5] Repeat forms of *anoint*

[6] Repeat *sins are forgiven*, *little*, vs. 47, 48

Chapter 7

48 And he said to that woman, "Your sins are forgiven."
49 And those who were sitting to eat began saying among themselves, "Who is this who even forgives sins?"[1]
50 But Jesus said to that woman, "Your faith has given you life. Go in peace."

Chapter 8

1 ^PAnd it happened [that] after these [things] Jesus was going around in the cities and in the villages and he was preaching and declaring the kingdom of God. And his twelve [were] with him
2 and those women who had been healed of sicknesses and of evil spirits: Mary who was called Magdalene, from whom seven demons had gone out,[2]
3 and Joanna the wife of Chuza, the steward of Herod, and Susanna, and many others who were ministering to them from their properties.
4 And when a large crowd had gathered and they were coming to him from all the cities, he spoke in parables:˥
5 ^{pb.}"A sower went to sow his seed, and as he sowed,[3] some fell by the side of the road and was trampled and a bird ate it.
6 And other ^e[seed] fell on rock. And immediately it sprang up, but because it did not have moisture, it withered.
7 And other ^e[seed] fell among thorns and the thorns sprang up with it and choked it.
8 And other ^e[seed] fell on good and fertile earth and sprang up and produced ^mfruit one hundred[fold]. When he had said these [things], he cried out, "He who has ears to hear should hear."˥
9 And his disciples asked him, "What is ^e[the meaning of] this parable?"
10 And **he** said to them, "⁴To you it is given to know the secret of the kingdom of God. But to the rest, it is spoken in comparisons: BECAUSE **ALTHOUGH THEY SEE, THEY WILL NOT SEE AND ALTHOUGH THEY HEAR, THEY WILL NOT UNDERSTAND.**

---

[1] Fig: erotesis – question to ponder
[2] OS (c): 'he had cast'
[3] Same root: *sow, seed*, vs. 6-8, 12-15, fig: ellipsis, emphasis on the seed
[4] Eastern txt: add 'for'

ARAMAIC PESHITTA NEW TESTAMENT
LUKE

Chapter 8

11 Now, this is ᵉ[the meaning of] the parable. ᵐᵉThe seed is the word of God.

12 ᵐᵉAnd those [seeds] that [fell] by the side of the road are those who hear the word, yet the enemy comes [and] takes the word from their heart[s] so that they will not believe and live.

13 ᵐᵉAnd those [seeds] that [fell] on rock are those that when they hear, receive the word with joy. But they have no root. On the contrary, their faith is for a while, yet in the ˢʸtime of temptation, they are offended.

14 ᵐᵉAnd that [seed] which fell among thorns are those who hear the word and are choked with the care and wealth and lusts of the world and they do not bear fruit.

15 ᵐᵉAnd that [seed] which [fell] on good ground are those who with an honest and good heart hear the word and adhere [to it] and bear fruit with patience.

16 ᵖᵇˡNo one lights a lamp and hides it in a vessel or places it under a bed.² On the contrary, he places it on a lamp stand, so that all who enter will see its light.

17 For there is not anything that is covered that will not be revealed or that is hidden that will not be known and come [out] openly.³

18 Take heed how you hear, for whoever has, it will be given to him,⁴ and whoever does not have, even that which he thinks he has, will be taken from him."

19 Now his mother and his brothers came to him and were not able to speak with him because of the crowd.

20 And they said to him, "Your mother and your brothers are standing outside and want to see you."

21 But **he** answered and said to them, "My mother and my brothers are those who hear the word of God and do it."

22 And it happened [that] on a certain day Jesus boarded [and] sat in a boat, he and his disciples, and he said to them, "Let us cross over to the other side of the lake."

---

¹ OS (c): add 'He told them another parable'
² OS (c): add 'or in a secret place'
³ Same root: *revealed, openly*
⁴ OS (c): 'it will increase for him'

ARAMAIC PESHITTA NEW TESTAMENT
LUKE

Chapter 8

23 And while they were journeying, Jesus was asleep. And there was a sudden wind storm on the lake[1] and the boat was about to sink.

24 And they came near [and] woke him and said to him, "Our Master, our Master,[2] we are being destroyed." And **he** stood up and rebuked the winds and the waves of the sea and they ceased and there was calm.

25 And he said to them, "Where is your faith?" And, being afraid, **they** were amazed and said one to another, "Who indeed is this [man] who commands even the winds and the waves and the sea and they obey him?"[3]

26 And they journeyed and came to the region of the Gadarenes[4] that is on the shore opposite Galilee.

27 And when he had come onto the land, he met a certain man from the city who had had a devil for a long time. And he did not wear clothes and did not live in a house, but in the tombs.[5]

28 And when he saw Jesus, he cried out and fell down before him and spoke with a loud voice, "What do we have in common, Jesus, Son of the Most High God? I beg you, do not torment me."

29 [pa]For Jesus was commanding the unclean spirit to go out of the man, for a long time had passed since he was [first] held captive by him. And he had been bound with chains and restrained with fetters, but he broke his bonds[6] and was driven by the demon into the wilderness.┐

30 And Jesus asked him, "What is your name?" He said to him, "Legion," because many devils had entered into him.

31 And they were begging him that he would not command them to go to the abyss.[7]

32 And there was there a herd of many pigs that was feeding on the mountain. And they were begging him to permit them to attack[8] the pigs and he permitted them.

---

[1] OS (c): add 'and the boat was filled by the waves'
[2] Fig: epizeuxis, solemn emphasis
[3] Fig: erotesis – question to ponder
[4] *Gadarenes* means, "pools"
[5] OS (c): add 'and called out all (manner of) curses and struck himself with stones'
[6] Same root: *bound, bonds*
[7] OS (c): *they*, 'those devils,' *abyss*, 'hell'
[8] Lit: enter in

Chapter 8

33 And the demons went out from the man and attacked the pigs and that whole herd rushed to a steep place and fell into the lake and was drowned.

34 And when the herdsmen saw what had happened, they fled and reported [it] in the cities and villages.

35 And the men came out to see what had happened. And they came to Jesus and found the man, whose demons had gone out, clothed and sober and sitting at the feet of Jesus, and they were afraid.

36 And those who had seen [it] reported to them how he healed the man possessed with a devil.

37 And all the assembly of the Gadarenes begged him to go away from them, because great fear had taken hold of them. And **Jesus** boarded a ship and turned away from them.

38 And that man from whom the demons went out begged him that he might remain with him. But Jesus sent him away and said to him,

39 "Return to your ᵐhouse and report what God has done for you." And he went and was preaching in the whole city what Jesus had done for him.

40 And when Jesus returned, a large crowd received him, for all were looking for him.

41 And a certain man whose name [was] Jairus, a chief of the synagogue, fell before the feet of Jesus and begged him to enter his house,

42 for he had an only daughter about twelve years old and she was about to die. And while Jesus went with him, a large crowd thronged him.

43 And a certain woman, whose blood had been flowing [for] twelve years, who had spent all her wealth among the doctors, but was not able to be healed by man,[1]

44 approached from behind him and touched the outer edge of his garment. And immediately the flow of her blood stopped.

---

[1] OS (c): add after *years*, 'and she had spent all her possessions for doctors', add at end of verse, 'and she thought to herself and said, If I go to the robe of Jesus and touch it, I will be healed,'

Chapter 8

45 And Jesus said, "Who touched me?" And while all were denying [it], Simon Peter and those with him said to him, "Our Master, the crowds are pressing and thronging you, yet you say, 'Who touched me?'"

46 And **he** said, "Someone touched me, for I know that power went out of me."

47 Now when that woman saw that she had not escaped his notice, she came trembling and fell down [and] worshipped him. And she declared before all the people for what reason she had touched [him] and how she was immediately healed.

48 And **Jesus** said to her, "Be encouraged, my daughter. Your faith has given you life. Go in peace."

49 And while he was speaking, a man from the house of the chief of the synagogue came and said to him, "Your daughter has died. Do not trouble the teacher."

50 But Jesus heard [it] and said to the father of the girl, "Do not fear, believe only and she will live."

51 And Jesus came to the house and did not allow anyone to enter with him, except Simon and James and John and the father of the girl and her mother.

52 And all were weeping and mourning over her. But Jesus said, "Do not weep, for she has not died, but sleeps."[1]

53 And they were laughing at him, because they knew that she had died.

54 And **he** put everyone outside and took her by her hand and called her and said, "Young girl, rise up."

55 And her spirit returned and immediately she rose up. And he commanded them to give her [something] to eat.

56 And her parents were astonished. And **he** warned them not to tell anyone what had happened.

Chapter 9

1   [P]And Jesus called his twelve and gave them power and authority over all demons and to heal sicknesses.

2   And he sent them to preach the kingdom of God and to heal the sick.

---

[1] OS (c): 'is sleeping a sleep'

ARAMAIC PESHITTA NEW TESTAMENT
LUKE

Chapter 9

3   And he said to them, "Do not take anything on the journey, neither staff nor bag[1] nor bread nor money nor should you have two coats.

4   And in whatever house you enter, remain there and leave from there.

5   And whoever does not receive you, when you leave that city, shake off even the dust from your feet for a witness against them."[2]

6   And the apostles left and were going around in the villages and cities and were preaching and healing in every place.⅂

7   Now Herod the tetrarch heard of all [the things] that were done by his ᵐhand and he was wondering, because some were saying that John had risen from the dead.

8   And others were saying that Elijah had appeared and others that a prophet from the first prophets had risen.

9   And Herod said, "**I** cut off the head of John, but who is this [man] about whom I hear these [things]?" And he wanted to see him.

10   And when the apostles returned, they reported to Jesus everything that they had done. And he took them privately to a desert place of Bethsaida.[3]

11   And when the crowds knew [it], they followed him. And he received them and spoke with them about the kingdom of God. And those who had a need for healing, he healed.

12   And when the day began to fade, his disciples came near and were saying to him, "Send away the crowds that they may go to the villages and to the towns around us to stay in them and to find food for themselves, because we are in a desert place.

13   Jesus said to them, "You give them [something] to eat." But **they** were saying, "We do not have more than five [loaves of] bread[4] and two fish, unless we go and buy food for all this people,"

14   for there were about five thousand men. Jesus said to them, "Cause them to sit to eat [in] groups, fifty men in a group."

15   And the disciples did so and caused them all to sit to eat.

---

[1] Culture: leather sack called a **tarmula** was a bag in which people carried their possession (similar to our "suitcase"); repeat *nor*

[2] OS (s): 'to you'

[3] OS (s): 'and went to the gate of the city called Bethsaida', OS (c): 'and went to a place of solitude'

[4] Lit: breads

Chapter 9

16 And Jesus took those five [loaves of] bread and two fish and gazed into heaven and blessed and broke [them] and gave [them] to his disciples to set before the crowds.

17 And all ate and were satisfied and they took up the fragments that were left over, twelve baskets.

18 And while he was praying alone and his disciples with him, he asked them and said, "What do the crowds say about me, who I am?"

19 They answered and were saying to him, "John the baptizer, and others, Elijah, and others, that a certain prophet from the first prophets has risen."

20 He said to them, "But who do **you** say that I am?" Simon answered and said, "The MESSIAH of God."

21 And **he** reproved them and warned them not to say this to anyone.

22 And he said to them that the Son of Man would suffer many things and he would be rejected by the elders and the chief priests and scribes and they would kill him and on the third day he would rise up.

23 And he said before everyone, "He who wants to follow me should deny himself and take up his ^mcross every day and follow me.

24 For he who wants to save his soul will lose it, but he who will lose his soul because of me, this one will save it.[1]

25 For what is a man helped who gains the whole world, but will lose or is deprived of his soul?[2]

26 And whoever will be ashamed of me and of my words, the Son of Man will be ashamed of him[3] when he comes in the glory of his Father with his holy angels.

27 *I say the truth to you, there are men who stand here who will not ^htaste death until they see the kingdom of God."

28 And it happened [that] about eight days after these words, Jesus took Simon and James and John and climbed a mountain to pray.

29 And while he was praying, the appearance of his face was changed and his clothes were whitened and made to shine.

30 And *behold, two men were talking with him, who were Moses and Elijah,

---

[1] Parallel structure, ABBA, could also be a proverb

[2] OS (c): add 'and perishes'; fig: erotesis – question to ponder

[3] Repeat *will be ashamed of*

ARAMAIC PESHITTA NEW TESTAMENT
LUKE

Chapter 9

31 who appeared in glory. And they were talking about his ^{eu}departure[1] that was about to be accomplished in Jerusalem.

32 And Simon and those who were with him were heavy with sleep and scarcely awake and they saw his glory and those two men who were standing with him.

33 And when they began to go away from him, Simon said to Jesus, "My Master, it is good for us that we were here. Yet let us make three booths, one for you and one for Moses and one for Elijah," and he did not know what he said.

34 And when he said these [things], a cloud came and overshadowed them. And they were afraid when they saw that Moses and Elijah entered into the cloud.

35 And a voice came from the cloud that said, "This is my beloved[2] Son. Hear him."

36 And after the voice came, Jesus was found alone and they kept silent and did not tell anyone in those days anything that they had seen.

37 And it happened [that] on the next day when they came down from the mountain, a large crowd met them.

38 And a certain man from that crowd cried out and said, "Teacher, I beg you, take notice of me. He is my only son

39 ᴾand a spirit quickly comes over him and suddenly he cries out and gnashes his teeth and foams and with difficulty does it go out of him when it has harassed him.⌐

40 And I begged your disciples to cast it out and they were not able."

41 And Jesus answered and said, "ᵈOh faithless and perverted generation! How long should I be with you and endure you? Bring your son here."

42 And while he was bringing him, that devil cast him down and convulsed[3] him. And Jesus rebuked that unclean spirit and he healed the young boy and gave him to his father.

43 And they were all amazed at the greatness of God. And while everyone was wondering about all that Jesus had done, he said to his disciples,

---

[1] Fig: euphemism, meaning "death"
[2] OS (s): 'chosen'
[3] OS (s): 'bruised'

Chapter 9

44 Set these words in your ^mears, for the Son of Man is about to be delivered into the ^mhands of men.

45 But they did not understand this saying, because it was hidden from them so that they did not know it, and they were afraid to ask him about this saying.

46 And the thought entered into them [as to] who was indeed great among them.

47 And Jesus knew the thought of their heart[s] and he took a young child and set him by him.

48 And he said to them, "He who receives a child like this in my name, receives me. And he who receives me, receives him who sent me. For whoever is least among all of you,[1] this one will be great."

49 And John answered and said, "Our Master, we saw a man who was casting out devils in your name and we prohibited him, because he did not follow you with us."

50 Jesus said to them, "Do not prohibit [him], for he who is not against you is for you."

51 And it happened that when the days of his offering up were fulfilled, he directed his face to go to Jerusalem.

52 And he sent messengers before his face and they went [and] entered a village of the Samaritans in order to prepare for him.

53 And they did not receive him because his face was set to go to Jerusalem.

54 And when James and John, his disciples, saw [it], they said to him, "Our Lord, do you want us to speak and have fire come down from heaven and consume them as also Elijah did?"

55 And he turned and rebuked them and said, "You do not know of what spirit you are.

56 For the Son of Man did not come to destroy souls, but to make [them] to live." And they went to another village.

57 And while they were traveling on the road, a man said to him, "I will follow you wherever you go, my Lord."

58 Jesus said to him, "Foxes have holes and a bird of heaven a shelter, but the Son of Man has no where to lay his head."

59 And he said to another, "Follow me." And he said to him, "My Lord, allow me first to go [and] bury my father."

---

[1] OS (s): add 'and a child among you', OS (c): add 'like this child'

Chapter 9

60 Jesus said to him, "Leave the ^{at}dead burying their dead and go [and] preach the kingdom of God."
61 Another said to him, "I will follow you, my Lord, but first allow me to go [and] say goodbye to my household and [then] I will come."
62 Jesus said to him, "No one places his hand on the handle of a plow and looks back and is useful for the kingdom of God."[1]

Chapter 10

1 After these [things], Jesus appointed from his disciples seventy[2] others and sent them two by two before his face to every region and city that he was about to go.
2 And he said to them, "The harvest is great and the workers are few. Therefore, pray the Lord[3] [of] the harvest to send out workers for his harvest.
3 Go! *Behold, I send you ^sas lambs among wolves.
4 Do not carry bags or sacks or shoes and do not greet anyone on the way.
5 And in whatever house you enter, first say, 'Peace to this house.'
6 And if there is there a man of peace,[4] your peace will rest on him, but if not, ⁵it will return on you.
7 And remain in the same house, eating and drinking from their [food], for the worker is worthy of his wage and do not move from house to house.
8 And in whatever city you enter and they receive you, eat what is placed before you.
9 And heal those who are sick in it and say to them, 'The kingdom of God has come near to you.'[6]
10 But in whatever city you enter and they do not receive you, go out in[7] the marketplace and say,

---

[1] Culture: if a laborer looked back when plowing, he would be unable to make straight furrows.
[2] OS (cs): 'seventy-two'
[3] OS (s): 'son'
[4] Lit: son of peace, meaning "harmony"
[5] Eastern txt: add 'your peace'
[6] Repeat *the kingdom of God has come near to you*, v. 11, Semitism: *come near* means "to be here, has arrived", Bivin, pp. 88-91.
[7] Eastern txt: ــ instead of ـ

Chapter 10

11 'Even the dust that sticks to us on our feet from your city, we shake off against you, but know this, that the kingdom of God has come near to you.'

12 *I say to you, it will be [more] pleasant for ^mSodom in that ^{sy}day than for that city.

13 ⁱWoe to you, ^mChorazin! ⁱWoe to you, ^mBethsaida! Because if the miracles that happened in you had happened in Tyre and Sidon, they would have long ago repented in sackclothes and in ash.

14 But for ^mTyre and ^mSidon it will be [more] pleasant in the judgment than for you.

15 And you, ^mCapernaum, who are lifted up to heaven will be brought down low to SHEOL.

16 He who hears you hears me. And he who rejects you rejects me and he who rejects me rejects[1] him who sent me."

17 And those seventy[2] whom he had sent returned with great joy and said to him, "Our Lord, even the demons were subject to us in your name."

18 And **he** said to them, "I was seeing SATAN fall ^slike lightning from heaven.

19 *Behold, I give to you authority to trample on ^mserpents and ^mscorpions and all the power of the enemy and nothing will hurt you.

20 But do not rejoice in this, that demons are subject to you, but rather rejoice that your names are written in heaven."

21 Immediately, Jesus was joyful in the Holy Spirit and said, "I thank you, my Father, Lord of heaven and earth, that you have hidden these [things] from wise and intelligent [ones] and have revealed them to infants, ⁱyes, my Father, because so was the will before you."

22 And he turned toward his disciples and said to them, "Everything is delivered to me from my Father and no man knows who is the Son, except the Father and who is the Father, except the Son and to whom the Son wants to reveal [him]?"

23 And he turned toward his disciples privately and said, "Blessed are the ^meyes that see what you see.[3]

---

[1] Repeat *rejects, he who*; OS (cs): *rejects* is 'cheats'

[2] OS (s): 'seventy-two'

[3] Repeat forms of *see, hear*, also v. 24

Chapter 10

24 For *I say to you, many prophets and kings have wanted to see what you see and have not seen, and to hear what you hear and have not heard."

25 And *behold, a certain scribe stood up to tempt him and said, "Teacher, what must I do to inherit eternal life?"

26 And **Jesus** said to him, "How is it written in the law? How do you read?"

27 He answered and said to him: YOU SHOULD LOVE THE LORD YOUR GOD WITH ALL YOUR HEART AND WITH ALL YOUR SOUL AND WITH ALL YOUR STRENGTH AND WITH[1] ALL YOUR MIND, and YOUR NEIGHBOR AS YOURSELF.

28 Jesus said to him, "You have spoken correctly; do this and you will live."

29 But wanting to justify himself, **he** said to him, "And who is my neighbor?"

30 Jesus said to him, pb."A certain man went down from Jerusalem to Jericho, and robbers fell on him and they stripped him and beat him and left him[2] when little life remained in him[3] and they went away.

31 And a certain priest happened to be going down on that road and he saw him and passed by.

32 And so also a Levite came [and] arrived at that place and saw him and passed by.

33 Now a Samaritan man, while he was journeying, came where he was, and he saw him and had compassion on him.

34 And he came near and bandaged his wounds and poured wine and oil[4] on them and placed him on his donkey and brought him to an inn and took care of him.

35 And at the break of the day he went away, he gave two denarii to the innkeeper and said to him 'Care for him. And if you spend anything more, when I return I will give [it] to you.'

36 Therefore, which of these three seems to you to have been a neighbor to him who fell into the hands of robbers?"

37 And **he** said, "The one who had compassion on him." Jesus said to him, "Go, you should also do the same."⌐

---

[1] Repeat *and with*

[2] Repeat suffix, *him*

[3] OS (cs): lit: 'between death and life'

[4] Culture: wine and oil were normal remedies for wounds, Freeman, p. 416.

ARAMAIC PESHITTA NEW TESTAMENT
LUKE

Chapter 10

38 And it happened that while they were journeying on the road, he entered a certain village and a woman whose name [was] Martha received him into her house.

39 And she had a sister whose name [was] Mary. And she came [and] seated herself at the feet of our Lord and was listening to his words.

40 But Martha was occupied with much service and came [and] said to him, "My Lord, do you not care that my sister has left me alone to serve? Tell her to help me."

41 But Jesus answered and said to her, "Martha, Martha,[1] you are anxious and troubled about many [things].

42 But there is one [thing] that is necessary and Mary has chosen that good part for herself that will not be taken from her."

Chapter 11

1 And it happened that while he was praying in a certain place, when he had finished, one of his disciples said to him, "Our Lord, teach us to pray, as John also taught his disciples."

2 Jesus said to them, "When you pray, you should speak so: Our Father who is in heaven, your name will be made holy, your kingdom will come, your desire will occur, as in heaven, even also on earth.

3 Give us the ᵐbread of our necessity every day,

4 and forgive us [of] our sins, for **we** also forgive all who have wronged us. And do not let us enter into temptation, but deliver us from the Evil [one]."

5 And he said to them, ᵖᵇ"Who is among you who has a friend and would go to him at midnight and say to him, 'My friend, lend me three loaves,

6 because a friend has come to me from a journey and I have nothing to place before him;'

7 and his friend would answer from within and say to him, 'Do not trouble me, for *behold, the door is shut and my children are with me in bed. I am not able to rise and give to you.'

8 *I say to you, if on account of friendship he will not give to him, because of his persistence, he will rise up and give to him as much as is needed by him.¬

---

[1] Fig: epizeuxis, solemn meaning; OS (s): omit *you are anxious and troubled about many things*

Chapter 11

9 *I say to you also, 'Ask and it will be given to you, seek and you will find, knock and it will be opened to you,'[1]

10 for everyone who asks will receive and whoever seeks will find and who knocks, it will be opened to him.

11 For what father among you whose son asks him for bread will offer him a stone? And if he asks him for a fish, instead of a fish will he offer him a serpent?[2]

12 And if he asks him for an egg, will he offer him a scorpion?

13 And if **you** who are evil know to give good gifts to your children, how much more will your Father from heaven give the Holy Spirit[3] to those who ask him?"[4]

14 And as he was casting out a demon because he was dumb, it occurred that after that demon went out that dumb [man] spoke and the crowds were amazed.

15 And some of them said, "This [man] casts out devils by BEELZEBUB, the prince of devils."

16 And others, tempting him, were asking him for a sign from heaven.

17 But Jesus, who knew their thoughts, said to them, "Every kingdom that is divided against itself will be ruined and a house that is separated from its essential [foundation][5] will fall.

18 And if SATAN is divided against himself, how will his kingdom stand?[6] For you say that I cast out devils by BEELZEBUB.

19 And if **I** cast out devils by BEELZEBUB, by whom do your sons cast [them] out? Because of this, they will be judges to you.

20 But if I cast out devils by the [m]finger of God, the kingdom of God has come near to you.

21 [al]When a strong man, being armed, guards his courtyard, his property is in quietness.

22 But if one who is stronger than him should come, he will conquer him [and] he will capture all of his armor on which he had relied and he will distribute his spoil.⌐

---

[1] Fig: climax, emphasis on the progression of actions
[2] Fig: erotesis, **lema** questions, obvious answer "no", vs. 11, 12
[3] OS (s): 'good things'
[4] Fig: erotesis, **kema** question, answer in the affirmative
[5] Lit: its essence
[6] Fig: erotesis – question to ponder

Chapter 11

23 He who is not with me is against me and he who does not gather with me actually scatters.[1]

24 When an unclean spirit leaves a man, it goes [and] wanders around in places in which there is no water to seek rest for itself. And when it does not find [rest], it says, "I will return to my house from where I left."

25 And if it comes [and] finds that it is swept and furnished,

26 then it goes [and] leads seven other spirits more evil that it and they enter and live there and the end [state] of that man becomes worse than his first [state]."

27 And while he was speaking these [things], a certain woman raised up her voice from the crowd and said to him, "Blessed is the womb that bore you and the breasts that nursed you."

28 He said to her, "Blessed are those who have heard the word of God and keep it."

29 And when the crowds were gathered, he began to say, "This evil generation seeks a sign and a sign will not be given to it, except the sign of Jonah the prophet.

30 For as Jonah was a sign to the Ninevites, so also the Son of Man will be [a sign] to this generation.

31 The queen of the south will stand in the judgment concerning the men of this generation and will condemn them, because she came from the far sides of the earth to hear the wisdom of Solomon, and *behold, one who is greater than Solomon [is] here.

32 The Ninevite men[2] will stand in the judgment concerning this generation and will condemn it, because they repented at the preaching of Jonah, and *behold, one who is greater than Jonah [is] here.

33 alNo one lights a lamp and places it in a hidden place or under a basket, but rather e[he places it] on a lamp stand, so that those who enter will see its light.

34 meThe lamp of your body is the eye. So when your eye is simple, your whole body will also be lightened. But if it is evil, your [whole] body will also be darkened.[3]

35 Therefore, beware that the light that is in you is not darkness.

---

[1] Fig: polyptoton, "scatters a scattering"

[2] Lit: men, the sons of Nineveh

[3] Culture: *simple* means to be generous, *evil* in this context means to be greedy

Chapter 11

36 Now if your whole body is lightened and does not have any dark portion, all of it will be giving light, ^sas a lamp by its flame gives you light."¹┐

37 And while he was speaking, a certain Pharisee asked him to eat with him and he entered [and] sat to eat.

38 And that Pharisee, when he saw him, was amazed that he had not washed first before his meal.

39 And Jesus said to him, "Now **you** Pharisees cleanse the outside of the cup and of the dish, but your inside is full of rape² and evil.

40 ⁱFools! Did not he who made the outside also make the inside?³

41 But what you have, give in alms, and *behold, everything will be clean to you.

42 But ⁱwoe to you, Pharisees,⁴ because you tithe of mint and rue and every herb, yet you pass over justice and the love of God. Now these [things] you ought to do and these [things] you should not leave out.

43 ⁱWoe to you, Pharisees, because you love the chief seats in the synagogues and a greeting in the streets.

44 ⁱWoe to you, scribes and Pharisees, hypocrites, because you are ^slike graves that are unknown and men walk over them and do not know [it]."

45 And one of the scribes answered and said to him, "Teacher, when you say these [things], you reproach us also."

46 And **he** said, "^{di}Woe also to you, scribes, because you make men carry heavy burdens, yet **you** do not touch the burdens with one of your fingers.

47 ⁱWoe to you, because you build tombs for the prophets whom your fathers killed.

48 Therefore, you bear witness to and approve of the works of your fathers, because **they** killed them and **you** build their graves.⁵

49 Because of this, the ^{pe}wisdom of God also said, '*Behold, **I** will send them prophets and apostles, some of whom they will persecute and kill,'

---

¹ OS (c): entire verse is different from (s) and Peshitta: 'And if the light that is in you is dark, how great will your darkness be!'

² Or can refer to any violent crime

³ Fig: erotesis – question to ponder

⁴ Repeat *woe to you*, vs. 42-44, 46, 47; OS (c): add 'scribes and', also v. 43

⁵ OS (s): 'you are the children', OS (c): 'you are the children of those murderers'

Chapter 11

50 so that the blood of all the prophets that was shed from when the world was established will be required from this generation,

51 from the blood of Abel up to the blood of Zacharias, who was killed between the temple [and] the altar, yes, *I say to you, it will be required from this generation.

52 [i]Woe to you, scribes, because you have taken away the [m]keys of knowledge. **You** have not entered and you have hindered those who were entering."

53 And while he was speaking these [things] to them,[1] the scribes and Pharisees began to be offended and they grew angry and were criticizing his words.

54 And they were plotting against him in many [ways], seeking to catch something from his [m]mouth in order to be able to accuse him.[2]

Chapter 12

1 And when very large crowds were gathered, so that they were trampling one another, Jesus began to say to his disciples, "First, beware among yourselves of the [h]leaven of the Pharisees, which is hypocrisy.

2 And there is not anything that is covered that will not be revealed or that is hidden that will not be known.[3]

3 For everything that you speak in darkness will be heard in the light, and what you murmur in closets into ears will be proclaimed on the roofs.

4 And *I say to you, my friends, 'Do not fear those who kill the body and afterwards have nothing more to do.'

5 But I will show you whom you should fear, him who after he has killed, has authority to send into GEHENNA, yes, *I say to you, 'Fear this [one].'

6 Are not five birds sold for two coins?[4] And one of them is not forgotten before God.

7 But even the separate hairs[5] of your head are all numbered. Do not fear, therefore, because you are more valuable than a multitude of birds.

---

[1] OS (s): add 'in the sight of all the people'
[2] OS (s): omit *in order to be able to accuse him*
[3] Parallel structure, opposites, ABAB
[4] Name for coin is **assarion,** see Appendix 2.
[5] Lit: hairs of the hair

Chapter 12

8 And *I say to you, whoever will confess me before men, the Son of Man also will confess him before the angels of God.

9 But he who denies me before men will be denied himself before the angels of God.

10 And whoever speaks a word against the Son of Man will be forgiven, but he who blasphemes against the Holy Spirit will not be forgiven.

11 And when they bring you to the synagogues before chiefs and rulers, do not be anxious how you should answer or what you should say,

12 for the Holy Spirit will teach you at that moment what you ought to say."

13 And one of that crowd said to him, "Teacher, tell my brother to divide the inheritance with me."

14 And Jesus said to him, "Man, who set me [as] a ᵸᵉʲudge and distributor over you?"

15 And he said to his disciples, "Beware of all greediness, because life is not in the abundance of possessions."

16 And he spoke a parable to them, ᵖᵇ"A certain rich man's land brought to him many crops.

17 And he thought within himself and said, 'What shall I do, because I do not have anywhere I can gather in my crops?'

18 And he said, 'I will do this. I will pull down my storehouses and I will build and enlarge them and I will gather in there all my harvest and my goods.'

19 And I will say to my soul, 'My soul,[1] you have many goods that are laid up for many years. Take rest, eat, drink [and] be merry.'

20 But God said to him, 'Fool! In this night they will require your soul from you, and those [things] that you have prepared, for whom will they be?'

21 So is he who lays up for himself treasures and does not abound in God."

22 And he said to his disciples, "Because of this, *I say to you, do not be anxious for yourselves, what you will eat or for your body, what you will wear,

23 for the soul is more than food, and the body than clothes.

---

[1] Fig: epizeuxis, solemn repetition

Chapter 12

24 Consider the ravens, for they neither sow nor reap and they do not have rooms and storehouses, yet God provides for them. Therefore, how much more important are **you** than birds?[1]

25 And which of you, being anxious, is able to add one cubit to his stature?

26 And if you are not even capable of a small [thing], why are you anxious about the rest?

27 Consider how the lilies grow, for they neither labor nor spin, but *I say to you, not even Solomon in all his glory was covered ᵇas one of these.

28 And if God so clothes the grass that today is in the field and tomorrow falls into the oven, how much more you, [oh] little of faith?

29 And **you** should not seek what you will eat and what you will drink and your mind should not wander in these [things].

30 For all these [things] the Gentiles of the world seek. Now your Father also knows that these [things] are necessary for you.

31 But seek the kingdom of God and all these [things] will be added to you.

32 Do not fear, little flock, because your Father wants to give you the kingdom.

33 Sell your possessions and give alms. Make for yourselves bags that do not grow old and a treasure that does not fail in heaven, where a thief does not approach and moth does not[2] corrupt.

34 For wherever your treasure is, there will your heart be also.

35 Your loins should be girded and your lamps lit.[3]

36 ᵃˡAnd you should be like men who wait for their lord at that time when he returns from the wedding feast, so that when he comes and knocks, they may immediately open [the door] for him.

37 Blessed are those servants whose lord comes and finds them awake. *Truly I say to you, he will gird up his loins and cause them to sit to eat and will cross over [and] serve them.

38 ⁴And if he comes in the second or third watch and finds [them] so, blessed are those servants.

---

[1] Fig: erotesis, **kema** question, answer in the affirmative, also v. 28; questions to ponder, vs. 25, 26

[2] Repeat *not*, 4x

[3] Culture: *loins girded and lamps lit* means, "to be ready for action."

[4] OS (c): add 'And if he comes in the first watch and finds them awake, blessed are they for he will seat them and serve them'

Chapter 12

39 Now know this, that if the lord of the house had known in what watch the thief would come, he would have watched and would not have allowed his house to be broken into.

40 Therefore, **you** should also be prepared, because the Son of Man will come at that moment that you do not expect."┐

41 Simon Peter said to him, "Our Lord, do you speak this parable to us or also to everyone?"

42 Jesus said to him, ᵖᵇ"Who indeed is the ʰᵉfaithful and wise steward, whose lord will place him over his service that he should give [him] a measured portion in its time?

43 Blessed is that servant whose lord comes [and] finds that he does so.

44 *Truly I say to you, he will place him over all his possessions.

45 But if that servant says in his heart, 'My lord delays to come,' and begins to beat the servants and the handmaids of his lord and begins to eat and to drink and to be drunk,

46 the lord of that servant will come in a ˢʸday that he does not expect and in an ˢʸhour that he does not know and will separate him and place his lot with those who are not faithful.

47 And the servant, who knows the will of his lord and does not prepare for him according to his will, will be beaten with many [stripes].

48 But **he** who did not know, yet did something that was worthy of stripes, will be beaten[1] with a few stripes, for anyone who is given much, much is required, and to whom they have committed much, they will require more by his ᵐhand.┐

49 I have come to send ᵐfire on the earth and I want to. ⁱOh that it was already kindled!

50 And I have a baptism that I am baptized [with] and I am greatly pressured, until it is fulfilled.

51 Do you think that I have come to bring[2] harmony on earth? *I say to you, 'No, but rather division.'

52 For from now on, there will be five in one house who are divided, three against two and two against three.

---

[1] Lit: swallowed
[2] Lit: throw

Chapter 12

53 For father will be divided against[1] his son and son against his father, mother against her daughter, and daughter against her mother, mother-in-law against her daughter-in-law, and daughter-in-law against her mother-in-law."

54 And he said to the crowds, "When you see a cloud that rises from the west immediately you say, 'Rain will come,' and it happens so.

55 And when the south [wind] blows, you say, 'There will be heat,' and it happens.

56 Hypocrites! You know [how] to distinguish the appearance of the earth and of heaven. So how do you not distinguish this time?

57 And why of yourselves do you not judge [with] truthfulness?[2]

58 For when you go with your adversary to the ruler, while you are on the road, make terms [with him] and be quit of him, so that he will not conduct you to the judge and the judge deliver you to the official and the official cast you in prison.

59 And *I say to you, you will not leave there until you give back the last coin."[3]

Chapter 13

1 Now at that time, men came [and] told him about those Galileans, whose blood Pilate had mingled with their sacrifices.

2 And Jesus answered and said to them, "Do you think[4] that these Galileans were sinners more than all the Galileans because it happened to them so?

3 'No! And *I say to you, but all of you will also be destroyed likewise, [if] you do [not] repent.

4 Or those eighteen, on whom the tower fell in Siloam and killed them, do you think that they were sinners more than all the men who lived in Jerusalem?

5 'No! And *I say to you, except all of you repent like them, you will be destroyed."

6 And he spoke this parable, pb"A man had a fig tree that was planted in his vineyard, and he came [and] looked on it for fruit and did not find [any].

---

[1] Repeat *against*, 6x

[2] Fig: erotesis – questions to ponder, vs. 56, 57

[3] Coin is **shamuna**, see Appendix 2.

[4] Repeat *do you think*, v. 4, repeat *no, and I say to you*, vs. 3, 5

Chapter 13

7   And he said to the laborer, '*Behold, [for] three years I have come [and] I looked for fruit on this fig tree and I have not found [any]. Cut it down. Why should the ground be wasted?'

8   The laborer said to him, 'My lord, leave it even this year, until I work with it and manure it[1]

9   and perhaps it will produce fruit. Yet if not, next year you may cut it down.'"ﬧ

10 And while Jesus was teaching on the SABBATH in one of the synagogues,

11 there was a woman there who had had a spirit of infirmity [for] eighteen years and she was bent over and was not able to straighten at all.

12 And Jesus saw her and called her and said to her, "Woman, you are free from your infirmity."

13 And he placed his hand on her and immediately she straightened and praised God.

14 And the ruler of the synagogue, being angered because Jesus had healed on the SABBATH, answered and said to the crowds, "There are six days in which you ought to work. You should come [and] be healed in them and not on the day of the SABBATH."

15 And Jesus answered and said to him, "ⁱHypocrite! What one of you on the SABBATH does not untie his ox or his donkey from the stall and go [and] water [it]?[2]

16 And this [woman], because she is a daughter of Abraham, and the ACCUSER[3] has bound her, *behold, eighteen years, is it not right that she should be freed from this bondage on the day of the SABBATH?"

17 And when he said these [things], all those who were opposing were ashamed and all the people were rejoicing at all the wonders that occurred by his ᵐhand.

18 And Jesus said, "What is the kingdom of God like and to what can I compare it?

19 ᵖᵖIt is like a grain of mustard seed, which a man took [and] threw into his garden. And it grew and became a large tree and a bird of heaven built a nest in its branches."ﬧ

20 Jesus again said, "To what can I compare the kingdom of God?

---

[1] Repeat suffix *it*, also v. 9
[2] OS (cs): add 'on the Sabbath day'
[3] OS (s): 'Satan'

Chapter 13

21 ^{pb}It is like leaven that a woman took and hid in three measures [of] flour until all was leavened."┐

22 And he traveled into the villages and cities while teaching and going to Jerusalem.

23 And a man asked him whether those who will live are few.

24 And Jesus said to them,[1] "Strive to enter through the narrow door, for *I say to you, many will seek to enter and not be able.

25 From the time that the lord [of] the house will rise and shut the door, then you will stand outside and knock on the door and begin to say, 'Our lord, our lord, open to us,' and he will answer and say, '*I say to you, I do not know you. From where are you?'

26 And you will begin to say, 'We have eaten and we drank before you and you have taught[2] in our streets.'

27 And he will say to you, 'I do not know you. From where are you? **DEPART FROM ME, WORKERS OF FALSEHOOD.'**

28 There will be there weeping and gnashing of teeth when you see Abraham and Isaac and Jacob and all the prophets in the kingdom of God, but **you** will be thrown outside.[3]

29 And they will come from the ^{mr}east and from the west and from the south and from the north and will sit to eat in the kingdom of God.

30 And *behold, there are last who will be first and there are first who will be last."[4]

31 On the same day, some of the Pharisees approached and were saying to him, "Go away, leave here, because Herod wants to kill you."

32 Jesus said to them, "Go, tell this ^hfox,[5] '*Behold, I will cast out demons and do healings today and tomorrow and on the third day I will be finished.'

33 Nevertheless, it is right for me to heal today and tomorrow and I will go on another day, because it is not possible that the prophet should be hurt outside of Jerusalem.

---

[1] Eastern txt: *And Jesus said to them* in v. 23; OS (s): *them* is 'him'

[2] OS (c): 'walked'

[3] Culture: *weeping and gnashing of teeth* means the whole range of emotions; OS (s): omit 'but you will be thrown outside'

[4] Parallel structure: ABBA

[5] Fig: hypocatastasis, *fox* means "a devious or crafty person"

ARAMAIC PESHITTA NEW TESTAMENT
LUKE

Chapter 13

34 Jerusalem, Jerusalem,[1] she has killed the prophets and stoned those who were sent to her. How many times did I want to gather your children ^sas a hen who gathers her chicks under her wings and you did not want [it]?[2]

35 *Behold, your house is left desolate, for *I say to you, you will not see me until you say, 'Blessed is he who comes in the name of the LORD.'"

Chapter 14

1 And it happened that when he entered the house of one of the rulers of the Pharisees to eat bread on the day of the SABBATH, they were watching him.

2 And *behold, there was a certain man before him who was swollen with water.

3 And Jesus spoke out and said to the scribes and Pharisees, "Is it lawful to heal on the SABBATH?"

4 And **they** were quiet and he took him and healed him and let him go.

5 And he said to them, "Which of you whose son or ox falls into a well on the day of the SABBATH does not immediately draw up [and] lift him out?"[3]

6 And they did not find an answer to give to him about this.

7 And he spoke a parable to those who were invited there because he saw those who were choosing the places that were the best seats.

8 ^{pb}When you are invited by someone to a banquet, do not go [and] seat yourself in the best seat, lest someone who is more honorable than you should be invited there,

9 And he who called you and him will come and say to you, 'Give place to this [man].' And you will be ashamed as you stand and take the last place.

10 On the contrary, when you are invited, go [and] seat yourself at the end, so that when he who called you comes, he will say to you, 'My friend, move yourself up higher and be seated,' and you will have praise before all who sit to eat with you,

11 because everyone who elevates himself will be humbled, and everyone who humbles himself will be raised up."[4]⌐

---

[1] Fig: epizeuxis, solemn repetition
[2] Fig: erotesis, "not" question, obvious answer "yes"
[3] OS (c): add 'immediately'
[4] Parallel structure, opposites, ABBA

Chapter 14

12 And he spoke also to him who invited him, ^{pb}"When you make a meal or a dinner, do not call your friends, not even your brothers or your kinsmen, and not your[1] rich neighbors, lest they also invite you and you have this payment.

13 On the contrary, when you make a feast, call the ^apoor, the hurt, the lame, [and] the blind.┐

14 And you ^e[will have] blessing, because they have nothing to repay you, for your payment will be in the resurrection of the just."┐

15 And when one of those who were seated to eat heard these [things], he said to him, "Blessed is he who will eat bread in the kingdom of God."

16 Jesus said to him, ^{pb}"A certain man made a great supper and called many.

17 And he sent his servant at the time of the supper to tell those who were called, '*Behold, everything is prepared for you. Come.'

18 And all began as one to excuse themselves. The first said to him, 'I have bought a field and I need to go out [and] see it. I beg you, allow me to be excused.'

19 Another said, 'I have bought five yoke [of] oxen and I am going to prove them. I beg you, allow me to be excused.'[2]

20 And another said, 'I have taken a wife and because of this, I am not able to come.'

21 And that servant came and told his lord these [things]. Then the lord of the house was angry and said to his servant, 'Go out quickly into the marketplaces and streets of the city and bring here the poor ^Pand the afflicted and the lame and the blind.'┐

22 And the servant said, 'My lord, it is as you commanded and yet there is room.'

23 And the lord said to his servant, 'Go out into the roads and among the hedges and urge them to enter, so that my house may be full,

24 for *I say to you, not one of those men who were called will taste of my supper.'"

25 And while large crowds were going with him, he turned and said to them,

---

[1] Repeat *your*, 3 times
[2] Repeat *I beg you, allow me to be excused*, from v. 18

Chapter 14

26 "He who comes to me and does not hate his father ᴾand his mother and his brothers and his sisters and his wife and his children and also himself⌐ is not able to be a disciple of me.

27 And he who does not bear his ᵐcross and follow me is not able to be a disciple of me.[1]

28 ᵃˡFor which of you who wants to build a tower does not first sit down [and] think about his expenses, whether he has [enough] to complete it,

29 so that when he has not laid the foundation and is not able to finish [it], all who see will mock him

30 and say, 'This man began to build and was not able to finish [it]'?⌐

31 ᵃˡOr what king who goes to war to fight with his neighboring king does not first think whether he is able to meet with ten thousand, him who comes against him with twenty thousand?

32 And if not, while he is far away from him, he will send an ambassador and ask for peace.

33 So, every one of you who does not forsake all his wealth is not able to be a disciple of me.⌐

34 Salt is good, but if even the salt should lose its flavor, with what will it be salted?[2]

35 It is fit neither for the land nor for the dung-heap. They put it outside. He who has ears to hear should hear."

Chapter 15

1 Now the tax collectors and sinners came near to him in order to hear him.

2 And the scribes and Pharisees were murmuring and saying, "This [man] receives sinners and eats with them."

3 And Jesus told them this parable.

4 ᵖᵇ"What man among you who has one hundred sheep and if one of them should be lost, does not leave the ninety-nine in the open country and go [and] seek that one which is lost until he finds it?

5 And when he has found it, he will rejoice and take it on his shoulders

---

[1] Repeat *is not able to be a disciple of me*, from v. 27, also v. 33
[2] Same root: *salt, be salted*, could be a proverb

Chapter 15

6 and come to his house and call to his friends and his neighbors and say to them, 'Rejoice with me, because I have found my sheep that was lost.'
7 *I say to you, so there will be [more] joy in heaven for one sinner who repents than for ninety-nine just [ones] who do not need repentance.
8 **pb**Or what woman, who has ten coins[1] and loses one of them, does not light a lamp and sweep the house and search for it carefully until she finds it?
9 And when she has found it, she will call her friends and her neighbors and say to them, 'Rejoice with me, because I have found my coin that was lost.'
10 *I say to you, so there will be joy before the angels of God over one sinner that repents."┐
11 And Jesus spoke again to them,, **pb**"A certain man had two sons.
12 And his younger son said to him, 'My father, give me the portion that is coming to me from your house, and he divided to them his wealth.'
13 And after a few days, his younger son gathered up everything that came to him and went to a region far away and there spent his wealth living wastefully.[2]
14 And when he had used up everything that he had, a great famine occurred in that region and he began to have need.
15 And he went [and] joined himself to one of the citizens of that land and he sent him into the field to tend the pigs.
16 And he desired to fill his stomach from the carob husks that the pigs were eating, and no one gave to him.
17 And when he came to himself, he said, 'How many hired servants are now [at] my father's house who have an abundance of bread and **I** am perishing here with my hunger?'
18 I will rise up [and] go to my father and say to him, 'My father, I have sinned against **m**heaven and before you,
19 and therefore I am not worthy to be called your son. Make me like one of your hired servants.'

---

[1] Coin is **zuza**, equal to ¼ shekel, see Appendix 2.
[2] OS (cs): add 'because he lived dissolutely with prostitutes'

Chapter 15

20   And he rose up [and] came to his father. And while he was far away, his father saw him and had compassion on him and ran [and] fell on his neck and kissed him.

21   And his son said to him, 'My father, I have sinned against ^mheaven and before you and I am not worthy to be called your son.'

22   And his father said to his servants, 'Bring out the best robe, clothe him, and place a ring on his hand and put shoes on him

23   and bring [and] kill the ox that is fattened and let us eat and be merry,

24   because this, my son, was dead and [now] is alive, and he was lost and [now] is found,' and they began to be merry.

25   Now his oldest son was in the field and when he arrived and came near to the house, he heard the sound of the singing[1] of many.

26   And he called to one of the boys and asked him, 'What is this?'

27   He said to him, 'Your brother has come and your father has killed the ox that is fattened, because he has received him [back] healthy.'

28   And he was angry and did not want to enter. So his father came out [and] begged him.

29   And **he** said to his father, '*Behold, how many years have I worked for you [in] service and never transgressed your commandment, yet during all this time you did not give me a goat to make merry with my friends.

30   But for this your son, after he has squandered your wealth with harlots and has come [home], you kill for him the ox that is fattened.'

31   His father said to him, 'My son, **you** always are with me and everything of mine is yours,

32   but it is right for us to make merry and to rejoice, because your brother was dead, yet [now] is alive and was lost, yet [now] is found.'"[2]⌐

Chapter 16

1   And he spoke a parable to his disciples, ^pb"There was a certain rich man, and he had a steward, and they had accused him of squandering his wealth.

---

[1] OS (s): add 'and piping'
[2] Parallel structure: ABAB

Chapter 16

2   And his lord called him and said to him, 'What is this that I hear about you? Give me an accounting of your stewardship, for you can no longer be a steward for me.'

3   That steward said to himself, 'What should I do, for my lord has taken from me the stewardship? I am not able to dig, and I am ashamed to beg.

4   I know what I will do so that when I am dismissed from the stewardship, they will receive me into their houses.'

5   And he called each one of his lord's debtors and said to the first, 'How much do you owe my lord?'

6   He said to him, 'One hundred measures [of] oil.' He said to him, 'Take your book and sit down quickly; write fifty measures.'

7   And he said to another, 'And what do **you** owe my lord?' He said to him, 'One hundred cors [of] wheat.' He said to him, 'Take your book and sit down; write eighty cors.'

8   And our Lord praised the unjust steward because he had acted wisely, for the sons of this world are wiser than the sons of light, in this, their generation.⌐

9   And also *I say to you, 'Make friends for yourself from this [an]wealth of evil[1] that when it is fully spent, they may welcome you into their everlasting shelters.'

10   He who is trustworthy in little also is trustworthy in much, and he who is unjust in little also is unjust in much.[2]

11   If therefore you are not trustworthy [ones] with the [an]wealth of evil, who will entrust the truth to you?

12   And if you have not been found trustworthy [ones] in that which is not yours, who will give to you your own?"[3]

13   There is no servant that is able to serve two masters, for either he will hate the one and love the other or honor the one and despise the other. You are not able to serve God and wealth.

14   Now the Pharisees, when they heard all these [things], because they loved money, were mocking him.

15   And Jesus said to them, "You are those who justify themselves before men. But God knows your hearts, because what is esteemed among men is abominable before God.

---

[1] Fig: antimeria, "evil wealth", also v. 11

[2] Repeat *little, much*

[3] Fig: erotesis – questions to ponder, also v. 11

Chapter 16

16 The law and the prophets [were] until John. Since then, the kingdom of God is preached and all crowd to enter it.[1]

17 And it is easier for heaven and earth to pass away than [for] one letter of the law to pass away.

18 Everyone who dismisses and marries another commits adultery, and everyone who marries a forsaken commits adultery.

19 [al]Now there was a certain rich man and he wore linen and purple. And every day he lived in pleasure splendidly.

20 And there was a certain poor man whose name was Lazarus. And he lay at the gate of that rich man, stricken with boils.

21 And he longed to fill his stomach from the crumbs that fell from the table of that rich man. But even the dogs came [and] licked his boils.

22 Now it happened and that poor [man] died and the angels carried him to the bosom of Abraham. And also that rich man died and was buried.

23 And while he was tormented in SHEOL, he [pr]lifted up his eyes[2] from far away and saw Abraham and Lazarus in his bosom.

24 And he cried with a loud voice and said, 'My father Abraham, have compassion on me and send Lazarus to dip the tip of his finger in water and to moisten my tongue for me, for, *behold, I am tormented in this flame.'

25 Abraham said to him, 'My son, remember that you received your good [things] during your life and Lazarus his bad [things] and now, *behold, he is refreshed here and you are tormented.

26 And with all these [things] a great chasm is placed between us and you, so that those who want to pass over from here to you are not able, nor from there to pass over to us.'

27 Then he said to him, 'I beg of you, my father, to send him to the house of my father,

28 for I have five brothers. Let him go [and] witness to them so that they will not also come to this place of torment.'

29 Abraham said to him, 'They have Moses and the prophets. They should hear them.'

30 And **he** said to him, 'No, my father Abraham, but if someone from the dead would go to them, they would repent.'

---

[1] OS (s): 'everyone is pressing toward it'
[2] OS (cs): add 'while he was in torment'

Chapter 16
31 Abraham said to him, 'If they will not hear Moses and the prophets, even if someone would rise from the dead, they will not believe him.'"ך

Chapter 17
1 And Jesus said to his disciples, "It is not possible that offenses not come, but ⁱwoe to him by whose ᵐhand they come!
2 It would be better for him if a millstone of a donkey were hung on his neck and he were thrown into the sea, than to cause one of these little ones to stumble.
3 Take heed to yourselves. If your brother sins, reprove him. And if he repents, forgive him.
4 And if he offends you seven times in a day and in a day seven times he turns to you and says, 'I repent,' forgive him."
5 And the apostles said to our Lord, "Increase faith to us."
6 He said to them, "If you have faith ˢlike a grain of mustard seed, you could say to¹ this tree, 'Be uprooted and be planted in the sea,' and it will obey you.
7 And which of you who has a servant who plows or tends a flock, and when he comes from the field says immediately to him, 'Pass through, sit down to eat?'
8 On the contrary, he says to him, 'Prepare something to eat for me and gird up your loins [and] serve me until I have eaten and drunk, and afterwards you also may eat and drink.'
9 Does that servant receive his thanks because he did what was commanded him?² I think not.
10 So also, when you do all these [things] that are commanded to you, say, 'We are unprofitable servant[s],' because what we ought to do we have done."
11 And it happened that when Jesus went to Jerusalem he passed through the Samaritans to Galilee.
12 And when he was about to enter a certain village, ten men, lepers, met him and stood at a distance.
13 And they ᵖʳlifted their voice[s] and said, "Our Master, Jesus, have compassion on us."

---

¹ OS (c): add 'a mountain to move from here and it would move or to a sycamore tree'; OS (s): slightly different variation
² Fig: erotesis, **lema** question, implied answer "no"

Chapter 17

14 And when he saw them, he said to them, "Go [and] show yourselves to the priests." And as they went, they were cleansed.

15 And one of them, when he saw that he was cleansed, returned and with a loud voice was praising God.

16 And he fell on his face before the feet of Jesus, giving him thanks, and this [man] was a Samaritan.

17 And Jesus answered and said, "Were there not ten who were cleansed? Where are the nine?

18 Did ᶜ[no one else] determine to come [and] give praise to God, except this [one] who is from a foreign nation?"[1]

19 And he said to him, "Stand up [and] go! Your faith has given you life."

20 And when some of the Pharisees asked Jesus when the kingdom of God would come, he answered and said to them, "The kingdom of God does not come with watching,"

21 nor should they say, '*Behold, here it is,' and '*behold, there it is,' for *behold, the kingdom of God is in the middle of you."

22 And he said to his disciples, "The days will come when you will desire to see one of the days of the Son of Man and you will not see.

23 And if they say to you, '*Behold, here he is,' and '*behold, there he is,' you should not go.

24 For ˢas lightning shines from heaven and all under heaven is lightened, so the Son of Man will be in his ˢʸday,

25 but first he is going to suffer many [things] and be rejected by this generation.

26 And as it was in the days of Noah, so will it be in the days of the Son of Man,

27 for they were eating ᴾand drinking and taking wives and being given to husbands,˥ until the day that Noah entered the ark and the flood came and destroyed everyone.

28 And [it will be] again as it was in the days of Lot, when they were eating ᴾand drinking and buying and selling and planting and building.˥

29 And on the day that Lot went out from Sodom, the LORD rained fire and sulphur from heaven and destroyed all of them.

30 So it will be in the ˢʸday that the Son of Man is revealed.

---

[1] Fig: erotesis, **lema** question, implied answer "no"

Chapter 17

31 In that day, he who is on the roof and his goods are in the house should not come down to take them, and he who is in the field should not turn back.

32 Remember the wife of Lot.

33 He who wants to save his soul will lose it, and he who loses his soul will save it.[1]

34 *I say to you, in that night, two will be in one bed. One will be taken and the other will be left.

35 Two [women] will be grinding together. One will be taken and the other will be left.

36 Two [men] will be in the field. One will be taken and the other will be left."[2]

37 They answered and said to him, "To where, our Lord?" He said to them, "Where the body [is], there the eagles will be gathered."

Chapter 18

1 And he also spoke to them a parable that at all times they should pray and not be weary.

2 pb"There was a certain judge in a certain city who did not fear God and did not reverence men.

3 And there was a certain widow in that city and she came to him and said, 'Avenge me of my adversary.'

4 And he did not want to [for] a long time, but afterwards he said to himself, 'Although I do not fear God and I do not reverence men,

5 yet, because this widow troubles me, I will avenge her, so that she is not coming continually [and] annoying me.'"

6 And our Lord said, "Hear what the unjust judge said.

7 And will not God perform vengeance even more for his chosen [ones], who call on him by mrday and by night, and be long-suffering with them?[3]

8 *I say to you, he will perform their vengeance quickly. Nevertheless, will the Son of Man come and will he indeed find faith on the earth?"[4]

---

[1] Parallel structure, ABBA, could be a proverb
[2] Repeat *one will be taken and the other will be left*
[3] Fig: erotesis, "not" question, answer in the affirmative
[4] Fig: erotesis – question to ponder

Chapter 18

9   And he spoke this parable against those men who were confident in themselves that they were just and were despising everyone.

10   ᵖᵇ"Two men went up to the temple to pray. One [was] a Pharisee and the other a tax collector.

11   And that Pharisee was standing by himself and so was praying, 'God, I thank you that I am not like the rest of men, extortioners ᵖand greedy [ones] and adulterers, nor like this tax collector.

12   On the contrary, I fast twice in a week and I tithe everything that I gain.'

13   But that tax collector was standing far away and did not even want to raise his eyes to heaven, but was beating on his breast[1] and saying, 'God, have mercy on me, a sinner.'

14   *I say to you, this [man] went down to his house more justified than that Pharisee, for everyone who raises himself up will be humbled, and everyone who humbles himself will be raised up."[2]

15   And they also brought him infants that he would touch them, and his disciples saw them and rebuked them.

16   And **Jesus** called them and said to them, "Let the children come to me, and do not hinder them, for the kingdom of ᵐheaven belongs to those who are like these.

17   *Truly I say to you, whoever does not receive the kingdom of God ˢas a child will not enter it."

18   And one of the rulers[3] asked him and said to him, "Good teacher, what must I do to inherit eternal life?"

19   Jesus said to him, "Why do you call me good?[4] There is none good, except one, God.

20   You know the commandments: **DO NOT KILL,** and **DO NOT COMMIT ADULTERY,** and **DO NOT STEAL,** and **DO NOT BEAR WITNESS THAT IS FALSE. HONOR YOUR FATHER AND YOUR MOTHER."**

21   He said to him, "All these [things] I have kept from my youth."

22   And when Jesus heard these [things] he said to him, "You lack one [thing]. Go [and] sell everything that you have and give to the poor and you will have a treasure in heaven and follow me."

23   But when he heard these [things], he was sad, for he was very rich.

---

[1] Culture: *beating on his breast* means to be very sorrowful
[2] Parallel structure: ABBA
[3] OS (c): add 'of the Pharisees'
[4] OS (c): add 'and why do you ask me about goodness?'

Chapter 18

24 And when Jesus saw that he was sad, he said, "How difficult [it is] for those who have possessions to enter the kingdom of God,

25 because it is easier for a camel[1] to enter through the eye of a needle, than [for] a rich man ᵉ[to enter] the kingdom of God."

26 Those who heard were saying to him, "Then who is able to have life?"

27 And Jesus said, "Those [things] that with men are not possible, with God are possible."

28 Simon Peter said to him, "*Behold, we have left everything and have followed you."

29 Jesus said to him, "*Truly I say to you, there is no man who has left houses or parents or brothers or wife or² children because of the kingdom of God

30 and will not receive doubly many [things]³ in this ˢʸtime, and in the age to come, eternal life."

31 And Jesus took his twelve and said to them, "*Behold, we go up to Jerusalem and all the things that are written in the prophets about the Son of Man will be fulfilled,

32 for he will be delivered to the Gentiles ᴾand they will mock him and they will spit in his face.

33 And they will beat him and they will despise him and they will kill him,⁴ and on the third day he will rise up."⌐

34 And they did not understand any of these [things], but this saying was hidden from them and they did not know these [things] that were spoken to them.

35 And when he was near to Jericho, a certain blind man was sitting by the side of the road, begging.

36 And he heard the sound of the crowd that was passing by and he asked, "Who is this [man]?"

37 They said to him, "Jesus the Nazarene is passing by."

38 And he cried out and said, "Jesus, Son of David, have compassion on me."

---

¹ Or "rope," see note on Mat 19:24.
² Repeat *or*, 4x
³ Or "many times more", OS (cs): 'one hundred fold'
⁴ Repeat suffix, *him*, vs. 32, 33

Chapter 18

39 And those who were preceding Jesus rebuked him that he should be silent, but **he** cried out all the more, "Son of David, have compassion on me."

40 And Jesus stopped and commanded that they bring him to him. And when he was near to him, he asked him

41 and said to him, "What do you want me to do for you?" And **he** said, "My Lord, that I may see."

42 And Jesus said to him, "See! Your faith has given you life."

43 And immediately, he saw and followed him and praised God. And all the people who saw [it] were giving glory to God.

Chapter 19

1 And when Jesus entered and passed through into Jericho,

2 there was a certain man whose name was Zacchaeus, a rich man and the chief of the tax collectors.

3 And he wanted to see who Jesus was, and was not able to from the crowd, because Zacchaeus was small in his stature.

4 And he ran before Jesus and climbed up a barren fig tree to see him, because he was going to pass by that way.

5 And when Jesus came to that place, he saw him and said to him, "Hurry, come down, Zacchaeus, for today I must be in your house."

6 And he hurried [and] came down and received him, rejoicing.

7 And when all of them saw, they were murmuring and saying that he had entered [and] lodged with a sinful man.

8 And Zacchaeus stood up and said to Jesus, "*Behold, my Lord, half of my possessions I give to the poor and to everyone I have defrauded anything I repay fourfold."

9 Jesus said to him, "Today life has come to this house, because this [man] also is a son of Abraham,

10 for the Son of Man is come to seek and to give life to him who was perishing."

11 And when they heard these [things], he went on to speak a parable because he was near to Jerusalem and they thought that the kingdom of God was going to be revealed at that time.

12 And he said, pb"A certain man, a great nobleman, went to a far country to receive a kingdom for himself and [then] to return.

13 And he called his ten servants and gave them ten coins, and said to them, 'Do business until I come.'

Chapter 19

14 But his citizens hated him, and sent ambassadors after him and were saying, 'We do not want this [man] to rule over us.'

15 And when he received the kingdom and was returning, he said that they should call to him those [of] his servants to whom he had given money, to know what each and every one of them had gained.

16 And the first came said, 'My lord, your coin has gained ten coins.'

17 He said to him, 'Well done, good servant. Because you have been found faithful with little, you will be a ruler over ten walled cities.'

18 And the second came and said, 'My lord, your coin has made five coins.'

19 He also said to this [man], 'You also will be a ruler over five walled cities.'

20 And another came and said, 'My lord, *behold, your coin has been with me since it was placed in a linen cloth,

21 for I feared you because you are a harsh man and you take up what you have not laid down and you reap what you have not sown.'

22 He said to him, 'From your ᵐmouth I will judge you, evil servant. You knew me, that I am a harsh man and [that] I take up what I have not laid down and [that] I reap what I have not sown.

23 Why did you not give my money to the exchange and I could come [and] demand it with its interest?'

24 And to those who were standing before him, he said, 'Take from him the coin and give [it] to the one who has ten coins.'

25 They were saying to him, 'Our lord, he has ten coins.'[1]

26 He said to them, '*I say to you, to whomever has, it will be given, and whoever does not have, even that which he has will be taken from him.

27 But my enemies, those who did not want me to rule over them, bring them and kill them before me.'"⌐

28 And when he had said these [things], Jesus left to travel on to Jerusalem.

29 And when he arrived at Bethphage and Bethany on the side of the mountain that is called the Mount of Olives, he sent two of his disciples.

30 And he said to them, "Go to the village that is opposite us, and when you enter it, *Behold, you will find a colt that is tied, on which a man has never ridden. Untie [and] bring it.

---

[1] OS (cs): omit verse

Chapter 19

31 And if anyone asks you, 'Why are you untying it,' say thus to him, 'Our Lord needs [it].'"

32 And those, who were sent, went and found [it] as he had told them.

33 And while they were untying the colt, its owners said to them, "Why are you untying that colt?"

34 And they said to them, "Our Lord needs [it]."

35 And they brought it to Jesus and they threw their garments on the colt and mounted Jesus on it.

36 And as he went along, they were spreading their garments on the road.

37 And when he came near to the descent of the Mount of Olives, the whole crowd of disciples began rejoicing and praising God with a loud voice for all the miracles that they had seen.

38 And they were saying: **BLESSED IS THE KING WHO HAS COME IN THE NAME OF THE** LORD. **PEACE IN HEAVEN AND GLORY IN THE HIGHEST.**

39 And some of the Pharisees from among the crowds were saying to him, "My Master, rebuke your disciples."

40 He said to them, "*I say to you, if these would be quiet, the stones would cry out."

41 And when he came near and saw the city, he wept over it.

42 And he said, "Would that you had known those [things] that were for your peace, even in this your ˢʸday, but now they[1] are hidden from your ᵐeyes.

43 But the days will come to you when your enemies will surround you ᵖand will pressure you on every side.

44 And they will overthrow you and your children within you and they will not leave a stone on a stone in you,˥ for you did not know the ˢʸtime of your visitation."[2]

45 And when he entered the temple, he began to throw out those who were selling and buying in it.

46 And he said to them, "It is written: **MY HOUSE IS A HOUSE OF PRAYER,**[3] but you have made it a ʰden of robbers."

47 And **he** taught everyday in the temple and the chief priests and scribes and elders of the people were seeking to destroy him.

---

[1] OS (s): 'it', OS (c): 'peace'

[2] OS (s): 'maker", OS (c): 'grandeur' or 'greatness'

[3] OS (c): completes quote from Is 56:7, add 'for all nations'

Chapter 19

48 And they were not able to find to do to him, for all the people were intent to hear him.

Chapter 20

1 And it happened [that] on one of the days when he was teaching to the people in the temple and preaching, the chief priests and scribes with the elders rose up against him.

2 And they were saying to him, "Tell us with what authority you do these [things] and who is it who gave you this authority?"

3 Jesus answered and said to them, "I will also ask you a question and [you] tell me,

4 the baptism of John, was it from ᵐheaven or from men?"

5 And **they** were reasoning among themselves and were saying, "If we say from ᵐheaven, he will say to us, 'Then why do you not believe him?'

6 And if we say from men, the people will stone us, for they all are convinced that John was a prophet."

7 And they said to him, "We do not know from where it is."

8 Jesus said to them, "Neither will **I** tell you with what authority I do these [things]."

9 And he began to speak this parable to the people. ᵖᵇ"A certain man planted a vineyard and handed it over to workers and stayed away [for] a long time.

10 And in time, he sent his servant to the workers that they should give him of the fruit of the vineyard. But the workers beat him and sent him away empty-handed.

11 And in addition he sent[1] another servant. And **they** also beat that one and shamefully treated him and sent him away empty-handed.

12 And in addition he sent a third. And also **they** wounded that one and threw him[2] out.

13 The lord of the vineyard said, 'What should I do? I will send my beloved son. Perhaps they will see him and respect [him].'

14 But when the workers saw him they were reasoning among themselves and were saying, 'This is the heir. Come, let us kill him and the inheritance will be ours.'

---

[1] Lit: he added and sent
[2] Repeat suffix, *him*, from v. 11

Chapter 20
15 And they threw him outside of the vineyard and killed him.
Therefore what should the lord of the vineyard do to them?
16 He will come and destroy those workers and will give the vineyard
to others." And when they heard [it] they said, "This should not be."[1]
17 And **he** gazed at them and said, "And what is that which is written:
THE STONE THAT THE BUILDERS REJECTED HAS BECOME THE HEAD
OF THE CORNER OF THE CORNERSTONE?
18 And whoever will fall on that stone will be bruised, and whomever it
falls on, it will blow him away ᵉ[as chaff]."⌐
19 And the chief priests and scribes were wanting to lay hands on him at
that time, yet they were afraid of the people, for they knew that he had
spoken this parable against them.
20 And they sent to him spies who were acting like just [men] to catch
him in speech and to deliver him to the judge and to the authority of the
governor.
21 And they asked him and said to him, "Teacher, we know that you
speak and teach rightly and do not respect persons, but rather you teach
the way of God with truthfulness.
22 Is it lawful for us to give the poll tax to Caesar or not?"
23 But **he** perceived their craftiness and said, "Why do you tempt me?
24 Show me a denarius. Whose image and inscriptions are on it?" And
they said, "That of Caesar."
25 Jesus said to them, "Give therefore that which is of Caesar to Caesar
and that which is of God to God."
26 And they were not able to capture a word[2] from him before the
people, and they marveled at his answer and were silent.
27 And some of the Sadducees came near, those who were saying that
there is no resurrection, and they asked him
28 and said to him, "Teacher, Moses wrote to us, 'If a brother of a man,
who has a wife, should die without children, he should take the wife of
his brother and raise up seed for his brother.'
29 ᵃˡNow there were seven brothers. The first took a wife and died
without children.
30 And the second took her for his wife, and this [one] died without
children.

---

[1] OS (s): omit *they said, this should not be*, add 'they knew that he had said the
parable about them' (in v. 19 in the Peshitta)
[2] Lit: to seize on his word

Chapter 20

31 And the third took her again, and so also the seven of them. And they died and did not leave children.

32 And finally the woman also died.

33 Therefore, in the resurrection, whose wife will she be, for seven of them married her?"ܗ

34 Jesus said to them, "The children of this world take women and women are [given] to men,

35 but those who are worthy of that world and of the resurrection that is from the dead neither take women nor are women [given] to men.

36 For neither are they able to die again, for they are ˢlike the angels and are sons of God, because they are sons of the resurrection.

37 Now that the dead will rise even Moses showed, for he mentioned [it] at the bush when he said: THE LORD, THE GOD OF ABRAHAM AND THE GOD OF ISAAC AND THE GOD OF JACOB.

38 And he is not the God of the dead, but of the living, for all are alive to him."

39 And some of the scribes answered and said to him, "Teacher, you have spoken well."

40 And they did not dare to ask him about anything again.

41 And he said to them, "In what way do the scribes say concerning the MESSIAH that he is the Son of David?

42 Even David said in the book of Psalms: THE LORD SAID TO MY LORD, SIT AT MY RIGHT [HAND]

43 UNTIL I PLACE YOUR ENEMIES[1] UNDER YOUR FEET.

44 If therefore David called him, 'My Lord,' how is he his son?"

45 And while all the people were listening, he said to his disciples,

46 "Beware of the scribes who want to walk in robes[2] and love a greeting in the streets and the chief places in the synagogues and the best seats at meals.

47 Those who devour the houses of widows with the pretext of lengthening their prayers, the same will receive a greater judgment."

Chapter 21

1 And Jesus looked at the rich [men] who were putting their gifts in the treasury.

---

[1] OS (s): add 'as a footstool'

[2] OS (s): 'porches'

Chapter 21

2 And he also saw a certain poor widow who put in two small coins.

3 And he said, "I speak the truth to you that this poor widow has put in more than everyone.

4 For all of these have put into the place of the offerings of God from what was left over to them, but this [widow] from her need has put in all that she owned."

5 And while some were speaking about the temple, how it was adorned with beautiful stones and with gifts, Jesus said to them,

6 These [things] that you see, the days will come in which [one] stone will not be left on [another] stone that is not pulled down.

7 And they asked him and said, "Teacher, when will these [things] be and what is the sign when these [things] are about to happen?"

8 And **he** said to them, "See [that] you are not deceived, for many will come in my name and will say, 'I am the MESSIAH, and the time draws near,' but you should not follow them.

9 And when you hear of wars and riots, do not fear, for these [things] are going to happen first, but the end will not yet have arrived,

10 for nation will rise against nation and kingdom against kingdom

11 and great earthquakes will occur in various places, [P]and famines and plagues,[1] and there will be fears and panic, and great signs from heaven will be seen and there will be much foul weather.[2]⌐

12 But before all these [things], they will lay hands on you and persecute you and deliver you to the synagogues and to prison, and they will bring you[3] before kings and governors on account of my name.

13 But it will happen to you for a testimony.

14 And put [it] in your heart[s] that you should not be learning to make a defense,

15 for **I** will give to you a [he]mouth and wisdom so that all your enemies will not be able to stand against it.

16 [P]And your fathers and your brothers and your kinsmen and your friends will betray you and they will kill some of you.

17 And you will be hated by everyone on account of my name,⌐

18 yet not a hair from your head will be hurt.

---

[1] OS (s): add '*plagues* in various places,' *and there...seen*, change to, 'and dreadful things from heaven and great signs will be seen.'

[2] OS (c): add 'and great storms,' agrees with Old Latin mss.

[3] Repeat suffix, *you*, 4x

Chapter 21

19 And by your patience you will gain your life.

20 And when you see Jerusalem [with] an army surrounding it, then know that its destruction draws near.

21 Then those who are in Judea should flee to the mountain and those who are within it should flee and [those] in the villages should not enter it,

22 because these are the ^{sy}days of vengeance that everything that is written will be fulfilled.

23 And ⁱwoe to those who are pregnant and to those who are nursing in those days, for there will be a great torment in the land and wrath on this people.

24 And they will fall by the edge of the sword and be led away captive to every land. And Jerusalem will be trampled by the Gentiles until the times of the Gentiles will be fulfilled.

25 And there will be signs in the sun ^Pand in the moon and in the stars, and on the earth the torment of the nations and anxiety from the roaring of [1] the sea,

26 and a shaking that draws out the lives of men from the fear of what is about to come on the earth, and the powers of heaven will be shaken.

27 And then they will see **THE SON OF MAN WHO WILL COME IN THE CLOUDS** with much power and great glory.

28 And when these [things] begin to happen, take heart and lift up your heads, because your deliverance is near."

29 And he told them a parable: ^{pb}"Look at the fig tree and all the trees,

30 because when they bud, you understand immediately from them that summer is near.

31 Likewise also, when **you** see these [things] that are happening, know that the kingdom of God is near.⌐

32 *Truly I say to you, this generation will not pass away until all these [things] happen.

33 Heaven and earth will pass away, yet my words will not pass away.

34 And take heed to yourselves that your hearts should never become heavy in excess and in drunkenness and in[2] the anxiety of the world, and that ^{sy}day should come suddenly on you.

---

[1] Lit: *roaring* of the voice
[2] Repeat *in*

ARAMAIC PESHITTA NEW TESTAMENT
LUKE

Chapter 21

35 For ˢas a snare it will ensnare[1] all those who live on the ᵐface of all the earth.
36 Therefore, watch always and pray that you will be worthy to escape these [things] that are going to happen and [that] you will stand before the Son of Man."
37 And in the daytime, he was teaching in the temple and at night he went out [and] was staying in the mountain that was called the Mount[2] of Olives.
38 And all the people were preceding him to the temple to hear his word.

Chapter 22

1 Now the Feast of Unleavened Bread, that is called the Passover, was near
2 and the chief priests and scribes were seeking how to kill him, for they were afraid of the people.
3 And SATAN entered into Judas, who was called Iscariot, who was from the number of the twelve.
4 And he went [and] talked with the chief priests and scribes and captains of the temple about how he might deliver him to them.
5 And they rejoiced and pledged to give him money.
6 And he promised them and sought an opportunity to deliver him to them apart from the crowd.
7 And the day of the Feast of Unleavened Bread[3] arrived, during which was the custom that the Passover be killed.
8 And Jesus sent Peter and John and said to them, "Go [and] prepare for us the Passover that we may eat."
9 And **they** said to him, "Where do you want us to prepare [it]?"
10 He said to them, "*Behold, when you enter the city, a man will meet you who is bearing a jar of water.[4] Follow him.
11 And where he enters, say to the lord of the house, 'Our Master says, Where is a place of lodging where I may eat the Passover with my disciples?'

---

[1] Same root: *snare, ensnare*
[2] Lit: house of
[3] OS (s): 'day of the Passover'
[4] Culture: it is unusual for a man to carry water, normally it was a woman's job.

213

Chapter 22

12 And *behold, he will show you a certain large upper room that is furnished. There make ready."

13 And they went [and] found [the man] as he had told them and they prepared the Passover.

14 And when the time was come, Jesus and the twelve apostles[1] with him came [and] sat to eat.

15 And he said to them, "I have greatly desired[2] to eat this Passover with you before I suffer.

16 For *I say to you, from now on I will not eat until it is fulfilled in the kingdom of God."

17 OMITTED IN PESHITTA TEXT[3]

18 OMITTED IN PESHITTA TEXT[4]

19 And he took bread and gave thanks and broke [it] and gave [it] to them and said, "meThis is my body that is given for your sakes. This do for my remembrance."

20 And likewise also, concerning the cup, after they had eaten supper he said, "meThis cup [is] the new covenant in my blood that is shed on behalf of you.

21 But, *behold, the mhand of my betrayer [is] on the table

22 and the Son of Man dies[5] as it was determined. But iwoe to that man by whose mhand he is betrayed!"

23 And they began to examine among themselves which one of them indeed it was who was going to do this.

24 And there was also a conflict among them about which of them was the greatest.

25 And **Jesus** said to them, "The kings of the Gentiles are their lords and those who are authorities over them are called workers of good.

26 But you are not so, but he who is the greatest among you must be as the least and he who is chief as a servant.

27 For who is greater, he who sits to eat or he who serves? Is it not he who sits to eat? But I am among you as one who serves.

---

[1] OS (s): 'his disciples', OS (c): 'his apostles'

[2] Fig: polyptoton, lit: desiring, I have desired

[3] OS (cs): add 'he took the cup and gave thanks over it and said, Take this, divide it among you', omit in v. 20

[4] OS (s): add 'for I say to you that from now on I will not drink of this fruit until the kingdom of God comes'

[5] Lit: goes

Chapter 22

28 But you are those who have continued with me in my trials.

29 And **I** promise to you, as my Father has promised a kingdom to me,

30 that you will eat and drink at the table of my kingdom and you will sit on thrones and you will judge the twelve tribes of Israel."

31 And Jesus said to Simon, "Simon, *behold, SATAN is resigned to sift you ˢlike wheat.

32 And **I** have prayed for you that your faith would not be lacking. You also in time will turn and strengthen your brothers."

33 And Simon said to him, "My Lord, I am ready [to go] with you even to prison and to death."

34 Jesus said to him, "*I say to you, Simon, that the rooster will not crow today[1] before you insist three times that you do not know me."

35 And he said to them, "When I sent you out without purses and without bags and shoes, what did you lack?"[2] They said to him, "Nothing."

36 He said to them, "From now on, he who has a purse should take [it] and likewise also a bag. And he who does not have a sword should sell his garment and buy a sword for himself.

37 For *I say to you, this also that was written must be fulfilled in me: I WILL BE NUMBERED WITH THE UNJUST, for all [things] that concern me will be fulfilled."

38 And they said to him, "Our Lord, *behold, here are two swords." He said to them, "They are sufficient."

39 And he left and traveled ᵖᵃ(as he was accustomed) to the Mount of Olives and his disciples also followed him.

40 And when he arrived at the place, he said to them, "Pray, so that you should not enter into temptation."

41 And he went away from them about ᵉ[the distance] one throws a stone and he knelt and was praying.

42 And he said, "Father, if you want, let this ᵐcup pass by me. Nevertheless, not my will, but yours be done."

43 And an angel from heaven appeared to him to strengthen him.

44 And being in fear, he prayed earnestly and his sweat was ˢas drops of blood and he fell down on the ground.

---

[1] OS (c): add 'two times'

[2] Fig: erotesis, **lema** question, implied answer "no"

Chapter 22

45 And he rose up from his prayer and came to his disciples and found them asleep from sorrow.

46 And he said to them, "Why are you sleeping? Rise up [and] pray, so that you should not enter into temptation."

47 And while he was speaking, *behold, a crowd with him who was called Judas, one of the twelve, came before them. And he came near to Jesus and kissed him, for he had given this sign to them, "Whomever I kiss is him."

48 Jesus said to him, "Judas, do you betray the Son of Man with a kiss?"

49 And when those who were with him saw what happened, they said to him, "Our Lord, should we strike them with swords?"

50 And one of them struck the servant of the chief priests and took off his right ear.

51 And Jesus answered and said, "This is enough." And he touched the ear of the one who was wounded and healed him.

52 And Jesus said to those who had come against him, the chief priests and the elders and the captains of the temple, "Do you come out against me 's'as against a robber with swords and with clubs to arrest me?

53 Every day I was with you in the temple and you did not lay hands on me. But this is your 'sy'hour and the power of darkness."

54 And they arrested [him and] brought him to the house of the high priest and Simon followed him from a distance.

55 And they kindled a fire in the middle of the enclosure and they were sitting around it and Simon also was sitting among them.

56 And a certain young woman saw him while he was sitting by the fire and she looked at him and said, "This [man] was also with him."

57 And **he** denied [it] and said, "Woman, I do not know him."

58 And after a little while another saw him and said to him, "**You** also are of them,"[1] but Peter said, "I am not."

59 And after one hour, another argued and said, "Truly this [man] also was with him, for he is also a Galilean."

60 Peter said, "Man, I do not know what you are talking about." And immediately while he was speaking, the rooster crowed.

---

[1] OS (s): add 'but he said to him, Leave (me) alone man, I do not know (him)', omit '*but Peter said, I am not*'

Chapter 22

61 And Jesus turned and looked at Peter, and Simon remembered the word of our Lord that he had spoken to him, "Before the rooster will crow[1], you will deny me three times."

62 And Simon went outside [and] cried bitterly.

63 And the men who held Jesus captive were mocking him [2]and were covering him

64 and were striking him[3] on his face and saying, "Prophesy who struck you."

65 And many other [things] they were reviling and saying against him.

66 And when [day] dawned, the elders and chief priests and scribes were gathered together and they took him to their council.[4]

67 And they said to him, "If you are the MESSIAH, tell us." He said to them, "If I tell you, you will not believe me.

68 And if I ask you, you will not restore or will you release me.

69 From now on, the Son of Man will be seated at the right [hand] of the power of God."

70 And all of them were saying, "Are you therefore the Son of God?" Jesus said to them, "**You** say that I am."

71 They said, "Why do we need more witnesses? For **we** have heard [it] from his ᵐmouth."

Chapter 23

1 And the whole company of them rose up and brought him to Pilate.

2 And they began to accuse him and say, "We have found that this [man] is deceiving our nation and he denies that the poll tax should be given to Caesar. And he says about himself that he is a king, the MESSIAH."

3 And Pilate asked him and said to him, "Are you the king of the Judeans?" He said to him, "You have said [it]."

4 And Pilate said to the chief priests and to the crowd, "I do not find any cause against this man."

5 And they were shouting and saying, "He incites our nation, teaching in all of Judea. And he began from Galilee up to here."

---

[1] OS (c): add 'two times'
[2] Eastern txt: begin v. 64 here
[3] Repeat suffix *him*, from v. 63, 3 times
[4] Eastern txt: one word for *council*

217

Chapter 23

6   And Pilate, when he heard the name of Galilee, asked if the man was a Galilean.

7   And when he knew that he was under the authority of Herod, he sent him to Herod, because he was in Jerusalem in those days.

8   And Herod, when he saw Jesus, was very glad, for he had wanted to see him for a long time because he had heard many [things] about him, and he thought that he might see some sign from him.

9   And he asked him many questions, but Jesus did not give him any answer.

10   And the chief priests and scribes rose up and were vehemently accusing him.

11   And Herod and his soldiers treated him with contempt and when he had mocked [him], he clothed him with garments of purple and sent him[1] to Pilate.

12   And in that day Pilate and Herod became friends with one another, for there had been a conflict between them from the start.

13   And Pilate called the chief priests and the rulers and[2] the people

14   and he said to them, "You have brought me this man as a rebel against of your nation and *behold, I have examined him before your eyes and I have not found any fault in this man of all you have accused him.

15   Not even Herod e[found anything], for I sent him to him and *behold, nothing that is worthy of death has been done by him.

16   I will therefore punish him and let him go."

17   paFor it was a custom that he would release one [prisoner] to them at the feast.⌐

18   And the whole crowd cried out and said, "Take this [man] away and release Barabbas to us,"

19   him who was thrown into prison because of insurrection and murder that had happened in the city.[3]

20   And again Pilate spoke to them, wanting to release Jesus.

21   But **they** cried out and said, "Crucify him, crucify him."[4]

---

[1] Repeat suffix *him*

[2] Eastern txt: 'of'

[3] OS (s): transpose v. 17 after v. 19

[4] Fig: epizeuxis, very solemn repetition

ARAMAIC PESHITTA NEW TESTAMENT
LUKE

Chapter 23

22 And the third time **he** said to them, "For what evil has this [man] done? I have not found any cause that is worthy of death in him. Therefore, I will punish him and let him go."

23 But **they** were insisting with a loud voice and asking him to crucify him. And their voice and [that] of the chief priests prevailed.

24 And Pilate commanded that their request be done.

25 And he released to them him who because of insurrection and murder was thrown into prison, whom they had requested, but he delivered Jesus to their will.

26 And as they were leading him, they took hold of Simon, a Cyrenian, who was coming from the country, and set the cross on him to carry [it] after Jesus.

27 And a large group of people were following him and women who were lamenting and mourning for him.

28 And Jesus turned to them and said, "Daughters of Jerusalem, do not weep for me, but weep for yourselves and for your sons.

29 For *behold, the days are coming in which they will say, 'Blessed are the barren and the wombs that have not given birth and the breasts that have not nursed.'

30 **THEN YOU WILL BEGIN TO SAY TO THE MOUNTAINS, 'FALL ON US,' AND TO THE HILLS, 'COVER US.'**

31 For if they do these [things] in a green tree, what will happen in the dry?"[1]

32 And two others, evildoers, were coming with him to be killed.

33 And when they had come to a certain place that was called 'The Skull,' they crucified him there, and those evildoers, one on his right and one on his left.

34 And **Jesus** said, "Father, forgive them, for they do not know what they are doing." And they divided his garments and cast a lot for them.

35 And the people were standing and observing and the rulers also were mocking him and saying, "He saved others. Let him save himself if he is the MESSIAH, the chosen of God."

36 And the soldiers were also mocking him, while drawing near to him and offering him vinegar.

37 And they were saying to him, "If you are the king of the Judeans, save yourself."

---

[1] Could be fig: proverb, meaning "if you do these things when things are going well, what happens when they are going badly?"

Chapter 23

38 And there was also an inscription that was written over him in Greek and Latin and Hebrew: "This is the king of the Judeans."

39 And one of those evildoers who was crucified with him was blaspheming against him and said, "If you are the MESSIAH, rescue yourself and rescue us also."

40 And his companion rebuked him and said to him, "Are you not afraid even of God, because indeed you are in the same judgment?

41 And we justly, for as we deserve and as we have done we have been repaid, but nothing that is hateful has been done by this [man]."

42 And he said to Jesus, "Remember me, my Lord, when you come in your kingdom."

43 Jesus said to him, "*Truly I say to you, today you will be with me in paradise."

44 Now it was about the sixth hour and darkness was on all the land until the ninth hour.

45 And the sun was dark and the veil of the temple was torn from the middle of it.

46 And Jesus cried out with a loud voice and said, "My Father, INTO YOUR HANDS I PLACE MY SPIRIT." He said this and died.

47 And when the centurion saw what had happened, he praised God and said, "Truly this man was just."

48 And all the crowds, who were gathered for this sight, when they saw what had happened, returned, beating their breast[s].[1]

49 And all the acquaintances of Jesus were standing at a distance, and the women, who had come with him from Galilee, and they saw these [things].

50 And a certain man, whose name [was] Joseph, a counselor from Arimathaea, a city of Judea, was a good and just man.

51 This [man] did not agree with their will and with their deed and was waiting for the kingdom of God.

52 This [man] came near to Pilate and asked for the body of Jesus.

53 And he took it down and wrapped it in a sheet of linen and placed it in a hewn tomb in which no man yet had been placed.

54 And it was the preparation day and the SABBATH was dawning.

55 And the women who had come with him from Galilee were near and they saw the grave and how his body had been placed.

---

[1] Culture: *beating their breasts* means "to be very sorrowful"

Chapter 23

56 And they returned [and] prepared spices and ointments and rested on the SABBATH as was commanded.

Chapter 24

1 Now on the first [day] of the week, at dawn while [it was] dark, they came to the tomb and brought the spices they had prepared, and there were with them other women.

2 And they found the stone that was rolled from the tomb.

3 And they entered, yet did not find the body of Jesus.

4 And it happened that while they were astonished about this, *behold, two men stood above them and their clothing was shining.

5 And they were in fear and bowed their faces to the ground. And they said to them, "Why do you seek the living with the dead?

6 He is not here. He has risen! Remember what he spoke to you while he was in Galilee

7 and he said that the Son of Man will be delivered into the ᵐhands of men [who are] sinners and would be crucified, and after three days would rise?"

8 And they remembered his words.

9 And they returned from the grave and told all these [things] to the eleven and to the rest.

10 Now there was Mary Magdalene and Joanna and Mary the mother[1] of James and the rest who were with them, who had told the apostles.

11 And these words seemed crazy in their eyes and they did not believe them.

12 And Simon stood up and ran to the grave and looked in [and] saw the linen clothes placed alone, and went away wondering in himself about what had happened.

13 And *behold, two of them on the same day went to a village by the name of Emmaus, and it was sixty furlongs[2] distant from Jerusalem.

14 And **they** were speaking with each other about all those [things] that had happened.

15 And while they were speaking and questioning one another, Jesus came and approached them and was walking with them.

16 And their eyes were closed so that they did not recognize him.

---

[1] OS (cs): 'daughter'

[2] See Appendix 2, sixty furlongs is approximately 10 miles.

Chapter 24

17 And he said to them, "What are these words that you are speaking with each other while you walk and are sad?"

18 One of them whose name was Cleopas answered and said to him, "Are you indeed only a stranger from Jerusalem that you do not know what has happened in it in these days?"

19 He said to them, "What [things]?" They said to him, "About Jesus who was from Nazareth, a man who was a prophet and was mighty in word and in deeds before God and before all the people.

20 And the chief priests and elders delivered him to the judgment of death and they crucified him.

21 But we had hoped that he was going to deliver Israel and *behold, three days ᵉ[have passed] since all these [things] happened.

22 But also [some of] our women astonished us, for they went early to the tomb

23 and when they did not find his body, they came [and] told us, 'We saw angels there and they said about him that he is alive.'

24 And also, [some of] our men went to the tomb and found the same as what the women had said, but they did not see him."

25 Then Jesus said to them, "ᵈOh fools and dull of heart to believe in all those [things] that the prophets spoke!

26 Were not for these [things] MESSIAH intended to endure and to enter into his glory?"

27 And he began from Moses and from all the prophets and expounded to them about himself from all the scriptures.

28 And they came near the village to which they were going and he caused them to think that he was going to a more distant place.

29 And they constrained[1] him and said to him, "Remain with us because the day now is at an end ᵉ[and it is starting] to become dark." And he entered to continue with them.

30 And it happened that while he sat to eat with them, he took bread and blessed [it] and broke [it] and gave [it] to them.

31 And immediately their eyes were opened and they knew him. And he was taken from them.

---

[1] Culture: *constrained him* means to ask at least 3 times and to be persistent, not taking no for an answer.

Chapter 24

32 And they said one to another, "Were not our heart[s] heavy within us while he talked with us along the road and expounded to us the scriptures?"

33 And they rose up immediately and returned to Jerusalem. And they found the eleven, who were gathered together and those who were with them,

34 saying, "*Truly our Lord has risen and appeared to Simon."

35 And those also related these [things] that had happened on the road and how he was made known to them while breaking bread.

36 And while they were saying these [things], Jesus stood among them and said to them, "Peace [be] with you. It is I. Do not be afraid."

37 And they were astonished and were in fear, for they supposed that they had seen a spirit.

38 And Jesus said to them, "Why are you troubled and why do thoughts well up in your hearts?

39 Look at my hands and my feet, for it is I. Touch me and know that a spirit has no flesh and bones as you see that I have."

40 And while he said these [things], he showed them his hands and his feet.

41 And while they did still not believe from their joy and were astonished, he said to them, "Do you have anything here to eat?"

42 And **they** gave him a portion of fish that was broiled and of a comb of honey.

43 And he took [and] ate [it] before them.[1]

44 And he said to them, "These are the words that I spoke to you while I was with you, that it was necessary that everything be fulfilled that was written in the law of Moses and in the prophets and in the Psalms about me."

45 Then he opened their minds to understand the scriptures.

46 And he said to them, "So it is written and so it was right that the MESSIAH should suffer and rise from the dead after three days

47 and that repentance will be preached through his name for the forgiveness of sins in all the nations and [that] the beginning will be from Jerusalem.

48 And you are a witness of these [things]

---

[1] OS (c): add 'and picked up what remained (and) gave it to them'

223

Chapter 24

49 and **I** will send to you the promise of my Father. But remain in the city, Jerusalem, until you be clothed with power from on ^mhigh."

50 And he took them out up to Bethany and raised his hands and blessed them.

51 And it happened that while he blessed them, he was separated from them and taken up to heaven.

52 And **they** worshipped him[1] and returned to Jerusalem with great joy.

53 And they were always in the temple, praising and blessing God. Amen.

---

[1] OS (s): omit *And they worshipped him*

ARAMAIC PESHITTA NEW TESTAMENT
JOHN

Chapter 1

1 In the beginning was the word and that word was with God and God was that word.

2 This ^e[word] was in the beginning with God.

3 Everything existed by his ^mhand and without him ^tnot even one [thing] existed [of] that which existed.[1]

4 ^{aT}In him was life and the life was the light of men.

5 And that light brought light[2] in the darkness and the darkness did not overtake it.

6 There was a man who was sent from God whose name [was] John.

7 This [man] came for a witness to bear witness[3] concerning the light that everyone would believe by his ^mhand.

8 He was not the light, but rather ^e[he came] to bear witness concerning the light.

9 For the light of truth was that which brings light to everyone who comes into the world.⌐

10 He was in the world and the world was by his ^mhand and the ^{sy}world did not know him.

11 He came to his own and his own did not receive him.

12 But those who did receive him, to those who believed in his name, he gave authority to be sons of God,

13 those who were birthed, not by blood, nor by the will of ^{sy}flesh, nor[4] by the will of man, but rather by ⁵God.

14 And the word became ^{sy}flesh and lived among us and we saw his glory, the glory as of the unique one who was from the Father, who is full of ^{he}grace and truthfulness.

15 John witnessed about him and cried out and said, "This is he, who I said would follow me, yet be before me, because he was earlier than me.

16 And from his fullness we all have received and grace on account of grace,

---

[1] OS (c): *of that which existed* is changed to the next verse, 'That which was made *in him was life'*

[2] Same root: *light, brought light,* repeat *light,* vs. 4-9, part of the allegory.

[3] Same root: *witness, bear witness,* also v. 8

[4] Repeat *nor,* lit: and not

[5] Fig: ellipsis, [the will of] *God*

ARAMAIC PESHITTA NEW TESTAMENT
JOHN

Chapter 1

17 because the law was given by way of Moses, but [he]truth and grace was by way of Jesus Christ.

18 No man has ever seen God. The unique one [of] God, who was in the [m]bosom of his Father,[1] has declared [him].

19 And this is the witness of John, when the Judeans from Jerusalem sent to him priests and Levites to ask him, "Who are you?"

20 And he confessed and did not deny, but confessed,[2] "I am not the MESSIAH."

21 And they asked him again, "Who then? Are you Elijah?" And he said, "I am not."[3] "Are you a prophet?" And he said, "No."

22 And they said to him, "Then who are you that we may give an answer to those who sent us? What do you say about yourself?"

23 He said, "I AM THE VOICE THAT CRIES IN THE WILDERNESS, MAKE SMOOTH THE WAY OF THE LORD, as Isaiah the prophet said."

24 And they who were sent were from the Pharisees.

25 And **they** asked him and said to him, "Why then do you baptize, if you are neither the MESSIAH nor Elijah nor[4] a prophet?"

26 John answered and said to them, "I baptize with water, but among you stands him whom **you** do not know.

27 This is he who will follow me, yet was before me, the straps of whose sandals I am not worthy to loosen."

28 These [things] happened in Bethany[5] at the crossing of the Jordan where John was baptizing.

29 And on the next day, John saw Jesus, who was coming towards him and said, "*Behold, the [m]Lamb of God who takes away the sin of the world.

30 This is he about whom I said, 'A man will follow me, yet he was before me, because he was earlier than me.'[6]

31 And I did not know him, except that he would be made known to Israel. Because of this, I have come to baptize with water."

---

[1] Word play: *in the bosom* **b'auba** ܟܣܐ, *of his Father* **d'abuhi** ܕܐܒܘܗܝ

[2] Repeat *confessed*

[3] OS (c): omit *again...not*

[4] Repeat *nor*, lit: *and not*

[5] OS (cs): 'Bethabara', this is a different location than the village near Jerusalem.

[6] Repeat *because he was earlier than me* from v. 15

ARAMAIC PESHITTA NEW TESTAMENT
JOHN

Chapter 1

32 And John testified and said, "I saw the [1]Spirit coming down from heaven [s]as a dove and it remained on him.

33 And **I** did not know him,[2] but he who sent me to baptize with water said to me, 'Him on whom you see the Spirit come down and remain, this [one] will baptize with the Holy Spirit.'

34 And **I** have seen and testify that this is the Son[3] of God."

35 And on another day John was standing, and two of his disciples,

36 and he looked at Jesus as he was walking and said, "*Behold,[4] the [m]Lamb of God."

37 And two of his disciples heard [him] when he spoke and they followed Jesus.

38 And Jesus turned and saw them who were following and said to them, "What do you want?" They said to him, "Our Master, where do you live?"[5]

39 He said to them, "Come and you will see." And they came and saw where he was and they were with him that day and it was about the tenth hour.

40 And one of those who had heard from John and followed Jesus was Andrew, the brother of Simon.

41 This [one] first saw Simon his brother[6] and said to him, "I have found the MESSIAH."

42 And he brought him to Jesus. And Jesus looked at him and said, "You are Simon, the son of Jonas. You will be called Peter."[7]

43 And on another day, Jesus wanted to go to Galilee. And he found Philip and said to him, "Follow me."

44 Now Philip was from Bethsaida, from the city of Andrew and of Simon.

45 And Philip found Nathaniel and said to him, "We have found him about whom Moses wrote in the law and the prophets, that he is Jesus the son of Joseph from Nazareth."

---

[1] OS (s): add 'Holy'

[2] Repeat phrase *And I did not know him*, from v. 31

[3] OS (cs): 'chosen'

[4] OS (s): add '*Behold* the Messiah, behold *the Lamb*'

[5] Lit: where are you?

[6] OS (s): add 'at the dawn of the day,' this addition testified in 2 Old Latin mss.

[7] OS (s): *Peter* is, 'Kepha, which is interpreted in Greek, Petros'

ARAMAIC PESHITTA NEW TESTAMENT
JOHN

Chapter 1

46 Nathaniel said to him, "Is it possible for anything good to be from Nazareth?" Philip said to him, "Come and you will see."

47 And Jesus saw Nathaniel coming towards him and said about him, "*Behold, truly a son of Israel in whom there is no deceit."

48 Nathaniel said to him, "From where do you know me?" Jesus said to him, "Before Philip called you, while you were under the fig tree, I saw you."

49 Nathaniel answered and said to him, "My Master, you are the Son of God. You are the King of Israel."

50 Jesus said to him, "Because I told you that I saw you under the fig tree, do you believe? For you will see greater [things] than these."

51 He said to him, "*Truly, truly I say to you, from now on you will see heaven opening and the angels of God ^{sy}ascending and descending to the Son of Man."

Chapter 2

1 And on the third day there was a wedding feast in Cana, a city of Galilee, and the mother of Jesus was there.

2 And Jesus and his disciples were also invited to the wedding feast.

3 And the wine was running out and his mother said to Jesus, "They have no wine."

4 Jesus said to her, "What do you want from me, woman? My ^{sy}hour has not yet come."

5 His mother said to the servants, "Whatever he tells you, do."

6 And there were there six water pots of stone, which were placed for the purification of the Judeans that each held two or three liquid measures.

7 Jesus said to them, "Fill the water pots [with] water." And they filled them up to the top.

8 He said to them, "Draw ^e[the wine] now and take [it] to the chief of the feast." And they took [it].

9 And when the chief of the feast had tasted that water that had become wine and did not know from where it came ^{pa}(but the servants knew, because they had filled the water) the chief of the feast called the bridegroom

10 and said to him, "Everyone first brings good wine and when they are drunk, then that which is inferior. But you have kept the good wine until now."

Chapter 2

11 This was the first sign that Jesus did in Cana of Galilee. And he made known his glory and his disciples believed in him.

12 After this, he went down to Capernaum, he ᴾand his mother and his brothers and his disciples and they stayed there a few days.⌐

13 And the feast of the Passover of the Judeans was near and Jesus went up to Jerusalem.

14 And he found in the temple those who were selling oxen ᴾand sheep and doves and moneychangers who were sitting.

15 And he made himself a whip from a rope and drove out all of them from the temple, even the sheep and oxen and the moneychangers. And he poured out their money and turned over their tables.

16 And to those who were selling doves, he said, "Take these away [from] here and do not make the house of my Father a house of merchandise."

17 And his disciples remembered that it was written: **THE ZEAL OF YOUR HOUSE HAS CONSUMED ME.**

18 Now the Judeans answered and said to him, "What sign do you show us, because you do these [things]?"

19 Jesus answered and said to them, "Tear down this temple and after three days, **I** will raise it."

20 The Judeans said to him, "This temple was being built for forty-six years and after three days **you** will raise it?"

21 But he was speaking about the ᵐtemple of his body.

22 And when he rose from the dead, his disciples remembered that he had said this and they believed the scriptures and the word that Jesus had said.

23 Now while Jesus was in Jerusalem at the feast of the Passover,[1] during the feast many believed in him when they saw the signs that he did.

24 But **Jesus** did not entrust himself to them, because he knew all men[2]

25 and he did not need a man to testify to him about anyone, for he knew what was in man.

---

[1] OS (s): 'unleavened bread'
[2] OS (s): omit *because he knew all men*

ARAMAIC PESHITTA NEW TESTAMENT
JOHN

Chapter 3

1 Now there was a certain man there from the Pharisees. His name was Nicodemus, a ruler of the Judeans.

2 This [man] came to Jesus at night and said to him, "My Master, we know that you were sent from God [as] a teacher, for no man is able to do these signs that **you** do, but he with whom God [is]."

3 Jesus answered and said to him, "*Truly, truly I say to you, if a man is not born again,[1] he is not able to see the kingdom of God."

4 Nicodemus said to him, "How is it possible for an old man to be born? Is it possible to enter the womb of his mother again a second time and to be born?"[2]

5 Jesus answered and said to him, "*Truly, truly I say to you, if a man is not born from water and Spirit, he is not able to enter into the kingdom of God.

6 What is born from the ˢʸflesh is ˢʸflesh and what is born from the Spirit is spirit.[3]

7 Do not marvel that I say to you that it is necessary for you to be born again.

8 The wind will blow where it wants and you hear its sound, but you do not know [from] where it comes and to where it goes. So is everyone who is born from the Spirit."[4]

9 Nicodemus answered and said to him, "How can these [things] be?"

10 Jesus answered and said to him, "You are a teacher of Israel and you do not know these [things]?

11 *Truly, truly I say to you, what we know, we speak, and what we see, we witness [to], and you do not receive our witness.

12 If I have spoken to you about [things] on the earth and you do not believe, how will you believe me if I speak to you about [things] in heaven?[5]

13 And no man has ascended into heaven, but he who descended from heaven, the Son of Man who is in[6] heaven.

---

[1] Lit: from the beginning, from the head, or all over again, anew

[2] Fig: erotesis, **lema** question, obvious answer "no"

[3] Repeat next word, *flesh, Spirit*; OS (s): add 'because God is a living spirit, OS (c): add 'and is born of God'

[4] OS (cs): add 'water and'; repeat at beginning and end of sentence, same word, *wind, Spirit*

[5] Fig: erotesis – question to ponder

[6] OS (s): 'from'

Chapter 3

14 And [s]as Moses raised up the serpent in the wilderness, so the Son of Man is going to be raised up,

15 so that everyone who believes in him will not be destroyed, but will have eternal life.

16 For God so loved the world, even that he would give his unique Son, that whoever will believe in him will not be destroyed, but will have eternal life,

17 for God did not send his Son into the world to condemn the world, but to give life to the world by his [m]hand.

18 He who believes in him is not judged and he who does not believe is judged[1] already, because he does not believe in the name of the unique Son of God.

19 Now this is the judgment, because the [m]light has come to the world and men loved [m]darkness more than the [m]light, for their works are evil.

20 For everyone who does hateful [things] hates the [m]light and does not come to the [m]light, so that his works will not be reproved.

21 But he who does truth[ful things] comes to the [m]light, so that his works may be known that they are done in God."[2]

22 After these [things] Jesus and his disciples went to the land of Judea and he was living with them there and baptizing.

23 Now John was also baptizing at Aenon, which was beside Salim, because there was plenty of water there and they were coming and being baptized,

24 for John had not yet been cast into prison.

25 Now there was a question with a certain Judean to one of the disciples of John about purification.

26 And they came to John and said to him, "Our Master, he who was with you at the crossing of the Jordan about whom **you** witnessed, *behold, he is also baptizing and many are coming to him."

27 John answered and said to them, "No man is able to receive anything of his own desire, except it be given to him from [m]heaven.

28 You are my witnesses that I said that I am not the MESSIAH, but I am a messenger who is before him.

---

[1] Same root: *condemn*, v. 17, *is judged*

[2] Parallel structure, opposites, ABCABC; same roots: *does, works,* and *hateful, hates*

ARAMAIC PESHITTA NEW TESTAMENT
JOHN

Chapter 3

29   He who has the bride is the bridegroom, but the friend of the bridegroom[1] who stands and listens for him rejoices [with] a great joy, because of the voice of the bridegroom. Therefore, this my joy,[2] *behold, is full.

30   It is necessary for him to increase and for me to decrease.

31   For he who has come from above is above all and he who is from the earth is from the earth and speaks from the earth. He who has come from heaven is above all.[3]

32   And what he has seen and heard he witnesses, yet no man receives his witness.[4]

33   But he who receives his witness confirms that God is true.

34   For he whom God sent speaks the words of God, for God did not give the Spirit with measure.

35   The Father loves the Son and has given everything into his [m]hands.

36   He who believes in the Son has eternal life and he who does not obey[5] the Son will not see life. On the contrary, the wrath of God will continue against him."

Chapter 4

1   Now Jesus knew that the Pharisees had heard that he made many disciples and was baptizing more than John,

2   [pa]although Jesus was not baptizing, but rather his disciples [were].⌐

3   And he left Judea and went again to Galilee

4   and he was planning to pass through Samaria.[6]

5   And he came to a city of the Samaritans that was called Sychar,[7] by the edge of the field that Jacob had given to Joseph, his son.

6   And there was there a well of water that [e][had belonged to] Jacob. And Jesus was tired from the toil of the journey and was sitting by the well and it was the sixth hour.

7   And a woman from Samaria came to draw water. And Jesus said to her, "Give me water to drink,"

---

[1] For further study regarding the friend of the bridegroom, Freeman, p. 423.

[2] Same root: *rejoice, joy*

[3] Repeat *above all, from the earth*

[4] Same root: *witnesses, witness*, as next word, also v. 33

[5] OS (cs): 'believe'

[6] Lit: house of the Samaritans

[7] OS (cs): 'Shechem'

ARAMAIC PESHITTA NEW TESTAMENT
JOHN

Chapter 4

8   for his disciples had entered the city to buy food for them.[1]

9   That Samaritan woman said to him, "How is it [since] you are a Judean, yet you ask to drink of me, who am a Samaritan woman? For the Judeans do not deal with the Samaritans."

10   Jesus answered and said to her, "If you were aware of the gift of God and who this is who said to you, 'Give me to drink,' you would ask him and he would give you living water."

11   That woman said to him, "My Lord, you have no water pot and the well is deep. Where [is] your living water?

12   Are you greater than our father Jacob, who gave us this well and from which he and his sons and his flocks drank?"[2]

13   Jesus answered and said to her, "Everyone who drinks from this water will thirst again,

14   but everyone who drinks from the water that I give him will not thirst forever. But that water that I give him will be in him a spring of water that will bubble up to eternal life."

15   That woman said to him, "My Lord, give to me from this water, so that I will not thirst again nor have to come [and] draw [water] from here."

16   Jesus said to her, "Go, call your husband and come here."

17   She said to him, "I have no husband." Jesus said to her, "You have spoken well, 'I have no husband,'

18   for you have had five husbands and this [one] that you have now is not your husband. This you have said [is] true."

19   That woman said to him, "My Lord, I perceive that you are a prophet.

20   Our fathers worshipped on this mountain, yet **you**[3] say that in Jerusalem is the place that it is proper to worship."

21   Jesus said to her, "Woman, believe me that the ˢʸhour comes, when not on this mountain, nor even in Jerusalem will they worship the Father.

22   **You** worship that which you do not know, but **we** worship what we know, because life is from the Judeans.

---

[1] Fig: epitrechon, parenthesis running along side, or, as OS (s): v. 7 between 8 and 9.

[2] Fig: erotesis, **lema** question, implied answer "no"

[3] Plural pronoun, meaning "the Judeans"

Chapter 4

23 But the ^{sy}hour comes and now is, when the true worshipper will worship the Father by the Spirit and with the truth,[1] for the Father also seeks worshippers who are like these.

24 For God is a Spirit and those who worship him must worship by the Spirit and with truth."

25 That woman said to him, "I know that the MESSIAH will come and when he comes, he will teach us[2] everything."

26 Jesus said to her, "I who speak with you am [he]."

27 And while he spoke, his disciples came and were amazed that he spoke with a woman, but no one said, "What do you ask?" or, "Why do you speak with her?"

28 And the woman left her water pitcher[3] and went to the city and told the men,

29 "Come, see the man who told me everything that I have done. Is he the MESSIAH?"[4]

30 And the men went out of the city and they were coming to him.

31 And in the middle of these [things] his disciples were begging him and saying to him, "Our Master, eat."

32 But **he** said to them, "I have food to eat that **you** do not know."

33 The disciples spoke among themselves, "Has someone brought him something to eat?"

34 Jesus said to them, "My food is to do the will of him who sent me and [that] I complete his work.

35 ^{al}Do you not say that after four months comes the harvest? *Behold, I say to you, 'Lift up your eyes and see the fields that are white and have arrived at the harvest already.'

36 And he who reaps receives a wage and gathers ^mfruit for eternal life and the sower and the reaper will rejoice together.

37 For in this is a ^{an}word of truth: SOMEONE SOWS AND ANOTHER REAPS.

38 I have sent you to reap in what you did not labor, for others labored and you have entered into their toil."⌐

---

[1] Same prefix, *by, with*; this phrase is not the figure hendiadys, but we should read each preposition separately.

[2] OS (s): 'give us', OS (c): 'declare to us', Var (H): 'make known to us'

[3] Culture: leaving her water pitcher showed how excited she was -- she would not normally have considered leaving it.

[4] Fig: erotesis, **lema** question, obvious answer "yes"

Chapter 4

39 And many Samaritans from that city believed in him, because of the word of that woman who had testified, "He told me everything that I have done."

40 And when those Samaritans came to him, they begged him to stay with them and he stayed with them [for] two days.

41 And many believed in him, because of his word.

42 And they were saying to that woman, "From now on, we do not believe in him [only] because of your word, for **we** have heard and know that this is truly the MESSIAH, the Savior of the world."

43 And after two days, Jesus went away from there and traveled to Galilee,

44 for **Jesus** had testified that a prophet is not honored in his [own] city.

45 And when he came to Galilee, the Galileans received him who had seen all the signs that he had done in Jerusalem during the feast, for they also had gone to the feast.

46 And Jesus came again to Cana of Galilee, where he had made the water wine. And in Capernaum there was a servant of a certain king whose son was sick.

47 This [man] heard that Jesus had come from Judea to Galilee, and he went to him and was begging him to come down and to heal his son, for he was close to dying.

48 Jesus said to him, "If you do not see ^{he}signs and wonders, you do not believe."

49 That servant of the king said to him, "My Lord, come down before the boy dies."

50 Jesus said to him, "Go! Your son is alive." And that man believed in the word that Jesus spoke to him and he went away.

51 And while he was going down, his servants met him and brought him good news and said to him, "Your son lives."

52 And he asked them at what time he was healed. They said to him, "Yesterday, in the seventh hour the fever left him."

53 And his father knew that [it was] at that moment in which Jesus had said to him, "Your son lives." And he and his whole house believed.

54 Furthermore, this [was] the second sign Jesus did after he came from Judea to Galilee.

Chapter 5

1   After these [things] was the feast of the Judeans and Jesus went up to Jerusalem.

2   Now there was in Jerusalem there a certain pool of baptizing, that is called in Hebrew, Bethesda, and it had five porches in it.

3   And many people were lying in these [porches] who were sick ᴾand blind and lame and crippled ¹┐ and they were waiting for the movement of the water,

4   for an angel came down at various times to the pool and moved the water. And whoever would go down first after the movement of the water was healed [of] every pain that he had.

5   Now there was there a certain man who had had an infirmity [for] thirty-eight years.

6   Jesus saw this [man] who was lying [there] and knew that he had been ᵉ[infirm] a long time. And he said to him, 'Do you want to be healed?"

7   That sick man answered and said, "Yes, my Lord, but I have no one to place me in the pool when the water is moved. But before I go [down], another comes down before me."

8   Jesus said to him, "Rise, pick up your bed and walk."²

9   And immediately that man was healed and he rose up, picked up his bed and walked. And that same day was the SABBATH.

10   And the Judeans said to him who was healed, "It is the SABBATH. It is not lawful for you to carry your bed."

11   But he answered and said to them, "He who made me whole said to me, 'Pick up your bed and walk.'"

12   And they asked him, "Who is this man who told you to pick up your bed and walk?"

13   And **he** who was healed did not know who he was, for Jesus had withdrawn from the large crowd that was in that place.

14   After a time, Jesus found him in the temple and said to him, "*Behold, you are whole. Do not sin again, lest something that is worse than before should happen to you."

15   And that man went and told the Judeans that it was Jesus who had healed him.

---

¹ OS (c): omit *and they...water*, and all v. 4, OS (s): not represented
² Culture: it was against the Jewish law (not the Torah, but the Rabbinical teaching) to pick up something of that size on the Sabbath.

Chapter 5

16 And because of this, the Judeans were persecuting Jesus and seeking to kill him, because he had done these [things] on the SABBATH.

17 But **Jesus** said to them, "My Father works until now. **I** also work."

18 And because of this, the Judeans were seeking to kill him even more, not only because he had broken the SABBATH, but also because he was saying about God that he was his Father and was equating himself with God.

19 Now Jesus answered and said to them, "*Truly, truly I say to you, the Son is not able to do anything by his own will, but what he sees the Father [do], that he does. For those [things] that the Father does, these also the Son does[1] likewise.

20 For the Father loves his Son and everything that he does, he shows him and he will show him greater than these works, so that you will marvel.

21 For as the Father raises the dead and makes them alive, so also the Son will make alive those whom he wants.

22 For the Father does not judge anyone, but has given all judgment to the Son,

23 so that everyone should honor the Son as he honors the Father. **He** who does not honor the Son does not honor the Father who sent him.

24 *Truly, truly I say to you, whoever hears my word and believes on him who sent me has eternal life and does not come to judgment, but has removed himself from death to life.

25 *Truly, truly I say to you, the ˢʸhour comes, even now is, when the dead will hear the voice of the Son of God and those who hear [it] will live.

26 For as the Father has life in himself, so he also gave to the Son to have life in himself[2]

27 and he gave him authority to also execute judgment.

28 Now because he is the Son of Man,[3] do not marvel at this, because the ˢʸhour will come when all those who are in the graves will hear his voice.

29 And those who have done good [things] will go out to the resurrection of life and those who have done evil [things] to the resurrection of judgment.

---

[1] Same root: *does, do*

[2] Lit: in his underlying substance, his person

[3] Eastern txt: this part of verse at end of v. 27

Chapter 5

30 I cannot do anything of my own will,[1] but as I hear, I judge, and my judgment is upright, for I do not seek my will, but the will of him who sent me.

31 If **I** testify about myself, my testimony[2] is not true.

32 There is another who bears testimony about me and I know that his testimony that he testifies about me is true.

33 **You** sent to John and he testified concerning the truth.

34 And **I** did not receive the testimony from man, but I say these [things] that you may live.

35 ^{me}That [man] was a lamp that shone and brought light and you were willing to boast for a time in his light.

36 But **I** have a testimony that is greater than [that] of John, for the works that my Father gave to me to finish, those works that I do, testify concerning me that the Father sent me.

37 And the Father who sent me testifies about me. You have not ever heard his voice, nor have you seen his appearance.

38 And his word does not remain in you, because **you** do not believe in him whom he sent.

39 Search the scriptures, because in them you think that you have eternal life and they testify about me.

40 And you are not desiring to come to me that you might have eternal life.

41 I do not receive praise from men,

42 but I know you, that the love of God is not in you.

43 **I** have come in the name of my Father and you have not received me. Yet if another would come in his own name, you would receive him.

44 How are you able to believe, who receive praise from one another, yet you do not seek the praise that is from God alone?

45 Do you think that I will accuse you before the Father?[3] There is one who accuses you, Moses, in whom you trust,

46 for if you believe in Moses, you would also believe in me, for Moses wrote about me.

47 And if you do not believe his writings, how will you believe my words?"[4]

---

[1] Lit: the will of my mind; repeat *will*

[2] Same root: *testify, testimony*, throughout vs. 31-39

[3] Fig: erotesis, **lema** question, obvious answer "no"

[4] Fig: erotesis – question to ponder, also v. 44

Chapter 6

1 After these [things], Jesus went to the other shore of the Sea of Galilee, which is Tiberias.

2 And large crowds followed him, because they had seen the signs that he did with the sick.

3 And Jesus went up to a mountain and was sitting there with his disciples.

4 And the feast of the Passover of the Judeans was near.

5 And Jesus ^{pr}raised his eyes and saw a large crowd that came towards him. And he said to Philip, "Where will we buy bread that these may eat?"

6 And he said this, testing him, for he knew what he was going to do.

7 Philip said to him, "Two hundred denarii [of] bread is not sufficient for them, [even] when each of them would [only] take a little."

8 Andrew, the brother of Simon Peter, one of his disciples, said to him,

9 "There is a certain boy here who has five loaves of barley and two fish with him, but what are these for all those [people]?"

10 Jesus said to them, "Make all the men to sit to eat." Now there was much grass in that place and the men sat to eat, five thousand in number.

11 And Jesus took the bread and blessed [it] and distributed [it] to those who sat to eat, and so also from the fish, as much as they wanted.

12 And when they were satisfied, he said to his disciples, "Gather the fragments that remain, so that nothing will be lost."

13 And they gathered [them] and filled twelve baskets [with] those fragments that remained to them who had eaten from the five loaves of barley.

14 Now those men who had seen the sign that Jesus had done were saying, "Truly this is the prophet who has come into the world."

15 But Jesus knew that they were going to come [and] grab him and to make him a king and he went out to a mountain alone.

16 And when evening came, his disciples went down to the sea.

17 And they took a ship and were going to the other shore, to Capernaum. And it was dark and Jesus had not come to them.

18 And the ^{pe}sea was lifted up against them, because a fierce wind was blowing.

Chapter 6

19 And they went onward about twenty-five or thirty furlongs[1] and they saw Jesus walking on the lake. And as he came near to their ship, they were afraid.

20 And **Jesus** said to them, "It is I. Do not be afraid."

21 And they wanted to receive him into the ship and immediately, that ship was at the land [to] which they were going.

22 And on the next day that crowd that remained on the other side of the sea saw that there was no other ship there, except that one which the disciples had boarded and that Jesus had not entered the ship with his disciples.

23 But other boats had come from Tiberias to the shore of the place in which they ate bread after Jesus had blessed [it],

24 and when that crowd saw that neither Jesus was there nor his disciples, they boarded these boats and came to Capernaum and were seeking Jesus.

25 And when they found him on the other shore of the sea, they said to him, "Our Master, when did you come here?"

26 Jesus answered and said to them, "*Truly, truly I say to you, you are seeking me, not because you saw the miracles, but because you ate bread and were satisfied.

27 Do not labor for food that is destroyed, but [for] food that lasts for life forever, that which the Son of Man will give to you, for this the Father, God, has confirmed."

28 They said to him, "What should we do to labor for the works of God?"

29 Jesus answered and said to them, "This is the work of God, that you should believe in him whom he sent."

30 They said to him, "What sign have you done that we may see and believe in you? What have you performed?

31 Our fathers ate manna in the wilderness, as it is written: HE GAVE THEM BREAD FROM HEAVEN TO EAT."

32 Jesus said to them, "*Truly, truly I say to you, Moses did not give you bread from heaven, but my Father gave you [an]the truthful bread[2] from heaven.

---

[1] *Furlong* is a stadia, 1/8 of a Roman mile, see Appendix 2.

[2] Lit: bread of truthfulness, OS (s): 'true bread', fig: metonymy, meaning "provision"

Chapter 6

33 For the ^mbread of God is he who has come down from heaven and gives life to the world."

34 They said to him, "Our Lord, give us this ^mbread always."

35 Jesus said to them, "^{..me}I am the ^{an}bread of life. He who comes to me will not hunger and he who believes in me will not thirst forever.

36 But I said to you, 'You have seen me, yet you do not believe.'

37 All whom my Father has given to me will come to me and whoever will come to me ^fI will not throw out,

38 because I came down from heaven, not to do my will, but to do the will of him who sent me.

39 And this is the will of him who sent me, that I do not lose anyone [of] all whom he has given me, but I will raise him up in the last ^{sy}day.[1]

40 For this is the will of my Father, that all who see the Son and believe in him will have eternal life and I will raise him up in the last ^{sy}day."

41 And the Judeans were murmuring against him, because he said, "^{..me}I am the ^mbread that came down from heaven."

42 And they were saying, "Is not this Jesus the son of Joseph, him whose father and mother we know? Yet how does this [man] say, 'I came down from heaven?'"

43 Jesus answered and said to them, "Do not murmur to each other.

44 No one is able to come to me, unless the Father who sent me draws him and I will raise him up in the last ^{sy}day,

45 for it is written in the prophet: ALL OF THEM WILL BE TAUGHT OF GOD. Everyone who hears, therefore, from the Father and learns from him will come to me.

46 There is no one who will see the Father, but rather he who is from God is that one [who] sees the Father.

47 *Truly, truly I say to you, he who believes in me[2] has eternal life.

48 ^{me}I am the ^{an}bread of life.[3]

49 Your fathers ate manna in the wilderness and they died.

50 ^{al}Now this is the ^mbread that came down from heaven, that a man may eat of it and not[4] die.

---

[1] Repeat phrase *I will raise him up in the last day*, vs. 40, 44, 54, as refrain

[2] OS (cs): 'God'

[3] OS (c): add 'which came down from heaven'

[4] OS (c): omit *not*, evidently refers to manna, not Christ

Chapter 6

51 ^{me}I am the living bread, who came down from heaven and if a man should eat of this bread, he will live forever. And the ^{me}bread that I give is my body, which I give for the life of the world."

52 And the Judeans were arguing with each other and saying, "How can this [man] give us his body to eat?"

53 And Jesus said to them, "*Truly, truly I say to you, ^{al}unless you eat the body of the Son of Man and drink his blood, you do not have life in yourselves.¹

54 And he who eats of my body and drinks of my blood has eternal life and I will raise him up in the last ^{sy}day.

55 For ^{me}my body truly is food and ^{me}my blood truly is drink.

56 He who eats my body and drinks my blood remains in me and I in him.

57 As the living Father has sent me and **I** live because of the Father, [so] he who eats me will also live because of me.

58 This is the bread that came down from heaven, not as your fathers ate manna and died. He who eats this bread will live forever."⌐

59 These [things] he said in the synagogue while teaching in Capernaum.

60 And many of his disciples who heard [him] said, "This saying is hard. Who is able to hear it?"

61 Now Jesus knew in himself that his disciples were murmuring about this [saying] and he said to them, "[Does] this offend you?

62 ^e[What]² if then you see the Son of Man ascending to the place where he was before?

63 It is the Spirit that makes alive. The body does not profit anything. The ^{me}words that I speak with you are ^{ht}spirit and they are life.³

64 But there are some of you who do not believe." ^{pa}(For Jesus knew previously who those were who did not believe and who it was who would betray him.)

65 And he was saying to them, "Because of this, I told you that no one is able to come to me, unless it is given to him by my Father."

66 Because of this saying, many of his disciples ^{pr}turned their back[s] and did not walk with him.

---

¹ Lit: underlying substance
² Fig: ellipsis, could add [What will you then believe]
³ Fig: heterosis, meaning "spiritual and living"

Chapter 6

67 And Jesus said to his twelve, "Do you also want to go?"[1]

68 Simon Peter answered and said, "My Lord, to whom would we go? You have the words of eternal life.

69 And **we** believe and know that you are the MESSIAH, the Son of the living God."

70 Jesus said to them, "Did not I choose you twelve? Yet one of you is an opponent."[2]

71 Now he was speaking about Judas, the son of Simon Iscariot, for he was going to betray him, one of the twelve.

Chapter 7

1 After these [things], Jesus was walking in Galilee, for he did not want to walk in Judea, because the Judeans were seeking to kill him.

2 And the Feast of Tabernacles of the Judeans was near.

3 And his brothers said to Jesus, "Leave here and go to Judea, so that your disciples may see the works that you are doing,

4 for there is no one who does anything secretly, yet desires that it be ᵉ[known] openly. If you do these [things], show yourself to the world."

5 For not even his brothers believed in Jesus.

6 Jesus said to them, "My ˢʸtime has not yet arrived, but your ˢʸtime has always been ready.

7 The world is not able to hate you, but it hates me, because **I** testify against it that its works are evil.

8 Go up to this feast. **I** will not go up to this feast now, because my ˢʸtime is still not finished."

9 He said these [things] and he stayed in Galilee.

10 Now after his brothers had gone up to the feast, then he also went up, not openly, but secretly.

11 And the Judeans were seeking him at the feast and were saying, "Where is he?"

12 And there was much murmuring in the crowd because of him, for there were [those] who said, "He is good," and others were saying, "Not so, but rather he deceives the people."

13 But no one was speaking openly about him, because of fear of the Judeans.

---

[1] Fig: erotesis, **lema** question, implied answer "yes"
[2] Same word as Satan

Chapter 7

14 Now when the days of the feast were half gone,[1] Jesus went up to the temple and was teaching.

15 And the Judeans were amazed and said, "How does this [man] know the writings, when he has not learned [them]?"

16 Jesus answered and said, "My teaching is not mine, but his who sent me.

17 He who wants to do his will, will understand my teaching, if it is from God or [if] I speak from my own will.

18 He who speaks from the will of his [own] mind seeks glory for himself. Now he who seeks the glory of him who sent him is true and has no wickedness in his heart.

19 Did not Moses give you the law?[2] Yet not one of you keeps the law.

20 Why do you seek to kill me?" The crowd answered and said, "You have a devil. Who wants to kill you?"

21 Jesus answered and said to them, "I have done one work and all of you are amazed.

22 On account of this, Moses gave you circumcision, not because it was from Moses, but because it was from the forefathers, and on the SABBATH you circumcise a man.

23 If a man is circumcised on the day of the SABBATH [and] because of [this] the law of Moses is not broken,[3] [why] are you murmuring against me, because I have healed the man on the day of the SABBATH?

24 Do not judge with respect of persons, but rather judge [with an] upright judgment."[4]

25 And some from Jerusalem were saying, "Is this not him whom they seek to kill?

26 And *behold, he speaks openly and they do not say anything to him. Do our elders know that this is truly the MESSIAH?[5]

27 But we know from where he is. And the MESSIAH, when he comes, no man will know from where he is."

28 And Jesus [pr]lifted up his voice as he taught in the temple and said, "You both know me and you know from where I [am]. And I did not

---

[1] Lit: were divided
[2] Fig: erotesis – question to ponder, also v. 23
[3] Lit: is loosed
[4] Same root: *judge, judgment*
[5] Fig: erotesis, **lema** question, implied answer "no"

Chapter 7

come by my own will, but he is true who sent me, whom **you** do not know.

29 But **I** know him, because I [am] from his presence and he has sent me."

30 And they wanted to arrest him, yet no one laid hands on him, because his ^{sy}hour had not yet come.

31 Now many from the crowd believed in him and said, "When the MESSIAH comes, will he do more than these miracles this [man] has done?"[1]

32 And the Pharisees heard the crowds who were saying these [things] about him and they and the chief priests sent guards to arrest him.

33 And Jesus said, "Yet a little time I [am] with you, and I will go to him who sent me.

34 And you will seek me and you will not find me and where I am ^e[going], you are not able to come."

35 The Judeans said among themselves, "Where is this [man] about to go that we cannot find him? Is he about to go, perhaps, to the regions of the Gentiles and to teach the heathens?

36 What is this saying that he said, 'You will seek me and you will not find me and where I am ^e[going], **you** are not able to come?'"

37 And on the high day, which is the last [day] of the feast, Jesus was standing and he cried out and said, "If anyone is thirsty, he should come to me and drink.

38 Whoever believes in me, as the scriptures have said,[2] rivers of living water will flow from his inner part."

39 Now he said this about the Spirit that those who believed in him were about to receive, for the Spirit was not yet given, because Jesus was not yet glorified.

40 And many from the crowds who heard his words were saying, "This is truly a prophet."

41 Others were saying, "This is the MESSIAH." Others were saying, "Does the MESSIAH come from Galilee?[3]

---

[1] Fig: erotesis, **lema** question, obvious answer "no"

[2] Fig: ellipsis [concerning Jerusalem, so shall it be], cf. Zech.14:8 (lesson read during the feast), Prov. 18:4. The *inner part* refers to the Lord by way of the Holy Spirit, "rivers of water" will flow to people.

[3] Fig: erotesis, **lema** question, obvious answer "no"

Chapter 7

42 Does not the scripture say that the MESSIAH will come from the seed of David and from Bethlehem, the village of David?"

43 And there was division in the crowds[1] because of him.

44 And there were some of them who wanted to arrest him, but no one laid hands on him.

45 And those guards came to the chief priests and the Pharisees and the priests said to them, "Why have you not brought him?"

46 The guards said to them, "Never has a man spoken so, as this man speaks."

47 The Pharisees said to them, "Are you also deceived?[2]

48 Have any of the leaders or of the Pharisees believed in him,

49 except only this cursed people, who do not know the law?"

50 Nicodemus, one of them, who had come to Jesus in the night, said to them,

51 "Does our law condemn a man, unless it hears from him first and knows what he has done?"

52 They answered and said to him, "Are **you** also from Galilee? Search and see that the prophet will not rise up from Galilee."

53 Then each one went to his house.[3]

Chapter 8

1 And Jesus went to the Mount of Olives.

2 And in the morning he came again to the temple and all the people came to him. And while he was sitting, he was teaching them.

3 And the scribes and Pharisees brought a woman who was caught in adultery. And placing her in the middle,

4 they said to him, "Teacher, this woman was caught openly in the act of adultery.

5 And in the law of Moses, he commanded that we stone those who are like these. Therefore, what do **you** say?"

6 They said this tempting him, so that they would have [cause] to accuse him. But Jesus, after he had stooped down, wrote on the ground.

7 And when they continued asking him, he straightened himself and said to them, "Whoever is without sin may throw a stone at her first."

---

[1] Eastern txt: singular *crowd*, also OS (cs):

[2] Fig: erotesis, **lema** questions, vs. 48-49, 51, 52, implied answers "no"

[3] Eastern txt: omit 7:53-8:11, also OS (cs):, some ancient Grk mss and Old Latin. This passage stands after Luke 21:38 in Ferrar group of Greek mss.

ARAMAIC PESHITTA NEW TESTAMENT
JOHN

Chapter 8

8   And again after he had stooped down, he wrote on the ground.

9   And when **they** heard [it], they went out one by one beginning with the elders. And the woman was left by herself, being in the middle.

10   And after Jesus straightened himself, he said to the woman, "Where are they? Does no man condemn you?"

11   And that [one] said, "No man, LORD." And Jesus said, "Neither do **I** condemn you. Go and from now on, do not sin again."

12   Now again Jesus spoke to them and said, "^{me}I am the light of the world. He who follows me will not walk in ^mdarkness, but he will find for himself the ^mlight of life."

13   The Pharisees said to him, "**You** testify concerning yourself. Your testimony is not true."[1]

14   Jesus answered and said to them, "Even if **I** testify concerning myself, my testimony is true, because I know from where I came and to where I am going. But **you** do not know from where I came or to where I am going.

15   **You** judge according to the ^{sy}flesh. I do not judge anyone.

16   Yet now if I do judge, my judgment is true, because I am not alone. But rather, I and my Father who sent me ^e[judge].[2]

17   And now in your law it is written that the testimony of two men is true.

18   I am [one] who testifies concerning myself and my Father who sent me testifies concerning me."

19   They said to him, "Where is your father?" Jesus answered and said to them, "You know neither me nor my Father. If you would know me, you would also know my Father."

20   He spoke these words [in] the treasury while he taught in the temple. And no one arrested him, for his ^{sy}hour had not yet come.

21   Again Jesus said to them, "**I** will go and you will seek me and you will die in your sins. And where **I** am going, **you** are not able to come."

22   The Judeans said, "Will he perhaps kill himself?"[3] because he said, "Where **I** am going, **you** are not able to come."

23   And he said to them, "**You** are from below and I am from above. **You** are from this world. I am not from this world.

---

[1] Same root: *testify, testimony*, repeat throughout vs. 13-18
[2] Repeat same root: *judge, judgment*, vs. 15, 16
[3] Fig: erotesis, **lema** question, implied answer "yes"

Chapter 8

24 I told you that you will die in your sins, for unless you believe that I am [he], you will die in your sins."

25 The Judeans said, "Who are you?" Jesus said to them, "Although I have [just] begun to speak to you,

26 I have much to say and to judge against you, but he who sent me is true and those [things] that I have heard from him, I speak in the world."

27 And they did not know that he spoke to them about the Father.

28 Jesus said to them again, "When you have ᵉᵘlifted up the Son of Man, then you will know that I am [he] and [that] I did not do anything of my own will, but as my Father has taught me, so I speak.

29 And he who sent me is with me and my Father does not leave me alone, because I always do that which pleases him."

30 While he was speaking these [things], many believed in him.

31 And Jesus said to those Judeans who believed in him, "If you will remain in my word, you [are] truly my disciples.

32 And you will know the truth and that truth will set you free."

33 They said to him, "We [are] the seed of Abraham and bondage has not ever been served by us to anyone. How can you say, 'You will be free men?'"

34 Jesus said to them, "*Truly, truly I say to you, everyone who commits sin is the servant of sin.[1]

35 And a servant does not remain in the house forever, but the Son remains forever.

36 Therefore, if the Son should free you, you will truly be free men.

37 I know that you [are] the seed of Abraham, but you are seeking to kill me, because you do not empty yourselves ᵉ[to make room] for my word.

38 What I have seen with my Father, I speak, and what you have seen with your father, you do."

39 They answered and said to him, "Our father is Abraham." Jesus said to them, "If you were the children of Abraham, you would do the works of Abraham.

40 But now, *behold, you are seeking to kill me, a man who has spoken the truth with you, that which I have heard from God. Abraham did not do this,

---

[1] Same root: *commits, servant*, OS (s): omit *of sin*, agrees with Codex Bezae.

Chapter 8

41 but **you** are doing the works of your father." They said to him, "**We** were not [born] of fornication. We have one Father, God."

42 Jesus said to them, "If God was your Father, you would love me, for **I** have gone out and I have come from God and it was not of my own will, but rather he sent me.

43 Why do you not understand my word concerning [this]? Because you are not able to hear my word.

44 **You** are from [your] father, the ACCUSER.[1] And you desire to do the lust of your father, he who from the beginning killed men and he [who] does not stand in the truth, because he has no truth. When he speaks a lie, he speaks from himself, because he [is] a liar, even its originator.[2]

45 Now because **I** speak the truth, you do not believe me.

46 Which of you rebukes me concerning sin? And if I speak the truth, why do **you** not believe me?[3]

47 He who is of God hears the words of God. Because of this, **you** do not hear, because you are not of God." [4]

48 The Judeans answered and said to him, "Did we not well say that you are a Samaritan and you have a devil?"

49 Jesus said to them, "I do not have a devil. But rather, I honor my Father and you curse me.

50 And **I** do not seek my [own] glory. There is one who seeks [it] and judges.

51 *Truly, truly I say to you, he who keeps my word will not [h]see death forever."

52 The Judeans said to him, "Now we know that you have a devil. Abraham and the prophets died and **you** say, 'Whoever keeps my word will not [h]taste death forever.'

53 Are you greater than our father Abraham who died and the prophets who died?[5] Whom do you make yourself?"

54 Jesus said to them "If **I** praise myself, my praise is nothing. My Father is the one who praises me, [of] whom you say, 'He is our God.'

---

[1] OS (s): *father the Accuser* is 'the evil one'

[2] Lit: the father of it

[3] Fig: erotesis – question to ponder

[4] Parallel structure: ABBA

[5] Fig: erotesis, **lema** question, implied answer

Chapter 8

55 And you do not know him, but **I** know him. And if I say that I do not know him, I would be a liar like you. But I know him and I keep his word.

56 Abraham, your father, was longing to see my ^{sy}day and he saw [it] and rejoiced."

57 The Judeans said to him, "You are not yet fifty years old and you have seen Abraham?"[1]

58 Jesus said to them, "*Truly, truly I say to you, before Abraham was, I was."

59 And they took up rocks to stone him, yet Jesus hid himself and went away from the temple and passed among them and left.

Chapter 9

1 And as he passed by, he saw a man who was blind from the womb of his mother.

2 And his disciples asked him and said, "Our Master, who sinned, this [man] or his parents, that he was born being blind?"

3 Jesus said to them, "He did not sin, nor his parents, but that the works of God may be seen in him.

4 It is necessary for me to work the works[2] of him who sent me while it is day. The night will come when no one will be able to serve.

5 As long as I am in the world, ^{me}I am the light of the world."

6 And while he said these [things], he spat on the ground and formed clay from his saliva and he rubbed [it] on the eyes of that blind man.

7 And he said to him, "Go [and] wash in the pool of Siloam." And he went [and] washed and he came seeing.

8 Now his neighbors and those who previously had seen him begging were saying, "Is this [man] not he who was sitting and begging?"

9 [There were] some who were saying, "This was he," yet [others] who were saying, "No, but he really resembles[3] him." Now he said, "I am [he]."

10 They said to him, "How were your eyes opened?"

---

[1] OS (s): 'has Abraham seen you?'

[2] Same root: *work, works*

[3] Fig: polyptoton, lit: resembling, he resembles

Chapter 9

11 He answered and said to them, "A man whose name is Jesus made clay and rubbed [it] on me, on my eyes, and said to me, "Go [and] wash in the water of Siloam." And I went, I washed and I began to see.[1]

12 They said to him, "Where is he?" He said to them, "I do not know."

13 And they brought him who previously was blind to the Pharisees.

14 Now it was the SABBATH when Jesus made the clay and opened his eyes for him.

15 And again the Pharisees asked him, "How did you begin to see?" And he said to them, "He placed clay on my eyes and I washed and I began to see."

16 And some of the Pharisees were saying, "This man is not from God, who does not keep the SABBATH." But others were saying, "How is a man [who is] a sinner able to do these miracles?" And there was division among them.

17 Again they said to that blind man, "What do **you** say about him who opened your eyes for you?" He said to them, "**I** say that he is a prophet."

18 But the Judeans did not believe that he was blind and [then] saw, until they called the parents of him who saw.

19 And they asked them, "Is this your son whom **you** say was born being blind? How does he now see?"

20 Now his parents answered and said, "We know that this is our son and that he was born being blind,

21 but how he now sees or who opened his eyes for him, we do not know. Indeed, he is of age. Ask him. He will speak for himself."

22 His parents said these [things], because they were afraid of the Judeans, for the Judeans had decided that if anyone would confess him, that he was the MESSIAH, they would put him out of the synagogue.

23 Because of this, his parents said, "He is of age. Ask him."

24 And they called the man who was blind a second time and said to him, "Give glory to God, for we know that this man is a sinner."

25 He answered and said to them, "If he is a sinner, I do not know, but one [thing] I do know, I was blind and now, *behold, I see."

26 Again they said to him, "What did he do to you? How did he open your eyes for you?"

---

[1] Lit: it was seen by me, or, it appeared to me

Chapter 9

27 He said to them, "I told you and you did not hear. What do you want
to hear again? Do you also want to become his disciples?"[1]

28 And they reviled him and said to him, "You are his disciple, but we
are disciples of Moses.

29 And we know that God spoke with Moses, but this [man], we do not
know from where he is."

30 That man answered and said to them, "In this there is therefore
[something] to be amazed at, because **you** do not know from where he is,
yet he opened my eyes.

31 Now we know that God does not hear the voice of sinners, but
whoever fears him and does his will, he hears.

32 Never before has it been heard that anyone has opened the eyes of
one who was born blind.

33 If this [man] was not from God, he would not be able to do this."

34 They answered and said to him, "You were born entirely in sins, yet
you teach us?" And they put him out.

35 And Jesus heard that they had put him out and he found him and said
to him, "Do **you** believe in the Son of God?"[2]

36 That one who was healed answered and said, "Who is he, my Lord,
that I may believe in him?"

37 Jesus said to him, "You have seen him and he who speaks with you
is him."

38 And he said, "I believe, my Lord." And he fell down [and]
worshipped him.

39 And Jesus said, "I have come for the judgment of this world, so that
those who do not see may see and those who see may become blind."

40 And those of the Pharisees who were with him heard these [things]
and said to him, "Are we also blind?"[3]

41 Jesus said to them, "If you were [only] blind, you would have no
sin." But now you say, "We see. Because of this, your sin is established."

---

[1] Fig: erotesis, **lema** question, obvious answer "no"

[2] OS (s): 'man'

[3] Fig: erotesis, **lema** question, obvious answer "no"

Chapter 10

1 ^{pb}*Truly, truly, I say to you, whoever does not enter the sheepfold of the flock by the gate,[1] but climbs up by another place, that [man] is a thief and a robber.

2 But he who enters by the gate is the shepherd of the flock,

3 and for this [man], the keeper of the gate opens the gate. And the flock hears his voice and he calls his sheep by their names and leads them out.

4 And when he leads out his flock, he goes before it and his sheep follow him, because they know his voice.

5 Now the flock will not follow a stranger, but rather it flees from him, because it does not know the voice of a stranger."┐

6 Jesus told them this parable, but they did not understand what he said to them.

7 Now again Jesus said to them, "*Truly, truly I say to you, ^{me}I am the gate of the flock.

8 And all ^{me}those who come are thieves and robbers, unless the flock hears them.

9 ^{me}I am the gate and if anyone should enter by me, he will live. And he will enter and he will go out and find pasture.[2]

10 A thief does not come, except to steal and to kill and to destroy. I have come that they may have life and [that] they may have that which is abundant.

11 ^{me}I am the good shepherd. A good shepherd lays down his life on behalf of his flock.

12 But a hired servant, who is not the shepherd nor are the sheep his, when he sees a wolf coming, leaves the flock and flees. And the wolf comes [and] plunders and scatters the flock.

13 Now a hired servant flees, because he is a hired servant and he does not care about the flock.

14 ^{me}I am the good shepherd and I know my own and I am known by my own,

15 as my Father knows me and I know my Father and I lay down my life on behalf of the flock.[3]

---

[1] Word play: *sheepfold* **tira** ܛܝܪܐ *gate* **tera** ܬܪܥܐ

[2] Same root: *shepherd, find pasture*, for further study about shepherds, see Van-Lennep, *Bible Lands,* p. 185; Mackie, *Bible Manners and Customs*, pp. 33-34.

[3] Repeat phrase, *I lay down my life on behalf of the flock,* from v. 11

Chapter 10

16 Now I also have other sheep, those that are not from this sheepfold, and it is also necessary for me to bring them. And they will hear my voice and all the flock will become one and [have] one shepherd.

17 Because of this, my Father loves me, because I lay down my life that I may take it up again.

18 No one takes it away from me, but rather I lay it down by my [own] will, for I have authority to lay it down and I have authority to take it up again, for I have received this command from my Father."

19 And again there was division among the Judeans, because of these words.

20 And many of them were saying, "He has a devil and is quite insane.[1] Why do you listen to him?"

21 But others were saying, "These are not the words of a possessed [man]. Is a devil able to open the eyes of a blind man?"[2]

22 Now the feast of dedication[3] was in Jerusalem and it was winter.

23 And Jesus was walking in the temple, in the porch of Solomon.

24 And the Judeans gathered around him and said to him, "How long will you keep us [waiting]?[4] If you are the MESSIAH, tell us openly."

25 Jesus answered and said to them, "I told you and you do not believe and the works that I do in the name of my Father testify about me.

26 But **you** do not believe, because you are not of my sheep, as I said to you.

27 My sheep hear my voice ᴾand I know them and they follow me.

28 And I give them eternal life and they will not be destroyed forever and no one will seize them out of my ᵐhands.⌐

29 For my Father who gave [them] to me is greater than all and no one is able to seize [them] out of the ᵐhand of my Father.

30 I and my Father are one."

31 And again the Judeans took up rocks to stone him.

32 Jesus said to them, "I have shown you many good works from my Father. Because of which work of them do you stone me?"

33 The Judeans said to him, "We do not stone you because of the good works, but rather because you have blasphemed, and being a man, you make yourself God."

---

[1] Fig: polyptoton, lit: "being insane, is insane"
[2] Fig: erotesis, **lema** question, obvious answer "no"
[3] OS (s): feast called 'Honor of the Sanctuary'
[4] Lit: will you take our breath (souls)

Chapter 10

34 Jesus said to them, "Is it not so written in your law: I HAVE SAID, YOU ARE GODS?

35 If he called those [people] gods, because the word of God was with them and the scripture is not able to be broken,

36 to him whom the Father made holy and sent to the world do you say, 'You blaspheme,' because I told you that I [am] the Son of God?

37 Unless I do the works of my Father, do not believe me.

38 But if I do, even if you do not believe me, believe the works, that you may know and believe that my Father [is] in me and I [am] in my Father."

39 And they were seeking to arrest him again, yet he escaped from their ᵐhands.[1]

40 And he went to the crossing of the Jordan, to the place where John had been previously when he was baptizing and he stayed there.

41 And many men came to him and were saying, "John did not even do one sign, but everything that John said about this man is true."

42 And many believed in him.

Chapter 11

1 Now there was a certain [man] who was sick, Lazarus from the town [of] Bethany, the brother of Mary and Martha.

2 And it was this Mary who anointed the feet of Jesus with perfume and wiped [them] with her hair.[2] Lazarus who was sick was the brother of this [one].

3 And his two sisters sent to Jesus and said, "Our Lord, *behold, he whom you love is sick."

4 Now Jesus said, "This sickness is not to death, but rather for the glory of God, so that the Son of God may be glorified because of him."

5 Now Jesus loved Martha and Mary and Lazarus.

6 And when he heard that he was sick, he remained in the place that he was [for] two days.

7 And afterwards he said to his disciples, "Come, let us go again to Judea."

8 His disciples said to him, "Our Master, the Judeans now are seeking to stone you and you are going there again?"

---

[1] Lit: from between their hands

[2] Could be fig: parenthesis, about Mary, because this had not happened yet.

Chapter 11

9 Jesus said to them, ^{pb}"Are [there] not twelve hours in a day? And if a man walks in the day he will not stumble, because he sees the light of this world.

10 But if a man should walk in the night, he will stumble, because he has no illumination."[1]

11 These [things] Jesus said and afterward he said to them, "Lazarus, our friend, sleeps, but I am going to wake[2] him."

12 His disciples said to him, "Our Lord, if he sleeps, he will be healed."

13 But **Jesus** spoke about his death, yet they thought that he spoke about sleeping on a bed.[3]

14 Then Jesus said to them plainly, "Lazarus has died.

15 And I rejoice that I was not there for your sakes, so that you may believe. But let us walk there."

16 [Then] Thomas, who was called the Twin, said to his fellow disciples, "Let us also go [and] die with him."

17 And Jesus came to Bethany and found him to have been in the tomb for four days.

18 Now Bethany was near to Jerusalem, being about fifteen furlongs away from it.

19 And many of the Judeans were coming to Martha and Mary to comfort their heart[s] because of their brother.

20 And Martha, when she had heard that Jesus had come, went out to meet him, but Mary was sitting in the house.

21 And Martha said to Jesus, "My Lord, if only you would have been here, my brother would not have died.

22 But even now, I know that whatever you ask God he will give to you."

23 Jesus said to her, "Your brother will rise up."

24 Martha said to him, "I know that he will rise up in the resurrection in the last ^{sy}day."

---

[1] Word play: *light* (v. 9), **nuhra** ܢܘܗܪܐ *illumination*, **nahira** ܢܗܝܪܐ, same root.

[2] Or "resurrect"

[3] Three different words: *sleeps* v. 11, can mean "died", *sleeps* v. 12, *sleeping on a bed,* v. 13 refers to natural sleep, clarifying what is meant.

Chapter 11

25 Jesus said to her, ""^{me}I am the ^{he}resurrection and the life.[1] He who believes in me, even if he should die, will live.

26 And everyone who is alive and believes in me will not ever die. Do you believe this?"

27 She said to him, "Yes, my Lord. I am a believer that you are the MESSIAH, the Son of God, who has come into the world."

28 And when she had said these [things], she went [and] called Mary her sister secretly and said to her, "Our Master has come and calls for you."

29 And Mary, when she heard [it], rose up quickly and came to him.

30 Now **Jesus** had not yet come into the village, but was in that place that he met Martha.

31 And those Judeans also who were with her in the house, who were comforting her, when they saw Mary, that she quickly rose [and] went out, followed her. For they thought that she was going to the grave to weep.

32 But **Mary**, when she came [to] where Jesus was and saw him, fell down at his feet and said to him, "If only you had been here, my Lord, my brother would not have died."

33 And when Jesus saw her weeping and those Judeans who had come with her who were weeping, he groaned in his spirit[2] and was moved [in] his soul.

34 And he said, "Where have you laid him?" And they said to him, "Our Lord, come [and] see."

35 And the tears of Jesus came.

36 And the Judeans were saying, "See how much he loved him."

37 Now some of them said, "Was not this [one] able, who opened the eyes of that blind man, to do ^e[something], so that this [man] would not have died also?"

38 And Jesus, groaning in himself, came to the tomb. And that tomb was a cave and a stone was placed on its entrance.

39 And Jesus said, "Take away this stone." Martha, the sister of that dead man, said to him, "My Lord, he already stinks, for it is the fourth day."

---

[1] Fig: hendiadys, "resurrected one who brings life"
[2] Or "was deeply moved in his spirit", see Black, pp. 240-243.

Chapter 11

40 Jesus said to her, "Did I not tell you that if you would believe, you would see the glory of God?"

41 And they took away that stone and Jesus raised up his eyes and said, "Father, I thank you that you have heard me.

42 And **I** know that you always hear me, but because of this crowd that stands [here] I have said these [things], so that they will believe that you have sent me."

43 And when he had said these [things], he cried out with a loud voice, "Lazarus, come outside."

44 And that dead man came out, his hands and feet being bound in swathing and his face bound in burial cloth. Jesus said to them, "Untie him and allow [him] to go."

45 And many of the Judeans who had come with Mary, when they saw what Jesus had done, believed in him.

46 And some of them went to the Pharisees and told them what Jesus had done.

47 And the chief priests and the Pharisees were gathered together and were saying, "What will we do? For this man does many signs,

48 and if we allow him [to continue] like this, all men will believe in him and the Romans will come [and] take away our land and our nation."

49 But one of them, whose name [was] Caiaphas, was the high priest for that year and he said to them, "**You** do not know anything.

50 And do you not realize that it is better for us that one man should die for the nation, than [that] the whole nation should be destroyed?"

51 Now he did not say this from his own will. But because he was the high priest for that year, he prophesied that Jesus was going to die for the nation,

52 and not only for the nation, but that he should also gather together into one the sons of God who are scattered.

53 And from that day, they decided to kill him.

54 Now **Jesus** did not walk openly among the Judeans, but he went from there to a place that was near the wilderness, to a walled city that was called Ephraim. And there he was staying with his disciples.

55 Now the Passover of the Judeans was near. And many from the villages went up to Jerusalem before the feast to purify themselves.

56 And they were seeking Jesus and were saying one to another in the temple, "What do you think? Will he not come to the feast?"[1]

---

[1] Fig: erotesis, "not" question, answer in the affirmative

Chapter 11

57 Now the chief priests and the Pharisees had commanded that if anyone knew where he was, he should show [it] to them, so that they could arrest him.

Chapter 12

1   Now six days before the Passover, Jesus came to Bethany where Lazarus was, whom Jesus had raised from the dead.

2   And they[1] made a dinner for him there and Martha was serving and Lazarus was one of the guests who [were] with him.

3   And Mary took an alabaster vase of perfume of the best spikenard, very expensive, and anointed the feet of Jesus and wiped his feet with her hair and the house was filled with the smell of the perfume.

4   And Judas Iscariot, one of his disciples, he who was about to betray him, said,

5   "Why was this oil not sold for three hundred denarii and given to the poor?"[2]

6   Now he said this, not because he cared for the poor, but because he was a thief and the bag was with him and he was carrying whatever fell into it.

7   But Jesus said, "Leave her. She has kept it for the day of my burial,

8   for you always have the poor with you, but you do not always have me."

9   And large crowds of the Judeans heard that Jesus was there and came, not because of Jesus alone, but also to see Lazarus who was raised from the dead.

10 And the chief priests were thinking that they should also kill Lazarus,

11 because many of the Judeans, on account of him, went away and were believing in Jesus.

12 And on the next day a large crowd that had come to the feast, when they heard that Jesus was coming to Jerusalem,

13 took branches of palm trees and went out to meet him. And they were crying out and saying: HOSANNA, **BLESSED IS HE WHO COMES IN THE NAME OF THE** LORD, **THE KING OF ISRAEL.**

14 And Jesus found a donkey and sat on it, as it was written:[3]

---

[1] OS (s): 'one' or 'he'
[2] Fig: erotesis, **lema** question, implied answer "yes, it should have been"
[3] OS (s): add 'by Zechariah the prophet'

Chapter 12

15 DO NOT FEAR, DAUGHTER OF ZION. *BEHOLD, YOUR KING COMES TO YOU AND IS MOUNTED ON A COLT, THE FOAL OF A DONKEY.

16 Now these [things] his disciples did not understand at that time, but when Jesus was glorified, his disciples remembered that these [things] were written about him and [that] they had done these [things] to him.

17 And the crowd that was with him was bearing testimony that he had called Lazarus from the grave and raised him from the dead.

18 And because of this, large crowds went out to meet him, because they heard that he had done this sign.

19 Now the Pharisees were saying to each other, "Do you see that you do not gain anything? For *behold, the whole ˢʸworld goes after him."

20 And there were also some of the Gentiles,¹ men among them who had gone up to worship at the feast.

21 These [men] came [and] drew near to Philip who [was] from Bethsaida of Galilee and asked him and said to him, "My lord, we want to see Jesus."

22 And Philip came and told Andrew and Andrew and Philip told Jesus.

23 And Jesus answered and said to them, "The ˢʸhour has come for the Son of Man to be glorified.

24 *Truly, truly I say to you, ᵃˡa grain of wheat, except it fall and die in the ground, remains alone. But if it dies, it will produce much fruit.²ꓶ

25 He who loves his life will lose it, and he who hates his life in this world will keep it to eternal life.

26 If anyone serves me, he should follow me. And wherever I am, there will my servant be also. He who serves me, the Father will honor him.

27 Now *behold, my soul is troubled. And what do I say, 'My Father, deliver me from this ˢʸhour?' On the contrary, because of this, I have come to this ˢʸhour.

28 ᵉ[I will say] 'Father, glorify your name.'" And a voice was heard from heaven, "I have glorified [it] and again I will glorify [it]."

29 And the crowd that was standing by heard [it] and said, "It was thunder." But others said, "An angel spoke with him."

30 Jesus answered and said to them, "This voice was not for me, but it was for you.

---

¹ OS (s): 'Arameans'
² Word play: *dies* **mita** ꝏꞙ *produces* **mitya** ꝏꞙ

ARAMAIC PESHITTA NEW TESTAMENT
JOHN

Chapter 12

31 Now is the judgment of this world. Now the ruler of this world is cast outside.

32 And when I am ^{pr}lifted up from the earth, I will draw all men to me."

33 And this he said to show by what death he would die.[1]

34 The crowds said to him, "We have heard from the law that the MESSIAH remains forever. How do you say that the Son of Man is going to be ^{pr}lifted up? Who is this Son of Man?"[2]

35 Jesus said to them, ^{al}"The light is with you a little while longer. Walk while you have light, so that the darkness will not overtake you. And he who walks in darkness does not know to where he goes.

36 While you have the light, believe in the light that you may become sons of light." Jesus spoke these [things] and went [and] hid from them.

37 And although he did all these miracles before them, they did not believe in him,

38 that the word of Isaiah the prophet would be fulfilled, who said: MY LORD, WHO HAS BELIEVED OUR REPORT AND TO WHOM HAS THE ARM OF THE LORD BEEN REVEALED?

39 Because of this, they were not able to believe, because again Isaiah said:

40 THEY HAVE BLINDED THEIR EYES AND HAVE DARKENED THEIR HEART[S], SO THAT THEY WOULD NOT SEE WITH THEIR EYES AND WOULD UNDERSTAND WITH THEIR HEART[S] AND WOULD REPENT AND I WOULD HEAL THEM.[3]

41 These [things] Isaiah said, when he saw his glory and spoke about him.

42 Now many of the rulers also believed in him, but because of the Pharisees, they did not confess [him], lest they should be [put] out of the synagogue,

43 for they loved the praise of men more than the praise of God.

44 Now Jesus cried out and said, "He who believes in me does not believe in me, but in him who sent me.

45 And he who sees me, sees him who sent me.

---

[1] Same root: *death, die*

[2] For further study regarding the attitude of the Rabbis about the Messiah, see Edersheim, *Sketches of Jewish Social Life*, pp. 63-70.

[3] Parallel structure: ABABC

Chapter 12

46 I have come [as] a ^mlight to the world that all who believe in me would not remain in ^mdarkness.

47 And he who hears my words, yet does not keep them, I do not judge, for I did not come to judge the world, but to give life to the world.

48 He who rejects me and does not receive my words, there is something that judges him. The word that I speak will judge[1] him in the last ^{sy}day,

49 because I do not speak from myself, but rather the Father who sent me gave me a command, what I [should] say and what I [should] speak.

50 And I know that his command is eternal life. Therefore, these [things] that I speak, as my Father told me, so I speak."[2]

Chapter 13

1 Now before the Feast of the Passover, Jesus knew that the ^{sy}hour had arrived that he would go out of this world to his Father. And he loved his own who were in this world and he loved them until the end.

2 And when it was supper, it was placed by SATAN in the heart of Judas, the son of Simon Iscariot, that he should betray him.

3 And Jesus, because he knew that the Father had given everything into his ^mhands and that he had proceeded from God and was going to God,

4 rose up from the supper and lay aside his garments and took a cloth [and] girded his loins.

5 And he poured water into a bowl and began to wash the feet of his disciples and he was wiping [them] with the cloth that girded his loins.

6 Now when he came to Simon Peter, Simon said to him, "My Lord, do **you** wash my feet for me?"

7 Jesus answered and said to him, "What I am doing **you** do not understand now, but afterwards you will understand."

8 Simon Peter said to him, "You will not ever wash my feet for me." Jesus said to him, "Unless I wash you, you have no portion with me."

9 Simon Peter said to him, "Then, my Lord, wash[3] not only my feet for me, but also my hands, even my head."

---

[1] Repeat *judge,* vs. 47-48

[2] Repeat forms of *speak*, vs. 49, 50

[3] Different word for *wash*, not ceremonial cleansing as in v. 5.

ARAMAIC PESHITTA NEW TESTAMENT
JOHN

Chapter 13

10 Jesus said to him, "He who has bathed does not need ᵉ[to wash his whole body], but to only wash his feet, for all of him is clean. Also, all of you are clean, but not all of you."

11 For Jesus knew him who would betray him. Because of this, he said, "Not all of you are clean."

12 And after he had washed their feet, he took up his garments and sat and said to them, "Do you know what I have done to you?

13 **You** call me 'our Master and our Lord' and you speak well, for I am.

14 If therefore I, your Lord and your Master, have washed your feet for you, how much more ought **you** to wash the feet of one another?[1]

15 For I have given you this example, that you should also do as I have done for you.

16 *Truly, truly I say to you, there is no servant who is greater than his lord and there is no[2] apostle who is greater than him who sent him.

17 If you understand these [things], you are blessed if you will do them.

18 I do not speak concerning all of you, for I know those whom I have chosen, but rather [I speak] because the scripture will be fulfilled: HE WHO EATS BREAD WITH ME HAS ᵖʳLIFTED HIS HEEL AGAINST ME.[3]

19 I tell you from now on before it happens, so that when it happens, you will believe that I am [he].

20 *Truly, truly I say to you, he who receives him whom I send receives me, and he who receives me receives him who sent me.

21 Jesus said these [things] and he groaned in his spirit and testified and said, "*Truly, truly I say to you, one of you will betray me."

22 And the disciples looked at each other, because they did not know about whom he spoke.

23 Now there was one of his disciples who was reclining on his bosom, he whom Jesus loved.

24 Simon Peter waved to this [one] that he should ask him who it was about whom he spoke.

25 And that disciple fell on the breast of Jesus and said to him, "My Lord, who is this [man]?"

---

[1] Fig: erotesis, **kema** question, answer in the affirmative
[2] Eastern txt: 'and not'
[3] Semitism: *lifted his heel* means 'to become an enemy'

ARAMAIC PESHITTA NEW TESTAMENT
JOHN

Chapter 13

26 Jesus answered and said, "He [is] the one to whom I give the bread that I dip." And Jesus dipped the bread and gave [it] to Judas, son of Simon Iscariot.

27 And after the bread, then SATAN entered him and Jesus said to him, "What you do, do quickly."

28 Now not one of those guests understood what he said to him.

29 For some thought because Judas had the bag with him that he had expressly commanded[1] him to buy something that was needed for the feast or to give something to the poor.

30 Now **Judas** took the bread immediately and went outside. And it was night when he went out.

31 And Jesus said, "Now the Son of Man is glorified and God is glorified[2] in him.

32 And if God is glorified in him, God also will glorify him in himself and will glorify him at once.

33 My sons, a little while longer I am with you and you will seek me and as I said to the Judeans, 'Where **I** go, **you** are not able to come,' yet even now I say to you.

34 A new commandment I give to you, be loving one to another. As I loved you, you should also love one another.

35 By this everyone will know that you [are] my disciples, if love be among you one toward another."

36 Simon Peter said to him, "Our Lord, where are you going?" Jesus answered and said to him, "Where I go you are not now able to follow me, but you will come ᵉ[after me] at the end."

37 Simon Peter said to him, "My Lord, why am I not able to follow you now? I will lay down my life for you."

38 Jesus said to him, "Will you lay down your life for me? *Truly, truly I say to you, the rooster will not crow until you deny me three times."

Chapter 14

1 "Let your heart not be troubled. Believe in God and believe in me.

2 There are many rooms [in] the house of my Father. And [if] not, I would have told you, for I go to prepare a place for you.

---

[1] Fig: polyptoton, lit: "commanding, he commanded"
[2] Repeat forms of *glorify*, vs. 31, 32

Chapter 14

3   And if I go [and] prepare a place for you, I will come again and I will take you with me, so that where I am you may be also.

4   And to where I go, you know and the way you know."

5   Thomas said to him, "Our Lord, we do not know where you are going and how are we able to know the way?"

6   Jesus said to him, "[me]I am the way and truth and life.[1] No one comes to my Father except by me.

7   If you knew me, you would also know my Father. And from now on, you will know him and you have seen him."

8   Philip said to him, "Our Lord, show us the Father and it will satisfy us."

9   Jesus said to him, "[Have] I [been] with you all this time and you do not know me, Philip? He who sees me sees the Father. And how do **you** say, 'Show us the Father?'

10   Do you not believe that I [am] in my Father and my Father [is] in me? These words that I speak, I do not speak of myself, but my Father who lives in me works these works.

11   Believe that I [am] in my Father and my Father [is] in me. Otherwise, believe also because of the works.

12   *Truly, truly I say to you, whoever believes in me, these works that I do, he also will do and more than these will he do, because **I** go to the Father.[2]

13   And whatever you ask in my name, I will do for you, so that the Father will be glorified by his Son.

14   And if you ask of me in my name, I will do [it].[3]

15   If you love me, keep my commandments.

16   And **I** will ask of my Father and he will give you another Deliverer,[4] who will be with you forever,

17   the Spirit of truth that the world is not able to receive, because it has not seen him and does not know him. But **you** know him, because he lives with you and he [is] in you.

---

[1] Fig: hendiatris, "the true (reliable) and living way (or lit: road)"

[2] Repeat, vs. 9-12: *Father, in me, believe, works, speak*

[3] OS (s): and Pal Syr: omit verse

[4] Root words for the "Comforter" are **peraq** ܦܪܩ deliver, and **leyta** ܠܝܛܐ the curse, meaning "one who ends the curse" or "curse breaker." The Holy Spirit is the deliverer from the curse of Adam on down.

Chapter 14

18 [I will not leave you [as] orphans, for I will come to you in a little while.

19 And the world will not see me, but you will see me. Because I live, you also will live.

20 In that [sy]day you will know that I [am] in my Father and you [are] in me and I [am] in you.

21 He who has my commandments with him and keeps them, that [one] loves me. And he who loves me will be loved by my Father and I will love him and I will show myself to him."

22 Judas, not Iscariot,[1] said to him, "My Lord, why is it you are going to show yourself to us and not to the world?"

23 Jesus answered and said to him, "He who loves me will keep my word and my Father will love him and we[2] will come to him and we will make a dwelling with him.

24 But **he** who does not love me will not keep my word. And this word that you have heard is not mine, but rather of the Father who sent me.

25 I have spoken these [things] with you while I am with you.

26 But that Deliverer, the Holy Spirit, whom my Father will send in my name, will teach you everything and will remind you of all that I said to you.

27 I leave you peace, my own peace I give to you. Not as the world gives, do **I** give to you. Let not your heart[s] be troubled and do not fear.

28 You have heard that I have said to you that I will go [away] and I will come to you. If you love me, you would have rejoiced that I go to my Father, because my Father is greater than I [am].

29 And now, *behold, I have told you before it happens, so that when it happens[3] you will believe.

30 After this, I will not speak many [things] with you, for the [pr]ruler of the world comes and he does not have anything in me.

31 But that the world may know that I love my Father and as my Father has commanded me, so I do. Rise up, let us go from here.

---

[1] OS (s): 'Thomas', Eusebius says that Thomas' name was Judas Thomas (i,13).
[2] OS (c): 'I'
[3] Repeat *happens*, or lit: is

ARAMAIC PESHITTA NEW TESTAMENT
JOHN

Chapter 15

1   [me]I am the [an]vine of truth and my Father is the vine-dresser.[1]

2   [al]Every branch that is on me [that] does not bear fruit he takes away. And that which bears fruit, he prunes, so that it may produce much fruit.

3   You are pruned already, because of the word that I have spoken with you.

4   Remain in me and I [e][will remain] in you. As the branch is not able to produce fruit of itself, unless it will remain in the vine, so neither [e][will] you, unless you remain in me.[2]

5   [me]I am the vine and you [are] the branches. He who remains in me and I in him, this [one] will bring much [m]fruit, because without me you are not able to do anything.

6   Now except a man remains in me, he is thrown outside [s]like a branch that has withered and they gather and place it in the fire that it may burn.

7   But if you remain in me and my words remain in you, whatever you want to ask, you will have.

8   In this the Father is glorified, that you bear much [m]fruit and be my disciples.⌐

9   As my Father has loved me, so also I have loved you. Remain in my compassion.

10 If you keep my commandments, you will remain in my love, as I have kept the commandments of my Father and remain in his love.

11 These [things] I have spoken with you, so that my joy would be in you and [that] your joy would be made full.

12 This is my commandment, that you love one another as I have loved you.

13 There is no love that is greater than this, that a man would lay down his life for[3] his friends.

14 You are my friends, if you do all that I command you.

15 No longer do I call you servants, because a servant does not know what his lord does, but I have called you my friends, because everything that I have heard from my Father I have made known to you.

---

[1] Lit: worker or cultivator
[2] Repeat *remain*, vs. 4-10
[3] Lit: on behalf of, for the sake of

Chapter 15

16 **You** did not choose me, but **I** have chosen you and I have appointed you that you also should go [and] bear ^mfruit and [that] your ^mfruit should remain, so that whatever you ask of my Father in my name, he will give to you.

17 These [things] I command you, that you should love one another.

18 And if the world hates you, know that it hated me before you.

19 Now if you are of the world, the world would love its own. But you are not of the world, for **I** have chosen you out of the world. Because of this, the world hates you.

20 Remember the saying that I told you, 'There is no servant who is greater than his lord.' If they persecute me, they will also persecute you. And if they keep my word, they will also keep yours.

21 But all these [things] they will do to you because of my name, because they do not know him who sent me.

22 If **I** had not come [and] spoken with them, they would have no sin. But now they have no excuse for their sin.[1]

23 He who hates me also hates my Father.

24 And if I had not done deeds before their eyes that another man did not do, they would have no sin. But now they have seen and have hated both me and also my Father,

25 that the word that is written in their law would be fulfilled: THEY HATED ME WITHOUT A CAUSE.

26 Now when the Deliverer comes, whom **I** will send to you from my Father, the Spirit of truth who has proceeded from my Father, he will testify about me.

27 **You** also will testify, because you [were] with me from the beginning.[2]

Chapter 16

1 These [things] I have spoken with you, so that you will not be offended.

2 For they will put you out of their synagogues and the ^{sy}hour will come when all who kill you will think that he offers an offering[3] to God.

---

[1] Lit: for the face of their sin

[2] Repeat *testify*, vs. 26, 27. See note on *Deliverer*, John 14:16.

[3] Same root: *offer, offering*

Chapter 16

3   And they will do these [things], because they do not know either my Father or me.[1]

4   These [things] I have spoken with you, so that when their time has come, you will remember that I told you. Now I did not tell you these [things] previously, because I was with you.

5   But now I go to him who sent me, yet not one of you asks me, 'Where are you going?'

6   For I have told you these [things] and sorrow has come and filled your hearts.

7   But *I tell you the truth, it is profitable for you that I go, for if **I** do not go, the Deliverer will not come to you. But if [I] go, I will send him to you.

8   And when he has come, he will reprove the ˢʸworld concerning sin and concerning justification and concerning[2] judgment--

9   concerning sin, because they do not believe in me,

10   and concerning justification, because I go to my Father and you will not see me again,

11   and concerning judgment, because the ruler of this world is judged.[3]

12   Again, I have much to say to you, but you are not able to accept [it] now.

13   But when the Spirit of truth comes, he will lead you into all truth, for he will not speak of his own mind. But everything that he hears, he will speak and he will make known to you future [things].

14   And he will glorify me, because he will receive from me and will show [it] to you.

15   Everything that belongs to my Father is mine. Because of this, I have told you that he will receive from me and will show [it] to you.

16   A little while and you will not see me and again a little while and you will see me, because I go to the Father."

17   And his disciples said to one another, "What is this that he tells us, 'A little while and you will not see me and again a little while[4] and you will see me,' and, 'I go to my Father?'"

18   And they were saying, "What is this little while that he spoke of? We do not understand what he says."

---

[1] OS (s): omit whole verse

[2] Repeat *concerning*, also vs. 9-11

[3] Same root: *judgment, judged*

[4] Repeat *a little while*, also vs. 18, 19

ARAMAIC PESHITTA NEW TESTAMENT
JOHN

Chapter 16

19 Now Jesus knew that they wanted to ask him and he said to them, "Are you questioning each other about this, because I said to you, 'A little while and you will not see me and again a little while and you will see me'?

20 *Truly, truly I say to you, you will weep and you will mourn, yet the world will rejoice. And you will have sadness, but your sorrow will become joy.

21 A woman, when she gives birth, has sadness, because the ˢʸday of her birthing has come. But when she has given birth to a son, she does not remember her ordeal, because of the joy that a man has been born into the world.

22 You also now have sadness, but I will see you again and your heart[s] will rejoice and no one will take your joy from you.[1]

23 And in that ˢʸday you will not ask me anything. *Truly, truly I say to you, everything that you ask of my Father in my name, he will give to you.

24 Until now you have not asked for anything in my name. Ask and you will receive, so that your joy may be full.

25 These [things] I have spoken with you with comparisons. But the ˢʸhour comes when I will not speak to you with comparisons, but I will openly make known to you about the Father.

26 In that ˢʸday, you will ask in my name and I will not say to you that I will ask the Father for you.

27 For the Father loves you, because you have loved me and you have believed that I proceeded from before God.[2]

28 I proceeded from before the Father and came to the world and again I will leave the world and I will go to the Father."

29 His disciples were saying to him, "*Behold, now you speak clearly and you do not speak one comparison.

30 Now we know that you know everything and have no need of a man to ask you.[3] In this we believe that you proceeded from God."

31 Jesus said to them, "Believe,

---

[1] Parallel structure: opposites, ABAB, vs. 20-22; same root: *sorrow, have sadness*, and *joy, rejoice*

[2] Eastern txt: 'the Father'

[3] OS (s): *have no...you* is 'and do not need that you should ask any man'

270

Chapter 16

32 for *behold, the ^{sy}hour comes and now has come, when you will be scattered, [each] man to his place and you will leave me alone. Yet I will not be alone, because the Father is with me.

33 These [things] I have told you, so that you may have peace about me. In the world you will have affliction, but take courage, **I** have conquered the world."

Chapter 17

1 These [things] Jesus spoke and he raised his eyes to heaven and said, "My Father, the ^{sy}hour has come. Glorify your Son, so that your Son may glorify you.[1]

2 According as you have given him authority over all ^{sy}flesh, to whomever you have given him, he will give eternal life.

3 Now this is eternal life, that they will know you, that you alone are the God of truth and he whom you have sent [is] Jesus the MESSIAH.

4 I have glorified you on the earth. The work that you gave me to do I have completed.

5 And now, my Father, glorify me with you with that glory that I had with you before the world was.

6 I have made known your name to the men whom you gave to me from the ^{sy}world. They were yours and you gave them to me and they have kept your word.

7 Now I know that whatever you gave me was from before you,

8 for the words that you gave me, I gave to them and they received [them] and they know truly that I have proceeded from before you and they believe that you sent me.

9 And **I** pray for them. I do not pray for the ^{sy}world, but for those whom you gave me, because they are yours.

10 And everything that is mine is yours and yours is mine and I am glorified by them.

11 From now on, I will not be in the world, yet these are in the world and **I** am coming to you, holy Father. Keep them in your name, [those] whom you gave me, so that they be one as we [are].

12 While I was with them in the world, **I** have kept them in your name. Those whom you gave me, I have kept and not one of them is lost, except for the ^{pr}son of destruction, that the scripture would be fulfilled.

---

[1] Repeat *glorify, glory,* vs. 1-10

Chapter 17

13 But now I come to you. And these [things] I speak in the world, so that my joy will be full in them.

14 **I** have given them your word and the ^{sy}world hates them, because they are not of the world, as **I** am not of the world.

15 I do not pray that you should take them from the world, but that you would keep them from the Evil [one],

16 for they are not of the world, as **I** am not of the world.

17 Father, set them apart by your truth, for your word is truth.

18 As you sent me into the world, so also I send them into the world.

19 And for their sakes I set myself apart, so that they also may be set apart in truth.[1]

20 And I do not pray for the sake of these only, but also for the sake of those who will believe in me through their word,

21 so that all of them may be one as you [are], my Father in me and I in you, so that they also may be one in us, so that the world may believe that **you** have sent me.[2]

22 And the glory that you gave me, **I** gave to them, so that they may be one as we are one,

23 I in them and you in me, that they be perfected into one, and that the world may know that **you** have sent me and that you have loved them, as also you have loved me.

24 Father, I desire that those whom you gave me may also be with me where I am, so that they may see my glory that you gave me, because you loved me from before the foundations of the world.

25 My upright Father, the world has not known you, but **I** know you and they know that **you** sent me.

26 And I have made known your name to them and I will make [it] known, so that the love [with] which you loved me will be in them and I will be in them."

Chapter 18

1 These [things] Jesus spoke and he went out with his disciples to the other side of the brook of Kidron, a place that had a garden, where he entered, he and his disciples.

---

[1] Repeat *send, set apart*, also v. 18

[2] Repeat, vs. 21-26, *you have sent me, you gave me, you loved me, one*

Chapter 18

2   Now Judas, the betrayer, also knew that location, because Jesus had gathered there many times with his disciples.

3   Therefore, **Judas** took a company of soldiers and he took guards from the chief priests and the Pharisees and came there with torches [P]and lamps and weapons.⌐

4   Now Jesus, because he knew everything that was coming concerning him, went out and said to them, "Whom do you seek?"

5   They said to him, "Jesus, the Nazarene." Jesus said to them, "I am [he]." Now Judas, the betrayer, was also standing with them.

6   And when Jesus said to them, "I am [he]," they went backwards and fell on the ground.

7   Jesus again asked them, "Whom do you seek?" And they said, "Jesus, the Nazarene."

8   Jesus said to them, "I told you that I am [he][1] and if you seek me, allow these to go,"

9   that the word that he had said would be fulfilled, "I have not lost any of those whom you gave me, not even one."

10 But Simon Peter had a sword on him and he drew it and struck the servant of the high priest and took off his right ear. Now the name of the servant [was] Malchus.

11 And Jesus said to Peter, "Place the sword into its sheath. Should I not drink the [m]cup that my Father has given to me?"

12 Then the company of soldiers [P]and the captains and the guards of the Judeans⌐ arrested Jesus and bound him.

13 And they brought him to Annas first, because he was the father-in-law of Caiaphas, who was the high priest of that year.[2]

14 [Pa](Now Caiaphas was he who had counseled the Judeans that it was expedient that one man should die on behalf of the people.)

15 Now Simon Peter and one of the other disciples were following Jesus. And that disciple knew the high priest and he entered the hall with Jesus.

16 But Simon was standing outside by the gate. And that other disciple, who knew the high priest, went out and spoke to the keeper of the gate and brought in Simon.

---

[1] Repeat *I am [he]*, 3x, vs. 5-8
[2] OS (s): sequence of verses: 13, 24, 14, 15, 19-23, 16-18, 25-31

Chapter 18

17 And the young woman, the keeper of the gate,[1] said to Simon, "Are you also [one] of the disciples of this man?" He said to her, "No."

18 And the servants and guards were standing and had made a fire to warm themselves because it was cold. Now Simon was also standing with them and warming himself.

19 And the high priest asked Jesus about his disciples and about his teaching.

20 And Jesus said to him, "I spoke openly with the people and I always taught in the synagogue[2] and in the temple, where all the Judeans are gathered and I did not say anything in secret.

21 Why do you ask me? Ask those who heard what I spoke with them. *Behold, they know everything that I have said."

22 And when he had said these [things], one of the guards who was standing [there] struck Jesus on his cheek[3] and said to him, "Do you give such an answer to the high priest?"

23 Jesus answered and said to him, "If I have spoken wickedly, bear witness against the wickedness,[4] yet if e[I have spoken] well, why do you strike me?"

24 Now Annas sent Jesus bound to Caiaphas, the high priest.

25 And Simon Peter was standing and warming himself and they said to him, "Are you not also one of his disciples?"[5] And he denied [it] and said, "I am not."

26 One of the servants of the high priest, a kinsman of him whose ear Simon had cut off, said to him, "Did I not see you with him in the garden?"

27 And again Simon denied [it] and immediately the rooster crowed.

28 Now they brought Jesus from Caiaphas into the judgment hall and it was daybreak. And they did not enter into the judgment hall, so that they would not be defiled before they had eaten the Passover.

29 And Pilate went outside to them and said to them, "What accusation do you have against this man?"

---

[1] OS (s): 'handmaid of the doorkeeper'; Culture: such an important position would not be given to a woman, see Black, p. 258.

[2] Same root: *gathered, synagogue*

[3] Culture: to strike on the cheek was to cause great shame, Lamsa, *Gospel Light*, p. 478.

[4] Same root: *wickedly, wickedness*

[5] Fig: erotesis, **lema** question, implied answer "yes"

ARAMAIC PESHITTA NEW TESTAMENT
JOHN

Chapter 18

30 They answered and said to him, "If he was not a doer of evil, we would not even have delivered him to you."

31 Pilate said to them, "Take him and judge him according to your law. The Judeans said to him, "It is not lawful for us to kill a man,"

32 that the word would be fulfilled that Jesus said when he made known with what death he was going to die.[1]

33 Now Pilate entered the judgment hall and called Jesus and said to him, "Are you the king of the Judeans?"

34 Jesus said to him, "Do you say this of yourself or have others told you about me?"

35 Pilate said to him, "Am I a Judean?[2] Your countrymen and the chief priests have delivered you to me. What have you done?"

36 Jesus said to him, "My kingdom is not of this world. If my kingdom were of this world, my servants would have fought, so that I would not be delivered to the Judeans. But now my kingdom is not from here."

37 Pilate said to him, "Then [are] you a king?" Jesus said to him, "**You** have said that I am a king. I was born for this and for this I came into the world that I would testify concerning the truth. Everyone who is of the truth hears my voice."

38 Pilate said to him, "What is truth?" And after he had said this, he went out again to the Judeans and said to them, "**I** do not find even one fault in him.

39 But you have a custom that I should release someone to you during the Passover. Therefore, do you want me to release to you this king of the Judeans?"

40 And all of them cried out and said, "Not this [man], but Barabbas." Now this Barabbas was a thief.

Chapter 19

1 Then Pilate scourged Jesus.

2 And the soldiers wove a crown of thorns and they placed it on his head and covered him with robes of purple.

3 And they were saying, "Peace [be] to you, king of the Judeans, and they were striking him on his cheeks."

---

[1] Same root: *death, die*

[2] Fig: erotesis, **lema** question, obvious answer "no"

Chapter 19

4 And Pilate went outside again and said to them, "*Behold, I will bring him outside to you, so that you may know that I can find not even one fault against him."

5 And Jesus went outside while the crown of thorns and robes of purple were on him and Pilate said to them, "*Behold, the man."

6 Now when the chief priests and guards saw him, they cried out and said, "Crucify him, crucify him."[1] Pilate said to them, "You take and crucify him, for I am not able to find a fault in him."

7 The Judeans said to him, "We have a law and according to that which is in our law, he is deserving of death, because he made himself the Son of God."

8 And when Pilate heard this saying, he was more afraid.

9 And he entered again into the judgment hall and said to Jesus, "Where [are] you from?" But Jesus did not give him an answer.

10 Pilate said to him, "Are you not speaking to me? Do you not know that I have the authority to release you and I have the authority to crucify you?"

11 Jesus said to him, "You would have no authority over me at all,[2] if it had not been given to you from above. Because of this, his sin who delivered me to you is greater than yours."

12 And because of this, Pilate wanted to release him, but the Judeans were crying out, "If you release this [man], **you** are not the friend of Caesar, for everyone who makes himself a king is an opponent of Caesar."

13 Now when Pilate heard this saying, he brought Jesus outside and sat on the judgment seat in a place that is called "The Pavement of Stones," but in Hebrew is called Gabbatha.[3]

14 And it was the day of preparation of the Passover and it was about the sixth hour. And he said to the Judeans, "*Behold, your king."

15 And they were crying out, "Take him away, take him away. Crucify him, crucify him."[4] Pilate said to them, "Should I crucify your king?" The chief priests were saying, "We have no king, except Caesar."

16 Then he delivered him to them that they might crucify him. And they led Jesus out and took him,

---

[1] Fig: epizeuxis, very solemn repetition, also v. 15

[2] Lit: not even one

[3] These two words for *pavement* are from two different Aramaic dialects.

[4] Repeat suffix *him*

Chapter 19

17 bearing his cross, to a place that was called 'The Skull,' but in Hebrew is called Golgotha,

18 where they crucified him and with him two others, one on one side and one on the other and Jesus in the center.

19 And Pilate also wrote a tablet and placed [it] on his cross. Now it was written like this, "Jesus, the Nazarene, the king of the Judeans."

20 And many of the Judeans read this board, because the place at which Jesus was crucified was near to the city and it was written in Hebrew and in Greek and in Latin.

21 And the chief priests said to Pilate, "Do not write that he is king of the Judeans, but rather, 'He said I [am] the king of the Judeans.'"

22 Pilate said, "What I have written, I have written."[1]

23 Now the soldiers, after they had crucified Jesus, took his garments and made four pieces, a piece for each of the soldiers. But his robe was without seam from the top, completely woven.

24 And they said to one another, "Let us not tear it, but let us cast lots[2] for it, whose it will be." And the scripture was fulfilled that said: **THEY DIVIDED MY GARMENTS AMONG THEMSELVES AND FOR MY CLOTHES THEY CAST A LOT.** These [things] the soldiers did.

25 Now standing at the cross of Jesus were his mother and the sister of his mother and Mary, who [was the wife] of Cleophas, and Mary Magdalene.

26 And Jesus saw his mother and the disciple whom he loved who was standing [there] and he said to his mother, "Woman, *behold your son."

27 And he said to that disciple, "*Behold, your mother." And from that time, that disciple took her with him.

28 After these [things], Jesus knew that everything was fulfilled. And so that the scripture would be fulfilled, he said, "I am thirsty."

29 And a vessel was placed [there] that was full of vinegar. And they filled a sponge with the vinegar and placed [it] on hyssop and brought [it] to his mouth.

30 And after he had taken that vinegar, Jesus said, "*Behold, it is finished." And he bowed his head and gave up his spirit.

---

[1] Repeat *I have written,* next word, exactly same form
[2] Fig: polyptoton, lit: casting, cast

Chapter 19

31 Now the Judeans, because it was the day of preparation, said, "These bodies should not remain on their crosses, because the SABBATH is dawning, for the day of that SABBATH was a high day. And they begged Pilate that they might break the legs of those [who were] crucified and take them down.

32 And the soldiers came and broke the legs of the first and of that other [one] who was crucified with him.

33 And when they came to Jesus, they saw that he was dead already and did not break his legs.

34 But one of the soldiers struck him in his side with a spear and immediately blood and water came out

35 and the one who saw [it] testified and his testimony[1] is true. And he knows that he spoke the truth that you also may believe.

36 For these [things] happened that the scripture would be fulfilled that said: A BONE OF HIM WILL NOT BE BROKEN.

37 And again another scripture that said: THEY WILL GAZE AT HIM WHOM THEY PIERCED.

38 After these [things], Joseph, who was from Arimathaea, requested from Pilate, because he was a disciple of Jesus and was hiding for fear of the Judeans, that he might take away the body of Jesus. And Pilate gave permission and he came and took the body of Jesus.

39 And Nicodemus also came, who previously had come to Jesus during the night, and he brought with him a mixture of spices of myrrh and of aloe, about one hundred Roman libras.[2]

40 And they took the body of Jesus and wrapped it in linen and with spices, as is the custom for the Judeans when they bury.

41 Now there was a garden in that location in which Jesus was crucified and in that garden, a new tomb in which no one had yet been placed.

42 And they placed Jesus there, because the SABBATH was beginning and because the grave was nearby.

---

[1] Same root: *testified, testimony*

[2] Culture: *libra* translated "pound" in KJV, approximately 75 pounds by U.S. measure, see Appendix 2.

Chapter 20

1 Now on the first of the week, Mary Magdalene came in the early morning while it was dark to the tomb. And she saw the stone that it was taken away from the grave.

2 And she ran [and] came to Simon Peter and to that other disciple whom Jesus loved and she said to them, "They have taken our Lord from the tomb and I do not know where they have put him."

3 And Simon went and that other disciple and they came to the tomb.

4 And both of them were running together, but that disciple ran before Simon and came to the tomb first.

5 And he looked in [and] saw the linen clothes laid [there], but he did not indeed enter.[1]

6 Now Simon came after him and entered the tomb and saw the linen clothes laid [there]

7 and the cloth that had been bound around his head, not with the linen clothes, but folded and placed aside in a certain place.

8 Then that disciple who had come to the tomb first entered also and he saw and believed,

9 for they did not yet know from the scriptures that he was going to rise from the dead.

10 And those disciples went away again to their place.

11 Now Mary was standing by the grave and was crying. And as she cried, she looked into the grave.

12 And she saw two angels in white who were sitting, one by his pillows and one at his feet, where the body of Jesus had been laid.

13 And they said to her, "Woman, why are you crying?" She said to them, "Because they have taken away my Lord and I do not know where they have put him."

14 She said this and she turned back and saw Jesus standing [there]. And she did not know that it was Jesus.

15 Jesus said to her, "Woman, why are you crying and whom do you seek?" Now she thought that he was the gardener and said to him, "My lord, if you have taken him, tell me where you have put him. I will go [and] take him away."

16 Jesus said to her, "Mary." And she turned around[2] and said to him in Hebrew, "RABBULI," which means Teacher.

---

[1] Fig: polyptoton, lit: entering, did enter

[2] OS (s): *turned around* is 'recognized him,' add 'and she ran to him that she might touch him'

Chapter 20

17 Jesus said to her, "Do not touch me, for I have not yet ascended to my Father. But go to my brothers and tell them [that] I ascend to my Father and your Father, and [to] my God and your God."

18 Then Mary Magdalene came and declared to the disciples that she had seen our Lord and that he had told her these [things].

19 Now when it was the evening[1] of that first day in the week and the doors were shut where the disciples were because of fear of the Judeans, Jesus came [and] stood among them and said to them, "Peace [be] with you."

20 He said this and showed them his hands and his side and the disciples rejoiced that they had seen our Lord.

21 And Jesus said to them again, "Peace [be] with you. As my Father has sent me, I also send you."

22 And when he had said these [things], he breathed on them and said to them, "Receive the Holy Spirit.

23 If you forgive sins of anyone, they will be forgiven him, and if you retain ʿ[the sins] of anyone, they will be retained."[2]

24 Now Thomas, one of the twelve who was called the Twin, was not there with them when Jesus came.

25 And the disciples told him, "We have seen our Lord." But he said to them, "Unless I see in his hands the locations of the nails and place my fingers in them and stretch out my hand on his side, I will not believe."

26 And after eight days the disciples again were inside and Thomas [was] with them. And while the doors were closed, Jesus came [and] stood in the middle and said to them, "Peace [be] with you."

27 And he said to Thomas, "Reach your finger here and see my hands. And reach your hand and stretch [it] out on my side and do not be an unbeliever, but a believer."

28 And Thomas answered and said to him, "My Lord and my God."

29 Jesus said to him, "Now that you have seen me, you have believed. Blessed [are] those who have not seen me and believe."[3]

30 Now Jesus did many other signs before his disciples that are not written in this book.

---

[1] OS (s): omit *when it was the evening*

[2] Repeat *forgive, retain*

[3] Repeat forms of *believe*, vs. 27-31

Chapter 20

31   But even these [things] were written that you would believe that Jesus is the MESSIAH, the Son of God, and [that] when you believe, you would have eternal life through his name.

Chapter 21

1   After these [things], Jesus showed himself again to his disciples by the sea of Tiberias. And he appeared like this.

2   There were together, Simon Peter and Thomas who was called the Twin, and Nathaniel, who was from Cana of Galilee, and the sons of Zebedee and two of the other disciples.

3   Simon Peter said to them, "I am going to catch fish." They said to him, "We will also come with you." And they went out and boarded a ship. And during that night they did not catch anything.

4   Now when it was morning, Jesus stood on the shore of the sea. And the disciples did not know that it was Jesus.

5   And Jesus said to them, "Children, do you have anything to eat?"[1] They said to him, "No."

6   He said to them, "Cast your net from the right side of the boat and you will find." And they cast [it] and they were not able to drag in the net from the great number of fish that it had caught.

7   And that disciple whom Jesus loved said to Peter, "This [man] is our Lord." Now Simon, when he heard that it was our Lord, took his garment [and] girded his loins, **Pa**because he was naked,¬ and threw himself in the sea to come to Jesus.

8   But the other disciples came in the boat, for they were not very far from the land, but [only] about two hundred cubits[2] and they were dragging in that net of fish.

9   And when they had climbed up to the land, they saw burning coals placed [there] and fish placed on them and bread.

10   And Jesus said to them, "Bring some of those fish that you have just now caught."

11   And Simon Peter boarded [the boat] and dragged the net to land, full of large fish, one hundred fifty-three. And with this entire load, that net was not torn.

---

[1] Fig: erotesis, **lema** question, obvious answer "no"
[2] See Appendix 2, approximately 250 feet from shore.

Chapter 21

12 And Jesus said to them, "Come [and] eat." And not one of the disciples dared to ask him who he was, because they knew that he was our Lord.

13 Now Jesus came near and took the bread and fish and gave to them.

14 This [was] the third time Jesus had appeared to his disciples after he had risen from the dead.

15 Now after they had eaten, Jesus said to Simon Peter, "Simon, son of Jonas, do you love me more than these?" He said to him, "Yes, my Lord, **you** know that I love you." He said to him, "Feed my lambs for me."

16 He said to him again a second time, "Simon, son of Jonas, do you love me?" He said to him, "Yes, my Lord, **you** know that I love you." Jesus said to him, "Feed my sheep[1] for me."

17 He said to him a third time, "Simon, son of Jonas, do you love me?" And Peter was sad, because he had said to him a third time, "Do you love me?" And he said to him, "My Lord, **you** know everything. **You** know that I love you." Jesus said to him, "Feed my ewes[2] for me.

18 *Truly, truly I say to you, ᵃˡwhen you were a boy, you girded your loins by yourself and you walked to where you wanted, but when you grow old, you will stretch out your hands and another will gird your loins for you and conduct you to where you do not want [to go]."˥

19 Now he said this to show by what death he would glorify God. And after he had said these [things], he said to him, "Follow me."

20 And Simon Peter turned and saw the disciple whom Jesus loved who followed him, who fell on the breast of Jesus during the supper and said, 'My Lord, who will betray you?"

21 When Peter saw this [man], he said to Jesus, "My Lord, and what [of] this [man]?"

22 Jesus said to him, "If I desire that this [man] should remain until I come, what is it to you? Follow me."

23 And this saying went out among the brothers that that disciple would not die. But Jesus did not say that he would not die, but rather, "If I desire that this [man] should remain until I come, what is it to you?"[3]

---

[1] OS (s): 'ewes'

[2] OS (s): 'sheep', shows a progression of those more helpless, to more mature. Fig: metonymy, *sheep* in this passage referring to people.

[3] Repeat *what is it to you* from v. 22, OS (c):, Old Latin, Pal Lex, omit

Chapter 21

24 This is the disciple who testified about all these [things] and also wrote them and we know that his testimony[1] is true.

25 Now there are also many other [things] that Jesus did, which if they were written one by one, not even the world [pa](as I suppose) would be sufficient for the books that would be written.

---

[1] Same root: *testified, testimony*

ARAMAIC PESHITTA NEW TESTAMENT
ACTS

Chapter 1

1 I wrote the former book, oh Theophilus, concerning all those [things] that our Lord Jesus Christ began to do and to teach,

2 until that day in which he was taken up, after he had commanded the apostles, those whom he had chosen by the Holy Spirit,

3 those to whom he also showed himself alive after he had suffered with many signs for forty days, while he was seen by them and spoke about the kingdom of God.

4 And as he ate bread with them, he commanded them that they should not leave Jerusalem, but that they should wait for the promise of the Father, about which [e][he said], "You have heard from me.

5 For John baptized with water, yet you will be baptized with the Holy Spirit after not many days."

6 Now while they were assembled, they asked him and said to him, "Our Lord, at this time will you restore the kingdom to Israel?"

7 He said to them, "This is not yours to know the [sy]time or these [sy]times that the Father has placed in his own authority.

8 But when the Holy Spirit comes on you, you will receive power [P]and you will be witnesses for me in Jerusalem and in all Judea and also among the Samaritans,┐ even to the ends of the earth."┐

9 And after he said these [things], while they watched him, he was taken up and a cloud received him and he was hidden from their [m]eyes.

10 And while they were staring into heaven as he was going away, two men were found standing near them in white clothing.

11 And they said to them, "Galilean men, why are you standing and staring into heaven? This Jesus, who was taken up[1] from you into heaven, will come in the same manner as you have seen him who went up to heaven."

12 And afterwards, they returned to Jerusalem from the mountain that is called the Mount[2] of Olives, which was near Jerusalem and distant from it about seven furlongs.[3]

13 And after they entered, they went up to an upper room, in which Peter [P]and John and James and Andrew and Philip and Thomas and Matthew and Bartholomew and James, the son of Alphaeus, and Simon, the zealot, and Judas, the son of James┐ were staying.

---

[1] Repeat *was taken up* from v. 9
[2] Lit: house
[3] Culture: seven furlongs is .875 miles, or 1.4 km, see Appendix 2.

Chapter 1

14   All of these as one were steadfast in prayer with one soul with the women [P]and with Mary, the mother of Jesus, and with[1] his brothers.

15   And among them in those days, Simon Peter stood up in the middle of the disciples [pa](now there was a gathering there of about one hundred and twenty men) and he said,

16   "Men, our brothers, it was right that the scripture should be fulfilled, which the Holy Spirit foretold by the [m]mouth of David, about Judas who was a guide to those who arrested Jesus,

17   because he was numbered with us and he had a portion in this ministry.

18   This is he who acquired a field for himself from the wage of sin and fell on his face on the ground and burst from his middle and all his insides poured out.

19   And this was known to all who lived in Jerusalem and so that field was called in the language of the country, "Akeldama," which [by] interpretation is, "Field of Blood."[2]

20   For it is written in the book of Psalms: **LET HIS HABITATION BE DESOLATE** and **LET NO ONE BE A DWELLER**[3] **IN IT AND LET ANOTHER TAKE HIS MINISTRY.**

21   It is right, therefore, for one of these men who were with us during this whole time in which our Lord Jesus entered and went out among us,

22   who began from the baptism of John until the day that he was taken up from [being] with us, to be a witness of his resurrection with us."

23   And they caused two to stand,[4] Joseph, who was called Barsabas, who was named Justus, and Matthias.

24   And when they prayed, they said, "LORD, you know what is in the hearts of all. Reveal the one that you have chosen of these two,

25   that he should receive a portion of the [he]ministry and apostleship from which Judas left to go to his place.

26   And they cast lots and it fell on Matthias and he was numbered with the eleven apostles.

---

[1] Repeat *with*, 4x

[2]. Culture: strangling in the East was accomplished as this verse describes, cf. Matt 27:3-10. For further study, see Wilcox, *The Semitisms of Acts*, pp. 87-88.

[3] Same root: *habitation, dweller*

[4] Or "proposed two"

ARAMAIC PESHITTA NEW TESTAMENT
ACTS

Chapter 2

1　And when the days of Pentecost were fulfilled as all were assembled together,

2　suddenly there was a sound from heaven ˢas a powerful wind and the whole house in which they were sitting was filled with it.

3　And tongues that were divided appeared to them ˢas fire and sat on each one of them.

4　And all of them were filled with the Holy Spirit and they began to speak in different languages, as the Spirit gave them to speak.

5　And there were men who were living in Jerusalem who feared God, Judeans from all the nations that are ᴾʳunder heaven.

6　And when that sound occurred, all the people gathered and were troubled, because each one of them heard that they were speaking in their [own] languages.

7　And all of them were amazed and wondered, saying to each other, "All these who are speaking, *behold, are they not Galileans?

8　How do **we** each hear the language into which we were born?

9　Parthians ᴾand Medes and Elamites, and those who dwell in Mesopotamia, Judeans and Cappadocians and those from the region of Pontus and of Asia,

10　and those from the region of Phrygia and of Pamphylia and of Egypt and of the regions of Libya that are near to Cyrene, and those who have come from Rome, Judeans and proselytes,

11　and those from Crete, and Arabians,┐ *behold, we hear them, that they are speaking in our languages the wonders of God."

12　And all of them were amazed and wondered,[1] saying to one another, "What is this event?"

13　And others were mocking them, saying, "These [men] have drunk new wine and are intoxicated."

14　Afterward, Simon Peter stood up with the eleven apostles and ᴾʳraised his voice and said to them, "Men, Judeans, and all who live in Jerusalem, let this be known to you and listen to my words.

15　For these [men] are not intoxicated, as you suppose, for *behold, it is still only the third hour.[2]

---

[1] Same root: *wonders* (v. 11), *wondered*

[2] Culture: on the feast days, they drank and ate nothing until noon, Freeman, pp. 440-441 (quote from Lightfoot).

ARAMAIC PESHITTA NEW TESTAMENT
ACTS

Chapter 2

16   But this is that which was spoken by Joel the prophet:

17   IT WILL BE IN THE LAST DAYS, said God, [THAT] I WILL ^cPOUR OUT MY SPIRIT ON ALL ^{sy}FLESH. YOUR SONS WILL PROPHESY ^PAND YOUR DAUGHTERS AND YOUR YOUNG MEN WILL SEE VISIONS, AND YOUR OLD MEN WILL DREAM DREAMS.[1]

18   AND ON MY SERVANTS AND ON[2] MY HANDMAIDENS I WILL ^cPOUR OUT MY SPIRIT IN THOSE DAYS AND THEY WILL PROPHESY.

19   AND I WILL GIVE SIGNS IN HEAVEN AND MIGHTY WORKS ON THE EARTH, BLOOD AND FIRE AND VAPOR OF SMOKE.

20   THE SUN WILL BE TURNED TO DARKNESS AND THE MOON INTO BLOOD BEFORE THE GREAT AND TERRIBLE ^{sy}DAY OF THE LORD WILL COME.

21   AND IT WILL BE [THAT] EVERYONE WHO CALLS ON THE NAME OF THE LORD WILL LIVE.⌐

22   Men, sons of Israel, hear these words! Jesus the Nazarene, a man who was shown to you by God with miracles ^Pand with signs and with[3] mighty works⌐ that God did among you by his ^mhand, as **you** know,

23   this [man], who was set apart for this by the foreknowledge and will of God, you delivered into the hands of ungodly [men] and you crucified and you killed.

24   But God raised him and released the cords[4] of SHEOL, because it was not possible that he should be held captive in SHEOL.

25   For David spoke about him, I FORESAW MY LORD AT ALL TIMES, FOR HE IS AT MY RIGHT HAND, SO THAT I WILL NOT BE MOVED.

26   BECAUSE OF THIS, MY HEART REJOICES AND MY PRAISE FLOURISHES AND ALSO MY BODY WILL LIE DOWN IN HOPE,

27   BECAUSE YOU WILL NOT LEAVE MY SOUL IN SHEOL, NEITHER WILL YOU ALLOW YOUR INNOCENT [ONE] TO SEE CORRUPTION.

28   YOU HAVE REVEALED TO ME THE WAY OF LIFE. YOU WILL FILL ME WITH GLADNESS WITH YOUR PRESENCE.

29   Men, our brothers, allow [me] to speak boldly with you about the patriarch David, who is dead and also buried and whose tomb is with us until today.

---

[1] Same roots: *see, visions,* and *dream, dreams*

[2] Repeat *and on*

[3] Repeat *with*

[4] *Cords* is homonym with "birth pangs" in Aramaic.

ARAMAIC PESHITTA NEW TESTAMENT
ACTS

Chapter 2

30   For he was a prophet and knew that God had sworn oaths to him: OF THEM ^mFRUIT OF YOUR LOINS I WILL ESTABLISH ^e[ONE] ON YOUR THRONE.¹

31   And he foresaw and spoke about the resurrection of Christ: HE WAS NOT LEFT IN SHEOL, NEITHER DID HIS BODY SEE CORRUPTION.

32   This Jesus has God raised and all of us are his witnesses.

33   And this is he who is elevated at the right hand of God and received from the Father the promise concerning the Holy Spirit. And he has ^cpoured out this gift that *behold, you see and you hear.

34   For David did not ascend into heaven, because he said, THE LORD SAID TO MY LORD, SIT AT MY RIGHT HAND

35   UNTIL I PLACE YOUR ENEMIES [AS] A FOOTSTOOL FOR YOUR FEET.

36   Therefore, all the house of Israel should truly know that God has made this Jesus, whom you crucified, LORD and Christ."

37   And when they heard these [things], they were moved in their heart[s] and said to Simon and to the rest of the apostles, "What should we do, our brothers?"

38   Simon said to them, "Repent and be baptized, each one of you, in the name of the LORD Jesus for the forgiveness of sins, so that you will receive the gift of the Holy Spirit.

39   For the promise is to you ^Pand to your children and to² all those who are far away,˺ those whom God will call."

40   And with many other words he testified to them and begged them, saying, "Live apart from this perverse generation."

41   And some of them willingly received his word and believed and were baptized. And there were added in that day about three thousand people.

42   And they were steadfast in the teaching of the apostles and were fellowshipping in prayer and in the breaking [of the bread] of communion.

43   And fear was to every person and many signs and mighty works occurred by way of the apostles in Jerusalem.

---

¹ Word play: *loins,* **karsakh** ܟܪܣܟ, *your throne,* **kursaikh** ܟܘܪܣܝܟ. Ellipsis could be [a king].

² Repeat *and to*, polysyndeton extends through v. 47.

Chapter 2

44 And all those who had believed were as one and everything that they had was held in common.

45 And those who had wealth sold it and distributed to each one according to whatever was needed.

46 And every day they were steadfast in the temple with one soul and at home they were breaking bread and were receiving food, rejoicing. And in the simplicity of their heart[s]

47 they were praising God, while giving mercies before all the people. And our Lord added every day those who were being given life in the church.

Chapter 3

1 And it happened that while Simon Peter and John were going up together to the temple at the time of prayer at the ninth hour,

2 and *behold, men were carrying a certain man who was lame from the womb of his mother. These [were men] who were accustomed to bringing and laying him at the gate of the temple, which was called Beautiful, so that he could ask alms from those who were entering the temple.

3 This [man], when he saw Simon and John entering the temple, begged them to give him alms.

4 And Simon and John looked at him and said to him, "Look at us."

5 And **he** looked[1] at them, expecting to receive something from them.

6 Simon said to him, "I have no gold and silver,[2] but what I have I will give to you. In the name of Jesus Christ the Nazarene, rise up [and] walk."

7 And he took him by his right hand and raised him up. And immediately his feet and his ankles were strengthened.

8 And he leaped up [and] stood and walked and entered with them into the temple, walking and leaping and praising God.

9 And all the people saw him walking and praising God.

---

[1] Repeat *looked, look* (v. 4)
[2] Culture: it was unlawful by rabbinical teaching to carry a purse into the temple, Bullinger, *Companion Bible*, p. 1582. *Gold and silver* could be metonymy, standing for "money" in general.

Chapter 3

10   And they recognized that he was that beggar who sat every day and asked alms at the gate that was called Beautiful. And they were filled with ^{he}amazement and wonder at what had happened.

11   And while he held Simon and John, all the people, being amazed, ran to them, to the porch that was called Solomon's ^e[Porch].

12   And when Simon saw [it], he answered and said to them, "Men, sons of Israel, why do you wonder at this [man]? Or why do you look at us as if by our own power or by our authority we did this, so that this [man] would walk?[1]

13   The God of Abraham and of Isaac and of Jacob, the God of our fathers, has glorified his Son Jesus, whom **you** delivered up and denied in the presence of Pilate, after he had thought it right to let him go.

14   But **you** denied the Holy and Just [one][2] and requested that a murderer[3] should be given to you.

15   And you killed that Prince of Life, whom God raised from the dead. And we all are his witnesses.

16   And by the faith of his name he has strengthened and healed this [man], whom you see and know, and faith that is in him has given him this wholeness before all of you.

17   But now, our brothers, I know that through ignorance you did this, as did your leaders.

18   And God, according to what he preached beforehand by the ^mmouth of all the prophets, that his Messiah would suffer, has fulfilled [it] in this manner.

19   Repent, therefore, and be converted, so that your sins will be blotted out and ^{sy}times of rest will come to you from the presence of the LORD.

20   And he will send to you him who was prepared for you, Jesus Christ,

21   whom it is required for ^mheaven to retain, until the fullness of the times of all those [things] that God spoke by the ^mmouth of his holy prophets of old.

---

[1] Fig: erotesis – question to ponder
[2] Fig: antonomasia, description given for a name, also for *Prince of Life*, v. 15
[3] Lit: murdering man

ARAMAIC PESHITTA NEW TESTAMENT
ACTS

Chapter 3

22 For Moses said: THE LORD WILL RAISE UP A PROPHET FOR YOU FROM YOUR BROTHERS LIKE ME. HEAR HIM IN WHATEVER HE SPEAKS TO YOU.

23 AND IT WILL BE [THAT] EVERY PERSON THAT DOES NOT HEAR THAT PROPHET, THAT PERSON[1] WILL PERISH FROM HIS PEOPLE.

24 And all the prophets from Samuel and those who were after him spoke and preached about those days.

25 You are the sons of the prophets and of the covenant that God established with our fathers, when he said to Abraham: IN YOUR SEED ALL THE FAMILIES OF THE EARTH WILL BE BLESSED.

26 He has first appointed to you and God has sent his Son to bless you, if you will be converted and repent from your evil [ways].[2]

Chapter 4

1 And while they were speaking these words to the people, the priests and the Sadducees and the rulers of the temple stood up against them,

2 being furious at them that they taught the people and preached about Christ concerning the resurrection from the dead.

3 And they seized them and kept them for the next day, because evening was drawing near.

4 And many who heard the word believed. And there were about five thousand men in number.

5 And on the next day, the rulers and elders and scribes were gathered together,

6 and also Annas, the high priest, and Caiaphas and John and Alexander and those who were of the family of the chief priests.

7 And after they had placed them in the middle, they asked them, "By what power or in what[3] name have you done this?"

8 Then Simon Peter was filled with the Holy Spirit and said to them, "Rulers of the people and elders of the house of Israel, hear [me].

9 If today **we** are judged by you concerning the good [thing] that happened to the sick man, by what [means] this [man] was healed,

10 let this be known to you and to all the people of Israel, that in the name of Jesus Christ the Nazarene, whom **you** crucified, whom God

---

[1] Repeat *person*, lit: soul
[2] Lit: evils
[3] Repeat *by what*, same as *in what*

Chapter 4

raised from the dead, by that same [one], *behold, this [man] stands before you whole.

11 This is **THE STONE THAT YOU BUILDERS REJECTED AND HE HAS BECOME THE HEAD OF THE CORNER.**

12 And there is no deliverance by another man, for there is no other name ᴾʳunder heaven that is given to men by which it is possible to have life."

13 And when they heard the word of Simon and of John that they spoke boldly, they perceived that they were unlearned and ignorant. And they marveled at them and recognized that they had associated with Jesus.

14 And they saw the lame [man], who had been healed, standing with them and they were not able to say anything against them.

15 Then they commanded that they should remove them from their assembly. And they were saying to each other,

16 "What should we do to these men? For *behold, a visible sign that has happened by their hands is known to all the inhabitants of Jerusalem and we are not able to deny [it].

17 But so that this rumor does not spread any more among the people, we should threaten them that they should not speak again to anyone among men in this name."

18 And they called them and commanded them that they should absolutely not speak or teach in the name of Jesus.

19 Simon Peter and John answered and said to them, "You judge if it is right before God that we should obey you more than God.

20 For we are not able not to speak what we have seen and heard."

21 And they threatened them and released them, for they did not find a cause for which to punish them[1] because of the people, for everyone was glorifying God for what had happened.

22 For that man, on whom this sign of healing happened, was more than forty years old.

23 And when they were released, they went to their brothers and told them all that the priests and elders had said.

24 And when they heard [it], they raised their voice as one to God and said, "LORD, you are God, who made the heaven ᴾand earth and seas and everything that is in them.⌐

---

[1] Lit: a cause to place on their head

ARAMAIC PESHITTA NEW TESTAMENT
ACTS

Chapter 4

25   And it is you who spoke by way of the Holy Spirit by the ^mmouth of David your servant: WHY DO THE NATIONS RAGE AND THE PEOPLE CONSIDER VANITY?

26   THE KINGS OF THE EARTH AND THE RULERS HAVE RISEN UP AND HAVE DELIBERATED AS ONE AGAINST THE LORD AND AGAINST HIS MESSIAH.

27   For truly Herod and Pilate with the Gentiles and the congregation of Israel were gathered together in this city against the Holy [one], your Son, Jesus, whom **you** anointed,

28   to do everything that your ^mhand and your will **foreordained** to be ^e[done].

29   And also now, LORD, look and see their threats and allow your servants to boldly preach your word,

30   while you extend your ^mhand for healings and mighty works and signs to be ^e[done] in the name of your holy Son, Jesus."

31   And after they had prayed and made [this] request, the place in which they were gathered was shaken and all of them were filled with the Holy Spirit and were boldly speaking the word of God.

32   And the assembly of men who believed had one soul and one mind and not one of them said concerning the possessions that he owned that they were his, but everything that they had was held in common.

33   And with great power the apostles witnessed about the resurrection of Jesus Christ and great grace was with all of them.

34   And there was no one among them who was lacking, for those who owned fields and houses sold [them] ^Pand brought the price of what was sold

35   and placed [it] at the feet of the apostles and it was given to each one according to what he needed.⌐

36   And Joseph, who was called Barnabas by the apostles, which is interpreted, "son of comfort," a Levite from the region of Cyprus,

37   had a field. And he sold it and brought its price and placed [it] before the feet of the apostles.

Chapter 5

1   And a certain man whose name was Ananias, with his wife, whose name was Sapphira, sold his field

293

Chapter 5

2   and took [some] of its price and hid [it], his wife being aware of it. And he brought a part of the money and placed [it] before the feet of the apostles.

3   And Simon said to him, Ananias, why is it that SATAN has so filled your heart that you should lie to the Holy Spirit and hide some of the money of the sale of the field?

4   Was it not yours before it was sold? And after it was sold, again **you** were in control of its sale. Why have you decided in your heart to do this thing?[1] You have not lied to men, but to God.

5   And when Ananias heard these words, he fell down and died. And there was great fear among all those who heard.

6   And those who were young among them rose up and gathered him up and took [and] buried him.

7   And after three hours had passed, his wife also entered, not knowing what had happened.

8   Simon said to her, "Tell me if you sold the field for this sale price?" And **she** said, "Yes, for this sale price."

9   Simon said to her, "Because you have agreed to tempt the Spirit of the LORD, behold, the feet of the grave diggers of your husband [are] at the door and they will take you out."

10   And immediately, she fell before their feet and died. And those young men entered and found her dead. And they gathered [her] up, took [and] buried her by the side of her husband.

11   And there was great fear in all the church and among all those who heard.

12   And by way of the apostles many signs and mighty works occurred among the people. And they were all assembled together in Solomon's Porch.

13   And of other men, no one dared to come near to them, but the people magnified them.

14   And more were added who believed in the LORD, a crowd of men and of women,

15   so that they brought out the sick into the streets, lying on pallets, that when Simon should come by, at least his shadow would cover them.

---

[1] Fig: erotesis – questions to ponder

Chapter 5

16 And many came to them from other cities that were around Jerusalem, bringing the sick and those who had unclean spirits and all of them were healed.

17 And the high priest and all who were with him who were of the teaching of the Sadducees were filled with envy.

18 And they seized the apostles and arrested [and] bound them [in] prison.

19 Then, during the night, an angel of the LORD opened the door of the prison and took them out and said to them,

20 "Go! Stand in the temple and speak to the people all these words of life."

21 And they went out at daybreak[1] and entered the temple and were teaching. And the high priest and those who were with him called for their companions and the elders of Israel and sent to the prison to bring out the apostles.

22 And when those who had been sent by them went, they could not find them [in] prison, and they turned [and] came [back],

23 saying, "We found the prison that was securely closed, and also the guards who were standing at the doors. And we opened [them], yet we did not find anyone there."

24 And when the chief priests and rulers of the temple heard these words, they were amazed at them and were reasoning, "What is this?"

25 Then a man came [and] told them, "Those men that you confined [in] prison, *behold, they are standing in the temple and teaching the people."

26 Then the rulers with the guards went to have them brought, [but] not with violence, for they feared lest the people would stone them.

27 And when they had brought them, they caused them to stand them before all the assembly and the high priest began to speak to them.

28 "Did we not particularly command[2] you that you should not teach anyone in this name? Now *behold, you have filled Jerusalem with your teaching. And you want to bring the blood of this man on us."

29 Simon answered with the apostles and said to them, "It is right to be persuaded by God, more than by men.

---

[1] Lit: at the moment of dawn
[2] Fig: polyptoton, lit: commanding, we commanded; fig: erotesis, "not" question, answer in the affirmative.

Chapter 5

30   The God of our fathers raised Jesus, whom **you** killed when you hung him on the [eu]tree.

31   God has established this [man as] a leader and savior and has elevated him by his right hand to give repentance and forgiveness of sins to Israel.

32   And **we** are witnesses of these words and [so] is the Holy Spirit that God gives to those who believe in him."

33   And when they heard these words, they were inflamed with anger and planned to kill them.

34   And one of the Pharisees stood up, whose name was Gamaliel, a teacher of the law and honored by all the people. And he commanded that they should take the apostles outside [for] a short time.

35   And he said to them, "Men, sons of Israel, take precaution among yourselves and look at what you ought to do about these men.

36   For before this time, Theudas rose up and said about himself that he was someone great. And about four hundred men followed him. And he was killed and those who followed him were scattered and became as nothing.

37   And Judas the Galilean rose up after him in the days that men were registered for the poll tax and caused many people to turn after him. And he died and all those who followed him were scattered.

38   And now *I say to you, 'Separate yourselves from these men and leave them alone,' for if this thought and this work is of men they will be dismissed and pass away.

39   But if it is from God, you are not able to stop it with your [m]hands, lest you should be found standing against God."

40   [P]And they were persuaded by him. And they called the apostles and beat them and commanded them that they should not speak in the name of Jesus and released them.

41   And they left their presence, rejoicing that they were worthy to be despised because of the name.

42   And they did not cease to teach every day in the temple and at home and to preach about our Lord Jesus Christ.⌐

Chapter 6

1   And in those days as the disciples multiplied, the Greek disciples were murmuring against the Hebrews that their widows were neglected in the daily service.

ARAMAIC PESHITTA NEW TESTAMENT
ACTS

Chapter 6

2   And the twelve apostles called the whole assembly of disciples and said to them, "It is not good that we should leave the word of God and serve tables.

3   Therefore, my brothers, search out and choose seven men from among you about whom there is a [good] testimony and [who] are full of the Spirit of the LORD and wisdom, and we will set them over this matter.

4   And **we** will be steadfast in prayer and in the ministering of the word."

5   And this saying was good before all the people, and they chose Stephen, a man who was full of faith and the Holy Spirit, ^Pand Philip and Prochorus and Nicanor and Timon and Parmenes and Nicolas, an Antiochene proselyte.⌐

6   These stood before the apostles and after they had prayed, they laid a hand[1] on them.

7   And the word of God grew and the number of disciples in Jerusalem multiplied greatly and many people of the Judeans were obedient to the faith.

8   Now Stephen was full of ^{he}grace and power and did ^{he}signs and wonders[2] among the people.

9   And men from the synagogue, which was called that of the Libertine,[3] rose up, along with the Cyrenians ^Pand Alexandrians and those from Cilicia and from Asia,⌐ and they were disputing with Stephen.

10   And they were not able to stand against the wisdom and the Spirit by which he spoke.

11   Then they sent men and instructed them to say, "We have heard him speak words of blasphemy against Moses and against[4] God."

12   And they stirred up the people ^Pand the elders and the scribes⌐ and came and stood against him and seized [and] brought him into the middle of the council.

13   And they set up false witnesses who said, "This man does not cease to speak words against the law and against this holy place.

---

[1] *Laid a hand on* could be translated "consecrated"

[2] Fig: hendiadys, "powerful grace" and "awe-inspiring signs"

[3] Culture: for further study regarding the *Libertines*, see Burder, vol. I, p. 340.

[4] Repeat *against*, also v. 13

Chapter 6

14   For **we** have heard him say that this Jesus, the Nazarene, will destroy this place and will change the customs that Moses delivered to you."

15   [P]And[1] all those who were sitting in the synagogue looked at him and saw his face [s]as the face of an angel.

Chapter 7

1   And the high priest asked him if these [things] were so.

2   And **he** said, "Men, our brothers and our fathers, listen. The God of glory appeared to our father Abraham when he was in Mesopotamia before he came to live in Haran.

3   And he said to him: DEPART FROM YOUR COUNTRY AND FROM AMONG YOUR KINSMEN, AND GO TO THE COUNTRY THAT I WILL SHOW YOU.

4   And then Abraham left the land of the Chaldeans and came [and] lived in Haran. And from there, after his father had died, God moved him to this land in which you live today.

5   And he did not give him an inheritance in it, not even a place to stand for [his] feet.[2] And he promised that he would give it to him to inherit it, to him and to his seed, when he had no son.

6   And God spoke with him, saying to him: YOUR [m]SEED WILL BE A SETTLER IN A STRANGE LAND, AND THEY WILL SUBJECT HIM AND TREAT HIM WICKEDLY [FOR] FOUR HUNDRED YEARS.

7   AND I WILL JUDGE THE PEOPLE WHOM THEY WILL SERVE [IN] BONDAGE, said God. AND AFTER THESE [THINGS] THEY WILL GO OUT AND SERVE ME IN THIS LAND.

8   And he gave him the covenant of circumcision. And then he fathered Isaac and circumcised him on the eighth day. And Isaac fathered Jacob and Jacob fathered[3] our twelve fathers.

9   And our fathers were jealous of Joseph and sold him into Egypt, yet God was with him.

10   And he delivered him from all of his adversities and gave him grace and wisdom before Pharoah, the king of Egypt, and he made him ruler over Egypt and over all his house.

---

[1] Fig: polysyndeton, extends to 7:35
[2] Fig: epitasis, or amplification
[3] Repeat *fathered*, repeat *our fathers*, vs. 9-15

Chapter 7

11 And there was a famine and great calamity in all of Egypt and in the land of Canaan and there was nothing to sustain our fathers.

12 And when Jacob heard that there was food in Egypt, he sent our fathers the first [time].

13 And as they were going away the second time, Joseph made himself known to his brothers and the family of Joseph was made known to Pharoah.

14 And Joseph sent and brought his father, Jacob, and all his family. And they were seventy-five people in number.

15 And Jacob went down to Egypt and died there, he and our fathers.

16 And he was moved to Shechem and placed in the grave that Abraham had bought with money from the sons of Hamor.

17 And when the time arrived for what God had promised to Abraham with oaths, the people had multiplied and grown strong in Egypt,

18 until another king rose up over Egypt, who did not know Joseph.

19 And he plotted against our family and dealt wickedly with our fathers and commanded that their infant boys should be cast away so that they would not live.

20 At that time Moses was born and he was loved by God. And he was nurtured three months [in] the house of his father.

21 And when he was cast away[1] by his mother, the daughter of Pharoah found him and raised him for herself as a son.

22 And Moses was instructed in all the wisdom of the Egyptians and he was prepared in his words and also in his actions.

23 And when he was forty years old, it came into his heart to visit his brothers, the sons of Israel.

24 And he saw one of the sons of his tribe[2] who was treated with violence and he avenged him and executed judgment on him and killed the Egyptian who had wronged him.

25 And he supposed that his brothers, the sons of Israel,[3] would understand that God by his [m]hand would give them deliverance, yet they did not understand.

26 And on another day, he was seen by them while they were quarreling with one another and he was persuading them to be reconciled, saying, 'Men, you are brothers. Why do you wrong one another?'

---

[1] Repeat *cast away* from v. 19
[2] Or "his family"
[3] Repeat *his brothers, the sons of Israel*, from v. 23

Chapter 7

27   But **he** who was wronging his neighbor, pushed him away from him and said to him: WHO HAS SET YOU OVER US [AS] A RULER AND JUDGE?

28   WILL YOU SEEK TO KILL ME AS YOU KILLED THE EGYPTIAN YESTERDAY?[1]

29   And Moses fled at this saying and was a settler in the land of Midian and he had two sons.

30   And after forty years were completed there, an angel of the LORD appeared to him in the wilderness of Mount Sinai in a fire that burned in a bush.

31   And when Moses saw [it] he was amazed at the vision and as he came near to see [it], the LORD said to him in a voice:

32   I AM THE GOD OF YOUR FATHERS, THE GOD OF ABRAHAM [P]AND OF ISAAC AND OF JACOB. And as he was trembling, Moses did not dare to look at the vision.

33   And the LORD said to him: LOOSEN YOUR SANDALS FROM YOUR FEET, FOR THE GROUND ON WHICH YOU STAND IS HOLY.

34   I HAVE INDEED SEEN[2] THE TORMENT OF MY PEOPLE WHO ARE IN EGYPT AND I HAVE HEARD THEIR GROANS AND I HAVE COME DOWN TO DELIVER THEM. AND NOW COME, I WILL SEND YOU TO EGYPT.

35   This [is] Moses, whom they denied, saying, 'Who set you over us [as] a ruler and judge? This [man] God sent to them [as] a ruler and deliverer by the hands of an angel who appeared to him in a bush.

36   This is he who brought them out after he had done signs and wonders and mighty works in the land of Egypt and in the sea of reeds and in the wilderness [for] forty years.

37   This is Moses, who said to the sons of Israel, 'The LORD God will raise up a prophet for you from your brothers like me. Hear him.'

38   This is he who was in the assembly in the wilderness with the angel who spoke with him and with our fathers in the mountain of Sinai. And he is the one who received the living words[3] to give to us.

---

[1] Fig: erotesis, **lema** question, implied answer "yes"
[2] Fig: polyptoton, lit: seeing, has seen
[3] Culture: in Hebrew thinking, *living words* described the excellency of the words, Bullinger, *Figures of Speech*, p. 831.

Chapter 7

39 And our fathers did not want to follow to him, but left him and in their hearts returned to Egypt,

40 saying to Aaron: MAKE US GODS TO PRECEDE US, BECAUSE THIS MOSES, WHO BROUGHT US OUT OF THE LAND OF EGYPT, WE DO NOT KNOW WHAT HAS HAPPENED TO HIM.

41 And they made for themselves a calf in those days and they sacrificed sacrifices[1] to the idols and they were rejoicing in the work of their hands.

42 And God turned away and delivered them to serve the powers of heaven, as it is written in the book of the prophets: [FOR] FORTY YEARS IN THE WILDERNESS DID YOU OFFER ME A SLAIN ANIMAL OR A SACRIFICE, SONS OF ISRAEL?

43 BUT YOU CARRIED THE TABERNACLE OF MOLOCH AND THE STAR OF THE GOD OF REPHAN, IMAGES THAT YOU MADE TO WORSHIP. I WILL REMOVE YOU BEYOND BABYLON.

44 *Behold, the tabernacle of the testimony of our fathers was in the wilderness, as he who spoke with Moses commanded to make it in the likeness that he showed him.

45 And our fathers, with Joshua, indeed brought[2] this tabernacle also into the land that God gave them [as] an inheritance from those nations that he threw out from before them. And it was carried about until the days of David,

46 who found mercy before God and requested that he find a tabernacle for the God of Jacob.

47 But Solomon built the house.

48 And the Most High does not dwell in a [pr]work of hands, as the prophet said:

49 HEAVEN [IS] MY THRONE AND EARTH A FOOTSTOOL THAT IS UNDER MY FEET. WHAT IS THE HOUSE THAT YOU WILL BUILD FOR ME? says the LORD. OR WHAT IS THE PLACE OF MY REST?

50 *BEHOLD, DID NOT MY [m]HAND MAKE ALL THESE [THINGS]?[3]

51 [i]Oh stiff of neck and without circumcision in their heart[s] and in their hearing! You always stand against the Holy Spirit. As your fathers [e][were], you [are] also.

---

[1] Same root: *sacrificed, sacrifices*

[2] Fig: polyptoton, lit: bringing, did bring

[3] Fig: erotesis – questions to ponder, vs. 49-52

Chapter 7

52 For which of the prophets have your fathers not persecuted and killed, those who foretold about the coming of the Just [one], whom you delivered up and killed?

53 And you have received the law by way of the command of angels and have not kept it."

54 And when they heard these [things], they were filled with anger in themselves, and they ^{pr}gnashed their teeth[1] against him.

55 And being full of faith and the Holy Spirit, **he** looked into heaven and saw the glory of God and Jesus standing at the right hand of God.

56 And he said, "*Behold, I see heaven opened and the Son of Man standing at the right hand of God."

57 And they cried out with a loud voice and closed their ^mears and all of them rushed on him.

58 And they arrested [and] took him outside of the city and stoned him. And those who witnessed against him laid their garments at the feet of a certain young man who was called Saul.

59 And they stoned Stephen while he prayed and he said, "Our Lord Jesus, receive my spirit."

60 And while he was kneeling down, he cried out with a loud voice and said, "Our Lord, do not cause this sin to stand against them." And after he said this, he ^{eu}fell asleep.

Chapter 8

1 And Saul was consenting and participating in his murder. And there was in that ^{sy}day a great persecution of the church that was in Jerusalem. And all were scattered into the villages of Judea and also among the Samaritans, except for the apostles only.

2 And faithful men gathered up [and] buried Stephen and they mourned over him greatly.

3 And Saul was persecuting the church of God, entering into houses and dragging away men and women and delivering [them] to prison.

4 And those who were scattered, traveled around and preached the word of God.

5 Now Philip went down to a city of the Samaritans and was preaching to them about Christ.

---

[1] Culture: *gnashing of teeth* means to be furious.

Chapter 8

6   And when they heard his word, the men who were there listened to him and were persuaded by all that he said, because they saw the signs that he did.

7   For many, who were possessed with unclean spirits, cried out with a loud voice, and they came out of them. And others, paralytics and lame, were healed.

8   And there was great joy in that city.

9   And there was there a certain man whose name was Simon. And he had lived in that city a long time. And he was seducing the nation of the Samaritans with his sorceries, magnifying himself and saying, "I am a great [man]."

10   And all of them were praying to him, [mr]great and small, and were saying, "This is the mighty power of God."

11   And all of them were persuaded by him, because he had astonished them a long time with his sorceries.

12   But when they believed Philip, who was preaching the kingdom of God in the name of our Lord Jesus Christ, they were baptized, men and women.

13   And even **Simon** believed and was baptized and was following Philip. And when he had seen the signs and the great miracles that happened by his [m]hand, he was amazed and marveled.

14   And when the apostles who were in Jerusalem heard that the nation of the Samaritans had received the word of God, they sent Simon Peter and John to them.

15   And they went down and prayed for them, so that they would receive the Holy Spirit.

16   For it was not yet on any of them, but they were only baptized in the name of our Lord Jesus.

17   Then they placed a hand on them and they received the Holy Spirit.

18   And when Simon saw that by the placing of a hand of the apostles the Holy Spirit was given, he offered them money,

19   saying, "Give me also this authority that on whom I place a hand, he will receive the Holy Spirit."

20   Simon Peter said to him, "Your money will go with you to destruction, because you thought that the gift of God could be obtained with the wealth[1] of the world.

---

[1] Same root: *obtained, wealth*

Chapter 8

21   You have no part or portion in this faith, because your heart is not straight before God.

22   But repent from this, your evil, and implore God that somehow the treachery of your heart will be forgiven you.

23   For I see that you are in bitter anger and in the [an]bonds of wickedness."

24   Simon answered and said, "Implore God on my behalf that none of these [things] you have said will come on me."

25   And Simon and John, when they had witnessed and taught the word of God, returned to Jerusalem and preached in many villages of the Samaritans.

26   And an angel of the LORD spoke with Philip and said to him, "Rise up [and] go to the south on the desert road that goes down from Jerusalem to Gaza."

27   And he rose up [and] went. And he met a certain eunuch, who had come from Ethiopia, an official of Candace, queen of the Ethiopians. And he was responsible for all of her treasure and had come to worship in Jerusalem.

28   And as he turned to go, he was sitting in a chariot and was reading[1] in Isaiah the prophet.

29   And the Spirit said to Philip, "Go near and follow the chariot."

30   And when he had gone near, he heard that he was reading in Isaiah the prophet and said to him, "Do you understand what you are reading?"

31   And **he** said, "How am I able to understand, unless someone instructs me?" And he begged Philip to come up and sit with him.

32   And the section of the scripture which he was reading was this, [s]AS A LAMB HE WAS LED TO THE SLAUGHTER AND [s]AS A SHEEP BEFORE THE SHEARER IS SILENT, EVEN SO HE DID NOT [pr]OPEN HIS MOUTH.

33   IN HIS HUMILITY HE WAS LED FROM PRISON AND FROM JUDGMENT AND HIS GENERATION, WHO WILL DECLARE [IT]? FOR HIS LIFE HAS BEEN TAKEN FROM THE EARTH.

34   And that eunuch said to Philip, "I ask of you, concerning whom did the prophet speak this, of himself or of another man?"

35   Then Philip [pr]opened his mouth and from this same scripture began to preach to him about our Lord Jesus.

---

[1] Culture: it was common to read out loud, even to oneself, Freeman, p. 441, quoted from Hackett, *Illustrations of Scripture.*

Chapter 8

36 And as they traveled on the road, they arrived at a certain place where there was water. And that eunuch said, "Behold, [here is] water. What is the hindrance that I may be baptized?"

37 OMITTED IN THE WESTERN PESHITTA TEXT[1]

38 And he commanded the chariot to stop and the two of them went down into the water and Philip baptized that eunuch.

39 And when they came up from the water, the Spirit of the LORD caught up Philip and that eunuch did not see him again, but went on his way, rejoicing.

40 And Philip was found at Azotus and from there was traveling around and preaching in all the cities, until he came to Caesarea.

Chapter 9

1 And Saul was still full of threatening and the [an]anger of murder against the disciples of our Lord.

2 And he asked for letters from the high priest to give to Damascus to the synagogues, that if he should find any who were following in this way, men or women, he could bind [and] bring them to Jerusalem.

3 And as he went and approached Damascus, suddenly a light from heaven shone on him.

4 And he fell on the ground and heard a voice that said to him, "Saul, Saul,[2] why are you persecuting me? It is hard for you to kick at the goads."[3]

5 He answered and said, "Who are you, my Lord?" And our Lord said, "I am Jesus, the Nazarene, whom **you** are persecuting.

6 But rise up, enter the city, and there you will be told about what you ought to do."

7 And the men who were traveling with him on the journey were standing amazed, because they were hearing a voice only, but no one was visible to them.

---

[1] Eastern txt: "And Philip said, 'If you believe with a whole heart, it is allowed.' 'I believe that Jesus Christ is the Son of God.'" This verse was first added in the Hutter edition (1599-1600).

[2] Fig: epizeuxis, very solemn repetition

[3] Culture: the goad is a long rod with an iron or sharp wood point at one end to prod and drive the oxen. As an ox is older, it learns not to kick against the pricks from the goad, Neil, *Everyday Life in Bible Lands*, p. 98, cf. Acts 26:14

Chapter 9

8 And Saul got up from the ground and he was not seeing anything, although his eyes were open. And holding [him] by his hands, they brought him to Damascus.

9 And he was not seeing [for] three days and he did not[1] eat or drink.

10 And there was a certain disciple in Damascus, whose name was Ananias. And the LORD said to him in a vision, "Ananias." And he said, "*Behold, I e[am here], my Lord."

11 And our Lord said to him, "Rise up! Go to the street that is called Straight and ask at the house of Judas for Saul, who is from the city [of] Tarsus, for *behold, while he was praying,

12 he saw in a vision that a man whose name [was] Ananias entered and placed a hand on him, so that his eyes would be opened."

13 And Ananias said, "My Lord, I have heard from many about this man, how many evil [things] he has inflicted on your holy [ones] in Jerusalem.

14 And *behold, also here, he has authority from the chief priests to bind all those who call on your name."

15 And the LORD said to him, "Rise up [and] go, because mehe is a chosen vessel for me to carry my name to the Gentiles and to kings and among the sons of Israel,

16 for I will show him how much he will suffer on account of my name."

17 Then Ananias went to him to the house and placed a hand on him and said to him, "Saul, my brother, our Lord Jesus, who appeared to you while you were coming on the road, has sent me, so that your eyes would be opened and you would be filled with the Holy Spirit."

18 And immediately, something slike scales fell from his eyes and his eyes were opened. And he rose up [and] was baptized

19 and he received food and was strengthened. And he was [some] days with the disciples who were in Damascus.

20 And immediately, he was preaching in the synagogues of the Judeans about Jesus, that he was the Son of God.

21 And all those who heard him were amazed and were saying, "Is this not he who persecuted all those who called on this name in Jerusalem? Also, he was sent here for this same e[thing],[2] to bind and bring them to the chief priests."

---

[1] Repeat *and not*

[2] Fig: ellipsis, could be [reason]

Chapter 9

22 But Saul was strengthened even more and confounded the Judeans, those who lived in Damascus, showing that this is the Christ.

23 And after he had been there many days, the Judeans planned treachery against him to kill him.

24 But the plot that they were seeking to do to him was made known to Saul. And they watched the gates of the city, ^{mr}day and night, to kill him.

25 Then the disciples placed him in a basket and let him down from the wall during the night.

26 And he went to Jerusalem and wanted to join himself to the disciples, yet all were afraid of him and did not believe that he was a disciple.

27 But Barnabas took him and brought him to the apostles and related to them, how on the road he had seen the LORD and how he spoke with him and how[1] in Damascus he had spoken boldly in the name of Jesus.

28 And he entered in and went out with them in Jerusalem.

29 And he was speaking in the name of Jesus boldly and disputing with the Judeans who understood in Greek. But **they** wanted to kill him

30 and when the brothers knew [this], they brought him to Caesarea by night and from there they sent him to Tarsus.

31 Nevertheless the church that was in all Judea ^Pand in Galilee and in Samaria⌐ had peace, being edified, and were proceeding in the fear of God and were abounding in the comfort of the Holy Spirit.

32 And it happened that as Simon was traveling around in the cities, he came down also to the holy [ones] who lived in the city [of] Lydda.

33 And he found a certain man whose name [was] Aeneas who was lying on a pallet and was paralyzed [for] eight years.

34 And Simon said to him, "Aeneas,[2] Jesus Christ heals you. Rise up and smooth out your pallet." And immediately he rose up.

35 And all who lived in Lydda and in Saron saw him and turned to God.

---

[1] Repeat *how*

[2] *Aeneas* has a shortened form, Anya ܐܢܝܐ meaning "afflicted or distressed one"

Chapter 9

36   And there was a certain disciple in the city [of] Joppa, whose name was Tabitha. This [one] was rich in good deeds and in the charitable works that she did.

37   And she became sick in those days and died. And they washed her and laid her in an upper room.

38   And the disciples heard that Simon was in the city [of] Lydda, which was near Joppa. And they sent two men to him to ask him to come with them, [if] it was not tedious for him.

39   And Simon rose up [and] went with them. And when he had come, they took him up to the upper room and all the widows gathered [and] stood around him, weeping and showing him the tunics and coats that Tabitha had given to them while she was alive.

40   Now Simon put all the people outside and he kneeled down and prayed. And he turned to the dead body and said, "Tabitha, rise up." And **she** opened her eyes and when she saw Simon, she sat up.

41   And he stretched out his hand to her and raised her up. And called for the holy [ones] and widows and presented her to them alive.

42   And this was known in all the city and many believed in our Lord.

43   And he was in Joppa ^tnot a few days, lodging in the house of Simon, a tanner.

Chapter 10

1   And there was a certain man in Caesarea, a centurion, whose name was Cornelius from the band of soldiers that was called the Italian.

2   And he was just and feared God, he and all his ^mhouse. And he did many charitable works among the people and was always seeking God.

3   This [man] clearly[1] saw an angel of God in a vision [about] the ninth hour of the day, who came toward him and said to him, "Cornelius."

4   And he looked at him and was afraid and said, "What, my Lord?" And the angel said to him, "Your prayers and your charity have come up for a remembrance before God.

5   And now send men to the city [of] Joppa and bring Simon, who is called Peter.

6   *Behold, he is living in the house of Simon, the tanner, which is on the shore of the sea."

---

[1] Lit: openly to his face

308

ARAMAIC PESHITTA NEW TESTAMENT
ACTS

Chapter 10

7 And as the angel who had talked with him was going away, he called two of his household and a certain servant, who feared God, one who obeyed him,

8 and told them everything that he had seen and sent them to Joppa.

9 And on the next day, while they were traveling on the journey and approaching the city, Simon went up to the roof to pray[1] at the sixth hour.

10 And he was hungry and wanted to eat. And while they were preparing for him, astonishment came on him

11 and he saw heaven opened and a certain garment being held by four corners. And it was ˢlike a large linen cloth and it was coming down from heaven to the earth.

12 And in it there were many four-footed animals and creeping things of the earth and birds of heaven.

13 And a voice came to him that said, "Simon, rise up, kill and eat."

14 And Simon said, "ᵈLet it not be so, my Lord, because I have never eaten anything that is corrupt and unclean."

15 And again a second time, a voice came to him, "That which God has cleansed, do not regard as corrupt."

16 And this happened three times and the garment was lifted up to heaven.

17 And while Simon wondered in himself what was the vision that he had seen, those men who had been sent by Cornelius arrived. And they asked for the house in which Simon lodged and they came and stood at the gate of the courtyard.

18 And they called there and asked, "Is Simon, who is called Peter, lodged here?"

19 And while Simon thought on the vision, the Spirit said to him, "*Behold, three men seek you.

20 Rise up, get down, and go with them, not letting your mind doubt, because **I** have sent them."

21 Then Simon went down to those men and said to them, "I am he whom you seek. What is the reason for which you have come?"

---

[1] Culture: worship often took place on the rooftops, *Scripture Manners & Customs*, p. 52.

ARAMAIC PESHITTA NEW TESTAMENT
ACTS

Chapter 10

22   They said to him, "A certain man whose name [is] Cornelius, a centurion, an upright [man] who fears God and about whom all the people of the Judeans give testimony, was told in a vision from a holy angel to send [and] bring you to his house and to hear a word from you.

23   And Simon brought them in and received them where he lodged. And he rose up on the following day and left [and] went with them. And some of the brothers of Joppa went with him.

24   And on the next day, he entered Caesarea and Cornelius was waiting for them, all his kinsmen and also beloved friends that he had being assembled with him.

25   And as Simon was entering, Cornelius met him and fell down [and] worshipped at his feet.

26   And Simon raised him up and said to him, "Stand up. I am a man also."

27   And while he was talking with him, he entered and found many who had come there.

28   And he said to them, "**You** know that it is not lawful for a Judean man to associate with an alien man who is not [of] his race, yet God showed me that I should not say about anyone that he is unclean or corrupt.

29   Because of this, I came promptly when you sent for me. But I ask you, 'Why did you send for me?'"

30   Cornelius said to him, "Four days have passed, since *behold, I was fasting, and in the ninth hour while I was praying in my house, a certain man stood before me, wearing white [clothes]."

31   And he said to me, "Cornelius, your prayer has been heard and there is a remembrance of your charity before God.

32   But send to the city [of] Joppa and bring Simon, who is called Peter. *Behold, he is living in the house of Simon, the tanner, which is on the shore of the sea. And he will come to speak to you.

33   And immediately I sent to you and you have done well that you came. Now *behold, all of us [are] before you and we want to hear all that has been commanded to you from God."

34   And Simon ᵖʳopened his mouth and said, "In truth, I perceive that God is not a respecter of persons,

35   but among all the nations, he who fears him and works uprightness is acceptable to him.

Chapter 10

36 For [this is] the word that he sent to the sons of Israel and declared to them: Peace and harmony by way of Jesus Christ, who is the LORD of all.

37 And **you** also know about the word that was in all Judea that went out from Galilee after the baptism that John preached

38 concerning Jesus, who was from Nazareth, whom God anointed with the Holy Spirit and with[1] power. And this is he who traveled around and healed those who were oppressed by the Evil [one], because God was with him.

39 And we are his witnesses concerning all that he did in all the region of Judea and of Jerusalem. This same [one] the Judeans hung on a ᵉᵘtree and killed.

40 And God raised him after three days and allowed him to be seen openly.[2]

41 Now [he was] not ᵉ[seen] by all the people, but by us, those who were chosen by God to be witnesses for him, for we ate and drank with him after his resurrection that was from the dead.

42 And he commanded us to preach and to witness to the people that he was the one who was appointed by God [as] the judge of the living and of the dead.

43 And concerning him all the prophets witness, so that whoever believes on his name will receive forgiveness of sins."

44 And while **Simon** was speaking these words, the Holy Spirit overshadowed all who were hearing the word.

45 And the circumcised brothers who had come with him were amazed and astonished that the gift of the Holy Spirit was poured out on the Gentiles also,

46 for they heard them speaking in various languages and magnifying God. And Simon said,

47 "Can anyone forbid water, so that those who, *behold, have received the Holy Spirit as we, should not be baptized?"[3]

48 Then he commanded them to be baptized in the name of our Lord Jesus Christ. And they begged him to stay with them [some] days.

---

[1] Repeat *with*

[2] Lit: with open (naked) eyes

[3] Fig: erotesis, **lema** question, implied answer "no"

Chapter 11

1   And it was heard by the apostles and the brothers who were in Judea that the Gentiles had also received the word of God.

2   And when Simon went up to Jerusalem, those who were from the ᵐcircumcision were arguing with him,

3   saying that he had gone in with uncircumcised men and eaten with them.

4   And Simon began in order to say to them,[1]

5   "While I was praying in Joppa, I saw in a vision a certain garment, which resembled a linen cloth, that came down. And it was held by its four corners and it was lowered down from heaven and came all the way to me.

6   And I looked at it and saw that in it there were four-footed animals and creeping things of the earth and also birds of heaven.

7   And I heard a voice that said to me, 'Simon, rise up, kill and eat.'

8   And I said, 'ⁱLet it not be so, my Lord, because that which is unclean and corrupt has never entered my mouth.'

9   And again a voice said to me from heaven, 'That which God has cleansed, do not regard as corrupt.'

10   This happened three times and everything was taken up to heaven.

11   And immediately, three men, who were sent to me by Cornelius of Caesarea, came and stood at the gate of the courtyard in which I lodged.

12   And the Spirit said to me, 'Go with them without doubt.' And these six brothers also came with me and we entered the house of the man.

13   And he related to us how he saw an angel in his house, who stood and said to him, 'Send to the city [of] Joppa and bring Simon, who is called Peter.

14   And he will speak to you words by which you will have life, you and all your ᵐhouse.'

15   And as I began to speak there, the Holy Spirit overshadowed them, as [it had] previously on us.

16   And I remembered the word of our Lord, who said, 'John baptized with water, but **you** will be baptized with the Holy Spirit.'

17   Therefore, if God equally gave the gift to the Gentiles that believed in our Lord Jesus Christ, as also to us, who was **I** that I should be able to hinder God?"[2]

---

[1] Repeats record exactly from Acts 10.

[2] Fig: erotesis – question to ponder

Chapter 11

18   And after they had heard these words, they were quiet and praised God and were saying, "Doubtless, God has also given repentance to life to the Gentiles."

19   Now those who were scattered by the persecution that happened on account of Stephen, approached as far as Phoenicia ^Pand also to the region of Cyprus and to Antioch,┐ speaking the word to no one, but to the Judeans only.

20   And there were men of them from Cyprus and from Cyrene. These entered Antioch and were speaking to the Greeks and preaching about our Lord Jesus.

21   And the ^mhand of the LORD was with them and many believed and turned to the LORD.

22   And this was heard by the ^mears of the clergy that were in Jerusalem. And they sent Barnabas to Antioch.

23   And when he came there and saw the grace of God, he rejoiced and begged them that with all their heart[s], they should follow our Lord,

24   because he was a good man and filled with the Holy Spirit and with[1] faith. And many people were added to our Lord.

25   And he went away to Tarsus to seek Saul.

26   And when he had found him, he brought him with him to Antioch. And they were gathered together with the church a whole year and they taught many people. From that time, the disciples were first called Christians in Antioch.

27   And in those days, prophets came there from Jerusalem.

28   And one of them, whose name was Agabus, stood up and informed them spiritually that a great famine would occur in all the land. And this famine happened in the days of Claudius Caesar.

29   But nevertheless, the disciples, each one of them according to what he had, determined to send to the assistance of the brothers who were living in Judea.

30   And they sent, by way of Barnabas and Saul, to the elders who were there.

Chapter 12

1   Now at that time, Herod the king, who was named Agrippa, ^{pr}laid hands on some who were in the church to wrongfully treat them.

---

[1] Repeat *with*

Chapter 12

2   And he killed James, the brother of John, with a sword.

3   And when he saw that this pleased the Judeans, he proceeded to arrest Simon Peter also. And [these] were the days of the Feast of Unleavened Bread.

4   And he arrested him and threw him in prison and delivered him [to] sixteen soldiers to keep him,[1] so that after the feast of the Passover, he could deliver him to the people of the Judeans.

5   And while Simon was kept in prison, steadfast prayer was offered to God by the church on his behalf.

6   And in that night toward daybreak [when] he was going to deliver him up, while Simon was asleep between two soldiers and was bound by two chains and others were keeping the doors of the prison,

7   an angel of the LORD stood above him and a light shown in all the building. And he hit him on his side and woke him and said to him, "Rise up quickly." And the chains fell from his hands.

8   And the angel said to him, "Gird up your loins and put on your sandals." And he did so. And again he said to him, "Wrap yourself in your outer garment and follow me."

9   And he went out and followed him, not knowing that what was occurring by way of the angel was true, for he supposed that he was seeing a vision.

10   And after they had passed the first watch and the second, they came up to the gate of iron and it was opened to them of its own accord. And after they had gone out and passed one street, the angel left him.

11   Then Simon realized [e][what happened] and said, "Now I know with truthfulness that the LORD sent his angel and delivered me from the [m]hand of Herod the king and from what the Judeans had planned against me."

12   And when he understood, he came to the house of Mary, the mother of John who was called Mark, because many brothers were gathered and praying there.

13   And he knocked at the gate of the courtyard and a young girl, whose name [was] Rhoda, went out to answer him.

14   And she recognized the voice of Simon and in her joy, she did not open the gate for him, but turned back quickly and said to them, "Behold, Simon is standing at the gate of the courtyard."

---

[1] Culture: there were four soldiers for each watch, two in the prison, and two as sentries at the door, Freeman, p. 442; Eastern txt: alt sp. STRYOYIN ܣܛܪܛܝܘܛܐ

ARAMAIC PESHITTA NEW TESTAMENT
ACTS

Chapter 12

15 They said to her, "You are indeed confused."[1] Yet **she** was affirming that this was so. They said to her, "Perhaps it is his angel."

16 And Simon was knocking at the gate and they went out, saw him, and were amazed.

17 And he motioned with his hand to them to be quiet. And he entered and told them how the LORD had brought him out of the prison. And he said to them, "Tell these [things] to James and the brothers." And he left [and] went to another place.

18 And when it was morning, there was a great uproar among the soldiers about Simon about what had happened to him.

19 And Herod, when he searched for him and could not find him, judged the keepers and commanded that they should die. And he went away from Judea and was in Caesarea.

20 And because he was angry at the Tyrians and at the Sidonians, they gathered together and came to him. And they persuaded Blastus, the chamberlain of the king and they asked him for a peace treaty, because the supply of their country was from the kingdom of Herod.

21 And on a particular day, Herod was clothed in the clothing[2] of the kingdom and sat on the judgment seat and was speaking to the crowd.

22 And all the people cried out and said, "These are the voices of a god and are not of men!"

23 And because he did not give glory to God, immediately the angel of the LORD struck him and he rotted with worms and died.

24 And the gospel of God was preached and it increased.

25 And Barnabas and Saul returned from Jerusalem to Antioch, after they had completed their service. And they took with them John who was called Mark.

Chapter 13

1 And there were in the church of Antioch, prophets and teachers, Barnabas, ᴾand Simon, who was called Niger, and Lucius who was from the city [of] Cyrene, and Manaen, a foster-brother[3] of Herod the tetrarch, and Saul.┐

---

[1] Fig: polyptoton, lit: confusing, are confused
[2] Same root: *clothed, clothing*
[3] Lit: son of the upbringer

315

Chapter 13

2 And while they were fasting and making intercession to God, the Holy Spirit said to them, "Appoint to me Saul and Barnabas for the work [to] which I have called them."

3 And after they had fasted and prayed, they laid a hand on them and sent them.

4 And being sent by the Holy Spirit, **they** went down to Seleucia and from there journeyed by sea up to Cyprus.

5 And after they entered the city [of] Salamis, they were preaching the word of our Lord in the synagogues of the Judeans. And John was ministering to them.

6 And when they had traveled around all the island as far as the city [of] Paphos, they found a certain man, a Judean sorcerer, who was a false prophet, whose name was Barshuma.

7 This [man] attended a wise man, who was the proconsul and was called Sergius Paulus. And the proconsul called for Saul and Barnabas and asked to hear the word of God from them.

8 And this sorcerer, Barshuma, whose name is interpreted Elymas, was standing against them, because he wanted to turn the proconsul away from the faith.

9 But Saul, who was called Paul, was filled with the Holy Spirit and looked at him

10 and said, "ⁱOh full of all treacheries and all evil [things], son of the Accuser and enemy of all uprightness, will you not cease to pervert the straight ways of the LORD?[1]

11 And now the ᶜhand of the LORD [is] on you and you will be blind and you will not see the sun for a time." And immediately a thick darkness and blindness fell on him and he wandered around and looked for one who would take [him] by his hand.

12 And when the proconsul saw what had happened, he was amazed and believed in the teaching of the LORD.

13 And Paul and Barnabas traveled by sea from the city [of] Paphos and came to Perga, a city of Pamphylia. And John separated from them and went to Jerusalem.

14 And **they** went away from Perga and came to Antioch, a city of Pisidia. And they entered the synagogue on a SABBATH day and sat down.

---

[1] Fig: erotesis – question to ponder

ARAMAIC PESHITTA NEW TESTAMENT
ACTS

Chapter 13

15   And after the law and the prophets were read, the elders of the synagogue sent for them and said, "Men, our brothers, if you have a ᵃⁿword of comfort, speak with the people."

16   And Paul stood up and waved his hand and said, "Men, sons of Israel and those who fear God, listen.

17   The God of this people chose our fathers and lifted up and multiplied them while they were settlers in the land of Egypt and with a strong arm he brought them out of it.

18   And he fed them in the wilderness [for] forty years.

19   And he destroyed seven nations in the land of Canaan and gave them their land for an inheritance.

20   And [for] four hundred and fifty years, he gave them judges until Samuel the prophet.

21   And then they asked for a king. And God gave them Saul, the son of Kish, a man from the tribe of Benjamin, [for] forty years.

22   And he removed him and raised up for them David the king. And he testified about him and said: I HAVE FOUND DAVID, THE SON OF JESSE, [TO BE] A MAN ACCORDING TO MY HEART. HE WILL DO ALL OF MY DESIRES.

23   From the seed of this [man], God raised up for Israel as was promised, Jesus the redeemer.

24   And he sent John before his coming to preach the baptism of repentance to all the people of Israel.

25   And while John was completing his ministry, he said, 'Whom do you think that I am? I am not ᵉ[he]. But *behold, he follows me, the straps of whose sandals I am not worthy to loosen.'

26   Men, our brothers, sons of the family of Abraham and those with you who fear God, to you is the ᵃⁿword of life sent.

27   For those inhabitants of Jerusalem and their rulers did not acknowledge him or even the writings of the prophets that are read on every SABBATH. But they condemned him and fulfilled those [things] that were written.

28   And although they could not find any cause for death, they asked ᵉ[permission] of Pilate to kill him.

29   And after they had completed everything that was written about him, they took him down from the cross and laid him in a tomb.

30   But God raised him from the dead.

ARAMAIC PESHITTA NEW TESTAMENT
ACTS

Chapter 13

31   And he appeared many days to those who had gone up with him from Galilee to Jerusalem. And they are now his witnesses to the people.

32   And also, *behold, **we** declare to you that the promise that was to our fathers,

33   *behold, God has fulfilled it to us, their sons, that he raised up Jesus, as it was written in the second Psalm: YOU ARE MY SON, THIS DAY I HAVE FATHERED YOU.

34   And so God raised him from the dead, so that he will not return again [and] see corruption as he said: I WILL GIVE YOU THE FAITHFUL GRACE OF DAVID.

35   And again he said in another place: YOU WILL NOT ALLOW YOUR INNOCENT [ONE] TO SEE CORRUPTION.

36   For David in his generation ministered the will of God ᴾand slept and was added to his forefathers and saw corruption.⌐

37   But this [man], whom God raised, did not see corruption.

38   Therefore know, my brothers, that by this [man]¹ forgiveness of sins is preached to you.

39   And by this [man], everyone who believes is justified from all that which you could not be justified² by the law of Moses.

40   Beware, therefore, so that what is written in the prophets should not come on you:

41   SEE [YOU] DESPISERS AND BE ASTONISHED AND BE DESTROYED, FOR I WILL WORK A WORK³ IN YOUR DAYS WHICH YOU WILL NOT BELIEVE, ALTHOUGH SOMEONE TELLS YOU."

42   And while they were leaving their presence, they begged them that on the next SABBATH they would speak to them these words.

43   And after the synagogue was dismissed, many Judeans followed them and also proselytes who feared God. And **they** were speaking and persuading them to be follower[s] of the grace of God.

44   And on the next SABBATH [day], the whole city was gathered to hear the word of God.

45   And when the Judeans saw the large crowd, they were filled with envy and stood against the words that Paul spoke and they were blaspheming.

---

¹ Or "this same [one]"
² Repeat *justified*
³ Same root: *work, a work*

Chapter 13

46   And Paul and Barnabas spoke boldly, "It was necessary that the word of God be spoken to you first, but because you have pushed it away from you and have decided about yourselves that you are not worthy of eternal life, *behold, we turn to the Gentiles.

47   For so our Lord commanded us, as it is written: I HAVE SET YOU [AS] A LIGHT TO THE GENTILES THAT YOU WOULD BE FOR LIFE TO THE ENDS OF THE EARTH."

48   And when the Gentiles heard, they rejoiced and praised God and those who were ordained to eternal life believed.

49   And the word of the LORD was spoken in that whole place.

50   But the Judeans stirred up the rulers of the city and the rich women, those who feared God with them and they instigated a persecution against Paul and against[1] Barnabas. And they expelled them from their borders.

51   And after they had gone out, they shook off the dust of their feet against them[2] and came to the city [of] Iconium.

52   And the disciples were filled with [he]joy and the Holy Spirit.[3]

Chapter 14

1   And they came and entered the synagogue of the Judeans. And they spoke with them such that many of the Judeans and of the Greeks believed.

2   But the Judeans who were not persuaded stirred up the Gentiles to mistreat the brothers.

3   And **they** were there a long time and were boldly speaking about the LORD. And **he** gave witness concerning the [an]word of his grace by the signs and by the wonders that he was doing by their [m]hands.

4   And all the multitude of the city was divided. Some of them were with the Judeans and some of them[4] were following the apostles.

5   And there was an assault against them by the Gentiles and by the Judeans and their rulers to disgrace them and to stone them with rocks.

---

[1] Repeat *against*

[2] Culture: *shook off the dust of their feet* refers to letting go of animosity and bitterness, Barnes, *People's Bible Encyclopedia,* p. 286.

[3] Fig: hendiadys, "spiritual joy"

[4] Repeat *some of them*

Chapter 14

6 And after they knew [it], they went away and took refuge in the cities of Lycaonia, Lystra, and Derbe and the villages that surrounded them.

7 And they were preaching there.

8 And a certain man was sitting in the city [of] Lystra, who was hurt in his feet, lame from the womb of his mother, who had never walked.

9 This [man] heard Paul speak. And when Paul saw him and knew that he had faith to have life,

10 he said to him in a loud voice, "To you, I say in the name of our Lord Jesus Christ, stand up on your feet." And he leaped up, stood, and walked.

11 And the crowd of people, when they saw what Paul had done, ^{pr}raised up their voice[s] in the language of the country and were saying, "The gods have put on the likeness of men and come down to us."

12 And they called Barnabas, Jupiter, and Paul, Hermes, because he began the speaking.

13 And the priest of Jupiter, who was outside of the city, brought ^{he}oxen and crowns¹ to the gate of the courtyard where they lodged and wanted to sacrifice to them.

14 But Barnabas and Paul, when they heard, tore their garments and leaped up, went out to the crowd and cried out

15 and were saying, "Men, what are you doing? **We** also are men ^e[having] feelings like you, who preach to you that you should turn from these idle [things] to the living God, who made heaven ^Pand earth and the seas and all that is in them,⌐

16 [This is] who in former generations allowed all the nations to go in their own ways,

17 although he did not leave himself without a testimony, in that he did for them good [things] from heaven and caused rain to fall on them and caused the fruit to mature in their seasons and filled their hearts with ^{he}food and gladness."²

18 And while they were saying these [things], with difficulty did they restrain the people, so that no one sacrificed to them.

---

¹ Fig: hendiadys, "garlanded oxen"

² Fig: hendiadys, "glad provision"

Chapter 14

19   But the Judeans from Iconium and from Antioch came there and stirred up the people against them and they stoned Paul and dragged him outside of the city, because they supposed that he was dead.

20   And the disciples gathered about him and he rose up [and] entered the city. And on the next day, he went away from there with Barnabas and they went to the city [of] Derbe.

21   And while they were preaching to the citizens, they made many disciples. And they returned [and] came to the city [of] Lystra and to Iconium and to Antioch,

22   establishing the lives of the disciples and begging them to remain in the faith and telling them that it is necessary to enter the kingdom of God with much trial.

23   And they ordained elders for them in every church, while they fasted with them and prayed and commended them to our Lord in whom they believed.

24   And after[1] they had traveled around in the region of Pisidia, they came to Pamphylia.

25   And after they had spoken the word of the LORD in the city [of] Perga, they went down to Attalia.

26   And from there they journeyed by sea and came to Antioch, because from there they had been commended to the grace of the LORD for the work that they had accomplished.

27   And after they had gathered the whole church, they were narrating everything that God had done with them and that he had opened a [m]door of faith to the Gentiles.

28   And they were there a long time with the disciples.

Chapter 15

1   And men came down from Judea and were teaching the brothers, [e][saying] "Unless you are circumcised according to the custom of the law, you are not able to have life."

2   And Paul and Barnabas had much strife and dispute with them. And it happened that they sent up Paul and Barnabas and others with them to the apostles and elders who were in Jerusalem, because of this dispute.

---

[1] Repeat *and after*, vs. 24, 25, 27

Chapter 15

3   And the church escorted [and] sent them. And they were traveling in all of Phoenicia and also among the Samaritans, narrating about the conversion of the Gentiles and causing great joy to all the brothers.

4   And when they came to Jerusalem, they were received by the church and by the apostles and by the elders and they narrated to them all that God had done with them.[1]

5   And some stood up, those from the doctrine of the Pharisees who had believed, and they were saying, "It is necessary for you to circumcise them and you should command them to keep the law of Moses."

6   And the apostles and elders were gathered to look into this matter.

7   And after there had been much debate, Simon stood up and said to them, "Men, our brothers, **you** know that from the first days, by my [m]mouth, God chose that the Gentiles should hear the word of the gospel and believe.

8   And God, who knows what is in hearts, gave testimony concerning them and gave them the Holy Spirit as [he did] to us.

9   And he made no distinction between us and them, because he cleansed their hearts by faith.

10   And now, why do **you** tempt God as you place a [m]yoke on the necks of these disciples, which neither our fathers nor we were able to bear?[2]

11   But by the grace of our Lord Jesus Christ, we believe to have life, as they [e][do]."

12   And the whole assembly was silent and listened to Paul and Barnabas who were narrating everything God, had done by their hands, signs and mighty works among the Gentiles.

13   And after they were silent, James stood up and said, "Men, our brothers, hear me.

14   Simon narrated to you how God began to choose from the Gentiles a people for his name.

15   And to this the words of the prophets agree, as it is written:

16   AFTER THESE [THINGS] I WILL RETURN AND SET UP THE TABERNACLE OF DAVID WHICH HAS FALLEN AND I WILL REBUILD WHAT HAS FALLEN OF IT AND I WILL RAISE IT UP,

---

[1] Repeat *all that God had done with them* from 14:27

[2] Fig: erotesis – question to ponder

Chapter 15

17 SO THAT THE REMNANT OF MEN WILL SEEK THE LORD, AND ALL THE GENTILES, ON WHOM MY NAME IS CALLED, SAYS THE LORD WHO DID ALL THESE [THINGS].

18 THE WORKS OF GOD ARE KNOWN FROM OLD.

19 Because of this, I say, 'They should not harass those have turned to God from the Gentiles.'

20 But let it be sent to them that they should stay away from the uncleanness of that which is sacrificed and from fornication and from that which is strangled and from blood.

21 For Moses, from the first generations, had preachers in the synagogues, in every city, who read him on every SABBATH."

22 Then the apostles and elders, with all the church, chose men from them and sent [them] to Antioch, with Paul and Barnabas, Judas who was called Barsabas, and Silas, men who were chiefs among the brothers.

23 And they wrote a letter by their hands, [e][saying] thus, "The apostles and elders and brothers, to those who are in Antioch and in Syria and in Cilicia, brothers who are from the Gentiles, peace.

24 It has been heard by us that men from us have gone out and disturbed you with words and have upset your souls, saying that you should be circumcised and keep the law, those [things] that we did not command them.

25 Because of this, all of us, being gathered together, purposed and chose men and sent [them] to you, with our beloved Paul and Barnabas

26 [pa](men who have committed themselves on behalf of the name of our Lord Jesus Christ).

27 And we have sent with them Judas and Silas, who will tell you these same [things] by word:

28 For it was the will of the Holy Spirit and also of us that a greater burden should not be placed on you, outside of those [things] that are necessary,

29 that you should stay away from that which is sacrificed [P]and from blood and from [that which] is strangled and from fornication,⌐ that as you keep yourselves from these [things], you will [do] well. Be steadfast in our Lord."

30 And those who were sent came to Antioch and gathered all the people and delivered the letter.

31 And after they had read [it], they rejoiced and were comforted.

Chapter 15

32   And with an abundance of the word Judas and Silas strengthened the brothers and established those of the ᵐhousehold, because they also were prophets.

33   And after they were there a while, the brothers dismissed them in peace to the apostles.

34   OMITTED IN THE WESTERN PESHITTA TEXT[1]

35   Now Paul and Barnabas remained in Antioch and were teaching and preaching the word of God with many others.

36   And after [some] days, Paul said to Barnabas, "Let us return and visit the brothers who are in every city in which we have preached the word of God and let us see what they are doing."

37   And Barnabas wanted to take John, who was called Mark.

38   But Paul did not want to take him with them, because he had left them while they were in Pamphylia and had not gone with them.

39   Because of this contention, they separated from each other and Barnabas took Mark and journeyed by sea and traveled to Cyprus.

40   Now Paul chose Silas and went away, being commended by the brothers to the grace of God.

41   And he traveled in Syria and in Cilicia and established the churches.

Chapter 16

1   And he arrived at the city [of] Derbe and of Lystra. And there was a certain disciple there, whose name [was] Timothy, the son of a certain faithful Judean woman and his father was an Aramean.

2   And all the disciples who were from Lystra and from Iconium gave testimony concerning him.

3   Paul wanted to take this [man] with him, so he took [and] circumcised him because of the Judeans that were in the place, for all of them knew his father was an Aramean.

4   And while they went among the cities, they were preaching and teaching them to be keeping the commandments which the apostles and elders who were in Jerusalem had written.

5   Yet the churches were established in faith and increased in number every day.

6   And they walked in the regions of Phrygia and of Galatia and the Holy Spirit hindered them from speaking the word of God in Asia.

---

[1] Eastern txt: add 'Nevertheless, it was the will of Silas to remain there.'

Chapter 16

7   And after they had come to the region [of] Mysia, they wanted to go from there to Bithynia, yet the Spirit of Jesus did not permit them.

8   And after they had gone out from Mysia, they went down to the region [of] Troas.

9   And in a vision during the night, there appeared to Paul **pa**(as [it were]) a certain Macedonian man who was standing and begging him, saying, "Come to Macedonia and help us."

10   And after Paul had seen this vision, immediately **ac**we wanted to leave for Macedonia, because we understood that our Lord had called us to preach to them.

11   And we traveled from Troas and headed straight for Samothracia and from there on the next day, we came to the city [of] Neapolis,

12   and from there to Philippi, which is the chief **e**[city] of Macedonia and is a colony. And we were in that city certain days.

13   And we went out on the day of the SABBATH outside of the gate of the city by the edge of a river, because a house of prayer was seen there.[1] And after we were seated, we were speaking with the women who were gathered there.

14   And a certain woman, a seller of purple cloth, who feared God **e**[was there]. Her name was Lydia, from the city [of] Thyatira. Our Lord opened the heart of this [woman] and she heard what Paul said.

15   And she was baptized, she and her household. And she begged us and was saying, "If you are truly confident that I believe in our Lord, come, lodge in my house." And she constrained us much.

16   And it happened that while we were going to the house of prayer, a certain young woman met us who had a spirit of divinations. And she earned a large profit for her masters by the divination that she was divining.[2]

17   And she was following Paul and us and was crying out and saying, "These men are the servants of the Most High God and are declaring to you the way of life."

18   And so she did many days. And Paul was provoked and said to that spirit, "I command you in the name of Jesus Christ to come out of her. And immediately it went away.

---

[1] Culture: this probably meant that there was no synagogue in the city, Freeman, p. 445.

[2] Same root: *divination, divining*

Chapter 16

19 And when her masters saw that the hope of their profit had gone out of her, they arrested Paul and Silas and dragged [and] brought them to the marketplace.

20 And they brought them to the magistrates and to the rulers of the city and were saying, "These men are troubling our city, because they are Judeans

21 and are preaching to us customs that are not permitted for us to receive and to do because we are Romans."[1]

22 And a large crowd gathered against them. Then the magistrates tore their garments[2] and commanded to beat them.

23 And after they had beaten them much, they threw them into prison and commanded the keeper of the prison to keep them carefully.

24 Now when he received this command, he brought [them] in [and] confined them in the inner room of the prison and fastened their feet in stocks.

25 [P]And in the middle of the night, Paul and Silas were praying and praising God and the prisoners were listening to them.

26 And suddenly, there was a great earthquake and the foundations of the prison were shaken[3] and immediately, all the doors were opened and the fastenings of all were released.

27 And when the keeper of the prison was awakened and saw that the doors of the prison were opened, he took a sword and wanted to kill himself, because he thought that the prisoners had fled.

28 And Paul called to him with a loud voice and said to him, "Do not do to yourself anything evil, because all of us are here."

29 And he lit a lamp for himself and sprang up and entered, trembling, and fell at the feet of Paul and of Silas.

30 And he brought them outside and said to them, "My lords, what is necessary for me to do, so that I may have life?"

31 And **they** said to him, "Believe in our Lord Jesus Christ and you will have life, you and your house."

32 And they spoke to him the word of the LORD and to all his household.

---

[1] Culture: they were violating a Roman law against the introduction of foreign religions, Conybeare & Howsen, p. 233.

[2] Culture: rending the mantle was an outward sign of inward anger or grief.

[3] Same root: *earthquake, shaken*

Chapter 16

33   And immediately in the night, he took [and] washed them of their wounds and immediately[1] he was baptized, he and all his household.

34   And he took [and] brought them up to his house and set a table for them and was rejoicing, he and his household, in the faith of God.

35   And when it was morning, the magistrates sent sergeants to say to the ruler of the prisoners, "Release those men."

36   And when the ruler of the prison heard about [it], he told Paul this message, "The magistrates have sent ᵉ[a message] that you should be released, and now leave, go in peace."⌐

37   Paul said to him, "They have beaten Roman men without fault before the eye of the whole world and have put [them] into prison and now secretly do they send us away?[2] ⁱIndeed not! Rather, they should come [and] send us away."

38   And the sergeants went and told the magistrates these words that were said to them. And when they heard that they were Romans, they were afraid.

39   And they came to them and begged them to go out and to leave the city.

40   And after they had gone out of the prison, they entered ᵉ[the house of] Lydia and saw the brothers there and comforted them and left.

Chapter 17

1   And they passed by the cities [of] Amphipolis and Apollonia and came to Thessalonica, where there was a synagogue of the Judeans.

2   And Paul, as he was accustomed, went in to them and [for] three SABBATHS, spoke with them from the scriptures,

3   explaining and demonstrating that Christ had to suffer and to rise from the dead and ᵉ[saying], "This Jesus is the MESSIAH whom I declare to you."

4   ᴾAnd some of them believed and followed Paul and Silas and many of the Greeks who feared God and also notable women, not a few, ᵉ[followed Paul].

---

[1] Repeat *immediately*

[2] Culture: they had treated them illegally as Roman citizens in 3 ways: 1) bound them in stocks, 2) beaten them, 3) had no trial, Freeman, p. 446.

Chapter 17

5   And the Judeans were jealous and gathered to themselves evil men from the streets of the city and formed a large mob and disturbed the city and came and assaulted the house of Jason and wanted to take them from there and deliver them to the mob.

6   And when they did not find them there, they dragged away Jason and the brothers who were there and brought them to the rulers of the city, crying, "These are they who have disturbed the whole region and *behold, they have come here also.

7   And this is Jason, their host, and all of these stand against the commandments of Caesar, saying, 'There is another king, Jesus.'"

8   And the rulers of the city and all of the people were troubled after they had heard these [things].

9   And they took bail from Jason and also from the brothers and then released them.┐

10   Now the brothers immediately in the night sent Paul and Silas to the city [of] Berea. And when they had come there, they entered the synagogue of the Judeans.

11   For those Judeans who were there were nobler than those Judeans in Thessalonica. And they gladly heard the word from them every day, discerning from the scriptures whether these [things] were so.

12   And many of them believed and likewise also from the Greeks, many men and notable women ᵉ[believed].

13   And when those Judeans who were from Thessalonica knew that the word of God was preached by Paul in the city [of] Berea, they came there also and did not cease to stir up and to trouble the people.

14   And the brothers sent Paul away to go down to the sea and Silas and Timothy remained in that city.

15   And those who escorted Paul went with him as far as the city [of] Athens. And when they went away from his presence, they took a letter from him to Silas and Timothy that they should travel to him quickly.

16   Now **Paul**, while waiting in Athens, was grieved in his spirit, when he saw that the whole city was full of idols.

17   And he spoke in the synagogue with the Judeans and with those who feared God and in the marketplace with those who were present every day.

ARAMAIC PESHITTA NEW TESTAMENT
ACTS

Chapter 17

18   And also philosophers, who were from the teaching of Epicurus and others who were called Stoics,[1] were debating with him. And every one of them were saying, "What does this babbler want?" And others were saying, "He preaches strange gods," because he was preaching[2] Jesus and his resurrection to them.

19   And they arrested him and brought him to the judgment hall that was called Areopagus, saying to him, "Can we know what this new teaching is that you preach?

20   For you are sowing strange words in our hearing and we want to know what these [things] are."

21   Now all the Athenians and those strangers who came there did not care for anything else, except to say and to hear something new.

22   And as Paul stood in the Areopagus, he said, "Men, Athenians, I see that in all [things] you are abundant in the worship of demons.

23   For while I was traveling around and seeing the place of your worship, I found a certain altar on which was inscribed, 'The unknown god.' Therefore, although you do not know whom you worship,[3] I will preach about this one to you.

24   For the God, who made the world and all that is in it and is the Lord of heaven and of earth, does not live in temples that hands have made.

25   And he is not served by the hands of men and he does not lack in anything, because he has given life and soul to every man.

26   And from one blood he made the whole world of men to be living on the [m]face of all the earth. And he appointed the seasons by his commandment and set boundaries for the habitation of men,

27   that they would seek and inquire after God and by his creations find him, because he is also not far from all of us.

28   For it is in him we live and move and are, as also one of the wise [men] who is with you said, 'From him is our origin.'[4]

29   Therefore, men, because our origin is from God, we ought not to think that the divine is likened to gold or to silver or[5] to stone that is engraved by the workmanship and by the knowledge of man.

---

[1] Eastern txt: alt sp, ܐܣܛܘܐܝܐ for further study, Freeman, p. 447.
[2] Same root: *preaches, preaching*
[3] Repeat *worship*, vs. 22, 23, 2x
[4] This is a quote from a secular astronomical work by Aratus, called *Phainomena*, 5th line of the poem.
[5] Repeat *or*

Chapter 17

30   For God has caused the ^{sy}times of ignorance to pass. And in this time he has commanded all men that every man in every[1] place should repent,

31   because he has established a ^{sy}day in which he is going to judge the whole earth with justice by way of the man whom he appointed. And he has caused everyone to turn to his faith, in that he raised him from the dead."

32   And when they heard of the resurrection that is from the dead, some of them mocked, and some of them[2] said, "At another time we will hear you about this."

33   And so Paul went away from among them.

34   And some of them followed after him and believed. And one of them was Dionysius of the judges of Areopagus, and a certain woman whose name was Damaris, and others with them.

Chapter 18

1   And after Paul went away from Athens, he came to Corinth.

2   And he found there a certain Judean man whose name was Aquila, who was from the region [of] Pontus, who in that time had come from the region of Italy, he and Priscilla his wife, because Claudius Caesar had commanded all the Judeans to leave Rome. And he approached them

3   and because he was their fellow craftsman, he lodged with them and was working with them. And by their craft, they were makers of tent cloth.

4   And he spoke in the synagogue on every SABBATH and persuaded the Judeans and heathens.

5   And after Silas and Timothy had come from Macedonia, Paul was pressured in the word because the Judeans were opposing him and blaspheming while he was witnessing to them that Jesus was the MESSIAH.

6   And he shook his garments and said to them, "From now on, I am clean. I am going to the Gentiles."

7   And he went away from there and entered the house of a man whose name [was] Titus, who feared God. And his house was attached to the synagogue.

---

[1] Repeat *every* (*all*), 3x
[2] Repeat *some of them*, also v. 34

Chapter 18

8   And Crispus, the ruler of the synagogue, believed in our Lord, he and all his household. And many Corinthians heard and believed in God and were baptized.

9   And the LORD said to Paul in a vision, "Do not fear, but speak and do not keep silent,

10   because I am with you, and no man is able to harm you, and I have many people in this city."

11   And he stayed in Corinth [for] one year and six months and taught them the word of God.

12   And when Gallio was proconsul of Achaia, the Judeans were gathered together against Paul. And they brought him before the judgment seat,

13   saying, "This [man] persuades men to be fearing God, beyond the law."

14   And while Paul was requesting to ᵖʳopen his mouth and to speak, Gallio said to the Judeans, "If you were accusing about a matter of evil or of deceit or[1] of hatred, oh Judeans, of necessity I would receive you.

15   But if the questions are about word[s] and about names and about[2] your law, you should understand [them] among yourselves, for I do not want to be a judge of these issues."

16   And he expelled them from his judgment seat.

17   And all the heathens arrested Sosthenes, an elder of the synagogue, and beat him before the judgment seat. And Gallio overlooked these [things].

18   And after Paul was there many days, he gave a farewell[3] to the brothers and journeyed by sea to go to Syria. And Priscilla and Aquila went with him, after he had shaved his head in Cenchrea, because a vow was vowed[4] by him.

19   And they arrived at Ephesus. And Paul entered the synagogue and was speaking with the Judeans.

20   And they begged him to extend the time with them, yet he was not persuaded,

---

[1] Repeat *or*
[2] Repeat *about*
[3] Lit: peace
[4] Same root: *vow, vowed*

Chapter 18

21   saying, "It is right for me certainly, that I should keep the feast that is coming in Jerusalem. But if God wills, I will return again to you." And he left Aquila and Priscilla in Ephesus.

22   And he journeyed by sea and came to Caesarea. And he went up and greeted the clergy and went to Antioch.

23   And after he was there some days, he went away and traveled around in order in the region of Galatia and of Phrygia, establishing all the disciples.

24   And a certain man whose name was Apollos, a Judean who was a native of Alexandria and was trained in speech and observant in the scriptures, came to Ephesus.

25   This [man] was instructed in the way of the LORD and was spiritually fervent and was speaking and teaching fully about Jesus, while not knowing anything except the baptism of John.

26   And he began to speak boldly in the synagogue. And when Aquila and Priscilla heard him, they brought him to their house and fully showed him the way of the LORD.

27   And when he wanted to go to Achaia, the brothers encouraged him and wrote to the disciples to receive him. And after he had gone, through grace, he greatly aided all the believers,

28   for he debated mightily against the Judeans before the crowds, showing from the scriptures concerning Jesus, that he is the MESSIAH.

Chapter 19

1   And while Apollos was in Corinth, Paul traveled around in the upper regions and came to Ephesus. And he asked the disciples whom he found there,

2   "Did you receive the Holy Spirit when you believed?" They answered and said to him, "We have not even heard if there is a Holy Spirit."

3   He said to them, "Then into what were you baptized?" They said, "Into the baptism of John."

4   Paul said to them, "John baptized the people with the baptism of repentance, telling [them] to believe in him who would follow him, who is Jesus Christ."

5   And after they heard these [things], they were baptized in the name of our Lord Jesus Christ.

Chapter 19

6   And Paul laid a hand on them and the Holy Spirit came on them and they spoke in different languages and prophesied.

7   And all the men were twelve.

8   And Paul entered the synagogue and spoke boldly [for] three months and was persuading [them] about the kingdom of God.

9   And some of them were hardened ^Pand were striving against and reviling the ^mway of God before the assembly of the Gentiles.⌐ Then Paul distanced [himself] and separated the disciples from them. And every day he was speaking to them in the school of a man whose name [was] Tyrannus.

10   And this continued [for] two years, until all who lived in Asia, Judeans and Arameans, heard the word of the LORD.

11   And God was doing great miracles by the ^mhand of Paul,

12   so that even from the coats that were on his body, handkerchiefs or pieces of cloth were brought and placed on the sick and the sicknesses went away from them[1] and demons also went out.

13   And some Judeans, who traveled about and exorcised demons, were also wanting to exorcise in the name of our Lord Jesus those who had unclean spirits, saying, "We exorcise you in the name of the Jesus whom Paul preaches."

14   And there were seven sons of a certain Judean man, a chief priest whose name was Sceva, who were doing this.

15   And that wicked demon answered and said to them, "Jesus I know and Paul I know,[2] but who are **you**?"

16   And that man who had the evil spirit leaped on them and overcame them and cast them down. And being naked and wounded, they fled from that house.

17   And this was known by all the Judeans and Arameans who lived in Ephesus. And fear fell on all of them and the name of our Lord Jesus Christ was lifted up.

18   And many of those who believed came and declared their faults and confessed what they had done.

---

[1] Culture: this was a common Eastern belief that a piece of clothing of a holy man had healing power, Hardy, p. 123; same root: *sick, sicknesses*

[2] Repeat *I know*

Chapter 19

19   And many sorcerers also gathered their books and brought [and] burned them before everyone. And they counted their price and the silver amounted to five thousand [pieces].

20   And so with great power the faith of God grew strong and increased.

21   And after these [things] had been accomplished, Paul set in his mind to travel around in all of Macedonia and in Achaia and [then] to go to Jerusalem. And he said, "When I have gone there, it is right for me to also see Rome."

22   And he sent two men from those who ministered to him to Macedonia, Timothy and Erastus. But **he** remained a time in Asia.

23   And during that time a great uproar occurred about the [m]way of God.

24   And there was there a certain worker of silver, whose name was Demetrius who was making shrines of silver for Artemis[1] and he brought great profit to his fellow craftsmen.

25   This [man] gathered all his fellow craftsmen and those who worked with them and said to them, "Men, you know that all our trade is from this occupation.

26   And **you** have also heard and you have seen that this Paul has persuaded and turned away, not only the citizens of Ephesus, but also a multitude of all of Asia, saying that those are not gods that are made by the hands of men.

27   And not only this business is being shamed and brought to nothing, but also the temple of the great goddess Artemis is counted as nothing, and also the goddess, whom all Asia and all the Gentiles worship, is despised."

28   And when they heard these [things], they were filled with fury and cried out and said, "Great is Artemis of the Ephesians."

29   And the whole city was stirred up. And they ran together and went to the theater. And they seized [and] took along with them, Gaius and Aristarchus, Macedonian men, the companions of Paul.

30   And Paul wanted to enter the theater, yet the disciples prevented him.

---

[1] Culture: this goddess was known among the Greeks as Artemis and among the Romans as Diana, Barnes, *People's Bible Encyclopedia*, p. 417.

Chapter 19

31   And also the chiefs of Asia, because they were his friends, sent [and] begged him not to give up his life to enter the theater.

32   And the crowds that were in the theater were very confused and were crying one thing and [then] another, for many of them did not know why they had been gathered.

33   And the people of the Judeans who were there put forward a Judean man of them whose name was Alexander. And when he stood up, he waved his hand and wanted to make a defense to the people.

34   And knowing that he was a Judean, all of them cried out with one voice [for] about two hours, "Great is Artemis of the Ephesians."

35   And the ruler of the city quieted them, saying, "Men, Ephesians, for who are the men who do not know that the ^{pe}city of the Ephesians is the priestess of the great Artemis and her image that came down from heaven?

36   Therefore, because no one can speak against this, you ought to be quiet and not do anything in haste,

37   for you have brought these men [here], although they have not stolen from the temples, nor reviled our goddess.

38   Now if this Demetrius and his fellow craftsmen have a controversy with someone, *behold, the proconsul [is] in the city. They are craftsmen, [so] they should go near and judge one with the other.

39   And if you are seeking something else, let it be settled in a place that is given by the law for an assembly,

40   because now we also stand in danger of being accused as troublemakers, because we are not able to give a reason for the crowd of this day, because we have been assembled[1] needlessly and made an uproar without a cause."

41   And after he had said these [things], he dismissed the crowd.

Chapter 20

1   And after the uproar had subsided, Paul called for the disciples and comforted them and kissed them and left [and] went to Macedonia.

2   And when he had gone about those regions and had comforted them with many words, he came to the country [of] Greece.

---

[1] Same root: *crowd, assembled*

Chapter 20

3 And he was there [for] three months. But the Judeans planned treachery against him when he was about to go to Syria and he thought that he should return to Macedonia.

4 And Sopater, who was from the city [of] Berea, and Aristarchus and Secundus, who were of the Thessalonians, and Trophimus and Gaius, who were from the city [of] Derbe, and Timothy, who was from Lystra, and Tychicus and Trophimus from Asia went away with him as far as Asia.

5 These went on before us and waited for us at Troas.

6 But [ac]**we** left Philippi, a city of the Macedonians, after the days of the Feast of Unleavened Bread, and traveled by sea and arrived at Troas in five days. And we were there [for] seven days.

7 And on the first day of the week when we were assembled to break [the bread of] communion, Paul spoke with them, because the next day he was going to leave and he continued to speak until the middle of the night.

8 And there were many lamps burning there in that upper room where we were gathered.

9 And a certain young man, whose name was Eutychus, was sitting in a window and listening. And he sunk into a deep sleep while Paul was continuing the speech, and in his sleep he fell from the third loft and was taken up as dead.

10 And Paul went down [and] fell on him and embraced him. And he said, "Do not be troubled, because his life is in him."

11 Now when he had gone [back] up, he broke bread and ate and continued speaking until the morning dawned. And then he left to go on by land.

12 And they led out the young man alive and rejoiced in him greatly.

13 And **we** went down to the ship and sailed to the port of Assos, because there we had arranged to meet Paul. For so he had commanded us, when he had gone on by land.

14 Now when we met him at Assos, we boarded the ship and came to Mitylene.

15 And from there, the next day we sailed toward the island [of] Chios. And again, the next day we came to Samos and remained at Trogyllium. And the next day we came to Miletus,

Chapter 20

16   for Paul was determined to pass by Ephesus, lest he should be delayed there, because he was hurrying, so that if possible, he would celebrate the day of Pentecost in Jerusalem.

17   And from Miletus, he sent to bring the elders of the church at Ephesus.

18   And when they came to him, he said to them, "**You** know, since the first day that I entered Asia, how I was with you all the time,

19   as I was serving God with great meekness and with tears and in[1] the trials that came on me by the treacheries of the Judeans.

20   And I did not avoid what was profitable for your lives to preach to you and teach in the streets and in houses,

21   witnessing[2] to the Judeans and to the Arameans concerning repentance towards God and the faith that is in our Lord Jesus Christ.

22   And now **I** am bound by the Spirit and I am traveling to Jerusalem and I do not know what will happen to me in it.

23   Nevertheless, the Holy Spirit witnesses in every city to me and has said, 'Bonds and trials are prepared for you.'

24   But I have not counted my life [as] anything, so that I may complete my [m]course and the ministry that I have received from our Lord Jesus, that I may witness concerning the gospel of the grace of God.

25   And now **I** know that you will not see my face again, all of you for whom I have traveled [and] preached the kingdom.

26   And because of this, I witness to you this very day that I am pure from the [m]blood of all of you.

27   For I have not refused to make known to you all the will of God.

28   [al]Watch, therefore, over yourselves and over all the [h]flock over which the Holy Spirit has appointed you overseers, to feed the church of God[3] that he purchased with his blood.

29   **I** know that after I am gone fierce [h]wolves will enter among you without mercy on the [h]flock.⌐

30   And also, from yourselves [there] will rise up men speaking perverse [things] to turn away the disciples to follow them.

---

[1] Repeat *with* (*in*), 3x
[2] Repeat forms of *witness*, vs. 21-26
[3] Eastern txt: *God* is "Christ"

Chapter 20

31 Because of this, you should be vigilant and remember that [for] three years I did not stop, ^{mr}by night and by day, admonishing each one of you with tears.

32 And now I commend you to God and to the word of his grace that is able to build you up and to give you an inheritance with all the holy [ones].

33 Silver or gold or[1] garments I have not desired.

34 And **you** know that these hands ministered to my necessity and to those who were with me.

35 And I demonstrated everything to you, that so it is right to labor and to care for those who are weak and to remember the words of our Lord Jesus, because **he** said, 'He who gives is more blessed than he who receives.'"

36 And when he said these [things], he kneeled down and prayed and everyone with him.

37 And there was great weeping among all of them and they embraced him and kissed him.

38 But they were most anguished about that word that he said, that they were not going to see his face again. And they accompanied him as far as the ship.

Chapter 21

1 And ^{ac}we separated from them and journeyed directly to the island [of] Coos. And the next day we came to Rhodes and from there to Patara.

2 And we found a ship there that was going to Phoenicia and we boarded it and proceeded.

3 And we came as far as the island [of] Cyprus and passed it by on the left hand and came to Syria. And from there we arrived at Tyre, for there the ship was to unload her cargo.

4 And finding disciples there, we remained with them seven days and they were saying every day to Paul spiritually that he should not go to Jerusalem.

5 And after those days, we left to go on the journey and they all accompanied us,[2] with their wives and their children, until [we were]

---

[1] Repeat *or*

[2] Culture: it was common to accompany a departing guest a distance on the way, Rice, *Orientalisms in Bible Lands*, p. 75.

Chapter 21

outside of the city. Then they kneeled down[1] by the shore of the sea and prayed.

6   And we kissed each other and we boarded the ship and they returned to their houses.

7   Now **we** sailed from Tyre and came to the city [of] Accho. And we greeted the brothers there and lodged with them one day.

8   And on the next day we left and came to Caesarea. And we entered [and] lodged in the house of Philip the evangelist, who was [one] of the seven.[2]

9   And he had four unmarried daughters who prophesied.

10   And while we were there many days, a certain prophet came down from Judea, whose name was Agabus.

11   And he came in to us and took the girdle of the loins of Paul and bound his own feet and his hands and said, "Thus says the Holy Spirit, so the Judeans in Jerusalem will bind the man [who is] the owner of this girdle and will deliver him into the hands of the Gentiles."

12   And when we heard these words, we and the residents begged him that he would not go to Jerusalem.

13   Then Paul answered and said, "What are you doing, that you are weeping and breaking my heart? For **I** am ready not to be bound only, but also to die in Jerusalem for the name of our Lord Jesus."

14   And when he was not persuaded by us, we ceased and we said that the will of our Lord will happen.

15   And after those days, we prepared ourselves and went up to Jerusalem.

16   And some of the disciples from Caesarea came with us, bringing with them a brother, one of the first disciples whose name was Mnason and was from Cyprus, so that he might receive us in his house.

17   And when we arrived at Jerusalem, the brothers received us gladly.

18   And the next day we went in with Paul to James, as all of the elders were with him.

19   And we greeted them and Paul was narrating to them in order all that God had done among the Gentiles by his ministry.

---

[1] Lit: bowed on their knees

[2] Fig: ellipsis, *seven* [original deacons]

Chapter 21

20   And after they heard, they praised God and said to him, "Our brother, you see how many thousands there are in Judea who have believed and all of these are zealots of the law.

21   Now it was said to them about you, that you are teaching that all of the Judeans who are with the Gentiles should break away from Moses, saying that they should not circumcise their children and they should not walk in the customs of the law.

22   Therefore, because they have heard that you have come here,

23   do what we tell you. We have four men who have made a vow to be purified.

24   Lead them and go, be purified[1] with them and pay the expenses with them, as they will shave their heads. And it will be known to everyone that what is said about you is false and [that] **you** fulfill and keep the law.

25   Now about those who believed of the Gentiles, we have written that they should be keeping themselves away from that which is sacrificed and from fornication and from [that which] is strangled and from blood."

26   Then Paul took these men the next day and was purified with them. And he entered [and] went into the temple, informing them [of] the completion of the days of purification, until the offering of each one of them was offered.[2]

27   And when the seventh day arrived, the Judeans who were from Asia saw him in the temple and incited all of the people against him and they laid hands on him,

28   crying out and saying, "Men of Israel, help! This is the man who is against our own people, teaching in every location against the law and against[3] this place. And he has also brought Arameans into the temple and defiled this holy place."

29   For previously they had seen Trophimus, an Ephesian, with him in the city, and were supposing that he had entered the temple with Paul.

30   And the city was stirred up and all of the people were gathered. And they took hold of Paul and dragged him outside of the temple and immediately the gates were shut.

31   And as the crowd was seeking to kill him, it was reported to the chiliarch of the military guard that all of the city was stirred up.

---

[1] Repeat *be purified* from v. 23
[2] Same root: *offering, was offered*
[3] Repeat *against*

Chapter 21

32   And immediately he took a centurion and many soldiers and they ran to them. And when they saw the chiliarch and the soldiers, they stopped beating Paul.

33   And the chiliarch came toward him and held him and commanded that they should bind him with two chains. And he asked about him, who he was and what he had done.

34   And some of the mob cried out various [things] about him, yet because of their noise, he was not able to know what was the truth. And he commanded that they should conduct him to the military camp.

35   And when Paul reached the stairs, the soldiers carried him because of the violence of the people.

36   For many people followed him and they cried out and were saying, "Take him away!"

37   And when he arrived at the entrance to the military camp, **Paul** said to the chiliarch, "Will you allow me to speak with you?" And **he** said to him, "Do you know Greek?

38   Are you not that Egyptian, who before these days stirred up and led out to the wilderness four thousand men, doers of evil [things]?"

39   Paul said to him, "I am a Judean man from Tarsus, the notable city of Cilicia in which I was born. I beg you [to] allow me to speak to the people."

40   And when he allowed him, Paul stood on the stairs and was motioning to them with his hand. And when they quieted down, he spoke with them in Hebrew and said to them,

Chapter 22

1   "Brothers and fathers, hear a defense that is to you."

2   And when they heard that he was speaking with them in Hebrew, they quieted down more. And he said to them,

3   "**I** am a Judean man and I was born in Tarsus of Cilicia, but I was educated in this city beside the feet of Gamaliel and was instructed perfectly in the law of our fathers. And I was zealous of God, even as also all of you are.

4   And I persecuted this ^m^way to the death, binding and delivering men and women to prison.

341

Chapter 22

5   As the chief priests and all of the elders witness about me, from them I received letters to go to the brothers that are in Damascus, that I should also bring those who were there to Jerusalem, being bound and to receive punishment.

6   And as I was traveling and began to approach Damascus in the middle of the day, suddenly a great light from heaven shone on me.

7   And I fell on the ground and I heard a voice that said to me, 'Saul, Saul,[1] why are you persecuting me?'

8   And I answered and said, 'Who are you, my Lord?' And **he** said to me, 'I am Jesus, the Nazarene, whom you are persecuting.'

9   And the men who were with me saw the light, but they did not hear the voice that was speaking with me.

10   And I said, 'What should I do, my Lord?' And our Lord[2] said to me, 'Stand up [and] go to Damascus and there it will be told you about everything that is commanded you to do.'

11   And when I did not see because of the glory of that light, those who were with me took hold of my hands and I entered Damascus.

12   And a certain man, Ananias, upright in the law, as all of the Judeans there witnessed about him,

13   came to me and said to me, 'Saul, my brother, open your eyes!' And immediately my eyes were opened and I looked at him.

14   And he said to me, 'The God of our fathers has appointed you to know his will and to see the Just [one][3] and to hear the voice from his ᵐmouth.

15   And you will be a witness for him to all men about all that you have seen and heard.

16   And now, why are you wasting time? Rise up [and] be baptized and be cleansed from your sins, as you call on his name.'

17   And I returned [and] came here to Jerusalem and I prayed in the temple.

18   And I saw in a vision as he said to me, 'Hurry and go out from Jerusalem, because they will not receive your witness concerning me.'

19   And I said, 'My Lord, they also know that I delivered to prison and beat those who believed in you in all our synagogues.

---

[1] Fig: epizeuxis, very solemn repetition

[2] Repeat *Lord* next word

[3] Fig: antonomasia, name change

ARAMAIC PESHITTA NEW TESTAMENT
ACTS

Chapter 22
20   And when the blood of Stephen[1] your witness was shed, **I** was also standing with them. And I approved the desire of the murderers and kept the garments of those who were stoning him.'
21   And he said to me, 'Go, for **I** am sending you to a far place to preach to the Gentiles.'"
22   And after they had listened to Paul up to this word, they [pr]raised their voice[s] and cried out, "This [one] should be cut off from the earth, for thus it is not right for him to live!"
23   And as they were calling out and putting off their garments and throwing dust up into the sky,[2]
24   the chiliarch commanded that they should carry him to the military camp and commanded that he should be interrogated with stripes, so that he would know for what cause they cried out against him.
25   And while they stretched him with leather straps, **Paul** said to the centurion who was standing over him, "Is it permissible for you to beat a Roman man who is not condemned?"
26   And when the centurion heard [this], he came near to the chiliarch and said to him, "What are you doing? For this man is a Roman."
27   And the chiliarch came near to him and said to him, "Tell me, are you a Roman?" And he said to him, "Yes."
28   And the chiliarch answered and said, "**I** obtained Roman citizenship with much money." Paul said to him, "But **I** was even born in it."
29   And immediately those who were wanting to beat him went away from him and the chiliarch was afraid after he learned that he was a Roman, because he had bound him.
30   And the next day, he desired to know truly, what the accusation was that the Judeans were bringing against him. And he released him and commanded that the chief priests and all the assembly of their rulers should come. And he took Paul and brought [him] down [and] put him forward among them.

Chapter 23
1   And when Paul looked at their assembly, he said, "Men, my brothers, in all good conscience, I have conducted myself before God up to this day."

---

[1] Eastern txt: alt sp DASYPNS ܐܣܛܦܢܘܣ
[2] Culture: throwing dust in the air shows their anger, Barnes, *People's Bible Encyclopedia*, p. 286.

ARAMAIC PESHITTA NEW TESTAMENT
ACTS

Chapter 23

2 And Ananias, the priest, commanded those who were standing by his side to strike Paul on his mouth.

3 And Paul said to him, "God is going to strike you, [h]whitened wall![1] And are you sitting [and] judging me according to the law when you are transgressing the law and commanding that they should strike me?"

4 And those who were standing there said to him, "Are you speaking evil of the priest of God?"

5 Paul said to them, "I did not know, my brothers, that he was a priest, for it is written: **YOU SHOULD NOT CURSE THE LEADER OF YOUR PEOPLE.**

6 And after Paul knew that some of the people were of the Sadducees and some [were] of the Pharisees, he cried out in the assembly, "Men, my brothers, I am a Pharisee, the son of Pharisees and concerning the hope of the resurrection of the dead, I am being judged."

7 And when he had said this, the Pharisees and Sadducees fell on one another and the people were divided.

8 For the Sadducees said that there was no resurrection and no angels and no spirit, but the Pharisees professed all of these.

9 And there was a loud cry and some scribes of the side of the Pharisees rose up and were striving with them and said, "We have not found anything that is evil in this man. Now if a spirit or an angel has spoken with him, what is in this?"

10 And as there was a huge uproar among them, the chiliarch was afraid lest they should tear Paul apart. And he sent Romans to go to seize him in the middle of them and bring him to the military camp.

11 And when it was night, our Lord appeared to Paul and said to him, "Be strengthened, because as you have witnessed about me in Jerusalem, so you are also going to witness in Rome."

12 And when it was daybreak, men from the Judeans were assembled and they vowed to themselves that they would neither eat nor drink until they had killed Paul.

13 Now there were more than forty men who had confirmed this pact by oaths.

---

[1] Fig: hypocatastasis, meaning a hypocrite, where the outside is painted and clean, but the inside is corrupt.

Chapter 23

14   And they approached the priests and the elders and said, "We have vowed a vow[1] to ourselves that we will taste nothing, until we have killed Paul.

15   And now you and the rulers of the synagogue request of the chiliarch, that he should bring him to you as if you were seeking to truly examine his circumstance, and we are prepared to kill him before he would arrive to you."

16   And the son of the sister of Paul heard of this plot. And he entered the military camp and informed Paul.

17   And Paul sent [and] called for one of the centurions and said to him, "Conduct this young man to the chiliarch, for he has something to say to him."

18   And the centurion took the young man and brought him to the chiliarch and he said, "Paul, the prisoner, called me and asked me to bring this young man to you, who has something to say to you."

19   And the chiliarch held the young man by the hand[2] and led him to one side and asked him, "What do you have to say to me?"

20   And the young man said to him, "The Judeans have purposed to ask you to bring Paul down tomorrow to their synagogue, as though they wish to learn something more from him.

21   However, **you** should not be persuaded by them, for *behold, more than forty men of them are watching for him in ambush and have vowed to themselves that they will neither eat nor drink until they will have killed him. And *behold, they are ready and are waiting for your promise."

22   And the chiliarch dismissed the young man after he had charged him, "Let no man know that you have shown me these [things]."

23   And he called two centurions and said to them, "Go [and] prepare two hundred Romans to go to Caesarea and seventy horsemen and two hundred archers with the right hand to leave at the third hour of the night.

24   And also provide a beast of burden to set Paul on and deliver him to Felix the governor."

25   And he wrote a letter [and] gave [it] to them in which was the following:

---

[1] Same root: *vow, vowed*

[2] Culture: to take the hand symbolizes a friendly and honorable reception, Neil, *Palestine Life*, p. 150.

ARAMAIC PESHITTA NEW TESTAMENT
ACTS

Chapter 23
26 Claudius[1] Lysias to Felix, the noble governor: "Greeting.
27 The Judeans arrested this man so that they could kill him and I aided [him] with Romans and rescued him when I learned that he was a Roman.
28 And as I was seeking to know the charge for which they accused him, I brought him to their synagogue.
29 And I found out that they accused him about questions of their law and there was not a charge toward him that was worthy of bonds or death.
30 And when I was informed of a plot by an ambush that the Judeans had planned against him, immediately I sent him to you and commanded his accusers to come and speak with him before you. Farewell."
31 Then the Romans, as they were commanded, led Paul by night and brought him to the city [of] Antipatris.
32 And the next day, the horsemen sent away the foot soldiers, their associates, to return to the military camp.
33 And they brought him to Caesarea and gave the letter to the governor and they placed Paul before him.
34 And when he read the letter, he asked him from what province he was. And when he learned that he was from Cilicia,
35 he said to him, "I will hear you, when your accusers are come." And he commanded that they should keep him in the judgment hall of Herod.

Chapter 24
1 And after five days, Ananias the high priest went down, with the elders and with Tertullus the orator, and they informed the governor concerning Paul.
2 And when he was called, Tertullus began to accuse him and said, "We live in ^{an}abundance of quietness because of you and many reforms have been [made] for this people in the discharge of your care.
3 And all of us in every place receive your favor, noble Felix.
4 But lest you should be wearied with many [things], I beg you to hear our humility with few words.
5 For we have found this man to be one who is corrupt and stirs up sedition among all the Judeans in all the land. For he is the leader of the teaching of the Nazarenes

---

[1] Eastern txt: omit *Claudius*

346

Chapter 24

6   and he wanted to defile our temple. After we arrested him, we wanted to judge him according to our law,

7   but Lysias the chiliarch came and with great violence, grabbed him out of our hands and sent him to you.

8   And he commanded his accusers to come before you. And you will find when you ask him, that you will learn from him about all these [things] of which we are accusing him."

9   And the Judeans also cried out against him, saying that these [things] were so.

10   And the governor signaled to Paul to speak. And Paul answered and said, "For many years, I know that you have been a judge of this people and because of this, I make a defense for myself gladly.

11   As you may know, there has not been more than twelve days since I went up to Jerusalem to worship.

12   And they did not find me speaking with anyone in the temple, nor gathering a crowd, not in their synagogue or in the city.

13   And they will not be able to prove before you what they are now accusing me.

14   Nevertheless, this I do confess, that in this teaching about which they speak, I serve the God of my fathers, believing all the things that are written in the law and in the prophets.

15   And I have hope of God, which they themselves also are hoping, that there is going to be a resurrection from the dead of the upright and of the wicked.

16   Because of this also, I am laboring to have a pure conscience before God and before men always.

17   Now after many years, I came to my own people to give charity and to bring an offering.

18   And these [men] found me in the temple as I was purifying myself, not with a crowd nor in a riot.

19   But if certain Judeans who came from Asia stirred up ᵉ[the riot], these ought to stand with me before you and accuse [me of] whatever they have ᵉ[against me].

20   Or **these** should say what offense they found in me, when I stood before their assembly.

21   ᵉ[There was no offense] except this one word that I cried out when I stood among them, 'Concerning the resurrection of the dead I am being judged before you today.'"

Chapter 24

22   Now Felix, because he knew of this [m]way fully, put them off, saying, "When the chiliarch comes, I will hear between you."

23   And he commanded a centurion to keep Paul at ease and that none of his associates would be forbidden to minister to him.

24   And after a few days, Felix and Drusilla his wife, who was a Judean, sent and called for Paul and heard from him about the faith of Christ.

25   And while he was speaking with them about justification and about sanctification and about[1] the judgment of the future, Felix was filled with fear. And he said, "Now go, and when I have time, I will send for you."

26   For he was hoping that a bribe would be given to him by Paul. Because of this, he also continually sent for him to come and speak with him.

27   And after two years were concluded, another governor came into his position, who was called Porcius Festus. Now Felix, so that he would gain favor with the Judeans, left Paul bound.

Chapter 25

1   And when Festus came to Caesarea, after three days, he went up to Jerusalem.

2   And the chief priests and the rulers of the Judeans informed him about Paul. And they begged him,

3   asking him this favor, that he would summon him to be brought to Jerusalem, as they were setting ambushes along the road to kill him.

4   And Festus gave an answer, "Paul will be kept at Caesarea and I will hasten to journey [there].

5   Therefore, those who are with you, who are able to come down with us, should accuse [him] concerning every offense that is in the man."

6   And when he had been there eight or ten days, he went down to Caesarea. And on the next day he sat on the judgment seat and commanded that they should bring Paul.

7   And after he arrived, the Judeans, who had come down from Jerusalem, surrounded him and the leaders brought many harsh [things] against him, which they were not able to prove,

---

[1] Repeat *about*

Chapter 25

8   and after Paul made a defense that he had not offended [in] anything, neither in the law of the Judeans, nor in the temple, nor[1] against Caesar.

9   But Festus, because he was willing to grant a favor to the Judeans, said to Paul, "Are you willing to go up to Jerusalem and there to be judged before me about these [things]?"

10   Paul answered and said, "I stand on the judgment seat of Caesar. Here it is right for me to be judged. I have not committed any sin against the Judeans, as **you** also know.

11   And if I had committed an offense or anything worthy of death, I would not refuse death. But if there is nothing against me of these [things] that they are accusing me, no one should give me to them [as] a gift. I make an appeal to Caesar."

12   Then Festus spoke with his counselors. And he said, "Have you made an appeal [to] Caesar? To Caesar[2] you will go."

13   And after there were [some] days, Agrippa the king and Bernice came down to Caesarea to greet Festus.

14   And after they were with him [some] days, Festus narrated the case of Paul to the king, saying, "A certain man was left a prisoner by the [m]hands of Felix.

15   And when I was in Jerusalem, the chief priests and elders of the Judeans informed me regarding him and desired that I would give them judgment against him."

16   And I said to them, "It is not the custom of the Romans to give a man [as] a gift for murder, until his opponent at law should come and charge him to his face and an opportunity is given to him to make a defense regarding that for which he is accused.

17   And when I came here, without delay, the next day I sat on the judgment seat and commanded them to bring me the man.

18   And his accusers stood with him and they were not able to prove any evil accusation against him, even as I had supposed.

19   But they had various questions to him concerning their religion and concerning Jesus, a man who died, whom Paul was saying was alive.

---

[1] Repeat *nor*, lit: and not

[2] Repeat *to Caesar*

Chapter 25

20   And because I did not establish [anything] about the dispute of these [things], I had said to Paul, 'Do you desire to go to Jerusalem and there to be judged concerning these [things]?'

21   But **he** requested to be kept for judgment before Caesar and I commanded that he should be kept until I would send him to Caesar."

22   And Agrippa said, "I desire to hear this man." And Festus said, "Tomorrow you will hear him."

23   And the next day Agrippa and Bernice came with great ceremony and entered the judgment hall with the chiliarchs and rulers of the city and Festus commanded and Paul came.

24   And Festus said, "Agrippa, the king, and all men who are with us, concerning this man whom you see, all the people of the Judeans have complained to me in Jerusalem and here, crying out that it is no longer right for this [man] to live.

25   But **I** have found that he has not done anything that is worthy of death. And because **he** requested to be kept for judgment before Caesar, I have commanded that he should be sent.

26   And I do not know what to write about him to Caesar. Because of this, I desired to bring him before you and especially before you, King Agrippa, that when his case will be examined, I will be able to write what [it is].

27   For it is not proper, when we send a man [as] a prisoner, not[1] to write his offense."

Chapter 26

1   And Agrippa said to Paul, "You are permitted to speak for yourself." Then Paul stretched out his hand and made a defense and said,

2   "Concerning all of which I am accused by the Judeans, King Agrippa, I consider myself blessed that I may make a defense before you today,

3   especially because I know that you are acquainted with all the questions and laws of the Judeans. Because of this, I beg you to hear me with long-suffering.

4   For those Judeans also know, if they were willing to testify, [that] my manner of life was from my childhood, from the beginning, among my people and in Jerusalem,

---

[1] Repeat *not*

Chapter 26

5   because from long ago they were aware of me and know that I lived in the best teaching of the Pharisees.

6   And now, concerning the hope of the promise that was [given] to our fathers from God, I stand and am judged.

7   For concerning this hope our twelve tribes hope to come, with diligent prayers ^{mr}by day and by night. And concerning this hope,[1] I am accused by the ^mhands of the Judeans, King Agrippa.

8   What are you judging? Is it not right that we believe that God raises the dead?[2]

9   For formerly, I had set in my mind that I would do many adverse [things] against the name of Jesus the Nazarene.

10   This I also did in Jerusalem and I threw many holy [ones] in prison by the authority that I received from the chief priests. And when they were killed by them, I shared fully with those who condemned them.

11   And in every synagogue I tortured them, compelling [them] to blaspheme in the name of Jesus. And with the great anger that I was filled with against them, I also went to other cities to persecute them.

12   And when I was going for this purpose to Damascus with the authority and permission of the chief priests,

13   in the middle of the day on the road, I saw from heaven, oh King, a light that was greater than the sun that shone on me and on[3] all who were with me.

14   And we all fell on the ground. And I heard a voice saying to me in Hebrew, 'Saul, Saul,[4] why are you persecuting me? It is hard for you to kick against the goads.'

15   And I said, 'Who are you, my Lord?' And our Lord said to me, 'I am Jesus, the Nazarene, whom **you** are persecuting.'

16   And he said to me, 'Stand on your feet. For I have appeared to you because of this, to ordain you [as] a minister and a witness that you have seen me and that you are going to see me.

17   And I will deliver you from the people of the Judeans and from other Gentiles, to whom I send you,

---

[1] Same root: (*this*) *hope, hope*
[2] Fig: erotesis, "not" question, answer in the affirmative
[3] Repeat *on*
[4] Fig: epizeuxis, very solemn repetition; see note on Acts 9:4.

Chapter 26

18 that you should open their eyes, so that they will turn from darkness to the light ^Pand from the authority of SATAN to God and they will receive forgiveness of sins and a portion with the holy [ones] by faith that [is] in me.'⌐

19 Because of this, King Agrippa, I did not oppose the heavenly vision with dispute,

20 but I preached from the first to those of Damascus ^Pand to those who were in Jerusalem and in all the villages of Judea and also to the Gentiles.⌐ I preached that they should repent and should turn back to God and should perform works that are suitable to repentance.

21 And on account of these [things],[1] the Judeans arrested me in the temple and desired to kill me.

22 But God helped me to this day and *behold, I stand and testify to the small and to the great, not saying anything outside of Moses and the prophets, but those [things] that they said that were going to happen,

23 that the Messiah would suffer and would become the first[fruit] of the resurrection from the dead and that he would preach light to the people and to the Gentiles."

24 And as Paul was thus making a defense, Festus cried out with a loud voice, "Paul, you are mad! Much learning has caused you to be mad!"

25 Paul said, "I am not mad,[2] noble Festus, but I am speaking words of ^{he}truth and integrity.[3]

26 And also, King Agrippa especially knows about these [things], and because of this, I speak boldly before him, because I think that not one of these words has escaped his notice, for it was not performed secretly.

27 Do you believe the prophets, King Agrippa? I know that you do believe."

28 Agrippa said to him, "You are very nearly persuading me to become a Christian."

29 And Paul said, "I have asked God ^{mr.}in little and in much, not only for you to be, but also all those who hear me today, that they should be like me, except for these bonds."

---

[1] Lit: the face of these [things]

[2] Repeat *mad* from v. 24

[3] Fig: hendiadys, "exact truth"

Chapter 26

30   And the king stood up and the governor and Bernice and those who were sitting with them.

31   And after they had gone out from there, they spoke with each other and said, "This man has not done anything that is worthy of death or bonds."

32   And Agrippa said to Festus, "It is possible that this man could have been freed, if he had not appealed to Caesar."

Chapter 27

1   And Festus[1] commanded concerning him that he should be sent to Caesar to Italy. And he delivered Paul and other prisoners with him to a certain man, a centurion from the Augustan cohort, whose name was Julius.

2   And when it was ready to sail, [ac]we went down to a ship that was from the city [of] Adramyttium and was traveling to the region of Asia. And Aristarchus, a Macedonian who was from the city [of] Thessalonica, came on the ship with us.

3   And the next day we arrived at Sidon. And the centurion treated Paul with compassion and allowed him to go to his friends and to be refreshed.

4   And we sailed from there and because the winds were contrary to us, we followed a course near Cyprus.

5   And we crossed over the sea of Cilicia and Pamphylia and arrived at the city [of] Myra, of Lycia.

6   And there the centurion found a ship from Alexandria that was traveling to Italy and they settled us on it.

7   And because we were sailing under heavy [seas], after many days we barely reached the island [of] Cnidus. And because the wind did not allow us to proceed by a straight course, we kept a heading near Crete towards the city [of] Salmone.

8   And after we had sailed around it with difficulty, we arrived at a place that was called Fair Havens, [that] was near to a city by the name of Lasea.

9   And we were there a long time until even the day of the fast of the Judeans was past. And it was dangerous for anyone to travel by sea and Paul counseled them

---

[1] Eastern txt: alt sp PHSYS ܦܗܣܝܣ

Chapter 27

10   and said, "Men, I perceive that our voyage will occur with calamity and with much loss, not only of the cargo of our ship, but also of our own lives."

11   But the centurion listened to the shipmaster and the captain of the ship, rather than the words of Paul.

12   And because that port was not suitable to winter in foul weather, many of us wanted to travel from there and if possible, to reach and winter in a certain port that was in Crete and was called Phenice and looked to the south.

13   And after the south wind blew and they thought that we would arrive according to their desire, they followed a course on the side of Crete.

14   And shortly after we left, a sudden blast of wind [came] on us that was called a typhoon Euroclydon.[1]

15   And the ship was caught up and was not able to bear up against the wind and we yielded control of it.

16   And as we passed by a certain island that was called Cauda, we were hardly able to keep hold of the longboat.

17   And after we had taken it up [on board], we undergirded and prepared the ship. And because we were afraid, lest we should fall in the downward rapids of the sea, we pulled down the sail and so we drifted.

18   And as the violent storm raged against us, the next day we threw goods in the sea.

19   And the third day, we cast overboard the ship's own riggings with our hands.

20   And as the tempest continued more days and the sun was not visible nor the moon nor[2] stars, all hope of our living was completely cut off.

21   And as no one had eaten anything, then Paul stood up among them and said, "If you had been persuaded by me, men, we would not have sailed from Crete and we would have been spared from loss and from this calamity.

22   And now, I counsel that you should be without distress, for not one of you will be destroyed, but only the ship.

23   For there appeared to me in this night, an angel of that God whose I am and whom I serve.

---

[1] Culture: this wind was from the E.N.E., for detailed explanation of the storm and the shipwreck, Conybeare & Howsen, pp. 644-658

[2] Repeat *nor*

Chapter 27

24   And he said to me, 'Fear not, Paul, it is prepared for you to stand before Caesar and *behold, God has given to you [as a] gift, all who sail with you.'

25   Because of this, be encouraged, men, for I believe in God that it will be so even as it was communicated with me.

26   Nevertheless, we have to be thrown on a certain island."

27   And after fourteen days that we were wandering and were buffeted in the Adriatic Sea, at midnight, the sailors thought that they were coming near land.

28   And they put out the anchors and found twenty fathoms, and again they went forward a little, and found fifteen fathoms.

29   And being afraid lest we should be found the places where there were rocks, they put out four anchors from the stern of the ship and prayed that it would be day.

30   Now the sailors tried to flee from the ship and they lowered the longboat to the sea on the pretext that they would go in it to secure the ship on the land.

31   And Paul seeing [this], said to the centurion and to the soldiers, "If these do not remain in the ship, you will not be able to be saved."

32   Then the soldiers cut off the ropes of the longboat from the ship and allowed it to go adrift.

33   But Paul, when it was almost daybreak, convinced all of them that to take [some] nourishment, saying to them, "*Behold, today [it has been] fourteen days since you have eaten anything on account of the danger.

34   Because of this, I beg you to take food for the strengthening of your life, for not a hair from the head of any of you will be hurt."[1]

35   And as he said these [things], he took bread and praised God before all of them and he broke [the bread] and began to eat.

36   And they were all comforted and they received sustenance.

37   Now there were two hundred and seventy-six people in the ship.

38   And when they were satisfied with the food, they lightened the ship and took the wheat and threw [it] in the sea.

39   And when it was day, the sailors did not recognize what land it was, but they saw by the shore of the dry land a certain bay of the sea, where they thought that, if possible, they could thrust the ship.

---

[1] Perhaps *not a hair from the head of any of you will be hurt* is a proverb

ARAMAIC PESHITTA NEW TESTAMENT
ACTS

Chapter 27

40 And they cut off the anchors from the ship and they left them in the sea. And they released the bands of the rudders[1] and hoisted the small sail to the wind that was blowing and they proceeded toward the dry land.

41 And the ship struck on a place that was high between two deep [parts] of the sea and it was stuck on it. And the forward part of it stayed on it and was not to be moved, but the back part of it was broken to pieces by the violence of the waves.

42 And the soldiers wanted to kill the prisoners, so that they would not jump in swimming and would escape from them.

43 And the centurion prevented them from this, because he wanted to save Paul. And those who were able to jump in swimming, he commanded to swim first and to pass over to the land.

44 And the rest crossed over on boards and on other wood pieces of the ship. And so all of them escaped safely to the land.

Chapter 28

1 And afterwards, they learned that the island was called Melita.

2 And the barbarians who were living on it showed us many kindnesses and they kindled a fire and called to all of us that we should warm ourselves, because there was a great rain and [it was] cold.

3 And Paul picked up a large bundle of sticks and placed [them] on the fire and a viper came out of them because of the heat of the fire and bit his hand.

4 And when the barbarians saw that it was hanging on his hand, they said, "Perhaps this man is a murderer, so that even though he was rescued from the sea, [pe]justice will not allow him to live."

5 But **Paul** shook his hand and threw the viper in the fire and it did not harm him.

6 Now the barbarians expected that immediately he would swell up and fall dying on the ground. And after they waited a long time and saw that it did not harm him, they changed their words and said, "He is a god."

---

[1] Culture: there were two rudders on the ship, Conybeare & Howsen, p. 625, Freeman, p. 455.

356

Chapter 28

7   Now there were fields in that place [that belonged] to a certain man, whose name was Publius, who was the ruler of the island. And he gladly received us in his house [for] three days.

8   Now the father of Publius was sick with fever and with pain in the bowels. And Paul went in to him and prayed and laid his hand on him and healed him.

9   And after this happened, the rest of those who were also sick on the island came to him and they were healed.

10   And they honored us [with] great honors[1] and after we left there, they supplied us with provisions.

11   Now after three months, we left and sailed in a ship [of] Alexandria that had wintered in the island and the sign of the Twins[2] was on it.

12   And we came to the city [of] Syracuse and remained there [for] three days.

13   And from there we took a course and arrived at the city [of] Rhegium. And after one day, the south wind blew for us and in two days we came to Puteoli, a city of Italy.

14   And we found brothers there and they asked us [to stay] and we were with them [for] seven days and then we went on to Rome.

15   And when the brothers who were there heard [of our coming], they went out to meet us as far as the square that was called Appii Forum and as far as the Three Taverns.[3] And when Paul saw them, he gave thanks to God and was strengthened.

16   And we entered Rome and the centurion allowed Paul to lodge where he wanted, with a soldier who guarded him.

17   And after three days, Paul sent [and] called for the rulers of the Judeans. And when they were gathered, he said to them, "Men, my brothers, although in nothing I stood against the people and the law of my fathers, I was delivered in bonds at Jerusalem into the ᵐhand of the Romans."

18   And after **they** examined me, they wanted to release me, because they did not find any fault against me that was worthy of death.

---

[1] Same root: *honored, honors*

[2] Culture: the Twins were two main stars from the constellation Gemini and were regarded as the special patrons of sailors, Freeman, p. 455.

[3] Culture: it was an Oriental custom to meet, welcome and escort an important visitor to his journey's end. Appii Forum was 43 miles and Three Taverns, 33 miles from Rome, Neil, *Peeps into Palestine*, p. 170.

Chapter 28

19 "And as the Judeans stood against me, I was compelled to appeal to Caesar, [but] not because I had anything of which I would accuse the sons of my people.

20 Because of this, I asked you to come and to see you and to narrate these [things] to you, for because of the ^mhope[1] of Israel, I am bound with this chain."

21 **They** said to him, "**We** have not received a letter about you from Judea and none of the brothers who have come from Jerusalem have told us anything that is evil about you.

22 Now we want to hear from you what you think, because we know that this teaching is not accepted by men."

23 And they appointed him a day and they gathered together. And many came to him where he was lodging and he made known to them about the kingdom of God, witnessing and persuading them about Jesus, from the law of Moses and from[2] the prophets, from morning until evening.

24 And some of them were convinced of his words and others were not convinced.[3]

25 And they left him, disagreeing with one another. And Paul said to them this word, "Well did the Holy Spirit speak by the ^mmouth of Isaiah the prophet against your fathers,

26 saying: **GO TO THIS PEOPLE AND SAY TO THEM, HEARING, YOU WILL HEAR AND YOU WILL NOT UNDERSTAND AND YOU WILL SEE AND YOU WILL NOT[4] COMPREHEND.**

27 **FOR THE HEART OF THIS PEOPLE HAS BECOME DENSE AND THEY HAVE MADE HEAVY THEIR HEARING AND THEY HAVE CLOSED THEIR EYES, LEST THEY SHOULD SEE WITH THEIR EYES AND HEAR WITH THEIR EARS AND SHOULD UNDERSTAND IN THEIR HEART[S] AND SHOULD RETURN TO ME AND I SHOULD FORGIVE THEM.**

28 Therefore, be this known to you, that to the Gentiles is this redemption of God being sent. For **they** also are hearing it."

29 OMITTED IN THE WESTERN PESHITTA TEXT[5]

---

[1] Fig: metonymy, hope stands for the Messiah

[2] Repeat *from*

[3] Repeat *convinced*

[4] Repeat *not*

[5] Eastern txt: 'And when he said these [things], the Judeans went out and many were reasoning among them.'

Chapter 28

30 And Paul hired a house for himself at his own [cost] and was in it [for] two years. And there he received all those who came to him.

31 And he was preaching about the kingdom of God and teaching boldly about our Lord Jesus Christ without hindrance.

ARAMAIC PESHITTA NEW TESTAMENT
ROMANS

Chapter 1

1 Paul, a servant of Jesus Christ, a called [one] and an apostle, who was set apart for the gospel of God

2 that he had promised previously by way of his prophets in the holy scriptures,

3 concerning his Son, who was born[1] in the flesh of the seed of the house of David

4 and was made known [as] the Son of God by power and by[2] the Holy Spirit, who raised Jesus Christ our Lord from the dead,

5 by whom we have received [he]grace and apostleship among all the Gentiles, so that they would obey the faith of his name,

6 that **you** also from them are called [ones] in Jesus Christ.

7 To all who are in Rome, beloved of God, called and holy [ones]: Peace and grace [be] with you from God our Father and from[3] our Lord Jesus Christ.

8 First, I thank my God in Jesus Christ for[4] all of you that your faith is heard in all the [sy]world.

9 For God is a witness to me, whom I am spiritually[5] serving in the gospel of his Son, that without ceasing at all times, I remember you in my prayers.

10 And I am imploring that perhaps even now a way would be opened to me by the will of God to come to you,

11 because I greatly long to see you and to give you a spiritual gift by which you may be strengthened

12 and together we will be comforted by your and my own faith.

13 Now I want you to know, my brothers, that many times I wanted to come to you [pa](yet I was hindered until now) that I would also have [m]fruit among you, as among the rest of the Gentiles,

14 Greeks and barbarians, the wise and the foolish, because [me]I am a debtor to preach to every man.

15 And so I am concerned that I should declare [e][the gospel] to you who are in Rome also.

---

[1] OS (Efr) 'who was seen'

[2] Repeat *by*; lit: by power and by the holiness Spirit, not normal construction for "Holy Spirit"

[3] Repeat *from*

[4] Var (SLM): 'on behalf of'

[5] Var (M): 'with my spirit'

ARAMAIC PESHITTA NEW TESTAMENT
ROMANS

Chapter 1

16 For I am not ashamed of the gospel,[1] because it is the power of God for the life of all who believe in it, whether [they are] from the Judeans first or from[2] the heathens.

17 For the uprightness of God is revealed in it from faith to faith,[3] as it is written: **THE UPRIGHT [ONE] WILL LIVE BY FAITH.**

18 For the [c]wrath of God is revealed[4] from [m]heaven on all the wickedness and the ungodliness of men, those who close off truthfulness with wickedness,

19 because the knowledge of God is revealed among them, for God revealed it among them.

20 For the hidden [things] of God were made evident from the foundations of the world by his created [things] in [e][his] wisdom [P]and his power and his Godhead that is eternal,┐ so that they would be without defense,

21 because they knew God [P]and they did not glorify him as God and give thanks to him, but rather they became fruitless in their reasonings, and their heart without understanding was darkened.

22 And while they were thinking in themselves that they were wise, they were foolish.

23 And they changed the magnificence of the incorruptible God into the [an]likeness of the image[5] of corruptible man and into the likeness of birds and of four-footed [animals] and of creeping things of the earth.┐

24 Because of this, God delivered them to the polluted desires of their heart[s] to dishonor[6] their bodies by them.

25 And they changed the truth of God into a lie and they reverenced and served the created [things] more than their creator, [be]to whom [be] our praises and our blessings, forever and ever. Amen.

---

[1] Fig: tapeinosis, means the opposite

[2] Repeat *from*

[3] Semitism: *from faith to faith*, means from the beginning of faith to the end of faith. This could also be explained as being born again to living faithfully.

[4] Repeat *is revealed*, vs. 17-19

[5] Fig: antimeria, "imaginative likeness"

[6] Same root: vs. 24-27: *dishonor, shame,* and *use, used*

ARAMAIC PESHITTA NEW TESTAMENT
ROMANS

Chapter 1

26 Because of this, God delivered them[1] to [an]passions of shame. For their women changed the [e][natural] use of their sex and used what was not natural.

27 And so also their men left the [e][natural] use of the sex of women and ran riotously in lust for each other. And male with male, they acted with shame and received in themselves[2] the payment for their error that was just.

28 And since they had not determined in themselves to know God, God delivered them to a [an]mind of emptiness, that they would do what is not right,

29 being filled with all wickedness [P]and fornication and bitterness and evil and greed and envy and murder and strife and deceit and evil reasonings

30 and murmuring and slander.￢ And [they are] [a]haters of God, insolent, prideful, boastful, inventors of evil [things], ignorant [ones],[3] who are not obedient to their parents￢

31 and who do not have stability, nor[4] love, nor quietness, nor is there tenderness[5] in them.

32 [They are] those who, [pa]although they know the judgment of God that those who act like this he condemns to death,￢ not only are doing these [things], but also fellowship with those who are doing[6] these [things].

Chapter 2

1 Because of this, you have no defense, [i]oh man [who] judges[7] his neighbor, for by that which you judge your neighbor, you condemn yourself. For you who judge are also occupied in these [things].

2 And [ac]we know that the judgment of God is with truthfulness against those who are occupied in these [things].[8]

---

[1] Repeat *because of this, God delivered them* from v. 24
[2] Lit: in their persons
[3] Semitism: we would say "mentally unbalanced"
[4] Repeat *nor*
[5] Lit: bowels
[6] Repeat *are doing*
[7] Same root: *judge, judgment,* vs. 1-3; repeat *are occupied in these things*
[8] Fig: this whole verse could be a parenthesis, instead of anacoluthon

Chapter 2

3   But what do you think, [i]oh man, you who judge those who are
occupied in these [things], while you also are occupied in these [things],
that you will escape from the judgment of God?[1]

4   Or are you presumptuous against[2] the [c]riches of his kindness and
against his long-suffering and against the advantage that he gave to you?
And do you not know that the kindness of God brings you to repentance?

5   But because of the hardness of your heart that does not repent, you
lay up for yourself a treasure of [m]wrath for the [sy]day of wrath and for the
revelation of the upright judgment of God,

6   who repays everyone according to his works.

7   To those, who in the patience of good works seek glory [p]and honor
and incorruptibility,⌐ [3] he gives eternal life.

8   But [to] those who are stubborn and do not obey the truth, but obey
wickedness, he will repay[4] wrath [p]and fury

9   and pressure and trouble,⌐ [5] to everyone who does evil [things], first
to the Judeans and [then] to the heathens.

10 But glory [p]and honor and peace⌐ [c][will be] to all who do good
[things], first to the Judeans and [then] to the heathens.

11 For there is no respect of persons with God.

12 For those who have sinned without the law will also be destroyed
without[6] the law, and those who have sinned in the law will be judged
from the law,

13 for the hearers of the law are not upright before God, but the doers of
the law are justified

14 [pa](for if the Gentiles, who did not have the law, naturally did [the
things] of the law, who although they did not have the law, have a law
for themselves

15 and they show the work of the law as it is written on their heart[s]
and their conscience testifies concerning them, while [pe]their reasonings
rebuke or defend each other)

---

[1] Fig: erotesis, vs. 3-5 – questions to ponder

[2] Repeat *against* (3x)

[3] Fig: could be hendiatris, which would then be translated, "incorruptible,
honorable glory"

[4] Repeat *repay* from v. 6

[5] Fig: synonymia, also v. 8, *wrath, fury*, could be hendiadys in both verses.

[6] Fig: ellipsis, add [being judged by]; repeat *law* (12x), vs. 12-18

ARAMAIC PESHITTA NEW TESTAMENT
ROMANS

Chapter 2
16 in the ^{sy}day when God judges the secret [things] of men according to my gospel by way of Jesus Christ.

17 Now if ^{ac}you who are called a Judean and you take rest in the law and you boast in God

18 that you know his will and you distinguish the proper [things] that you learned from the law

19 and are confident about yourself that you are a leader of the blind and a light for those who are in darkness

20 and a guide of ignorant [ones] and a teacher of children and you have an example of knowledge and of truth in the law,

21 then **you** who teach others, do you not teach yourself?[1] And you who preach that they should not steal, do **you** steal?

22 And you who say that they should not commit adultery, do **you** commit adultery? And you who despise idols, do you spoil the sanctuary?

23 And you who boast in the same law when you transgress the law, do you dishonor God?

24 **FOR BECAUSE OF YOU THE ^mNAME OF GOD IS DEFAMED AMONG THE GENTILES,** as it is written.

25 For circumcision is beneficial if you thoroughly perform the law, but if you transgress the law, your ^mcircumcision becomes ^muncircumcision.[2]

26 Now if the ^muncircumcision keeps the commandment of the law, *behold, should not the ^muncircumcision be counted ^mcircumcision?

27 And the ^muncircumcision, which fulfills the law by its nature, will judge you who with the scripture and with circumcision transgress the law.

28 For he is not a Judean who is one in appearance, nor [is] what is made visible in the flesh circumcision.

29 But that one is a Judean, who is one secretly and circumcision is that of the heart spiritually and not literally, whose praise is not from men, but from God.

---

[1] Fig: erotesis, vs. 21-23 – questions to ponder; vs. 17-23, repeat *you*; vs. 21-22, repeat forms of *teach, steal, commit adultery*

[2] Fig: oxymoron, meaning you become like the Gentiles

364

Chapter 3

1 Therefore, what is the advantage of the Judean or what [is] the profit of circumcision?

2 Much in everything. [It is] that they were first entrusted with the words of God.

3 For if some of them did not believe, did they make void the faith of God in that they did not believe?[1]

4 [i]Let it not be so! For God is true and every man [is] false, as it is written: **YOU SHOULD BE UPRIGHT IN YOUR WORDS AND BE INNOCENT WHEN THEY JUDGE YOU.**

5 But if our wickedness establishes the uprightness of God, what should we say? Is God wicked who brings his wrath? [pa](I speak as a man.)

6 [i]Let it not be so! Yet if not,[2] how will God judge the [sy]world?

7 For if the truth of God was increased by my falsehood for his glory, am I therefore judged as a sinner?

8 Or perhaps [e][we should say], [pa]as they[3] blaspheme about us and say that we say,⌐ "We will do evil, so that good may come." Their judgment is kept for justice.

9 What then? Do we have the superiority, although we previously determined about the Judeans and about[4] the heathens that they were all under sin?

10 As it is written: **THERE IS NO ONE UPRIGHT, NOT EVEN ONE,**

11 **NOR ONE WHO UNDERSTANDS, NOR WHO SEEKS GOD.**

12 **ALL OF THEM HAVE TURNED ASIDE TOGETHER AND HAVE REJECTED [e][GOD] AND THERE IS NO ONE WHO DOES GOOD, NOT EVEN ONE.** [5]

13 [me]**THEIR THROATS [ARE] OPEN GRAVES AND THEIR [m]TONGUES ARE DECEITFUL AND THE [h]POISON OF THE ASP [IS] UNDER THEIR [m]LIPS.**

14 **THEIR [m]MOUTH IS FULL OF [he]CURSING AND BITTERNESS**

15 **AND THEIR [sy]FEET ARE SWIFT TO SHED BLOOD.**

---

[1] Fig: erotesis, **lema** question, implied answer "no", also v. 5, 7

[2] OS (Afr) (Efr): *Yet if not* is 'but therefore'

[3] Var (SLM): add 'men' *blaspheme*

[4] Repeat *about*

[5] Repeat *not even one* from v. 12

Chapter 3

16 ^{he}ADVERSITY AND MISERY [ARE] IN THEIR PATHS[1]

17 AND THEY DO NOT KNOW THE PATH OF PEACE

18 AND THERE IS NO FEAR OF GOD BEFORE THEIR ^mEYES.

19 ^{pe}But we know that what the law[2] said, it said to those who are in the law, so that every ^mmouth may be shut and all the ^{sy}world may be found guilty before God,

20 because by the deeds of the law no ^{sy}flesh is justified before him, for by the law sin is known.

21 But now, without the law, the uprightness of God is revealed and the law and the prophets testify about it.

22 But the uprightness of God is by way of the faith of Jesus Christ to everyone, even on everyone[3] who believes in him, ^{pa}(for there is no distinction,

23 because all have sinned and are deficient compared to the glory of God)

24 and they are freely justified by grace and by the redemption that is in Jesus Christ

25 ^{pa}(this [one] whom God determined beforehand [to be] a pardon by the faith of his ^{mt}blood because of our sins that we had previously sinned).

26 [It is] by the advantage that God in his long-suffering gave to us for the clear showing of his uprightness that is at this ^{sy}time, that he would be upright and would justify with uprightness[4] him who is in the faith of our Lord Jesus Christ.

27 Then where is boasting? It has been stopped. By what? The law of works? No, but by the law of faith.

28 Therefore, ^{ac}we conclude that a man is justified by faith and not by the works of the law.

29 For is he the God of the Judeans only and not of the Gentiles?[5] Yes,[6] also of the Gentiles,

---

[1] Fig: metalepsis, meaning "lifestyle"

[2] Fig: personification, *law*, vs. 19-21

[3] Repeat *everyone*; Pal Lect: omit *even on everyone*

[4] Same root: *upright, uprightness*

[5] Fig: erotesis, **lema** questions, vs. 29, 31, implied answers "yes" and "no"

[6] Fig: ellipsis, add [he is the God]

Chapter 3

30 because there is one God who justifies the ^mcircumcision by faith [and] also¹ the ^muncircumcision by the same faith.
31 Therefore, do we make the law of none effect by faith? ⁱLet it not be so! Rather, we establish the law.

Chapter 4

1 What then? Are we saying about Abraham the patriarch that he obtained ^e[justification] by the flesh?
2 For if Abraham was justified by works, he had ^e[a reason for] boasting, but not toward God.
3 For what does the scripture say? **ABRAHAM BELIEVED IN GOD AND IT WAS COUNTED TO HIM FOR JUSTIFICATION.**
4 Now to him who labors, his wage is not counted to him as by grace, but as that which is owed to him.
5 But to him who does not labor, but believes only in him who justifies sinners, his faith is counted to him for uprightness.
6 As David also said concerning the blessing of the man to whom God counts justification without works, saying:
7 **BLESSED ARE THEY WHOSE WICKEDNESS IS FORGIVEN AND WHOSE SINS ARE COVERED**
8 and **BLESSED IS THE MAN TO WHOM GOD WILL NOT COUNT HIS SIN.**
9 Therefore, [is] this blessing on the ^mcircumcision or on the ^muncircumcision? For we say that his faith was counted to Abraham for uprightness.
10 How then was it counted to him, in circumcision or in uncircumcision? It was not in circumcision, but in uncircumcision.
11 For **he** received circumcision [as] a sign and seal of the uprightness of his faith that was in uncircumcision, so that he would become the father to all those who believe from the ^muncircumcision ^{pa}(that it would be counted to them for uprightness also)
12 and the father to the ^mcircumcision, not to those who are from the ^mcircumcision only, but also to those who follow in the footsteps of the faith of the uncircumcision of our father Abraham.

---

¹ Fig: ellipsis, add [justifies]

Chapter 4

13 For the promise to Abraham and to his ^mseed that he would be the heir to the ^{sy}world was not by the law, but by the uprightness of his faith.

14 For if those who are from the law become heirs, faith becomes void and the promise is being made of no effect.

15 For ^{pe}the law is a worker of wrath, for where there is no law, neither [is there] transgression of the law.

16 Because of this, [it is] by faith that we will be justified by grace and[1] the promise will be sure to all his ^mseed, not to those who are from the law only, but also to those who are from the faith of Abraham, who is the father of all of us.

17 As it is written: **I HAVE PLACED YOU [AS] A FATHER TO A MULTITUDE OF THE GENTILES, BEFORE GOD IN WHOM YOU BELIEVED, WHO MAKES ALIVE THE DEAD AND CALLS THOSE [THINGS] THAT ARE NOT AS THOUGH THEY ARE.**

18 ^PAnd without hope, he believed for the hope[2] that he would be a father to a multitude of the Gentiles, as it is written: **SO YOUR ^mSEED WILL BE.**

19 And he was not weak in his faith,[3] considering his dead body that was one hundred years old and the dead womb of Sarah.

20 And he did not doubt the promise of God as [one] lacking faith, but was strong[4] in faith and gave praise to God.

21 And he was convinced that God was able to complete what he had promised to him.⌐

22 Because of this, it was counted to him for uprightness.

23 And not on his behalf only was this written: **HIS FAITH WAS COUNTED FOR UPRIGHTNESS,**

24 but also on our behalf, because he is also prepared to count ^e[uprightness to] those who believe in him who raised our Lord Jesus Christ from the dead,

25 who was delivered up[5] for our sins and rose in order to justify us.

---

[1] Var (SLM): 'that' *the promise*

[2] Repeat *hope*, next word

[3] Fig: tapeinosis, opposite meaning; repeat vs. 18-24, *faith, believe*

[4] Fig: pleonasm, *he did not doubt...but was strong*

[5] Fig: ellipsis, add [to die]

Chapter 5

1 Therefore, because we are justified[1] by faith, we have peace[2] toward God by our Lord Jesus Christ,

2 by whom we were brought by faith to this grace in which we stand and boast in the [an]hope of the glory of God.

3 And not only so, but we also boast[3] in our adversities, because we know that adversity perfects patience in us,

4 and patience,[4] experience, and experience, hope.

5 And [t]hope does not put [us] to shame, because the love of God is [c]poured out in our hearts by the Holy Spirit that was given to us.

6 Now if Christ at this time, because of our weakness, died for the ungodly,

7 [pa](for seldom does anyone die for the ungodly, although for good [ones] perhaps some would dare to die)

8 here God has manifested his love that is toward us, because if when we were sinners, Christ died for us,

9 then how much more will we be justified now by his [mt]blood and be rescued from wrath by him?[5]

10 For if when we were enemies God was reconciled with us by the death of his Son, then how much more will we by his reconciliation live by his life?[6]

11 And not only so, but also we boast in God by way of [7] our Lord Jesus Christ, in whom we have now received reconciliation.

12 For as by way of one man sin entered the world and by way of sin, death,[8] even so death passed on all men, in that all of them have sinned.

13 For until the law, sin, although it was in the [sy]world, was not counted sin, because there was no law.

14 But [pe]death reigned from Adam until Moses, even over those who had not sinned in the likeness of the transgression of the law[9] of Adam, who was the likeness of him who was to come.

---

[1] Same root: *justified, justify*, 4:25

[2] Pal Lect: 'we should have peace,' v. 2, 'in whom we have an entrance'

[3] Repeat *boast* from v. 2

[4] Fig: ellipsis, add [perfects]; fig: climax

[5] Fig: erotesis, **kema** question, answer in the affirmative, also v. 10, 15

[6] Same root: *live, life*

[7] Repeat *by way of*, 3x; lit: by the hand of

[8] Fig: ellipsis, add [entered the world]; same root, vs. 12-21: *sin, sinned, sinner*

[9] Var (L): 'command,' Murdock agrees

Chapter 5

15 But not as the offense, so also was the gift. For if because of the offense of one, many died, then how much more the grace of God and his gift, because of one man, Jesus Christ, will be made to increase[1] in many?

16 And not as the error of one, so also [was] the gift. For the judgment that was from one resulted in condemnation, but the gift[2] resulted in uprightness from many sins.

17 For if because of the error of one, [pe]death reigned, much more those who receive the [as]abundance of grace[3] and of the gift and of uprightness will reign in life by way of one, Jesus Christ.

18 In like manner, therefore, because of the error of one, condemnation was to all men, so also because of the uprightness of one, the victory for life will be to all men.

19 For as because of the disobedience of one man, many became sinners, so also because of the obedience of one, many will become upright [ones].

20 [pe]Now the entrance that the law had [was] that sin should be multiplied. And where[4] sin multiplied, there grace increased,

21 because as [pe]sin reigned in death, so also [pe]grace will reign in uprightness to eternal life by way of our Lord Jesus Christ.

Chapter 6

1 What then should we say? Should we continue in sin that grace would increase?[5]

2 [i]Let it not be so! For [e][we are] those who are dead to sin. How can we live in it again?

3 Or do you not know that we who are baptized in Jesus Christ are baptized in his death?

4 We are buried with him in baptism[6] to death, that as Jesus Christ rose up from the dead in the glory of his Father, so **we** will also walk in new life.

---

[1] Same root: *much more, increase*, also v. 17; fig: antithesis, vs. 15-19.

[2] Fig: ellipsis, add [that was from one]

[3] Fig: antiptosis, "abounding grace"

[4] Var (SL): 'when'

[5] Fig: erotesis – obvious answer "no", series of 2 questions, also 6:15, 7:7, 7:13

[6] Same root: *baptism, baptized*, v. 3

Chapter 6

5   For if we were [h]planted together with him in the likeness of his death, so we will also be in [e][the likeness of] his resurrection.

6   For we know that our [h]old man was crucified with him that the [an]body of sin should be annulled, so that we should no longer serve sin.

7   For he who is dead[1] is set free from sin.

8   If then we are dead with Christ, we should believe that we will live with[2] Christ.

9   For we know that Christ rose up from the dead and will not die again and [pe]death does not have authority over him.

10   For in dying, he died to sin one time, and in living, he lives to God.

11   So also **you** should count yourselves that you are dead to sin and alive to God in our Lord Jesus Christ.

12   Therefore, [pe]let not sin reign in your dead body, so that you would obey its desires.

13   And also do not present your members [s]as an instrument of wickedness for sin, but present yourselves to God as men who have life from the dead and let your members be an instrument for the uprightness of God.

14   And [pe]sin will not have authority over you, for you are not under the law, but under[3] grace.

15   What then? Should we sin because we are not under the law but under grace? [i]Let it not be so!

16   Do you not know that you must obey him to whom you present yourself for his service?[4] You are the servants of that one whom you obey, whether to sin or to the obedience of uprightness.

17   But [i]thanks [be] to God, because [me]you were a servant of sin, yet [now] you have obeyed from the heart the likeness of the teaching to which you are committed.

18   And when you were freed from sin, you were made subject to uprightness

---

[1] Repeat forms, vs. 7-13: *die, dying, dead,* and *life, live, alive*

[2] Repeat *with,* 3x, see Interlinear

[3] Repeat *under*

[4] Fig: erotesis – question to ponder; fig: personification of sin, vs. 14-23

Chapter 6

19 [pa](I speak as among men, because of the weakness of your flesh) that in the same manner that you presented your members for the service of uncleanness and of wickedness, so also now present your members for the service of uprightness and of holiness.[1]

20 For when you were the servants of sin, you were free from uprightness.

21 And what kind of result did you have at that time of which today you are ashamed?[2] For its end is death.

22 And now that you have been freed from sin and you are servants to God, you have holy [m]fruit, whose end [is] eternal life.

23 Now the [pe]wage of sin is death and[3] the gift of God [is] eternal life in our Lord Jesus Christ.

Chapter 7

1 Or do you not know, my brothers, [pa](for I speak to learned [ones] of the law) that the law has authority over a man as long as he is alive?

2 [al][It is] as a woman who is bound by the law to her husband as long as he is alive, but if her husband dies, she is freed from the law of her husband.

3 And if while her husband is alive, she has intercourse with another man, she becomes an adulteress. But if her husband dies, she is freed from the law and she is not an adulteress if she marries another man.

4 And now, my brothers, you are also dead to the law in the body of Christ that you would be [e][married] to another, him who rose up from the dead, so that you would bear [m]fruit to God.⌐

5 For while we were in the [sy]flesh, the [an]passions of sins that are by the law[4] were working in our members, so that we would bear [m]fruit to death.

6 But now we are absolved from the law and we are dead to that which was holding us captive, that from now on, we should serve in the newness of the Spirit and not in the oldness of the [sy]writing.

---

[1] OS (LG): 'presented your members (as) implements to sin, so be prepared to hear justice.'

[2] Fig: erotesis – question to ponder

[3] Fig: ellipsis, add [the wage of]

[4] OS (Afr) omit *that are by the law*

Chapter 7

7 What then are we saying? Is the law sin? [i]Let it not be so! But I did not learn sin, except by way of the law. For I had not known lust, except that the law said: **DO NOT LUST.**

8 And by this commandment, [pe]sin found opportunity and perfected in me every lust,[1] for without the law sin was dead.

9 Now **I** was alive previously without the law. But when the commandment came, sin lived and I died.

10 And I found that commandment of life [to be] to death.

11 For sin, by the opportunity that it found by way of the commandment, caused me to err and by it killed me.

12 Then the law is holy and the commandment is holy [P]and upright and good.

13 Did a good [thing] therefore become death to me? [i]Let it not be so! But sin, that it would be seen as sin, perfected death in me by a good [thing], so that sin would be more condemned by the commandment.

14 For we know that the law is spiritual, but **I** am of the flesh and I am sold to sin.

15 For that which I perform,[2] I know not. And that which I desire, I do not do, but that which I hate, that I do.

16 And if I do that which I do not desire, I am testifying concerning the law that it is good.

17 But now, **I** am not performing this, but sin[3] that lives in me.

18 For I know that good does not live in me [pa](but that is in my flesh). For to desire the good is easy for me, but to perform it, I am not able.

19 For I do not do the good that I desire to do,[4] but the evil that I do not desire to do, I do it.

20 And if that which I do not desire, I do, **I** am not doing [it], but sin that lives in me.

21 Therefore, I find a law that agrees with my mind that desires to do good, because evil is near to me.

22 For I rejoice in the law of God in the inward man.

23 But I see another law in my members that wars against the law of my mind and makes me captive to the law of sin that is in my members.

---

[1] Fig: personification, sin portrayed as a manipulating person that rules, 7:8-8:4.

[2] Repeat forms: *do, perform*, vs. 15-20

[3] Fig: ellipsis, add [does it] or [works evil], same in v. 20

[4] Var (M): omit *to do*, Murdock agrees

Chapter 7

24 [1]I am a miserable man! Who will rescue me from this [an]body of death?[1]

25 I thank God by way of our Lord[2] Jesus Christ. Now therefore, in my mind, **I** am a servant of the law of God, but in my [sy]flesh, I am a servant of the law of sin.

Chapter 8

1 From now on, there is no condemnation to those who in Jesus Christ do not walk in the [sy]flesh.[3]

2 For the [an]law of the Spirit of life that is in Jesus Christ has freed [ac]you from the law of sin and of death.

3 For because the law was weak by way of the frailty of the [sy]flesh, God sent his Son in the likeness of the [an]flesh of sin, because of sin, to condemn sin in the [sy]flesh,

4 so that the uprightness of the law would be completed in us, who do not walk carnally but[4] spiritually.[5]

5 For those who are [e][walking] carnally[6] are carnally minded and those who are [e][walking] spiritually are spiritually minded.

6 For the [an]thinking of the [sy]flesh is death, yet the [an]thinking of the Spirit [is] [he]life and peace,

7 because the thinking of the [sy]flesh is an enemy to God, for it is not subject to the law of God, because it is impossible.

8 And those who are carnal are not able to please God.

9 Now **you** are not [e][walking] carnally, but spiritually, if truly the Spirit of God lives in you. But if anyone does not have the Spirit of Christ, this [one] is not his.

10 Now if Christ [is] in you, the body is dead because of sin, but the Spirit is life because of uprightness.

---

[1] Culture: this was a mode of capital punishment where a criminal had a dead body fastened to him and was left to die with the corpse, Freeman, p. 455.

[2] OS (LG): *by way of our Lord* is 'by the grace of God that is in our Lord'

[3] Repeat *in the flesh,* vs. 3, 4, 5, 8, 12

[4] Fig: ellipsis, add [walk]

[5] Fig: antithesis, vs. 4-15

[6] Lit: in the flesh, vs. 5-9

Chapter 8

11 And if the Spirit of that [pr]one who raised our Lord[1] Jesus Christ from the dead lives in you, that one who raised Jesus Christ from the dead will also make alive your dead bodies because of his Spirit that lives in you.

12 Now, my brothers, [me]we are not debtors to the flesh that we should walk in the [sy]flesh.

13 For if you live by the [sy]flesh, you are going to die. And if spiritually you put to death the habits[2] of the body, you will have life.

14 [al]For those who are led by the Spirit of God are the sons of God.

15 For you have not received the spirit of bondage again to fear, but you have received the Spirit of adoption by which we call, "Father, our Father."[3]

16 And the Spirit gives testimony to our spirit that we are the sons of God.

17 And if [e][we are] sons, [then] also heirs, heirs[4] of God and fellow-heirs of Jesus Christ, that if we suffer with him, we will also be glorified with him.⌐

18 For I consider that the sufferings of this time are not equal to the glory that will be revealed in us.

19 For all the [pe]creation hopes and waits for the revelation of the sons of God.[5]

20 For the creation was made subject to emptiness, [pa]not by its will, but because of him who subjected it,⌐ to the hope

21 that also the creation will be freed from the [an]bondage of corruption to the [an]freedoms of the glory of the sons of God.

22 For we know that all created [things] groan and labor in childbirth until today.

23 And they are not alone, but **we** also who have the first[fruit] of the Spirit groan within ourselves and we wait for the adoption and[6] the redemption of our bodies,

---

[1] Var (S): omit *our Lord*

[2] Lit: walkings

[3] Culture: adoption had two parts, private and public (v. 23). We are waiting for the formal public declaration, Freeman, pp. 455-456. Fig: allegory, vs. 14-17, portrayal of sons in a family. "Abba" is an intimate term similar to "Daddy."

[4] Repeat *heirs*, next word, same root, *fellow-heirs*

[5] Fig: personification, creation, including man, is portrayed as a woman subjected to a corrupt husband and is in childbirth, vs. 19-25

[6] Var (SLM): omit *and*

Chapter 8

24 because we live in hope. But hope that is seen is not hope. For if we see it, why do we wait for it?[1]

25 But if we hope for something that is not seen, we continue with endurance.

26 So also, the Spirit aids our weakness, for we do not know what is right to pray for. But the Spirit prays on our behalf with groans that are not describable.

27 Now he who searches the hearts knows what is the thinking of the Spirit that prays on behalf of the holy [ones] according to the will of God.

28 But we know that those who love God, he aids in everything for good, those whom he determined beforehand to be called [ones].

29 And from the first he knew them and marked them out with the likeness of the image of his Son, that he would be the firstborn of many brothers.

30 And those whom he marked out beforehand, he called, and those whom he called, he justified, and those whom he justified, he [ht]glorified.[2]

31 What then should we say about these [things]?[3] If God [is] for us, who is against us?

32 And if he did not spare his Son, but delivered him up for all of us, how will he not give us everything with him?

33 Who can accuse the chosen [ones] of God? God justifies.

34 Who condemns? Christ died and rose and is at the right hand of God and makes petition on our behalf.

35 What will separate me from the love of Christ? [e][Is it] trial or[4] distress or persecution or famine or nakedness or peril or [m]sword?

36 As it is written: **BECAUSE OF YOU EVERY DAY WE ARE DYING AND WE ARE COUNTED [s]AS LAMBS TO SLAUGHTER.**

37 On the contrary, in all these [things] we are victorious by way of him who loved us.

38 For I am persuaded that neither death nor life nor angels nor authorities nor powers nor those [things] present nor future

---

[1] Repeat forms of *wait, hope*, vs. 19-25
[2] Fig: climax
[3] Fig: erotesis – questions to ponder (7 questions), vs. 31-35
[4] Repeat *or*, repeat *nor*, v. 39

Chapter 8

39   nor height nor depth, neither any other created [thing] will be able to separate me from the love of God that is in our Lord Jesus Christ.

Chapter 9

1   I am speaking [with] truthfulness in Christ[1] and I am not lying and [pe]my mind bears witness concerning me by the Holy Spirit

2   that I have great sorrow and the grief that is from my heart does not cease.

3   For I have prayed that I myself would be cursed from Christ,[2] instead of my brothers and my kinsmen who are in the [sy]flesh,

4   who are the sons of Israel, to whom belong the adoption [P]and the glory and the covenants and the law and the service that is in it[3] and the promises

5   and the fathers and from whom Christ was seen in the [sy]flesh.⌐ [be]He who is God who is over all, to him [be] our praises and our blessings forever and ever. Amen.

6   Now the word of God has indeed not failed,[4] for not all who are from Israel are Israel.

7   Neither are all of them sons because [they are] from the seed of Abraham, because it was said: **IN ISAAC THE [m]SEED WILL BE CALLED TO YOU.**

8   Now this is [e][the truth]: the sons of [5] the [sy]flesh are not the sons of God, but the sons of the promise are counted for the [m]seed.

9   For the word of promise is this: **IN THIS SEASON I WILL COME AND SARAH WILL HAVE A SON.**

10   And not this only, but also when Rebecca had intercourse with one [man], our father Isaac,

11   before her sons were born and they had not done good or evil, the calling of God was already made known that it should not remain by works, but by way of him who called.

---

[1] Fig: deasis, oath
[2] OS (LG): 'you are a witness for me, God, that I wished to die'
[3] Var (SM): omit *that is in it*
[4] Fig: polyptoton, "failing, has not failed"
[5] Repeat *sons of*

Chapter 9

12 For it was said: **THE ELDER WILL BE A SERVANT TO THE YOUNGER.**

13 As it is written: **JACOB ^cI HAVE LOVED AND ESAU I HAVE HATED.**[1]

14 What then should we say? Is there wickedness with God?[2] ⁱLet it not be so!

15 *Behold, to Moses he also said: **I WILL HAVE MERCY ON WHOM I WILL HAVE MERCY AND I WILL PITY WHOM I PITY.**[3]

16 Therefore ^e[it is][4] not by the hands of him who wills, nor by the hands of him who strives, but by the hands of the merciful God.

17 For he said in the scripture to Pharaoh: **FOR THIS I HAVE APPOINTED YOU, THAT I MAY DEMONSTRATE MY POWER BY YOU AND THAT MY ^mNAME MAY BE PREACHED IN THE WHOLE EARTH.**

18 Then with whom he wills, he has mercy, and with whom he wills, he deals harshly.

19 And perhaps you will say, "Why does he complain? For who can stand against his will?"[5]

20 Therefore, who are you, oh man, that you are giving an answer to God? ^{al}Does [the thing] formed ^{pe}say to him who formed it, "Why have you so formed me?"

21 Or does not the potter have authority over his clay, that from the [same] lump[6] he makes utensils, one to honor and another to dishonor?

22 Now if God wanted to display his wrath and to make known his power, he would have brought, in the abundance of his long-suffering, wrath on the utensils of wrath that were made for destruction

23 and poured out his mercy on the utensils of mercy that were prepared by God for glory,⌐

24 which we are, the called [ones], not only from the Judeans, but also from the Gentiles.

25 As also he said in Hosea: **I WILL CALL THOSE WHO WERE NOT MY PEOPLE, MY OWN PEOPLE,**[7] **AND TO WHOM I HAVE NOT SHOWN MERCY, I WILL SHOW MERCY.**

---

[1] Or "put aside", see Lamsa, *New Testament Light*, pp. 187-188.

[2] Fig: erotesis – obvious answer "no"

[3] Repeat *mercy, pity*

[4] Fig: ellipsis, or [the election is]; repeat *by the hands of,* 3x

[5] Fig: erotesis – questions to ponder, vs. 19-21

[6] Same root: *formed [thing]* v. 20, *lump*; see Bowen, pp. 114-118, regarding utensil of wrath and mercy.

[7] Repeat *people, mercy*

Chapter 9

26 For it will be [that] in the place where they were called "NOT MY PEOPLE," there they will be called the sons of the living God.

27 And Isaiah preached concerning the sons of Israel: EVEN THOUGH THE NUMBER OF THE SONS OF ISRAEL SHOULD BE [s]AS THE SAND THAT IS IN THE SEA, [ONLY] A REMNANT OF THEM WILL BE SAVED.

28 HE HAS DECIDED AND DETERMINED THE MATTER AND THE LORD WILL ACCOMPLISH IT ON THE EARTH.

29 And [it is] as what Isaiah previously said: IF THE LORD OF HOSTS HAD NOT LEFT US A SURVIVOR, WE WOULD HAVE BEEN [s]AS SODOM AND WOULD HAVE RESEMBLED GOMORRAH.

30 What then should we say? The Gentiles who were not following[1] after uprightness have obtained uprightness, even the uprightness that is from faith.

31 But Israel, who was following after the law of uprightness, did not obtain the law of uprightness.

32 Because of what? Because it was not from faith, but from the works of the law, for they stumbled at the stone of stumbling.[2]

33 As it is written: *BEHOLD, I HAVE SET IN ZION A [an]STONE OF STUMBLING AND A [an]STONE OF OFFENSE AND HE WHO BELIEVES IN IT[3] WILL NOT BE ASHAMED.

Chapter 10

1 My brothers, the desire of my heart and my request to God for them [is] that they would be saved.

2 For I testify about them that they have the zeal of God, but not with knowledge.

3 For they do not know the uprightness[4] of God, but they seek to establish an uprightness of their own, and because of this, they are not subject to the uprightness of God.

4 For Christ is the consummation of the law for uprightness to all who believe.[5]

5 For Moses so wrote [about] the uprightness that is by the law: HE WHO DOES THESE [THINGS] WILL LIVE BY THEM.

---

[1] Lit: running; repeat next word, *uprightness*
[2] Same root: *stumbled, stumbling*
[3] Pal Lect: 'on him'
[4] Repeat *uprightness*, vs. 3-6
[5] Var (SL): add 'in it'; Pal Lect: 'God's end of the Law is Christ'

Chapter 10

6 Now the uprightness that is by faith so says: DO NOT SAY IN YOUR HEART, "WHO HAS ASCENDED TO HEAVEN AND BROUGHT DOWN CHRIST?

7 AND WHO HAS GONE DOWN TO THE DEPTH OF SHEOL AND BROUGHT UP CHRIST FROM THE DEAD?"

8 BUT WHAT DOES IT[1] SAY? THE ANSWER IS NEAR TO YOU, TO YOUR [m]MOUTH AND TO YOUR HEART, which is the word of faith that we preach.

9 And if you confess with your [m]mouth our Lord Jesus[2] and you believe in your heart that God raised him from the dead, you will have life.

10 For the heart that believes in him is justified and the mouth that confesses him has life.

11 For the scripture said: ALL WHO BELIEVE IN HIM WILL NOT BE ASHAMED.

12 And in this it does not discriminate either against Judeans or against the heathens, for the LORD of all of them is one who is abundant with all who call on him.

13 For ALL WHO WILL CALL [ON] THE NAME OF THE LORD WILL HAVE LIFE.

14 How then will they call who have not believed in him? Or how will they believe on him whom they have not heard? Or how will they hear without a preacher?

15 Or how will they preach if they are not sent?[3] As it is written: HOW BEAUTIFUL [ARE] THE [sy]FEET OF THE MESSENGERS OF PEACE AND OF THE MESSENGERS OF GOOD [THINGS].

16 But not all of them have obeyed the message of the gospel. For Isaiah said: MY LORD, WHO HAS BELIEVED OUR REPORT?

17 Then, faith is by obedience and obedience[4] by the word of God.

18 But I say, "Have they not heard?"[5] And *behold, THEIR REPORT HAS GONE OUT INTO ALL THE EARTH AND THEIR WORDS INTO THE OUTMOST BORDERS OF THE INHABITED WORLD.

---

[1] Pal Lect: 'the scripture'

[2] Pal Lect: 'confess that Jesus is Lord'

[3] Fig: climax, vs. 14, 15; repeat *messengers*

[4] Repeat *obedience*, lit: hearing of the ear

[5] Fig: erotesis -- questions to ponder, vs. 14-18; repeat *But I say*, 10:18, 19, 11:1, 11

ARAMAIC PESHITTA NEW TESTAMENT
ROMANS

Chapter 10

19 But I say, "Did not Israel know?" First Moses so said: ^{mi}I WILL MAKE YOU JEALOUS BY A NATION THAT IS NOT A NATION, AND BY A NATION[1] THAT IS DISOBEDIENT, I WILL ANGER YOU.

20 And Isaiah was bold and said: I WAS SEEN BY THOSE WHO DID NOT SEEK ME AND I WAS FOUND BY THOSE WHO DID NOT ASK FOR ME.[2]

21 But to Israel he said: I HAVE STRETCHED OUT MY HANDS ALL DAY TOWARD A NATION WHO IS ^{he}CONTENTIOUS AND DISOBEDIENT.

Chapter 11

1 But I say, "Has God rejected his people?" ⁱLet it not be so! For I am also from Israel. I am from the seed of Abraham, from the tribe of Benjamin.

2 God has not rejected his people, who previously were known by him. Or do you not know what he said in the scripture about Elijah when he was complaining to God about Israel? And he said:

3 MY LORD, THEY HAVE KILLED YOUR PROPHETS AND HAVE PULLED DOWN YOUR ALTARS AND I AM LEFT ALONE AND THEY SEEK MY LIFE.

4 And it was said to him by revelation:[3] *BEHOLD, I HAVE RESERVED[4] FOR MYSELF SEVEN THOUSAND MEN WHO HAVE NOT KNEELED ON THEIR KNEES AND HAVE NOT WORSHIPPED BAAL.

5 So also in this time, a remnant is left[5] by the calling of grace.

6 Now if by grace, it is not by works, unless grace is not grace. And if by works, it is not by grace, unless work is not work.

7 What then? Israel did not find what it was seeking, but the called [ones] found [it] and the rest of them were blinded in their heart[s].

8 As it is written: GOD GAVE THEM A BLINDING SPIRIT AND EYES THAT THEY WOULD NOT EXAMINE AND EARS THAT THEY WOULD NOT HEAR UNTIL THIS VERY DAY.

9 And David again said: THEIR ^{me}TABLE WILL BE A SNARE BEFORE THEM AND THEIR REWARD ^e[WILL BE] STUMBLING.[6]

---

[1] Repeat *nation*, also v. 21

[2] Fig: oxymoron

[3] Var (M): 'boldly'

[4] Same root: *reserved, left* (v. 3), and *kneeled, knees*

[5] Word play: *remnant*, **sharkana** ܫܪܟܢܐ *is left* **ashtekhar** ܐܫܬܚܪ

[6] Var (SL): *stumbling* (pl); repeat *stumble, stumbling*, vs. 9-12

Chapter 11

10 THEIR EYES WILL BE DARKENED, SO THAT THEY WILL NOT SEE AND [pr]THEIR BACK WILL ALWAYS BE BOWED.[1]

11 Now I say, "Have they stumbled so as to fall?" [i]Let it not be so! But in their stumbling, life has come to the Gentiles for their jealousy.

12 And if their stumbling became riches for the world, and their loss,[2] riches to the Gentiles, how much more then their fullness?[3]

13 But I speak to you Gentiles,[4] I who am the apostle of the Gentiles. I am glorifying my ministry,

14 so that perhaps I may provoke my kinsmen to jealousy and may give life to some of them.

15 For if their rejection was reconciliation to the [sy]world, then how much more their return, but life that is from the dead?[5]

16 [al]Now if the original part [is] holy, the thing formed [e][is holy] also. And if the root is holy, the branches [are] also.

17 And if some branches were broken off [6] and **you** who are a wild olive [tree] were grafted into their places and became a sharer of the root and of the fatness of the olive [tree],

18 do not pride yourself about the branches. Now if you pride yourself, you are not bearing the root, but the root bears you.

19 And it may be [that] you should say of the branches that were broken off, "**I** will be grafted in their places."

20 These [things] are good. They were broken off because they did not believe, but **you** stand by faith. Do not be elevated in your mind, but have reverence,

21 for if God did not spare the natural branches, perhaps he will also not spare you.

22 See then the gentleness and the harshness of God. On those who fell, harshness. But on you, gentleness, if you remain in the gentleness, and if not, **you** will also be broken off.[7]

---

[1] Fig: periphrasis, meaning "they will always be slaves"
[2] Fig: ellipsis [became]
[3] Fig: erotesis, **kema** question, answer in the affirmative, also v. 15
[4] Fig: apostrophe or antimetathesis, change of narration to the Gentiles
[5] Fig: erotesis – questions to ponder, "how much more", also v. 24
[6] Repeat *broken off*, vs. 17-24
[7] Parallel structure: ABBAC, concluding phrase

Chapter 11

23 And those, if they do not remain in their lack of faith, will also be grafted in, for God is able to graft them in[1] again.

24 For if you, who are from the olive [tree] that was wild by your nature, were cut off and were grafted contrary to your nature in the good olive [tree], then how much more those, if they be grafted in their natural olive [tree]?ך [2]

25 For I want you to know this mystery, my brothers, so that you will not be wise in your own mind, that blindness of the heart in part has happened to Israel until the fullness of the Gentiles should come in.

26 And then all Israel will have life, as it is written: **FROM ZION A DELIVERER WILL COME AND TURN WICKEDNESS FROM JACOB.**

27 **AND THEN** THEY WILL HAVE **THE COVENANT THAT IS FROM ME, WHEN I FORGIVE THEM THEIR SINS.**

28 Now in the gospel, they are enemies because of you, and in the calling, they are beloved because of the fathers,

29 for [c]God does not repent in his gift and in his calling.

30 For as **you** were also disobedient to God previously and now have obtained favor because of their disobedience,

31 so also these are disobedient now to the mercies that are on you, that mercies may also be on them.

32 For God has confined everyone in disobedience,[3] so that he could have mercy on everyone.

33 [i]Oh the depth of the [c]riches and wisdom and knowledge[4] of God, because no one has explored his judgments and his ways are untraceable!

34 **FOR WHO KNOWS THE MIND OF THE LORD? OR WHO IS A COUNSELOR TO HIM?**

35 And **WHO FIRST GIVES TO HIM AND THEN RECEIVES FROM HIM?**[5]

36 Because all [is] from him, and all [is] by him, and all [is] by his [m]hand, [be]to whom [be] our praises and our blessings forever and ever. Amen.

---

[1] Repeat *graft in*, vs. 23, 24
[2] Fig: erotesis, **kema** question, answer in the affirmative
[3] OS (LG): 'them that they are not persuaded'
[4] Fig: hendiatris, "richly wise understanding"
[5] Fig: erotesis – questions to ponder

ARAMAIC PESHITTA NEW TESTAMENT
ROMANS

Chapter 12

1   Therefore, I beg you, my brothers, by the mercies of God, to present your bodies a living [P]and holy and acceptable sacrifice to God in reasonable service. [1]

2   And do not imitate this [sy]world, but be turned the other way by the renewal of your minds and distinguish what is the good [P]and acceptable and perfect⌐ will of God.

3   Now I say by the grace that was given to me for all of you, you should not think outside of what is right to think, but everyone should think[2] soberly, according to faith in the measure God has distributed to him.

4   For as in one body we have many members and all members do not have one function,

5   so also [me]we who are many are one body in Christ and each one of us are members of one another.

6   But we have various gifts according to the grace that is given to us. There is [e][giving] of prophecy according to the measure of his faith,

7   and there is [e][giving] of ministering one has in his ministering, and there is [e][giving] of a teacher in his teaching,

8   and there is [e][giving] of a comforter in his comforting, and of one who gives, with simplicity, and of one who presides,[3] with diligence, and of one who is merciful, with cheerfulness.

9   And let not your love be deceitful, but hate evil and adhere to good.

10   Be[4] compassionate to your brothers and love one another. Prefer one another in honor.

11   Be diligent and not lazy. Be fervent in spirit. Labor for your Lord.

12   Rejoice in your hope. Endure your trials. Be steadfast in prayer.

13   Share toward the need of the holy [ones]. Be compassionate [to] strangers.

14   Bless your persecutors. Bless and do not curse.

15   Rejoice with [those] who are rejoicing and weep with [those] who are weeping.[5]

---

[1] Culture: Lamsa, *New Testament Light*, means "to keep your body pure and unblemished," p. 192; Pal Lect: 'a service which is orderly'

[2] Repeat *should think*

[3] Lit: stands at the head

[4] Repeat *be...*, same forms of verbs, vs. 10-13

[5] Word play, *rejoice, rejoicing,* **khedo, khedin,** ܚܕܘ ܚܕܝܢ *weep, weeping,* **beco, becin,** ܒܟܘ ܒܟܝܢ

ARAMAIC PESHITTA NEW TESTAMENT
ROMANS

Chapter 12

16 And what you think about yourself, also ᵉ[think] about your brothers. And do not think [with] a proud mind, but associate with those who are meek. And do not be wise in your own mind.

17 And do not repay anyone evil [things] for evil [things], but be diligent to do good [things] before all men.

18 And if it is possible, according to what is in you, be at peace with everyone.

19 And do not avenge yourselves, my beloved, but give place to anger, for it is written: **IF YOU WILL NOT PERFORM JUDGMENT FOR YOURSELF, I WILL PERFORM YOUR JUDGMENT**, says God.

20 And **IF YOUR ENEMY IS HUNGRY, FEED HIM AND IF HE IS THIRSTY, GIVE HIM DRINK AND IF YOU DO THESE [THINGS] TO HIM, YOU WILL HEAP COALS OF FIRE ON HIS HEAD.**[1]

21 Do not let evil [things] overcome you, but overcome evil [things] with good [things].

Chapter 13

1 Every one should be subject to greater authorities,[2] for there is no authority that is not from God and these who are authorities were ordained by God.

2 Therefore, he who stands against an authority stands against an ordinance of God and those who stand against them will receive judgment.

3 For judges are not fearful for good works, but for evil.[3] So do you want to not be afraid of an authority? Do good and you will have praise from him.

4 For he is a minister of God, but to you for good. And if you do evil [things], fear, for he is not girded with the ᵐsword in vain. For he is a minister of God and an avenger of wrath to those who do evil [things].

5 And because of this, it is necessary for us to be subject, not only because of ᵐwrath, but also because of our conscience.

---

[1] Culture: *heap coals of fire on his head* means to "warm him with your love" because in the morning, people would share "coals" from their fires with those who needed to light their fires.

[2] Repeat *authority*, vs. 1-3

[3] Fig: ellipsis [works]

Chapter 13

6 Because of this, you should also give tribute, for they are the ministers of God, who for these same [things] are established.

7 Therefore, repay everyone as is owed to him, to whom tribute ^e[is due], tribute, and to whom tax ^e[is due], tax, and to whom reverence ^e[is due], reverence, and to whom honor [is due], honor.[1]

8 And do not owe anyone anything, but to love each other. For he who loves his neighbor has fulfilled the law.

9 For this [is] also what is said: **DO NOT COMMIT ADULTERY AND DO NOT KILL AND DO NOT STEAL AND DO NOT LUST,** and if there is another commandment, it is fulfilled in this saying: **LOVE YOUR NEIGHBOR AS YOURSELF.**

10 Love does not do evil [things] to his neighbor, because love is the fulfillment of the law.

11 ^{al}And also know this, that it is the time and the ^{sy}hour that from now on we should be awakened from our sleep. For now our life has come nearer to us than when we believed.

12 Then the night is passed and the day is near. So we should lay aside from us the works of darkness and we should put on the ^marmor of light.⌐

13 And we should walk in [this] manner, ^sas in the day, not in[2] reveling ^Pand not in drunkenness and not in a defiled bed and not in envy and in strife.⌐

14 But put on our Lord Jesus Christ and do not have regard for the desires that are in your flesh.

Chapter 14

1 Now to him who is weak in faith, give a hand, and do not have doubt in your reasonings.

2 For there is one who believes that he may eat[3] everything, yet he who is weak eats herbs.

3 Now that one who eats should not treat with contempt him who does not eat, and that one who does not eat should not judge him who eats, for God has received him.

---

[1] Repeat as next words: *tribute, tax, reverence, honor*

[2] Repeat *not in*, 4x

[3] Repeat *eat*, vs. 1-3, 6

Chapter 14

4 Who are you that you judge a servant who is not your own, who, if he stands, stands before his lord and if he falls, falls before his lord? But he will indeed stand,[1] for it will be by the hands of his lord that he will be established.

5 There is one who judges a day[2] from a day and there is one who judges all days. But everyone should be assured in his own mind.

6 He who is mindful[3] of a day is mindful [of it] before his Lord. And everyone who is not mindful of a day is not mindful [of it] before his Lord. And whoever eats, eats before his Lord and thanks God. And he who does not eat, does not eat before his Lord and thanks God.

7 For there is not one of us who lives for himself and there is not one who dies for himself,

8 because if we live, we live for our Lord and if we die, we die for our Lord. And therefore, whether we live or whether we die, we belong to our Lord.[4]

9 Because of this, Christ also died and is alive and is risen that he would be the LORD for the dead and for the living.

10 Now why do you judge your brother? Or why do you also treat your brother with contempt?[5] For all of us are going to stand before the judgment seat of Christ,

11 as it is written: **I LIVE**, says the LORD, **EVERY ˢʸKNEE WILL BOW TO ME AND EVERY ᵐTONGUE WILL CONFESS ME.**

12 So then, every one of us will give an answer for himself to God.

13 So then, we should not judge each other, but rather determine[6] this more, that you will not place a stumbling block before your brother.

14 For I know and am persuaded in the LORD Jesus that there is not anything that is defiled of itself. But to him who thinks that something is unclean, to him alone it is unclean.

15 And if you grieve your brother because of food, you are not walking in love. Do not hurt him by your food for whose sake Christ died.

16 And let not our good be defamed.

---

[1] Fig: polyptoton, "standing, will stand"; repeat *stand, fall*
[2] Fig: ellipsis [more holy] than...*judges all days* [alike]
[3] Repeat *is mindful*
[4] Repeat *live, die*, as encircling the passage
[5] Fig: erotesis – questions to ponder
[6] Lit: judge

Chapter 14

17 For the kingdom of God is not ^{mr}food and drink, but uprightness and peace and joy[1] by the Holy Spirit.

18 For he who serves Christ in these [things] pleases God and stands approved [before] men.

19 Now we should follow after peace and after edifying each other.

20 And we should not depart from the works[2] of God because of food. For everything is pure, but it is wrong for a man who eats with stumbling.

21 It is good that we should neither eat flesh nor[3] drink wine nor ^{e}[do] anything by which our brother stumbles.

22 You who have faith, keep it in yourself before God. Blessed is he who does not judge himself in what he distinguishes.

23 For he who doubts and eats is condemned, because it is not in faith, for everything that is not from faith is sin.

Chapter 15

1 Therefore, we, the strong [ones], ought to bear the infirmity of the weak [ones] and not to please ourselves.

2 But, each of us should please his neighbor in good [things] for edification,

3 because Christ also did not please himself. But as it is written: THE REVILING OF YOUR REVILERS HAS FALLEN ON ME.

4 For everything that was previously written is for our instruction. It was written so that by the patience and by the comfort of the scriptures we would have hope.

5 Now the God of patience and of comfort[4] grant you to think in harmony with each other, in Jesus Christ,

6 that with one mind and with one[5] mouth you may praise God, the Father of our Lord Jesus Christ.

7 Because of this, draw near to and bear up each other, as also Christ has drawn near to you for the glory of God.

8 Now I say that Jesus Christ served the ^{m}circumcision on behalf of the truth of God to confirm the promise of the fathers

---

[1] Fig: hendiatris, "joyfully whole uprightness"

[2] Var (LM): 'work' (singular)

[3] Repeat nor

[4] Repeat patience and comfort from v. 4

[5] Repeat one

Chapter 15

9   and [that] the Gentiles[1] would glorify God for the mercies that came on them. As it is written: **I WILL CONFESS YOU AMONG THE GENTILES AND I WILL SING TO YOUR NAME.**

10   And again he said: **REJOICE, GENTILES, WITH HIS PEOPLE.**

11   And again he said: **PRAISE THE LORD, ALL YOU GENTILES. PRAISE HIM, ALL PEOPLE.**

12   And again Isaiah said: **THERE WILL BE A [m]ROOT TO JESSE AND HE WHO WILL RISE UP WILL BE A RULER TO THE GENTILES AND ON HIM THE GENTILES WILL HOPE.**

13   Now the God of hope fill you with all joy and peace in faith, so that you may abound in his hope[2] by the power of the Holy Spirit.

14   Now I also am persuaded concerning you, my brothers, that you are also full of goodness and are completed with all knowledge and are also[3] able to admonish others.

15   Now I have written somewhat boldly to you, my brothers, to remind you of the grace that was given to me from God,

16   that I should be a minister to Jesus Christ among the Gentiles and I should labor for the gospel of God, so that the offering of the Gentiles would be acceptable and made holy by the Holy Spirit.

17   Therefore, I have boasting in Jesus Christ to God.

18   For I do not presume to speak of anything that Christ has not accomplished by my hands for the obedience of the Gentiles, in word and in deeds,

19   by the power of signs [P]and of wonders and by the power of the Spirit of God.⌐ From Jerusalem I have traveled all the way to Illyricum and I have fulfilled the gospel of Christ,

20   being careful not to preach where the name of Christ was called, so that I would not build on a strange foundation,

21   but rather, as it is written: **THOSE WHO WERE NOT TOLD ABOUT HIM WILL SEE HIM AND THOSE WHO HAVE NOT HEARD WILL BE PERSUADED.**

22   Because of this, I have been prevented many times [from] coming to you.

---

[1] Repeat *Gentiles*, vs. 9-12
[2] Repeat *hope*
[3] Repeat *also*, (3x)

Chapter 15

23 But now, because I have no place in these regions and I have desired for many years to come to you,

24 when I go to Spain, I hope to come and see you and [that] you will accompany me there when I have been a little refreshed by the sight of you.

25 But now, I am going to Jerusalem to minister to the holy [ones],

26 for those who are in Macedonia and in Achaia desired to be a partner with the poor[1] holy [ones] who are in Jerusalem.

27 They desired [this], because they are also indebted to them. For if the Gentiles have partnered with them in spiritual [things], they are indebted also to serve them in fleshly [things].

28 Therefore, when I have finished this and have impressed on them this fruit, I will cross over to you ᵉ[on my way] to Spain.

29 And I know that when I come to you, I will come in the fullness of the blessing of the gospel of Christ.

30 Now I beg you, my brothers, by our Lord Jesus Christ and by love of the Spirit, to labor with me in prayer to God for me,

31 that I may be delivered from those who are not persuaded who are in Judea, and [that] the service that I carry to the holy [ones] that are in Jerusalem will be received well,

32 and [that] I may come to you with joy by the will of God and be refreshed with you.

33 ᵇᵉNow the God of peace be with all of you. Amen.

Chapter 16

1 Now I commend to you Phoebe, our sister, who is a minister of the church of Cenchrea,

2 that you should receive her in our Lord as is just for holy [ones] and you should assist her in every matter that she asks of you, because she has been an assistant both to many [and] also to me.

3 Greet Priscilla and Aquila, workers with me in Jesus Christ,

4 because these same ones risked their necks for my life. And not only I am thankful for them, but also all the churches of the Gentiles ᵉ[are thankful].

5 And greet the church that is in their house. Greet my beloved Epaenetus, who was the ᵐfirst[fruit] of Achaia in Christ.

---

[1] Var (S): add 'and'

Chapter 16

6 Greet Mary who has toiled much among you.

7 Greet Andronicus and Junia, my brothers, who were captives with me and are known by the apostles and were in Christ before me.

8 Greet Amplias, my beloved in our Lord.

9 Greet Urbane, a worker who is with us in Christ, and my beloved Stachys.

10 Greet Apelles, chosen in our Lord. Greet the household of Aristobulus.

11 Greet Herodion, my kinsman. Greet the household of Narcissus, who are in our Lord.

12 Greet Tryphena and Tryphosa who labor in our Lord. Greet my beloved Persis, who labored much in our Lord.

13 Greet Rufus, chosen in our Lord, and his own mother and mine.

14 Greet Asyncritus and Phlegon and Hermas and Patrobas and Hermes and the brothers who are with them.

15 Greet Philologus and Julia and Nereus and his sister and Olympas and all of the holy [ones] who are with them.

16 Greet each other with a holy kiss.[1] All of the churches of Christ greet you.

17 Now I beg you, my brothers, to beware of those who cause [he]divisions and scandals outside of the teaching that you have learned, that you keep away from them.

18 For those who are like this do not serve our Lord Jesus Christ, but their [sy]belly. And with sweet words and with blessings, they turn away the hearts of the simple.

19 But your obedience is known to everyone. I rejoice, therefore, in you and want you to be wise to good [things] and innocent to evil [things].

20 And the God of peace will soon crush SATAN under your [sy]feet. The grace of our Lord Jesus Christ be with you.

21 Timothy, a worker with me, greets you, and Lucius and Jason and Sosipater, my brothers.

22 I, Tertius, who wrote the letter, greet you in our Lord.

23 Gaius, my host and [e][a host] of all the church, greets you. Erastus, the steward of the city, and Quartus, a brother, greet you.

24 [be]Now to God, who is able to establish you in my gospel that is proclaimed about Jesus Christ by the revelation of the mystery that was hidden from the times of the ages,

---

[1] Culture: men and women would kiss only other men, or other women, respectively, Bullinger, *Figures of Speech*, p. 62, Freeman, p. 456.

25 but is revealed in this time by way of the writings of the prophets, and by the commandment of the eternal God is made known to all the Gentiles for the obedience of the faith,

26 who alone is wise, [be] glory by way of Jesus Christ forever and ever. Amen.

27 ^{be}The grace of our Lord Jesus Christ [be] with all of you. Amen.

Chapter 1

1   Paul, a called [one] and an apostle by Jesus Christ by the will of God, and Sosthenes, a brother,

2   to the church of God that is in Corinth, called [ones] and holy [ones] who are made holy in Jesus Christ, and to all who call on the name of our Lord Jesus Christ in every place, theirs and ours:

3   Grace [be] with you and peace from God our Father and from our Lord Jesus Christ.

4   I give thanks to my God at all times on behalf of you for the grace of God that was given to you in Jesus Christ,

5   that in everything you may grow rich in him in every word and in all knowledge,

6   as the witness of Christ is established in you,

7   so that you do not lack in any one of his gifts, but you are waiting for the appearance of our Lord Jesus Christ,

8   who will establish you up to the end, so that you may be without blame in the [sy]day of our Lord Jesus Christ.

9   God is faithful, by whom you were called to the fellowship of his Son, Jesus Christ, our Lord.

10   Now I beg you, my brothers, in the name of our Lord Jesus Christ, that you have one word to all and [that] there should be no divisions among you, but [that] you may be perfected in one purpose and in one[1] mind.

11   For they sent a message to me about you, my brothers, from the house of Chloe, that there are disputes among you.

12   Now I say this because there is one[2] of you who says, "I am of Paul," and there is one who says, "I am of Apollos," and there is one who says, "I am of Peter," and there is one who says, "I am of Christ."

13   Is Christ divided? Or was Paul crucified for your sake?[3] Or were you baptized in the name of Paul?

14   I thank God that I did not baptize any of you, except Crispus and Gaius,

15   so that no one would say that I baptized[4] in my name.

16   Now I also baptized the household of Stephanas. But besides [them], I do not know if I baptized anyone else.

---

[1] Repeat *one*, 3x

[2] Repeat *there is one*

[3] Fig: erotesis, **lema** questions, obvious answer "no"

[4] Repeat *I baptized* next word, v. 16

Chapter 1

17 For Christ did not send me to baptize, but to preach, not with wisdom of words, so that the ^{mt}cross of Christ would not be made void.

18 For the word regarding the ^{mt}cross is foolishness to the perishing [ones], but to us who are living, it is the power of God.

19 For it is written: **I WILL DESTROY THE WISDOM OF THE WISE AND I WILL TAKE AWAY THE UNDERSTANDING OF THE INTELLIGENT.**

20 Where is the wise? Or where is the scribe? Or where is[1] the analyzer of this world? *Behold, has not God made foolish the wisdom of this world?[2]

21 For because in the wisdom of God, the world by wisdom did not know God, God desired to give life to those who believe by the foolishness of preaching,

22 because the Judeans ask for signs and the Arameans seek wisdom.

23 But **we** preach Christ crucified, a stumbling block to the Judeans, and to the Arameans, foolishness.

24 But to those who are called, Judeans and Arameans, Christ [is] the power of God and the wisdom[3] of God,[4]

25 because the foolishness of God is wiser than men and the weakness of God is stronger than men.[5]

26 For consider also your calling, my brothers, that not many among you ^e[are] wise in the ^{sy}flesh and not many among you ^e[are] mighty and not many among you ^e[are] of noble birth.[6]

27 But God chose the foolish [ones] of the world to shame the wise and he chose the weak [ones] of the world to shame the strong,

28 and he chose[7] those in the world whose birth was inferior and despised [ones] and those who are nothing to make of none effect those who are [something],

29 so that no ^{sy}flesh should boast before him.

30 But **you** also are in Jesus Christ, by whom we have wisdom from God ^Pand justification and sanctification and redemption,¬

---

[1] Repeat *where is*, 3x
[2] Fig: erotesis – questions to ponder
[3] Same roots: *power, stronger* (v. 25); *wisdom, wiser* (v. 25)
[4] Pal Lect: Father
[5] Parallel structure: ABAB, also vs. 27, 28
[6] Repeat *and not many among you*; fig: ellipsis, add [are called]
[7] Repeat *chose*, from v. 27

ARAMAIC PESHITTA NEW TESTAMENT
I CORINTHIANS

Chapter 1
31 as it is written: **HE WHO BOASTS SHOULD BOAST IN THE** LORD.

Chapter 2
1   And my brothers, when I came to you, **I** declared to you the mystery of God, not with excellent speech nor with wisdom.

2   And I did not judge myself among you as though I knew anything, except Jesus Christ and him crucified.

3   And **I** was with you in much fear and in trembling.

4   And my speech and my preaching were not by persuasion of words of wisdom,[1] but by demonstration of the Spirit and of power,

5   so that your faith would not be by the wisdom of men, but by the power of God.

6   Now we speak wisdom among the mature [ones], not the wisdom of this world, nor of the authorities of this world who come to nothing,

7   but we speak the wisdom of God in a mystery, which was hidden and [which] God determined beforehand, from before the ages, for our glory.

8   Not one of the authorities of this world knew, for if they had known it, they would not have crucified the Lord of glory.

9   But as it is written: **THE EYE HAS NOT SEEN AND THE EAR HAS NOT HEARD AND INTO THE HEART OF MAN HAS NOT ENTERED WHAT GOD HAS PREPARED FOR THOSE WHO LOVE HIM.**

10   But God has revealed [it] to us by his Spirit, for the Spirit searches everything, even the deep [things] of God.

11   For who is the man who knows what is in a man, except the spirit of the man[2] that [is] in him? So also, no man knows what is in God, except the Spirit of God.

12   Now **we** have not received the spirit of the world, but the Spirit that is[3] from God, so that we would know the gifts that were given to us from God,

13   which also we speak, not in the teaching of the words of the wisdom of men, but in the teaching of the Spirit and to spiritual men, we compare spiritual [things].[4]

---

[1] Repeat *wisdom*, vs. 4-7
[2] Var (L): *man* is two words
[3] Fig: ellipsis, add [received]
[4] Same root: *Spirit, spiritual men, spiritual [things]*, vs. 13-15

Chapter 2

14 For a man who is natural[1] does not receive spiritual [things], for they are foolishness to him, and he is not able to know that which is judged spiritually.

15 Now the spiritual man[2] judges everything and is judged by no one.

16 **FOR WHO KNOWS THE MIND OF THE LORD TO TEACH HIM?** But we have the mind of Christ.

Chapter 3

1 And my brothers, I was not able to speak with you as with spiritual men, but as with carnal [ones] and as to babies in Christ.

2 I gave you milk to drink and I did not give you food, for you were not yet able ᵉ[to eat]. But not even now are you able,

3 for you are yet in the ˢʸflesh. For where there is among you envy ᴾand contention and divisions,┐ *behold, are you not carnal [ones] and are you walking in the ˢʸflesh?

4 For when each one of you says, "I am of Paul," and another says, "I am of Apollos," *behold, are you not carnal [ones]?[3]

5 For who is Paul or who is Apollos, but the ministers by whose hands you believed and each one as the LORD gave to him?

6 ᵃˡI planted and Apollos watered, but God caused increase.

7 Therefore, he who plants is nothing, nor he who waters, but God who causes increase.

8 Now he who plants and he who waters are one and each receives his wage according to his labor.┐

9 ᵃˡFor we work with God and ᵃᶜyou are the work of God and the building of God.

10 And according to the grace of God that was given to me, I laid the foundation as a wise master-builder, but another builds on it. Now everyone should consider how he will build on it.

11 For no one is able to lay another foundation other than this that is laid, which is Jesus Christ.

---

[1] Lit: *a man* who is in his soul
[2] OS (Afr) 'man of the Spirit'
[3] Repeat *behold are you not carnal [ones]* from v. 3; fig: erotesis -- questions to ponder

Chapter 3

12 Now if anyone builds on this foundation, gold or[1] silver or precious stones or pieces of wood or grass or straw,

13 the work of everyone is revealed. For that [sy]day will reveal it, because it is revealed[2] by fire. And the fire will distinguish the work of everyone, according to what it is.

14 And he who builds, whose work will endure, will receive his reward.

15 And he whose work will burn will suffer loss. Now **he** will escape, but so [s]as from fire.⌐

16 Do you not know that [me]you are the temple of God and [that] the Spirit of God lives in you?[3]

17 And[4] he who corrupts the temple of God, God will corrupt,[5] for the temple of God is holy, because you are [e][holy].

18 No one should delude himself. He among you who thinks that he is wise in this world, should be foolish, so that he may become wise.[6]

19 For the wisdom of this world is foolishness with God, for it is written: **HE APPREHENDS THE WISE IN THEIR CRAFTINESS.**

20 And again [he says]: **THE** LORD **KNOWS THE REASONINGS OF THE WISE THAT THEY ARE FRUITLESS.**

21 Because of this, no one should boast in men, for everything is your own,

22 whether Paul or[7] Apollos or Peter or the world, whether life or death, whether present [things] or future [things], everything is your own.

23 And you are of Christ and Christ [is] of God.

Chapter 4

1 So we should be regarded by you as ministers of Christ and stewards of the mysteries of God.

2 Now then it is required in stewards that a man should be found faithful.

3 Now this is a little matter to me that I should be judged by you or by any man, since **I** do not even judge myself.

---

[1] Repeat *or*, 5x

[2] Repeat forms of *revealed*

[3] Fig: erotesis – question to ponder

[4] Var (SLM): omit *and*

[5] Repeat *corrupt*

[6] Fig: oxymoron; repeat forms of *wise, foolish*, vs. 18-20

[7] Repeat *or*, 4x

Chapter 4

4 ^{pa}For I am guilty of nothing in myself,⌐ but I am not justified by this, for the LORD is my judge.

5 Because of this, do not judge before the ^{sy}time until the LORD comes, who will bring to light the hidden [things] of darkness and reveal the reasonings of the hearts. And then there will be praise to each one from God.

6 Now these [things], my brothers, because of you I have decided concerning my own person and that of Apollos, so that by us you should learn not to think more than what is written and [that] no one should be elevated above his neighbor because of anyone.

7 For who has examined you or what do you have that you did not receive? And if you received, why are you boasting as one who did not receive?[1]

8 Already you have been satisfied and you have grown rich and without us you have reigned.[2] ⁱOh that you had reigned, so that **we** would also reign with you!

9 For I think that God has placed the apostles last, as though for death, since ^{me}we have become a spectacle to the ^{sy}world ^pand to angels and to men.⌐ [3]

10 We are fools on account of Christ, but you are wise in Christ. We are weak and you are strong. You are glorified and we are despised.[4]

11 Until this time, we are hungry ^pand thirsty and are naked and are mistreated and we have no stable dwelling⌐

12 and we labor, working with our hands. They despise us and we bless. They persecute us and we endure.

13 They revile us and we entreat them. We have become as the filth of the world and the refuse of all men until now.

14 I do not write these [things] to shame you, but as beloved sons, I am warning [you].

15 For even if you have a large number of instructors in Christ, surely not many fathers, for in Jesus Christ **I** have fathered you by the gospel.

16 Therefore, I beg you to be like me.

---

[1] Fig: erotesis – questions to ponder

[2] Repeat suffix ending: *you have...*

[3] Culture: in the Roman games, prisoners at the last were not given any weapons, Freeman, p. 456, and Kitto, vol I, pp. 728-735.

[4] Parallel structure, antithesis, vs. 10-13

Chapter 4

17 Because of this, I sent you Timothy, who is my beloved son and faithful in the LORD, that he would remind you of my ways that are in Christ, according to what I teach in all the churches.

18 Now some of you are puffed up, as though I am not coming to you.

19 But if the LORD wills, I will come quickly to you, and I will know, not the word of those who elevate themselves, but their power.

20 For the kingdom of God is not in word, but in power.

21 In what manner do you want [e][me to come]? Should I come to you with a rod or in love and with a humble spirit?[1]

Chapter 5

1 Actually, fornication has been reported among you and such fornication as this which is not even named among the heathen, insomuch that a son would take the wife of his father.

2 And **you** are puffed up and you did not rather sit in grief, that he who did this deed should be cut off from among you.

3 For while **I** am distant from you in body, yet I am spiritually near to you. I have already, as though present, judged him who did this,

4 that all of you should be gathered in the name of our Lord Jesus Christ and I with you spiritually with the power of our Lord Jesus Christ,

5 and [that] you should deliver this [one] to SATAN for the ruin of his body, so that he will live spiritually in the [sy]day of our Lord Jesus Christ.

6 Your boasting is not pleasing.[2] [al]Do you not know that a little leaven leavens the whole mass?

7 Purge from you the old leaven, so that you will be a new mass [of] unleavened bread. For our Passover[3] is Christ, who was sacrificed on our behalf.

8 Because of this, we should celebrate the feast, not with old leaven and not with the [h]leaven of wickedness and of bitterness, but with the [h]leaven[4] of purity and of holiness.⌐

9 I wrote to you in a letter that you should not associate with fornicators.

---

[1] Fig: erotesis – questions to ponder
[2] Var (S): add 'my brothers'
[3] Fig: ellipsis, add [Lamb]
[4] Var (S): 'with the unleavened bread'; see Smith, p. 170 for uses of this figure of leaven.

Chapter 5

10 Now I was not speaking about fornicators who are in this world or[1] about wrong-doers or about extortioners or about idol worshipers, otherwise you would be required indeed to go out of the world.

11 But this [is] what I wrote to you, that if there is one who is called a brother and he is a fornicator or a wrong-doer or an idol worshiper or a reviler or a drunkard or an extortioner, you should not associate with one who is so, not even to eat bread.

12 For what [is it] to me to judge ones outside?[2] You judge those who are within,

13 but God judges the ones outside. **YOU SHOULD CUT OFF THE WICKED [ONE] FROM AMONG YOU.**

Chapter 6

1 Does anyone among you dare, when he has a dispute with his brother, to go to trial before the unrighteous and not before the holy [ones]?

2 Or do you not know that the holy [ones] will judge[3] the world? And if the world is being judged by you, are you not worthy to judge judgments of small [things]?

3 Do you not know that you will judge angels? How much more these [things] that are of this world?[4]

4 But if you have a dispute about a worldly issue, you should cause those who are despised in the church to sit in judgment for you.[5]

5 Now I say [this] for a reproach to you. So do you not have even one wise [person] who is able to cause agreement between a brother and his brother?

6 But a brother is judged against his brother, and moreover, [i]before those who do not believe!

7 Already therefore, you have condemned yourselves, because you have a dispute with one another. For why should you not be taken advantage of? And why should you not be defrauded?

8 But **you** take advantage of and you defraud even your brothers.

---

[1] Repeat *or*, vs. 10, 11, 8x

[2] Fig: erotesis, begins series of questions, 6:1, 2, 3, 5, 7, 9, 15, 16, 19, often beginning with *or* – questions to ponder

[3] Repeat forms of *judge, judgment* vs. 2-6

[4] Fig: erotesis, **kema** question, answer in the affirmative

[5] Fig: irony, we would use the word "sarcastic"

Chapter 6

9 Or do you not know that wicked [ones] will not[1] inherit the kingdom of God? Do not err. Neither fornicators nor idolaters nor adulterers nor corrupt [ones] nor homosexuals

10 nor wrong-doers nor thieves nor drunkards nor revilers nor extortioners, these will not inherit the kingdom of God.

11 And these [things] have been in some of you, but you are washed and you are made holy and you are justified in the name of our Lord Jesus Christ and by the Spirit of our God.

12 Everything is lawful to me, but everything is not profitable to me. Everything[2] is lawful to me, but no one will have authority over me.

13 Food [is] for the stomach and the stomach [is] for food, but God makes both void. Now the body [is] not for fornication, but[3] for our Lord and our Lord for the body.

14 Now God raised our Lord and raises[4] us by his power.

15 [al]Do you not know that [me]your bodies are members of Christ? Should one take a member of Christ [and] make it a member of a prostitute? [i]Let it not be so!

16 Or do you not know that he who joins to a prostitute is one body? For it is said: **THE TWO OF THEM WILL BE ONE FLESH.⌐**

17 Now he who joins to our Lord becomes one spirit with him.

18 Flee from fornication. Every sin that a man may do is outside of his body. But he who commits fornication sins in his body.

19 Or do you not know that [me]your body is the temple of the Holy Spirit that lives in you that you received from God and [that] you are not your own?

20 For you are bought with a price. Therefore, glorify God in your body and in your spirit, which are of God.

Chapter 7

1 Now about those [things] that you wrote to me, it is good for a man not to touch a woman.

2 But because of fornication, a man should hold fast to his [own] wife and a woman should hold fast to her [own] husband.

---

[1] Repeat *not,* double negative, *nor,* also v. 10

[2] Repeat *everything,* lit: all

[3] Fig: ellipsis, add [the body is]; parallel structure: ABCCBA

[4] Var (SL): will raise

Chapter 7

3   A husband should pay to his wife the love that is owed. So also, the wife[1] to her husband.

4   The wife [has] no authority over her body, but her husband. So also, the man [has] no authority over his body, but his wife.

5   Therefore, do not deprive one another, except when both of you consent for a time to be devoted to fasting and to prayer and return again to the same arrangement, so that SATAN will not tempt you because of the desire of your body.

6   But this I say as though to weak [ones], not by commandment.

7   For **I** want all men to be like me in purity. But everyone is given a gift from God, some in one manner and some in another.

8   But I speak to those who do not have wives and to widows, that it is profitable to them if they would remain like me.

9   But if they are not enduring, they should marry, for it is more profitable[2] to take a wife than to burn with desire.

10   But to those who have wives, I command, not I, but my Lord, that a wife should not separate from her husband.

11   And if she separates, she should remain without a man or she should be reconciled to her husband. And a man should not leave his wife.

12   But to the rest I say, I, not my Lord, if there is a brother who has a wife who is not a believer, yet she wants to live with him, he should not leave her.

13   And a woman who has a husband that does not believe, yet he wants to live with her, should not leave her husband.

14   For the husband who does not believe is made holy by the wife who is a believer, and the wife who is not a believer is made holy by the husband who believes. Otherwise, their children are impure, but now they are pure.

15   Now if one who does not believe separates, let him separate. A brother or sister is not bound in these [things]. God has called us to peace.

16   For how do you know, wife, if you may give life to your husband? Or you, husband, [how] do you know if you may give life to your wife?[3]

---

[1] Fig: ellipsis, add [should pay] *to her husband* [the respect that is owed]

[2] Repeat *it is profitable* from v. 8

[3] Fig: erotesis – questions to ponder

Chapter 7

17 But each one as the LORD has distributed to him and each as God has called him, so he should walk. And so also, I am commanding all the churches.

18 If a man was called while circumcised, he should not return to ᵐuncircumcision. And if he was called in ᵐuncircumcision, he should not be circumcised.

19 For ᵐcircumcision is not anything, neither ᵐuncircumcision, but the observances of the commandments of God.[1]

20 Everyone should remain in the calling in which he was called.[2]

21 If you were called [being] a servant, it should not concern you. But even if you are able to be freed, choose to work.

22 For he who was called in our Lord [being] a servant is a freeman of God. So also, he who was called a free man is a servant of Christ.

23 You were bought with a price. You should not become servants of men.

24 Everyone, my brothers, should remain with God in that ᵉ[calling] in which he was called.

25 Now concerning virginity, I do not hold fast to a commandment from God, but I give counsel as a man who has obtained mercy from God to be faithful.

26 And I think that this is good, because of the urgency of time. ᵉ[I think] that it is better for a man to be like this.

27 Are you bound with a wife? Do not seek a divorce. Are you divorced from a wife? Do not seek a wife.

28 Yet if you take a wife, you are not sinning. And if an unmarried woman gets married, she does not sin. Now those who are so will have trouble in the body, but I ᵉ[want to] spare you.

29 And *this I say, my brothers, that the time is now shortened, so that those who have wives should be as though they do not have [any],

30 and those who weep, as not weeping, and those who rejoice, as not rejoicing, and those who buy, as not acquiring,[3]

---

[1] Fig: ellipsis, add [are everything]

[2] Same root: *calling, called*, vs. 20-24; repeat verse as conclusion, v. 24.

[3] Same roots: *weep, weeping; rejoice, rejoicing; buy, acquiring*; fig: ellipsis, add [should be] before *as not*, 3x

Chapter 7

31 and those who are occupied with this world, not outside of what is just for use,[1] for the fashion of this world passes away.

32 Because of this, I desire for you to be without anxiety, for he who does not have a wife is concerned with the one who is his Lord, how he should please his Lord.

33 And he who has a wife, cares about the world, how he should please his wife.

34 Now there is also a difference between a wife and an unmarried woman. She who is not married is concerned with her Lord, so that she will be holy in her body and in her spirit. And she who has a husband is concerned with the world, how she should please her husband.

35 Now I say this for your own advantage. I am not laying a snare for you, but rather that you may be faithful toward your Lord in a pleasing manner, while not being concerned with the world.

36 But if a man thinks that he is mocked by his unmarried [daughter] who is past her time and he has not given her to a man and it is fitting that he should give her, he should do as he desires. He does not sin [if] she would be married.

37 But he who has firmly decided in his mind and is not compelled by the matter and has power over his will and so judges in his heart to keep his unmarried [daughter], he does well.

38 And therefore, he who gives his unmarried [daughter] does well. And he who does not give his unmarried [daughter] does very well.

39 A wife, while her husband lives, is bound by the law. But if her husband should [eu]sleep, she is free to be [married] to whom she wants, only in our Lord.

40 But she is blessed if she should remain so, according to my own mind. And I am also convinced that the Spirit of God is in me.

Chapter 8

1 Now concerning the sacrifices of idols, we know that in all of us there is knowledge and knowledge[2] makes [one] proud, but love builds.

2 Now if anyone thinks that he knows anything, he does not know anything yet, as he ought to know it.

3 But if anyone loves God, this [one] is known by him.

---

[1] Same root: *occupied, use*

[2] Repeat *knowledge*, next word; repeat forms of *know, knowledge,* vs. 1-11

ARAMAIC PESHITTA NEW TESTAMENT
I CORINTHIANS

Chapter 8

4   Therefore, concerning the food of the sacrifices of idols, we know that an idol is nothing in the world and that there is no other God, except one.

5   For although there are [those] who are called gods, either in heaven or on earth, ᵖᵃas there are many gods and many[1] lordships,ך

6   but to us ourselves, [there] is one God, the Father, from whom [are] all [things] and by whom we are, and one LORD, Jesus Christ, by way of him [are] all [things] and we are also by way of him.

7   But not everyone has [this] knowledge, for there are some who in their conscience until now eat that which is sacrificed to idols. And because their conscience[2] is weak, it is defiled.

8   Now food does not bring us near to God, for if we eat, we do not grow, and if we do not eat, we do not lack.

9   But watch, so that this authority of yours should not become a stumbling block to the weak.

10   For if someone sees you in whom there is knowledge, that you are sitting to eat [in] the temple[3] of idols, *behold, is not his conscience, because he is weak, encouraged to eat what is sacrificed?

11   And he who is feeble, on account of whom Christ died, will be hurt by your knowledge.

12   And if you are injuring your brothers in this manner and you are wounding the consciences [of] the feeble, you are injuring Christ.

13   Because of this, if food causes offense to my brother, I will not eat flesh forever, so that I should not cause offense to my brother.

Chapter 9

1   Am I not a free man?[4] Or am I not an apostle? Or have I not seen Jesus Christ our Lord? Or[5] are you not my work in my Lord?

2   And if I am not an apostle to others, yet I am to you and you are the seal of my apostleship.

3   And my defense to those who judge me is this:

4   Is it not lawful for us to eat and to drink?

---

[1] Repeat *many*

[2] Repeat *conscience*, vs. 7-12

[3] Lit: house

[4] Fig: erotesis, **lema** questions, vs. 1, 4, 5, 8, 9, obvious answer "no", total of 20 questions from vs. 1-24.

[5] Repeat *or*

Chapter 9

5 And[1] is it not lawful for us to lead a sister with us, a wife, as the rest of the apostles and as the brothers of our Lord and as Peter?

6 Or I only and Barnabas, do we not have the authority not to work?

7 Who is he who does military service[2] at his own expense? Or who is he who plants a vineyard and does not eat from its fruit? Or who is he who tends the flock and does not eat from the milk of his flock?

8 Am I saying these [things] as a man? *Behold, the law also says these [things].

9 For it is written in the law of Moses: YOU SHOULD NOT MUZZLE THE OX THAT THRESHES. Is it a concern to God about oxen?

10 On the contrary, it is known that because of us he said [it] and because of us it was written, because the plowman ought to plow for hope and he who threshes[3] for the hope of harvest.

11 If **we** have sown [things] of the Spirit among you, is it a great [thing] if **we** reap [things] of the body from you?

12 And if others have authority over you, ought we not [to have] more? Yet we have not used this authority, but we have endured everything, so that we would not hinder the gospel of Christ in anything.

13 Do you not know that those who serve in the sanctuary are sustained from the sanctuary and those who serve at the altar have a portion of the altar?

14 So also, our Lord commanded that those who are preaching his gospel should live from his gospel.

15 But **I** have not used one of these [things] and I have not written because of this, that it would be so [done] to me, for it is better for me that I should indeed die,[4] than that anyone should make my boasting void.

16 For although I preach, I have no boasting, for necessity is laid on me and 'woe to me if I do not preach!

17 For if I do this willingly, I have a reward, but if not willingly, I am entrusted with a stewardship.

---

[1] Var (SL): 'or'

[2] Same root: *does, military service*

[3] Same root: *plowman, plow*; fig: ellipsis, add [ought to thresh]

[4] Fig: polyptoton, lit: dying, I should die

Chapter 9

18 What then is my reward? [It is] that when I am preaching, I make the gospel of Christ without cost and I do not use the authority that he gave me in the gospel.

19 For although I am free from all [things], I have subjected myself to everyone, that I may gain many.[1]

20 And with the Judeans I was as a Judean, that I would gain Judeans, and with those who are under the law, I was as those under the law, so that I would gain those that are under the law.

21 And to those who have no law, I was as without the law [pa](although I am not without the law to God, but in the law of Christ), so that I would also gain those who are without the law.

22 I was with the weak [ones] as weak, so that I would gain the weak. I am all [things] to everyone, so that I may give life to everyone.

23 And I am doing this in order to be a participant of the gospel.

24 [al]Do you not know that those who run in a contest all run, but one receives the victory? So, run that you may obtain.[2]

25 Now everyone who participates in a contest controls his mind in every way. And those are running to receive a crown that is corruptible, but we,[3] one that is incorruptible.

26 Therefore, **I** so run, not as for something unknown, and I so fight, not [s]as one who beats the air,

27 but I subdue my body and I subject [it], so that when **I** have preached to others, I myself will not be rejected.⌐

Chapter 10

1 But I want you to know, my brothers, that our fathers were all under the cloud [P]and all passed through the sea

2 and all were baptized by way of Moses in the cloud and in the sea

3 and all ate of the same food of the Spirit

---

[1] Parallel structure, vs. 19-23,; repeat *gain, law, weak,* vs. 19-23

[2] Fig: ellipsis, add [the victory]

[3] Fig: ellipsis, add [are running to receive]; Culture: the crown refers to the laurel wreath which was given to victors in the Greek and Roman games, Freeman, p. 457.

Chapter 10

4   and all drank of the same drink of the Spirit,⌐ for they were drinking[1] from the rock of the Spirit that came with them and ^{me}that rock was Christ.

5   But with many of them God was not well pleased, for they fell in the wilderness.

6   Now these [things] were an example for us, so that we should not lust after evil [things] as those lusted.

7   And neither should we be worshipping idols, as some of them also worshipped,[2] as it is written: **THE PEOPLE SAT TO EAT AND TO DRINK AND THEY ROSE UP TO PLAY.**

8   Neither should we commit fornication, as some of them committed fornication, and they fell in one day, twenty-three thousand.

9   And we should not tempt Christ, as some of them tempted, and serpents destroyed them.

10 Neither should you murmur, as some of them murmured, and were destroyed by the hands of the Violator.

11 Now all these [things] that happened to them were for our example[3] and it was written for our instruction, on whom the end of the ages has come.

12 Therefore, he who thinks that he stands should watch, so that he does not fall.

13 No temptation has come on you, except of men, but God is faithful, who will not allow you to be tempted more than what you are able, but will make a way out for your temptation, so that you will be able to endure [it].

14 Because of this, my beloved [ones], flee from the worship of idols.

15 I am speaking as to the wise. You judge what I am saying.

16 That cup of thanksgiving that we bless, ^{me}is it not the fellowship of the blood of Christ? And that bread that we break, ^{me}is it not the fellowship of the body of Christ?[4]

17 ^{al}As that bread is one, so all of us are one body, for all of us have taken from that one bread.⌐

---

[1] Same root: *drank, drink, drinking*

[2] Repeat, vs. 7-14: *worship, commit fornication, tempt, temptation, murmur, some of them*

[3] Repeat from v. 6

[4] Fig: erotesis – questions to ponder, also vs. 18, 19

Chapter 10

18 Look at Israel who are in the ^{sy}flesh. Do not those who eat the sacrifices become participants of the altar?

19 Therefore, what am I saying? That an idol is anything or a sacrifice of an idol is anything? No.

20 But what the heathen sacrifice, they sacrifice to demons and not to God. And I do not want you to be participants with demons.

21 You are not able to drink the cup of our Lord and the cup of demons and you are not able to participate with the table of our Lord and with the table of demons.

22 Or are we especially provoking[1] our Lord to jealousy? Are we stronger than him?[2]

23 Everything is lawful to me, but not everything is profitable. Everything is lawful for me, but not everything builds up.

24 No one should seek his own [things], but everyone also ^e[should seek] the ^e[things] of his neighbor.

25 Everything that is sold in the marketplace, eat without a question on account of conscience,[3]

26 **FOR THE EARTH IS OF THE LORD IN ITS FULLNESS.**

27 But if one of the heathen invites you and you want to go, eat everything that is set before you without a question on account of conscience.

28 But if anyone should say to you that this is that which is sacrificed, you should not eat, because of him who told you and on account of conscience.

29 Now the conscience I speak [of] is not your own, but his who told [you]. For why is my liberty judged by the conscience of others?[4]

30 If I apply grace, why am I reproached for what I give thanks?

31 Therefore, whether you eat or drink or do anything, do everything to the glory of God.

32 Be without offense to Judeans ^Pand to Gentiles and to the church of God,⌐

33 even as I please everyone in everything and I do not seek what is profitable to me, but what is profitable to many, that they may have life.

---

[1] Fig: polyptoton, lit: provoking, have provoked
[2] Fig: erotesis, **lema** questions, obvious answer "no"
[3] Repeat *on account of conscience*, vs. 27, 28
[4] Fig: erotesis, also v. 30 – questions to ponder

ARAMAIC PESHITTA NEW TESTAMENT
I CORINTHIANS

Chapter 11

1   Be like me, as also I am in Christ.

2   Now I commend you, my brothers, that in everything you are mindful of me and you hold fast the commandments, even as I delivered [them] to you.

3   Now I want you to know that the head[1] of every man is Christ and the head of the woman is the man and the head of Christ is God.

4   Every man who prays or prophesies while his ^{at}head is covered dishonors his head.

5   And every woman who prays or prophesies while her ^{at}head is uncovered dishonors her head, for she is on a level with her whose head is shaven.

6   For if a woman is not covered, she should also be shorn. But if it is disgraceful for a woman to be shorn or to be shaven, she should be covered.

7   For a man ought not to cover his head, because he is the likeness and glory of God, but the woman is the glory of the man.

8   For a man is not from the woman, but the woman from the man,

9   for neither was the man made for the woman, but the woman for the man.

10   Because of this, the woman is obliged to have authority[2] on her head, because of the angels.

11   Nevertheless, the man [is] not outside of the woman, nor the woman outside of the man in our Lord.

12   For as the woman [was] from the man, so also the man [was] by way of the woman and everything is from God.

13   Judge among yourselves, for yourselves. Is it proper for a woman to pray to God while her head is uncovered?[3]

14   Does not even nature teach you that it is a shame for a man when his hair grows long?

15   And [for] a woman, it is a glory to her when her hair is abundant, because her hair is given to her for a covering.

16   But if anyone contends about these [things], we have no custom as this and not for the church of God.

---

[1] Repeat *head*, vs. 3-11, see figure: antanaclasis
[2] Could be a figure of speech for "covering of"
[3] Fig: erotesis – questions to ponder, also v. 14

ARAMAIC PESHITTA NEW TESTAMENT
I CORINTHIANS

Chapter 11

17 Now this which I command [is] not as though I am praising you, because you have not progressed, but rather you have fallen behind.

18 For in the first place, when you are gathered in the church, I hear that there are divisions among you and I believe some [of these things].

19 For there are also going to be contentions among you, that those who are approved among you may be known.

20 Then when you are gathered, you do not eat and drink[1] as is proper for the [sy]day of our Lord.

21 But each man eats his meal beforehand and it happens [that] one is hungry and one is drunk.

22 Do you not have houses [in] which you may eat and drink?[2] Or do you despise the church of God and shame those who do not have? What can I say to you? Should I praise you in this? I do not praise [you].

23 For I have received from our Lord what I committed to you, that our Lord Jesus in that night [in] which he was betrayed took bread

24 and blessed [it] and broke [it] and said, "Take, eat, [me]this is my body, that is broken on your behalf.[3] Do so for my memorial."

25 Likewise, after they had eaten, he also gave the cup and said, "This [me]cup is the new covenant in my [mt]blood. Do so, whenever you drink, for my memorial."

26 For whenever you eat this bread and drink this cup, you call to remembrance the death of our Lord until his coming.

27 Therefore, whoever eats of the bread of the LORD and drinks from his cup and is not worthy, he is indebted to the blood of the LORD and to his body.

28 Because of this, a man should examine himself and then eat from this bread and drink from this cup,

29 for he who eats and drinks from it, being unworthy, eats and drinks condemnation to himself, because he has not discerned the body of the LORD.

30 Because of this, many among you [are] sick [P]and weak and many are [eu]asleep.⌐

---

[1] Repeat *eat and drink*, vs. 20-29

[2] Fig: erotesis, **lema** question (1st), obvious answer "yes", other questions to ponder

[3] Pal Lect: omit *take, eat, broken*; fig: ploce, "word-folding" *broke, broken*

Chapter 11

31 For if we judge ourselves, we are not judged.[1]

32 But when we are judged by our Lord, we are indeed instructed,[2] so that we should not be condemned with the world.

33 From now on, my brothers, when you are gathered to eat, wait for one another.

34 And he who is hungry should eat in his house, so that you will not be gathering together to condemnation. Now concerning the rest, I will charge you when I come.

Chapter 12

1 Now about spiritual [things], my brothers, I want you to know

2 that you were heathens and were led to idols that have no distinct voice.

3 Because of this, I make known to you that there is no one who speaks by the Spirit of God and says that Jesus is cursed. And neither is anyone able to say that Jesus is LORD, except by the Holy Spirit.

4 And there are distributions of gifts, but the Spirit is one.

5 And there are distributions of services,[3] but the LORD is one.

6 And there are distributions of powers, but God is the one who works all in everyone.

7 Now the manifestation of the Spirit is given to each one as it is profitable for him.

8 There is a word of wisdom that is given to him by the Spirit, now for another,[4] a word of knowledge by the same Spirit,

9 for another, faith by the same Spirit, for another, gifts of healing by the same Spirit,

10 now for another, miracles, now for another, prophecy, now for another, discerning of spirits, now for another, kinds of tongues, now for another, the interpretation of tongues.

11 Now all these [things] the one Spirit works and distributes to everyone as he wills.

12 For as the body is one and there are many members in it and all the members of the body, although they are many, are one body, so also [is] Christ.

---

[1] Repeat forms of *judge*, also v. 32

[2] Fig: polyptoton, lit: instructing are instructed

[3] Var (SL): *service* (singular)

[4] Fig: ellipsis, add [profiting] or [profitability], from v. 7

Chapter 12

13 For all of us also are baptized in one spirit into one body, whether Judean or Gentile, whether slave or free men. And all of us drink of one Spirit.

14 For also the body is not one member, but many.

15 For if the foot should say, "Because I am not the hand, I am not a part of the body," because of this, is it not a part of the body?[1]

16 And if the ear should say, "Because I am not the eye, I am not a part of the body," because of this, is it not a part of the body?

17 For if all the body were eyes, where would the hearing be? And if all of it were hearing, where would the smelling be?

18 But now God has placed every one of the members in the body, as he willed.

19 Now if they were all one member, where would the body be?

20 But now, there are many members, but it is one body.

21 The eye is not able to say to the hand, "You are not necessary to me." Nor is the head able to say to the feet, "You are not necessary to me."[2]

22 But more, there is a necessity for those members that are thought to be weak.

23 And to those that we think are despised in the body, we give more honor. And for those that are modest, we make more decoration.

24 Now those members that we have that are honored do not require honor. For God has joined together the body and he has given more honor to the member who is least,

25 so that there would not be division in the body, but rather [that] all the members would care for one another equally,

26 so that when one member was hurt, all of them would suffer, and if one member was praised, all the members would be praised.

27 Now ᵐᵉyou are the body of Christ and members in your place.

28 For God set in his church, first apostles, after them, prophets, after them, teachers, after them, workers of miracles, after them,[3] gifts of healing ᴾand helpers and leaders and kinds of tongues.⌐

---

[1] Repeat *because of this, is it not a part of the body*, v. 16; fig: erotesis – questions to ponder, also vs. 16, 17, 19

[2] Repeat *you are not necessary to me*

[3] Repeat *after them*, 4x

413

Chapter 12

29 [Are] all of them apostles?[1] [Are] all of them prophets? [Are] all of them teachers? [Are] all of them doers of miracles?

30 Do all of them have gifts of healing? Do all of them speak in tongues? Or do all of them interpret?

31 Now if you are zealous about the best gifts, **I** will also show you a way that is of more value.

Chapter 13

1 If I should speak in every tongue of men and with [tongues] of angels and not have love, [me]I would be[2] brass that sounds or a cymbal that gives out noise.

2 And if I would have prophecy and I would know all mysteries and all knowledge and if I would have all faith so that I could move a mountain[3] and I do not have love, I am nothing.

3 And if I would feed the poor all that I have and if I would deliver my body to be burned and I do not have love, I am not profiting anything.

4 [pe]Love is long-suffering and kind. Love does not envy. Love is not ruffled [P]and is not puffed up

5 and does not do that which is shameful and does not seek its own and is not enraged and does not think what is evil,⌐

6 does not rejoice in wickedness, but rejoices with truthfulness.

7 [Love] [a]endures everything, believes everything, hopes all, bears all.⌐

8 Love never fails. For prophecies will be made void [P]and tongues will be silent and knowledge will be made void.⌐

9 For we know in part and we prophesy in part.

10 Now when what is completed comes, then what is partial will be made void.

11 When I was a child, I spoke as a child [P]and I thought as a child and I reasoned as a child.⌐ But when I became a man, I stopped these [things] of youth.

---

[1] Fig: erotesis, **lema** questions (6x in vs. 29, 30), obvious answer "no"

[2] Var (S): add 'as'

[3] Var (LM): *mountains* (plural)

ARAMAIC PESHITTA NEW TESTAMENT
I CORINTHIANS

Chapter 13
12 Now ˢas in a mirror,[1] we see in an illustration, but then face to face. Now I know in part, but then I will know as I am known.
13 For there are these three that remain, faith ᴾand hope and love,⌐ but the greatest of these is love.

Chapter 14
1 Pursue love and be zealous about the gifts of the Spirit, but especially to prophesy.
2 For he who speaks in a tongue does not speak to men, but to God, for no one understands anything that he speaks, but spiritually he speaks a mystery.
3 Now he who prophesies speaks to men edification ᴾand encouragement and comfort.⌐
4 He who speaks in a tongue builds himself up and he who prophesies builds up the church.
5 Now I am desiring that all of you would speak in tongues and especially that you would prophesy. For greater is he who prophesies than he who speaks in a tongue, unless he interprets. Now if he interprets, he edifies the church.
6 And now, my brothers, if I come to you and speak with you in tongues, what am I profiting you, unless I speak with you either by revelation or by knowledge or by prophecy or by[2] teaching?
7 For even those things that have no life and give out sound, whether flute or harp, if they do not make a distinction between one tone and the other, how is what is sung or what is played known?[3]
8 And if the trumpet should sound a sound[4] that is not distinct, who will prepare for the battle?
9 Likewise also, if **you** speak a message in a tongue and it will not be interpreted, how is what you spoke known? You will be as if you are speaking to the air.
10 For *behold, there are many kinds of tongues in the world and there is not one of them without meaning.

---

[1] Culture: ancient mirrors were not polished as today, so the reflection was shadowy and not completely clear, Freeman, pp. 75-76, 458.
[2] Repeat *or by*, 4x
[3] Fig: erotesis – questions to ponder, vs. 6, 8, 9
[4] Same root: *sound, a sound*

Chapter 14

11 But if I do not know the significance of the sound,[1] I will be a barbarian to him who speaks, and also he who speaks will be a barbarian[2] to me.

12 Likewise also, because **you** are zealous of the gifts of the Spirit, seek to excel for the building up of the church.

13 And he who speaks in a tongue should seek to interpret [it].

14 For if I was to pray in a tongue, my spirit prays, but my understanding is without fruit.

15 What then should I do? I will pray in my spirit and I will pray also with my understanding. And I will sing in my spirit and I will sing with my understanding also.

16 Otherwise, if you bless spiritually, how will he who fills the place of the unlearned say "Amen" at your thanksgiving, because he does not know what you said?

17 For **you** are blessing well, but your associate is not built up.

18 I thank God that I speak in tongues more than all of you.

19 But in the church I desire to speak five words with my understanding, so that I would also teach others, rather than a great number of words in a tongue.

20 My brothers, do not be children in your minds. But rather, be babies to evil [things] and be mature in your minds.[3]

21 In the law it is written: **WITH A STRANGE SPEECH AND WITH ANOTHER** [m]**TONGUE I WILL SPEAK WITH THIS PEOPLE. EVEN SO, THEY WILL NOT HEAR ME,** says the LORD.

22 Then tongues are placed for a sign, not to believers, but to those who do not believe. And prophecies are not to those who do not believe, but to those who believe.

23 If therefore all the church is gathered and all would speak in tongues and unlearned [ones] or those who do not believe should enter, will they not say, "These [people] are crazy"?

24 And if all of you would prophesy and an unlearned [one] or one who does not believe enters, he is examined by all of you [P]and reproved by all of you

---

[1] Lit: power of the voice

[2] Lit: son of the wilderness, or son of a foreigner, **bar brea;** culture: "everyone not a Greek is a barbarian" was a common Greek definition, Smith, p. 33.

[3] Repeat *in your minds*

ARAMAIC PESHITTA NEW TESTAMENT
I CORINTHIANS

Chapter 14

25 and the hidden [things] of his heart are revealed. And then he will fall on his face and will worship God and will say, "Truly God is with you."⸗

26 Therefore, my brothers, I say that when you are gathered, whoever of you has a psalm should speak. ᴾAnd he who has a teaching and he who has a revelation and he who has a tongue and he who has an interpretation, all of them should be for building up.

27 And if someone speaks in a tongue, two should speak and at the most three. And they should speak one by one and [that] one should interpret.

28 And if there is not one to interpret, he who speaks in a tongue should keep silent in the church and should speak to himself and to God.

29 And the prophets should speak, two or three, and the rest should discern.[1]

30 And if ᵉ[something] is revealed to another while he sits, the first should be silent.⸗

31 For all of you can prophesy one by one, so that everyone may learn and everyone may be comforted.

32 For the spirit of the prophets is subject to the prophets,

33 because God is not ᵉ[one][2] of confusion, but of peace, as in all the churches of the holy [ones].

34 Your wives should be silent in the church, for they are not allowed to speak, but they are to be subject, as the law also says.

35 And if they want to learn anything, they should ask their husbands at home, for it is a shame that wives should speak in the church.

36 Did the word of God go out from you?[3] Or did it only arrive to you?

37 Now if one of you thinks that he is a prophet or that he is ᵉ[prophesying] of the Spirit, he should acknowledge that these [things] that I write to you are the commandments of our Lord.

38 Now if someone does not know, he will not know.

39 Therefore, my brothers, earnestly desire to prophesy and to speak in tongues. Do not hold back.

40 Now everything should be [done] with decency and order.

---

[1] Var (P14470): 'should interpret' or 'should explain'
[2] Or [God]
[3] Fig: erotesis, **lema** question, obvious answer "no", second question to ponder

417

Chapter 15

1   Now I make known to you, my brothers, the gospel that I preached to you ^Pand [that] you received and in which you stand

2   and by which you have life.⌐ With what word I preached to you,[1] you remember, unless you have believed fruitlessly.

3   For I committed to you from the first according to what I received, that Christ died for our sins, as it is written,

4   ^Pand that he was buried and rose after three days, as it is written.[2]

5   And he appeared to Peter and after him, to the twelve.

6   And after that, he appeared to more than five hundred brothers together, many of whom remain until now, yet some of them sleep.

7   And after these, he appeared to James and after him, to all the apostles.

8   And last of all, he appeared to me also, ^sas one of an untimely birth.⌐

9   For I am the least of the apostles and am not worthy to be called an apostle,[3] because I persecuted the church of God.

10 But by the grace of God, I am what I am. And his grace that is in me was not fruitless. But I worked more than all of them, not I, but his grace that is with me.

11 Whether I, therefore, or they, so we preach and so you have believed.

12 And if Christ is preached that he rose from the dead, how are there some among you who say [that] there is no resurrection of the dead?

13 And if there is no resurrection of the dead, not even Christ has been raised.

14 And if Christ did not rise, our preaching is fruitless. Your faith [is] also fruitless.[4]

15 And we are also found [to be] false witnesses of God, because we have witnessed about God that he raised Christ, when he did not raise [him] up.

16 For if the dead do not rise, not even Christ has been raised.[5]

17 And if Christ did not rise, your faith is void and you are still in your sins

---

[1] Repeat *I preached to you* from v. 1

[2] Repeat *as it is written* from v. 3

[3] Fig: meiosis, "belittling"

[4] Repeat *fruitless* from v. 10

[5] Repeat *not even Christ has been raised* from v. 13

Chapter 15

18 and doubtless also, those who sleep in Christ have perished.

19 And if in this life only we hope in Christ, we are most miserable of all men.

20 But now Christ has risen from the dead and has become the first of those asleep.[1]

21 And as by way of a man came death, so also by way of a man came the resurrection of the dead.

22 For as in Adam all men die, so also in Christ all live,

23 each in his order. Christ was the first [and] after that, those who are of Christ at his coming.

24 And then will be the end, when he delivers the kingdom to God the Father, when every ruler [P]and every authority and all powers cease.⌐

25 For he is going to reign, until he places all his enemies under his [m]feet.[2]

26 And the last enemy, death, will be abolished.

27 **FOR HE HAS SUBJECTED ALL UNDER HIS [m]FEET.** But when he says that everything has been made subject to him, it is evident that it is apart from him who subjected[3] all to him.

28 And when everything is subjected to him, then the Son will be made subject to the one who subjected all to him, so that God will be all in all.

29 And if not, what will those who are baptized do for the dead, if the dead do not rise? Why are they baptized? For the dead?[4]

30 And why do **we** also stand in danger in every [sy]hour?

31 I swear by your boasting that I have in our Lord Jesus Christ, my brothers, that I am dying daily.

32 If as among men I was thrown to the beasts in Ephesus, what did I gain, if the dead do not rise? **LET US EAT AND DRINK, FOR TOMORROW WE WILL DIE.**

33 Do not err. Evil conversations corrupt good minds.

34 Stir up your heart justly and do not sin, for there are some who do not have the knowledge of God. [pa]I am speaking to your shame.⌐

---

[1] Fig: ellipsis, add [to be raised]

[2] Culture: *under his feet* refers to the custom of trampling on the vanquished enemy. Putting the feet on the necks of a conquered enemy symbolized the victory, Freeman, p. 459; see Joshua 10:24.

[3] Repeat forms of *subjected*

[4] Fig: erotesis – questions to ponder, also v. 30

Chapter 15

35 One of you will say, "How do the dead rise? And in what body will they come?"

36 [i]Fool! [al]The seed that you sow does not live unless it dies.

37 And what you sow, you are not sowing that body that it is going to be, but the naked kernel of wheat or of barley or of the rest of the grains.

38 Now God gave it a body as he willed and to each one of the grains its natural body.⌐

39 Now every body is not the same, for the body of a man is one [kind] and another[1] of a beast and another of a bird and another of a fish.

40 And there are heavenly bodies and there are earthly bodies, but the glory of the heavenly is one [kind] and another of the earthly.

41 And the glory of the sun is one [kind] and the glory of the moon [is] another and the glory of the stars another and [one] star is greater than [e][another] star in glory.

42 So also [is] the resurrection of the dead. They are sown in corruption. They are raised without corruption.[2]

43 They are sown in disgrace. They are raised in glory. They are sown in weakness. They are raised in power.

44 It is sown a natural[3] body. It rises a spiritual body. For there is a physical body and there is a spiritual body.

45 So also it is written: **ADAM, THE FIRST MAN, BECAME A LIVING SOUL.** And the last Adam [e][became] a life-giving spirit.

46 But the spiritual was not first, but the natural and then the spiritual.

47 The first man [was] dust from the earth. The second man [was] the LORD from heaven.

48 As he was [of] dust, so also [are those of] dust.[4] And as he who was from heaven, so also [are] the heavenly [ones].

49 And as we have worn the likeness of him who is from dust, so we will wear the likeness of him who is from heaven.

50 And I am saying this, my brothers, that [sy]flesh and blood cannot inherit the kingdom of [m]heaven, nor [can] [sy]corruption inherit [sy]incorruption.

---

[1] Repeat *and another*, vs. 39-41

[2] Parallel structure, antithesis, vs. 42-49

[3] Lit: of the soul

[4] Lit: dust [ones]

Chapter 16

51 *Behold, I am telling you a mystery. Not all of us will ^{eu}sleep, but all of us will be changed,

52 suddenly, ^sas the twinkling of an eye, at the last trumpet sounding, and the dead will rise without corruption and **we** will be changed.

53 For this [one] that was going to be corrupted will put on[1] incorruption. And this [one] that ^e[was going to] die will put on immortality.

54 Now when this [one] that is corrupted puts on incorruption, and this [one] that dies, immortality, then the saying will happen that is written: **DEATH IS SWALLOWED IN VICTORY.**

55 ^{pe}**WHERE IS YOUR STING, DEATH? OR WHERE IS YOUR VICTORY, GRAVE?**[2]

56 Now the sting of death is sin and the power of sin is the law.

57 ^{be}But blessed [be] God who gives us the victory by way of our Lord Jesus Christ.

58 Therefore, my brothers and my beloved [ones], be steadfast and do not be moved, but excel always in the work of the LORD, knowing that your labor is not fruitless in the LORD.

Chapter 16

1 Now concerning that which is gathered for the holy [ones], as I commanded to the churches of the Galatians, so **you** should do also.

2 On every first of the week, each of you in his home should lay aside and keep what he has prepared ^e[to give], so that when I come, then collections will not occur.

3 And when I come, I will send those whom you choose with a letter to carry your ^mgrace to Jerusalem.

4 And if the situation is proper for me to also go, they may go with me.

5 Now I will come to you when I have crossed over from the Macedonians, for I will cross over Macedonia.

6 And perhaps also I will remain with you or winter with you, so that you may escort me to wherever I may go.

7 For I do not want to see you now as I pass by the road. For I am trusting to remain a time with you, if my Lord allows me.

---

[1] Lit: wear (like clothes)

[2] Fig: erotesis – questions to ponder. It seems as though the grave has victory, but not ultimately.

Chapter 16

8   Now I will remain in Ephesus until Pentecost,

9   for a great ᵐdoor has opened to me that is full of opportunities and the adversaries are many.

10 Now if Timothy should come to you, see that he may be with you without fear, for he does the work of the LORD as I [do].

11 Therefore, no one should despise him, but should accompany him in peace, so that he may come to me, for I am waiting for him with the brothers.

12 Now about Apollos, my brothers, I begged him much to come to you with the brothers and it may be [his] desire was not to come to you, but when he will have an opportunity, he will come to you.

13 Watch and stand in the faith. Act mature. Be strong.

14 And all your affairs should be [done] with love.

15 Now I beg you, my brothers, concerning the house of Stephanas, because you know that they are the first[fruit] of Achaia and have committed themselves to the service of the holy [ones],

16 that you should also listen to those who are so and to everyone who works hard with us and helps.

17 Now I am rejoicing at the arrival of Stephanas ᴾand of Fortunatus and of Achaicus,⌐ because what you have neglected regarding me, they have filled,

18 for they have refreshed my spirit and yours. Therefore, acknowledge those who are likewise.

19 All the churches that are in Asia greet you. Aquila and Priscilla greet you much in our Lord¹ with the church that is in their house.

20 All the brothers greet you. Greet one another with a holy kiss.

21 [This] greeting [is] in the handwriting of my own hand, Paul.

22 Whoever does not love our Lord Jesus Christ will be cursed. Our Lord comes.

23 ᵇᵉThe grace of our Lord Jesus Christ [be] with you.

24 And my love [be] with all of you in Christ Jesus.

---

¹ Var (L): in the LORD

ARAMAIC PESHITTA NEW TESTAMENT
II CORINTHIANS

Chapter 1

1 Paul, an apostle of Jesus Christ by the will of God, and Timothy, a brother, to the church of God that is in Corinth and to all the holy [ones] that are in all Achaia:

2 Grace [be] with you and peace from God our Father and from our Lord Jesus Christ.

3 Blessed be God, the Father of our Lord Jesus Christ, the Father of mercies and the God of all comfort,

4 he who comforts us in all our pressures, so that **we** would also be able to comfort those who are in all pressures with that comfort [with] which **we** are comforted by God.

5 For as the sufferings of Christ are increased in us, so also by way of Christ our comfort also is increased.

6 Now even if we are pressured, it is for your comfort and [if] we are pressured, [it is] for your life and if we are comforted, [it is] on account of you. You should be comforted and have an earnest care to endure the sufferings that **we** also suffer.

7 ᵖᵃAnd our hope for you is steadfast,˺ for we know that if you are participants in the sufferings, you are also participants[1] in the comfort.

8 Now we want you to know, our[2] brothers, about the pressure that we had in Asia. We were greatly pressured beyond our strength, to the point that our lives were about to end.

9 And we resigned ourselves to death, that we should not have confidence in ourselves, but in God who raises the dead ᵉ[and it was]

10 he who rescued us from violent deaths. And we trust that he will rescue us[3] again

11 with the aid of your prayer for us, that his gift toward us may be a blessing that is done on behalf of many and many[4] will give thanks to him for us.

12 For our boasting is this, the testimony of our mind, that we have conducted ourselves in the world in simplicity ᵖand in purity and in the grace of God and not in the wisdom of the flesh and especially toward you yourselves.˺

---

[1] Repeat *participants*
[2] Var (WSLM): 'my'
[3] Repeat forms of *rescue us*
[4] Repeat *many*

ARAMAIC PESHITTA NEW TESTAMENT
II CORINTHIANS

Chapter 1

13 We do not write anything else to you, but these [things] that you know [and] also acknowledge. And I trust that you will acknowledge[1] [them] to the end,

14 as even you have acknowledged in part that we are your boasting, as also you are ours in the [sy]day of our Lord Jesus Christ.

15 And in this confidence I wanted to come to you before, so that you would doubly[2] receive grace,

16 and [e][I wanted] to pass by you [e][on the way] to the Macedonians and to come to you again from Macedonia and [so that] **you** would accompany me to Judea.

17 This [thing] therefore that I had determined, did I determine [it] hastily?[3] Or perhaps are these [things] that I decided of the flesh? Because it is proper that there should be yes, yes, and no, no.[4]

18 God is faithful, so that our word to you was not [mr]yes and no.

19 For the Son of God, Jesus Christ, who was preached to you by way of us, by me [P]and by Silvanus and by Timothy,⌐ was not yes and no, but was yes in him.

20 For all the promises of God in him, in Christ, are yes. Because of this[5] by way of him, we give an "Amen" to the glory of God.

21 Now **God** establishes [ac]us with you in Christ, who anointed us[6]

22 [P]and has sealed us and has placed the downpayment of his Spirit in our hearts.⌐

23 And **I** give testimony before God concerning myself that I did not come to Corinth in order to spare you,

24 not because we are lords of your faith, but we are helpers of your joy, for you stand by faith.

Chapter 2

1 And I determined this in myself, that I would not come to you again with sadness.

---

[1] Repeat *acknowledge*

[2] Or 'a second time'

[3] Repeat *determine*; fig: erotesis, **lema** question, obvious answer "no", next question to ponder

[4] Fig: epizeuxis, solemn repetition; repeat *yes, no*, vs. 17-20

[5] Repeat *because of this*, 2:8, 4, 16, 5:8, introduces new sections

[6] For further explanation of anointing, see Kitto, vol I, pp. 152-153.

ARAMAIC PESHITTA NEW TESTAMENT
II CORINTHIANS

Chapter 2

2   For if **I** cause you sadness, who will make me rejoice, but he whom **I** made sad?[1]

3   And [e][I determined] that I would write to you this, so that when I come, you will not make me sad, those who ought to make me rejoice. And I am confident about all of you, that my joy is [e][the joy] of all of you.

4   And from great distress and from anguish of heart I wrote to you these [things] with many tears, not that you should be sad, but that you would know the abundant love that I have for you.

5   And if anyone has caused sorrow, he has not caused sorrow to me [only], but almost to all of you, lest the word should be heavy for you.

6   And this reproof from many is sufficient for him.

7   And from now on the contrary, you ought to forgive him and to comfort him, so that he who is such should not be swallowed up in excessive sorrow.

8   Because of this, I am begging you to confirm your love with him.

9   For because of this, I have also written [you], so that I would know with proof if you are being obedient[2] in everything.

10 Now whom **you** forgive, I also [e][forgive]. For also what **I** forgave whom I forgave[3] because of you, I forgave[4] in the presence of Christ,

11 so that SATAN[5] should not take advantage of us, for we know his devices.

12 Now when I came to Troas with the gospel of Christ and a [m]door was opened to me by the LORD,

13 I had no rest in my spirit, because I did not find Titus, my brother. So I left them and went to the Macedonians.

14 [al]Now thanks be to God who always brings to pass triumph for us in Christ and by us makes evident the [h]fragrance of the knowledge of him in every place.[6]

---

[1] Fig: erotesis – question to ponder
[2] Var (WS): 'to me'
[3] Var (WS) omit *whom I forgave*
[4] Repeat forms of *forgive*
[5] For further explanation of the name Satan, see Kitto, vol. II, pp. 692-696.
[6] Culture: refers to the comparison with a Roman military procession, Freeman, pp. 460-461, Dake, p. 193.

ARAMAIC PESHITTA NEW TESTAMENT
II CORINTHIANS

Chapter 2
15 For ^{me}we are a sweet fragrance in Christ to God with those who live and with those who are lost.

16 To those ^e[who are lost], [we are] a fragrance of death to ^{at}death, and to them ^e[who live], a fragrance of life to ^{at}life.¬ [1] And who is equal to these [things]?[2]

17 For we are not like the rest who dilute the words of God, but as in truth and as from God, we speak before God in Christ.

Chapter 3
1 Are we starting again from the beginning to show you who we are? Or do you, as others, need letters of recommendations to be written to you concerning us? Or ^e[do we need] you to write [and] recommend us?

2 ^{al}Now ^{me}you are our own letter that is written on our heart[s] and known and read aloud by everyone.

3 For you know that ^{me}you are a letter of Christ that was ministered by us, written not with ink, but by the Spirit of the living God, not on tablets of stone, but on tablets[3] of the ^{an}heart of flesh.¬

4 And we have such confidence in Christ toward God,

5 not that **we** are sufficient to think anything as though from ourselves, but our power is from God,

6 who made us worthy to be ministers of the new covenant, not by ^{sy}writing, but by the Spirit, for ^{sy}writing kills, but the Spirit gives life.[4]

7 Now if the ^{pr}ministering of death was engraved in writing on stones ^{pa}(and was so magnificent that the sons of Israel were not able to look on the face of Moses because of the glory of his face) which ended,

8 how then will not the ministering of the Spirit be more glorious?

9 For if the ministering of condemnation had glory, how much more will the ministering of justification be increased in glory?[5]

10 For that which was glorified [was] as if not worthy of glory, in comparison to this surpassing glory.

11 For if what has ended was glorious, that which remains will be increasingly glorious.

---

[1] Fig: antanaclasis, *to death, to life* is substituted for "with the result being death eternally or life eternal."

[2] Fig: erotesis – questions to ponder, also 3:1

[3] Repeat *on tablets*

[4] Fig: hypocatastasis, *writing* implying the Law and shows contrast between Law and Spirit

[5] Fig: erotesis, **kema** question, answer in the affirmative

ARAMAIC PESHITTA NEW TESTAMENT
II CORINTHIANS

Chapter 3

12 Therefore, because we have this hope, we conduct ourselves more boldly,

13 and [we are] not ˢas Moses, ᵃˡwho put a veil over his face so that the sons of Israel would not look at the fullness of that which was abolished.

14 But they were blinded in their understanding,[1] for until this day when the Old Covenant is read, that veil rests on them and it is not known that it is abolished by Christ.

15 And until this day when Moses is read, a veil is lying over their heart[s],

16 yet when one of them turns to the LORD, the veil is lifted from him.

17 Now the LORD is the Spirit and where the Spirit of the LORD [is], there is freedom.

18 But **all** of us, with open faces, see the magnificence of the LORD ˢas in a mirror and we are being changed into that likeness from glory to glory, as by the LORD, the Spirit.⌐

Chapter 4

1 Because of this, we are not weary in this ministry that we are holding, according to the mercies that are on us.

2 But we have rejected ᵃⁿthe hidden [things] of shame and we do not walk with cunning, nor are we deceitful with the word of God, but we show ourselves by the ᵃⁿevidence of the truth to all the minds of men before God.

3 Now if our gospel is hidden, it is hidden[2] to those who are lost,

4 ᵃˡthose whose minds[3] the god of this age has blinded so that they would not believe, in order that the light of the ᵃⁿgospel of the glory of Christ, who is the likeness of God, should not ʰdawn on them.

5 For we do not preach ourselves, but Christ Jesus our Lord, and ᵉ[we preach] of ourselves that we are your servants because of Jesus,

6 because God, who said: **FROM DARKNESS LIGHT SHOULD SHINE**, has shined in our hearts, so that we would be enlightened[4] with the knowledge of the glory of God in the presence of Jesus Christ.⌐

---

[1] Var (LM, some P): 'their understanding was blinded'

[2] Repeat *is hidden*

[3] OS (LG) add 'of the impious' or 'of the wicked'

[4] Same root: *light, enlightened*; repeat forms of *shine*

427

ARAMAIC PESHITTA NEW TESTAMENT
II CORINTHIANS

Chapter 4

7 Now we have this treasure in a [an]utensil of earth that the greatness of the power would be from God and not from us.

8 For in everything, we are pressured, but are not overwhelmed.[1] We are harassed, but are not overcome.

9 We are persecuted, but are not left alone. We are thrown down, but are not destroyed.

10 We always bear the death of Jesus in our bodies, so that the life of Jesus may also be revealed in our bodies.

11 For if we are alive, we are delivered to death because of Jesus, so that the life of Jesus may also be revealed in this mortal body.[2]

12 Now death works in us, yet life[3] in you.

13 Even **we**, therefore, have one Spirit of faith, as it is written: **I BELIEVED. BECAUSE OF THIS, I ALSO SPOKE.** We believe. Because of this, we also speak.

14 And we know that he who raised our Lord Jesus will also raise us by way of Jesus and will bring us with you to him.

15 For everything is on account of you, so that as grace increases by way of many, thanksgiving would multiply to the glory of God.

16 Because of this, we are not weary, for even if our outer man is corrupted, yet that which [is] inside is renewed day by day.

17 For the adversity of this time, being very small and little,[4] prepares for us a great glory, without end forever,

18 because we do not rejoice[5] in these [things] that are seen, but in these that are not seen. For [e][the things] that are seen are for a time, but [e][the things] that are not seen are eternal.[6]

Chapter 5

1 [al]For we know that if our [h]house that is on earth, this of the body, should be broken down, yet we have a [h]building that is from God, a house that is not by the work of hands, eternal in heaven.

---

[1] Parallel structure: vs. 8, 9, antithesis; repeat suffix endings, making words rhyme

[2] Lit: body of death; repeat *death, life*, vs. 10-12

[3] Fig: ellipsis, add [works]

[4] Fig: redundancy

[5] Var (SL): 'gaze at'

[6] Parallel structure, ABBA; repeat *that are seen*

Chapter 5

2   Indeed also because of this, we groan and long to be clothed with our [h]house that is from heaven,[1]

3   since indeed when we are clothed, we will [e][not] be found naked.

4   For while we are now in this [h]house, we groan from its burden and we do not desire to put it off, unless we should be clothed over it, so that its mortality would be swallowed by life.⌐

5   And he who prepares us for this is God, who has given us the [h]downpayment of his Spirit.

6   Therefore, because we know and are persuaded that while we live in the body, we are [eu]absent from our Lord

7   [pa](for we walk by faith and not by sight).

8   Because of this, we are confident and we long to be absent from the body and to be with our Lord.

9   And we are diligent that whether we are absent [ones] or dwellers [e][in our body],[2] we would please him.

10 For all of us are going to stand before the judgment seat of Christ that each one may be rewarded [for] what was done by him in his body, whether of good or of evil.

11 Therefore, because we know the fear of our Lord, we persuade men and we are revealed to God and I think that also we are revealed to your own minds.

12 We do not praise ourselves again to you, but we give you cause to be boasting about us to those who are boasting in appearances and not in heart.

13 For if we are foolish, [e][it is] for God. And if we are ordained, [e][it is] for you.

14 For the love of Christ compels us to determine this, that one died on behalf of everyone, so then everyone is dead in him.

15 And he died on behalf of everyone, so that those who live should not live for themselves, but for him who died and rose for them.

16 And from now on, **we** do not know anyone in the [sy]flesh. And even if we have known Christ in the [sy]flesh, yet now we do not know [him].

17 Everyone who is in Christ is therefore a new creation. Old [things] have passed away

---

[1] Fig: hypocatastasis, vs. 1-4, *house* meaning a body, either earthly or heavenly

[2] Repeat *absent*, from v. 6, 8; repeat *dwell* from v. 6 (*live*); word play: *absent [ones]* enoda ﻻﻬﻼ *dwellers* emora ﻻﻬﻼ

Chapter 5

18 and everything has become new from God, who reconciled us to himself in Christ and has given us the ministry of reconciliation.

19 For God was in Christ, the one who reconciled the [sy]world with his majesty and did not count to them their sins. And he placed in us[1] the word of reconciliation.

20 Therefore, [me]we are ambassadors on behalf of Christ and [it is] as if God were begging you by way of us on behalf of[2] Christ. Therefore, we beg [e][you], "Be reconciled to God."

21 For that one who had not known sin, he has made [to be] sin[3] on your account, that **we** would become the justification of God in him.

Chapter 6

1 And as helpers, we beg you, that the grace of God that you received should not be fruitless in you.

2 For he has said: IN AN ACCEPTABLE [sy]TIME, I HAVE ANSWERED YOU AND IN THE [sy]DAY OF SALVATION, I HAVE HELPED YOU.[4] *Behold, now [is] an acceptable [sy]time and *behold, now [is] the [sy]day of salvation.

3 Give no one a cause for stumbling in anything, so that there will be no blemish in our ministering.

4 But in everything we should show ourselves that we are ministers of God with much endurance, [a]in trials, in necessities, in[5] difficulties,

5 in beatings, in imprisonments, in riots, in labor, in watching, in fasting,

6 by purity, by knowledge, by long-suffering, by kindness, by the Holy Spirit, by love without deceit,

7 by the truthful word, by the power of God, by the [m]armor of justification that is on the right hand and on the left,

8 in honor and in disgrace, in good report and in a struggle, as [e][between] deceivers and true.⌐

9 As though unknown, yet we are known,[6] as though dying, yet *behold, we are living, as chastised, yet we are not dying,

---

[1] Lit: in us ourselves

[2] Repeat *on behalf of*

[3] Fig: antanaclasis, 2nd word for *sin* means "sin offering"

[4] Word play: *answered you* **enithakh** ꭒꮞ *helped you* **edirthakh** ꭒꮞ

[5] Repeat *in, by* ꭎ, vs. 4-8, 22x

[6] Repeat participle endings, *we are...* vs. 9, 10; parallel structure, antithesis

ARAMAIC PESHITTA NEW TESTAMENT
II CORINTHIANS

Chapter 6

10   as though having sorrow, yet we are rejoicing always, as though poor, yet we are causing many to increase, as though not having anything, yet we are holding everything.

11   Our [m]mouth is opened to you, [oh] Corinthians,[1] and our heart is enlarged.

12   You are not pressured by us, but you are pressured by your [m]bowels.

13   Now I speak as to children, pay me my [h]debt that is for you. Expand your love to me.

14   And you should be not yoke-fellows to those who do not believe. For what fellowship has justification with wickedness or what communion has light with darkness?[2]

15   Or what agreement has Christ with SATAN? Or what part has he who believes with him who does not believe?

16   And what alliance has the [h]temple of God with demons? But **you** are the temple of the living God, as it is said: **I WILL LIVE WITH THEM AND [c]I WILL WALK WITH THEM AND I WILL BE THEIR GOD AND THEY WILL BE MY PEOPLE.**

17   Because of this, **GO OUT FROM AMONG THEM AND BE SEPARATED FROM THEM,** says the LORD. **AND DO NOT COME NEAR UNCLEAN [THINGS] AND I WILL RECEIVE YOU,**

18   **AND I WILL BE A FATHER TO YOU AND YOU WILL BE SONS AND DAUGHTERS TO ME,** says the LORD, the Almighty.

Chapter 7

1   Therefore, because we have these promises, my beloved [ones], we should purify ourselves from all defilement of the [sy]flesh and of the spirit and we should serve with holiness with reverence for God.

2   Bear [with us], our[3] brothers, we have caused no one harm, we have corrupted no one, we have wronged no one.[4]

3   I am not speaking to make you guilty, for I have said before that you are in our heart, to die and to live together.

---

[1] Fig: apostrophe, direct speech
[2] Fig: erotesis – questions to ponder, vs. 14-16
[3] Var (WSLM): 'my'
[4] Repeat *no one*, 3x

Chapter 7

4   I have great boldness to you and I have great boasting in you and I am full of comfort and a great[1] amount of joy abounds in me, in all my trials.

5   For even after we came to the Macedonians, we had no rest for our body, but we were pressured in everything, from without, conflict, and from within, fear.

6   But God, who comforts the meek, comforted[2] us by the coming of Titus,

7   and not only by his coming, but also by the rest [with] which he was refreshed[3] by you. For he told us about your love to us and about your grief and your zeal for us. And when I heard it, my joy was great.

8   For although I made you sad by a letter, I am not sorry, even though I was sorry. For I see that the letter, even if it made you sad for a ˢʸtime,[4]

9   yet produced great joy for me, not because it made you sad, but because your sorrow brought you to repentance. For you had godly sorrow, so that you should lack in nothing from us.

10   For sorrow because of[5] God produces repentance of the soul that is not reversed and turns to life, but the sorrow of the world produces death.

11   For *behold this, that you were distressed because of God. How much did it produce in you? Diligence ᴾand defense and anger and fear and love and zeal and vindication.⌐ And in everything you have shown that you are being pure in the matter.

12   Now let this be [so]. For I wrote to you, not because of the wrong-doer, not even because of that one who was wronged, but so that your diligence because of us would be known before God.

13   Because of this, we were comforted and with our comfort,[6] we rejoiced greatly in the joy of Titus, for his spirit was refreshed with all of you,

14   so that I was not ashamed of what I boasted to him about you. But as we spoke everything [with] truthfulness with you, so also our boasting to Titus was found [to be] with truthfulness.[7]

---

[1] Repeat *great*

[2] Repeat forms of *comforted*

[3] Same root: *rest, refreshed*

[4] Lit: an hour; repeat same root, *sorry, sorrow*, vs. 8-10

[5] Repeat *because of*, vs. 10-13, 6x

[6] Same root: *comfort, comforted*

[7] Repeat *truthfulness*

ARAMAIC PESHITTA NEW TESTAMENT
II CORINTHIANS

Chapter 7

15 His compassion has also increased greatly concerning you, when he recalls the obedience of all of you [and] that you received him with reverence and with [h]trembling.

16 I rejoice that in everything I am confident about you.

Chapter 8

1 But we make known to you, our brothers, the grace of God that was given by the churches of the Macedonians,

2 that in the great [an]trial of their adversity, there was an increase to their joy and the [as]depth of their poverty was increased by the [as]riches of their simplicity.[1]

3 For I testify that, [pa]according to their ability and greater than their ability,┐ voluntarily [in] themselves,

4 they begged us with much begging[2] to take part in the [m]grace of the service of the holy [ones].

5 And not as we had expected, but they gave themselves first to our Lord and also to us by the will of God,

6 so that **we** requested Titus, that as he had begun, so he would complete this [m]grace with you also.

7 But according as you increase in everything, in faith [P]and in word and in knowledge and in all diligence and in our love to you,┐ so you should increase[3] in this grace also.

8 I do not actually command[4] you, but by the exhortation of your fellow [believers], I am testing the genuineness of your love.

9 For you know the grace of our Lord Jesus Christ, who on account of you became poor when he was rich, so that you by his poverty would be made rich.[5]

10 Now I highly recommend[6] to you this that is profitable to you, because a year ago, you began not only to will, but also to do.

11 But now, complete with action what you willed, that as you have an eagerness to will, so you would fulfill [it] in action out of what you have.

---

[1] Or generosity, fig: oxymoron

[2] Same root: *begged, begging*

[3] Repeat *increase*, also *in*

[4] Fig: polyptoton, lit: commanding, we commanded

[5] Same roots: *became poor, poverty*; *rich, made rich*

[6] Fig: polyptoton, lit: recommending, we recommended

Chapter 8

12 For if there is a willingness, so he is accepted according to what he has, not according to what he does not have.

13 For it is not that others should have relief and you ᵉ[should have] pressure,

14 but [that] you should be in balance at this time, that your abundance may be for their need, so that also their abundance may be for your need, so that there will be a balance.¹

15 As it is written: **HE WHO RECEIVED MUCH DID NOT HAVE EXCESS AND HE WHO RECEIVED LITTLE DID NOT LACK.**

16 But ⁱthanks be to God who put this care for you in the heart of Titus.

17 For he received our exhortation and because he was very concerned, he went out to you willingly.

18 And we sent with him our brother, him whose praise in the gospel [is] in all the churches.

19 So also, he was especially chosen² by the churches to go out with us with this ᵐgrace that is ministered by us for the glory of God and for our own encouragement.

20 And by this we were avoiding ᵉ[a situation] that no one should put a blemish on us regarding this high position that is ministered by us.

21 For we were careful [to do] the right things, not before God only, but also before men.

22 And we also sent with them our brother who by us has always in many [things] been proven that he is diligent, but now he is especially diligent with the great confidence that [he has] about you.

23 Therefore, if Titus ᵉ[is asked about], he is my companion and assistant among you, or if our other brothers, they are sent [ones] of the churches of the glory of Christ.

24 From now on, in the presence of all the churches, show them a demonstration of your love and our boasting about you.

Chapter 9

1 Now concerning the service of the holy [ones], it would be excessive if I wrote to you.

---

¹ Parallel structure, ABBA

² Fig: polyptoton, lit: choosing, was chosen; it is unusual to have 3 uses of this figure so close together.

ARAMAIC PESHITTA NEW TESTAMENT
II CORINTHIANS

Chapter 9

2   For I know the [an]goodness of your mind[1] and because of this, I boasted of you to the Macedonians that Achaia was ready a year ago and your zeal has excited many.

3   Now I sent the brothers, so that our[2] boasting that we boasted of you would not be empty about this matter, that as I said, you would be prepared,

4   that the Macedonians would not come with me and find you not ready and we should be embarrassed [pa](should we not say that you would be embarrassed) by the boasting that we boasted.[3]

5   Because of this, I was concerned to request these my brothers, that they should come before me to you and prepare the bounty that you were previously advised to have prepared, so it is [s]as a bounty, not as greediness.

6   Now this [e][I say], [al]"He who sows sparingly will also reap sparingly and he who sows bountifully will reap bountifully,[4]

7   everyone according to what is in his mind, not from sadness or from constraint, for **GOD[5] LOVES A JOYOUS GIVER.**"

8   Now all [m]grace comes by the hands of God who causes [it] to increase in you, so that always, in everything, you will have what is sufficient for you and will increase[6] in every good work.

9   As it is written: **HE HAS DISTRIBUTED AND GIVEN TO THE POOR AND HIS JUSTIFICATION IS VALID FOREVER.**

10 Now he who gives seed to the sower and bread for food will give and will multiply your seed and will increase the [m]fruit of your justification,⌐

11 so that you may be enriched in everything in all simplicity, so that thanksgiving to God is completed by way of us,[7]

12 because the work of this service not only supplies the needs of the holy [ones], but also increases with much thanksgiving to God.

---

[1] Fig: antimeria, could be translated "your thoughtful goodness"
[2] Var (WSLM): omit *our*
[3] Same root: *boasting, boasted*
[4] Repeat *sparingly*; repeat next word, *bountifully*
[5] Var (WS) 'the LORD'
[6] Repeat forms of *increase*, vs. 8-12
[7] Lit: by our hands

Chapter 9

13 For on account of the trial of this service, we glorify God that you have subjected yourselves to the acknowledgment of the gospel of Christ and [that] you have shared fully in your simplicity with them and with everyone.

14 And they offer prayer for you with great love, because of the ^{as}abundance of the grace^l of God that is concerning you.

15 ⁱNow thanks be to God for his unspeakable gift.

Chapter 10

1 Now I, Paul, beg you by the quietness and by the meekness of Christ, that although in presence, I am meek toward you, yet being absent, I am confident about you.

2 Now I beg you, that when I come I may not be compelled by the confidence that I have to be bold ^{pa}(as I consider [it]) to those who think that we are walking according to the ^{sy}flesh.

3 For although we walk in the ^{sy}flesh, we do not serve of the ^{sy}flesh.

4 ^{al}For the equipment of our service is not of the ^{sy}flesh, but of the power of God and by it, we overcome rebellious strongholds.

5 And we pull down reasonings and all pride that elevates [itself] against the knowledge of God and we lead captive all thoughts to the obedience of Christ.

6 And we are prepared to execute justice on those who are disobedient, when your obedience is finished.⌐

7 Are you looking on appearances?[2] If anyone is confident of himself that he is of Christ, let him know of himself that as he is of Christ, so also are we.

8 For if I also boast[3] more about the authority that our Lord gave to me, I am not ashamed, because he gave [it] to us for your building up and not for your tearing down.

9 Now I hold back, so that I should not be considered that I especially terrified[4] you by my letters,

10 because there are some who say, "The letters are weighty and very hard, but his bodily presence is weak and his speech, worthless."

---

[1] Fig: antiptosis, "abundant grace"; same root: *great, abundance*

[2] Fig: erotesis – question to ponder

[3] Repeat *boast*, vs. 8-18

[4] Fig: polyptoton, lit: terrifying, I terrified

Chapter 10

11 But he who speaks so should consider this, that as we are in the ᵃⁿword of our letter[1] while we are absent, so also we are in action when we are present.

12 For we dare not value or compare ourselves with those who are boasting in themselves, but because those are comparing themselves with themselves,[2] they do not understand.

13 ᵃˡBut **we** will not boast more than our measure,[3] but according to the measure of the boundary that God distributed to us, so that we should also reach all the way to you.

14 For we are not stretching ourselves as if we were not reaching you, for we reach all the way to you with the gospel of Christ.

15 And we are not boasting beyond our measure about the labor of others, but we have the hope that when your faith is grown, we will be magnified by you as our measure and [that] it would be increased

16 also to preach far beyond you. Not in the measure of others do we boast about things that are prepared.⌐

17 **BUT HE WHO BOASTS, LET HIM BOAST IN THE** LORD,

18 for he who praises himself, that [one] is not approved, but he whom the LORD will praise.

Chapter 11

1 ˡOh that you would bear with me a little that I may speak foolishly, only indeed bear with me!

2 ᵃˡFor I am jealous of you with the jealousy[4] of God, for I have espoused you to a husband, a pure young woman, whom I present to Christ.⌐

3 But I fear, that even ˢas the serpent lead Eve astray by his deceit, so your minds will be corrupted from the simplicity that is to Christ.

4 For if he who came to you had preached to you another Jesus whom **we** had not preached[5] or you had received another spirit that you had not received or another gospel that you had not accepted, you would have been persuaded well.

---

[1] Fig: antimeria, "written word"

[2] Repeat *themselves*

[3] Repeat *measure*, vs. 13-16, comparison to an assigned area, such as a "territory" would be to a sales representative

[4] Same root: *jealous, jealousy*

[5] Repeat *had preached*

Chapter 11

5 For I think that I am no less than those apostles who most excel.

6 For although I am unskilled in my speech, yet not in my knowledge, but in everything we are being made evident to you.

7 Or did I actually cause offense[1] when I humbled myself so that you would be elevated and [superscript e][when I] freely preached to you the gospel of God?

8 And I robbed other churches[2] and received payments for your service.

9 And when I came among you and had lack,[3] I was not burdensome to any of you, for the brothers who came from Macedonia supplied my need and in everything I kept myself and I keep [superscript e][myself], so that I would not burden[4] you.

10 The truth of Christ is in me, that this boasting will not be stopped by me in the regions of Achaia.

11 Why? Because I do not love you?[5] God knows.

12 But this that I am doing, I will also do, so that I may cut off the occasion of those who seek an occasion,[6] so that they who are boasting in this may be found as we [are].

13 For these are false apostles and crafty workers and they liken themselves to apostles of Christ

14 and there is not [anything] to marvel at in this. For if SATAN became an imitator of an angel of light,

15 it is not a great thing, if his ministers also become imitators[7] of ministers of justification, whose end will be according to their works.

16 But again I speak. Should anyone think of me as though I am a fool and if otherwise, receive me as a fool, that also, I may boast a little?[8]

---

[1] Fig: polyptoton, lit: causing offense, caused offense; fig: erotesis, **lema** question, obvious answer "no"

[2] Fig: hyperbole, exaggeration

[3] Var (WS): omit *and had lack*

[4] Same verb: *burdensome, burden*

[5] Fig: erotesis, "not" question, answer in the affirmative

[6] Repeat *occasion*

[7] Repeat *imitator*, from v. 14

[8] Fig: erotesis, **lema** question, obvious answer "no"

Chapter 11

17 What I am speaking, I do not speak in our Lord, but as in folly, in this matter of boasting.

18 Because many boast in the flesh, **I** will also boast,

19 for you are content to hear fools, since you are wise.[1]

20 And you adhere to him who enslaves you and to him who devours you and to him who takes from you and to him who elevates himself over you and to him who strikes you on your face.[2]

21 I am speaking as if in shame. I am speaking as if **we** were weak through foolishness, for in everything [in] which anyone is bold, **I** am also bold.

22 If they are Hebrews, I am also. If they are Israelites, I am also. If they are the seed of Abraham, I am also.[3]

23 If they are ministers of Christ **pa**(I am speaking foolishly), I am greater than them, in labor more than them, in beatings more than them, in prisons more than them,[4] in deaths, many times.

24 Of the Judeans, five times I was beaten, each time forty [lashes] lacking one.

25 Three times I was beaten with rods, one time I was stoned, three times I was shipwrecked, a day and a night I was without a ship in the sea,

26 in many journeys, in danger of rivers, in danger of robbers, in danger from my relatives, in danger from the Gentiles. I was in danger in the cities, I was in danger in the wilderness, in danger in the sea, in danger[5] from false brothers,

27 in toil and in weariness, in much watching, in hunger and in thirst, in much fasting, in cold and in[6] nakedness,

28 besides familiar [things] and the crowd that is around me daily and my care on behalf of all the churches.

29 Who was weakened and **I** was not weakened? Who was offended and **I** did not burn?[7]

---

[1] Fig: irony

[2] Repeat *and to him*; culture: striking on the face causes great shame.

[3] Repeat *I am also* as a refrain, lit: also I am

[4] Repeat *more than them*

[5] Repeat *in danger*, 8x

[6] Repeat *in*, 7x

[7] Fig: erotesis – questions to ponder; *burn* (as with anger)

ARAMAIC PESHITTA NEW TESTAMENT
II CORINTHIANS

Chapter 11

30 If it is necessary to boast, I will boast in my weaknesses.[1]

31 God, [pa]the Father of our Lord Jesus Christ, blessed forever,ⁿ knows that I do not lie.

32 In Damascus, the commander of the army of Aretas, the king, was guarding the city of the Damascenes to arrest me.

33 And they let me down from the wall from a window in a basket and I escaped from his hands.[2]

Chapter 12

1 To boast is necessary, but not profitable, for I will come to visions and to revelations of our Lord.

2 I knew a man in Christ fourteen years ago [pa](but whether with a body or without a body I do not know, God knows) who was caught up to the third heaven.[3]

3 And I knew this man [pa](but whether with a body or without a body I do not know, God knows)

4 who was caught up to paradise and heard unspeakable words that are unlawful for a man to speak.

5 About this I will boast, but I will not boast about myself, except in weaknesses.

6 For if I desired to boast, I would not be crazy, for I am speaking the truth. But I refrain, so that no one should think of me more than what he sees in me and what he hears from me.

7 And so that I should not be elevated by the abundance of the revelations, a [m]thorn to my flesh was delivered to me, a messenger of SATAN, to buffet me, so that I should not be elevated.[4]

8 And concerning this, three times I requested from my Lord that it would go away from me.

9 And he said to me, "My grace is sufficient for you, for my power is perfected in weakness." Therefore, I will gladly boast in my weaknesses, so that the power of Christ will rest on me.[5]

---

[1] Repeat forms of *boast*, again in 12:1ff.

[2] Culture: the wall of the house was probably attached to the city wall, see Acts 9:25, Freeman, p. 461.

[3] Var (WSLM): 'to the third part of heaven'

[4] Repeat *so that I should not be elevated*, at beginning and end of sentence

[5] Same roots: *power, strong; weak, weaknesses*

Chapter 12

10 Because of this, I have pleasure ^ain weaknesses, in reproaches, in
adversities, in persecutions, in distresses⌐ that are on behalf of Christ,
for at what time I am weak, then I am strong.
11 *Behold, I became a fool in my boasting, because you pressured me.
For you ought to give testimony about me, because I am no less than the
apostles who most excel, even though I was nothing.
12 I performed the signs of the apostles among you with all patience
^Pand with exploits and with wonders and with mighty works.⌐
13 For in what were you made less than other churches, except in this,
that I did not burden you? Forgive me this fault.
14 *Behold, this is the third time that I am ready to come to you, and I
will not burden you, because I do not seek yours, but you, for children
ought not to lay up treasures for parents, but parents for their children.
15 And **I** will both cheerfully pay the expenses and also give myself for
you, although the more I love you, the less **you** love me.
16 And perhaps **I** did not burden you, but ^slike a cunning man, I robbed
you by trickery.
17 Why? [Was it] by way of another man that I sent to you [and] was
greedy of [the things] concerning you?¹
18 I begged Titus ^e[to go to you] and I sent the brothers with him. Was
Titus greedy of anything belonging to you? Did we not walk in one spirit
and in the same footsteps?
19 Do you again suppose that we should make a defense to you? Before
God, we speak in Christ, and all these [things], my beloved, [are] for
your building up.
20 For I fear, will I come to you and not find you as I desire and be
found by you even as you do not desire? [Will there be] contention ^Pand
envying and anger and obstinacy and slandering and murmuring and
pride and confusion?⌐
21 When I come to you, will my God humble me and will I mourn over
many who have sinned and have not repented from the uncleanness and
from the fornication and from the wantonness that they committed?

---

¹ Fig: erotesis, **lema** question, obvious answer "no", also vs. 19, 20, 21

ARAMAIC PESHITTA NEW TESTAMENT
II CORINTHIANS

Chapter 13

1   This is the third time that I will come to you: **BY THE MOUTH OF TWO OR THREE WITNESSES, EVERY WORD WILL BE ESTABLISHED.**

2   I have told you previously and again **I** tell you beforehand **Pa**(as if I was with you the second time, I tell you and now also while I am absent, I write to those who have sinned and to the others[1]) that if I come again, I will not refrain,

3   because you seek proof that it is Christ who speaks by me, who has not been weak among you, but powerful among you.

4   For although he was crucified in weakness, yet he is alive by the power of God. And if we are weak[2] with him, yet we are alive with him by the power of God that is in you.

5   Examine yourselves, whether you stand fast in the faith. Prove yourselves. Or do you not acknowledge that Jesus Christ is in you? And if [you do] not, you are rejected.[3]

6   But I am trusting that you will know that **we** are not rejecting **e**[you].

7   But I beg God that there may be no evil in you, so that our proof may be seen, nevertheless, that **you** may do good [things] and [that] **we** may be as rejected.

8   For we are not able to do anything contrary to truthfulness, but for truthfulness.[4]

9   Now we rejoice when we are weak and you are strong. For this we also pray, that **you** would be mature.

10 Because of this, when I am absent I write these [things], so that when I come, I should not act severely according to the authority that my Lord gave me for your building up and not for your tearing down.

11 From now on, my brothers, rejoice **P**and be mature and be comforted and there will be agreement and harmony among you and the God of love and of peace will be with you.⌐

12 Greet one another with a holy kiss.

13 All the holy [ones] greet you.

14 **be**The peace of our Lord Jesus Christ and the love of God and the fellowship of the Holy Spirit [be] with all of you. Amen.

---

[1] Lit: to the rest of the others
[2] Same root: *weak, weakness*
[3] Repeat *rejected [ones]*, vs. 5-7
[4] Repeat *truthfulness*

ARAMAIC PESHITTA NEW TESTAMENT
GALATIANS

Chapter 1

1 Paul an apostle, not from men and not by way of man, but by way of Jesus Christ and God his Father, who raised him from the dead,

2 and all the brothers who are with me to the churches that are in Galatia:

3 Grace and peace [be] with you from God the Father and from our Lord Jesus Christ,

4 who gave himself for our sins to deliver us from this evil world, according to the will of God our Father,

5 to whom [be] glory forever and ever. Amen.

6 [i]I am amazed at how quickly you are being turned from Christ, who called you by his grace, to another gospel

7 that is not [e][a true gospel]. But there are some who are troubling you and want to pervert the gospel of Christ.

8 Now even if **we** or an angel from heaven should declare to you [anything] outside of what we have declared to you, he will be cursed.[1]

9 As I said before and now I am saying again, "If anyone declares to you [anything] outside of what you have received, he will be cursed."

10 For now do I persuade men, or God? Or do I seek to please men?[2] For up to now, if I had pleased men, I would not have been a servant of Christ.

11 But I make known to you, my brothers, that the gospel that was declared by me was not from man.

12 For also **I** did not receive it and learn it from man, but [e][I received it] by the revelation of Jesus Christ.

13 For you have heard of my previous way of life that was in Judaism, that I had greatly persecuted the church of God and ruined it.

14 And I excelled in Judaism more than many [of] my contemporaries who were my countrymen. And I was very[3] zealous in the teaching of my fathers.

15 Now when it pleased him, who had set me apart from the womb of my mother and called me by his grace,

16 to reveal his Son in me, that I should declare him among the Gentiles, I did not immediately reveal [this] to [sy]flesh and blood

17 and I did not go to Jerusalem to the apostles who were before me. But I went to Arabia and returned again to Damascus.

---

[1] Repeat whole sentence, v. 9; same root: *gospel, declare*, vs. 8, 9, 11, 16

[2] Fig: erotesis – questions to ponder; repeat forms of *pleased*

[3] Same root: *excelled, very*

ARAMAIC PESHITTA NEW TESTAMENT
GALATIANS

Chapter 1

18   And after three years, I went to Jerusalem to see Peter and remained with him [for] fifteen days.

19   But I did not see the rest of the apostles, except James, the brother of our Lord.

20   Now these [things] that I write to you, *behold, before God, ⁱI am not lying!

21   After these [places], I came to the regions of Syria and of Cilicia.

22   And the churches in Judea that were in Christ did not know me personally.¹

23   But they had heard this only, "He who previously was persecuting us, *behold, now is preaching the faith that he was overthrowing in a previous time."

24   And they were glorifying God on account of me.

Chapter 2

1   Now after fourteen years, I went up again to Jerusalem with Barnabas and took Titus with me.

2   Now I went up by revelation and I made known to them the gospel that I was preaching among the Gentiles. And I showed it to those who were considered to be something privately, lest somehow I had ^hrun or would run in vain.

3   Even Titus, who was an Aramean with me, was not compelled to be circumcised.

4   Now because of false brothers who had entered among us to spy on the freedom that we have in Jesus Christ in order to enslave us,

5   not even for a minute² did we submit to their oppression, so that the truth of the gospel would remain with you.

6   Now those who were considered to be something ^{pa}(now what they were did not concern me, for God does not have respect of persons) now³ these did not add anything to me.

7   But [it was] otherwise, for they saw that I had been entrusted with the gospel of the ^muncircumcision, as Peter had been entrusted with⁴ the ^mcircumcision.

---

¹ Lit: by face
² Lit: for the fulness of an hour, fig: synecdoche
³ Repeat *now*
⁴ Repeat *entrusted with*

Chapter 2

8   For he who worked in Peter in the apostleship of the ^mcircumcision also worked in me in the apostleship of¹ the Gentiles.

9   And when they knew of the grace that was given to me, James and Peter and John, those who were considered to be ^hpillars, gave to me and to Barnabas the right hand of fellowship that we [should work]² among the Gentiles and they among the ^mcircumcision.

10   ^e[They asked] only that we should remember the poor and I was concerned to do this.

11   But when Peter came to Antioch, I reproved him to his face, because they were offended by him.

12   Before some men came from James, he ate with the Gentiles, but after they came, he withdrew and separated himself, because he was afraid of those who were from the circumcision.

13   And the rest of the Judeans also submitted to this with him, so that even Barnabas was led to respect persons.

14   And when I saw that they were not walking correctly in the ^{as}truth of the gospel, I said to Peter in front of all of them, "If **you** who are a Judean live as a heathen and not as a Judean, how can you compel the Gentiles to live as a Judean?"

15   For **we**, who by nature are Judeans and are not sinners of the Gentiles,

16   because we know that a man is not justified by the works³ of the law, but by the faith of Jesus Christ, we also believe in Jesus Christ, so that we may be justified by the faith of Christ and ⁴ not by the works of the law, because by the works of the law, **NO ^{sy}FLESH IS JUSTIFIED**.

17   But if while we are seeking to be justified by Christ, we are also found [that] we are sinners, then is Jesus Christ the minister of sin?⁵ ⁱLet it not be so!

18   ^{al}For if I build up again those [things] that I have broken down, I show about myself that I am a transgressor of the commandment.

19   For by the law **I** died to the law⁶ that I would live for God⌐

---

¹ Repeat *in the apostleship of*

² Fig: ellipsis, or [should carry the gospel], also after *they*

³ Var (M), 'work' (sing.)

⁴ Fig: ellipsis, add [is justified]

⁵ Fig: erotesis, obvious answer "no"

⁶ Repeat *law*, next word; fig: allegory, comparing law to a building in which one lives

ARAMAIC PESHITTA NEW TESTAMENT
GALATIANS

Chapter 2

20 and I am crucified with Christ. And from now on, I am not living, but Christ lives in me, and this ᵉ[life] that I am now living in the ˢʸflesh, I am living¹ by the faith of the Son of God, who loved us and gave himself for us.

21 I am not denying the grace of God. For if justification is by way of the law, Christ died without cause.

Chapter 3

1 ⁱOh stupid Galatians! Who has made you envious?² For *behold, ˢas a portrait, Jesus Christ being crucified was portrayed³ before your eyes.

2 I want to know this only from you. Did you receive the Spirit by the works of the law or by the hearing of faith?

3 Are you so foolish that you began by the Spirit, yet now you are finishing in the flesh?

4 Have you endured all these [things] without result? ⁱBut oh that [it were] without result!

5 Therefore, he who imparts the Spirit in you and works miracles among you ᵉ[does he do these] by the works of the law or by the hearing of faith?⁴

6 In like manner, **ABRAHAM BELIEVED GOD AND IT WAS COUNTED TO HIM FOR JUSTIFICATION.**

7 Therefore, know that ᵐᵉthose who are of faith are the sons of Abraham.

8 For because God knew beforehand that the Gentiles would be justified by faith, he foretold [it] to Abraham, as the holy scripture says: **ALL THE GENTILES WILL BE BLESSED IN YOU.**

9 So then, believers are blessed with Abraham, the believer.⁵

10 For those who are of the works of the law are under the curse, for it is written: **CURSED⁶ IS EVERYONE WHO WILL NOT DO ALL THAT IS WRITTEN IN THIS LAW.**

---

¹ Repeat *I am living*, forms of *live*, vs. 19, 20
² Fig: erotesis – questions to ponder, vs. 1-5
³ Same root: *portrait, portrayed*
⁴ Repeat *works of the law or by the hearing of faith* from v. 2
⁵ Repeat *believer*
⁶ Repeat forms of *curse, cursed*, vs. 10-13

Chapter 3

11 Now that a man is not justified to God by the[1] law is evident, because it is written: **THE JUST [ONE] WILL LIVE BY FAITH.**

12 Now the law was not of faith. But whoever will do those [things] that are written in it will live by them.

13 And Christ redeemed us from the curse of the law and became a curse for us, for it is written: **CURSED IS EVERYONE WHO IS HUNG ON A ^mTREE**

14 that the blessing of Abraham would be on the Gentiles by Jesus Christ and [that][2] we would receive the ^{as}promise of the Spirit by faith.

15 My brothers, ^{pa}I speak as among men,⌐ because a covenant of man that is established, no man sets aside or changes anything in it.

16 Now the promise was promised[3] to Abraham and to his ^mseed. And he did not say to him, "To your ^mseeds" as to many, but **TO YOUR ^mSEED** as to one, who is the Messiah.[4]

17 And this I say, that the covenant, which was previously established by God in Christ, the law, which was four hundred and thirty years after, is not able to set it aside and make the promise void.

18 Now if the inheritance was by the law, then it was not by promise. But God gave it to Abraham by promise.

19 Why then [was] the law? It was added because of transgression until that ^mseed should come to whom was the promise. And the law was given by way of angels, by the ^mhand of a mediator.

20 Now a mediator is not of one, but God is one.

21 Therefore, is the law opposite to the promise of God?[5] ⁱLet it not be so! For if a law had been given that was able to give life, truly justification would have been from the law.

22 But ^{pe}the scripture has confined everything under sin, so that the promise by the faith of Jesus Christ would be given to those who believe.

23 ^{al}Now until faith came, ^{pe}the law was guarding us, while we were confined from the faith that was going to be revealed.

24 Therefore, the ^{me}law was a tutor[6] for us for Christ, that we would be justified by faith.

---

[1] Fig: ellipsis, add [the works of]

[2] Var (WSL): omit *and*, add 'that'

[3] Same root: *promise, promised*, different word than v. 14

[4] Repeat *seed*, 3x

[5] Fig: erotesis, obvious answer "no"

[6] Var (M): 'gate'

ARAMAIC PESHITTA NEW TESTAMENT
GALATIANS

Chapter 3

25 Now when faith came, we were not under tutors.⌐ [1]

26 For all of you are sons of God by the faith of Jesus Christ.

27 For those who were baptized in Christ have put on Christ.

28 There is neither Judean nor heathen, there is neither servant nor free man, there is neither male nor[2] female, for all of you are one in Jesus Christ.

29 And if you are of Christ, then [me]you are the [m]seed of Abraham and heirs in the promise.

Chapter 4

1 [al]Now I am saying that as long as the heir [is] a child, he is no different from the servants,[3] although he is lord of all.

2 But he is under guardians and stewards[4] until the time that his father sets.

3 So also, while **we** were babies, we were made subject to the elements of the world.

4 But when the fulfillment of the time came, God sent his Son. And he was from a woman and was under the law,[5]

5 so that he would redeem those who are under the law and [that] we would receive adoption.

6 And now that you are sons, God sent into your hearts the Spirit of his Son that calls, "Father, our Father."

7 From now on, [me]you are not servants, but sons, and if sons, [you are] also heirs of God[6] by way of Jesus Christ.[7]

8 For then, when you did not know God, you served [pr]those that by their nature are not gods.

9 But now that you know God, or rather that you are known by God, you have returned again to those weak and poor elements and desire to be made subject to them again.

---

[1] Culture: a tutor was a guide or guardian from age six until puberty. A tutor carries the idea of severity of discipline, more than a father, Barnes, *People's Bible Dictionary*, pp. 981-982. Var (WSL): 'tutor' (sing.)

[2] Repeat *neither... nor*

[3] Var (WM): 'servant' (sing.)

[4] Culture: manager of household, Barnes, *People's Bible Dictionary*, p. 1054

[5] Repeat *under the law*, v. 5

[6] Pal Lect: omit *of God*

[7] Fig: climax

ARAMAIC PESHITTA NEW TESTAMENT
GALATIANS

Chapter 4

10 You observe days ^Pand months and times and years.⸗

11 ⁱI am afraid that I have labored among you without result.

12 Become like me, because I have also been like you. My brothers, I am begging you. You have not offended me [in] anything.

13 For you know that in the weakness of my ^{sy}flesh, I declared the gospel to you at the first

14 and you did not despise or reject the temptation of my ^{sy}flesh, but you received me ^sas a messenger of God and as Jesus Christ.

15 Therefore, where is your happiness? For I testify concerning you that if it had been possible, you would have picked out your eyes and given [them] to me.¹

16 Have I become an enemy to you, because I preached to you the truth?²

17 They are not zealous of you for good, but they desire to confine you, so that **you** would be zealous³ of them.

18 Now it is good that you should be zealous in good [things] at all times and not only when I am with you.

19 ^e[You are] my sons, those for whom ^hI labor in birth again until Christ is formed in you.

20 And I wanted to be with you now and to change my report, because I am astonished at you.

21 Say to me, you who desire to be under the law, do you not hear the law?⁴

22 ^{al}For it is written, "Abraham had two sons, one from the bond woman and one from the free [woman]."⁵

23 But the one from the bond woman was born according to the flesh and the one from the free [woman] was ^e[born] according to the promise.

24 Now these ^e[women] are illustrations of the two covenants. ^{me}The one that is from Mount Sinai gives birth to bondage, which is Hagar.

25 For ^{me}Hagar⁶ is the mountain of Sinai that is in Arabia and corresponds to this Jerusalem and serves [in] bondage, she and her sons.

26 But that ^{me}Jerusalem above is the free ^e[woman], who is our mother.

---

¹ Fig: hyperbole, means that they would do anything for Paul
² Fig: erotesis, **lema** question, obvious answer "no"
³ Repeat *zealous*, also v. 18, could be fig: antanaclasis
⁴ Fig: erotesis – question to ponder; *hear* implies obedience
⁵ Repeat *bond woman, free [woman]*, vs. 22-31
⁶ Repeat *Hagar* as next word

Chapter 4

27 For it is written: TAKE DELIGHT, BARREN [WOMAN] WHO BEARS NOT. AND REJOICE AND SHOUT [YOU] WHO HAVE NOT LABORED IN BIRTH, BECAUSE THE SONS OF THE DESOLATE [WOMAN] ARE MANY MORE THAN THE SONS OF THE MARRIED WOMAN.

28 Now we, my brothers, ⁵like Isaac, are the sons of the promise.

29 And as then, he who was born by the flesh persecuted the one who ᵉ[was born] by the Spirit, so also now.

30 But what does the scripture say? THROW OUT THE BOND WOMAN AND HER SON, BECAUSE THE SON OF THE BOND WOMAN WILL NOT SHARE AN INHERITANCE WITH THE SON OF THE FREE [WOMAN].

31 Therefore, my brothers, we are not sons of the bond woman, but¹ sons of the free [woman].⌐

Chapter 5

1 Stand fast, therefore, in the freedom [for] which Christ freed² us and do not be subjected again³ with the ʰyoke of bondage.

2 *Behold, I, Paul, say to you, that if you should be circumcised, Christ does not profit you anything.

3 Now I testify again to everyone who is circumcised that ᵐᵉhe is a debtor to do the whole law.

4 You have made Christ ineffectual, those who would be justified by the law and you have fallen from grace.

5 For we, by the Spirit that is from faith, wait for the hope of justification.

6 For in Christ Jesus neither is circumcision anything nor uncircumcision, but faith that is matured by love.

7 You were ʰrunning well. Who disturbed you to not be persuaded by the truth?⁴

8 Your persuasion⁵ is not from the one who called you.

9 A little ʰleaven leavens the whole lump.

10 I am confident in you in our Lord that you will not think other things and [that] the one who troubled you will bear his judgment, whoever he is.

---

¹ Fig: ellipsis, add [we are]

² Same root: *freedom, freed us, free [woman]*

³ Var (WS): omit *again*

⁴ Fig: erotesis – question to ponder, also v. 11

⁵ Same root: *persuasion, persuaded*, v. 7

ARAMAIC PESHITTA NEW TESTAMENT
GALATIANS

Chapter 5

11 Now, my brothers, if **I** was still preaching circumcision, why am I persecuted? Has the offense of the ^{mt}cross ceased?[1]

12 ⁱOh that those who are troubling you would also be actually cut off![2]

13 Now **you** were called to freedom, my brothers. Only your freedom should not be an occasion for the ^{sy}flesh, but you should be serving one another in love.

14 For the whole law is fulfilled in one word, in this: **YOU SHOULD LOVE YOUR NEIGHBOR AS YOURSELF.**

15 Now if you bite and devour one another, be careful[3] that you are not devoured by one another.[4]

16 *But I say, "Walk by the Spirit and never serve the desire of the ^{sy}flesh."

17 For the ^{sy}flesh desires what is opposed to the Spirit and the Spirit desires what is opposed to the ^{sy}flesh, and the two of them are opposites to each other, so that you are not doing what you want.

18 Now if you are led by the Spirit, you are not under the law.

19 For the works of the ^{sy}flesh are known, which are ^afornication, uncleanness, filthiness,

20 the worship of idols, magic, animosity, contention, jealousy, anger, insolence, divisions, discords,

21 envy, murder, drunkenness, rioting and all that are similar to these.˥ And those who do these [things], as I told you before, even now I say that they will not inherit the kingdom of God.

22 But the ^mfruit of the Spirit is ^alove, joy, peace, long-suffering, kindness, goodness,[5] faith,

23 meekness, patience,˥ concerning which the law was not established.

24 Now those who are of Christ have ^hcrucified their flesh with all its passions and its desires.

25 Therefore, we should live by the Spirit and we should follow the Spirit.

26 And we should not be ^e[seeking] empty glory, so that we ridicule one another and are jealous of one another.

---

[1] Fig: erotesis, **lema** question, obvious answer "no"

[2] Fig: polyptoton, *cutting, would be cut off*

[3] Lit: see

[4] Fig: anti-personification, people portrayed as vicious animals

[5] Var (WS): 'grace'

Chapter 6

1   My brothers, if one of ^{ac}you should be overtaken in an offense, you who are spiritual should correct him with a humble spirit and you should be watchful so that **you** are not tempted also.

2   And bear the burden[1] of one another, so that you may complete the law of Christ.

3   For if anyone thinks that he is something when he is not, he deceives himself.

4   But a man should examine his work and then his boasting will be privately to himself and not with others,

5   for everyone should carry his own load.

6   Now he who has heard the word should communicate to him who instructs him in all good [things].

7   Do not err. ^cGod is not mocked, for ^{al}what a man sows, that he reaps.

8   He who sows in the ^{sy}flesh reaps decay from the ^{sy}flesh and he who sows spiritually will reap eternal life from the Spirit.

9   And when we do that which is good, we should not be weary. For the time will come when we will reap and we will not be weary.[2] ⌐

10   Now therefore, while we have time, we should do good to everyone, especially to the ^{an}household of faith.[3]

11   See, I have written these writings to you with my ^{sy}hands.

12   Those who want to boast in the flesh are compelling you to be circumcised, only so that they would not be persecuted for the ^{mt}cross of Christ.

13   For not even those who are circumcised keep the law, but rather they want you to be circumcised, so that they may boast in your flesh.

14   But [as] for me, I will have nothing to boast about except the ^{mt}cross of our Lord Jesus Christ, by whom the world is crucified to me and **I** am crucified to the world.

15   For neither circumcision is anything, nor uncircumcision, but a new creation.

16   And those who follow this path, peace and mercies will be on them and on the ^mIsrael of God.

---

[1] Fig: anti-personification, a person compared to a camel or donkey bearing a large amount of weight

[2] Repeat *be weary*

[3] Fig: antimeria, "faithful household"

Chapter 6

17 So then, no one should pour trouble on me, for **I** bear the marks of our Lord Jesus[1] in my body.

18 [be]The grace of our Lord Jesus Christ [be] with your spirit, my brothers. Amen.

---

[1] Var (WSLM) add 'Christ"

ARAMAIC PESHITTA NEW TESTAMENT
EPHESIANS

Chapter 1

1   Paul, an apostle of Jesus Christ, by the will of God, to those who are in Ephesus, holy [ones] and faithful [ones] in Jesus Christ:

2   Peace [be] with you and grace from God our Father and from our Lord Jesus Christ.

3   Blessed be God, the Father of our Lord Jesus Christ, who has blessed us with all spiritual blessings[1] in heaven in Christ,

4   even as he chose us beforehand in him, from before the foundations of the world, that we should be holy [ones] and without blemish before him. And in love, he marked us out beforehand[2] for himself

5   and he adopted us in Jesus Christ, as was pleasing to his will,

6   that the [as]glory of his grace would be glorified,[3] which he has poured on us by way of his beloved [one],

7   in whom we have redemption and remission of sins by his blood, according to the [as]wealth of his grace,

8   which he caused to abound in us with all wisdom and with all[4] understanding.

9   And he made known to us the [as]mystery of his will that he had determined beforehand to accomplish in him,

10   in the administration of the fullness of times, that everything that is in heaven and in earth should be made new again in Christ.

11   And **we** were chosen in him, even as he marked us out beforehand[5] and he desired, he who performs everything according to the [as]purpose of his will,

12   that **we**, those who first trusted in Christ, should be for the [as]esteem of his magnificence.

13   In him also, [ac]**you** heard the [an]word of truthfulness, which is the gospel of your life, and in him, you believed and you were sealed with the Holy Spirit that was promised,

14   which is the guarantee of our inheritance to the redemption of those who have life and to the [as]glory of his honor.

---

[1] Same root: *blessed, blessings*

[2] Repeat *beforehand*, also vs. 9, 11

[3] Same root: *glory, glorified*; fig: antiptosis, 6x, vs. 6-14, "his glorious grace," "his rich grace," "his secret purpose," "his intended will," "his honorable glory," "his glorious honor"

[4] Repeat *with all*; Var (WSLM): add 'spiritual'

[5] Repeat *marked us out beforehand* from v. 4; word picture: *marked out* is "to engrave as a tattoo"

ARAMAIC PESHITTA NEW TESTAMENT
EPHESIANS

Chapter 1

15 Because of this, *behold, I also, since I heard of your faith that is in our Lord Jesus Christ and your love that is toward the holy [ones],

16 have not ceased to give thanks for you and to remember you in my prayers,

17 that the God of our Lord Jesus Christ, the [an]Father of glory, would give you the Spirit of wisdom and of revelation in his knowledge[1]

18 and [that] the [m]eyes of your hearts would be enlightened, so that you would know what is the hope of his calling and what is the [an]wealth of the glory of his inheritance in the holy [ones]

19 and what is the [an]abundance of the greatness of his power in us, in those who believe, according to the [an]working of the might of his power.

20 [This is] he who worked in Christ and raised him from the dead and seated him at his right hand in heaven,

21 higher than all rulers [P]and authorities and powers and lordships and higher than every name that is named,┐ not only in this world, but in the coming [one] also.

22 And **HE SUBJECTED EVERYTHING UNDER HIS [sy]FEET** and he gave him who is higher than all [to be] the [h]head of the church,

23 [me]which is his body and the fullness of him who is filling all in all.[2]

Chapter 2

1 And [e][God is filling] even you who were dead in your sins and in your transgressions,

2 in which you had walked previously, according to the worldliness of this world [3] and according to the will of the chief authority of the air and of that[4] spirit that operates in the sons of disobedience.

3 We also were occupied in those deeds previously, in the desires of our [sy]flesh, and we were doing the will of our [sy]flesh and of our mind and we were the sons of wrath [as] fully as the rest.

4 But God, who is rich in his mercies, because of his great love [with] which he loved us, [5]

5 while we were dead in our sins, gave us life with Christ and, by his grace, redeemed us

---

[1] Or "by the knowledge of him"

[2] Repeat all; same root: *fullness, filling*

[3] Same root: *worldliness, world*; repeat *previously*, vs. 3, 10, 11

[4] Var (WSLM): omit *that*

[5] Same root: *love, loved*; repeat *us* as suffix, vs. 4-6

Chapter 2

6 ᴾand raised us with him and seated us┐ with him in heaven in Jesus Christ,

7 so that he could show to the ages that are coming the ᵃˢgreatness of the wealth of his grace and his goodness that is to us in Jesus Christ.

8 For by his grace we were redeemed by faith ᵖᵃand this was not from yourselves, but is the gift of God,┐

9 not from works, so that no one would boast.

10 For we [are] his own creation, who are created in Jesus Christ for good works, those ᵉ[works] which God prepared previously that we should walk in.

11 Because of this, remember that ᵃᶜyou were previously Gentiles in the ˢʸflesh and you were called the ᵐuncircumcision by that which is called the ᵐcircumcision and is ᵖʳthe work of the hands in the flesh.

12 And at that time, you were without Christ ᴾand you were aliens from the customs of Israel and you were strangers to the covenant of the promise and you were without hope and without¹ God in the world.┐

13 But now, in Jesus Christ, **you** who previously ²were far have become near by the ᵐᵗblood of Christ.

14 ᵃˡFor ᵐᵉhe was our peace treaty, who made the two of them one and has broken down the ʰwall that stood in the middle³

15 and the conflict, by his flesh. And he brought to an end the law of commandments with its commandments,⁴ so that [from] the two of them he would create in himself one ʰnew man, and he made a peace treaty.┐

16 And he reconciled the two of them with God in one ʰbody and, by his ᵐᵗcross, he destroyed the conflict.

17 And he came [and] HE DECLARED PEACE TO YOU, [BOTH] THE FAR AND THE NEAR,

18 because in him we both have access in one spirit to the Father.

19 From now on, you are neither strangers nor foreigners, but citizens who are holy [ones] and [of] the household of God.

---

¹ Repeat *without*, 3x

² Repeat *previously* from vs. 10, 11

³ Fig: hypocatastasis, *wall* stands for the law, comparing it to the wall separating the Jews and Gentiles in the temple

⁴ Repeat *commandments*

Chapter 2

20 ^{al}And you are built on the foundation of the apostles and of the prophets and Jesus Christ is the head of the corner of the building.[1]

21 And in him the whole building is fit together and is growing into a holy temple in the LORD,

22 while **you** also are built in him for a dwelling of God spiritually.┐

Chapter 3

1 Because of this, **I**, Paul, am a prisoner of Jesus Christ for you Gentiles,

2 even as you have heard of the administration of the grace of God that was given to me among you,

3 that by revelation the mystery was made known to me ^{pa}(as I have written to you in few [words],

4 so that you may be able, while you are reading, to understand my knowledge that is in the mystery of Christ),

5 which in other generations was not made known to men, as that which now has been revealed to his holy apostles and to his prophets spiritually,

6 that the Gentiles should be his heirs and participants of his ^hbody and of [2] the promise that was given in him, by way of the gospel,

7 ^{pa}of which **I** became a minister according to the gift of the grace of God that was given to me by the working of his power.┐

8 To me, ^twho am the least of all the holy [ones], this grace was given, that I should declare among the Gentiles the wealth of Christ that is untraceable

9 and [that] I should bring light to everyone what is the administration of the mystery that was hidden from the ages in God, who created all [things],

10 so that by way of the church, the extraordinary[3] wisdom of God would be made known to the rulers and to the authorities that are in heaven,

11 which ^e[wisdom] he had prepared from the ages and has performed in Jesus Christ our Lord,

---

[1] Same root: *built, building*, vs. 20-22; lit: **he** is the head of the corner of the building, Jesus Christ

[2] Var (WS): 'in' or 'by'

[3] Lit: full of distinctions

Chapter 3

12 in whom we have [he]boldness and access in the confidence of his faith.

13 Because of this,[1] I am petitioning that I will not be weary in my trials that are for you, because this is your glory,

14 and [pr]I bow my knees to the Father of our Lord Jesus Christ,

15 from whom all the family which is in heaven and on earth is named,

16 that he would allow[2] you, according to the [an]wealth of his glory, to be strengthened with power by his Spirit, that in your inner man

17 Christ would dwell in faith and in your hearts in love, as your [h]root and your [h]foundation becomes strong,

18 that you would be able to understand with all the holy [ones] what is the height [P]and depth and length and breadth⌐

19 and would know the [as]greatness of the knowledge[3] of the love of Christ and would be filled with all the fullness[4] of God.

20 [be]Now to him who is able, by surpassing power, to do even more for us than what we ask and think, according to his power that is performed in us,

21 to him [be] glory in his church by Jesus Christ in all generations, forever and ever. Amen.

Chapter 4

1 I, therefore, a prisoner in our Lord, beg you that you should walk as is proper for the calling that you were called,[5]

2 with all humbleness of mind and quietness and long-suffering. And hold up one another in love

3 and be diligent to keep the alliance of the Spirit with the [m]girdle of peace,[6]

4 so that you will be in one body and by one Spirit, even as you are called in one hope of your calling.

5 For [there] is one LORD and one faith and one baptism

---

[1] Repeat *because of this* from v. 1, ties the passage to a new context; vs. 1-12 could also be a long parenthesis.

[2] Lit: give

[3] Var (WS): omit *of the knowledge*; same root: *know, knowledge*

[4] Same root: *filled, fullness*

[5] Same root: *calling, called*, also v. 4

[6] Fig: metonymy, the Spirit is the bond or tie that brings peace

Chapter 4

6   and one God, the Father of all and above all and by all and in us all.[1]

7   Now to each one of us is given grace according to the measure of the gift of Christ.

8   Because of this, it is said, HE ASCENDED TO THE HEIGHT AND CAPTURED CAPTIVITY AND GAVE GIFTS[2] TO MEN.

9   [pa](Now what is it that he ascended, unless he had also first descended to the depths of the earth?

10   He who descended is he who also ascended higher than all the heaven, that he would complete all.)

11   And he gave some apostles and some prophets and some evangelists and some pastors and some[3] teachers,

12   for the maturity of the holy [ones], for the work of the ministry, for the building up of the [h]body of Christ,

13   until we all become one in the faith and in the knowledge of the Son of God and one mature man, in the [an]measure of the standing of the fullness of Christ.[4]

14   And we should not be babies, who are shaken and blown about by every wind[5] of the deceitful teachings of men, who in their craftiness are plotting to deceive.

15   But we should be steadfast in our love, so that [in] everything [al]we ourselves may grow up in Christ, who is the head.

16   And from him the whole body is fit together and is knit together in all the joints, according to the gift that is given by measure to each member for the growth of the body, that its building up would be accomplished in love.⌐

17   Now *this I say and I bear witness in the LORD, that from now on you should not walk as the rest of the Gentiles, who walk in the emptiness[6] of their mind[s]

18   [P]and are dark in their thoughts and are strangers from the life of God, because there is no knowledge in them and because of the blindness of their heart[s],⌐

---

[1] Repeat *one, all*, vs. 5, 6

[2] Same root: *capture, captivity* and *gave, gifts*

[3] Repeat *and some*

[4] Fig: antimeria, with 2 nouns, could be translated "the full, high, measure", or with 1 noun, it would be "the measure of the full standing"

[5] Fig: antiprosopaeia, comparing babies to ships blown about in a storm

[6] Or "worthlessness"

Chapter 4

19 those who have cut off their hope and have surrendered themselves to perversion and to the ^{an}work of all uncleanness[1] in their greediness.

20 But **you** did not so learn about Christ,

21 ^{pa}if truly you have heard him and by him you have learned, as truthfulness is in Jesus.⌐

22 But ^e[you have learned] that you should strip off your former ways of life, the ^hold man who was corrupted by the ^{an}lusts of deceit,

23 and you should be renewed by the Spirit, that is, your minds.

24 And you should put on the ^hnew man, who was created by God by justification and by the ^{an}pardoning of truthfulness.

25 Because of this, strip off[2] lying and **SPEAK [WITH] TRUTHFULNESS, EACH ONE WITH HIS NEIGHBOR,** for ^{me}we are members of one another.

26 **BE ANGRY AND DO NOT SIN** and the sun should not go down on your anger.[3]

27 And do not give place[4] to the ACCUSER.

28 And he who was stealing should no longer steal,[5] but he should work with his ^{sy}hands and should do good [things], so that he may have to give to him who has need.

29 No hateful word should come out of your mouth, but that which is pleasing and useful for building up, so that it may give grace to those who hear.

30 And you should not grieve the sanctified Spirit of God, by whom you were sealed until the ^{sy}day of redemption.

31 All bitterness ^Pand wrath and anger and contention and reviling⌐ should be taken away from you with all wickedness.

32 And be kind to one another ^Pand merciful and be forgiving to one another,⌐ as God in Christ forgave ^{ac}us.

Chapter 5

1 Therefore, imitate God as beloved sons.

2 And walk in love, as Christ also loved[6] us and delivered himself up for us, an ^{he}offering and a sacrifice to God for a sweet smell.

---

[1] Fig: antimeria, could be translated "unclean practice"

[2] Repeat *strip off* from v. 22

[3] Same root: *angry, anger*

[4] Or "opportunity"

[5] Repeat forms of *steal*

[6] Same root: *love, loved*

Chapter 5

3   But fornication and all uncleanness and greed should also especially not be named[1] among you as is proper to holy [ones],

4   and neither obscenities nor words of foolishness or of reproach or[2] of nonsense that are not necessary, but instead of these, [e][words of] thanksgiving.

5   But this you should know, that everyone who is a fornicator or unclean or greedy, who is an idol worshipper, does not have an inheritance in the kingdom of Christ and of God.

6   [e][I say this], so that no one deceives you with empty words, for because of these [things] the [c]wrath of God will come on the sons of disobedience.[3]

7   Therefore, do not become partners with them,

8   [al]for you were first of all [in] darkness, but now [me]you are light in our Lord. Therefore, so walk as sons of light,

9   for the [m]effects[4] of the light are in all goodness [P]and justification and truthfulness.⌐ [5]

10   And determine what is pleasing before our Lord

11   and do not fellowship with the works of darkness that have no [e][good] [m]effects, but reprove them,

12   for what they do in secret is abominable even to speak,

13   for everything is exposed and is revealed by the light and everything that reveals[6] is light.

14   Because of this, it is said, "Awake, sleeper, and rise up from the dead, and Christ will enlighten you." ⌐

15   Therefore, see how you should walk accurately, not as fools, but as wise [ones]

16   who buy their opportunity,[7] because the days are evil.

17   Because of this, do not be stupid, but understand what is the will of God.

18   And do not be drunk with wine, in which is excess, but be filled with the Spirit,

---

[1] Fig: polyptoton, lit: naming, be not named

[2] Repeat *nor, or*, also v. 5

[3] Or "disobedient [ones]"

[4] Lit: fruit, also v. 11

[5] Fig: hendiatris, meaning "true, just, goodness"

[6] Repeat forms of *revealed* and *light*

[7] Cf Grk: **karsos**; we would say "make the best use of your time."

Chapter 5

19 and speak among yourselves with psalms and with hymns. And sing in your hearts to the LORD with songs of the Spirit.

20 And give thanks always for everyone in the name of our Lord Jesus Christ to God the Father.

21 And be subject[1] to one another in the love of Christ.

22 Wives, be subject to your husbands as to our Lord,

23 because the [me]man is the head of the wife, as also [me]Christ is the head of the church and he is the life-giver of the [h]body.

24 But even as the church is subject to Christ, so also wives [e][should be subject] to their husbands in everything.

25 Men, love your wives [al]as also Christ loved his church and delivered himself up for it,

26 to make it holy and to cleanse it by the washing of [m]water and by the word

27 and to establish the church for himself, being glorious and having no spot and no wrinkle and nothing like these, but rather to be holy [and] without blemish.⌐

28 So it is right for men to love their wives as their [own] bodies, for he who loves his wife loves himself,

29 for no one ever hates[2] his body, but nourishes it and cares for his own [e][body]. [It is] even as Christ [e][nourishes and cares] for his church,[3]

30 because [me]we are members of his body, and we are of his flesh and of his bones.

31 Because of this, A MAN SHOULD LEAVE HIS FATHER [P]AND HIS MOTHER AND SHOULD BE JOINED TO HIS WIFE AND THE TWO OF THEM SHOULD BECOME ONE [sy]FLESH.⌐

32 This mystery is great, but I am speaking about Christ and about[4] his church.

33 Nevertheless, you also, each and every one of you, should so have compassion for his wife as for himself and the wife should have respect for her husband.

---

[1] Repeat *be subject*, vs. 21-24
[2] Lit: a man never hates
[3] Var (WSLM): 'the church'
[4] Repeat *about*

Chapter 6

1 Children, obey your parents in our Lord, for this [is] upright.

2 And this is the first commandment that has a promise: **HONOR YOUR FATHER AND YOUR MOTHER,**

3 **THAT IT MAY BE WELL FOR YOU AND YOUR LIFE MAY BE LONG ON THE EARTH.**

4 Parents, do not anger your children, but rear them in the instruction and in[1] the teaching of our Lord.

5 Servants, be obedient to your masters that are in the [sy]flesh, with reverence and with [h]trembling and with simplicity of heart, as to Christ,

6 not with what is seen by the eye[2] as if you were pleasing men, but [s]as servants of Christ, who are doing the will of God.

7 And minister to them from your whole life in love, as to our Lord, and not as to men,

8 knowing that what someone does that is good will be rewarded from our Lord, whether he is a servant or a free man.

9 Also, **you** masters, so serve your servants.[3] Forgive them an error,[4] because you also know that your own Master is in heaven and there is no respect of persons with him.

10 From now on, my brothers, be strong in our Lord and in the [as]immensity of his power

11 [al]and put on the whole armor of God, so that you may be able to stand against the tactics of the Accuser,

12 because your struggle is not with [sy]flesh and blood, but with rulers [P]and with authorities and with the possessors of this dark world and with the evil spirits that are under heaven.⌐ [5]

13 Because of this, put on the whole armor of God, so that you will be able to engage the Evil [one] and, being prepared in everything, you will stand firm.

14 Therefore, stand[6] and **GIRD UP YOUR WAIST WITH TRUTHFULNESS** and **PUT ON THE BREASTPLATE OF JUSTIFICATION**

15 and **BIND [AS A SANDAL] ON YOUR FEET THE GOODNESS OF THE GOSPEL OF PEACE.**

---

[1] Repeat *in*

[2] Lit: the sight of the eye

[3] Same root: *serve, servants*

[4] Var (W): *errors* (pl)

[5] Repeat *and with*

[6] Repeat *stand* as next word from v. 13

Chapter 6

16 And with these, take to you the ^mshield of faith,[1] by which you will be empowered with strength to quench all the fiery ^harrows of the Evil [one].

17 And SET ON [YOUR HEAD] THE HELMET OF REDEMPTION and take hold of the ^msword of the Spirit, which is the word of God.⌐

18 And with all prayers and with all petitions, pray at all times spiritually, and in prayer, be watchful in every season, praying continually and interceding for all[2] the holy [ones],

19 [and] also for me, that the word may be given to me in the ^{pr}opening of my mouth, that I would boldly preach the mystery of the gospel,

20 for which ^{me}I am its ambassador in chains, that with frankness I may speak, as I ought to speak[3] it.

21 Now that you also may know about me[4] and what I am doing, *behold, Tychicus, a beloved brother and faithful minister in our Lord, will make known ^e[these things] to you,

22 whom I sent to you especially for this,[5] that you would know how [it is] with me[6] and [that] he would comfort your hearts.

23 ^{be}Peace [be] with our brothers and love with faith, from God the Father and from our Lord Jesus Christ.

24 Grace [be] with all those who love our Lord Jesus Christ without corruption. Amen.

---

[1] Var (S): 'hope of faith'
[2] Repeat *all*, 5x; same root: *pray, prayer*
[3] Repeat *speak*
[4] Lit: what to me
[5] Lit: for it, for this
[6] Lit: how to me

ARAMAIC PESHITTA NEW TESTAMENT
PHILIPPIANS

Chapter 1

1 Paul and Timothy, servants of Jesus Christ, to all the holy [ones] who are in Jesus Christ, who are at Philippi, with the elders and ministers:

2 Grace [be] with you and peace from God our Father and from our Lord Jesus Christ.

3 I thank my God for constant remembrance of you,[1]

4 because in all my petitions that are for you and as I rejoice, I make intercession

5 for your fellowship that is in the gospel from the first day until now,

6 because I am confident about this, that he who has begun good works in you will complete [them] until the [sy]day of our Lord Jesus Christ.

7 For so it is right for me to think about all of you, because you are established[2] in my heart. And in my bonds and in my defense that is concerning the truth of the gospel, you are my partners in grace.

8 [i]For God is my witness, how I love you with the compassion of Jesus Christ.

9 And this I pray, that again your love may increase and grow in knowledge and in all spiritual understanding,

10 so that you may distinguish those [things] that are profitable and [that] you may be pure, without offense in the [sy]day of Christ,

11 and [that] you may be full of the [m]fruit of justification that is by Jesus Christ, to the glory and to the honor of God.

12 Now I want you to know, my brothers, that my circumstance has increasingly led to advancement in the gospel,

13 so that even my bonds in Christ are publicized in all the Praetorium and to everyone else.

14 And many of the brothers who are in our Lord have become confident on account of my bonds and are increasingly[3] bold to speak the word of God without fear.

15 And some are preaching Christ out of envy and controversy, but others with good will and in love,

16 because they know that I am appointed for the defense of the gospel.

17 Now those who are preaching Christ with controversy are not [e][doing it] purely, but they hope to add pressure to my [m]bonds.

---

[1] Or "your constant remembrance"
[2] Lit: you are seated
[3] Repeat *increasingly* from v. 12

ARAMAIC PESHITTA NEW TESTAMENT
PHILIPPIANS

Chapter 1

18 And in this I rejoiced and am rejoicing,[1] that in every way, whether in pretext or with truthfulness, Christ is preached.

19 For I know that these [things] will be found for life to me by your prayer[2] and by the gift of the Spirit of Jesus Christ,

20 since I am hoping and expecting that I will not be ashamed in anything, but with boldness [pa](as at all times even so now), Christ will be magnified in my body, whether in life or in death,

21 for my life is[3] Christ and if I die, I have gain.

22 Now if in this life of the [sy]flesh I also have the [m]fruit of my works, I do not know what to choose.

23 For the two [e][choices] press closely on me. I desire to [eu]depart, so that I may be with Christ, and this would be very profitable for me.

24 But also, the matter concerning you urges me to remain in my body.

25 And this I confidently know, that I will wait and will remain for your joy and for the growth of your faith,

26 so that when I come again to you, your boasting that is in Jesus Christ alone will increase with me.

27 Conduct yourselves as is becoming to the gospel of Christ, so that if I come, I may see you and if I am distant, I may hear about you, that you are standing in one spirit and in one soul and [that] you are conquering together[4] in the faith of the gospel.

28 And do not be shaken by anything from those who stand against us, [which is] the evidence of their loss and of your life.

29 And this is given to you by God, that you would not only indeed believe[5] in Christ, but also that you would suffer for him

30 and [that] you would endure the [h]contest as you saw in me and now hear concerning me.

Chapter 2

1 Therefore, if you have encouragement in Christ or if [e][you have] consolation in love or if [e][you have] fellowship of the Spirit or if [e][you have] loving-kindness and[6] mercies,

---

[1] Repeat forms of *rejoice*

[2] Var (WSL): plural

[3] Fig: ellipsis, add [to serve]

[4] Lit: as one; repeat *one*, notice throughout this book

[5] Fig: polyptoton, lit: believing, should believe

[6] Var (WS): add, 'or if'

Chapter 2

2 complete my joy, so that you will have one mind [P]and one love and one soul and one purpose.⅂

3 And do not do anything with controversy or with empty boasting, but[1] with humbleness of mind. Everyone should count his associate as better than himself.

4 And a man should not be concerned for himself [only], but each one [should] also [e][be concerned] for his associate.

5 And think this in yourselves which Jesus Christ also [e][thought],

6 who, as he was in the likeness of God, did not consider it extortion to be the equal of God.

7 But he emptied himself [2] and took on the likeness of a servant and was in the likeness[3] of men and was found in fashion as a man.

8 And he humbled himself and became obedient until death, even the death[4] of the cross.

9 Because of this, God also elevated him highly and gave him a name that is greater than all names,[5]

10 that at the name of Jesus [pr]every knee should bow that is in [mr]heaven and on earth and that is under the earth,

11 and every [m]tongue should confess that Jesus Christ is the LORD, to the glory of God his Father.

12 From now on,[6] my beloved [ones], as you have been obedient at all times, not only when I was near to you, but [also] now that I am far from you, increasingly work the work[7] of your life with reverence and with [h]trembling.

13 For God energizes you to will as well as to perform what you desire.[8]

14 Do everything without murmuring and without[9] division,

15 so that you will be innocent and without blemish, as pure sons of God who are living in a [he]perverted and crooked generation. And be seen among them as lights in the world,

---

[1] Fig: ellipsis, add [do everything]

[2] Fig: catabasis, steps downward (7 phrases)

[3] Repeat *likeness*

[4] Repeat *death*, next word

[5] Repeat *name*, also v. 10

[6] Repeat *from now on*, marking sections, 3:1, 4:1, 4:8

[7] Same root: *work, the work*

[8] Same verb: *to will, desire*

[9] Repeat *without*

Chapter 2

16 so that you will be to them in place of life, for my glory in the ^{sy}day of Christ, so that I have not ^hrun at random nor worked hard fruitlessly.

17 But if I am offered for the sacrifice and the service of your faith, I am rejoicing and I am glad with all of you.

18 So also, rejoice and be glad[1] with me.

19 Now I expect in our Lord Jesus to send Timothy to you shortly, so that I may also have rest when I learn about you.

20 For I have no others here who are like myself, who earnestly care for your ^e[affairs].

21 For all seek themselves and not Jesus Christ.

22 But you know the proof of him, that as a son with his father, so he has served with me in the gospel.

23 I expect to send him[2] to you shortly, when I see how [it is] with me.

24 And I trust in my Lord that I will also come to you shortly.

25 But now, a matter urges me to send Epaphroditus to you, a brother who is a helper and worker with me, but your own apostle and a minister for my need,

26 because he was longing to see all of you and was distressed, for he knew that you had heard that he was sick.

27 For he was indeed sick almost to death, but God had mercy on him and not on him only, but also on me, so that I would not have distress on distress.[3]

28 Therefore, I have sent him to you promptly, so that when you see him again, you would rejoice and [that] I would have a little refreshment.[4]

29 Therefore, receive him in the LORD with all joy and hold those who are so in honor.

30 For because of the work of Christ, he came near to death and despised danger regarding himself, so that he could supply what you had neglected in service to me.

Chapter 3

1 From now on, my brothers, rejoice in our Lord. That I should write these [things] to you is not wearisome to me, because they caution you.

---

[1] Repeat *rejoice, glad*, from v. 17
[2] Lit: this [one]
[3] Repeat *distress*
[4] Word Picture: from root, "to breathe"

Chapter 3

2 Beware of [h]dogs, beware of evil doers, beware of [1] the [pr]cutting of flesh.

3 For [me]we are the circumcision, who serve God by the Spirit and boast in Jesus Christ and are not confident about the flesh,

4 although I did have confidence also about the flesh. For if anyone thinks that his confidence is in the flesh, I [should have confidence] more than he.

5 [I was] circumcised [when] eight days old, [a]from the family of Israel, from the tribe of Benjamin, a Hebrew, the son of Hebrews, in the law, of the Pharisees,

6 in zeal, a persecutor of the church, and in the justification of the law, I was without blame.⌐

7 But those [things] that were a gain to me I counted a loss because of Christ.

8 I[2] also count all of these [things] a loss[3] because of the [as]greatness of the knowledge of Jesus Christ, my Lord, because of whom I have forfeited everything and have counted [it] [s]as dung, so that I would gain Christ

9 and be found in him, not having justification of myself that is from the law, but that which is from the faith of Christ, which is the justification[4] that is from God,

10 so that by it I would know Jesus and the power of his resurrection and would be made a participant in his sufferings and would be conformed to his death,

11 that it may be I would be able to arrive at the resurrection that is from the dead.

12 [al]I have not yet received [e][the victory], nor yet been made perfect, but I am [h]running, so that I will attain what Jesus Christ attained[5] [for] me.

13 My brothers, I do not consider myself to have attained. But one [thing] I know, that I am forgetting what is behind me and I am reaching out before me.

---

[1] Repeat *beware of*

[2] Var (WSL): add, 'and'

[3] Repeat *I counted a loss*, from v. 7

[4] Repeat *justification*

[5] Repeat forms of *attain*, vs. 12, 13

Chapter 3

14 And I am running toward the goal,[1] so that I would receive the victory of the high calling of God in Jesus Christ.⌐

15 Therefore, those who are mature should think these [things] and if you think anything otherwise, God will also reveal this to you.

16 Nevertheless, to reach this, we should follow in one path and with one[2] agreement.

17 Imitate me, my brothers, and consider those who so walk as an example that you have seen in us.

18 For there are many who walk otherwise, those whom I have told you about many times, and now weeping, I am saying that they are enemies of the [mt]cross of Christ,

19 whose end is destruction, whose god [is] their stomach and whose glory [is] their shame, whose thinking is on the earth.

20 But our work is in heaven and from there we are expecting the Savior,[3] our Lord Jesus Christ,

21 who will change the [an]body of our humiliation that it would be in the likeness of the [an]body of his glory, according to his great power by which all is made subject to him.

Chapter 4

1 From now on, my beloved and dear brothers, my joy and my [m]crown, so stand fast in our Lord, my beloved.[4]

2 I beg Euodias and Syntyche to have one mind in our Lord.

3 I beg you also, my true yoke-fellow, that you would help those who are toiling with me in the gospel, with Clement and with the rest of my helpers, whose names are written in the book of life.

4 Rejoice in our Lord at all times, and again I say, "Rejoice."[5]

5 And let your meekness be known to everyone. Our Lord is near.

6 Do not be distressed about anything, but at all times, by prayer [P]and by petition and with thanksgiving,⌐ your requests should be made known before God.

7 And the peace of God that is greater than all knowledge will guard your hearts and your minds in Jesus Christ.

---

[1] Or "finish line"

[2] Repeat in (or with) one

[3] Lit: Life-giver

[4] Repeat my beloved

[5] Repeat rejoice, at beginning and end of verse, also referring back to 3:1

Chapter 4

8   From now on, my brothers, those [things] that are[1] true [P]and those [things] that are modest and those [things] that are upright and those [things] that are pure and those [things] that are lovely and those [things] that are praiseworthy and those works of glory and of commendation, think these [things].⌐

9   Those [things] that you have learned [P]and received and heard and seen in me,⌐ these do and the God of peace will be with you.

10   Now I rejoice greatly in our Lord that you have begun [again] to care for me, as also you were caring, but you did not have sufficiency.

11   Now I do not say [this] because I am in need, for I have learned that what I have will be sufficient for me.

12   I know [how] to be humble. I also know [how] to abound in every [situation] and I am disciplined in everything, whether in plenty or in famine, in abundance or in[2] need.

13   I find strength for everything in Christ who strengthens me.

14   [al]Nevertheless, you have done well to have shared in my difficulties.[3]

15   Now **you** know also, Philippians, that in the beginning of the gospel when I left Macedonia, not even one of the churches shared with me in the accounting of receiving and giving, but you only,

16   so that even at Thessalonica, once and again, you sent to me[4] for my use.

17   It is not that I am requesting a gift, but I am requesting[5] that [m]fruit should multiply to you.

18   I have received everything and I have abundance and I am full. And I have accepted all that you sent to me by way of Epaphroditus, a sweet [h]fragrance and an acceptable sacrifice that is pleasing to God.

19   And my God will supply all your need according to his riches in the glory of Jesus Christ.⌐

20   [be]Now to God our Father [be] glory and honor, forever and ever. Amen.

21   Greet all the holy [ones] who are in Jesus Christ. The brothers who are with me greet you.

---

[1] Repeat *those [things] that are*, 6x
[2] Repeat *in*, 6x in this verse
[3] Fig: allegory, vs. 14-19 are an extended hypocatastasis regarding financial giving and comparing giving to the records of an accounting ledger.
[4] Var (WS): omit *to me*
[5] Repeat *I am requesting*

Chapter 4

22 All the holy [ones] greet you, especially those who are from the household of Caesar.

23 The grace of our Lord Jesus Christ [be] with all of you. Amen.

ARAMAIC PESHITTA NEW TESTAMENT
COLOSSIANS

Chapter 1

1   Paul, an apostle of Jesus Christ by the will of God, and Timothy, a brother,

2   to those who are at Colosse, brothers, holy [ones] and faithful [ones] in Jesus Christ: Peace [be] with you and grace from God, our Father.

3   We give thanks at all times to God the Father of our Lord Jesus Christ and we pray for you,

4   ever since we heard of your faith that is in Jesus Christ and your love that is toward all the holy [ones]

5   because of the ^mhope that is kept for you in heaven, that which you previously heard in the ^{an}word of truthfulness of the gospel,

6   that is preached to you as also to all the world. And it grows and yields ^mfruit, as also ^e[it has] in you from the ^{sy}day that you heard and acknowledged the grace of God with truthfulness,

7   as you learned from Epaphras, our beloved fellow-servant, who is for you a faithful minister of Christ

8   and who has made known to us your love that is by the Spirit.

9   Because of this, **we** also, from the ^{sy}day that we heard, do not cease to pray for you and to ask that you may be filled with knowledge of the will of God with all wisdom and with all[1] spiritual understanding,

10 that you may walk as is just and may please God with all good works and may bear fruit and may[2] grow up in the knowledge of God

11 and may be strengthened with all strength,[3] according to the ^{as}greatness of his glory. With all patience and long-suffering and with joy,

12 you should give thanks to God the Father, who has made us worthy for a portion of the inheritance of the holy [ones] in light

13 and has delivered us from the ^{an}authority of darkness and has transferred us to the kingdom of his beloved Son,

14 in whom we have redemption[4] and forgiveness of sins,

15 who is the image of the God who is not seen[5] and the firstborn of all created [ones].

---

[1] Repeat *with all*

[2] Repeat *may...*, same forms of imperfect verb, also v. 11

[3] Same root: *strengthened, strength*

[4] Same root: *redemption, delivered,* v. 13

[5] Repeat *is seen*, 3x, vs. 15, 16

Chapter 1

16 And in him everything that is in ^{mr}heaven and on earth was built, all that is seen and all that is not seen, whether thrones or lordships or rulers or[1] authorities, everything [is] by way of him and was built in him.

17 And he is in front of all and everything stands in him.

18 And he is the head of the body, the church, for he is the ^{he}beginning and the firstborn[2] from the dead in order that he would be the first in all [things].

19 For in him, he desired all fullness to live

20 and by way of him[3] to reconcile everything to him. And he made peace by the blood of his cross by his hands, whether in earth or in heaven.

21 For ^{ac}**you** also, who previously were strangers and enemies in your minds because of your evil works, he has now made peace[4]

22 by the ^{an}body of his ^{sy}flesh and by his death, so that he would establish you before him, holy, without blemish, and without[5] blame.

23 Since ^e[this is so], continue in your faith, your ^hfoundation being firm, and be not shaken from the hope of the gospel that you heard [and] that was preached in all the creation that is under heaven, of which **I**, Paul, am a minister.

24 And I rejoice in the sufferings that are for you and I supply the need because of the adversities of Christ in my ^{sy}flesh on behalf of his ^hbody, which is the church,

25 of which I am a minister,[6] according to the administration of God that was given to me among you, that I should fully supply[7] the word of God,

26 the mystery that was hidden from ages and from generations, but now is revealed to his holy [ones].

27 To them, God wanted to make known what is the ^{an}wealth of the glory of this mystery among the Gentiles, which is the MESSIAH who is in you, the hope of our glory,

---

[1] Repeat *or*

[2] Fig: hendiadys, "firstborn leader"

[3] Lit: by his hand, repeat from v. 16

[4] Lit: "peaced you", repeat from v. 20

[5] Repeat *without*

[6] Repeat *I am a minister*

[7] Same root: *fully supply, supply*, v. 24

ARAMAIC PESHITTA NEW TESTAMENT
COLOSSIANS

Chapter 1

28 [It is] him **we** preach [P]and teach and make known to every man with all wisdom,⌐ so that we may present every man mature in Jesus Christ.

29 For in this also I am working hard and striving with the help of the power that was given to me.

Chapter 2

1 Now I want you to know the kind of struggle I have for you and for them who are in Laodicea and for the rest of those who have not seen my face in the [sy]flesh.

2 [e][The struggle is] that their[1] hearts would be comforted and would be brought near in love to all the [as]wealth of assurance and to the understanding of the knowledge of the mystery of God the Father and of Christ,

3 in whom are hidden all the treasures of wisdom and of knowledge.

4 Now I say this, so that no one should deceive you by the persuasiveness[2] of words.

5 For even if I am physically separated from you, nevertheless I am with you spiritually and I rejoice to see your orderliness and the steadfastness of your faith that is in Christ.

6 Therefore,[3] as you have received Jesus Christ our Lord, walk in him,

7 your [h]roots being strengthened and built up in him and established in the faith that you have learned, in which you should abound with thanksgiving.

8 Beware, so that no one will [h]rob you by philosophy and by empty deception, according to the teachings of men and according to the elements of the world and not according to[4] Christ,

9 in whom all the fullness of divinity lives bodily.

10 [P]And in him also you are absolutely completed, him who is the head of all rulers and authorities.

11 And in him[5] you were circumcised with the circumcision that is not by our hands in the putting off of the [an]flesh of sins, [e][but] by the circumcision of Christ.

---

[1] Var (M): 'your'

[2] Same root: *persuasiveness, assurance*, v. 2

[3] Repeat *therefore*, marks sections, 2:16, 3:1, 5, 12

[4] Repeat *according to*

[5] Repeat *in him*, from v. 10, also v. 12

Chapter 2

12 And you were buried with him in baptism and in him you have risen with him, for you believed in the power of God who raised him from the dead.

13 And **you**, who were dead in your sins and in the uncircumcision of your flesh, he has made alive with him and he has forgiven [ac]us all our sins.

14 And he has blotted out, by his commandments, the handwriting of our [h]debts that was against us and he took it from the middle and fastened it to his cross.

15 And by the putting off of his body, he exposed rulers and authorities and shamed them openly in his person.⌐

16 Therefore, no one should disturb you about food and drink or about the distinctions of feasts [P]and of new moons and of Sabbaths,⌐

17 which are shadows of things that are to come. But [me]the body is the MESSIAH.

18 And no one should desire, by [e][false] humility of mind, to make you guilty, in order to subject you to the worship of angels, by presuming about something that he has not seen. And he is puffed up fruitlessly in the [an]mind of his flesh

19 [al]and does not hold the head [in honor], from whom the whole body is fit together [P]and established with joints and with members and grows [with] the growth[1] of God.⌐

20 For if you died with Christ to the elements of the world, are you judged as though you live in the world?[2]

21 [Those say], "Do not touch and do not taste and do not[3] associate with [these]."

22 For these [things] are a custom that is corrupted and are the commands and teachings of men,

23 and they appear to have a word of wisdom with a [an]face of humility[4] and of the reverence of God and of depriving the body, not about anything of value, but rather about those [things] that are a custom of the [sy]flesh.

---

[1] Same root: *grows, growth*

[2] Fig: erotesis, **lema** question, obvious answer "no"

[3] Repeat *and not*

[4] Fig: antimeria, "humble presence"

ARAMAIC PESHITTA NEW TESTAMENT
COLOSSIANS

Chapter 3

1   Therefore, if you have risen with Christ, seek what is above, where Christ sits at the right hand of God.

2   Think what is above and not what is on the earth,

3   for you are dead[1] and your life is hidden with Christ in God.

4   And when Christ, who is our life, is revealed, then you also will be revealed with him in glory.

5   Therefore, put to death your members that are of the earth, fornication [P]and uncleanness and passions and evil desire and greed,¬ which is the reverence of idols.

6   For because of these [things] the wrath of God will come on the sons of disobedience.

7   And in these [things] also, you were previously walking, when you were occupied with them.

8   But now, cease all these [things], [a]anger, fury, wickedness, reviling, unclean speech.¬

9   [al]And do not lie to one another, but rather strip off the [h]old man with all his practices[2]

10   and put on the [h]new [man] that is renewed[3] in knowledge in the likeness of his Creator,

11   where there is not Judean and Aramean, not circumcision and uncircumcision, not Greek and barbarian, not servant and free[men], but Christ is all and in all[4] men.

12   Therefore, as the chosen [ones] of God, holy and beloved, put on mercies [P]and loving-kindness and gentleness and humbleness of mind and quietness and long-suffering.¬

13   [P]And be forbearing to one another and forgiving to one another. And if someone has a complaint against his associate, as Christ forgave you, so also **you** forgive.

14   And with all these [things], [e][put on] love, which is the [m]girdle of maturity.¬

15   And the peace of Christ will govern your hearts, for to him you were called in one body. And be thankful to Christ,

---

[1] Lit: it is dead to you

[2] Same root: *practices, occupied*, v. 7; fig: allegory, vs. 9-14, comparison of putting off the old man and putting on the new man as putting on clothes.

[3] Same root: *new, renewed*

[4] Repeat *all*; repeat *not*

Chapter 3

16 that his word may live in you richly with all wisdom. And teach and instruct yourselves in psalms and in hymns and in[1] songs of the Spirit and sing with grace in your hearts to God.

17 And everything that you do in word and in work, do in the name of our Lord Jesus Christ and give thanks by way of him to God the Father.┐[2]

18 Wives, be subject to your husbands as is right in Christ.

19 Men, love your wives and do not be bitter against them.

20 Children, be obedient to your parents in everything, for so it is pleasing before our Lord.

21 Parents, do not anger your children, so that they will not be discouraged.

22 Servants, be obedient in everything to your masters of the flesh, not with what is seen by the eye as those who please men, but with a generous heart and in the reverence of the LORD.

23 And all that you do, do with your whole self as to our Lord and not as to[3] men.

24 And know that from our Lord you will receive a reward in the inheritance, for you serve the LORD the MESSIAH.

25 But the evil-doer is rewarded according to what he did wrong[4] and there is no respect of persons.

Chapter 4

1 Masters, serve equality and justice to your servants and know that you also have a Master[5] in heaven.

2 Be steadfast in prayer ᴾand be vigilant in it and give thanks.

3 And pray also for us that God will open a door of speech for us to speak the mystery of Christ,┐ because of whom I am imprisoned,

4 that I may reveal him and speak of him, as it is right for me ᵉ[to do].

5 Walk with wisdom toward outsiders ᴾand buy out your opportunity.

6 And your speech at all times should be with grace, ˢas though seasoned with salt. And know how you ought to give an answer to every man.┐

---

[1] Repeat *in*

[2] Fig: polysyndeton, vs. 13-17

[3] Repeat *as to*

[4] Same root: *evil-doer, wrong,* and *rewarded, reward,* v. 24

[5] Var (W): 'the LORD'

Chapter 4

7 Now what concerns me,[1] Tychicus, a beloved brother [P]and faithful minister and our fellow-servant˥ in the LORD, will make known to you.

8 I have sent him to you for this [reason], that he would know what concerns you and would comfort your hearts,

9 with Onesimus, a faithful and beloved brother, who is one of you. They will make known to you what concerns us.

10 Aristarchus, a captive with me, greets you and Mark, the cousin of Barnabas, concerning whom you received commandment that if he came to you, you should receive him,

11 and Jesus who is called Justus. These who are from the [m]circumcision and they only have assisted me in the kingdom of God and they have been a comfort to me.

12 Epaphras greets you, who is one of you, a servant of Christ, laboring at all times for you in prayer, that you would stand, mature [ones] and complete [ones] in all the will of God.

13 For I witness about him that he has great zeal for you and for those who are in Laodicea and in Hierapolis.

14 Luke, our beloved physician, greets you and Demas.

15 Greet the brothers who are in Laodicea and Nymphas and the church that is in his house.

16 And when this letter is read among you, cause it to be read also in the church of the Laodiceans, and that which is written from Laodicea, read.

17 And tell Archippus, "Take care of the ministry that you have received in our Lord to fulfill it."

18 This greeting [is] by my own hand, Paul. Remember my [m]bonds. [be]Grace [be] with you. Amen.

---

[1] Lit: the thing that is with (or toward) me, repeat vs. 8, 9

ARAMAIC PESHITTA NEW TESTAMENT
I THESSALONIANS

Chapter 1

1   Paul and Silvanus and Timothy to the church of the Thessalonians, which is in God the Father and in our Lord Jesus Christ: Grace [be] with you and peace.

2   We give thanks to God at all times for all of you and we remember you in our prayers continually.

3   And we recall before God the Father the [an]works of your faith and the [an]labor of your love and the [an]endurance of your hope that is in our Lord Jesus Christ.

4   For we know your calling, my brothers, beloved of God,

5   because our preaching to you was not only in words, but also with power and with the Holy Spirit and with[1] true conviction. Also, **you** know how we were among you on your account.

6   And **you** became imitators of us and of our Lord, in that you received the word in great trial and in the joy of the Holy Spirit.

7   And you were an example to all the believers who are in Macedonia and in Achaia.

8   For from you the word of our Lord was heard, not only in Macedonia and in Achaia, but in every place your faith that is in God was heard, so that it was not necessary to say anything about you.

9   For **they** report what kind of entrance we had to you and how you turned to God from reverence of idols to serve the [he]living and true God,

10 while you wait for his Son from heaven, Jesus, whom he raised from the dead, who has delivered us from the wrath that is coming.

Chapter 2

1   And **you** know, my brothers, that our entrance to you was not fruitless,

2   but first we suffered and were dishonored in Philippi, as you know, and then with a great struggle, with the boldness of our God we spoke to you the gospel of Christ.

3   For our exhortation was not from deception, nor from uncleanness, nor[2] with treachery.

4   But as we were approved of God to be entrusted with his gospel, so we speak, not to please men, but [e][to please] God, who searches our hearts.

---

[1] Repeat *with*, 4x

[2] Repeat *nor*

Chapter 2

5 For we never used flattering speech, [pa]as you know, nor with a plan of greediness.⌐ [i]God [is] witness.

6 And we did not seek praise from men, nor from you, nor from others, although we could have been honored [ones] as the apostles of Christ.

7 But we were meek among you, and [s]as a nurse who loves her children,

8 so also **we** were loving and were desiring to give to you, not only the gospel of God, but also ourselves, because you were beloved.[1]

9 For you recall, our brothers, that we were laboring and toiling by the work of our hands, [mr]by night and by day, so that we would not burden one of you.

10 You and God are witnesses how we preached to you the gospel of God, [he]purely and uprightly, and we were without blame to all the believers.

11 As you know, we were entreating each one of you as a father [e][entreats] his children and we were comforting your heart [2]and were charging you

12 that you should walk as is becoming to God, who called you to his kingdom and to his glory.

13 Because of this also, **we** give thanks continually to God that you received the word of God that you received from us, not as the word of men, but as it is truly, the word of God, and is effectively working[3] in you who believe.

14 But **you**, my brothers, became imitators of the churches of God that are in Judea, they that are in Jesus Christ. For so you also suffered from your countrymen, as they also[4] from the Judeans,

15 who killed our Lord Jesus Christ [P]and persecuted their own prophets and us and are not pleasing God and are acting contrary[5] to all men.⌐

16 [These are they] who forbid us to speak with the Gentiles that they would have life, concluding their sins at all [other] times. But [m]wrath will come on them to the fullest extent.

---

[1] Same root: *loving, beloved*
[2] Eastern txt: v. 12 begins here
[3] Var (WSL): add 'and'
[4] Fig: ellipsis, add [suffered]
[5] Var (WSLM): 'contrary [things]', plural

ARAMAIC PESHITTA NEW TESTAMENT
I THESSALONIANS

Chapter 2

17 But ^{me}**we**, our brothers, have been orphans away from you for a short time,[1] in our presence, yet not in our heart. And we have been especially concerned to see your ^mfaces with great love.

18 And we wanted to come to you ^{pa}(I, Paul, once and again,[2] yet SATAN hindered me).

19 For what is our hope and our joy and the ^{an}crown of our glory,[3] except you, before our Lord Jesus at his coming?[4]

20 For ^{me}you are our praise and our joy.

Chapter 3

1 And because we could not hold out against ^e[knowing],[5] we were willing to remain in Athens[6] alone

2 and to send to you Timothy, our brother and a minister of God and our helper in the gospel of Christ, so that he would strengthen you and would inquire of you concerning your faith,

3 so that none of you should be disheartened by these trials, for you know that we are appointed to this.

4 For even while we were with you, we previously said to you that we were going to be tried,[7] ^{pa}as you know happened.⌐

5 Because of this also, I could not hold out against [it], until I sent to know of your faith, so that the Tempter would not tempt[8] you and our effort would be fruitless.

6 But now, from when Timothy came to us from among you and told us about your faith and about your love and that you have a good memory of us continually and [that] you are longing to see us, as also we ^e[long to see] you,

7 because of this, we were comforted by you, our brothers, concerning all our adversities and our trials, because of your faith.

8 And now we live, if you stand fast in our Lord.

---

[1] Lit: for the time of an hour

[2] Fig: idiom, *once and again* means numerous times, not just twice

[3] Fig: metonymy, *crown* means "reward"

[4] Fig: erotesis – question to ponder

[5] Fig: ellipsis, could add [knowing how it was with the saints] or [our inquiry]

[6] Var (P14470): alt sp. ܐܬܢܘܣ Var (WSL): alt sp. ܐܬܢܘܣ

[7] Same root: *tried, trials*, v. 3

[8] Same root: *Tempter, tempt*

Chapter 3

9 For what thanks are we able to repay on behalf of you to God concerning all the joy that we rejoice[1] because of you,

10 but that we petition God earnestly, [mr]by night and by day, that we may see your [m]faces and [that] we may make whole what your faith is lacking?[2]

11 [be]Now may God our Father and our Lord Jesus Christ direct our way to you.

12 And may he [he]multiply and increase your love to one another and to everyone, even as **we** love you.

13 And may he establish your hearts without blame in holiness before God our Father at the coming of our Lord Jesus Christ with all his holy [ones].

Chapter 4

1 Therefore, my brothers, we beg you and we entreat you in our Lord Jesus, that as you received from us how you ought to walk and to please God, that you would increasingly do more.

2 For you know those commandments we gave to you in our Lord Jesus.

3 For this is the will of God, your holiness, and that you should stay away from all fornication,

4 and [that] each one of you would know [how] to possess his [h]vessel in holiness and in honor

5 and not with the [as]passions of desire, as the rest of the Gentiles who do not know God.

6 And no one should dare to transgress against and oppress his brother in this matter, because our Lord is the avenger concerning all these [things], even as also we previously said and testified to you.

7 For God did not call you to uncleanness, but to holiness.

8 So then, he who rejects [this] does not reject man, but[3] God who gave his sanctified Spirit to you.

9 Now concerning love of the brothers, you do not need me to write to you, for **you** yourselves are taught of God to love one another.

10 So also, you are serving all the brothers who are in all of Macedonia. But I beg you, my brothers, that you should increase in [e][love]

---

[1] Same root: *joy, rejoice*

[2] Fig: erotesis – question to ponder

[3] Fig: ellipsis, add [rejects]

Chapter 4

11 ^Pand be diligent to be quiet and to be occupied with your business. And work with your hands as we commanded you,˥

12 so that you would walk in a proper manner toward outsiders and you should not be dependent on anyone.

13 But I want you to know, my brothers, that you should not have sorrow concerning those who are ^{eu}asleep, even as others who have no hope.

14 For if we believe that Jesus died and rose, so also God[1] will bring with him, by Jesus, those who are asleep.

15 Now this we say to you, by the word of our Lord, that we who remain at the coming of our Lord who are living will not overtake those who are asleep,

16 because our Lord, with a command ^Pand with the voice of the archangel and with the trumpet of God, will come down from heaven and the dead who are in Christ will rise up first.

17 And then we who remain who are living will be caught up with them as one in the clouds for the meeting[2] of our Lord in the air and so we will always be with our Lord. ˥

18 Therefore, comfort one another with these words.

Chapter 5

1 Now concerning the times and the seasons, my brothers, you do not need me to write to you.

2 For **you** know truly that the ^{sy}day of our Lord will so come ^sas a thief in the night,

3 when they say, "Peace and harmony." And then suddenly, destruction will come on them ^sas birth pains on a pregnant woman and they will not escape.

4 ^{al}But **you**, my brothers, are not in darkness so that ^{sy}day should overtake you ^sas a thief.

5 For all of ^{me}you are sons of light and sons of the day. And you are not sons of the night, nor sons of darkness.

6 We should not sleep, therefore, as others, but we should be watchful and be wise,

---

[1] Pal Lect: add 'will raise and'

[2] Culture: this *meeting* happens when an important person such as a king comes to a city, where the people go out to meet him and escort him back, Gaebelein, *The Expositor's Bible Commentary*, vol 11, p. 279, cf. Acts 28:15

Chapter 5

7   for those who are asleep are asleep in the night and those who are drunk are drunk[1] in the night.

8   But **we** who are sons of the day should be watchful in our mind and be clothed with the [h]breastplate of faith and of love and should put on the [h]helmet of the [an]hope of life,

9   because God has not appointed us to wrath, but to the possession of life in our Lord Jesus Christ,

10   who died for us, that whether we are awake or asleep, we will live together with him.

11   Because of this, comfort one another and build[2] one another up, as also you have done.

12   And we beg you, my brothers, recognize those who toil among you and stand before you in our Lord[3] and teach you,

13   that they may be regarded by you with abundant love. And because of their work, come to agreement with them.

14   Now we beg you,[4] my brothers, instruct the wrong-doers [P]and encourage the faint-hearted [ones] and bear the burden of weak [ones] and be long-suffering to everyone.

15   And beware that none of you should repay evil for evil, but always pursue[5] good [things] to one another and to everyone.

16   Rejoice at all times

17   and pray unceasingly.

18   And in everything give thanks, for this is the will of God in Jesus Christ for you.

19   Do not extinguish the Spirit.

20   Do not reject prophecies.[6]

21   Search everything and hold that which is good

22   and flee from every evil affair.

23   [be]Now may the God of peace make all of you holy completely [P]and may he keep your whole spirit and your life and your body without blame until the coming of our Lord Jesus Christ.

24   Faithful is he who called you who will do [this].

25   My brothers, pray for us.

---

[1] Repeat *asleep, drunk*
[2] Var (M): 'beseech'
[3] Var (WS): omit *in our Lord*
[4] Repeat *we beg you* from v. 12
[5] Lit: run after
[6] Var (WSL): *prophecy* (singular)

Chapter 5

26 Greet all our brothers with a holy kiss.

27 I charge you by our Lord that this letter should be read to all the holy brothers.

28 [be]The grace of our Lord Jesus Christ [be] with you. Amen.

ARAMAIC PESHITTA NEW TESTAMENT
II THESSALONIANS

Chapter 1

1 Paul and Silvanus and Timothy, to the church of the Thessalonians that is in God, our Father, and our Lord Jesus Christ:

2 Grace [be] with you and peace from God our Father and from our Lord Jesus Christ.

3 We are indebted to give thanks to God always for you, my brothers, as is right, because your faith grows abundantly and the love of each one of you increases for his associate,

4 so that **we** will also be boasting about you among the churches of God concerning your faith and concerning your endurance in all your persecution and your trials that you are enduring.[1]

5 [This is] the evidence of the upright judgment of God, that you should be worthy of his kingdom, for which you suffer.

6 And surely it is upright before God that he should repay oppression to your oppressors.[2]

7 And you who are oppressed, he will make alive with us at the appearance of our Lord Jesus Christ, who [e][will appear] from heaven with the [as]power of his messengers,

8 when he will execute vengeance with the [as]burning of fire on those who do not know God and on those who do not acknowledge the gospel of our Lord Jesus Christ.

9 For in the judgment, **they** will be repaid with eternal destruction[3] from the presence[4] of our Lord and from the [as]glory of his power,

10 after he comes to be glorified with his holy [ones] and shows his wonders in his faithful [ones], [pa]because our testimony about you will be believed[5] in that [sy]day.⌐

11 Because of this, we pray always for you that God will count you worthy of your calling and will fill you with all desire for good [things] and [for] the works of faith by power,

12 that in you the name of our Lord Jesus Christ will be glorified [and that] you also [e][will be glorified] in him, according to the grace of our God and our Lord Jesus Christ.

---

[1] Same root: *enduring, endurance*

[2] Same root: *oppression, oppressors, oppressed*, v. 7

[3] Fig: ellipsis, add [driven out]

[4] Lit: face

[5] Same root: *believed, faithful [ones]*

Chapter 2

1   Now we beg you, my brothers, concerning the coming of our Lord Jesus Christ and concerning our own gathering to him,

2   that you should not be quickly shaken in your minds, nor be troubled, not by word, nor by a spirit, nor[1] by a letter, as though from us, [saying] namely, "*Behold, the [sy]day of our Lord has arrived."

3   Will anyone deceive you in any way?[2] Because [e][it will not come] except a rebellion[3] should come first and the man of sin should be revealed, the son of destruction,[4]

4   who is an opponent of [e][God] and elevates himself above all that is called God and that is reverenced, so that he will even sit in the temple of God as God and will portray himself as though he is God.[5]

5   Do you not remember that while I was with you I told you these things?[6]

6   And now, you know what holds back [e][this day][7] that he should be revealed in its time.

7   For the mystery of wickedness has already begun to work, however, [e][it will work] by itself when that which now holds [it] back is taken away from the middle.

8   And then the unjust [one] will be revealed, whom our Lord Jesus will consume by the [h]breath of his mouth, and he will put a stop to him with the manifestation of his coming.

9   For the coming of that [one] is by[8] the working of SATAN, with all power [P]and signs and lying wonders

10   and with all the [as]deception of wickedness that is in the perishing [ones],⅂ because they did not receive the love of the truth by which they should have life.

11   Because of this, God will send them the [as]working of deception that they should believe the lie

12   and [that] all of them would be condemned, those who did not believe with truthfulness, but delighted in wickedness.

---

[1] Repeat *nor*

[2] Fig: erotesis, **lema** question, obvious answer "no"

[3] Var (WSLP): 'discipline' or 'instruction' ܡܪܕܘܬܐ

[4] Or "the destructive [one]"

[5] Repeat *God*

[6] Fig: erotesis, obvious answer "yes"

[7] Or [the man of sin]

[8] Var (WS): omit *by*

Chapter 2

13 But **we** are indebted to give thanks to God always for you,[1] our brothers, beloved of our Lord, because God chose you from the beginning to life by the holiness of the Spirit and by the [an]faith of the truth.

14 For to these [things] he[2] called you by our preaching to be a glory for our Lord Jesus Christ.

15 Therefore, my brothers, stand fast and hold firmly to the commandments that you learned, whether by word or by our letter.

16 [be]Now our Lord Jesus Christ and God our Father, who loved us and gave us everlasting comfort and good hope by his grace,

17 comfort your hearts and establish [you] in every word and in every good work.

Chapter 3

1 For now, our brothers, pray for us that the [pe]word of our Lord may run [e][its course] and be glorified in every place as [it is] with you

2 and that we may be delivered from [he]evil and dishonest men, for not everyone has faith.

3 But the LORD is faithful,[3] who will keep you and rescue you from the Evil [one].

4 And we are confident about you in our Lord that the things that we have commanded you, you have done [and] also, you will do.

5 And may our Lord direct your hearts to the love of God and to the endurance of Christ.

6 And we command you, my brothers, in the name of our Lord Jesus Christ, to stay away from every brother who walks very evilly and not according to the commandments that he received from us.

7 For **you** know how you ought to be imitators of us, for we did not walk very evilly [4]among you.

8 But rather, we ate bread without an expense for any of you, but with toil and with labor, [mr]by night and by day, we worked, so that we would not burden any of you,

9 not because we are without authority, but that we would give you an example, in ourselves so that you would imitate us.

---

[1] Repeat *we are indebted...you* from 1:3

[2] Var (WS): add 'God'

[3] Same root: *faithful, faith*, v. 2

[4] Repeat *very evilly* from v. 6, also v. 11

Chapter 3

10 For even when we were with you, we commanded you this, that everyone who does not want to work should also not[1] eat.

11 For we hear that there are men among you who walk very evilly and are not doing anything except unprofitable [things].

12 Now to those we command, and we beg them by our Lord Jesus Christ, that they should work in quietness and eat their [own] bread.

13 Now **you**, my brothers, should not be weary of doing what is good.

14 And if anyone does not obey our words [pa](these that are in this letter), he should be separated from you. And do not associate with him so that he may be ashamed.

15 Yet do not consider him as an enemy, but reprove him as a brother.

16 [be]And the Lord of peace give you peace always in everything. Our Lord [be] with all of you.

17 The salutation [is] in my handwriting. I, Paul wrote [it], which is the sign that is in all my letters. So I write.

18 [be]The grace of our Lord Jesus Christ [be] with all of you. Amen.

---

[1] Fig: ellipsis, add [want to]

490

ARAMAIC PESHITTA NEW TESTAMENT
I TIMOTHY

Chapter 1

1   Paul, an apostle of Jesus Christ by the commandment of God, our Life-giver, and of Christ Jesus our hope,

2   to Timothy, a true son in the faith: Grace and mercy and peace from God our Father and Christ Jesus our Lord.

3   I begged you, when I went to Macedonia, to remain in Ephesus and to charge each one that they should not teach different doctrines[1]

4   and [that] they should not pay attention to fables and to accounts of endless[2] genealogies. These [things] increasingly bring about controversies and not edification in the [an]faith of God.

5   But the end of the commandment is love that is from a pure heart [P]and from a good conscience and from the true faith.⌐

6   And from these [things], some have erred and have turned aside to empty words,

7   in that they seek to be teachers of the law, not understanding what they speak, nor about which they dispute.

8   But we know that the law[3] is good if a man conducts himself in it according to it lawfully,

9   knowing that the law was not established for the upright [ones], but for the wicked [P]and for the rebellious and for the ungodly and for the sinners and for the deceitful and for those who are not pure and for those who wound their fathers and for those who wound[4] their mothers and for murderers

10   and for fornicators and for homosexuals and for kidnappers of free men and for liars and transgressors concerning oaths and for everything that is contrary to sound teaching

11   of the [an]gospel of the glory of the blessed God, [with] which I am entrusted.⌐

12   And I thank him who strengthened me, our Lord Jesus Christ, who counted me a faithful[one] and ordained me to his service,

13   me who previously was a reviler [P]and a persecutor and a scorner,⌐ but I received mercy, because when I was ignorant, I acted without faith.

14   Now the grace of our Lord and the faith and love that are in Jesus Christ abounded in me.

---

[1] Same root: *teach, doctrines*
[2] Lit: that have no end, repeat *end,* v. 5
[3] Repeat forms of *law*, vs. 7-9
[4] Repeat *for those who wound*

Chapter 1

15   The word is faithful[1] and it is worthy to receive, that Jesus Christ came into the world to give life to sinners, [mi]of whom I am chief.

16   But because of this, he had mercy on me, that in me first, Jesus Christ would display all his long-suffering as an example to those who were going to believe in him to eternal life.

17   [be]And to the King of the ages, to him who is [he]incorruptible and invisible, who is one God, [be] [he]honor and glory, forever and ever. Amen.

18   This commandment I am entrusting to you, my son, Timothy, according to the first prophecies that were about you, that you should work this good work[2]

19   in faith and in a good conscience. For those, who have rejected this, are destitute of faith,

20   like Hymenaeus and Alexander, those whom I have delivered to SATAN to be disciplined,[3] so that they would not be blaspheming.

Chapter 2

1   I beg you, therefore, that before everything you should offer petition to God [P]and prayer and intercession and thanksgiving on behalf of all men,┐

2   on behalf of[4] kings and princes, that we may live a [he]peaceful and restful life with all reverence for God and purity,

3   for this is good and acceptable before God, our Life-giver,

4   who wants all men to have life and to turn to the [an]knowledge of the truth.

5   For God is one and the mediator of God and of men is one,[5] the man, Jesus Christ,

6   who gave himself [as] a ransom for everyone, a witness that arrived in its time,

7   [of] which I was ordained its preacher and its apostle. [pa]I speak [with] truthfulness and I do not lie,┐ for I became a teacher of the Gentiles in the [an]faith of the truth.

---

[1] Repeat *the word is faithful*, throughout Timothy and Titus, marks sections, 3:1, 4:9, 2Ti 2:11, Tit 3:8

[2] Same root: *work, work*

[3] Var (WS): omit *to be disciplined*

[4] Repeat *on behalf of* from v. 1; same root: *live, life*

[5] Repeat *one*

ARAMAIC PESHITTA NEW TESTAMENT
I TIMOTHY

Chapter 2

8 Therefore, I want men to pray in every place, lifting up their hands purely, without anger and without[1] arguments.

9 So also, women e[should dress] in a moderate style of clothing. Their adornment should be with modesty and with moderation,[2] not with braiding [of the hair] or with gold or with pearls or with[3] beautiful outer garments,

10 but with good works, as it is proper for women who profess reverence for God.

11 A wife should learn in quietness with all submission,

12 for I do not allow a wife to teach nor to be presumptuous[4] over the husband, but she should be at peace.

13 For Adam was formed first and then Eve,

14 and Adam did not err, but the woman erred[5] and transgressed the commandment.

15 But she has life by way of her children, if they remain in faith Pand in love and in holiness and in sobriety.⌐

Chapter 3

1 The word is faithful. For if a man desires the office of an elder, he desires good works.[6]

2 Now it is proper for an elder to be one in whom no blemish is found Pand is the husband of one woman, who [is] of a watchful mind and sober and orderly and loving of strangers and able to teach

3 and does not transgress concerning wine and is not swift to strike [with] his hand.⌐ But he should be humble Pand not quarrelsome and not loving of money

4 and should lead his mhouse well and keep his children in submission with all purity.⌐

5 For if he does not know how to lead his own mhouse well, how is he able to lead the church of God?[7]

6 And his discipleship should not be recent, so that he should not be Prlifted up and fall into the judgment of SATAN.

---

[1] Repeat *without*

[2] Same root: *moderate, moderation*

[3] Repeat *or with*

[4] Lit: teach against

[5] Repeat forms of *erred*

[6] Var (M): 'good work,' Var (WSL): 'beautiful work'

[7] Fig: erotesis – question to ponder

493

Chapter 3

7 And also he ought to have a good testimony from those without, so that he should not fall into reproach and into the ^hsnares[1] of SATAN.

8 And so also, ministers should be pure ^Pand should not be double-tongued and should not be inclined to much wine and should not[2] love corrupt profits,¬

9 but they should adhere to the mystery of the faith with a pure conscience.

10 And these should be proven first and then they may serve, when they are without blame.

11 So also, the women should be sober ^Pand should be watchful in their minds and should be faithful in everything and should not be slanderers.¬

12 Ministers should be he who has one wife ^Pand leads his children and his ^mhouse well.¬

13 For those who have ministered well obtain recognition for themselves and much boldness in the faith of Jesus Christ.

14 These [things] I am writing to you, ^{pa}although I am hoping to come to you soon,

15 and even if I should delay,¬ so that you may know how you ought to behave in the house of God, ^{he}which is the church of the living God. The ^{he}pillar and foundation of truth

16 and truly great is this ^{an}mystery of uprightness, which was revealed in the flesh ^Pand was justified spiritually and was seen by angels and was preached among the Gentiles and was believed in the world and was taken up in glory.¬

Chapter 4

1 Now the Spirit plainly says that in the last times some will depart from the faith ^Pand will follow deceiving spirits and doctrines[3] of demons,

2 those who deceive by false appearance and are speaking a lie and are seared in their conscience

3 and forbid to marry. And they keep away from foods,¬ which God created for use and for thanksgiving for those who believe and know the truth,

---

[1] Var (WSLP): *snare* (singular)
[2] Repeat *and should not*; repeat *and should be*, v. 11
[3] Var (WSL): *doctrine* (singular)

Chapter 4

4   because everything that was created by God is good and there is not anything that should be rejected, if it is received with thanksgiving,

5   for it is made holy by the word of God and by prayer.

6   If you teach these [things] to your brothers, you will be a good minister of Jesus Christ, as you grow up in the words of faith and in the good teaching that you were taught.[1]

7   Now withdraw from the foolish tales of old [women] and train yourself in uprightness.

8   For the training[2] of the body profits a little [time], but uprightness profits in everything and has the promise of the life of this time and of the future.

9   The word is faithful and it is worthy to receive,

10   for because of this, we labor and suffer blame, because we trust in the living God, who is the Life-giver of all men, especially of the believers.

11   These [things] teach and command.

12   And no one should despise your youth, but be an example to the believers in word and in conduct and in love and in faith and in[3] purity.

13   Until I come, be diligent in reading Pand in petition and in teaching.ᒣ

14   And do not despise the gift that you have that was given to you by prophecy and by the laying on of the hand of the eldership.

15   Meditate on these [things] and be in them, that it may be known to everyone that you are going forward.

16   And watch yourself and your teaching and persevere in them.[4] For as you do these [things], you will give life to yourself and to those who hear you.

Chapter 5

1   You should not reprove an elder, but should persuade him ˢas a father and those who are younger ˢas your brothers

2   and the elder women ˢas mothers and those who are younger ˢas your sisters with all purity.

3   Honor widows, who are truly widows.[5]

---

[1] Same root: *teaching, taught*
[2] Same root: *training, train,* v. 7
[3] Repeat *and in,* beginning sound, also v. 13
[4] Repeat *in them* from v. 15, meaning, "practice these things"
[5] Repeat *widows, truly,* vs. 3-16

Chapter 5

4   And if there is a widow who has children or grandchildren, they should first learn that they should act rightly in their households and they should repay the obligations to their parents, for this is acceptable before God.

5   Now she who truly is a widow and alone, her trust is in God and she is faithful in prayers and in petitions ᵐʳby night and by day.

6   But she who serves luxury is dead while alive.

7   Command them these [things], so that they may be without blame.

8   For if [there is] a man who does not take care of those who are his own and especially those who are [of] the household of faith, this [one] has denied the faith and is more evil than those who do not believe.

9   Therefore, you should choose a widow ᵉ[to honor] who is not less than sixty years [old], who was [married] to one man

10   and has a reputation of good works, whether she brought up children or received strangers or washed the feet of holy [ones] or relieved troubled [ones] or¹ walked in every good work.

11   But from those widows who are young, excuse yourself, for they may be wanton against Christ and seek to have husbands.

12   And their judgment is established, because they have set aside their former faith.

13   And they also learn laziness while circulating among the houses, and not only laziness, but also to talk too much and to distract themselves with fruitless [things] and to speak what is not proper.

14   Therefore, I want those who are young to marry ᴾand to bear children and to direct their homes and not give to the enemy even one cause for reproach.⌐

15   For at this time some have begun to turn aside after SATAN.

16   If any believing [man] or believing [woman] have widows, they should support them and they should not be a burden on the church, so that there may be a sufficiency for those who are truly widows.

17   Those elders who conduct themselves well should be esteemed worthy of double honor,² especially those who work hard in the word and in teaching,

18   for the scripture says: **YOU SHOULD NOT MUZZLE THE OX IN THE THRESHING** and **THE LABORER IS WORTHY OF HIS WAGE.**

---

¹ Repeat *or*

² Culture: *double honor* means the highest or most liberal honor, double denoting full compensation, Bullinger, *Figures of Speech*, p. 586

Chapter 5

19   Do not accept an accusation against an elder, except by the mouth of two or three witnesses.

20   Reprove those who sin before everyone, so that the rest of the people would also have respect.

21   I charge you before God and our Lord Jesus Christ and his chosen messengers that you observe these [things]. And your mind should not be preoccupied with anything and do not do anything with respect of persons.

22   Do not lay a hand quickly on anyone and do not participate in strange sins. Guard yourself with purity.

23   And from now on, do not drink water, but drink a little wine because of your stomach and because of your continuing infirmities.

24   There are men whose sins are well-known and precede them to the house of judgment and there are ᵉ[some] whose ᵉ[sins][1] follow after them.

25   So also, good works[2] are well-known and those that are otherwise are not able to be hidden.

Chapter 6

1   Those who are under the ʰyoke of bondage should hold their masters in all honor, so that the name of God and his teaching will not be reviled.

2   And those who have faithful masters should not despise them, because they are their brothers. But rather, they should especially minister to them, because they are believers and beloved, in whose service they are refreshed. These [things] teach and require from them.

3   But if there is a man who teaches another doctrine and does not apply himself to the sound words of our Lord Jesus Christ and to the doctrine[3] of reverence for God,

4   this [one] is proud, knowing nothing. But [he is] sick with controversy and with questioning about words, from which come envy ᴾand contention and reviling and the setting of evil in the mind[4]

5   and the strife of men,˥ those whose mind is corrupted and [who] are deprived of truthfulness. And they suppose that reverence for God is gain. But you, avoid these [things],

---

[1] Fig: ellipsis, or [the knowledge of their sins]
[2] Var (WS): 'men'
[3] Same root: *doctrine, teaches*
[4] Or, "premeditation of evil"

Chapter 6

6   for our own gain[1] is great in the [an]use of our sufficiency, because it is reverence for God.

7   For we did not bring anything into the world and it is evident that we also cannot carry [anything] out of it.

8   Because of this, food and clothing are sufficient for us.

9   But those who want to grow rich fall into temptations [P]and into snares and into many pleasures, which are foolish and are hurtful and are drowning men in corruption and loss.⌐

10   For the [h]root of all evil [things] is the love of money. And there are some who have longed for it and have erred from the faith and have brought to themselves many miseries.

11   But you, [i]oh man of God, flee from these [things] [P]and pursue after justification and after uprightness and after faith and after love and after patience and after[2] meekness.

12   And struggle in the good contest of faith and obtain eternal life,⌐ to which you were called and confessed a good confession[3] before many witnesses.

13   I am charging you before God, who gives life to all, and Jesus Christ, who testified a good testimony[4] before Pontius Pilate,

14   that you keep the commandment without spot and without blemish until the appearance of our Lord Jesus Christ,

15   [be]whom God is going to show in its time, the blessed and only powerful [one], King of kings and Lord of lords,[5]

16   who alone is incorruptible and lives in light, to whom no one is able to draw near and no one from men has seen, nor is even able to see, to whom [be] [he]honor and authority, forever and ever. Amen.

17   Command the rich of this world that they should not be elevated in their minds and that they should not trust in wealth that is not trustworthy, but rather in the living God, who gave us everything richly[6] for our rest.

---

[1] Repeat from v. 5

[2] Repeat *and after*

[3] Same root: *confessed, confession*

[4] Same root: *testified, testimony*

[5] Repeat *kings, lords,* meaning that Jesus is "the greatest King and the greatest Lord." A noun is repeated in the genitive plural to express the superlative degree, Bullinger, *Figures of Speech*, p. 243.

[6] Same root: *richly, rich, wealth* and *trust, trustworthy*

Chapter 6

18   And ᵉ[command that] they should do good works ᴾand should increase in pleasing occupations and should be ready to give and to fellowship,

19   and they should lay up for themselves a good foundation for that which is to come, that they may obtain true life.⌐

20   ⁱOh Timothy, watch over what was entrusted to you and flee from fruitless reports and from the contrary principles of false knowledge,

21   for those who profess[1] it have erred from the faith. ᵇᵉGrace [be] with you. Amen.

---

[1] Same root: *profess, knowledge,* v. 20

ARAMAIC PESHITTA NEW TESTAMENT
II TIMOTHY

Chapter 1

1   Paul, an apostle of Jesus Christ, by the will of God and by the promise of life that is in Jesus Christ,

2   to Timothy, a beloved son: Grace and mercy and peace from God the Father and from our Lord Jesus Christ.

3   I give thanks to God, whom I serve from my fathers with a pure conscience, that I continually remember you in my prayers ^{mr}by night and by day.

4   And I long to see you and I recall your tears, that I may be filled with joy

5   by the remembrance I have about your steadfast faith that lived first in your grandmother, Lois, and in your mother, Eunice, and I am persuaded is also in you.

6   Because of this, I remind you to stir up the gift of God that you have by ^{pr}the laying on of my hand.

7   For God has not given us a spirit of fear, but ^e[a Spirit] of power and of love and of instruction.

8   Therefore, do not be ashamed about the testimony of our Lord, nor about me, his prisoner, but endure evil [things] connected with the gospel by the power of God,

9   who gave us life and called us with a holy calling,[1] not according to our works, but according to his will and his grace that was given to us by Jesus Christ from before the ^{sy}time of the ages

10   and now has been revealed by the appearance of our Life-giver, Jesus Christ, who made death of no effect and made ^{he}life and incorruptibility evident by the gospel,

11   of which **I** was appointed a preacher and an apostle and a teacher of the Gentiles.

12   Because of this, I endure these [things] and I am not ashamed, for I know in whom I have believed and I am persuaded that he is able by his hands to keep my ^hdeposit for me until that ^{sy}day.

13   You should continue the pattern of sound words, which you heard from me in the faith and in the love that is in Jesus Christ.

14   Keep the good ^hdeposit by the Holy Spirit that lives in us.

15   This you know, that all those who were in Asia have turned from me, among whom are Phygellus and Hermogenes.

16   May our Lord give mercies to the house of Onesiphorus, who refreshed me many times and was not ashamed of the chains of my bonds.

---

[1] Same root: *called, calling*

500

ARAMAIC PESHITTA NEW TESTAMENT
II TIMOTHY

Chapter 1

17   But also, when he came to Rome, he searched for me with diligence and found me.

18   May our Lord allow him to find mercies with our Lord in that ^{sy}day. And you know well how he ministered to me in Ephesus.

Chapter 2

1   You, therefore, my son, be strong in the grace which is in Jesus Christ.

2   And those [things] that you have heard from me by way of many witnesses, these entrust to faithful men, who are able by their ^mhands to teach others also.

3   ^{al}And endure evil [things] as a good worker of Jesus Christ.

4   No man works and is entangled with the matters of the world, so that he may please the one who chose him.

5   And if a man competes, he is not crowned, if he does not compete according to the rule.

6   The husbandman who labors ought to be the first fed from his fruits.⌐

7   Consider closely what I say. May our Lord give you wisdom in everything.

8   Remember Jesus Christ, who rose from the dead who is from the ^mseed of David, according to my gospel,

9   in which I am suffering evil [things], even unto ^mbonds, as though [I was] an evil-doer. But the word of God is not bound.[1]

10   Because of this, I endure everything on account of the chosen [ones], so that **they** may also find life that is[2] in Jesus Christ, with glory that is forever.[3]

11   The word is faithful. For if we died with him, we will also live with him.

12   And if we endure, we will also reign with him. But if we deny him, **he** will also deny us.

13   And if we do not believe in him, **he** continues in his faithfulness, for he is not able to deny himself.

14   Remind them of these [things] and give witness before our Lord, that they should not be disputing about words without profit to the overthrow of those who listen to them.

---

[1] Same root: *bonds, bound* and *evil, evil-doer*
[2] Var (WSL): omit *that is*
[3] Pal Lect: 'with his glory that is from heaven'

501

Chapter 2

15   And you should be diligent to present yourself maturely before God, a worker without shame, who is rightly proclaiming the [an]word of truth.

16   And avoid empty words that have no usefulness in them, for they add more and more to the irreverence of those who are occupied with them.

17   And their word, [s]as gangrene, has spread to many. And one of these is Hymenaeus and another, Philetus,

18   who have erred from the truth, saying that the resurrection of the dead has happened. And they are turning away the faith of some.

19   But the [h]foundation of God stands steadfast and it has this [m]seal: AND THE LORD KNOWS THOSE WHO ARE HIS OWN. And EVERYONE WHO CALLS ON THE NAME OF THE LORD SHOULD WITHDRAW FROM WICKEDNESS.

20   [al]Now in a great house, there are not only vessels of gold or of silver, but there are [e][vessels] also of wood and of pottery, some for honor and some for dishonor.

21   Therefore, if a man will cleanse himself from these [things], [me]he will be a pure vessel for honor that is profitable for the use of his Lord and prepared for every good work.⌐

22   Flee from all the desires of youth and pursue uprightness [P]and faith and love and peace,⌐ with those who call on our Lord with a pure heart.

23   Avoid foolish controversies [with] those who are without instruction, for you know that they generate disputes.

24   Now a servant of our Lord should not dispute,[1] but he should be meek to everyone and adept at teaching and long-suffering,

25   so that he may guide those who argue against him with meekness, so that God will give them repentance and they will know the truth

26   and will recall [e][the truth] to themselves and will break away from the [h]snare of SATAN, by whom they were caught for his desire.

Chapter 3

1   But know this, that in the last days difficult times will come.

2   And men will be lovers of themselves and [a]lovers of money, boastful, proud, revilers, those who are not obedient to their parents, ungrateful, wicked,

3   slanderers, slaves to desire, cruel, haters of good [things],

4   traitors, unrestrained, haughty, attached to desires, more than the love of God,

---

[1] Same root: *dispute, disputes,* v. 23

Chapter 3

5   those who have the form of reverence for God, yet are far removed from his power.¬ [1] Push away from you those who are so.

6   For of them are they who [h]creep from house to house and captivate women who are steeped in sins and are led away by various desires,

7   who are always learning and are never able to come to the knowledge of the truth.

8   But [s]as Jannes and Jambres stood against Moses, so they are also standing against the truth, one whose mind is corrupt and [who] rejects the faith.

9   But they will not go in front of them, for their folly is made known to everyone, as also theirs was made known.

10   But **you** have followed after my teaching and after my ways and after my will and after my faith and after my long-suffering and after my love and after my[2] patience

11   and after my persecution and after my sufferings. And you know those [things] I endured in Antioch [P]and in Iconium and in Lystra,¬ what persecution I endured. And from all of these my Lord delivered me.

12   Now all those who desire to live in reverence for God in Jesus Christ will be persecuted.

13   But [he]evil and deceiving men will add to their evil, while deceiving and being deceived.[3]

14   Now **you** remain in those [things] that you learned and were assured of, for you know from whom you[4] learned [them],

15   and that from your youth you were taught the holy writings, which are able to make you wise for life by the faith of [5] Jesus Christ.

16   Every writing that was written by the Spirit is profitable for teaching [P]and for reproof and for correction and for instruction that is about uprightness,¬

17   so that the man of God may be mature and complete for every good work.

Chapter 4

1   I charge you before God and our Lord Jesus Christ, who is ready to judge the dead and the living at the appearing of his kingdom.

---

[1] Var (WSL): add 'of God'
[2] Repeat *and after*, also v. 11
[3] Repeat forms of *deceiving*
[4] Repeat *you*, also v. 15
[5] Var (WSLM): 'that is in'

Chapter 4

2   Proclaim the word and stand with diligence [mr]in season and out of season. Admonish and reprove with all long-suffering and teaching,

3   for the time will come when they will not hear sound teaching, but according to their desires, they will multiply teachers to themselves in the [h]itching of their hearing

4   and they will turn their [m]ear[s] away from the truth and they will turn aside to fables.

5   But you, be vigilant in everything and endure evil [things] and do the work of an evangelist and complete your ministry.

6   For from now on, I am being poured out [e][as a drink offering] and the time that I should [eu]depart is coming.

7   [al]I have fought a good contest and I have completed my course and I have kept my faith.

8   And now a [m]crown of uprightness is reserved for me that my Lord, who is the upright judge, will reward me in that [sy]day, and not only me, but also those who love his appearing.⌐

9   Be diligent to come to me quickly.

10   For Demas has left me and loved this world and gone to Thessalonica, Crescens[1] to Galatia and Titus to Dalmatia.

11   Only Luke is with me. Take Mark and bring him with you, for he is profitable to me for the ministry.

12   And I have sent Tychicus to Ephesus.

13   And when you come, bring the book-carrier that I left in Troas with Carpus and the books, especially the rolls of parchments.

14   Alexander, the silversmith, showed me many evil [things]. Our Lord will reward him according to his works.

15   Now also, **you** beware of him, for he is very [h]puffed up against our words.

16   In my first defense, no man was with me, but all of them left me. Do not count this to them.

17   But my Lord stood by me and strengthened me, that by me, the preaching would be completed and all the Gentiles would hear that I was rescued from the [m]mouth of the lion.

18   And my Lord will rescue me from every evil work and will give me life in his kingdom that is in heaven. [be]To him [be] glory, forever and ever. Amen.

19   Greet Priscilla and Aquila and the house of Onesiphorus.

---

[1] Var (WSLM): 'Crispus'

Chapter 4

20   Erastus stayed in Corinth and I left Trophimus sick in the city of Miletus.

21   Be diligent to come before winter. Eubulus greets you ᴾand Pudens and Linus and Claudia and all the brothers.┐

22   ᵇᵉOur Lord Jesus Christ [be] with your spirit. Grace [be] with you. Amen.

ARAMAIC PESHITTA NEW TESTAMENT
TITUS

Chapter 1

1   Paul, a servant of God and an apostle of Jesus Christ, according to the faith of the chosen [ones] of God and the knowledge of the truth that is by reverence for God,

2   concerning the hope of eternal life, which the true God promised before the times of the age

3   and manifested his word in its time by way of our preaching, [with] which I was entrusted by the commandment of God our Life-giver,

4   to Titus, a true son in the common faith: Grace and peace from God the Father and from our Lord Jesus Christ, our Life-giver.

5   Because of this, I had left you in Crete, that you would set in order those [things] that were lacking and [that] you would ordain elders in every city as I commanded you.

6   [He should be] one who is without blame and is the husband of one wife and has faithful children, who are not speaking evil and are not unruly with intemperance.

7   For it is required that an elder should be without blame as a steward of God and should not be led by his own mind[1] and should not be full of rage and should not be a transgressor concerning wine and should not be swift to strike [with] his hand and should not be[2] a lover of corrupt profits.

8   But he should be a lover of strangers and he should be a lover of good [things] and he should be sober[3] and he should be upright and he should be pure and keeping himself from passions

9   and being diligent concerning the teaching of the ^{an}word of faith, so that he may also be able to encourage by his sound teaching and to reprove those who are quarrelsome.

10   For there are many who are not submissive and their words are empty and they are deceiving the minds of men, especially those who are from the ^mcircumcision.

11   Their ^mmouth[s] ought to be shut closely, for they are corrupting many ^mfamilies[4] and are teaching what is not right because of corrupt profits.

---

[1] Or "self-willed"

[2] Repeat *and should not be*, repeat *and should be*, v. 8

[3] Var (M): omit *and he should be sober*

[4] Lit: houses

Chapter 1

12   One of them, their own prophet, said, "^{me}The Cretans are always liars, evil beasts and idle gluttons,"[1]

13   and this testimony is truthful. Because of this, reprove them sharply that they should be sound in the faith

14   and [that] they should not yield to the fables of the Judeans and the commandments of men who hate the truth.

15   For everything is pure to the pure, but those who are corrupted and unbelieving do not have what is pure, but their mind is corrupted and their conscience.[2]

16   And they profess to know God, but by their works they deny him and they are detestable ^Pand disobedient[3] and rejecters of every good work.⌐

Chapter 2

1   But you, speak what is suitable to sound teaching.

2   ^PAnd teach[4] the elders that they should be watchful in their minds and should be sober and should be pure and should be[5] sound in faith and in love and in patience.

3   And also [teach] the elder women likewise that they should be in behavior as is suitable for reverence to God and should not be slanderers and should not be enslaved to much wine and [that] they should be teachers of good [things]

4   and moderating[6] those who are younger [women], so that they love their husbands and their children

5   and they should be ^{he}moderate and holy and should be good caretakers of their houses and should be subject to their husbands, so that no one will profane the word of God.

6   And likewise, request those who are young [men] to be sober.⌐

7   Now in everything, show yourself as an example in all good works. And in your teaching, you should have sound speech

---

[1] Fig: could be a proverb; Jerome said that this was a quote by Epiminedes, Bullinger, *Figures of Speech*, p. 801.

[2] Fig: ellipsis, add [is corrupted also]; repeat *pure, corrupted,* vs. 11-15

[3] Or "not persuadable"

[4] Same root: *teach, teaching*, v. 1

[5] Repeat *and should be*, repeat *and should not be*, v. 3

[6] Same root: *moderating, moderate*, vs. 5, 8

Chapter 2

8   that is moderate and not corrupt. And [let] no one despise it, so that he who stands against us will be ashamed, not being able to say anything hateful against us.

9   Servants should serve[1] their masters in everything [P]and should be pleasing and not be disputing

10   and not stealing.┐ But they should demonstrate their integrity in everything, so that in everything they may adorn the teaching of God, our Life-giver.

11   For the grace of God, the Life-giver of all, is revealed to all men

12   and instructs us to deny irreverence and the [an]passions of the world and to live in this world with moderation [P]and with justice and with reverence for God,┐

13   looking for the blessed hope and for the [an]manifestation of the glory of the great God and our Life-giver, Jesus Christ,

14   who gave himself for us, so that he could deliver us from all wickedness and would purify for himself a new people who are zealous in good works.

15   Speak these [things] and entreat and reprove with all authority and let no one despise you.[2]

Chapter 3

1   And remind them that they should obey [P]and should be subject to rulers and to authorities and that they should be prepared for every good work

2   and they should not revile anyone and should not be contentious, but rather they should be humble and they should demonstrate their kindness to all men in everything.┐

3   For [ac]we were also previously without sense [P]and we were disobedient and we were erring and we were serving various passions and we were occupied with wickedness and with envy and we were being hateful.┐ [3] We were even hating one another.

4   But when the kindness and compassion of God, our Life-giver, was revealed,

---

[1] Same root: *servants, serve*

[2] Repeat *no one despise you* from v. 8

[3] Repeat endings of verbs (passive participles), repeat *and with*

Chapter 3

5   not by works of justification that we did, but by his own mercies, he gave us life by the washing of the birth from above and[1] by the renewing of the Holy Spirit,

6   which he ᶜpoured out on us abundantly by way of Jesus Christ, our Life-giver,

7   that we would be justified by his grace and would be heirs in the hope of eternal life.

8   The word is faithful. And these [things] I want you also to affirm to them, so that those who have believed in God may be diligent to perform good works. These [things] are good and profitable for men.

9   But withdraw from foolish questioning[2] and from accounts of genealogies and from contentions and from[3] disputes of the scribes. For there is no profit in them and they are fruitless.

10   Withdraw from a heretical man after you have instructed him once and again.

11   And know that he who is so is perverse and sinful and he has condemned himself.

12   When I send to you Artemas or Tychicus, be diligent to come to me at Nicopolis, for I have decided to winter there.

13   But concerning Zenas, the scribe, and concerning Apollos, be diligent to escort them well ᵉ[on their journey], so that they should lack nothing.

14   And those who are our own should also learn to perform good works in matters that are pressing, so that they will not be without ᵐfruit.

15   All those who are with me greet you. Greet all those who love us in the faith. ᵇᵉGrace [be] with all of you. Amen.

---

[1] Var (WS): omit *and*

[2] Var (WL): *questionings* (plural)

[3] Repeat *and from*; repeat *withdraw* at end of vs. 9, 10

ARAMAIC PESHITTA NEW TESTAMENT
PHILEMON

1   Paul, the prisoner of Jesus Christ, and Timothy, a brother, to Philemon, beloved and a worker who is with us,

2   and to our beloved Apphia, and to Archippus, a worker who is with us, and to the church that is in your house:

3   Grace [be] with you and peace from God our Father and from our Lord Jesus Christ.

4   I thank my God always and I remember you in my prayers,

5   since I heard of your faith and the love that you have toward our Lord Jesus and toward all the holy [ones],

6   that the fellowship of your faith may yield [m]fruit in works and in the knowledge of all the good [things] that you have in Jesus Christ.

7   For we have great joy and comfort, because by your love the [m]bowels of the holy [ones] are refreshed.

8   Because of this, I have great boldness in Christ to command you [e][to do] those [things] which are just.

9   But because of love, I earnestly beg[1] you, **I**, Paul, who am old, as you know, and now also am a prisoner of Jesus Christ.

10   And I am begging you concerning my son, whom I have born in my bonds, Onesimus,

11   in whom at one time you had no profit, but now is very profitable[2] both to you and also to me.

12   And I have sent him to you. So now,[3] receive him as one born by me.

13   For I wanted to keep him with me that he should minister to me instead of you during [my] [m]bonds for the gospel.

14   But I did not want to do anything without your counsel, so that your goodness would not be with compulsion, but by your [e][free] will.

15   Now perhaps, even because of this, he went away for a time, so that you may keep him forever,

16   from now on, not as a servant, but [as] more than a servant, my own beloved brother, how much more your own, both in the [sy]flesh and in our Lord.[4]

17   Therefore, if you are a partner with me, receive him as [e][you would] me.[5]

---

[1] Fig: polyptoton, lit: begging, I beg you

[2] Same root: *profitable, profit*

[3] Lit: now you, as one born by me, so receive him

[4] Fig: erotesis, **kema** question, answer in the affirmative

[5] Lit: as my own [self]

18   And if he has harmed you or he owes [you] anything, count this to me.

19   **I**, Paul, have written with my hands [that] **I** will repay. I will not say to you that you also owe your life to me.

20   Yes, my brother, **I** [want] to be refreshed by you in our Lord. Refresh[1] my ᵐbowels in Christ.

21   Because I am confident that you will obey me, I have written to you and I know that you will do more than I say.

22   And one ᵉ[more thing] also, prepare for me a guest house, for I hope that by your prayers I will be given to you.

23   Epaphras, a captive who is with me in Jesus Christ, greets you,

24   ᵖand Mark and Aristarchus and Demas and Luke, my helpers.┐

25   ᵇᵉThe grace of our Lord Jesus Christ [be] with your spirit. Amen.

---

[1] Repeat forms of *refreshed*

ARAMAIC PESHITTA NEW TESTAMENT
HEBREWS

Chapter 1

1   In all ways and in all[1] forms, God spoke previously with our fathers by the prophets.

2   And in these last days, he has spoken to us by his Son, whom he appointed heir of everything and by whom he made the ages,

3   who is the [an]radiance of his glory and the [an]image of his being[2] and almighty by the power of his word. And in his person, he accomplished the cleansing of our[3] sins and sat down at the right hand of [h]majesty in the high places.

4   And this [one] is greater than the angels in every way, even as the name that he inherited is greater than theirs.

5   For to which of the angels did God ever say: YOU ARE MY SON, THIS DAY I HAVE FATHERED YOU, and again, I WILL BE A FATHER TO HIM AND HE WILL BE A SON TO ME?

6   And again, when he brought the firstborn into the world, he said: LET ALL THE ANGELS OF GOD WORSHIP HIM.

7   But about the angels he spoke so: HE MADE HIS ANGELS A WIND AND HIS MINISTERS A [h]FLAMING FIRE.

8   But concerning the Son he said: YOUR THRONE, GOD, [IS] FOREVER.[4] AN UPRIGHT SCEPTER [IS] THE SCEPTER OF YOUR KINGDOM.

9   YOU LOVE UPRIGHTNESS AND HATE WICKEDNESS. BECAUSE OF THIS, GOD, YOUR [c]GOD, HAS ANOINTED YOU WITH THE OIL OF GLADNESS MORE THAN YOUR COMPANIONS.

10   And again: FROM THE BEGINNING YOU HAVE LAID THE FOUNDATIONS OF THE EARTH AND HEAVEN, [WHICH] ARE THE WORK OF YOUR HANDS.

11   THEY WILL PASS AWAY, YET YOU WILL ENDURE, AND ALL OF THEM WILL GROW OLD [s]AS A GARMENT

12   AND [s]AS AN OVERCOAT YOU WILL ROLL THEM UP. THEY WILL BE CHANGED, YET YOU WILL BE AS YOU ARE AND YOUR YEARS WILL NOT END.

---

[1] Repeat *in all*

[2] Pal Lect: for *and the image of his being*, 'of the Father who is at the right hand of God'

[3] Var (WS): omit *our*

[4] Pal Lect: 'of the ages'

ARAMAIC PESHITTA NEW TESTAMENT
HEBREWS

Chapter 1
13 And to which of the angels did he ever say:[1] SIT AT MY RIGHT HAND UNTIL I PLACE YOUR ENEMIES [AS] A FOOTSTOOL UNDER YOUR FEET?
14 *Behold, are they not all spirits of service[2] who are sent in service on account of those who are about to inherit life?

Chapter 2
1 Because of this, we ought to be especially cautious in what we have heard, so that we will not fall.
2 For if the word that was spoken by way of angels was confirmed and all who heard it and transgressed against it received a reward with uprightness,
3 how will **we** escape, if we despise [pa]those [things] that are our life, those that began to be spoken by our Lord and were confirmed in us by those who heard,┐ [3]
4 God being a witness about them with signs and with wonders and with various miracles and with[4] distributions of the Holy Spirit that were given according to his will?
5 For he did not subject the age that is to come, about which we speak, to angels.
6 But as the scripture witnesses and says: WHAT IS MAN THAT YOU REMEMBER HIM AND THE SON OF MAN THAT YOU VISIT HIM?[5]
7 YOU HUMBLED HIM LOWER THAN THE ANGELS. YOU PLACED ON HIS HEAD [he]GLORY AND HONOR AND GAVE HIM AUTHORITY OVER THE WORK OF YOUR HANDS
8 AND YOU SUBJECTED EVERYTHING UNDER HIS FEET. Now in that he subjected everything to him, he did not leave out anything that was not subjected. But now, we do not yet see that everything is subjected to him.
9 But we see him, who was humbled lower than the angels, to be [this] Jesus, because of the suffering of his death. And [he]glory and honor are placed on his head,[6] for by the grace of God, he [h]tasted death in place of everyone.

---

[1] Repeat from v. 5
[2] Repeat *service*
[3] Lit: those who heard from him
[4] Repeat *with*
[5] Fig: erotesis – question to ponder
[6] Repeat *glory and honor...head* from v. 7

Chapter 2

10 For it was proper for him, by whose ^mhand everything [was] and for whose sake everything [was] and [who] brought many sons into[1] glory, that he should perfect the prince of their life by his suffering.

11 For he who makes holy and those who are made holy[2] are all of one. Because of this, he is not ashamed to call them his brothers,

12 saying: I WILL ANNOUNCE YOUR NAME TO MY BROTHERS AND I WILL PRAISE YOU WITHIN THE CHURCH.

13 And again: I WILL BE CONFIDENT ABOUT HIM, and again, *BEHOLD, I AND THE CHILDREN THAT GOD HAS GIVEN ME.

14 For because the sons share in ^{mr}flesh and blood, he also in the same manner shared of the same,[3] that by his death he would put a stop to him who held the authority of death,[4] who is SATAN,

15 and would release those who by fear of death were subjected to bondage all their lives.

16 For he did not assume ^e[a nature] from the angels, but he assumed death from the seed of Abraham.[5]

17 Because of this, it is right that he should be made like his brothers in everything, so that he would be a merciful and faithful high priest in the things of God and would make atonement for the sins of the people.

18 For in that which he [himself] suffered and was tempted, he is able to help those who are tempted.

Chapter 3

1 Therefore, my holy brothers, who are called with a calling[6] that is from heaven, consider this apostle and high priest of our confession, Jesus Christ,

2 who was faithful to him who made him, as [was] Moses with all his ^mhouse.

3 ^{al}For the glory of this [man] is much greater than that of Moses, just as the honor of the builder of the house [is] much greater than [that of] his building.

---

[1] Var (WSL): add 'his'

[2] Repeat forms of *made holy*

[3] Pal Lect: for *of the same*, 'in sufferings'

[4] Repeat *death*, perhaps as antanaclasis

[5] Var (WSLM): omit *death*; Pal Lect: 'For not upon angels did he take hold, that He might declare God; but upon the seed of Abraham He took hold, that He might declare (Him).'

[6] Same root: *called, calling*

ARAMAIC PESHITTA NEW TESTAMENT
HEBREWS

Chapter 3

4   For every house is built by someone, but he who builds[1] all is God.

5   And Moses, as a servant, was faithful in all his house, for a witness of those [things] that were going to be, [that] were spoken by way of him.

6   Now Christ, as the Son, [is] over his house. And [me]we are his [m]house, if we hold fast the boldness and the boasting of his hope to the end.⌐

7   Because the Holy Spirit said, TODAY IF YOU WILL HEAR HIS VOICE,

8   DO NOT HARDEN YOUR HEARTS TO ANGER HIM AS THE REBELS AND AS [IN] THE [sy]DAY OF TEMPTATION IN THE WILDERNESS,

9   WHEN YOUR FATHERS TEMPTED AND TESTED ME [AND] SAW MY WORKS [FOR] FORTY YEARS.

10   BECAUSE OF THIS, I WAS WEARIED WITH THAT GENERATION AND I SAID, "[THIS] IS A PEOPLE WHOSE HEART WANDERS AND THEY DO NOT KNOW MY WAYS,"

11   SO THAT I SWORE IN MY ANGER THAT THEY WOULD NOT ENTER INTO MY [m]REST.[2]

12   Watch, therefore, my brothers, so that an evil heart that does not believe will not be in any of you and you should go away from the living God.

13   But examine yourselves all days until the [sy]day that is called, "The day," so that none of you will be hardened by the [as]deception of sin.

14   For we take part with Christ, if we persist from the beginning even to the end in this true covenant,

15   as it is said: TODAY IF YOU WILL HEAR HIS REPORT, DO NOT HARDEN YOUR HEARTS TO ANGER HIM.

16   But who were those who heard and angered him?[3] Not all those who came out of Egypt by way of Moses [e][angered him].

17   And with whom was he wearied [for] forty years, but with those who sinned and whose [sy]bones fell in the wilderness?

18   And about whom did he swear that they would not enter into his rest, but about those who were not persuaded?

19   We see that they were not able to enter, because they did not believe.

---

[1] Same root: *builder, building, built*, vs. 3, 4
[2] Repeat *enter into rest*, 3:11-4:11
[3] Fig: erotesis – questions to ponder, vs. 16-18

515

Chapter 4

1   Therefore, we should fear, so that while the promise of an entrance into his ^mrest is firm, none of you will be found to fall short when ^e[it is time] to enter.

2   For **we** also were brought the gospel, as they were, but the word did not profit those who heard, because it was not mixed with faith by those who heard it.

3   But we who believe are entering into rest. But as he said: AS I SWORE IN MY ANGER, "THEY WILL NOT ENTER INTO MY ^mREST." For *behold, the works of God were from the beginning of the world.

4   As he said about the SABBATH: GOD RESTED ON THE SEVENTH DAY FROM ALL HIS WORKS.

5   And here again, he said: THEY WILL NOT ENTER INTO MY ^mREST.

6   Therefore, because there was a place that each one should enter and those first [ones] who were brought the gospel did not enter since they were not persuaded,

7   again he set another ^{sy}day after a long time, as it was written above, for David said: TODAY IF YOU WILL HEAR HIS VOICE, DO NOT HARDEN YOUR HEARTS.

8   For if Joshua, the son of Nun, had given them rest, he would not have spoken afterwards about another ^{sy}day.

9   Therefore, it is established for the people of God to be given a rest.[1]

10   For he who enters into his ^mrest has also rested from his works, as God [rested] from his.

11   Therefore, we should be diligent to enter into that rest, so that we will not fall in the likeness of those who were not persuaded.

12   For the word of God is living ^Pand completely effective and sharper than a two-edged sword and enters all the way to the separation of soul and of spirit, and of the joints and of the marrow and of the bones, and judges the reasonings and the thoughts of the heart.⌐

13   And there is no created [thing] that is hidden before him, but everything is naked and evident before of the eyes of him to whom we give an account.

14   Therefore, because we have a great high priest, Jesus Christ, the Son of God, who went up to heaven, we should persist in confession of him.

15   For we do not have a high priest who is not able to feel our weakness, but one who was tempted in everything like us, ^e[yet] without sin.

---

[1] Lit: given a Sabbath

ARAMAIC PESHITTA NEW TESTAMENT
HEBREWS

Chapter 4

16   Therefore, we should boldly come near the throne of his grace to receive mercies and to find grace for help in [sy]time of adversity.

Chapter 5

1   For every high priest who is ordained of men for men, concerning those [things] that are of God, to offer offerings[1] and sacrifices for sins,

2   he who is able to humble himself and to feel with those who do not know and [who] err, because he also is clothed with weakness.

3   And because of this, it is necessary for the people, so also for himself, that he should offer [e][an offering] for his sins.

4   And no man takes the honor for himself, except he who was called by God, as [was] Aaron.

5   So also, Christ did not glorify himself to become the high priest, but he who said to him: **YOU ARE MY SON. TODAY I HAVE FATHERED YOU.**

6   As he said also in another place: **YOU ARE A PRIEST FOREVER IN THE LIKENESS OF MELCHISEDEC.**

7   Also, while he was clothed with [sy]flesh, he offered [he]petition and intercession with strong crying and with tears to him who was able to make him alive from death and he was heard.

8   And although he was a Son, from the fear and the sufferings that he bore, he learned obedience.

9   And so he was matured and became for all those who obey him the cause[2] of eternal life.

10   And he was named of God, the high priest in the likeness of Melchisedec.

11   Now concerning this Melchisedec, we have a great speech to say, yet it is difficult to explain it, because you are weak in your hearing.

12   For you ought to be teachers because of the time you have had in teaching, but now again you are needing to learn what are the first principles of the beginning of the words of God. [al]And you have need for milk and not for solid food.

13   But everyone whose food is milk is not persuaded in the word of uprightness, because [me]he is a baby.

14   But solid food belongs to the mature, those who, because they are trained, have exercised their senses to distinguish good and evil.⌐

---

[1] Same root: *offer, offerings*

[2] Or "source"

Chapter 6

1   Because of this, we should leave the starting point of the word of Christ and we should come to maturity. Or will you again lay another foundation for repentance from dead works [P]and for the faith that is in God

2   and for the doctrine of baptism and of the laying on of a hand and for the resurrection from the dead and for eternal judgment?⌐ [1]

3   If the LORD permits, we will do this.

4   But they are not able, those who once have gone down into baptism and have [h]tasted the gift that is from [m]heaven and have received the Holy Spirit

5   and have [h]tasted the good word of God and the power of the age that is to come,

6   to sin again and to be renewed to repentance from the beginning and to crucify and to disparage the Son of God from the beginning.

7   [al]For the earth, which drinks the rain that comes to it many times and produces the green herb that is useful to those because of whom it was cultivated, receives a blessing from God.

8   But if it produces thorns and thistles, it is rejected and is not far away from a curse, but rather its end is a fire.⌐

9   Now concerning you, my brothers, we are persuaded of those [things] that are proper and [that] are approaching life, even though we speak so.

10   For God is not wicked, that he forgets your works and your love that you have shown in his name, for you have ministered and do minister to the holy [ones].

11   But we want each one of you to show this diligence to the completion of your hope up to the end

12   and to not be discouraged, but to be imitators of those who by faith and long-suffering have become heirs of the promise.

13   For when God promised Abraham, because he had no one who was greater than himself by whom he could swear, he swore by himself

14   and said: I WILL CERTAINLY BLESS YOU AND I WILL GREATLY MULTIPLY[2] YOU.

15   And so he was long-suffering and received the promise.

16   For men swear by that which is greater than them and concerning every controversy that happens among them, the certain end of it is by oaths.

---

[1] Repeat *and for*; fig: erotesis, **lema** question, obvious answer "no"
[2] Fig: polyptoton, *certainly bless, greatly multiply*

ARAMAIC PESHITTA NEW TESTAMENT
HEBREWS

Chapter 6
17 Because of this, God especially wanted to show to the heirs of the promise that his promise would not change, so he bound it with oaths,[1]
18 that by two things that are unchangeable in which God is not able to lie, we who have sought refuge in him may have great comfort and may hold fast to the hope that was promised to us,
19 which we have ˢas an anchor that holds our soul, so that it is not shaken and it enters within the veil,
20 where Jesus previously entered for us and became a priest forever in the likeness of Melchisedec.

Chapter 7
1 Now this Melchisedec was king of Salem, a priest of the Most High God. And he met Abraham returning from the slaughter of the kings and blessed him.
2 And Abraham separated out to him tithes of everything that was with him. Now his name is interpreted, "king of uprightness," and again, "king of Salem," that is, "king of peace,"
3 whose father and mother are not written in the genealogies, nor the beginning of his days, nor the completion of his life. But in the likeness of the Son of God, his priesthood remains forever.
4 Now consider how great this [man was], to whom Abraham the patriarch gave tithes of the first [things].
5 For those of the sons of Levi who received the priesthood have the commandment of the law, that they should receive tithes from the people, from their brothers, when **they** also came from the ᵐloin[s] of Abraham.
6 But this [man], who is not written in their genealogies, took tithes from Abraham and blessed him who had received the promise.
7 And without controversy, he who is less is blessed by him who is greater than him.
8 And here men who die receive tithes. But there he [is] about whom the scripture testifies that he is alive.
9 And as one may say, by way of Abraham, even Levi who received the tithes also paid tithes.
10 For he was yet in the ᵐloin[s] of his father when he met Melchisedec.

---

[1] Repeat *oaths*, vs. 16, 17; *promise, his promise*, are two different words; Var (WSL): *oath* (singular)

519

Chapter 7

11   Therefore, if perfection is by way of the priesthood of Levi, by which the law was established for the people, why was it necessary that another priest should be raised up in the likeness of Melchisedec? Then he [would have] said, "He will be in the likeness of Aaron."

12   But in the same way as a change took place in the priesthood, so a change[1] also took place in the law.

13   For he about whom these [things] were spoken was born of another tribe, from which no man ever[2] ministered at the altar.

14   For it is revealed that our Lord rose up from Judah, from a tribe about which Moses did not say anything concerning the priesthood.

15   And yet it is further known in that he said that another priest will rise up in the likeness of Melchisedec,

16   who was not according to the law of fleshly commandments, but was according to the power of life that is endless.

17   For he testified about him: YOU ARE A PRIEST FOREVER IN THE LIKENESS OF MELCHISEDEC.

18   Now the change that happened to the first commandment [was] because of its lack of power and because it had no profit.

19   For the law did not perfect anything. But a hope that is greater than it entered in its place, by which we are drawn near to God.

20   And he confirmed it to us with oaths.[3]

21   For **they** became priests without oaths, but this [one] with oaths, as he said to him by way of David: THE LORD HAS SWORN AND WILL NOT LIE, THAT YOU ARE A PRIEST FOREVER IN THE LIKENESS OF MELCHISEDEC.

22   [In] all of this is this covenant better, for Jesus was the security in it.

23   And those priests were many, because they died and were not allowed to continue.

24   But this [one], because he remains forever, his priesthood does not pass away.

25   And he is able to give life forever to those who come near to God by way of him, for he is always alive and sends up prayer[4] for them.

26   For a priest like this [one] is also right for us, [one who is] pure, without evil and without impurity, one who is separated from sins and elevated higher than heaven

---

[1] Repeat *a change*
[2] Lit: never
[3] Repeat *oaths*, vs. 20, 21
[4] Var (WSL): *prayers* (plural)

Chapter 7

27 and has no need daily, like the high priests, to first offer sacrifices for his sins and then for the people, for this he did one time, in that he offered himself.

28 For the law established weak men [as] priests, but the word of the oaths[1] that was after the law [e][established] the Son [as] perfect forever.

Chapter 8

1 Now the first [point] of all these [things is that] we have a high priest who is seated on the right hand of the throne of the [h]majesty in heaven.

2 And he is a minister of the sanctuary and of the [an]tabernacle of truth that God pitched and not man.

3 For every high priest is ordained to offer offerings[2] and sacrifices. Because of this, it was right for this [one] to have something to offer also.

4 And if he were on earth, he would not even be a priest, because there are priests who offer offerings as in the law,

5 those who minister for a type and for shadows[3] of those [things] that are in heaven, as was said to Moses while he was making the tabernacle: SEE AND MAKE EVERYTHING ACCORDING TO THE TYPE THAT WAS SHOWN TO YOU IN THE MOUNTAIN.

6 And now, Jesus Christ has received a ministry that is more excellent than that, as also that covenant in which he was made the mediator is more excellent. So [it is] with the promises that are more excellent[4] than what was given.

7 For if the first [e][covenant] was without fault, there would be no place for this second.

8 For he found fault with them and said: *BEHOLD, THE DAYS COME, says the LORD, WHEN I WILL COMPLETE FOR THE HOUSEHOLD OF ISRAEL AND FOR THE HOUSEHOLD OF JUDAH, A NEW COVENANT,

9 NOT LIKE THAT COVENANT THAT I GAVE TO THEIR FATHERS IN THE DAY THAT I HELD [THEM] BY THEIR HAND AND BROUGHT THEM OUT OF THE LAND OF EGYPT. BECAUSE THEY DID NOT REMAIN IN MY COVENANT, I ALSO REJECTED THEM, says the LORD.

---

[1] Var (WSL): *oath* (singular)
[2] Same root: *offer, offerings*, also v. 4
[3] Var (WSLM): *shadow* (singular); repeat *type*, lit: likeness
[4] Repeat *more excellent*

Chapter 8

10 AND THIS [IS] THE COVENANT THAT I WILL GIVE TO THE HOUSEHOLD OF ISRAEL AFTER THOSE DAYS, says the LORD. I WILL PUT MY LAW IN THEIR MINDS AND I WILL WRITE IT ON THEIR HEARTS AND I WILL BE GOD TO THEM AND THEY WILL BE A PEOPLE TO ME.

11 AND A MAN WILL NOT TEACH HIS FELLOW-CITIZEN OR EVEN HIS BROTHER AND SAY, 'KNOW THE LORD,' BECAUSE ALL WILL KNOW ME, FROM THE YOUNGEST OF THEM UP TO THE OLDEST.

12 AND I WILL FREE THEM FROM THEIR WICKEDNESS AND I WILL NOT REMEMBER THEIR SINS AGAIN.

13 By that which he called new, he made the first old, and that which is outdated and old is near to corruption.

Chapter 9

1 Now in the first [e][covenant] there were ordinances of service and an earthly sanctuary.

2 For the first tabernacle that was made had a candlestick and a table and show-bread, and it was called the sanctuary.

3 And the inner tabernacle that was behind the second veil was called the holy of holies.

4 And in it there was the censer of gold and the ark of the covenant that was completely overlaid with gold and it had a pot of gold that had the manna [P]and the rod of Aaron that sprouted and the tablets of the covenant,

5 and on top of it, cherubim of glory that were overshadowing the mercy seat.⌐ But there is not time to speak about each one of these [things] that were so arranged.

6 And into the outer tabernacle the priests were always entering and performing their service.

7 But into the inner tabernacle once a year the high priest entered alone with the blood that he offered for himself and for the wrong-doing[1] of the people.

8 Now by this, the Holy Spirit was making known that the way to the holy [things] was not yet revealed, as long as the first tabernacle was standing.

9 This was a symbol for that time, in which offerings and sacrifices were offered that were not able to perfect the conscience of him who offered[2] them,

---

[1] Var (WL): *wrong-doings* (plural)
[2] Same root: *offerings, offered*

Chapter 9

10   but [were] only in food and drink and in washings of various kinds that are commandments of the flesh that were established until the [sy]time of a reformation.

11   Now Christ who has come [was] a high priest of the good [things] that he did. And he entered[1] the [he]great and perfect tabernacle that was not made by hands and was not of these created [things].

12   And he did not enter with the blood of goats or of calves, but with his own blood, he entered the sanctuary[2] one time and obtained redemption forever.

13   For if the blood of goats and of calves and the ash of a heifer was sprinkled on those who were defiled and it made them holy to the cleansing of their flesh,

14   then how much more will the blood of Christ, who by the eternal[3] Spirit offered himself without spot to God, cleanse our conscience from dead works that we may serve the living God?[4]

15   Because of this, he became the mediator of the new covenant, so that by his death he would become the deliverance for those who have transgressed against the first covenant, that those who were called to the eternal inheritance should receive the promise.

16   For where there is a covenant, it shows the death of him who made it,

17   but it is established only concerning a dead [person], because as long as he who made it is alive, there is no usefulness in it.

18   Because of this, neither was the first [e][covenant] established without blood.

19   For when the whole commandment had been commanded by Moses to all the people according to the law, Moses took the blood of a heifer and water, with wool of scarlet and hyssop, and he sprinkled [it] over the scrolls and over all the people

20   and said to them: [me]**THIS IS THE BLOOD OF THAT COVENANT THAT IS COMMANDED TO YOU BY GOD.**

21   He also sprinkled part of the blood over the tabernacle and over all the vessels of the service,

22   because everything is cleansed by blood in the law, and without the shedding of blood there is no forgiveness.

---

[1] Repeat *entered*, vs. 11, 12
[2] Pal Lect: *the sanctuary* is, 'the house of the Holy of Holies'
[3] Pal Lect: 'Holy'
[4] Fig: erotesis, **kema** question, answer in the affirmative

Chapter 9

23   For it was necessary that these that are a type of the heavenly [things] should be purified with those [things], and these heavenly [things][1] by sacrifices that are more excellent than those.

24   For Christ did not enter the sanctuary that was made by hands that was a type of that true [one], but he entered into heaven to appear before the presence of God for us.

25   Neither e[was it necessary] to offer himself many times, as the high priest did when he entered the sanctuary every year with blood that [was] not his own.

26   Otherwise, it would be required that he should suffer many times since the beginning of the age. But now in the end of the age, he has offered himself one time by his sacrificing to abolish sin.

27   And as it is appointed to men that they should die one time, and after their death [is] the judgment,

28   so also Christ was offered one time. And in his person he sacrificed [for] the sins of many and he will appear a second time without sins for the life of those who wait for him.

Chapter 10

1   For the law had a shadow of good [things] to come, not the substance of the things themselves. Because of this, although these same sacrifices were offered every year, they were never able to perfect those who offered them.

2   For if they had perfected [them], then doubtless they would have stopped their offerings, because their conscience would no longer trouble them with sins once they have been cleansed.

3   But by the sacrifices, they brought their sins to remembrance every year,

4   for the blood of bulls and of goats is not able to cleanse sins.

5   Because of this, when he entered the world he said, "You are not pleased with sacrifices and offerings, but you have clothed me with a body.

6   And you have not asked for burnt offerings[2] that are for sins."

7   Then I said: *BEHOLD, I COME. FOR IN THE BEGINNING OF THE sywRITINGS IT IS WRITTEN ABOUT ME, I WILL DO YOUR WILL, [OH] GOD.

---

[1] Repeat *heavenly [things]*

[2] Lit: peace burnings

Chapter 10

8   Above he said: YOU DO NOT DESIRE SACRIFICES [P]AND OFFERINGS AND BURNT OFFERINGS THAT ARE FOR SINS,] THOSE THAT ARE OFFERED ACCORDING TO THE LAW.

9   And after that he said: *BEHOLD, I HAVE COME TO DO YOUR WILL, [OH] GOD.[1] By this he annulled the first, so that he would establish the second.

10   For in this, his will, we are made holy by the offering of the body of Jesus Christ one time.

11   For every high priest who stood and served daily offered these same sacrifices that were never able to cleanse sins.

12   But this [one] offered one sacrifice for sins and SAT DOWN AT THE RIGHT HAND OF GOD FOREVER.

13   And he remains [there] from now on, until his enemies will be placed [as] a [h]footstool under his feet.

14   For with one offering he perfected those who were made holy by him forever.

15   Now the Holy Spirit also [is] a witness to us for he said:

16   THIS IS THE COVENANT THAT I WILL GIVE TO THEM AFTER THOSE DAYS, says the LORD. I WILL PLACE MY LAW IN THEIR MINDS AND I WILL WRITE IT ON THEIR HEARTS,

17   AND I WILL NOT REMEMBER THEIR WICKEDNESS AND THEIR SINS.

18   Now where there is forgiveness of sins, an offering for sins is not required.

19   We have, therefore, my brothers, boldness in the entering of the sanctuary by the blood of Jesus

20   and a [an]way of life that is now made new for us by the veil that [me]is his [sy]flesh.

21   And we have a high priest over the [m]house of God.

22   Therefore, we should come near with a steadfast heart and with the confidence of faith, our hearts being [h]sprinkled and pure from an evil conscience and our body [h]washed with pure water.

23   And we should persist in the confession of our hope and we should not waver, for he is faithful who promised us.

24   And we should gaze on one another with an encouragement to love and good works.

---

[1] Repeat from v. 7

Chapter 10

25   And we should not forsake our assembly, as is the custom for some, but we should desire [to be with] one another, especially the more you see that [sy]day approach.

26   For if by his will a man should sin after he has received knowledge of the truth, there is no longer a sacrifice that may be offered for sins,

27   but a terrible judgment is prepared and the [as]zeal of fire that will devour the adversaries.

28   For if he who transgressed against the law of Moses died at the [m]mouth of two or three witnesses without mercy,

29   how much more do you suppose will he receive capital punishment, who has [h]trampled on the Son of God and has counted the blood of his covenant, by which he was made holy like that of any man, and has despised the Spirit of grace?

30   We know him, who said: **VENGEANCE IS MINE AND I WILL REPAY,** and again, **THE** LORD **WILL JUDGE HIS PEOPLE.**

31   There is a great fear to fall into the [c]hands of the living God.

32   Remember, therefore, the first days, those in which you received baptism and endured a great contest of sufferings, with reproach and with[1] adversities,

33   and that [me]you were spectacles and also were associated with men who endured these [things].

34   And you were sorry for those who were imprisoned and you endured the robbery of your possessions with joy, because you knew that you had a possession[2] in heaven that is greater and does not pass away.

35   Therefore, do not lose the boldness that you have, for it will have a great reward.

36   For endurance is necessary for you to do the will of God and to receive the promise:

37   **BECAUSE IT IS A LITTLE, EVEN A VERY SHORT**[3] **TIME, THAT HE WHO COMES WILL COME**[4] **AND HE WILL NOT DELAY.**

38   **NOW THE UPRIGHT WILL LIVE BY MY FAITH AND IF HE SHOULD BE DISCOURAGED, I WILL NOT BE PLEASED WITH HIM.**

39   But **we** are not of the drawing back that leads to loss, but of the faith that obtains for us our life.

---

[1] Repeat *with*

[2] Repeat *possession*

[3] Fig: pleonasm, redundancy

[4] Repeat *come*

Chapter 11

1   Now faith is the persuasion concerning those [things] that are in hope, as if they had in fact happened, and the evidence of those [things] that are not seen.

2   And in this there is a testimony about the ancient [ones].

3   For by faith[1] we understand that the ages were prepared by the word of God and [that] those [things] that are seen were from those [things] that are not seen.[2]

4   By faith, Abel offered a sacrifice that was more excellent than that of Cain to God, and because of it, there is a testimony about him that he was upright. And God testified[3] to his offering and because of it, although [he is] dead, he speaks.

5   By faith, Enoch was removed and did not [h]taste death. And he was not found, because God had removed him, for before he removed him, there was a testimony about him that he pleased God.

6   Now without faith, no one is able to please God. For he who comes near to God is required to believe that he is and [that] he is a rewarder of those who seek him.

7   By faith, Noah, when it was told to him about those [things] that are not seen, feared and made for himself an ark for the life of his household, by which he condemned the world and became heir of the uprightness that is by faith.

8   By faith, Abraham, when he was called to leave for a place that he was going to receive for an inheritance, obeyed and went out, not knowing where he was going.

9   By faith, he was a settler in the land that was promised to him as in a foreign country and he lived in tents with Isaac and Jacob, his fellow-heirs of the promise,[4]

10   for he was waiting for a city that had a foundation, whose [c]craftsman and maker is God.

11   By faith also, Sarah, who was barren, received strength to receive seed and when her years were past, she gave birth, because she was convinced that he who had promised her was faithful.

12   Because of this, from one who was failing in old age, many [people] were born, [s]as the stars in heaven and [s]as the sand on the shore of the sea that has no number.

---

[1] Repeat *by faith*, 19x, vs. 3-33

[2] Repeat *that are seen*

[3] Same root: *testify, testimony*, also v. 5

[4] Same root: *promise, promised*, vs. 9-13

Chapter 11

13 These all died in faith and did not receive their promise, but they saw it from a distance and rejoiced in it and confessed that they were strangers and settlers on the earth.

14 Now those who say these [things] demonstrate that they seek their city.[1]

15 And if they were seeking that city from which they came out, they had an opportunity to return again [and] to go to it.

16 But now it is evident that they were longing for a better e[city] than that, for the [one] that is in heaven. Because of this, God was not ashamed to be called their God, for he has prepared a city for them.

17 By faith, Abraham in his trial offered Isaac and lifted up his only [son] on the altar, whom he had received by promise,

18 for it was said to him: IN ISAAC YOUR mSEED WILL BE CALLED.

19 And he reasoned in himself that God was able[2] even to raise [him] from the dead, and because of this, he was given back to him [as] in a parable.[3]

20 By faith regarding what was going to be, Isaac blessed Jacob and Esau.

21 By faith,[4] when he was dying, Jacob blessed each one of the sons of Joseph and worshipped e[leaning] on the top of his staff.

22 By faith, Joseph, when he was dying, remembered[5] the departure of the sons of Israel and directed [them] concerning his bones.

23 By faith, the parents of Moses hid him after he was born [for] three months, because they saw that he was a special child and they were not afraid of the commandment of the king.

24 By faith, Moses, when he was a man, insisted that he should not be called a son of the daughter of Pharaoh.

25 And he chose to be in adversity with the people of God and, not even for a short time, to be merry in sin.

26 And he considered that the aswealth of the reproach of Christ was more excellent than the treasures of Egypt, for he looked at the payment of the reward.

27 By faith, he left Egypt and was not afraid of the fury of the king. And he endured as one who has seen God, who is not visible.

---

[1] Repeat *city* from v. 10, also vs. 14-16
[2] Lit: was prepared by his hands
[3] Or "symbol"
[4] Var (M): add 'also'
[5] Fig: ellipsis, add [the promise of]

Chapter 11

28 By faith, he[1] kept the Feast of Passover and the sprinkling of blood, so that he who destroyed the firstborn should not approach them.

29 By faith, they crossed over the Red Sea, as on dry ground, in which the Egyptians were drowned when they dared to enter it.

30 By faith, the walls of Jericho fell after they had been surrounded [for] seven days.

31 By faith, Rahab, the harlot, was not destroyed with those who did not obey, because she received the spies in peace.

32 And what more can I say? For the time is [too] short for me to tell about Gideon Pand about Barak and about Samson and about Jephthah and about David and about Samuel and about the rest of the prophets,

33 those who by faith overcame kingdoms and worked [with] uprightness and received the promises and shut the mouth[s][2] of lions

34 and quenched the power of fire and were delivered from the edge[3] of the msword and were strengthened of weaknesses and became mighty in battle and routed the armies of the enemies

35 and gave [back] to women their children by raising of the dead. And others[4] died in tortures and did not expect to escape, so that they would have the better resurrection.⅂

36 Now aothers entered into jeering and beatings, others were delivered to prisons and to captivities,

37 others were stoned, others were sawed apart, others died by the edge of the sword, others wandered about clothed with the skins of lambs and of goats and were needy and troubled and wearied,⅂

38 men of whom the world was not worthy. And they were sas forgotten [ones] in the wilderness Pand in the mountains and in the caves and in the holes of the earth.⅂

39 And all these, about whom there is a testimony[5] by their faith, did not receive the promise,

40 because God had considered beforehand our benefit, that they should not be perfected without us.

---

[1] Var (WS): 'they'

[2] Var (WSL): *mouths* (plural)

[3] Lit: mouth, also v. 37

[4] Repeat *others*, 7x, vs. 35-37

[5] Repeat *testimony* from v. 4

Chapter 12

1   Because of this also, we, who have all these witnesses that surround us [s]like a cloud,[1] should unfasten all our burdens from us, even the sin that is always prepared for us, and we should [h]run with patience this race that is set for us.

2   And we should look at Jesus, who was the [mr]initiator and finisher of our faith, who for the joy there was for him endured the cross and discounted the shame and sat down at the right hand of the throne of God.

3   See, therefore, how much he endured from sinners who are contrary to themselves, so that you should not be weary or your soul become faint.

4   You have not yet come to [e][shedding of] blood in the contest that is against sin.

5   And you have forgotten the instruction, which says to you [s]as to children: **MY SON, DO NOT DISREGARD THE DISCIPLINE OF THE LORD, NOR LET YOUR SOUL FAINT WHEN YOU ARE REPROVED BY HIM.**

6   **FOR THE LORD DISCIPLINES HIM WHOM HE LOVES AND SCOURGES THE SONS WITH WHOM HE IS PLEASED.**

7   Therefore, endure discipline, because God is dealing with you [s]as [2]with sons. For what son is there whom his father does not discipline?[3]

8   And if you are without the discipline with which everyone is disciplined, [me]you have become strangers and not sons.

9   And if our [an]fathers of the flesh disciplined us and we respect them, how much more then ought we to obey our spiritual Father and live?[4]

10   For those for a short time disciplined us according to what they wanted, but God [e][disciplines us] for our benefit, so that we will share in his holiness.

11   Now at the time, no discipline is thought to be [e][a matter] of joy, but of sorrow. But in the end it bears the [m]fruit of peace and of justification to those who are trained by it.

12   [al]Because of this, strengthen your weak hands and your trembling knees

13   and make straight paths for your feet, so that the leg that is limping will not stumble, but be healed.

---

[1] Var (WSL): *clouds* (plural)
[2] Fig: ellipsis, add [a father deals]
[3] Fig: erotesis – question to ponder
[4] Fig: erotesis, **kema** question, answer in the affirmative

Chapter 12

14   Run after peace with everyone and after holiness, without which a man does not see our Lord.⌐

15   And be watchful, so that no one will be found among you who lacks the grace of God, or ^{al}so that a root of bitterness will not produce a flower and harm you and by it, many should be corrupted,

16   or [so that] no one will be found among you who is a fornicator and a careless [one], such ^sas Esau, who sold his birthright for one meal.

17   For you know that also afterwards he wanted to inherit the blessing, but was rejected, for he did not find a place of repentance, although he begged for it with tears.⌐

18   ^{al}For you have not come near to the fire ^e[of the mountain] that burned and was tangible, nor even to the darkness and mist and storm,

19   nor to the sound of the trumpet and the ^{as}voice of words, which those who heard asked that it should not continue to be spoken to them.

20   For they were not able to bear what they were commanded: **IF EVEN AN ANIMAL SHOULD COME NEAR TO THE MOUNTAIN, IT SHOULD BE STONED.**

21   And the sight was so terrible that Moses said: **I AM AFRAID AND I AM TREMBLING.**

22   But **you** have come near to the mountain of Zion and to[1] the city of the living God, to the Jerusalem that is in heaven, and to the multitudes of numbers of angels

23   and to the church of the firstborn, who are written in heaven, and to God, the judge of all, and to the spiritual [things] of the upright [ones] who are matured,

24   and to Jesus, the mediator of the new covenant, and to the ^hsprinkling of his blood that speaks more than that of Abel.⌐

25   Watch, therefore, so that you will not refuse ^e[to hear] him who speaks to you. For if those who refuse him who speaks with them on earth are not delivered, how much more we,[2] if we refuse[3] him who speaks with us from ^mheaven,

26   whose voice shook the earth? But now he has promised and said: **AGAIN, ONCE MORE, I WILL SHAKE,[4] NOT ONLY THE EARTH, BUT ALSO HEAVEN.**

---

[1] Repeat *and to*, 9x, vs. 22-24

[2] Fig: ellipsis, add [will not be delivered]; fig: erotesis, **kema** question, answer in the affirmative

[3] Repeat *refuse*

[4] Same root: *shaken, unshakeable*, vs. 26-28

Chapter 12

27   Now this that he said, "Once more," indicates a change of those [things] that are shaken, because they are ^e[things that are] made, so that those that are unshakable may remain.

28   Therefore, because we have received a kingdom that is unshakable, we should hold fast to the grace, by which we may serve and may please God, with reverence and with fear.

29   FOR OUR ^{me}GOD IS A DEVOURING FIRE.

Chapter 13

1   Love of the brothers should continue in you.

2   And do not forget ^e[to have] compassion to strangers, for by this some have been worthy to receive angels, being unaware [of it].

3   Remember those who are imprisoned, as if you are imprisoned with them. Remember those who are troubled, because you [also] are ^hclothed with ^{sy}flesh as a man.

4   Marriage is honorable in all and their bed is pure, but God will judge fornicators and adulterers.

5   Your mind should not love money, but what you have should be sufficient for you. For the LORD has said: **I WILL NOT LEAVE YOU AND I WILL NOT** LET GO OF YOU.[1]

6   And we can say confidently: MY LORD **IS MY HELPER. I WILL NOT BE AFRAID. WHAT DOES A MAN DO TO ME?**

7   Remember your leaders who have spoken the word of God with you. Consider the result of their manners of life and imitate their faith.

8   Jesus Christ is ^e[the same] yesterday ^Pand today and forever.┐

9   Do not be led away by ^{he}strange and diverse teachings, ^{pa}for it is good that we strengthen our hearts with grace and not with things to eat,┐ because those who have walked in them have not been benefited.

10   And we have an altar from which those who serve in the tabernacle have no right to eat.

11   For the animals, those whose blood the high priests brought into the sanctuary for sins, their flesh was burned outside of[2] the camp.

12   Because of this also, Jesus, so that he would make holy his people by his blood, suffered outside of the city.

13   And also **we**, therefore, should go out to him outside of the camp, bearing his reproach.

---

[1] Lit: my hands will not relax hold of you
[2] Repeat *outside of,* 3x, vs. 11-13

Chapter 13

14   For we have no city that remains here, but we expect one to come.

15   And by way of him, we should always offer up the sacrifices of praise to God, which is the ᵐfruit of ᵐlips that give thanks to his ᵐname.

16   And do not forget lovingkindness and sharing with the poor, for with these sacrifices a man pleases God.

17   Be convicted by your leaders and obey them, for **they** watch for your lives ˢas men who give an accounting of you, so that with joy they may do this and not with groanings, because that is not profitable for you.

18   Pray for us, for we trust that we have a good conscience, that in everything we want to conduct ourselves well.

19   I am begging you to do this especially, that I may be returned to you quickly.

20   ᵇᵉNow may the God of peace, who brought up from the dead the great ᵐShepherd of the flock by the blood of the everlasting covenant, who is Jesus Christ our Lord,

21   mature you in every good work to do his will and to perform in us what is pleasing before him, by way of Jesus Christ, to whom [be] glory forever and ever. Amen.

22   And I am begging you, my brothers, to be long-suffering in [this] word of encouragement, because I have written to you in few [words].

23   And know that our brother Timothy is set free, and if he comes soon, I will see you with him.

24   Greet all your leaders and all the holy [ones]. All who are from Italy greet you.

25   ᵇᵉGrace [be] with all of you. Amen.

Chapter 1

1   James, a servant of God and of our Lord Jesus Christ, to the twelve tribes that are scattered among the nations: Peace.

2   You should have all joy, my brothers, when you enter into various and numerous[1] trials,

3   for you know that the experience of faith causes you to obtain patience.

4   Now patience should have a full work that you may be [he]mature and complete and not lacking in anything.[2]

5   Now if any of you lacks wisdom, he should ask [for it] from God, who gives generously[3] to all and does not reproach and it will be given to him.

6   But he should ask in faith, not doubting,[4] for he who doubts is like the waves of the sea that the wind stirs up.

7   And that man should not expect to receive anything from the LORD,

8   who doubts in his mind and is troubled in all his ways.

9   And the humble brother should boast in his lifted position

10   and the rich in his humility, because [s]as the flower of an herb, likewise he passes away.

11   For the sun will rise with its heat and will dry up the herb and its flower will fall and the beauty of its appearance will be destroyed. So also the rich [man] withers in his ways.

12   Blessed [is] the man who endures trials, so that when he is examined, he may receive the [m]crown of life that God promised to those who love him.

13   No one should say when he is tempted, "I am tempted by God," for God is not tempted with evil [things] and does not tempt[5] anyone.

14   But each man is tempted by his [own] desire and he desires and is dragged away

15   and this desire conceives and produces sin. And sin, when it is matured, produces death.[6]

16   Do not err, my beloved brothers.

---

[1] Var (SLM): reverse order: *numerous and various*

[2] Repeat *patience* from v. 3; fig: climax, vs. 3, 4

[3] Lit: simply, ܟܫܝܛܐܝܬ from **peshita**

[4] Lit: being divided, also v. 8

[5] Repeat *tempted,* also v. 14

[6] Fig: climax, vs. 14, 15; repeat *sin* as next word; word play: *desire* ܪܓܬܐ *desires* ܡܬܪܓܪܓ *dragged* ܘܢܓܕ

Chapter 1

17   Every [he]good and complete gift [is] from above, coming down from the [m]Father of lights, with whom there is not any inconstancy, not even a shadow of change.

18   It is he [who] desired and fathered us by the [an]word of truthfulness that we would be the first[fruit] of his created [ones].

19   And you, my beloved brothers, everyone of you should be quick to hear and slow to speak and slow[1] to be angry.

20   For the anger of man does not serve the justification of God.

21   Because of this, put away from you all uncleanness [P]and the abundance of wickedness and receive with meekness the word that is implanted in our nature that is able to give life to your souls.

22   And be doers of the word and not hearers only and do not deceive yourselves.⌐

23   For if anyone is a hearer of the word and not a doer of it, this [one] is [s]like him who sees his face in a mirror,

24   for he sees himself [P]and passes on and forgets what kind [of man] he was.

25   And everyone who looks into the fulfilled law of liberty and remains in it is not a hearer of a report that is forgotten, but a doer of deeds. And this [one] will be blessed in his deed.[2]

26   And if a man supposes that he serves God and he does not hold his tongue, but the heart of this [man] deceives him, [then] his service is unprofitable.⌐

27   For the service that is [he]pure and holy before God the Father is this, to visit orphans and widows in their troubles and to keep oneself [3] without [h]spot from the world.

Chapter 2

1   My brothers, do not hold to the [an]faith of the glory of our Lord Jesus Christ with respect of persons.

2   For if a man should enter your assembly with rings of gold[4] or with beautiful garments and a poor man should enter with filthy garments,

---

[1] Repeat *and slow*

[2] Same root: *deed, deeds, doer*

[3] Lit: his soul

[4] Culture: among the Romans, the upper classes were distinguished from the common people by wearing a gold ring, Burder, vol II, p. 381.

Chapter 2

3 and you look at that one clothed with beautiful garments[1] and say to him, "Sit here [in] a good [place]," and to the poor man you say, "Stand back or sit here before the footstool,"

4 *behold, are you not discriminating among yourselves and have you [not] become expounders of evil reasonings?[2]

5 Hear, my beloved brothers, was it not the poor of the world, but [who are] rich in faith [that] God chose to be heirs in the kingdom that God promised to those who love him?

6 But **you** have rejected the poor. *Behold, do not rich [men] elevate themselves over you and drag you to court?

7 *Behold, do **they** not[3] reproach the good name that was called on you?

8 And if you fulfill the law of God in this, as it is written: YOU SHOULD LOVE YOUR NEIGHBOR AS YOURSELF, you are doing well.

9 But if you are respecting persons, you commit sin and you are reproved by the law as transgressors of the law.

10 For he who keeps the whole law and offends in one [thing] is found guilty of the whole law.

11 For he who said: DO NOT COMMIT ADULTERY, said, DO NOT KILL. Now if you do not commit adultery, but you kill, you have become a transgressor[4] of the law.

12 So speak and so act, as people who are going to be judged by the law of liberty.[5]

13 For judgment will be without mercy on that one who has not practiced mercy. By mercy,[6] you will be elevated above judgment.

14 What is the profit, my brothers, if someone says, "I have faith," and has no works? Is his faith able to give him life?

15 And if a brother or a sister should be naked and lacking food for the day

---

[1] Repeat *with beautiful garments* from v. 2

[2] Fig: erotesis – questions to ponder, vs. 4-7, also, vs. 14, 16

[3] Var (LM): omit *not*

[4] Repeat *transgressor* from v. 9

[5] Repeat *law of liberty* from 1:25

[6] Repeat *mercy*, 3x

Chapter 2

16   and one of you says to them, "Go in peace, be warm and be satisfied," and you do not give them what is necessary for the body, what is the profit?[1]

17   So also, faith alone without works is dead.

18   For a man will say to you, "You have faith," and to me, "I have works." Show me your faith without works and I will show you my faith by my works.

19   You believe that God is one. [i]You do well! Even the demons believe and [h]tremble.

20   Now do you want to understand, oh frail man,[2] that faith without works is dead?

21   Was not our father Abraham justified[3] by works when he offered Isaac his son on the altar?

22   You see that his faith aided his works and [that] by works, his faith was matured.

23   And the scripture was fulfilled that said: **ABRAHAM BELIEVED IN GOD AND IT WAS COUNTED TO HIM FOR JUSTIFICATION**, and he was called the friend of God.

24   You see that by works[4] a man is justified and not by faith alone.

25   So also, was not Rahab the harlot justified by works when she took in the spies and sent them out by another way?

26   As the body without the spirit is dead, so also faith without works is dead.[5]

Chapter 3

1   You should not have many teachers among you, my brothers, but know that we are liable [e][to have] a greater judgment.

2   For we all offend [in] many [things]. Anyone who does not offend in word, this [one] is a mature man who is also able to subject his whole body.

3   [al]For *behold, we place bits in the mouths of horses, so that they may be tamed by us and we turn their whole body.

---

[1] Repeat *what is the profit* from v. 14, encircling passage

[2] Fig: apostrophe; fig: erotesis – questions to ponder, vs. 20, 21, also v. 25

[3] Repeat *justified*, vs. 21-25

[4] Var (M): *work* (singular)

[5] Repeat *faith without works is dead* from v. 17

Chapter 3

4   Also, the mighty boats, although harsh winds drive them, are turned by a small piece of wood to the place that the pilot wants to see.

5   So also, the tongue is a small member and it elevates itself. Also, a small fire causes large forests to burn.

6   And the ᵐᵉtongue is a fire and the ᵃⁿworld of sin is ˢlike a forest. And the tongue, although it is [one] among the members, marks our whole body and sets on fire the successions of our generations that roll on ˢas wheels and it also burns with fire.¬

7   For all the natures of animals ᴾand of birds and reptiles,¬ of the sea and of dry land, are subjected to the nature of mankind.

8   But the tongue, no one is able to subdue. This evil, when it is not restrained, is full of the ᵃⁿpoison of death.

9   With it we bless the LORD and Father and with it we curse men, who are made in the likeness of God.

10   And from the same mouth proceed blessings and cursings. My brothers, it is not right that these [things] be done so.

11   ᵃˡCan sweet and bitter water come out of one fountain?¹

12   Or can a fig tree, my brothers, produce olives, or a vine, figs? So also, you cannot make salty water sweet.¬

13   Who is wise and instructed among you? He should show his works with praiseworthy actions, with humble wisdom.

14   But if you have bitter envy or contention in your hearts, do not elevate yourselves above the truth and lie,

15   because this wisdom does not come down from above, but is earthly, from the reasonings of the soul and from demons.

16   For where there is envy and contention, there also [is] confusion and everything that is evil.

17   Now the wisdom that is from above is pure ᴾand full of peace and humble and obedient and full of mercy and good fruits and is without division and does not respect persons.¬

18   And the ᵐfruit of justification is sown in quietness by those who serve peace.

---

¹ Fig: erotesis, **lema** questions, vs. 11, 12, obvious answer "no"

Chapter 4

1 From where are wars[1] and arguments among you? Is it not from the desires that war in your members?

2 You desire and you do not have. And you perish and are zealous,[2] yet it does not come into your hands. And you strive and cause wars, yet you have not, because you have not asked.[3]

3 You ask and do not receive, because you ask wrongly, so that you may nourish your desires.

4 Adulterers, do you not know that the friendship of this world is in opposition to God? Therefore, he who wants to be a friend of this world becomes an opponent of[4] God.

5 Or do you think that the scripture fruitlessly said: **THE SPIRIT THAT LIVES IN US DESIRES WITH ENVY?**[5]

6 But our Lord has given abundant grace to us. Because of this, he said: **GOD HUMBLES THE PROUD AND GIVES GRACE TO THE HUMBLE.**

7 Therefore, be subject to God and stand against SATAN and he will flee from you.

8 And come near to God and he will come near to you. Cleanse your hands, [you] sinners. Set apart your hearts, doubters of self.

9 Humble yourselves and mourn. And your laughter will be changed to mourning and your joy to sorrow.

10 Humble yourselves[6] before the LORD and he will elevate you.

11 Do not speak against one another, my brothers, for he who speaks against his brother or judges his brother, speaks against the law and judges the law. And if you judge the law, you are not a doer of the law, but its judge.[7]

12 There is one lawgiver and judge, who is able to give life and to destroy. But who are **you** that you are judging your neighbor?

13 Now what will we also say about those who say, "Today or tomorrow we will go to a certain city and we will work there [for] one year and we will do business and increase?"[8]

---

[1] Could be fig: hyperbole

[2] Var (M): 'are burdened'; repeat pronoun *you*, 11x, vs. 2-5

[3] Repeat *ask*, vs. 2, 3

[4] Var (SLM): 'to'

[5] Fig: erotesis, **lema** question, obvious answer "no"

[6] Repeat *humble yourselves* from v. 9

[7] Same root: *judge, judges*

[8] Culture: going from city to city is a common way for merchants to do business, Freeman, p. 457.

ARAMAIC PESHITTA NEW TESTAMENT
JAMES

Chapter 4

14   And they do not know what will happen tomorrow. For ^{me}what is our life, except a vapor that is seen a little while ^Pand [then] vanishes and is gone?⌐

15   Instead, they should say, "If the LORD wills and we live, we will do this or that."

16   They boast in their pride. All boasting[1] like this is[2] evil.

17   And he who knows good and does not do it, to him it is sin.

Chapter 5

1   ⌐Oh rich [men], wail and weep for the miseries that will come on you,

2   for your wealth is corrupted and is rotten and your garments have been eaten by a moth.

3   And your gold and your silver have tarnished and their tarnish[3] will be a witness against you and it is going to eat your ^{sy}flesh. You have gathered a ^mfire for you for the last days.

4   *Behold, the ^{pe}wage of the laborers who have reaped your lands, which you have withheld, cries out. And the crying of the reapers has entered the ^cears of the LORD of Hosts.[4]

5   For you have lived in pleasure on the earth and have been greedy and have nourished your bodies as in the ^{sy}day of slaughter.

6   You have condemned and killed the Just [one] and he did not stand against you.

7   But **you**, my brothers, be long-suffering[5] until the coming of the LORD, ^sas the farmer who waits for the precious ^mfruit of his ground and is long-suffering about it, until he receives the early and latter rain.

8   So also be long-suffering and establish your hearts, for the coming of our Lord draws close.

9   Do not murmur against one another, my brothers, so that you should not be judged, for *behold, judgment stands before the door.

10   Take the prophets [as] an example, my brothers, for long-suffering with respect to your trials, those who spoke in the name of the LORD.

---

[1] Same root: *boast, boasting*
[2] Var (S): add 'from'
[3] Same root: *tarnished, tarnish*
[4] Or "heavenly armies"
[5] Repeat *long-suffering,* vs. 7, 8, 10

Chapter 5

11 For *behold, we give a blessing to those who have endured. You have heard of the endurance of Job and have seen the result that the LORD brought to pass for him, because the LORD is merciful and compassionate.

12 Now above everything, my brothers, do not swear, neither by heaven, nor by earth, not even by [any] other oath.[1] But rather, your word should be, "Yes, yes, and no, no,"[2] so that you should not be condemned under judgment.

13 And if one of you should be in a trial, he should pray,[3] and if he is glad, he should sing psalms.

14 And if one is sick, he should call for the elders of the church and they should pray for him and anoint him [with] oil in the name of our Lord.

15 And the prayer of faith will heal him who is sick and our Lord will raise him, and if [any] sins were committed by him, they will be forgiven.

16 Now confess your faults to one another and pray for one another to be healed, for great is the power of prayer that a just man prays.

17 Elijah was also a passionate man like us and he prayed that the rain would not fall on the earth. And it did not fall [for] three years and six months.

18 And again he prayed and the heaven[4] gave rain and the earth produced its [m]fruit.

19 My brothers, if one of you errs from the [an]way of truthfulness and someone causes him to repent from his error,[5]

20 he should know that he who turns back a sinner from the error of his way will give life to his soul from death and will blot out a multitude of his sins.

---

[1] Var (S): *oaths* (plural)
[2] Fig: epizeuxis, very solemn repetition
[3] Same root: *pray, prayer*, vs. 13-18
[4] Var (SL): *heavens* (plural)
[5] Same root: *errs, error*, also vs. 20

ARAMAIC PESHITTA NEW TESTAMENT
I PETER

Chapter 1

1   Peter, an apostle of Jesus Christ, to the chosen [ones] [P]and settlers who are scattered in Pontus and in Galatia and in Cappadocia and in Asia and in Bithynia,⌐

2   those who were chosen by the foreknowledge of God the Father by the holiness of the Spirit to be to the obedience and the purifying by [h]sprinkling of the [mt]blood of Jesus Christ: Grace and peace be multiplied to you.

3   [be]Blessed be God, the Father of our Lord[1] Jesus Christ, who by his great mercy has fathered us anew to the [an]hope of life by the resurrection of Jesus Christ,

4   and to an incorruptible and undefiled and unfailing[2] inheritance that is prepared for you in heaven,

5   being kept by the power of God and by faith for the life that is prepared to be revealed in the last times,

6   in which you will rejoice[3] forever. Even though in this time you are discouraged a little by the various trials that have happened to you,

7   [it is] so that the testing of your faith may appear more precious than refined gold that is refined by fire, for the glory and honor and praise[4] at the appearing of Jesus Christ.

8   You have not seen him, yet love, and by his faith, you rejoice with glorious joy that is unspeakable,

9   that you would receive the reward of your faith, the life of your souls.

10   [It is] that life that the prophets investigated when they prophesied about the grace that was to come that has been given to you.

11   And they searched for what time [that] the Spirit of Christ that was living in them showed and testified, when the sufferings of Christ and his glory that followed would come to pass.

12   And it was revealed to all who were seeking that they were not seeking[5] for themselves, but they were prophesying these [things] for us that now are revealed to you, by way of those [things] that we announced by the Holy Spirit that was sent from [m]heaven, into which [things] even the angels desired to investigate.

---

[1] Var (M): omit *our Lord*

[2] Repeat *and not*, 3x

[3] Var (M): 'you will live'

[4] Fig: hendiatris, "glorious weighty praise"

[5] Repeat *seeking*

ARAMAIC PESHITTA NEW TESTAMENT
I PETER

Chapter 1

13 Because of this, ^{pr}gird up the loins of your thinking and be completely watchful and hope for the joy that will come to you at the appearing of our Lord Jesus Christ

14 ^sas obedient children. And do not associate again with your[1] former desires that you ignorantly desired.[2]

15 Rather, be holy in all your ways, as he who called you is holy,[3]

16 because it is written: **BE HOLY, EVEN AS I AM HOLY.**

17 And if you call on the Father, before whom there is no respect of persons and [who] judges everyone according to his works, conduct yourself with reverence during this time of your ^{pr}dwelling in a foreign country,

18 knowing that you were not redeemed with silver that is corruptible, nor with gold, by your empty works that you received from your fathers,

19 but with the precious ^{mt}blood of the ^hlamb,[4] who has no ^hspot or blemish, who is Christ.

20 He was previously appointed to this before the foundations of the world and was revealed in the end of times for you,

21 who by way of him have believed in God, who raised him from the dead and gave him glory, that your faith and your hope would be in God.

22 Your lives are becoming holy by the obedience of the truth and becoming full of love without respect of persons, so that you may love one another out of a ^{he}pure and mature heart.

23 Like a man, you were born anew, not of ^mseed that is corruptible, but of that[5] which is not corruptible, by the living word of God that stands forever.

24 Because, ^{me}**ALL** ^{sy}**FLESH [IS] GRASS AND ALL ITS BEAUTY** ^s**AS A FLOWER OF THE FIELD. THE GRASS DRIES UP AND THE FLOWER WITHERS,**

25 **YET THE WORD OF OUR GOD STANDS FOREVER.** And this is the word that was preached to you.

---

[1] Var (SLM): omit *your*
[2] Same root: *desires, desired*
[3] Repeat *holy*, also v. 16
[4] Var (M): omit *of the lamb*
[5] Fig: ellipsis, add [seed]

Chapter 2

1   Therefore, put away from you all wickedness [P]and all deceit and respect of persons and envy and accusation.˥

2   And be [s]like young infants and desire the word, as for pure and spiritual milk by which you are nourished to life,

3   since you have [h]tasted and seen that **THE LORD IS GOOD.**

4   The [me]one to whom you are drawn is the living stone[1] that men have rejected, yet with God [is] chosen and honored.

5   [al]And you also, [s]as living stones, are built up and [me]are spiritual temples and holy priests to offer spiritual[2] sacrifices that are acceptable before God by way of Jesus Christ.

6   For it is told in the scripture: *BEHOLD, I LAY IN ZION AN APPROVED AND PRECIOUS STONE IN THE HEAD OF THE CORNER AND HE WHO BELIEVES ON HIM WILL NOT BE ASHAMED.

7   Therefore, this honor is given to you who believe. But to those who are not convinced,

8   HE IS A [an]STONE OF STUMBLING AND A ROCK OF OFFENSE. And they stumbled at him,[3] in that they were not persuaded by the word to which they were appointed.˥

9   Now **you** are a chosen generation that serves as a priest for the kingdom, a holy people, a redeemed assembly, to declare the praises of him who called you from [m]darkness to his excellent [m]light,

10   you who previously were not counted a people, but now [are] the people of God. There were even no mercies on you, but now mercies[4] are poured out on you.

11   My beloved [ones], I beg you, [s]as strangers and [s]as settlers, be separate from all the desires of the body, those that wage a war [5] against the soul.

12   And your conduct should be proper before all men, [so that] those who speak evil words against you may see your good works and may praise God in the [sy]day of testing.

---

[1] Orientalism: *living* was used by the Hebrews to express the excellency of something, Bullinger, *Figures of Speech*, p. 831; cf. John 4:10, 11, Acts 7:38, Heb. 10:20, Rev. 7:17.

[2] Eastern txt: omit *spiritual*, see Etheridge translation

[3] Var (SL): 'it' (feminine, referring to the stone); same root: *stumbling, stumbled*

[4] Repeat *people, mercies*

[5] Var (SL): *wars* (plural)

Chapter 2

13 And be subject to all men because of God, to kings because of their authority

14 and to judges because they are sent by him for the punishment of wrong-doers and for the praise of the workers of good [things].

15 For so is the will of God, that by your good works you would ᵖʳshut the mouth of the foolish who do not know God.

16 [You are] ˢas free men, and not as men whose freedom is made a ᵐveil to them for their wickedness, but ˢas servants of God.

17 Honor everyone. Love your brothers and reverence God and honor kings.

18 And those who are servants among you, be subject to your lords with reverence, not only to the good and to the humble, but also to the hard and difficult,

19 for they will have grace before God, who because of a good conscience endure sorrows that come on them wrongfully.

20 But what praise will they have who endure pressures because of their transgressions? But when you do what is good and they pressure you and you endure, then your praise is great with God.

21 For to this you were called, because even Christ died for us and left us this example that **you** should walk in his footsteps:

22 **HE DID NOT COMMIT SIN, NEITHER WAS DECEIT FOUND IN HIS ᵐMOUTH,**

23 who was reviled, yet did not revile,[1] and was suffering, yet did not threaten, but delivered his case to the ᵃⁿjudge of uprightness.

24 And ᵖʳhe carried all our sins and lifted them in his body to the cross, so that being dead to sin, we would have life by his justification, for by his wounds you were healed.

25 For you were wandering ˢlike sheep, yet you are now returned to the ʰᵉshepherd and overseer of your souls.

Chapter 3

1 So also, wives, be subject to your husbands, so that those who are not persuaded by the word will be restored without difficulty by your good behavior,

2 when they observe that you behave with reverence and with modesty.

---

[1] Repeat *revile*

Chapter 3

3   And do not adorn yourselves with outer adornments[1] of the braiding of your hair or of ornaments of gold or of costly clothes.

4   But adorn yourselves with the hidden [h]man of the heart with a humble spirit, without corruption, an adornment that is costly before God.

5   For so also previously, holy women who trusted in God adorned themselves and were subject to their husbands,

6   as Sarah was subject to Abraham and called him, "My lord," whose daughters you are by good works, when you are not troubled by any fear.

7   And you men, likewise, live with your wives with knowledge. And hold them with honor [s]as delicate vessels, because they will also inherit the gift[2] of eternal life with you, for you should not be hindered in your prayers.

8   Now the conclusion [is] that all of you should be in agreement and you should suffer with those who suffer[3] and be compassionate to one another and you should be [he]merciful and humble.

9   And you should not repay anyone evil for evil, nor abuse for abuse, but in contrast to these [things], bless, for you were called to this, so that you may inherit a blessing.[4]

10   **THEREFORE, HE WHO DESIRES LIFE AND LOVES TO SEE GOOD DAYS SHOULD KEEP HIS [m]TONGUE FROM EVIL AND HIS [m]LIPS SHOULD SPEAK NO DECEIT.**

11   **HE SHOULD TURN AWAY FROM EVIL AND DO GOOD AND SHOULD SEEK PEACE AND PURSUE IT,**

12   **BECAUSE [c]THE EYES OF THE LORD [ARE] ON THE JUST [ONES] AND HIS EARS TO HEAR THEM AND THE FACE OF THE LORD [IS] AGAINST EVIL [ONES].**

13   And who is he who can do evil to you, if you are zealous of good [things]?[5]

14   And if you should suffer on account of uprightness, you are blessed. And do not be afraid of those who frighten you and do not be troubled.

---

[1] Same root: *adorn, adornments*, also v. 4, 5; culture: braiding of the hair was a common way of adorning oneself, Burder, vol II, p. 382, Freeman, p. 468.

[2] Var (M): *gifts* (plural)

[3] Repeat *suffer*

[4] Repeat *evil, abuse*; same root: *bless, blessing*

[5] Fig: erotesis – question to ponder

Chapter 3

15   But make holy the LORD Christ in your hearts and be ready to make a defense to all who ask you a word concerning the hope of your faith, with meekness and with fear,

16   having a good conscience, so that they who speak about you as about evil[1] men will be ashamed, as men who belittle your good behavior that is in Christ.

17   For it is profitable to you that you suffer evil [things] while you do good works ᵖᵃ(if therefore it is the will of God) and not while you do evil [things].

18   For even Christ died one time for our sins, the just [one] for sinners, that he would bring you to God. And he died bodily, but lives spiritually.

19   And he preached to those souls who were held captive in SHEOL,

20   those who previously were disobedient in the days of Noah, when [in] the long-suffering of God he commanded an ark to be made, in hope of their repentance, yet only eight souls entered it and were kept alive on the water.

21   For **you** also live in the same type by baptism ᵖᵃ(not when you wash the body of filth, but when you confess God with a pure conscience) and by the resurrection of Jesus Christ,

22   who was raised up to heaven ᴾand is at the right hand of God and angels and authorities and powers are subject to him.⌐

Chapter 4

1   If Christ therefore suffered for you in the ˢʸflesh, **you** also should arm yourselves with this mind, for whoever dies in his ˢʸflesh has ceased from all sins,

2   so that from now on, he should not live for the desires of men for as long as he is in the body, but for the will of God.

3   For the time that has passed by is sufficient when you served in the will of the pagans, in excess ᴾand in drunkenness and in filthiness and in revelry and in the service of demons.⌐

4   And *behold, now they marvel and criticize you, in that you do not burn with passion with them in that former excess.

5   They will give an account to God, who is going to judge the dead and the living.

---

[1] Repeat *evil*, vs. 16, 17

Chapter 4

6 For because of this, it was announced also to the dead, so that they should be judged as men in the flesh and [that] they should live in God spiritually.

7 But the end of all approaches. Because of this, be sober and be watchful in prayer.

8 And before everything, have keen love for one another, for love covers a multitude of sins.

9 And be compassionate to strangers without murmuring.

10 And everyone of you should minister the gift that he received from God to his friends, [s]as good stewards of the diverse grace of God.

11 All who speak should speak according to the word of God and all who serve [e][should serve] as from the strength that God has given to him, so that in all you do, God will be glorified by way of Jesus Christ, whose glory and honor is forever and ever. Amen.

12 My beloved [ones], do not be amazed at the trials that have come to you, as though something strange had happened to you, because they are for your experience.

13 But rejoice because you share in the sufferings of Christ, that so you will also rejoice and be glad at the [an]appearing of his glory.

14 And if you are reproached on account of the name of Christ, you are blessed, because the glorious Spirit of God rests on you.

15 Only none of you should suffer as a murderer or as a thief or as[1] a worker of evil [things].

16 But if he suffers as a Christian, he should not be ashamed, but he should glorify God in this name.

17 For it is the time when judgment will begin from the house of God and if it begins with us, what is the end of those who are disobedient to the gospel of God?[2]

18 And **IF THE JUST SCARCELY WILL LIVE, WHERE WILL THE WICKED AND THE SINNER BE FOUND?**

19 Because of this, those who suffer according to the will of God should commend to him their souls by good works, as to a faithful Creator.

---

[1] Repeat *or as*

[2] Fig: erotesis – question to ponder

ARAMAIC PESHITTA NEW TESTAMENT
I PETER

Chapter 5

1   Now I ask of the elders who are among you, I, an elder, your friend and a witness of the sufferings of Christ and a participant of his glory that is going to be revealed,

2   ^{al}feed the ^hflock of God that has been committed to you and perform [it] spiritually, not by necessity, but willingly, not for corrupt profits, but from your whole heart,

3   You should not be ^sas lords of the ^hflock, but ^sas a good example for them,

4   so that when the chief of the shepherds[1] is revealed, you will receive a ^{an}crown of glory from him that will not fade.⌐

5   And you, young ones, be subject to your elders and be clothed diligently with humbleness of mind toward one another, because **GOD IS OPPOSED TO THOSE WHO ELEVATE THEMSELVES, BUT HE GIVES GRACE TO THE HUMBLE.**

6   Therefore, humble yourselves under the mighty ^mhand of God, so that he will elevate you in the time that is right.

7   And throw all your care on God, because he is concerned for you.

8   Be watchful and remember, because your enemy, SATAN, roars ^sas a lion and walks about and seeks whom he may swallow.

9   Therefore, stand against him, being steadfast in faith and know that these sufferings also happen to your brothers who are in the world.

10   ^{be}Now the God of grace who has called us to his eternal glory by way of Jesus Christ, who has given us, while we endure these few trials, to be strengthened ^Pand to be made steadfast and to be established by him forever,⌐

11   to him [be] glory and dominion and honor, forever and ever. Amen.

12   These few [things], as I think of [them], I wrote to you by way of Silvanus, a faithful brother. And I am persuading[2] and bearing witness that this is the true grace of God in which you stand.

13   The chosen church that is in Babylon and Mark, my son, greet you.

14   Greet one another with a holy kiss. ^{be}Peace [be] with all those[3] who are in Christ. Amen.

---

[1] Culture: one shepherd was over all the others when there were many flocks, Freeman, p. 469.

[2] Var (SL): 'I am being persuaded'

[3] Var (SLM): 'all of you'

Chapter 1

1   Simon Peter, a ^{he}servant and apostle of Jesus Christ, to those who
have been made worthy of the equally[1] precious faith with us by the
justification of our Lord and our Savior, Jesus Christ:

2   Grace and peace be multiplied to you in the acknowledgment of our
Lord Jesus Christ.

3   [It is] he who has given all these [things] of divine power, for life
and the reverence of God, by way of the acknowledgment[2] of him who
called us into his glory and excellence.

4   For by him he has given you[3] great and precious promises, that by
way of these, you would be sharers of the divine nature, having escaped
from the corruption of the desires that are in the world.

5   Now while you are applying all this diligence, add to[4] your faith,
excellence, and to excellence, knowledge,

6   and to knowledge, self-control, and to self-control, endurance, and
to endurance, reverence of God,

7   and to reverence of God, brotherly kindness, and to brotherly
kindness, love.

8   For when these are found in you and increase, they establish you
[as] neither worthless, nor without ^mfruit in the acknowledgment of our
Lord Jesus Christ.

9   For he in whom these [things] are not found is blind so that he does
not see, because he has forgotten the cleansing of his former sins.

10   And concerning that, be especially diligent, my brothers, that by
way of your good works, you would make your calling and your
approval certain, for when you do these [things], you will never falter.

11   For so an entrance will be readily given to you to the eternal
kingdom of our Lord and our Savior, Jesus Christ.

12   And concerning this, I did not give up reminding you continually
about these [things], although you also know [them] well and are settled
concerning this truth.

13   And I think that it is right that as long as I am in this body, I should
stir you up by remembrance,

14   since I know that the ^{eu}absence of my body will be soon, as also our
Lord Jesus Christ has made known to me.

---

[1] Same root: *made worthy, equally*

[2] Repeat *acknowledgement* from v. 2, also v. 8

[3] Var: 'us', see Lamsa translation

[4] Repeat *to*, 7x, vs. 5-7; fig: climax, vs. 5-7

ARAMAIC PESHITTA NEW TESTAMENT
II PETER

Chapter 1

15   And I am concerned that you will also continually have [e][this care], that even after my [eu]departure, you will have remembrance of these [things].

16   For it was not following after sayings that were formed with skill [that] we made known to you the power and the coming of our Lord Jesus Christ, but after [me]we were spectators of his [h]majesty.

17   For after he received [he]honor and glory from God, the Father, when a voice came to him that [was] like this from glory, splendid in its greatness, "This is my beloved Son, in whom I am pleased,"

18   **we** also heard this voice from heaven that came to him, when we were with him on the holy mountain.

19   And we also have a word of prophecy that is certain, which you do well when you look at it [pa](as to a lamp that shines in a dark place until the day should dawn and the sun should rise) in your hearts,

20   knowing this first, that all prophecy was not a sending out of its own writing.

21   For prophecy never came by the will of man, but as they were being led by the sanctified[1] Spirit, men of God spoke sanctified [e][words].

Chapter 2

1   But there were also false prophets among the people, as also false teachers will be among you, who will introduce [an]heresies of destruction and deny the Lord who bought them, bringing on themselves swift destruction.

2   And many will follow their uncleanness, because of whom the [an]way of truth will be reproached.

3   And with fraud and with babbling words they will exploit you, whose previous condemnation has not stopped and whose [pe]destruction does not sleep.

4   For indeed God did not spare the angels who sinned, but cast them down in [as]chains of darkness into the low [regions] and delivered them to be kept for the [an]judgment of torment.

5   And he did not spare the former world, but protected Noah, the eighth [person], a preacher of uprightness, when he brought a flood over the world of the wicked.

---

[1] Repeat *sanctified*; double negative in this verse

Chapter 2

6   And when he burned the cities of Sodom and of Gomorrah and condemned them by an overthrow, setting an example to the wicked who were to come,

7   he also delivered just Lot, who was oppressed by the unclean conduct of those who were lawless,

8   for as that upright [man] was living among them, in seeing and in hearing ^{sy}day after day, his just soul was tormented by [their] lawless works.

9   The LORD knows how to deliver from trial those who reverence him, but he will keep the unjust for the ^{sy}day of judgment, when they will be tormented,

10   especially those who follow after the flesh with the ^{an}desire of defilement and rebel against lordship. [These are] daring [ones] and proud [ones], because they are not troubled when they blaspheme against the glory,

11   whereas angels that are greater than them in power and in might do not bring on themselves the ^{an}judgment of blasphemy from the LORD.

12   But these, ^sas dumb animals [that] are by nature for ^{he}slaughter and corruption, while blaspheming those [things] they do not know, will be corrupted in their own corruption,[1]

13   being those who have wickedness [as] the wage of wickedness.[2] To them, making merry that happens in the daytime is considered pleasure. [These are] defiled and full of blemishes, for they indulge themselves, while they are making merry in their idleness,

14   having eyes that are full of adultery and sins that do not come to an end, enticing people that are unstable and having a heart that is practiced in fraud, children of a curse,

15   who, having left the straight way, have swerved and gone in the way of Balaam, the son of Beor, who loved the wage of wickedness.[3]

16   And the reproof that he had for his transgression [was] an ass, without a voice, who spoke with the voice of men [and] restrained the foolishness of the prophet.

17   ^{me}These [men] are wells without water, clouds that are driven by a whirlwind, those for whom the ^{as}blackness of darkness is reserved.

---

[1] Same root: *corrupted, corruption*

[2] Repeat *wickedness*

[3] Repeat *wage of wickedness*, from v. 13

Chapter 2

18   For while they speak ^{an}vehement [words] of emptiness, they entice [again] with unclean desires of the flesh, those who had fled for a short time from these [men] who are living in error.

19   And they promise them liberty, while **they** are ^{pe}slaves of corruption, for by what a man is overcome, to this he is also enslaved.

20   For if, after they have fled from the ^{an}pollutions of the world by the acknowledgment of our Lord Jesus Christ, even our Savior, when they are entangled again in the same [and] are overcome, their end will be worse than the beginning.

21   For it would have been better for them not to have known the way of justification, than having known [it], to turn backwards from the holy commandment that was committed to them.

22   But these [sayings] of a true proverb have happened to them, "A dog has returned to his vomit[1] and the sow that was washed to wallowing in mud."

Chapter 3

1   This second letter, my beloved [ones], I write to you now, in which I stir up by remembrance your proper thinking,

2   so that you will recall the words that were spoken before by the holy prophets and the commandment of our Lord and our Savior by way of the apostles,

3   knowing this first, that at the end of days mockers will come who will mock,[2] walking according to their own desires

4   and saying, "Where is the promise of his coming? For since our fathers have slept, everything continues the same from the beginning of the creation."

5   For this is forgotten by them willingly, that the heaven[s] were from before, and the earth rose up out of the water and by way of water,[3] by the word of God.

6   Then by way of these e[waters] the world overflowed with water and was destroyed.

---

[1] Quoted from Prov. 26:11, became a proverb.

[2] Same root: *mockers, mock*

[3] Repeat *water, by way of,* vs. 5, 6

Chapter 3

7 But the heaven and the earth that are now are kept in store by his word, being reserved for fire on the [sy]day of the judgment and of the destruction of wicked men.

8 Now this one [thing] do not forget, my beloved [ones], that one day to the LORD is [s]as a thousand years and a thousand years [s]as one day.

9 The LORD does not delay in his promises as men consider delay, but he is long-suffering because of you, in that he does not want anyone to be destroyed, but rather [that] everyone should come to repentance.

10 But the [sy]day of the LORD will come [s]as a thief, in which the heaven[s] will suddenly pass away and the elements, while burning, will dissolve and the earth and the works that are in it will [not][1] be found.

11 Since therefore all these [things] will be dissolved, how ought you to be in your conduct? [e][You should be] holy [ones] and with reverence for God,

12 while you expect and you desire the coming of the [sy]day of God, in which the heaven[s], being [h]tried by fire, will be dissolved and the elements, while burning, will melt.

13 But we expect a new heaven and a new earth, according to his promise, in which justification will live.

14 Because of this, my beloved [ones], while you expect these [things], be diligent to be found by him without [h]spot and without blemish in peace.

15 And you should consider the long-suffering of the LORD [as] redemption, even as also our beloved brother Paul wrote to you according to the wisdom that was given to him.

16 As in all his letters, he speaks in them about these [things] [pa](in which there are some [things] hard to understand) that those who are without instruction and are unstable pervert, as they also [e][pervert] the writings of the rest to their own loss.

17 **You** therefore, my beloved [ones], since you know [these things] beforehand, guard yourselves, so that you should not fall from your commitment, following after the error of those who are lawless.

18 But grow in grace and in the knowledge of our Lord and our redeemer, Jesus Christ, and of God the Father, to whom [be][be] glory, both now and always, even for the days of eternity. Amen.

---

[1] Eastern txt: add 'not'

ARAMAIC PESHITTA NEW TESTAMENT
I JOHN

Chapter 1

1   We preach to you that which was from the beginning, which we have heard and seen with our eyes, sensed and touched with our hands, which is the [an]word of life.[1]

2   [pa]And life was revealed and we saw [it] and testify and preach to you the eternal life that was with the Father and was revealed to us.⌐

3   And what we have seen and heard, we also make known to you, so that you would have fellowship with us. And our fellowship is with the Father and with his Son, Jesus Christ.

4   And these [things] we write to you, so that our joy that is in you would be full.

5   And this is the gospel that we heard from him and we preach to you, that [c]God is light and there is no [m]darkness in him at all.

6   And if we say that we have fellowship with him and walk in [m]darkness, we are liars and we do not proceed in the truth.

7   But if we walk in the [m]light as he is in the light, we have fellowship with one another and the [mt]blood of Jesus his Son cleanses us from all of our sins.

8   And if we say that we have no sin, we deceive ourselves and the truth is not in us.

9   And if we confess our sins, he is faithful and just to forgive us our sins and to cleanse us from all our wickedness.

10   And if we say that we do not sin, we make him a liar and his word is not with us.

Chapter 2

1   My sons, I am writing these [things] to you so that you do not sin. Yet if someone should sin, we have a defense attorney with the Father, Jesus Christ, the Just [one].

2   For he is the payment for our sins and not on behalf of ours only, but also on behalf of [e][the sins of] the whole world.

3   And by this we perceive that we know him, if we keep his commandments.

4   For he who says, "I know him," and does not keep his commandments is a liar and the truth is not in him.

5   But he who keeps his word, in this [one] truly the love of God is completed, for in this we know that we are in him.

---

[1] Fig: anabasis, emphasis on *word of life*

Chapter 2

6　He who says, "I am in him," ought to conduct himself according to his own conduct.[1]

7　My beloved [ones], I am not writing a new commandment to you, but an old commandment that you have had from the beginning. And the old commandment is the word that you have heard.

8　[al]Again, I am writing a new commandment to you that is true in him and in you, because the [m]darkness has passed and the true [m]light[2] has begun to be seen.

9　Therefore, he who says that he is in the [m]light and hates his brother is in [m]darkness until now.

10　But he who loves his brother remains in the [m]light and there is no stumbling in him.

11　But he who hates his brother is in [m]darkness and walks in [m]darkness and does not know where he is going, because the [m]darkness has blinded his eyes.⌐

12　I am writing to you, sons, because your sins are forgiven on account of his name.

13　I am writing to you, fathers, because you have known him who is from the beginning. I am writing to you, young men,[3] because you have overcome the Evil [one]. I have written to you, young boys, because you have known the Father.

14　I have written to you, fathers, because you have known him who was from the beginning. I have written to you, young men, because you are strong and the word of God lives in you and you have overcome the Evil [one].

15　Do not love the [sy]world and not anything that is in it, for he who loves the [sy]world does not have the love of the Father.

16　For everything that is in the [sy]world, the desire of the body and the desire[4] of the [m]eyes and the boasting of the world, is not from the Father, but is from the [sy]world itself.

17　And the [sy]world and its desire pass away, but he who does the will of God remains forever.

18　My sons, it is the last time and according to what you have heard, a false Messiah will come. Even now there are many false Messiahs and from this we know that it is the last time.

---

[1] Same root: *conduct himself, conduct*

[2] Repeat *light, darkness,* vs. 8-11

[3] Repeat *fathers, young men,* vs. 13, 14

[4] Repeat *desire, world,* vs. 15-17

ARAMAIC PESHITTA NEW TESTAMENT
I JOHN

Chapter 2

19   They have gone out from us, but they are not of us, for if they had been of us they would have stayed with us, but they went out from us that it would be known that they were not of us.

20   And [ac]**you** have an anointing[1] from the holy [one] and are distinguishing between everyone.

21   I have not written to you because you do not know the truth, but because you do know it and because no falsehood is of the truth.

22   Who is a liar, except he who denies that Jesus is the Messiah?[2] This one is a false Messiah. He who denies the Father also denies the Son.

23   And he who denies the Son, also does not believe in the Father. He who confesses the Son, also confesses[3] the Father.

24   And what **you** have heard previously should remain with you, for if what you have heard previously remains with you, you will also remain[4] in the Father and in the Son.

25   And this is the promise that he has promised[5] to us, eternal life.

26   And these [things] I have written to you on account of those who seduce you.

27   And you also, if the anointing that you have received from him remains with you, will not need anyone to teach you. But as the anointing is from God, it teaches you about everything and it is the truth and there is no falsehood in it. And as he has taught you, remain in him.

28   And now, my sons, remain in him, so that when he is revealed, we will not be ashamed before him, but we will have boldness at his coming.

29   If you know that he is just, know that also everyone who does a just [thing] is from him.

Chapter 3

1   And see how great [is] the love of the Father toward us, because he has called us, even made us, sons. Because of this, the [sy]world does not know us, because it did not even know him.

2   My beloved [ones], now we are the sons of God and it does not yet appear what we are going to be, but we know that when he is revealed, we will be in his likeness and we will see him as he is.

---

[1] Same root: *anointing, Messiah* from v. 18, also vs. 22, 27

[2] Fig: erotesis – question to ponder

[3] Repeat *confesses*

[4] Repeat forms of *remain*, also, vs. 27, 28, 3:6, 14, 15

[5] Same root: *promise, promised*

Chapter 3

3   And everyone who has this hope concerning him purifies himself, as he is pure.

4   Now he who commits sin performs wickedness, for all sin is wickedness.[1]

5   And you know him who was revealed to take away our sins and there was no sin in him.

6   And everyone who remains in him does not sin and everyone who sins has not seen him and does not know him.

7   My sons, no man should deceive you. He who does a just [thing] is just, as also Christ is just.[2]

8   [3]He who performs sin is from SATAN, because from the beginning SATAN was a sinner.[4] And because of this, the Son of God appeared to destroy the works of SATAN.

9   Everyone who is born of God does not practice sin, because his seed is in him and he is not able to sin, because he is born of God.

10   By this the sons of God are separated from the sons of SATAN. Everyone who does not do[5] a just [thing] and does not love his brother is not from God.

11   For this is the commandment that you have heard previously, that you should love one another,

12   not as Cain, who was from the Evil [one] and killed his brother. And because of what did he kill him? Because his works were evil and those of his brother were just.

13   And do not wonder, my brothers, if the [sy]world hates you.

14   **We** know that we have moved from death to life in this, that we love our brothers. He who does not love his brother remains in death.

15   For everyone who hates his brother is a murderer and you know that everyone who is a murderer is not able to remain in eternal life.

16   In this we know his love toward us, for he gave himself for us. And it is also right for us to give ourselves for our brothers.

17   And whoever has property of the world and sees his brother who has a need and withholds his compassion from him, how is the love of God in him?

---

[1] Repeat *wickedness*

[2] Repeat *just*, vs. 7-12

[3] Var (SLM): add 'and'

[4] Same root: *sin, sinner, sins*, vs. 8, 9

[5] *Do* is same word as *practice*, v. 9

Chapter 3

18 My sons, do not love one another with words and with the [m]tongue, but with works and in truth.

19 And in this we recognize that we are from the truth and we will persuade our heart[s] before he comes.

20 Because if our heart condemns us, how much greater [is] God than our heart?[1] And he knows everything.

21 My beloved, if our heart does not condemn us, our faces are open before God,

22 and everything that we ask, we will receive from him, because we keep his commandments and do pleasing [things] before him.

23 And this is his commandment, that we believe on the name of his Son, Jesus Christ, and love one another as he commanded us.

24 And he who keeps his commandments is kept[2] by him and he lives in him. And by this we understand that he lives in us, from his Spirit that he gave to us.

Chapter 4

1 My beloved [ones], do not believe all the spirits, but discern whether the spirits are from God, because many false prophets have gone out in the [sy]world.[3]

2 By this the Spirit of God is known, [for] every spirit that confesses that Jesus Christ has come in the [sy]flesh is from God.

3 And every spirit that does not confess that Jesus[4] has come in the flesh is not from God, but this [e][spirit] is from the false Messiah, about whom you have heard that he would come and is now already in the [sy]world.

4 Now **you** children, are of God and you have overcome them, because greater [is] he who is in you than he who is in the [sy]world.

5 And these are from the [sy]world. Because of this, they speak from the [sy]world and the [at]world hears them.

6 But **we** are from God and he who knows God hears us and he who is not from God will not hear us. By this we know the [an]Spirit of truth and the [as]spirit of deception.

7 My beloved [ones], we should love one another, because love is from God and everyone who loves is born of God and knows God,

---

[1] Fig: erotesis, **kema** question, emphasizing how much greater God is.

[2] Repeat forms of *keep*

[3] Repeat *world*, vs. 1-5, 9

[4] Var (L): 'the Messiah'

Chapter 4

8   because God is love. And everyone who does not love, does not know God.

9   By this the love of God toward us is known, because God sent his unique Son into the [sy]world that we would have life by him.

10   In this is love, not that **we** loved God, but [that] he[1] loved us and sent his Son [as] a payment for our sins.

11   My beloved [ones], if God so loved us, we also ought[2] to love one another.

12   No one has ever seen God, but if we love one another, God remains[3] in us and his love is completed in us.

13   And by this we know that we remain in him and he remains in us, because he has given us his Spirit.

14   And **we** have seen and testify that the Father sent his Son [as] the Redeemer for the [sy]world.

15   Everyone who confesses Jesus, that he is the Son of God, God remains in him and he remains in God.

16   And **we** believe and we know the love that God has toward us, for God is love, and everyone who remains in love remains in God.

17   And in this his love is completed with us, so that we would have boldness in the [sy]day of judgment, because as he was, so are **we** in this [sy]world.

18   There is no fear in love, but complete love throws out fear, because fear is dangerous. Now he who fears is not completed in love.[4]

19   Therefore, we should love God, because he first loved us.

20   But if someone should say, "I love God," yet hates his brother, he is a liar. For he who does not love his brother, whom he has seen, how can he love God, whom he has not seen?[5]

21   And we have received this commandment from him, that everyone who loves God should also love his brother.

Chapter 5

1   Everyone who believes that Jesus is Christ is fathered of God and everyone who loves the one fathering loves also the one who is fathered[6] by him.

---

[1] Var (SLM): 'God'

[2] Var (M): omit *we ought*

[3] Repeat *remains* (again), vs. 12-16

[4] Repeat *love, fear, hate, seen,* vs. 18-21

[5] Fig: erotesis – question to ponder

[6] Same root: *one fathering, is fathered*

Chapter 5

2   And by this we know that we love the children of God, when we love God and do his commandments.

3   For this is the love of God, that we should keep his commandments. And his commandments are not difficult,

4   because everyone who is born of God has overcome the ^{sy}world and this is the victory that overcomes[1] the ^{sy}world, our faith.

5   For who is he who overcomes the ^{sy}world, but he who believes that Jesus is the Son of God?[2]

6   This is he who came by way of water and blood, Jesus Christ. He was not by water alone, but by water and blood.

7   And the Spirit bears witness, for the Spirit is truth.[3]

8   And there are three witnesses,[4] Spirit and water and blood and the three of them are as one.

9   If we receive the testimony of men, how much more[5] the testimony of God that is greater? And this is the testimony of God that he testified concerning his Son.

10   Whoever believes in the Son of God has this testimony in himself. Everyone who does not believe has made God a liar, in that he did not believe the testimony that God testified concerning his Son.

11   And this is the testimony, that God has given us eternal life and the life is in his Son.

12   Everyone who holds fast to the Son also holds fast to life. And everyone who does not hold fast[6] to the Son of God does not have life.

13   These [things] I have written to you, those who believe in the name of the Son of God, that you would know that you have eternal life.

14   And we have this confidence toward him, for everything that we ask of him according to his will, he hears us.

15   And if we are persuaded that he hears us concerning what we request of him, we are confident that we have already received our requests that we requested [7] of him.

---

[1] Repeat forms of *overcome*, vs. 4, 5

[2] Fig: erotesis – question to ponder

[3] Var (SM): add 'for there are three that bear witness in heaven, the Father, the Word and the Holy Spirit, and these three are one.'

[4] Var (SM): add 'on earth'

[5] Fig: ellipsis, add [should we receive]; fig: erotesis, **kema** question, answer in the affirmative; same root: *testimony, testified*, vs. 9-11

[6] Repeat *holds fast*

[7] Same root: *requests, requested*

Chapter 5

16 If someone should see his brother when he sins a sin that is not guilty of death, he should ask and life will be given to those who do not sin as to death. **ᵖᵃ**For there is a sin of death, [but] I do not say that anyone should pray for this **ᵉ**[sin].┐ ¹

17 For all wickedness is sin and there is a sin that is not of death.

18 And we know that everyone who is born of God does not sin, for he who is born of God guards himself and the Evil [one] does not come near him.

19 We know that we are of God and all the **ᵖᵉ**world is seated in wickedness.

20 And we know that the Son of God has come and has given us knowledge that we would know the true [one] and be in him, in the true [one],² in his Son, Jesus Christ. This is the true God and eternal life.

21 My sons, keep yourselves from idolatry.

---

¹ Repeat *sin, death, wickedness*, vs. 16-19
² Repeat *true [one]*

1   The elder, to the chosen lady[1] and to her children, those whom I love in truth, and not I alone, but all those who know the truth,

2   because of the truth that remains in us and is with us forever:

3   [be]Grace be with us[2] and mercy and peace from God the Father and from our Lord Jesus Christ, the Son of the Father, in truth and in love.

4   I rejoiced greatly that I found some of your children walking in truth, as we received commandment from the Father.

5   And now I persuade you, [my] lady, not as though I am writing a new commandment to you, but that which we had from the beginning, that we love one another.

6   And this is love, that we should walk according to his commandments. This is the commandment as [ac]you heard from the beginning that you should walk in it.

7   For many deceivers have gone out into the world, those who do not confess that Jesus Christ has come in the flesh. This [one] is a deceiver and an antichrist.

8   Be watchful of yourselves, so that you do not lose that for which you worked, but rather [that] you may be paid the full reward.

9   Everyone who transgresses and does not remain in the teaching of Christ does not have God. He who remains in his teaching, this [one] has both the Father and the Son.

10   If anyone comes to you and does not bring this teaching, do not receive him in the house and do not say to him, "Joy to you,"

11   for he who says to him, "Joy to you," is sharing in his evil works.

12   Since I have many [things] to write to you, I do not want [e][to write] with paper and ink, but I am hoping to come to you and to speak [m]mouth to mouth, that our joy may be complete.

13   The children of your sister, a chosen [one], greet you. [be]Grace [be] with you. Amen.

---

[1] Could be name of lady, Kuria ܟܘܪܝܐ

[2] Var (Murdock): 'you'

ARAMAIC PESHITTA NEW TESTAMENT
III JOHN

1   The elder, to Gaius, a beloved [one], whom **I** love in truth:

2   Our beloved [one], in everything I pray for you that you would prosper and would be healthy, even as your life prospers.[1]

3   For I rejoiced greatly when the brothers came and testified about your integrity, even as **you** walk in integrity.[2]

4   For I have no greater joy than this, than to hear that my children walk in integrity.

5   Our beloved [one], you are doing in faith what you perform toward the brothers and especially those who are strangers,

6   who have given testimony concerning your love before all the church, to whom you are doing well, because you supply them according to what is proper to God.

7   For they went out on behalf of his name, taking nothing from the Gentiles.

8   Therefore, [ac]we ought to receive those who are like these that we may be helpers for the truth.

9   I wanted to write to the church, but he who loves to be first among them, Diotrephes, did not receive us.

10   Because of this, if I come, I will remember his works that he did, that he tore us down with evil words. And when these [things] did not satisfy him, he did not receive the brothers and he hindered and threw out of the church those who were receiving [them].

11   Our beloved [one], do not imitate evil, but good. He who does good is of God. He who does evil has not seen God.[3]

12   About Demetrius, there is a testimony from everyone and from the church and from the truth. And also **we** bear [him] testimony and you know that our testimony[4] is true.

13   I have many [things] to write to you, but I do not want to write to you with ink and pen,

14   but I am hoping to see you soon and we will speak [m]mouth to mouth.

15   [be]Peace be with you. The friends greet you. Greet the friends, everyone by his name.

---

[1] Repeat *prosper*

[2] Repeat *integrity*, vs. 3, 4, same word as "truth"

[3] Parallel structure: ABBA

[4] Same root: testimony, bear testimony, *from v. 6*

ARAMAIC PESHITTA NEW TESTAMENT
JUDE

1   Jude, a servant of Jesus Christ, and the brother of James, to the called nations, who are loved by God, the Father, and are kept in Jesus Christ:

2   Mercy ^Pand peace and love⌐ be multiplied to you.

3   My beloved [ones], while I am being completely diligent to write to you about our own salvation that is common, there is a need for me to write to you, persuading you to ^hcontend in the struggle on behalf of the faith that was once delivered to the holy [ones].

4   For men have gained entrance, who from the beginning were previously described in this condemnation, wicked men who turn the grace of our God to uncleanness and deny him who is the only Lord God and our Lord Jesus Christ.

5   And I want to remind you, although you all know [it], that God, having rescued the people from Egypt at one time, at a second [time] destroyed those who did not believe.

6   And the angels who did not keep their first estate, but left their own dwelling, he has reserved in chains, unknown, under ^mdarkness, for the judgment of the great ^{sy}day.

7   [It is] as Sodom and Gomorrah and the cities of the surrounding area, which committed fornication in the same manner as these and followed other flesh, [which] are placed under a ^{an}demonstration of fire that is eternal, being condemned to judgment.

8   In the same manner also, these who are fantasizing in dreams are indeed polluting the flesh and rejecting lordship and blaspheming against the glory.

9   Now Michael, the archangel, who, when he was debating with the ACCUSER, spoke about the body of Moses, did not dare to bring on him the ^{as}judgment of blasphemy,[1] but said, "The LORD will rebuke you."

10   And these [men] are blaspheming about those [things] that they do not know. And in those [things] that they are familiar with naturally ^sas dumb animals, in these they are corrupted.

11   ⁱWoe to them, for they have gone in the ^{an}way of Cain, and after the ^{an}error of Balaam they have burned with passion for reward, and by the ^{an}stubbornness of Core they are destroyed.

---

[1] Same root: *blasphemy, blaspheme*, vs. 9, 10

12   They are those who in their idleness feast in excess, as they are defiled, feeding themselves without fear. ^{me}[They are] clouds without rain that are moved by the winds, ^{me}trees whose produce has ceased, that are without ^{m}fruit, that die a second time and are pulled up from their roots,^{1}

13   ^{me}raging waves of the sea that by way of their foam demonstrate their shame, ^{me}wandering stars, for which the ^{as}blackness of darkness is reserved forever.

14   And Enoch, who was the seventh from Adam, also prophesied of these, saying, "*Behold, the LORD will come with multitudes of holy [ones]

15   to execute judgment on all and to reprove all people because of all these works that they have impiously practiced and because of all the hardened words that the impious^{2} sinners have spoken."

16   These are they who murmur and complain about all matters, walking according to their own desires. And their ^{m}mouth speaks shocking [things] and they flatter the appearances of people on account of profits.

17   But ^{ac}you, my beloved [ones], remember the words that were spoken before by the apostles of our Lord Jesus Christ,

18   because they told you that at the end of the times there would be those who were mocking, who would follow wickedness according to their own desires.

19   They are those who are marked out, natural [men] who do not have the Spirit.

20   But you, my beloved [ones], be built up anew in your holy faith by the Spirit, sanctified while [you] pray.

21   And we should keep ourselves in the love of God, looking for the mercy of our Lord Jesus Christ for our life that is eternal.

22   And indeed, snatch some of them out of the ^{m}fire.

23   And when they repent, have compassion on them with fear, hating even the garment that is ^{h}spotted by the ^{sy}flesh.

24   ^{be}Now to him who is able to keep us faultless and without ^{h}spot and to establish [us] without blemish,

25   the only God, our Redeemer, by way of Jesus Christ our Lord, in the presence of his glory with joy, to him [be] glory ^{P}and dominion and honor and majesty,⅂ both now and in all ages. Amen.

---

^{1} Fig: metaphor, series, vs. 12, 13, could be a parenthesis

^{2} Same root: *impiously practiced, impious*

ARAMAIC PESHITTA NEW TESTAMENT
REVELATION

Chapter 1

1   The revelation of Jesus Christ that God gave to him to show to his servants what is right to happen soon. And he made [this] known when he sent by way of his angel to his servant John,

2   who gave witness to the word of God and to the witness[1] of Jesus Christ, all that he saw.

3   ^{be}Blessed [be] he who reads and those who hear the words of this prophecy and keep those [things] that are written in it, for the time has drawn near.

4   John,[2] to the seven churches that [are] in Asia: ^{be}Grace [be] to you and peace from him who is and was and comes and from the seven spirits that are before his throne

5   and from Jesus Christ, the faithful witness, the firstborn of the dead and the ruler of the kings of the earth, who loved us and released us[3] from our sins by his ^{mt}blood

6   and made us a priestly kingdom to God, even his Father. ^{be}To him [be] glory and dominion, forever and ever. Amen.

7   *Behold, he comes with clouds and all eyes will see him, even those who pierced him, and all the tribes of the earth will mourn concerning him. ^fYes and amen.

8   "I am Aleph and Tau," says the LORD God, "He who is and was and comes, who is the Almighty."

9   **I**, John, your brother and companion with you in the trial and in the endurance that is in Jesus, was on the island that is called Patmos because of the word of God and because of the witness of Jesus Christ.

10   And I was ^e[seeing] spiritually on the first day of the week[4] and I heard from behind me a loud voice ^sas a trumpet[5]

11   that said, "These [things] that you see, write in a book[6] and send to the seven churches, to Ephesus ^pand to Smyrna and to Pergamos and to Thyatira and to Sardis and to Philadelphia and to Laodicea."_٦

12   And I turned to know the ^mvoice that spoke with me and when I turned, I saw seven lampstands of gold.

---

[1] Same root: *witness, gave witness*

[2] See extensive background information on book, Kitto, vol II, pp. 612-627.

[3] Repeat suffix *us*

[4] Var (Mr): 'lordly day'

[5] Culture: most of the uses of *trumpet* in Revelation are equivalent to the Hebrew **shofar,** Kitto, vol II, p. 375.

[6] Same root: *write, book*

ARAMAIC PESHITTA NEW TESTAMENT
REVELATION

Chapter 1

13   And in the middle of the lampstands [was one] like the form of a man clothed with an ephod[1] and his breasts girded with a girdle[2] of gold.

14   Now his head and his hair [were] white ˢlike wool and ˢlike snow, and his eyes [were] ˢlike a flame of fire

15   and his feet [were] in the form of Lebanese brass that is burned in a furnace[3] and his voice [was] ˢlike the sound of many waters.

16   And he had in his right hand seven stars and a sharp spear came out of his mouth and his appearance [was] like the sun showing its power.[4]

17   And when I saw him, I fell at his feet ˢas [one] dead. And he laid his right hand on me, saying, "Fear not. I am the ᵐʳfirst and the last[5]

18   and he who is alive and was dead. And *behold, I am alive forever and ever. Amen. And I have the ᵐkey of death and of SHEOL.

19   Therefore, write what you saw and these [things] that are and are going to happen after these,

20   the mystery of the seven stars that you saw in my right [hand] and the seven lampstands. ᵐᵉThe seven stars are the angels of the seven churches and ᵐᵉthe seven lampstands of gold that you saw are the seven churches."

Chapter 2

1   "And to the angel of the church[6] of Ephesus, write, 'So says he who holds the seven stars in his hand, he who walks among the lampstands of gold.

2   I know your works ᴾand your labor and your endurance and that you are not able to bear evil [ones]. And you have tested those who say about themselves that they are apostles and are not and you have found them [to be] liars.

3   And you have endurance and you bear a burden because of my name and you have not become weary.⌐

---

[1] Var (Mr): 'tunic' cf. Greek, **poderes**

[2] Same root: *girded, girdle*; Var (Mr): *girdle* is ܐܣܪ, cf. Greek, **zone**

[3] Culture: Lebanese brass was famous for its fine quality and strength, Lamsa, *New Testament Commentary*, p. 549.

[4] Var (Mr): 'his countenance was like the sun shining power'

[5] Semitism: *the first and the last* means, 'I am the only messenger,' Lamsa, *New Testament Commentary*, pp. 550-551.

[6] Culture: in the synagogue, the priest who spoke prayers and led the worship was called the "angel" or "messenger of the assembly", sometimes also called the "speaker," Kitto, vol II, p. 806, Burder, p. 387, Moseley, p.9.

ARAMAIC PESHITTA NEW TESTAMENT
REVELATION

Chapter 2

4   But I have [something] against you, because you have left your former love.

5   Remember from where you came and do the former works, but if not, I will come to you and I will remove your lampstand, unless you repent.

6   But this you have, that you hate the works of the Nicolaitans,[1] those that I hate.'

7   He who has ears should hear what the Spirit says to the churches.[2] And to him who overcomes, I will allow [him] to eat of the tree of life which is in the paradise of God."

8   "And to the angel of the church of Smyrna, write, 'So says the first and the last, he who was dead and lives.

9   I know your trial and your poverty[3] pa(but you are rich) and the reproach from those who say of themselves [that they are] Judeans when they are not Judeans,[4] but the assembly of SATAN.

10   Do not be afraid of anything, of those [things] that you are going to suffer. *Behold, the ACCUSER is going to throw some of you into the detention hall, so that you may be tried and you will have torment [for] ten days. Be faithful [ones] until death and I will give to you the ancrown of life.'

11   He who has ears should hear what the Spirit says to the churches. 'He who overcomes will not be hurt by the second death.'"

12   "And to the angel that is in the church of Pergamos, write, 'So says he who has the sharp sword of two edges.

13   I know[5] where you live, the place of the throne of SATAN. And you hold fast to my name and you have not denied my faith, even in the days [when] you were watched and my faithful witness pa(because every witness of mine is faithful) was killed among you.

14   But I have a few [things] against you. You have there those who hold the doctrine of Balaam, who taught Balak to set a stumbling stone before the sons of Israel to eat the sacrifices of idols and to commit fornication.

15   So also you have those who adhere in the same manner to the doctrine of the Nicolaitans.

---

[1] Lit: 'pourers of the curse'
[2] Repeat exact phrase, 2:11, 17, 29, 3:6, 13, 22
[3] Var (Mr): 'I know your works and your suffering'
[4] Repeat *Judeans*, as next word
[5] Var (Mr): add 'your works and'; add at end of verse, 'where Satan dwells'

569

Chapter 2

16 Repent therefore.[1] And if not, I will come to you immediately and I will wage war with them with the sword of my mouth.'

17 And[2] he who has ears should hear what the Spirit says to the churches. 'To him who overcomes, I will give from the manna that is hidden and I will give to him a white pebble and on the pebble a new name written that no man knows, except him who receives.'"

18 "And to the angel that is in the church that is in Thyatira, write, 'So says the Son of God, he who has eye[s] ˢlike a flame of fire and his feet ˢlike Lebanese brass.

19 I know your works ᴾand your love and your faith and your service and your endurance and your last works are greater than the former [ones].˥

20 But I have much against you, because you allowed your wife, Jezebel, who says concerning herself that she is a prophetess and teaches and deceives my servants, to commit fornication and to eat sacrifices of idols.

21 And I gave her a time for repentance and she does not desire to repent[3] of her fornication.

22 *Behold, I will cast her on a bed and those who commit adultery with her into great torment, unless they repent of their works.

23 And I will kill her sons with death[4] and all the churches will know that I am searching the emotions and the heart[5] and I will give to all of you according to your works.'

24 *I say to you, to the rest who are in Thyatira, all those who do not have this teaching, those who have not known the deep [things] of SATAN ᴾᵃ(as they say), 'I will not place another burden on you.

25 Therefore, that which you have, hold fast until I come.

26 And he who overcomes and keeps my works, to him I will give authority over the nations

27 **TO RULE THEM WITH A ROD OF IRON AND ˢAS VESSELS OF A POTTER, THEY WILL BE BROKEN.** For thus I received from my Father.

28 And I will give him the star of the morning.'

29 He who has ears should hear what the Spirit says to the churches."

---

[1] Var (Mr): *repent therefore* is included in v. 15

[2] Var (Mr): omit *and*

[3] Same root: *repent, repentance*, also vs. 21, 22

[4] Fig: pleonasm, redundancy

[5] Var (Mr): *hearts* (plural)

Chapter 3

1 "And to the angel that is in the church of Sardis, write, 'So says he who has the seven spirits of God and the seven stars. I know your works ᴾand the name that you have and that you live and that you are dead.

2 And be watchful and establish the rest of those who are going to die,⌐ for I have not found that your works are complete before[1] God.

3 Remember how you heard and you received. Beware and repent. And if you do not watch, I will come to you ˢas a thief and you will not know [in] what ˢʸhour [he] comes to you.

4 But I have a few names in Sardis, those who have not defiled their clothes and walk before me in white and are worthy.

5 He who overcomes will be so dressed with white clothes[2] and I will not blot out his name from the scroll of life and I will confess his name before my Father and before his angels.'

6 He who has ears should hear what the Spirit says to the churches."

7 "And to the angel of the church of Philadelphia, write, 'So says the holy [one], the true [one], he who has the ᵐkeys[3] of David, the one who opens and no one shuts and [who] shuts and no one opens.

8 I know your works and *behold, I have set before you an open door that no one is able to shut, because you have little strength and you have kept my word and you have not denied my name.

9 And *behold, I will give those from the assembly of SATAN, who say concerning themselves that they are Judeans and they are not, but they lie, *behold, I will make them to come and to worship before your feet and to know that I have loved you.

10 Because you have kept the word of my patience, I will keep you from the trial that is going to come on all the earth to try[4] all the inhabitants of the earth.

11 I am coming quickly. Hold fast what you have, so that no man will take your ᵐcrown.

12 And I will make him who overcomes a ʰpillar in the temple of[5] God and he will not go outside again and I will write on him the name of my God and the name of the new city, Jerusalem, that comes down from my God, and my own new name.'

---

[1] Var (Mr): add 'my'

[2] Culture: if the Sanhedrin judged a priest fit for service, he was clothed in white, Burder, vol II, p. 387.

[3] Var (Mr): *key* (singular)

[4] Same root: *try, trial*

[5] Var (Mr): add 'my', add *comes down* 'from heaven'; repeat *name*

Chapter 3

13 And he who has ears should hear what the Spirit says to the churches."

14 "And to the angel of the church of Laodicea, write, 'So says the true [one], the faithful and true witness and the first[fruit] of the creation of God.

15 I know your works. You are neither cold nor hot. You ought[1] to be either cold or hot.

16 And you are lukewarm and neither cold nor hot. I am going to vomit you from my mouth,

17 because you have said that you are rich,[2] 'and I have grown rich and I am not in need of anything,' and you do not know that you are weak ᴾand miserable and poor and naked.⌐

18 I counsel you to buy gold from me that is tried by fire, so that you may become rich, and white garments to clothe yourself, so that the shame of your nakedness should not be revealed. And apply eye salve to the eyelids, so that you may see.

19 **I** reprove and I correct those whom I love. Be zealous, therefore, and repent.

20 *Behold, I stand at the door and knock. If anyone hears my voice and will open the door, I will enter and I will eat supper with him and he[3] with me.

21 And to him that overcomes, I will allow [him] to sit with me on my throne, even as **I** overcame and sat with my Father on his throne.'

22 He who has ears should hear what the Spirit says to the churches."

Chapter 4

1 After these [things], I looked and *behold, [there was] an open door in heaven. And the voice that I heard [was] ˢlike a trumpet speaking with me saying, "Come up here and I will show you what must happen after these [things]."

2 [4]And immediately I was [seeing] spiritually. And *behold, a throne was placed in heaven and [someone] was sitting on the throne.[5]

---

[1] Var (Mr): 'O that'

[2] Var (Mr): 'I am rich', instead of *poor*, 'blind'

[3] Fig: ellipsis, add [will eat supper]

[4] Fig: polysyndeton, after this point in the book, there are lengthy passages where all the phrases are connected with *and*...These are not marked because they are easily confused in the text with the shorter uses of this figure.

[5] Repeat *throne(s)*, vs. 2-10

ARAMAIC PESHITTA NEW TESTAMENT
REVELATION

Chapter 4

3 And he who was sitting [was] ˢlike the appearance of a stone of jasper and of sardius, and the rainbow around the throne [was] ˢlike the appearance of emeralds.

4 And around the throne [were] twenty-four thrones. And on the thrones, twenty-four elders were sitting, clothed in white garments. And on their heads [were] ᵃⁿcrowns of gold.

5 And thunderings ᴾand lightning bolts and shouts⌐ came out from the thrones and seven burning lights [were] before the throne that are the seven spirits of God.

6 And before the throne [was] a sea of glass ˢlike crystal. And between the throne and around the throne [were] four living creatures full of eyes in front and behind.

7 The first living creature was ˢlike a lion and the second living creature [was] ˢlike a calf and the third living creature had a face ˢas a man and the fourth living creature [was] ˢlike an eagle that was flying.

8 Each one of the four living creatures stood and had from its claws and upward,[1] six wings full of eyes around [it] and from within. And they have no rest, ᵐʳday or night, saying, "Holy, holy, holy, LORD God Almighty, he who was and is and comes."

9 And when the four living creatures give glory ᴾand honor and thanksgiving⌐ to him who sits on the throne and to him who truly lives forever and ever,

10 the twenty-four elders would fall down before him who sits on the throne and worship him who truly lives forever and ever. And they would throw their crowns before the throne, saying,

11 "Worthy is our Lord and our God to receive glory ᴾand honor and power,⌐ because you created all, and by way of your will, they came to be and were created."

Chapter 5

1 And I saw on the right hand of him who sat on the throne a book inscribed from within and from without and sealed with seven seals.

2 And I saw another strong angel who proclaimed with a loud voice, "Who is worthy to open the book and to loosen its seals?"

3 And there was no one who was able, in heaven or on earth or under the earth, to open the book and to loosen its seals and to see it.

4 And I was weeping very much, because there was no one who was found who was worthy to open the book and to loosen its seals.

---

[1] Var (Mr): omit *from its claws and upward*

Chapter 5

5   And one of the elders said to me, "Do not weep. *Behold, the [h]lion from the tribe of Judah, the [h]root of David, has conquered. He will open the book and its seals."

6   And I saw in the middle of the throne and of the four living creatures and of the elders a lamb that stood as if it was being sacrificed. And it had seven horns and seven eyes that are the seven spirits of God that are sent to all the earth.

7   And he came and took the book from the hand of him who sat on the throne.

8   And when he took the book, the four living creatures and the twenty-four elders fell down before the lamb, each one of them having a harp and a bowl of gold filled with perfumes, which are the prayers of the holy [ones],

9   who were praising a new praise-hymn[1] and saying, "You are worthy to take the book and to loosen its seals, because you were sacrificed and you bought us with your blood for God from all the tribes [P]and[2] nations and peoples.┐

10   And you made them a kingdom for our God [P]and priests and kings┐ and they will reign on the earth."

11   And I saw and I heard [e][a sound] [s]like the voice of many angels around the throne and of the living creatures and of the elders. And their number was a multitude of multitudes and a thousand of thousands.[3]

12   And they were saying with a loud voice, "Worthy is the sacrificed Lamb to receive power [P]and wealth and wisdom and strength and honor and glory and blessing

13   and the whole creation that is in heaven and on the earth and under the earth and is in the sea and all that is in them." ┐ And I heard them saying to him who sits on the throne and to the Lamb, "Blessing [P]and honor and praise and dominion,┐ forever and ever."

14   And the four living creatures were saying, "Amen." And the elders fell down and worshipped.

Chapter 6

1   And I saw when the Lamb opened one of the seven seals and I heard one of the four living creatures that spoke [s]as the sound of thunderings, "Come and see."

---

[1] Same root: *praising, praise-hymn*

[2] Var (Mr): add 'tongues and'

[3] Semitism: *multitude of multitudes* means the greatest amount, or innumerable

Chapter 6

2   And I heard and I saw and *behold, [there was] a white horse and he who sat on it had an archery bow and a crown was given to him and he went out a conqueror, both conquering and to conquer.[1]

3   And when he opened the second seal, I heard the second living creature, saying, "Come."

4   And a red horse went out and it was given to him who sat on it to take peace from the earth that they would slaughter one another and there was given to him a large sword.

5   And when the third seal was opened, I heard the third living creature, saying, "Come." And *behold, [there was] a black horse and he who sat on it had a balance in his hand.

6   And I heard a voice from among the living creatures, saying, "A measure[2] of wheat for a denarius and three measures of barley for a denarius and do not hurt the wine and the oil."

7   And when he opened the fourth seal, I heard the voice of the living creature, saying, "Come."

8   And I saw a pale horse and the name of him who sat on it [was] Death and SHEOL followed him. And authority was given to him over one-fourth of the earth to kill by the sword ᴾand by famine and by death and by the wild animal of the earth.┐ [3]

9   And when he opened the fifth seal, I saw under the altar the people that were killed because of the word of God and because of the testimony of Jesus that they had.

10   And they cried with a loud voice and said, "How long, LORD, ʰᵉholy and true, do you not judge and require our blood of the inhabitants of the earth?"

11   And there was given to each one of them a white robe[4] and it was said that they should rest for a short period of time until it should be completed, even their fellows and their brothers who were going to be killed, as also they ᵉ[had been].

12   And I saw when he opened the sixth seal and there was a great earthquake. And the sun was ˢas sackcloth of black hair and the whole moon was ˢas blood.

---

[1] Var (Mr): 'conquering that he would conquer'

[2] Var (Mr): 'choenix' (from Greek); a choenix was ½ a cab and normally would cost 1/8 denarius. This shows that there was extreme famine, Bullinger, *Commentary on Revelation*, pp. 257-258, see appendix 2.

[3] Var (Mr): 'the toothed creature' referring to the Antichrist, Rev. 13:1ff.

[4] Culture: white robes were given as rewards of honour, Burder, vol II, p. 270.

Chapter 6

13   And the stars of heaven fell on the earth, ˢas a fig tree that casts its unripe figs when it is shaken by a powerful wind.

14   And heaven was parted, ˢas scrolls that are rolled out, and every mountain and every island were moved out of their place[s].

15   And the kings of the earth ᴾand the great and the rulers of thousands and the rich and the strong [ones] and all the servants and the free men┐ hid themselves in caves and in the rocks of the mountains.

16   And they were saying to the mountains and the rocks: FALL ON US AND HIDE US FROM THE FACE OF THE LAMB,[1]

17   BECAUSE THE GREAT ˢʸDAY OF THEIR[2] ANGER HAS COME AND WHO IS ABLE TO STAND?

Chapter 7

1   And after this, I saw four angels standing on the four corners[3] of the earth and holding back the four winds, so that the wind would not blow on the earth, nor on the sea, nor[4] on any tree.

2   And I saw another angel who came up from the rising of the sun and he had the seal[5] of the living God. And he cried out with a loud voice to the four angels to whom it was given to hurt the earth and the sea.

3   And he said, "Do not hurt the earth nor the sea, not even the trees, until we seal the servants of God on their foreheads."

4   And I heard the number of the sealed [ones], one hundred and forty-four thousand from all the tribes of Israel,

5   from the tribe of[6] Judah, twelve thousand, from the tribe of Reuben, twelve thousand, from the tribe of Gad, twelve thousand,

6   from the tribe of Asher, twelve thousand, from the tribe of Naphtali, twelve thousand, from the tribe of Manasseh, twelve thousand,

7   from the tribe of Simeon, twelve thousand, from the tribe of Issachar, twelve thousand, from the tribe of Levi, twelve thousand,

8   from the tribe of Zebulun, twelve thousand, from the tribe of Joseph, twelve thousand, from the tribe of Benjamin, twelve thousand sealed [ones].

---

[1] Var (Mr): *hide us from* 'the presence of him who sits on the throne and form the wrath of the Lamb'

[2] Var (Mr): 'his'; fig: erotesis – question to ponder

[3] Var (Mr): **gunitha** ܓܘܢܝܬܐ cf. Greek, also 20:8

[4] Repeat lit: 'and not on'

[5] Culture: bearing of the seal is token of a high office, Burder, vol II, pp. 388-389

[6] Repeat *from the tribe of, twelve thousand,* vs. 4-8

Chapter 7

9   And afterwards, I saw a large crowd, which no one was able to number, from every nation ᴾand tribe and peoples and languages,˥ that stood before the throne and before the Lamb and were clothed with white robes and [with] palm branches in their hands.[1]

10   And they were crying out with a loud voice and saying, "Deliverance to our God and to him who sits on the throne and to the Lamb."

11   And all the angels were standing around the throne and the elders and the four living creatures. And they fell down before the throne on their faces,

12   saying, "Amen. ᵇᵉGlory ᴾand blessing and wisdom and thanksgiving and honor and power and strength˥ [be] to our God, forever and ever. Amen."

13   And one of the elders answered and said to me, "Who are those who are clothed with white robes and from where did they come?"

14   And I said to him, "My lord, **you** know." And he said to me, "They are those who came from great torment and have washed their robes and whitened them in the ᵐᵗblood of the Lamb.

15   Because of this, they are before the throne of God and serve him ᵐʳday and night in his temple. And he who sits on the throne will dwell with them.

16   They will not hunger ᴾand not thirst and the sun will not fall on them and not any heat,˥ [2]

17   because the Lamb who is in the middle of the throne will feed them and will guide[3] them to life and to the fountains of water and will wipe away all the tears from their eyes."

Chapter 8

1   And when he opened the seventh seal, there was silence in heaven for about half an hour.[4]

2   And I saw seven angels who were standing before God. Seven trumpets were given to them.

---

[1] Culture: carrying palm branches symbolized victory, Freeman, p. 471.

[2] Var (Mr): 'burning heat,' cf. Greek, **kauma**

[3] Var (Mr): 'lead'

[4] Culture: this may be an allusion to the period of silence that occurred when the high priest offered the incense in the Holy Place, Burder, vol II, p. 390.

Chapter 8

3   And another angel came and stood by the altar and he had a censer of gold. And much incense was given to him to offer with the prayers of all the holy [ones] on the altar that is before the throne.

4   And the smoke of the incense went up with the prayers of the holy [ones] from the hand of the angel before God.

5   And the angel took the censer and filled it from the fire on the altar and threw [it] on the earth[1] and there were thunderings [P]and shouts and lightning bolts and an earthquake.⌐

6   And the seven angels who [had] the seven trumpets on them prepared themselves to sound.[2]

7   And that first [angel] sounded and there was hail and fire mingled with water and [these] were thrown on the earth. And a third of the earth was burned and a third[3] of the trees were burned and all the grass of the earth was burned.

8   And the second [angel] sounded and it was [s]as a huge mountain that was burning. It fell into the sea and a third of the sea became blood.

9   And a third of all the created [ones] that are in the sea that have life died and a third of the ship[s] were destroyed.

10   And the third [angel] sounded and a large star fell from heaven that was burning [s]as a flame and it fell on a third of the rivers and on the fountains of waters.

11   And the name of the star was called Wormwood and a third of the waters became [s]as wormwood and a great number of men died, because the waters were made bitter.

12   And the fourth [angel] sounded and a third of the sun was struck and a third of the moon and a third of the stars and a third of them became dark. And the day did not show [for] a third part of it and the night likewise.

13   And I heard one eagle flying in heaven that said,[4] "[i]Woe, woe, woe, to the inhabitants of the earth, because of the sound of the trumpets of the three angels that are going to sound!"

---

[1] Compare Ezekiel 10:2ff.

[2] Var (Mr): 'blow a horn,' also v. 7

[3] Repeat *a third*, 12x, vs. 7-12

[4] Var (Mr): 'I looked and heard an eagle flying in the middle of heaven that said with a loud voice'; Lamsa: 'an eagle having a tail red as it were blood,' *New Testament Commentary*, p. 575.

ARAMAIC PESHITTA NEW TESTAMENT
REVELATION

Chapter 9

1   And the fifth [angel] sounded and I saw a star that fell from heaven on the earth and the key of the pits of the abyss was given to him.

2   And smoke went up from the pits, ^sas the smoke of a large furnace that was heated up. And the sun was darkened and the air [also] from the smoke of the pits.

3   And from the smoke, locusts went out on the earth and the authority that belongs to the scorpions of the earth was given to them.

4   And it was told to them that they should not harm the grass of the earth or any herb, not even the trees, but only the men who did not have the seal of God on their foreheads.

5   And it was given to them that they should not kill them, but [that] they should be tormented [for] five months. And their torment [was] ^slike the torment[1] of a scorpion when it falls on a man.

6   And in those days, men will seek death and will not find it. And they will earnestly desire to die and death will flee from them.

7   And the form of the locusts [was] ^slike horses that are prepared for battle. And on their heads [it was] ^slike a crown with the form of gold and their faces [were] ^slike the face of a man.

8   And they had[2] hair ^slike the hair of women and their teeth [were] ^slike [those] of lions.

9   And they had a breastplate ^slike a breastplate of iron and the sound of their wings [was] ^slike the sound of the chariots of many horses that are running to battle.

10   And they had tails ^slike a scorpion and stings in their tails and their authority [was] to hurt men [for] five months.

11   And there was a king over them, the angel of the abyss, whose name in Hebrew [is] Abaddon, and in Aramaic, his name is "Breaker."[3]

12   One woe is past. *Behold, there are still two woe[s].[4]

13   After these [things], the sixth angel sounded and I heard one voice from the four horns of the altar of gold that was before God

14   that said to the sixth angel that had the trumpet, "Release the four angels that are bound at the great river Euphrates."

15   And the four angels were released, who were prepared for an ^{sy}hour and for a day and for a month and for a year[5] to kill a third of mankind.

---

[1] Same root: *torment, tormented*

[2] Repeat *and they had,* vs. 9, 10

[3] Var (Mr): instead of *and in Aramaic…* 'and in Greek his name is Apollyon'

[4] Var (Mr): alt sp. ܠܐܐ

[5] Fig: extended synecdoche, meaning an undetermined point of time

ARAMAIC PESHITTA NEW TESTAMENT
REVELATION

Chapter 9

16 And the number of the hosts of the cavalry[1] was two thousand thousands. I heard their number.

17 And so I saw the horses in the vision and those sitting on them had a [an]breastplate of fire and chalcedony[2] and sulfur. And the heads of the horses [were] ⁵like the heads of lions and from their mouth[s] came out fire and sulfur and smoke.

18 And by these three plagues, a third of mankind was killed, even by the fire and by the sulfur and by[3] the smoke that came out of their mouth[s],

19 because the power of the horses [was] in their mouth[s] and also in their tails.[4]

20 And the rest of the men who were not killed by these plagues did not repent of the work of their hands that they should not worship demons ᴾand images of gold and of silver and of brass and of wood and of stone,ㄱ those that are not able to see, nor to hear or to walk.

21 And they did not repent of their murders or of their sorceries or of their fornication.[5]

Chapter 10

1 And I saw another angel who came down from heaven and was clothed with a cloud and a rainbow of heaven [was] on his head and his appearance [was] ⁵like the sun and his feet[6] [were] ⁵like pillars of fire.

2 And he had in his hand a little open book and he placed his right foot on the sea and the left on the land.

3 And he cried out with a loud voice ˢas a roaring lion. And when he had cried out, the seven thunders spoke with their voices.

4 And when the seven thunders spoke, I was preparing to write. And I heard a voice from heaven of the seven, saying, "Seal up what the seven thunders have said and do not write it."

5 And the angel that I saw standing on the sea and on the dry land, who lifted his hand to heaven,

---

[1] Var (Mr): 'horsemen'

[2] Var (Mr): 'jacinth'

[3] Repeat *and by*

[4] Var (Mr): add 'for their tails were like serpents and had heads, and with them they do harm'

[5] Repeat *or of*; Var (Mr): *fornication* is 'thefts'

[6] Or "legs"

ARAMAIC PESHITTA NEW TESTAMENT
REVELATION

Chapter 10

6   even he swore by him who lives forever and ever, he who created the heaven and that which is in it and the earth and that which is in it,[1] that there should not be any more time.

7   But in the days of the seventh angel, when he is about to sound, the mystery of God will be completed that he announced to his servants, the prophets.

8   And I heard a voice from heaven again speaking with me and saying, "Go [and] take the little book that is in the hand of the angel who stands on the land and on the sea."

9   And I came near to the angel, telling him to give the little book to me. And he said to me, "Take and eat it and it will be bitter to your stomach, but in your mouth it will be ˢlike honey."

10   And I took the little book from the hand of the angel and I ate[2] it. And it was in my mouth sweet ˢas honey. And when I ate it, my stomach became bitter.

11   And he said to me, "You must prophesy another time about the nations ᴾand peoples and languages and many kings."¬

Chapter 11

1   And a reed was given to me ˢlike a rod and the angel stood and said, "Rise up and measure the temple of God and the altar and those who worship in it,

2   and leave out the court within the temple and do not measure it, because it is given to the Gentiles and they will trample down the holy city [for] forty-two months.

3   And I will give my two witnesses ᵉ[authority] to prophesy, one thousand, two hundred and sixty days, being clothed with sackcloth.

4   ᵐᵉThese are two olive [trees] and two lampstands who stand before the Lord of the whole earth.

5   And [if] one seeks to harm them, fire comes out of their mouth[s] and consumes their enemies. And [if] anyone wishes to harm them, so they must be killed.

6   And these have authority to shut heaven, so that rain will not fall in the days of their prophecy. And they have authority to turn the waters to blood and to strike the earth with all plagues, as much as they desire.

---

[1] Repeat *that which is in it*

[2] Semitism: *eating* means to receive knowledge or understanding, Bullinger, *Commentary on Revelation*, p. 342.

Chapter 11

7   And when they have completed their testimony, the creature[1] who came up from the sea will wage war with them and will conquer them and will kill them.

8   And their corpses [will be] on the streets of the great city that is spiritually called Sodom and Egypt, where their Lord was crucified.

9   And some of the peoples ᴾand tribes and languages and nations⌐ see their corpses [for] three and a half days and they will not allow their corpses to be placed in graves.

10   And the inhabitants of the earth will rejoice over them and will be glad and they will send gifts to one another, because of the two prophets who tormented the inhabitants of the earth."

11   And after three and a half days, the living Spirit from God entered into them and they rose up on their feet and the Spirit of life fell on them and great fear was on those who saw them.

12   And they heard a loud voice from heaven that said to them, "Come up here." And they went up to heaven in a cloud and their enemies gazed at them.

13   And in that ˢʸhour there was a huge earthquake and one-tenth of the city fell and they were killed in the earthquake. The names of the men [were] seven thousand and the remainder were in fear and gave praise to God who is in heaven.

14   *Behold, two woe[s] have come and *behold, the third woe comes quickly.

15   And the seventh angel sounded and there were loud voices in heaven, saying, "The kingdom of the age has become ᵉ[the kingdom] of our God and of his MESSIAH and he reigns forever and ever."

16   And the twenty-four elders, who were sitting before God on their thrones, fell on their faces and worshipped God,

17   saying, "We praise you, LORD God Almighty, who is and was, because you have taken your great power and you have reigned.

18   And the nations were angry, yet your anger has come and the ˢʸtime of the dead that they should be judged. And you will give a reward to your servants, the prophets, and to the holy [ones] and to those who reverence your name, ᵐʳthe small with the great. And you will corrupt those who corrupted the earth.

19   And the temple was opened in heaven and the ark of his covenant was seen in the temple. And there were lightning bolts ᴾand thunderings and shouts and an earthquake and large hail.⌐

---

[1] Var (Mr): 'beast of prey'

Chapter 12

1   And a great sign was seen in heaven, a woman clothed with the sun and the moon under her feet and a crown of twelve stars on her head,

2   and [she was] pregnant and crying and laboring in childbirth, also being in pain to give birth.

3   And another sign was seen in heaven, and *behold, [I saw] a great ^{an}dragon of fire that had seven heads and ten horns and seven crowns on its heads.

4   And its tail drew away[1] a third of the stars that were in heaven and threw them on the earth. And the dragon was standing before the woman who was about to give birth, so that when she gave birth, he would devour her son.

5   And she gave birth to a male child who was going to rule all the nations with a rod of iron and her son was caught up to God and to his throne.

6   And the woman fled to the wilderness, where she had a place that was prepared there by God, so that they would nourish her [for] one thousand, two hundred and sixty days.

7   And there was a war in heaven and Michael and his angels were warring with the dragon, and the dragon and his angels warred.

8   And they did not prevail and no place was found for them in heaven.

9   And the great dragon was thrown out, that chief serpent, who is called the ACCUSER [2] and SATAN, who deceived the whole earth. And he was thrown out on the earth and his angels were thrown out with him.

10   And I heard a loud voice from heaven saying, "*Behold, there is deliverance and power and the kingdom of our God, because the Despiser of our brothers is thrown out, who despised[3] them, ^{mr}night and day, before our God.

11   And they overcame by the blood of the Lamb and by way of the word of his testimony and they did not love their own lives, until death.

12   Because of this, ^{pe}rejoice, [oh] heaven and those who live in them! ⁱWoe to the earth and to the sea, because the ACCUSER, who has great fury, has come down to them, knowing he has a short time."

13   And when the dragon saw that he was thrown on the earth, he persecuted the woman who gave birth to the male child.

---

[1] Var (Mr): 'cut off'

[2] Var (Mr): 'the Deceiver', same root as *thrown out*, ܐܬܪܡܝ

[3] Var (Mr): 'accuser,' 'accused,' cf. Greek, **katargeo**; same root: *despiser, despise*

Chapter 12

14   And two wings of a large eagle were given to the woman, so that she would fly to the wilderness to her place to be fed there [for] a time, times, and half of a time, from before the face of the serpent.[1]

15   And the serpent threw water [s]as a river out of his mouth after the woman, so that the water would cause her to be carried away.

16   And the earth helped the woman and the earth opened its mouth and swallowed the river that the dragon threw out of its mouth.

17   And the dragon was furious about the woman and he went to wage war with the rest of her seed, those who keep the commandments of God and have the testimony[2] of Jesus.

Chapter 13

1   And I stood on the sand of the sea. And I saw a creature[3] coming up from the sea that had ten horns and seven heads, and on his horns, ten crown headbands, and on his head, the [an]name of blasphemy.

2   And the creature that I saw was [s]like a leopard and his feet [were] [s]like those of a bear and his mouth [was] [s]like that of lions. And the dragon gave him his power and his throne and great authority.

3   And one of his heads [was] as wounded to death and the deadly wound was healed and the whole world was amazed at the creature.

4   And they worshipped the dragon who gave authority to the creature and they worshipped the creature, saying, "Who is like this creature and who is able to make war with him?"

5   And a [m]mouth was given to him for speaking great [things] and blasphemy and authority was given to him to act [for] forty-two months.

6   And he [pr]opened his mouth to blaspheme in the presence of God, to blaspheme the name and the dwelling of those who dwell in heaven.

7   And it was given to him to wage war with the holy [ones] and to conquer them and authority was given to him over all the tribes [P]and peoples and languages and nations.⌐

8   And all the inhabitants of the earth will worship him, **those** who are not written in the book of life of the slain Lamb before the foundations of the world.

---

[1] Semitism: meaning a great way away from the serpent, Bullinger, *Figures of Speech*, p. 407

[2] Repeat *testimony* from v. 11

[3] Var (Mr): 'savage beast', lit: "beast of tooth", used throughout Revelation to distinguish this creature or beast from the four living creatures around the throne; Jennings documents that the Lee manuscript uses this phrase 33x, p. 227.

Chapter 13

9   He who has ears should hear.

10   He who leads into captivity will go into captivity and he who kills with the sword will be killed with the sword.[1] Here is the [he]faith and the patience of the holy [ones].

11   And I saw another creature coming up from the earth and he had two horns [s]like a lamb and he was speaking [s]as the dragon.

12   And he will exercise all the authority of the first creature before him and he will cause the earth and those who live in it to worship the first creature, whose deadly wound was healed.

13   And he will do great signs, such as, he will make fire to come down from heaven on the earth before men.

14   And he will seduce those who are living on the earth by way of the signs that are given to him to do in the presence of the creature, telling those who are living on the earth to make an image for the creature who had the wound of the sword and lived.

15   And it was given to him to give breath to the image of the creature and to cause all who would not worship the image of the creature to be killed,

16   and to cause all, [mr]small and great, rich and poor, lords and servants, to be given a mark on their right hands or on their foreheads,

17   so that no one could buy or sell again, except those who had the mark of the name of the creature or the number of his name.

18   Here is wisdom. And he who has understanding should count the number of the creature, for it is the number of a man, six hundred and sixty-six.

Chapter 14

1   And I saw, and *behold, a lamb was standing on the mountain of Zion and with him [were] one hundred and forty-four thousand who had his name and the name of his Father written on their foreheads.

2   And I heard a sound from heaven [s]as the sound of many waters and [s]as the sound of great thunder. The sound that I heard [was] [s]as a harpist who strikes on his harps.

3   And they were praising as a new praise song[2] before the throne and before the four living creatures and before the elders. And no one was able to learn the praise song, except the one hundred and forty-four thousand purchased [ones] from the earth.

---

[1] Repeat *sword, go into captivity, killed*

[2] Same root: *praising, praise song*, also v. 2, *harpist, harps*

Chapter 14

4   These are they who have not defiled themselves with women, for they are virgins, they who followed the Lamb everywhere he would go. These were purchased from mankind, the first[fruit] to God and to the Lamb,

5   in whose mouth falsehood was not found, for they are without blemish.

6   And I saw another angel flying in the middle of heaven and he had the everlasting gospel with him to preach to the inhabitants of the earth and to all the people [P]and nations and tribes and language[s],⌐

7   saying with a loud voice, "Fear God and give him glory, because the [sy]hour of his judgment has come, and worship him who made heaven [P]and earth and the sea and the fountains of waters."⌐

8   And another, a second [angel], followed him and said, "Babylon, the great, has fallen, has fallen,[1] she who gave all the nations to drink of the [as]fury of her fornication."

9   And another, a third angel, followed them, saying with a loud voice, "He who worshipped the creature and his image and took his mark on his forehead

10   will also drink of the [an]wine of the fury of the LORD that is poured without mixture into the [m]cup of his anger.[2] And he will be tormented with fire and with sulfur before the holy angels and before the Lamb

11   and the smoke of their torment will rise forever and ever. And they will not have relief, [mr]day or night, those who were worshipping the creature and his image and who took the mark of his name."[3]

12   Here is the patience of the holy [ones], who keep the commandments of God and the faith of Jesus.

13   And I heard a voice from heaven saying, "Write. Blessed [are] the dead who [eu]depart in our Lord from now on. 'Yes,' says the Spirit, because they will rest from their labors."[4]

---

[1] Fig: epizeuxis, very solemn repetition

[2] Var (Mr): 'fury of God that is mixed in the cup'; Lamsa: 'mixed with bitterness'; culture: one type of sentence of death was to drink a cup of poison, Burder, vol II, p. 391.

[3] Var (Mr): omit *and who took the mark of his name*

[4] Var (Mr): *who depart in our Lord* is 'that die in God', add at end of verse, 'for their works accompany them'

Chapter 14

14 And *behold, [there was] a white cloud and on the cloud sat [one]
^slike the Son of Man and he had on his head a crown of gold and in his
hand [was] a sharp sickle.[1]

15 And another angel came out from the temple and cried out with a
loud voice to him who sat on the cloud, "Send your sickle and harvest,
because the ^{sy}hour to harvest has come."

16 And that [one] who sat on the cloud cast out his sickle on the earth
and the earth was harvested.

17 And another angel came out from the temple that is in heaven and a
sharp sickle was on him.

18 And another angel came out from the altar, who had authority over
fire and cried out with a loud voice to him who had the sharp sickle,
"Send your sharp sickle and gather the clusters of the vineyard of the
earth, because of the ripeness[2] of her grapes."

19 And the angel cast out his sickle on the earth and gathered the
vineyard of the earth and he cast [it] into the great winepress of the fury
of God.

20 And the winepress was trodden outside the city and blood came out
from the winepress to the bridles of the horses for one thousand and two
hundred furlongs.

Chapter 15

1 And I saw another sign in heaven, ^{he}great and marvelous, angels
who had the seven last injuries, for in them the fury of God is completed.

2 And I saw ^sas a sea of glass mingled with fire and those who had
conquered over the creature and over his image and over the number of
his name were standing on top of the sea of glass and they had the harps[3]
of God.

3 And they were praising the praise song[4] of Moses, the servant of
God, and the praise song of the Lamb and were saying, "Great and
wondrous [are] your works, LORD God Almighty, upright and true [are]
your works, King of the ages.

4 Who will not fear you, LORD, and glorify your name? Because you
alone are innocent, because all the nations will come and will worship
before you, because you are right."

---

[1] Repeat *sickle*, vs. 14-19

[2] Var (Mr): 'because her grapes are full-grown'

[3] Var (Mr): **qithrosa,** cf. Greek, **kithara**

[4] Same root: *praising, praise song*

ARAMAIC PESHITTA NEW TESTAMENT
REVELATION

Chapter 15

5   And after these [things], I looked and the temple of the [an]tabernacle of witness was opened in heaven.

6   And the seven angels came out from the temple, who had the seven injuries, being clothed with pure and shining linen cloth and girded on their breasts [with] a girdle[1] of gold.

7   And one of the four living creatures gave to the seven angels seven bowls filled with the fury of God, who is alive forever and ever. Amen.

8   And the temple was filled with the smoke of the glory of God and with his power and there was no one who was able to enter the temple until the seven injuries of the seven angels were completed.

Chapter 16

1   And I heard a loud voice from the temple that said to the seven angels, "Go and pour the seven bowls[2] of the fury of God on the earth."

2   And the first went and poured his bowl on the earth and an evil and painful ulcer came on the men who had the mark of the creature and [on] those who were worshipping his image.

3   And the second angel poured his bowl into the sea and the sea became [s]as dead and every living creature died in the sea.

4   And the third angel poured his bowl into the rivers and into the fountains of waters and they became blood.[3]

5   And I heard the angel of the waters[4] saying, "You are just, who is and was, and innocent, for you have judged these,

6   because they have shed the blood of the prophets and the holy [ones]. And you have given them blood to drink, [which] they deserve."

7   And I heard [e][another] at the altar who said, "Yes, LORD God Almighty, true and just [are] your judgments."

8   And the fourth angel poured his bowl on the sun and it was given to him to scorch men with fire.

9   And men were scorched by the great heat and they reviled the name of God, who has authority over these injuries, and they did not repent, to give him glory.

---

[1] Same root: *girded, girdle*

[2] Var (Mr): 'cups', used 7x in chapter, cf. Greek, **phialen**

[3] Repeat *blood*, vs. 4-6

[4] Culture: *the angel of the waters* was the priest of the Jews who was in charge of wells, fountains and ditches in Jerusalem, Burder, vol II, p. 391.

Chapter 16

10   And the fifth angel poured his bowl on the throne of the creature and his kingdom became dark and they were biting their tongues from pain.

11   And they reviled the name of the God of heaven because of their pains and because of their ulcers and they did not repent of their works.

12   And the sixth angel poured his bowl on the great river, Euphrates, and its water dried up to prepare the road for the kings from the east.

13   And I saw [coming] out of the mouth of the dragon and out of the mouth of the creature and out of the mouth of the false prophet, three unclean spirits, **s**like frogs,

14   **pa**for they are the spirits of demons that do signs,¬ that are going against the kings of the inhabited earth to gather them for the battle of that great **sy**day of God Almighty.

15   **pa***Behold, he comes as a thief.¬ **be**Blessed [is] he who watches and keeps his garments, so that he should not walk naked and they should see his shame.[1]

16   And he gathered them to a place that is called Megiddo[2] in Hebrew.

17   And the seventh angel poured his bowl into the air and a loud voice came out of the temple from before the throne that said, "It is [done]."

18   And there were lightning bolts and thunderings and there was a huge earthquake, the like of which had not happened since men had been on the earth, for so great was this shaking.

19   And the great city became three parts and the cities of the nations fell, and Babylon the great was remembered before God to give to her the **m**cup of the **an**wine of his fury and of his anger.

20   And every island fled away and the mountains were not found.

21   And large hail, **s**as a talent, came down from heaven on men and the men reviled God because of the injury of the hail, because the injury[3] of it was very great.

Chapter 17

1   And one of the seven angels who had the seven bowls came and spoke with me, saying, "Follow me. I will show you the judgment of the harlot who sits on many waters,

---

[1] Var (Mr): lit. 'his spreading'; culture: when a priest on watch was found asleep in the temple, his clothes were stripped and burned, Burder, vol II, pp. 391-392.

[2] Var (Mr): 'Armageddon,' cf. Greek.

[3] Repeat *injury,* cf. 15:1

Chapter 17

2   with whom the kings of the earth fornicated and all the inhabitants of the earth became drunk from the wine of her fornication."

3   And he led me to the wilderness spiritually and I saw a woman who was sitting on the red creature that was full of the names of blasphemy that had seven heads and ten horns.

4   And the woman was clothed with purple and scarlet [garments] that were gilded with gold and precious stones and pearls and she had a cup of gold in her hand and it was full of the abomination and pollution of her fornication.

5   And on her forehead it was written, "Mystery, Babylon[1] the great, mother of harlots and of pollutions of the earth."

6   And I saw that the woman was drunk from the blood of the holy [ones] and from the blood of the witnesses of Jesus. And I wondered [with] great wonder[2] when I saw her.

7   And the angel said to me, "Why do you wonder?[3] **I** will tell you the mystery of the woman and of the creature that carries her that has seven heads and ten horns.

8   The creature that you saw was and is not [and] is going to come up from the sea and go to destruction. And [those] living on the earth will wonder, whose names are not written in the scroll of life from the foundations of the world, when they see the creature that was and is not and approaches.

9   Here [is] understanding for him who has wisdom. [me]The seven heads are seven mountains on which the woman sits.

10   And [me]there are seven kings, five have fallen and one is [and] the other has not yet come. And when he comes, he must continue [for] a little while.

11   And the dragon and [me]the creature that was and is not, even he is the eighth and is one of the seven and goes to destruction.

12   And [me]the ten [m]horns that you saw are ten kings who have not yet received a kingdom, but they take authority as kings [for] one [sy]hour with the creature.

13   These have one will, and they give their own power and authority to the creature.

---

[1] Culture: Babylon was founded by Nimrod, a rebel against God and founder of idolatry, cf. Genesis 10:8, Bullinger, *Commentary on Revelation*, pp. 506-509.

[2] Same root: *wonder, wondered*

[3] Fig: erotesis, **lema** questions, obvious answer "yes"; question could be translated, "Are you wondering?"

Chapter 17

14   These will make war with the Lamb and the Lamb will conquer them, because he is Lord of lords and King of kings[1] and those with him [are] the called and chosen and faithful [ones]."

15   And he said to me, "The [me]waters that you saw, on which the harlot sits, are nations [P]and multitudes and peoples and languages.⌐

16   And the ten [m]horns that you saw of the creature will hate the harlot and they will make her [he]desolate and naked and they will eat her flesh and they will burn her with fire.

17   For God has put in their hearts to do his will and they will do their one will and they will give their kingdom to that creature until the words of God are fulfilled.

18   And the [me]woman whom you saw [is] the great city which has dominion over the kings of the earth."

Chapter 18

1   And after these [things], I saw another angel who came down from heaven who had great authority and the earth was shining from his glory.

2   And he cried out with a loud voice, "Babylon the great has fallen, has fallen,[2] and has become a dwelling for demons and a garrison for all unclean and hateful spirits,

3   because [pe]she has mixed the wine of her fornication[3] for all the nations, and the kings of the earth have fornicated with her and the merchants of the earth have grown rich from the power of her madness."

4   And I heard another voice from heaven, saying, "Come out from within her, my people, so that you do not share in her sins, so that you do not receive of her injuries,

5   because her sins have reached up to heaven[4] and God has remembered her wicked [deeds].

---

[1] Semitism: *Lord of lords and King of Kings* means "the greatest Lord and the greatest King." The superlative degree is shown in this way, also 19:16, Bullinger, *Figures of Speech*, p. 283

[2] Fig: epizeuxis, solemn repetition

[3] Var (Mr): 'wrath'; word play in Mosul text: wine **khemra,** wrath, **khimtha**

[4] Semitism: *her sins have reached up to heaven* means judgment is imminent, cf. Jeremiah 51:9, could be fig: hyperbole

Chapter 18

6   Render to her, even as also she has rendered, and double to her double for her works. In the ^{m}cup that she mixed, mix for her double.[1]

7   About what she glorified herself and was arrogant, likewise ^{e}[give her] ^{he}torment and sorrow, because in her heart, she said, 'I sit [as] a queen and ^{t}I am not a widow and I will see no sorrow.'

8   Because of this, in one ^{sy}day injuries will come on her, death and sorrow and famine, and she will be burned by fire, because the LORD [is] mighty who has judged her.

9   And the kings of the earth will cry and wail over her, those who fornicated with her and were arrogant, when they see the ^{an}smoke of her burning,

10   while standing away from [her] out of fear of her torment. And they will say, '^{i}Woe, woe, woe,[2] [to] the great city, Babylon, the powerful city,[3] because in one ^{sy}hour your judgment has come!'

11   And the businessmen of the earth will cry and will mourn over her and there is no one who will buy their merchandise any more,

12   the merchandise of gold ^{P}and of silver and of precious stones and of pearls and of fine linen and of purple clothing and silk of scarlet and every aromatic wood and every vessel of ivory[4] and every vessel of precious wood and brass and iron and marble

13   and cinnamon and perfumes[5] and myrrh and incense and wine and oil and fine flour and sheep and horses and chariots and the bodies and souls of men.⌐

14   And your ^{m}fruit, the desire of your soul, has gone away from you and everything luxurious and celebrated has gone away from you and you will not see them any more,

15   nor find them. The businessmen of these [things], who were made rich by her, will stand away from [her] out of fear of her torment, crying and wailing

16   and saying, '^{i}Woe, woe, [to] the great city that was clothed with fine linen and purple and scarlet [clothes] that were gilded with gold and precious stones and pearls,

---

[1] Repeat *double, render*; semitism: *double to her double* means to give her full compensation, Bullinger, *Commentary on Revelation*, p. 543.

[2] Var (Mr): omit third *woe*; fig: epizeuxis, very solemn repetition

[3] Var (Mr): 'prevailing *city*', *away from* is 'afar off'

[4] Var (Mr): compound word, lit: 'bone of an elephant,' cf. Greek

[5] Var (Mr): add 'and spices'

Chapter 18

17 because in one ^{sy}hour wealth like this is laid waste!'[1] And all the masters of ships and all those traveling to places in ships and the sailors and all those who do business by sea stood a distance away.

18 And they cried over it as they were watching the smoke of its burning and saying, 'What [city] is like the great city?'

19 And ^{pr}they threw dust on their heads and cried out, crying and wailing and saying, 'Woe, woe, [to] the great city, in which those who had ship[s] in the sea became rich from her greatness, for in one ^{sy}hour she is devastated!'

20 ^{be}Exult over her, [oh] heaven and holy [ones] and apostles and prophets, because God has judged your judgment[2] on her."

21 And one of the mighty angels took a huge stone ^slike a millstone and threw [it] into the sea and said, "So with violence Babylon, the great city, will be thrown down and you will not find [it] any more.[3]

22 And the sound of the harp ^Pand of the shofar and of all kinds of music and trumpeters¬ [4] will not be heard in you any more.

23 And the light of the lamp will not be seen in you any more ^Pand the voice of the bridegroom and the voice of the bride will not be heard in you any more,¬ because your merchants were the great [ones] of the earth, because you seduced all the nations with your enchantments,

24 and the blood of the prophets and the holy [ones] who were killed on the earth was found in her."

Chapter 19

1 And after these [things], I heard a loud voice of a large multitude in heaven who were saying, "Hallelujah! Deliverance and glory and power [be] to our God,

2 because ^{he}true and upright [are] his judgments, because he has judged the great harlot who has corrupted the earth with her fornication and has avenged the blood of his servants from her hands."

3 A second [time] they said, "Hallelujah!" And her smoke went up, forever and ever.

---

[1] Var (Mr): this phrase is in v. 17; *sailors*, alt sp. ܢܵܘܛܹܐ, cf. Greek, **nautes**

[2] Same root: *judged, judgment*

[3] Repeat *in you any more*, 4x, vs. 21-23

[4] Or "loud prayers"; Var (Mr): 'harp and of musicians and trumpeters'; Lamsa: "harpers and musicians and singers and trumpeters'

Chapter 19

4   And the twenty-four elders and the four living creatures fell down and worshipped our God who sat on the throne and said, "[i]Amen. Hallelujah!"

5   And a voice [came] from the throne saying, "Praise our God, all his servants and all those who reverence his name, [mr]the small with the great."

6   And I heard a voice, [s]as of a large crowd and [s]as the voice of many waters and [s]as the voice of mighty thunderings, saying, "[i]Hallelujah, because the LORD God Almighty reigns!

7   We are glad and rejoice. We will give him praise, because the marriage feast of the Lamb has come and his wife has made herself ready."

8   And it was given to her to be clothed with [me]fine linen, clean and shining, for the fine linen represents the straight[1] ways of the holy [ones].

9   And they said to me, "Write. [be]Blessed [are] those who are invited [ones] to the supper of the marriage feast of the Lamb." And he said to me, "These are the true words of God."

10   And I fell at his feet and worshipped him. And he said to me, "No. I am your fellow-servant and one of your brothers, those who have the testimony of Jesus. Worship God abundantly, for the testimony of Jesus is the Spirit of prophecy."

11   And I saw heaven opened, and *behold, [I saw] a white stallion and he who sat on it was called [he]faithful and true and with uprightness he judges and makes war.

12   And his eyes [were] [s]like a flame of fire and on his head [were] many crown headbands. And he had a name written [on him] that no [one] knew, except he.

13   And he was clothed with a garment dipped in[2] blood and his name was called "The Word of God."

14   And the armies in heaven were following him on white horses and were clothed with fine linen, [he]white and pure.

15   And from their[3] mouth[s] a sharp sword came out, with which to kill the nations. And he will rule them with a rod of iron and he will tread the winepress of the anger of God Almighty.

16   And he had a name written on his garments, on his thighs,[4] "King of kings and Lord of lords."

---

[1] Var (Mr): 'just'

[2] Var (Mr): 'sprinkled with'

[3] Var (Mr): 'his'

[4] Suggested variant reading as 'his banner,' Charles Torrey, *Documents of the Primitive Church*, pp. 221-222.

Chapter 19

17   And I saw another angel standing in the sun and he cried out with a loud voice and said to the bird[s] that fly in the middle of heaven, "Come, gather together for the great supper of God,

18   that you may eat the [sy]flesh of[1] the kings [P]and the [sy]flesh of the rulers of thousands and the [sy]flesh of the powerful [ones] and the [sy]flesh of the horses and of those who sit on them and the [sy]flesh of the free [men] and of the servants and of the small and of the great."[⌐]

19   And I saw the creature and his hosts[2] and the kings of the earth and their soldiers gathering to wage war with him who sits on the stallion and with his armies.

20   And the creature was captured and the false prophet with him, who performed signs before him by which he seduced those who received the mark of the creature and those who worshipped his image. And both of them went down and they were thrown into the lake of burning fire and of sulfur.

21   And the rest were killed by the sword of him who sat on the stallion, by that [sword] that came out of his mouth, and every bird of prey was full of their [sy]flesh.

Chapter 20

1   And I saw another angel that came down from heaven, who had the [m]key of the abyss and a great chain in his hand.

2   And he grabbed the dragon, the ancient serpent, who is the ACCUSER [3] and SATAN, and bound him [for] one thousand years.

3   And he threw him into the abyss and closed and sealed the top over him, so that he would not seduce all the nations any more. [pa]After these [things], he must release him [for] a short time.[⌐]

4   And I saw seats and they sat on them and judgment was given to them. And [I saw] the souls, those who were cut off because of the testimony of Jesus and because of the word of God and those who did not worship the creature nor his image, neither received the mark on their foreheads or on their hands, that they [he]lived and reigned with the Messiah [for] one thousand years.

5   And this is the first resurrection.

---

[1] Repeat *the flesh of*

[2] Var (Mr): omit *and his hosts*

[3] Var (Mr): instead of *the Accuser and Satan*, 'the Deceiver and Satan who seduced all the inhabited earth'

Chapter 20

6   Blessed and holy is he who has a part in the first resurrection. And on them the second death has no authority, but they will be priests of God and of Christ and will reign with him [for] one thousand years.

7   And when one thousand years is completed, SATAN will be released from his imprisonment

8   and will go out to seduce all the nations in the four corners of the earth, to Gog and to Magog, and to assemble them for battle, whose number [is] [s]as the sand of the sea.

9   And they went up on the space of the land and surrounded the city of the camp of the holy [ones] and the beloved city and fire came down from heaven from God and consumed them.

10   And the ACCUSER, their seducer, was thrown into the lake of [he]fire and sulfur, where the creature and the false prophet [were]. And they will be tormented, [mr]day and night, forever and ever.

11   And I saw a large white throne and him who sat on top of it, from before whose face the earth and heaven fled away, and a place was not found for them.

12   And I saw the dead, [mr]great and small, who stood before the throne, and the scrolls were opened. And another scroll was opened that is [the one] of judgment, and the dead were judged from those [things] that were written in the scroll,[1] according to their works.

13   And the sea gave up the dead in it and death and SHEOL gave up the dead with them and each one of them was judged according to their works.

14   And death and SHEOL were thrown into the lake of fire. This is the second death.

15   And he who was not found inscribed in the book of life was thrown into the lake of fire.

Chapter 21

1   And I saw a new heaven and a new earth, for the former heaven and the former earth had gone away and there was no more sea.

2   And I saw the holy city, the new Jerusalem, come down from heaven from God, prepared [s]as a bride adorned for her husband.

3   And I heard a loud voice from heaven that said, "*Behold, the dwelling[2] of God [is] with men, and he [will] live with them and they will be his own people and God is with them and will be a God to them.

---

[1] Repeat *scroll, judge, judgment, dead, death*, vs. 12-15

[2] Var (Mr): 'tabernacle'

Chapter 21

4   And he will wipe all tears from their eyes and there will no longer be death, neither sorrow, nor crying, nor[1] will there be any more pain on account of him,"

5   and it went away. And he who sat on the throne said to me, "*Behold, I am making all [things] new." And he said to me, "Write. These words are [he]faithful and true."

6   And he said to me, "I am Aleph and I am Tau, the beginning and the completion. To the thirsty, **I** will give from the fountain of living water, freely.

7   And he who overcomes will inherit these [things] and I will be God to him and he will be a son to me.

8   But for the fearful [P]and the unbelieving and the wicked and the defiled and murderers and sorcerers[2] and fornicators and idolaters and all liars,⌐ their portion [will be] in the lake burning with fire and sulfur, which is the second death."

9   And one of the seven angels came, who had the seven bowls filled with the seven last injuries, and spoke with me, saying, "Come, I will show you the bride, the wife of the Lamb."

10   And he carried me spiritually to a [he]great and high mountain and showed me the holy city, Jerusalem, coming down out of heaven from God.

11   And it had the glory of God and its light [was] [s]like a precious stone such as jasper, [s]like crystal.

12   And it had a great and high wall and it had twelve gates. And on the gates [were] twelve angels and the names written on them were the names of the twelve tribes of Israel.

13   On the east [were] three gates and on the north [were] three gates and on the south [were] three gates and on the west [were] three gates.

14   And the wall of the city had twelve foundations and on them [were] the twelve names of the apostles of the Son.

15   And that [one] who was speaking with me had a measuring rod of gold with him to measure the city and its wall.

16   And the city was laid out four-square[3] and its length [was] as its width. And he measured the city with the rod, about twelve thousand furlongs. Its length and its width and its height were equal.

---

[1] Repeat *nor*

[2] Var (Mr): omit *and sorcerers; fornicators,* alt sp. ܪܟܝܢܐ cf. Greek, "habitual fornicators"

[3] Var (H): alt sp ܠܠܟܝܢܐܘܘ cf. Greek, **tetragonos**

Chapter 21

17   And he measured its wall, one hundred and forty-four cubits, by the measure of a man, that is, of the angel.

18   And the structure of its wall [was of] jasper and the city [was] of pure gold with the appearance of pure glass.

19   And the foundations of the wall[1] of the city were adorned with precious stones. And the first foundation [was] jasper[2] and the second, sapphire and the third, chalcedony and the fourth, emerald

20   and the fifth, sardius and onyx[3] and the sixth, sardius and the seventh, chrysolite and the eighth, beryl and the ninth, topaz and the tenth, chrysoprasus, the eleventh, jacinth,[4] the twelfth, amethyst.

21   And the twelve gates and the twelve pearls, one for each and every one of the gates, were from one pearl. And the broad street of the city [was] of pure gold, [s]as though glass were in it.

22   And I saw no temple in it, for the LORD God Almighty was its temple,

23   and the Lamb. And for the city, neither the sun, nor the moon, was needed to illuminate it, for the glory of God will illuminate it and the lamp of it was the Lamb.

24   And the nations were walking in his light and the kings of the earth were bringing him praise.

25   And its gates will not be shut by day, for there will be no night there.

26   And they will bring the glory and honor of the nations into it.

27   And there will not be there any[one] unclean, nor he who practices [he]corruption[5] and falsehood, but only those who are written in the book of the Lamb.

Chapter 22

1   And he showed me a pure river of living water, also shining [s]as crystal, coming out from the throne of God and of the Lamb.

2   And in the middle of its broad streets, on this side and on that side by the river, was the tree of life that produced twelve fruits and in every month gave its fruits. And its leaves [were] for the healing of the nations.

---

[1] Culture: the foundations were actually ornamented rows of stones, which were inserted between the layers of rough stone, Burder, vol II, pp. 393-394

[2] Var (H): alt sp. ܩܘܣܐܝܣ

[3] Var (Mr): 'sardonyx'

[4] Var (H): alt sp. ܗܘܩܝܢܬܘܣ

[5] Var (Mr): 'uncleanness'

Chapter 22

3   And there will be no devoted [thing]¹ there and the throne of God and of the Lamb will be in it and his servants will minister to him.

4   And they will see his face and his name [will be] on their foreheads.

5   And there will be no night there and light will not be needed for them or a lamp or the light of the sun, because the LORD God illuminates them and their king, forever and ever.

6   And he said to me, "These words [are] faithful and true and the LORD God of the spirits of the holy prophets sent his angel to show his servants what must happen soon.

7   And *behold, I am coming soon. ᵇᵉBlessed [is] he who keeps the words of the prophecy of this book."

8   I am John who saw and heard these [things]. And when I saw and heard, I fell down to worship before the feet of the angel who showed me these [things].

9   And he said to me, "See, [do] not [worship me]. I am your fellow-servant and of your brothers the prophets and of those who keep these words of this book. Worship God."

10   And he said to me, "Do not seal the words of the prophecy of this book, for the time is near.

11   And he who does evil will do evil again and he who is filthy will be filthy again and the just will practice justification again and the holy will be holy² again.

12   *Behold, I am coming quickly and my reward [is] with me and I will give to everyone according to his work.

13   I am Aleph and I am Tau, the ᵐʳfirst and the last and the starting point and the completion.

14   ᵇᵉBlessed [are] they who do his commandments. Their authority will be over the tree of life and they will enter into the city by the gate.

15   And the fornicators ᴾand the murderers and the idolaters [will be] outside and the unclean and the sorcerers and all observers and doers of falsehood.˥

16   I, Jesus, have sent my angel to testify these [things] with you before the churches. I am [of] the ʰroot ᴾand the tribe of David and his people and the bright star of the morning.˥

17   And the Spirit and the bride say, 'Come.' And he who hears should say, 'Come.' And he who is thirsty should come and take the living water, freely.

---

¹ Or 'curse'; Var (Mr): 'fallen fruit or leaves'; Lamsa: 'that which withers'
² Same roots: *filthy, be filthy; just, justification; holy, be holy*

Chapter 22

18   I testify to all who hear the word of the prophecy of this book, that whoever will add to them, God will add to him the injuries that are written in this book.

19   And whoever takes away from the words of the book of this prophecy, God will take away his portion of the tree of life and of the holy city [and of] those [things] that are written in this book."

20   He said, testifying these [things], "Yes, I am coming soon." [i]Come, LORD Jesus.

21   [be]The grace of our Lord Jesus Christ [be] with all his holy [ones]. Amen.

APPENDIX 1
FIGURES OF SPEECH

Designed Emphasis

All language is ruled by laws, but to convey special emphasis of a word or group of words, these general laws of language are purposefully departed from, and other laws of language are invoked, giving the single word or group of words a new form. The Greeks called these departures from normal language use, *schemata*, meaning "a change of forms," from which the term "figure of speech" originated. When a word or words fail to be true to fact, they are figures of speech and bring an added emphasis to the basic truth of a sentence.

E. W. Bullinger stated in the beginning note of his book, *Figures of Speech Used in the Bible:*

> ...whenever and wherever it is possible, the words of Scripture are to be understood *literally,* but when a statement appears to be contrary to our experience, or to known fact, or revealed truth; or seems to be a variance with the general teaching of the Scriptures, then we may reasonably expect that some figure is employed. And as it is employed only to call our attention to some specially designed emphasis, we are at once bound to diligently examine the figure for the purpose of discovering and learning the truth that is thus emphasized.

One phrase above that should be noted is ***specially designed emphasis.*** The study of figures of speech needs to be integrally linked with a search for this emphasis. In *How to Enjoy the Bible,* Bullinger clarified how important this emphasis was: "the Figures, when used in connection with the 'words which the Holy Ghost teacheth,' give us the Holy Spirit's own *marking*, so to speak, of our Bible... calling our attention to what He desires us to notice for our learning, as being emphatic, and conveying His own special teaching." Every author has used figures for emphasis of what is important, but it is crucial to our understanding of the Bible to know what God intended to be emphasized in any particular passage. Thus, the search in this field should be to find out what each type of figure emphasizes and how it is used in a verse or passage.

APPENDIX 1
FIGURES OF SPEECH

Types of Figures

The Peshitta New Testament Translation is filled with footnotes and markings in the text itself of the common figures of speech. It does not mark every single figure of speech possible, but marks the ones that contribute to an added emphasis of the text. Light of the Word Ministry is developing a simple classification system that will clear up many of the misunderstandings in this field and enable the Bible student to understand what is the emphasis from the Holy Spirit in a particular passage. A figure is always used to add force to the truth presented, emphasis to the word or words and depth of meaning to the entire context. The type of figure determines the emphasis in the following five general ways:

1.	Illustration	This category includes all types of comparisons. The emphasis is on the points of comparison.
2.	Repetition	The repeated word is what is emphasized. The closer the repetition, or the more frequently it is used, the greater is the degree of emphasis.
3.	Meaning	Although this category is broad, the underlying meaning is always emphasized.
4.	Grammar	This category covers all uses that have a grammatical basis. Each figure has an individual emphasis, but it is always employed with consistency.
5.	Rhetoric	The general rule of this category is that the word or phrase used with the figure is what is emphasized.

Now that we have looked at the general categories, please study the Table of Figures code chart and pay particular attention to the column about emphasis. We have listed both the Greek/Latin name and also the English name in order to help with this study.

APPENDIX 1
FIGURES OF SPEECH

Table of Figures						
Category	Figure	English Name	Definition	Emphasis	Notes	Code
Grammar	Asterismos	Indicating	Employing some word which directs special attention to some particular point of subject	Calls attention to what follows	Examples include the phrase, "truly I say to you."	*
Grammar	Asyndeton	No-Ands	An enumeration of things without conjunctions	The whole unit	It is important to view the group as a whole unit and there may be climactic emphasis on last item in list.	a
Rhetoric	Anacoluthon	Non-Sequence	A breaking off the sequence of thought	The new pronoun	Beginning of the change of pronoun is important to note.	ac
Illustration	Allegory	Allegory	Continued comparison by representation or implication	Points of comparison	Allegory is a broader term in Semitic languages.	al
Meaning	Antimeria	Exchange of Parts of Speech	The exchange of a noun for an adjective or adverb	The changed word	The second noun is the adjective.	an
Meaning	Antiptosis	Exchange of Cases	One Case is put for another Case, the governing Noun being used as the Adjective instead of the Noun in regimen	The changed word	The first noun is the adjective.	as
Repetition	Antanaclasis	Word-Clashing	Repetition of the same word in the same sentence, with different meanings	1st meaning used is more important	Homonym - same word has more than one usage.	at
Rhetoric	Benedictio	Blessing	An expression of feeling by way of Benediction or blessing	The act of blessing and the blessing itself	The phrase may end with "Amen."	be

APPENDIX 1
FIGURES OF SPEECH

Table of Figures						
Category	Figure	English Name	Definition	Emphasis	Notes	Code
Meaning	Anthropo-patheia	Condescension	The ascribing of human attributes to God	God's diversity and greatness	Hebrew name is Derech Benai Adam, "the way of the sons of man."	c
Rhetoric	Ellipsis	Omission	Words omitted from a sentence or phrase that are necessary to complete the grammar, but not the sense	The omitted word or concept	There are many kinds of ellipsis.	e
Meaning	Euphemismos	Euphemism	Change of what is unpleasant for pleasant	The reality of what is meant	Emphasis is on the unpleasant concept.	eu
Illustration	Hypocatastasis	Implication	A declaration that implies the resemblance or representation, comparison by implication	What is compared	There is an implication of similar qualities. Can be a verb or noun.	h
Meaning	Hendiadys	Two for One	Two words used, but one thing meant	The combination of concepts	The one thing meant is greater than the individual meanings of the two words.	he
Meaning	Heterosis	Exchange	Exchange of one accidence of part of speech for another	The correct form	This is especially used with verb tenses.	ht
Rhetoric	Interjectio	Interjection	A parenthetic addition complete in itself, thrown in between, an exclamation	What follows the exclamation	This is a broad figure, covering many kinds of interjections and exclamations.	i
Meaning	Metonymy	Change of Noun	The change of one noun for another related noun	The related noun	There are several types.	m
Illustration	Metaphor	Representation	A declaration that one thing is (or represents) another, or comparison by representation	Quality that is compared	Usually has form of the verb "to be."	me

APPENDIX 1
FIGURES OF SPEECH

Table of Figures						
Category	Figure	English Name	Definition	Emphasis	Notes	Code
Rhetoric	Meiosis	Belittling	A belittling of something in order to magnify something else	The true meaning	Compare tapeinosis.	mi
Meaning	Merismos	Distribution	An enumeration of the parts of a whole that has been mentioned	The whole	Example: "morning and evening" means the whole day.	mr
Meaning	Metalepsis	Double Metonymy	Two metony-mies, one contained in the other, but only one expressed	The meaning underneath	There are at least two steps to discover the meaning.	mt
Grammar	Polysyndeton	Many-Ands	The repetition of the word "and" at the beginning of successive clauses or sentences	Each connected noun or phrase	Consider each word connected with "and" carefully.	p
Rhetoric	Parenthesis	Parenthesis	A parenthetic addition complete in itself, but needs context to be understood	The following sentence	This is the true figure of parenthesis used as an explanation or description.	pa
Illustration	Parabola	Parable	Comparison by continued resemblance	Points of comparison	Can be an extended simile with more than one point of comparison. Parable is a broader term in Semitic languages.	pb
Illustration	Prosopopoeia	Personification	Things or ideas represented as persons	The action	Human characteristics or actions are given to inanimate objects or abstract ideas.	pe
Meaning	Periphrasis	Circumlocution	When a description is used instead of the name	The action	Example: "lifted up his voice"	pr

APPENDIX 1
FIGURES OF SPEECH

Table of Figures						
Category	Figure	English Name	Definition	Emphasis	Notes	Code
Illustration	Simile	Resemblance	A declaration that one thing resembles another, comparison by resemblance	Quality that is compared	Uses "like" or "as" in comparison.	s
Meaning	Synecdoche	Transfer (or Part for Whole)	The exchange of one idea for another associated idea	The implied idea	This figure is often used of time.	sy
Rhetoric	Tapeinosis	Demeaning	A lessening of a thing in order to increase it	The superlative meaning	Differs from meiosis - the word(s) emphasized are the same.	t
					Marks the end of longer figures: allegory, asyndeton parable, parenthesis polysyndeton,.	ר

Several figures require further explanation, such as erotesis, metonymy, synecdoche and allegory. The latest articles with examples can be found on the Light of the Ministry website: www.lightofword.org.

APPENDIX 2
MONEY, WEIGHTS & MEASURES

MONEY

Value based on one denarius = $100, a day's wage

Unit	Type	Dictionary Number	Aramaic Word	Monetary Value	Equivalent	Translation Notes
Talent	Hebrew	1166	Kakra ܟܟܪܐ	$120,000	3000 shekels, weight of 75.6 lb	"Talent"– weight of gold and value today would be a much greater monetary value
Minah	Hebrew	1397	Manya ܡܢܝܐ	$10,000	100 denarii, 100 drachmas	"Mina" (not used in translation)
Shekel	Hebrew		None	$400	4 days' wage, 1/3000 talent, 1/50 minah	"Shekel" (not used in translation)
Stater	Greek	0168	Estira ܐܣܬܝܪܐ	$400	4 zozas, 4 drachmas	"Stater"
Drachma	Greek	0651	Zoza ܙܘܙܐ	$100	1 denarius, ¼ shekel	"Drachma" (2 drachmas were tribute money for temple)
Denarius	Roman	0519	Dinara ܕܝܢܪܐ	$100	1 drachma, one day's wage	"Denarius," pl. denarii
Assarion (as)	Roman	0166	Asra ܐܣܪܐ	$10	1/10 denarius	"Roman copper coin," "small coin"
Kodrantes	Roman		None	$2.50	¼ assarion, 2 mites	Translated "farthing" in KJV
Mite	Hebrew	2541	Shemona ܫܡܘܢܐ	$1.00	½ kodrantes, 1 lepton	"Small coin"
Lepton	Greek	1397	Manya ܡܢܝܐ	$1.00	½ kodrantes, 1 mite	"Lepton," same spelling of word in Aramaic for minah

APPENDIX 2
MONEY, WEIGHTS & MEASURES

MEASURES OF LENGTH

Unit	Type	Dictionary Number	Aramaic Word	Monetary Value	Equivalent
Roman mile	Roman	1352	Mila	4858 feet, 8 stadia	"Mile"
Stadion	Roman	0141	Estada	1/8 Roman mile, about 202 yards	Translated "furlong" as in KJV
Fathom	Hebrew	2170	Qauma	About 6 feet	Translated "fathom" as in KJV, from root verb "to stand up"
Cubit	Hebrew	0118	Amtha	15-18 inches	"Cubit", measure of arm from elbow to tip of middle finger

DRY MEASURES AND WEIGHTS

Unit	Type	Dictionary Number	Aramaic Word	Monetary Value	Equivalent
Kor	Hebrew	1158	Kura	6.25 bushels, 1 homer, 10 ephahs	Translated "cor" or "measure"
Ephah	Hebrew		None	1/10 homer	"Ephah"
Seah	Hebrew	1583	Satha	1/3 ephah, 6 2/3 dry quarts, 7.33 liters	Translated "seah" or "measure"
Cab	Hebrew	2132	Qaba	1.11 qts, 1/6 seah	Translated "measure," see also liquid measures
Pound	Roman	1295	Litra	12 oz., ¾ lb.	Grk: libra

LIQUID MEASURES

Unit	Type	Dictionary Number	Aramaic Word	Equivalent	Translation Notes
Kor	Hebrew	1158	Kura	60 gallons	Translated "cor"
Firkin	Roman	2286	Revea	About 10 gallons	Translated "liquid measure," cf Greek: metretes
Bath	Hebrew		None	6 gallons	
Hin	Hebrew		None	1 gallon	
Cab	Hebrew	2132	Qaba	2 quarts, ½ gallon	"cab"

BIBLIOGRAPHY

<u>Aramaic Sources</u>
_____Khaboris Manuscript. Yonan Codex Foundation

_____*Syriac New Testament & Psalms*. Istanbul, Turkey: United Bible Societies, 1985.

_____*The New Covenant*. Jerusalem: Aramaic Scriptures Research Society in Israel, 1986.

_____*The Elements of Syriac Grammar*. London: Samuel Bagster & Sons, 1906.

Aland, Barbara and Juckel, Andreas. *Das Neue Testament in Syrischer Uberlieferung*. Arbeiten zur Newtestamentlichen Textforschung: Bd 7, 2 vol. Berlin: W. deGruyter, 1986.

Bernstein, Georgio Henrico. *Lexicon Syriacum*. Lipsiae: 1836

Black, Matthew. *An Aramaic Approach to the Gospel & Acts*. Peabody, Massachusetts; Hendrickson Publishers, Inc., 1998.

Brockelmann, Carolo. *Lexicon Syriacum*. Edinburgh: T & T Clark, 1895.

Brown, Francis, S.R. Driver, Charles A. Briggs, eds. *The New Brown-Driver-Briggs-Gesenius Hebrew and English Lexicon*. Christian Copyrights, Inc., 1983.

Burkitt, F. Crawford. *Evangelion Da-Mepharreshe*. 2 vols. Cambridge University Press, 1904.

Burney, Charles Fox. *The Aramaic Origin of the Fourth Gospel*. Oxford: Clarendon Press, 1922.

Casey, Maurice. *Aramaic Sources of Mark's Gospel*. Edinburgh: Cambridge University Press, 1998

Chase, Frederic. *The Syro-Latin Text of the Gospels*. New York: MacMillan & Co., 1895.

_____*.The Old Syriac Element in the Text of Codex Bezae*. London: MacMillan & Co, 1893.

Cureton, William. *Remains of a Very Antient Recension of the Four Gospels in Syriac*. London: John Murray, 1858.

Errico, Rocco A. *Classical Aramaic*, Irvine: Noohra Foundation, 1992.

Etheridge, J. W. *the New Testament Translated from the Peshitta*, 2 vol. London: Longman, Green, Brown & Longmans.

Fitzmyer, Joseph A. and Daniel J. Harrington. *Manual of Palestinian Aramaic Texts*. Rome: Biblical Institute Press, 1978.

Fitzmyer, Joseph A. *The Semitic Background of the New Testament*. Grand Rapids, Michigan: William B. Eerdmans Publishing, 1997.

Goshen-Gottstein, M. H. *A Syriac-English Glossary with Etymological Notes*, Wiesbaden: Otto Harrasowitz, 1970.

Henderson, E. *Aegidii Gutbirii Lexicon Syriacum*. Eugene, Oregon: Wipf & Stock Publishers, 2004.

Hutchinson, Enock. *Uhlemann's Syriac Grammar*. New York: D. Appleton & Co, 1855.

Jahn, Herb. *The Aramaic New Covenant*. Orange, California: Exegeses Bibles, 1996.

Jennings, William. *Lexicon to the Syriac New Testament*. London: Oxford University Press, 1926.

Kerschensteiner, Josef. *Der Altsyrische Paulustext*. Corpus Scriptorum Christianorum Orientalium, Louvain: 1970.

Kiraz, George Anton. *Comparative Edition of the Syriac Gospels*, 4 vol. New York: E. J. Brill, 1996.

Lamsa, George M. *The Modern New Testament*, . Marina del Rey, California: DeVorss Publications, 1998.

Lewis, Agnes Smith. *A Palestinian Syriac Lectionary*. London: C. J. Clay & Sons, 1897.

_____*.A Translation of the Four Gospels from the Syriac of the Sinaitic Palimpsest*. London: MacMillan and Co., 1894.

_____*.Light on the Four Gospels from the Sinaitic Palimpsest*. London: Williams & Norgate, 1912.

MacLean, Arthur J. *Grammar of the Dialects of Vernacular Syriac*. Amsterdam: Philo Press, 1971.

Margoliouth, Rev. G. *The Palestinian Syriac Version of the Holy Scriptures*, London: Society of Biblical Archaeology, 1897.

Muller-Kessler, Christa and Sokoloff, Michael. *A Corpus of Christian Palestinian Aramaic*, 3 vol. Groningen: Styx Publications, 1998.

Murdock, James, trans. *The New Testament*. New York: Stanford and Swords, 1852.

Nestle, Eberhard. *Syriac Grammar*. Eugene, Oregon: Wipf and Stock Publishers, 2002.

Noldeke, Theodor. *Compendious Syriac Grammar*. London: Williams & Norgate, 1904.

Norton, William. *A Translation, of the Peshito-Syriac Text, and of the Received Greek Text of Hebrew, James, I Peter and I John*. London: W. E. Bloom, 1889.

Pashka, Joseph. *The Aramaic Gospels and Acts*. Xulon Press, 2003.

609

BIBLIOGRAPHY

Pusey, Philippus and Gwilliam, G. H. *Tetreuangelium Sanctum*. Oxford: Clarendon Press, 1901.

Phillips, George. *A Syriac Grammar*. London: Bell & Daldy, 1866.

Robinson, Theodore H. *Paradigms and Exercises in Syriac Grammar*. London: Oxford at the Clarendon Press, 1962.

Sokoloff, Michael. *A Dictionary of Jewish Palestinian Aramaic*. Israel: Bar Ilan University Press, 1990.

Smith, J. Payne. *A Compendious Syriac Dictionary*. London: Oxford at the Clarendon Press, 1967.

Stevenson, Wm B. *Grammar of Palestinian Jewish Aramaic*. Eugene, Oregon: Wipf & Stock, 1999.

Torrey, Charles Cutler. *Documents of the Primitive Church*. New York: Harper & Brothers, 1941.

Trimm, James Scott. *Hebraic-Roots Version "New Testament."* Hurst, Texas: Society for the Advancement of Nazarene Judaism, 2001.

_____.*The Semitic Origin of the New Testament*. Hurst, Texas: Hebrew/Aramaic New Testament Research, 1996.

Voobus, Arthur. *Studies in the History of the Gospel Text in Syriac*. Corpus Scriptorum Christianorum Orientalium, Louvain, 1951.

Wilcox, Max. *The Semitisms of Acts*. London: Oxford University Press, 1965.

Whish, Henry F. *Clavis Syriaca*. London: George Bell & Sons, 1883.

Wilson, E. Jan. *The Old Syriac Gospels*, 2 vol. Louaize, Lebanon: Notre Dame University and Gorgias Press, 2002.

Younan, Paul. *Holy Scriptures, The Good News of our Lord Jesus the Messiah*. Interlinear version, www.peshitta.org.

Manners and Customs

_____*Scripture Manners and Customs*. London: Society for Promoting Christian Knowledge, n.d.

Alexander, David. *Eerdman's Handbook to the Bible*. Grand Rapids, Michigan: William B. Eerdmans Publishing, 1973.

Barnes, Charles Randall, ed. *The People's Bible Encyclopedia*. Chicago: The People's Publication Society, 1921.

Bell, Albert A., Jr. *A Guide to the New Testament World*. Scottsdale, Pennsylvania: Herald Press, 1994.

Benton, Henry. *The Manners and Customs of the Jews*. Hartford Publishers, 1839.

Berrett, LaMar C. *Discovering the World of the Bible*. Provo, Utah: Brigham Young University Press, 1973.

Bissell, Edwin Cone. *Biblical Antiquities*. Philadelphia: American Sunday School Union, 1888.

Bivin, David and Roy Blizzard Jr. *Understanding the Difficult Words of Jesus*. Austin, Texas: Center for Judaic-Christian Studies, 1984.

Bouquet, A. C. *Everyday Life in New Testament Times*. New York: Charles Scribner's Sons, 1953.

Bowen, Barbara M. *Strange Scriptures That Perplex the Western Mind*. Grand Rapids, Michigan: William B. Eerdmans Publishing, 1973.

Breasted, James Henry. *Ancient Times, a History of the Early World*. Boston: Ginn & Co., 1944.

Burder, Samuel. *Oriental Customs: Or An Illustration of the Sacred Scriptures,* 2 vols. London: Longman, Hurst, Rees & Orme, 1808.

Conybeare, W. J. and Howson, J. S. *The Life and Epistles of St. Paul*. Grand Rapids, Michigan: Wm. B. Eerdmans Publishing, 1992.

Dalman, Gustaf. *The Words of Jesus*. Minneapolis: Klock & Klock Christian Publishers, 1981.

Dana, H. E. *The New Testament World*. Nashville: Broadman Press, 1937.

Daniel-Rops, Henri. *Daily Life in the Times of Jesus*. New York: Hawthorn Books, Inc., 1962.

_____.*Jesus and His Times.* 2 vols. New York: Image Books, 1958.

Duckat, Walter. *Beggar to King: All the Occupations of Biblical Times*. New York: Doubleday & Company, 1969.

Edersheim, Alfred. *Sketches of Jewish Social Life*. Grand Rapids, Michigan: William B. Eerdmans Publishing, 1982.

BIBLIOGRAPHY

_____.*The Life and Times of Jesus the Messiah*. McLean, Virginia: MacDonald Publishing Company, 1886 reprint.

_____.*The Temple*. Peabody, Massachusetts: Hendrickson Publishers, Inc., 1994.

Ehrlich, Eugene and David H. Scott. *Mene Mene, Tekel*. New York: HarperCollins Publishers, 1990.

Errico, Rocco A. *Aramaic Light of the Gospel of Matthew*. Santa Fe, New Mexico: Noohra Foundation, 2000.

Finegan, Jack. *Light From the Ancient Past*. Princeton, New Jersey: Princeton University Press, 1946.

Freeman, James M. *Manners and Customs of the Bible*. Plainfield, New Jersey: Logos International, 1972.

Gower, Ralph. *New Manners and Customs of the Bible*. Chicago: Moody Press, 1987.

Grant, Frederick C. *The Early Days of Christianity*. New York: The Abingdon Press, 1922.

Hardy, E. J. *The Unvarying East*. London: T. Fisher Unwin, 1912.

Huffman, J. A. *Voices From Rocks and Dust Heaps of Bible Lands*. Winona Lake, Indiana: The Standard Press, 1949.

Jamieson, Robert. *Eastern Manners Illustrative of the Old Testament History*. Philadelphia: Presbyterian Board of Publication, 1841.

Jeremias, Joachim. *Jerusalem in the Time of Jesus*. Philadelphia: Fortress Press, 1969.

Kitto, John. *Nations of the World: Palestine*. New York: Peter Fenelon Collier & Son, n.d.

_____.*The Cyclopedia of Biblical Literature*, 2 vol. New York: Ivison & Phinney, 1854.

Knight, William Allen. *The Song of Our Syrian Guest*. Westwood, New Jersey: Fleming H. Revell Co., 1964.

Lamsa, George M. *Gospel Light*. Philadelphia: A. J. Holman Co., 1936.

_____.*Idioms in the Bible Explained and a Key to the Original Gospels*. San Francisco: Harper & Row, Publishers, 1985.

_____.*My Neighbor Jesus*. St. Petersburg, Florida: Aramaic Bible Society, 1932.

_____.*New Testament Commentary*. Philadelphia: A. J. Holman Company, 1945.

_____.*New Testament Light*. San Francisco: Harper & Row, Publishers, 1968.

_____.*New Testament Origin*. St Petersburg, Florida: Aramaic Bible Society.

Lightfoot, John. *A Commentary on the New Testament from the Talmud and Hebraica*, 4 vols. Peabody, Massachusetts: Hendrickson Publishers, 1989.

_____.*Notes on the Epistles of St. Paul*. Winona Lake, Indiana: Alpha Publications, 1979.

Mackie, George M. *Bible Manners and Customs*. New York: Fleming H. Revell Co., 1898.

Mathews, Basil. *The World in Which Jesus Lived*. New York: The Abingdon Press, 1938.

Mathews, Shailer. *A History of New Testament Times in Palestine*. New York: The Macmillan Company, 1914.

Matthews, Victor H. *Manners and Customs in the Bible*. Peabody, Massachusetts: Hendrickson Publishers, 1988.

Miller, Madeleine S. *Encyclopedia of Bible Life*. New York: Harper & Brothers Publishing, 1944.

Moseley, Ron. *Yeshua*. Baltimore: Lederer Books, 1996.

National Geographic Society, ed. *Everyday Life in Bible Times*. New York: National Geographic Society, 1967.

Neil, James. *Everyday Life in the Holy Land*. London: Church Missions to Jews, 1953.

_____.*Palestine Explored*. London: James Nisbet & Co, 1881.

_____.*Peeps into Palestine*. London: Henry E. Walter, n.d.

_____.*Pictured Palestine*. London: James Nisbet & Co., 1893.

Nevin, John W. *A Summary of Biblical Antiquities*. Philadelphia: American Sunday School Union, 1849.

Packer, J.C. and Merrill C. Tenney. *Illustrated Manners and Customs of the Bible*. Nashville: Thomas Nelson Publishers, 1980.

Packer, J.C. and Merrill C. Tenney and William White Jr. *Nelson's Illustrated Encyclopedia of Bible Facts. Vol. 3. New Testament Times*. Baltimore, Maryland: Halo Press, 1980.

_____.*The Bible Almanac*. Carmel, New York: Guideposts, 1980.

611

BIBLIOGRAPHY

_____.*The Land of the Bible*. Nashville: Thomas Nelson Publishers, 1985.

Peloubet, F. N., ed. *Peloubet's Bible Dictionary*. Philadelphia: The John C. Winston Co, 1925.

Pillai, Bishop K. C. *Light Through an Eastern Window*. New Knoxville, Ohio: American Christian Press, 1986.

_____.*Orientalisms of the Bible*, 2 vols. New Knoxville, Ohio: American Christian Press, 1984.

Reader's Digest Association Inc. *Great People of the Bible and How They Lived*. New York: Reader's Digest Association Inc., 1974.

Renan, Ernest. *The Life of Jesus*. New York: Doubleday & Company, n.d.

Rice, Edwin W. *Orientalisms in Bible Lands*. Philadelphia: American Sunday-School Union, 1910.

_____.*People's Dictionary of the Bible*. Philadelphia: American Sunday-School Union, 1904.

Rihbany, Abraham Mitrie. *The Syrian Christ*. Boston: Houghton Mifflin Company, 1916.

Schor, Samuel. *Palestine and the Bible*. Ft. Washington, Pennsylvania: Christian Literature Crusade, 1934.

Smith, William. *Smith's Bible Dictionary*. Westwood, New Jersey: Barbour Books, 1987.

Thompson, J. A. *Handbook of Life in Bible Times*. Leicester, England: Inter-Varsity Press, 1986.

Thomson, W. M. *The Land and the Book*. Grand Rapids, Michigan: Baker Book House, 1954.

Tristram, H. B. *The Natural History of the Bible*. London: Society for Promoting Christian Knowledge, 1880.

Trumbull, H. Clay. *Studies in Oriental Social Life*. Philadelphia: J.D. Wattles & Company, 1894.

Tucker, T. J. *Life in the Roman World of Nero and St. Paul*. New York: The Macmillan Company, 1929.

Van Der Woude, A. S. *The World of the Bible*. Grand Rapids, Michigan: William B. Eerdmans Publishing, 1986.

Van Deursen, A. *Illustrated Dictionary of Bible Manners and Customs*. New York: Philosophical Library Inc., 1967.

Van-Lennep, Henry J. *Bible Lands: Their Modern Customs and Manners*. New York: Harper & Brothers, 1875.

Walker, Winifred. *All the Plants of the Bible*. New York: Harper & Brothers, 1957.

Weiss, G. Christian. *Insights Into Bible Times and Customs*. Chicago: Moody Press, 1974.

Wight, Fred H. *Manners and Customs of Bible Lands*. Chicago: Moody Press, 1953.

Wright, Ruth V. and Robert L. Chadbourne. *Crystals, Gems, and Minerals of the Bible*. New Canaan, Connecticut: Keats Publishing Inc., 1970.

General

Angus, Joseph and Green, Samuel G. ed. *The Bible Hand-Book: An Introduction to the Study of Sacred Scripture*. New York: Fleming H. Revell Co, 1902.

Barker, Kenneth, et al. *The NIV Study Bible*. Grand Rapids, Michigan: Zondervan Publishing House, 1995.

Barrett, C. K. *The New Testament Background: Selected Documents*. New York: Harpers & Row, Publishers, 1961.

Brown, Raymond E., Joseph A. Fitzmyer, Roland E. Murphy. *The Jerome Biblical Commentary*. Englewood Cliffs, New Jersey: Prentice-Hall, Inc., 1968.

Bruce, F. F. *New Testament History*. New York: Doubleday & Company, 1969.

Bullinger, E.W. *Commentary on Revelation*. Grand Rapids, Michigan: Kregel Publications, 1984.

_____.*Figures of Speech Used in the Bible*. Grand Rapids, Michigan: Baker Book House, 1968.

_____.*Number in Scripture*. Grand Rapids, Michigan: Kregel Publications, 1979.

Butler, Trent C. *Holman Bible Dictionary*. Nashville, Tennessee: Holman Bible Publishers, 1991.

Douglas, J. D, ed. *New Bible Dictionary*. Wheaton, Illinois: Tyndale House Publishers, 1987.

Fairweather, William. *The Background of the Epistles*. Minneapolis: Klock & Klock Christian Publishers, 1977.

Gaebelein, Frank E. *The Expositor's Bible Commentary*. Grand Rapids, Michigan: Zondervan Publishing House, 1984.

BIBLIOGRAPHY

Girdlestone, Robert Baker. *Synonyms of the Old Testament*. Grand Rapids, Michigan: William B. Eerdmans Publishing, 1897 reprint.

Hallock, G. B. F., ed. *The Evangelistic Cyclopedia*. New York: George H. Doran Company, 1922.

Halley, Henry H. *Halley's Bible Handbook*. Grand Rapids, Michigan: Zondervan Publishing House, 1965.

Harris, R. Laird, Gleason L. Archer, Jr., Bruce K. Waltke, eds. *Theological Wordbook of the Old Testament. 2 vols.* Chicago: Moody Press, 1980.

Hartman, Louis F., ed. *Encyclopedic Dictionary of the Bible*. New York: McGraw-Hill Book Co., 1963.

Jacobus, Melancthon W. and Elbert C. Lane, Andrew C. Zenos, ed. *Funk & Wagnall's New Standard Bible Dictionary*. Garden City, New York: Garden City Books, 1936.

Kaiser, Walter. *The Messiah in the Old Testament*. Grand Rapids, Michigan: Zondervan Publishing House, 1995.

Nave, Orville J. *The New Nave's Topical Bible*. Grand Rapids, Michigan: Zondervan Publishing House, 1969.

Pentecost, J. Dwight. *The Parables of Jesus*. Grand Rapids, Michigan: Zondervan Publishing House, 1982.

Tenney Merrill C. *New Testament Survey*. Grand Rapids, Michigan: William B. Eerdmans Publishing, 1961.

Thiele, Edwin R. *A Chronology of the Hebrew Kings*. Grand Rapids, Michigan: Zondervan Publishing House, 1977.

ABOUT THE AUTHOR

Janet Magiera is an ordained minister and the founder of Light of the Word Ministry, an educational ministry dedicated to teaching and making known the understanding of the Aramaic language, figures of speech and customs of the Bible. In 1979, under the tutelage of a student of Dr. George M. Lamsa, Jan began pursuing a course of study of the Aramaic of the Peshitta New Testament. For over 25 years, she has taught Bible fellowships and churches in Michigan, Ohio, Kansas, Tennessee, California and New Mexico, using the insight from her work with the language. Many articles and teachings of interest to the layman, as well as to biblical scholars, are on the Light of the Word Ministry website, www.lightofword.org, for those desiring to know more about these fields.

In 1990, Jan began compiling a database of the Aramaic Peshitta New Testament. As computer technology increased over the past 16 years, she expanded and developed the database to generate a series of research tools to study the New Testament. The entire database is being published by BibleWorks software as a module with their newest version 7. This translation is the first book being published in a complete *Aramaic Peshitta New Testament Library*. The library will include an interlinear, lexicon, concordance and parallel translations.

Jan has helped to publish several books. In conjunction with The Aramaic Bible Society, she edited footnotes and explanatory remarks for Dr. Lamsa's book, *Gospel Light.* On Amazon.com, published under LWM Publications, she has listed her first book in The Searchlight Series, called *Enriched in Everything*, which is a topical study on giving. Parallel editions of the Gospels are also available for purchase on Amazon.com.

Jan and her husband Glen currently live in Truth or Consequences, New Mexico and work with Christian Faith International Ministries.